Why You Need This New Edition?

The sixteenth edition of this classic anthology includes many new high interest readings, all written by leading scholars in the field. Here is a sampling of some of the topics covered in the new selections:

1. The startling changes in women's lives over the past fifty years, and why they happened when they did.
2. A comparison of family ideals and practices in contemporary Finland and Spain.
3. A comparison of today's "hooking up" culture on college campuses with the older pattern of dating, and how the new sexual patterns affect women and men.
4. An exploration of the paradoxical contrasts between "red" and "blue" states in their sexual attitudes and behavior.
5. A report on the new marriage norms among young adults in different parts of the country.
6. The contrast between the findings of divorce researchers the way those findings are presented in the media.
7. A look at how the unhealthy behaviors of some fathers and other adult men help shape the emotional and physical health of young people.
8. A discussion of how the "delayed adulthood" phenomenon is interpreted in the different cultures of Western Europe and Japan.
9. An exploration of the tensions between the younger generation of Chinese immigrants and their parents, and how these tensions are resolved.

PEARSON

Family in Transition

SIXTEENTH EDITION

Arlene S. Skolnick

New York University

Jerome H. Skolnick

New York University

Allyn & Bacon

Boston Columbus Indianapolis New York San Francisco
Upper Saddle River Amsterdam Cape Town Dubai London Madrid Milan
Munich Paris Montreal Toronto Delhi Mexico City Sao Paulo
Sydney Hong Kong Seoul Singapore Taipei Tokyo

Publisher: *Karen Hanson*
Editorial Assistant: *Alyssa Levy*
Executive Marketing Manager: *Kelly May*
Marketing Assistant: *Gina Lavagna*
Associate Production Project Manager: *Maggie Brobeck*
Production Manager: *Fran Russello*
Cover Administrator: *Jayne Conte*
Editorial Production and Composition Service: *Jogender Taneja/Aptara®, Inc.*
Cover Designer: *Bruce Kenselaar*

Credits appear on Page 543, which constitutes an extension of the copyright page.

Library of Congress Cataloging-in-Publication Data

Family in transition / [edited by] Arlene S. Skolnick, Jerome H. Skolnick.—16th ed.
p. cm.
Includes bibliographical references.
ISBN-13: 978-0-205-74730-6
ISBN-10: 0-205-74730-2
1. Families. I. Skolnick, Arlene S., II. Skolnick, Jerome H.
HQ518.F336 2011
306.85—dc22 2010035615

10 9 8 7 6 5 4 3 2 —DOH—14 13 12 11

Allyn & Bacon
is an imprint of

www.pearsonhighered.com

ISBN-10: 0-205-74730-2
ISBN-13: 978-0-205-74730-6

Contents

Preface

Once again, this new edition of *Family in Transition* has three aims. First, we looked for articles that help the reader make sense of current trends in family life. Second, we tried to balance excellent older articles with newer ones. Third, we have tried to select articles that are scholarly yet readable for an audience of undergraduates.

Among the new readings are the following:

- Gail Collins describes the startling changes in women's lives over the past fifty years, and why they happened when they did.
- Eriikka Oinonin compares family ideals and practices in contemporary Finland and Spain.
- Kathleen Bogle compares today's "hooking-up" culture on college campuses with the older pattern of dating, and how the new sexual patterns affect women and men.
- Margaret Talbot explores the paradoxical contrasts between "red" and "blue" states in their sexual attitudes and behavior.
- Maria Kefalas, Frank Furstenberg, and Laura Napolitano report on the new marriage norms among young adults in different parts of the country.
- Virginia Rutter looks at the contrast between the findings of divorce researchers—the way those findings are presented in the media.
- William Marsiglio argues that the unhealthy behaviors of some fathers and other adult men help shape the emotional and physical health of young people. But social pressure and financial struggles limit these men's ability to make better choices.
- Katherine Newman examines how the "delayed adulthood" phenomenon is interpreted in the different cultures of Western Europe and Japan.
- Min Zhou explores the tensions between the younger generation of Chinese immigrants and their parents, and how these tensions are resolved.

We would like to thank all those who have helped us with suggestions for this edition, as well as past ones. Thanks once more to Pamela Kaufman, an NYU doctoral candidate who helped to review the family research literature. And thanks also to Rifat Salam, recently awarded her NYU Ph.D. for her suggestions on revising the previous edition. Also, many thanks to the reviewers who offered many good suggestions for this edition: Dennis McGrath, *Community College of Philadelphia* and Rosalind Fisher, *University of West Florida*.

Introduction
Family in Transition

The aim of this book is to help the reader make sense of American family life in the early years of the twenty-first century. Contrary to most students' expectations, "the family" is not an easy topic to study. One reason is that we know too much about it, because virtually everyone has grown up in a family. As a result there is a great temptation to generalize from our own experiences.

Another difficulty is that the family is a subject that arouses intense emotions. Not only are family relationships themselves deeply emotional, but family issues are also entwined with strong moral and religious beliefs. In the past several decades, "family values" have become a central battleground in American politics. Abortion, sex education, single parenthood, and gay rights are some of the issues that have have been debated since the 1980s.

Still another problem is that the current state of the family is always being compared with the way families used to be. The trouble is, most people tend to have an idealized image of families in "the good old days." No era ever looked like a golden age of family life to people actually living through it. That includes the 1950s, which many Americans now revere as the high point of American family life.

Finally, it is difficult to make sense of the state of the family from the statistics presented in the media. For example, just before Father's Day in 2003, the Census Bureau issued a press release with the following headline: "Two Married Parents the Norm." It went on to state that, according to the Bureau's most recent survey, about 70 percent of children live with their two parents. Two months earlier, however, a report by a respected social science research organization contained the following headlines: "Americans Increasingly Opting Out of Marriage" and "Traditional Families Account for Only 7 Percent of U.S. Households."

These are just a few examples of the confusing array of headlines and statistics about the family that the media are constantly serving up. Most often, the news tells of yet another fact or shocking incident that shows the alarming decline of the family. But every once in a while, the news is that the traditional family is making a comeback. No wonder one writer compared the family to a "great intellectual Rorschach blot" (Featherstone, 1979).

Everyone agrees that families have changed dramatically over the past several decades, but there is no consensus on what the changes mean. The majority of women, including mothers of young children, are now working outside the home. Divorce rates have risen sharply (although they have leveled off since 1979). Twenty-eight percent of children are living in single-parent families. Cohabitation—once called "shacking up" or "living in sin"—is a widespread practice. The sexual double standard—the norm that demanded virginity for the bride, but not the groom—has largely disappeared from mainstream American culture. There are mother-only families, father-only families, grandparents raising grandchildren, and gay and lesbian families.

Indeed, the growing public acceptance of homosexuals is one of the most striking trends of recent time, despite persisting stigma and the threat of violence. Local governments and some leading corporations have granted gays increasing recognition as domestic partners entitled to spousal benefits. In June 2003, the Supreme Court struck down the last state laws that made gay sex a crime. The following November 18, the Massachusetts Supreme Judicial Court ruled that gays have the right to marry. These rulings have set off a national debate and a demand by conservatives to sponsor a Constitutional amendment forbidding same-sex marriage.

Does all of this mean the family is "in decline"? In crisis? Are we witnessing a moral meltdown? Why is there so much anxiety about the family? Why do so many families feel so much stress and strain? We can't answer these questions if we assume that family life takes place in a social vacuum. Social and economic circumstances have always had a profound impact on families, and when the world outside changes in important ways, families must also reshape themselves.

All these shifts in family life are part of an ongoing global revolution. All industrialized nations, and many of the emerging ones, have experienced similar changes. In no other Western country, however, has family change been so traumatic and divisive as in the United States. For example, the two-earner family is the most common family pattern in the United States; 75 percent of mothers of children under 18 and more than 60 percent of those with young children work outside the home. Yet the question of whether mothers *should* work is still a fiercely debated issue—except if the mother is on welfare.

Thus, the typical pattern for public discussion of family issues is a polarized, emotional argument. Lurching from one hot topic to another, every issue is presented as an either–or choice: Which is better for children—two parents or one? Is divorce bad or good for children? Should mothers of young children work or stay home?

This kind of argument makes it difficult to discuss the issues and problems facing the family in a realistic way. It doesn't describe the range of views among family scholars, and it doesn't fit the research evidence. For example, the right question to ask about divorce is "Under what circumstances is divorce harmful or beneficial to children?" How can parents make divorce less harmful for their children? (Amato, 1994). In most public debates about divorce, however, that question is never asked, and the public never hears the useful information they should.

Still another problem with popular discourse about the family is that it exaggerates the amount of change that has actually occurred. For example, consider the previous statement that only 7 percent of American households fit the model of the traditional family. This number, or something like it, is often cited by conservatives as proof that the institution is in danger of disappearing unless the government steps in to restore marriage and the two-parent family. At the opposite end of the political spectrum are those who celebrate the alleged decline of the traditional family and welcome the new family forms that have supposedly replaced it.

But is it true that only 7 percent of American households are traditional families? It all depends, as the saying goes, on how you define *traditional.* The statement is true if you count only families with children under 18 in which only the husband works outside the home. But if the wife works too, as most married women now do, the family doesn't count as "traditional" by that definition. Neither does the recently married couple who do not have children yet. The couple whose youngest child turns 18 is no longer counted as a "traditional" family either.

Despite the current high divorce rates (actually down from 1979), Americans have not abandoned the institution of marriage. The United States has the highest marriage rate in the industrial world. About 90 percent of Americans marry at some point in their lives, and virtually all who do either have, or want children. Further, surveys repeatedly show that family is central to the lives of most Americans. Family ties are their deepest source of satisfaction and meaning, as well as the source of their greatest worries (Mellman, Lazarus, and Rivlin, 1990). In sum, family life in the United States is a complex mixture of continuity and change, satisfaction and trouble.

While the transformations of the past three decades do not mean the end of family life, they have brought a number of new difficulties. For example, although most families now depend on the earnings of wives and mothers, the rest of society has not caught up to the new realities. For example, most schools are out of step with parents' working hours—they let out at 3:00, and still maintain the long summer vacations that once allowed children to work on the family farm. Most jobs, especially well-paying ones, are based on the male model—that is, a worker who can work full-time or longer without interruptions. An earnings gap persists between men and women in both blue-collar and white-collar jobs. Employed wives and mothers still bear most of the workload in the home.

UNDERSTANDING THE CHANGING FAMILY

During the same years in which the family was becoming the object of public anxiety and political debate, a torrent of new research on the family was pouring forth. The study of the family had come to excite the interest of scholars in a range of disciplines—history, demography, economics, law, and psychology. We now have much more information available about families of the past, as well as current families, than we have ever had before.

The main outcome of this research has been to debunk myths about family life, both past and present. Nevertheless, the myths persist and help to fuel the cultural wars over family change.

The Myth of Universality

In some ways, families are the same everywhere. Yet families also vary in many ways—in who is included as a family member, emotional environments, living arrangements, ideologies, social and kinship networks, and economic and other functions. Although anthropologists have tried to come up with a single definition of family that would hold across time and place, they generally have concluded that doing so is not useful (Geertz, 1965; Stephens, 1963).

For example, although marriage is virtually universal across cultures, the definition of marriage is not the same. Although many cultures have weddings and notions of monogamy and permanence, some lack one or more of these attributes. In some cultures, the majority of people mate and have children without legal marriage and often without living together. In other societies, husbands, wives, and children do not live together under the same roof.

In U.S. society, the assumption of universality has usually defined what is normal and natural both for research and therapy and has subtly influenced our thinking to regard deviations from the nuclear family as sick, perverse, or immoral. As Suzanne Keller (1971) once observed, "The fallacy of universality has done students of behavior a great disservice by leading us to seek and hence to find a single pattern that has blinded us to historical precedents for multiple legitimate family arrangements."

The Myth of Family Harmony

"Happy families are all alike; each unhappy family is unhappy in its own way." This well-known quotation from Leo Tolstoy is a good example of the widespread tendency to divide families into two opposite types—happy or unhappy, good or bad, normal or abnormal. The sitcom families of the 1950s—*Ozzie and Harriet*, *Leave It to Beaver*, and the rest—still serve as "ideal" models for how families should be.

But few families, then or now, fit neatly into either category. Even the most loving relationships inevitably involve negative feelings as well as positive ones. It is this ambivalence that sets close relationships apart from less intimate ones. Indeed, from what we have learned about the Nelson family over the years, the real Ozzie and Harriet did not have an Ozzie and Harriet family.

Only in fairly recent times has the darker side of family life come to public attention. For example, child abuse was only "discovered" as a social problem in the 1960s. In recent years, family scholars have been studying family violence such as child or spousal abuse to better understand the normal strains of family life. More police officers are killed and injured dealing with family fights than in dealing with any other kind of situation. In addition, of all the relationships between murderers and their victims, the family relationship is most common. Studies of family violence reveal that it is much more widespread than had been assumed, cannot easily be attributed to mental illness, and is not confined to the lower classes. Family violence seems to be a product of psychological tensions and external stresses that can affect all families at all social levels.

The study of family interaction has also undermined the traditional image of the happy, harmonious family. About three decades ago, researchers and therapists began to bring schizophrenic patients and their families together to watch how they behaved with one another. Oddly, researchers had not studied whole family groups before. At first, the family interactions were interpreted as pathogenic: a parent expressing affection in words but showing nonverbal hostility; alliances being made between different family members;

families having secrets; or one family member being singled out as a scapegoat to be blamed for the family's troubles. As more and more families were studied, however, such patterns were found in many families, not just in those families with a schizophrenic child. Although this line of research did not uncover the cause of schizophrenia, it revealed that normal, ordinary families can often seem dysfunctional, or, in the words of one study, they may be "difficult environments for interaction."

The Myth of Parental Determinism

The kind of family a child grows up in leaves a profound, lifelong impact. But a growing body of studies shows that early family experience is not the all-powerful, irreversible influence it has sometimes been thought to be. An unfortunate childhood does not doom a person to an unhappy adulthood. Nor does a happy childhood guarantee a similarly blessed future (Emde and Harmon, 1984; Macfarlane, 1964; Rubin, 1996).

Any parent knows that child rearing is not like molding clay or writing on a blank slate. Rather, it's a two-way process in which both parent and child influence each other. Children come into this world with their own temperaments and other characteristics. Moreover, from a very early age, children are active perceivers and thinkers. Finally, parents and children do not live in a social vacuum; children are also influenced by the world around them and the people in it—relatives, family friends, their neighborhoods, other children, their schools, as well as the media.

The traditional view of parental determinism has been challenged by the extreme opposite view. Psychologist Judith Rich Harris asserts that parents have very little impact on their children's development. In her book, *The Nurture Assumption: Why Children Turn Out the Way They Do* (1998), Harris argues that genetics and peer groups, not parents, determine how a child will develop. As in so many debates about the family, both extremes oversimplify complex realities.

The Myth of a Stable Past

Laments about the current state of decay of the family imply some earlier era when the family was more stable and harmonious. Historians have not, in fact, located a golden age of the family. Nor have they found any time or place when families did not vary in many ways from whatever the standard model was. Indeed, they have found that premarital sexuality, illegitimacy, and generational conflict can best be studied as a part of family life itself rather than as separate categories of deviation.

The most shocking finding of recent years is the prevalence of child abandonment and infanticide throughout European history. It now appears that infanticide provided a major means of population control in all societies lacking reliable contraception, Europe included, and that it was practiced by families on legitimate children (Hrdy, 1999).

Rather than being a simple instinctive trait, having profound love for a newborn child seems to require two things: the infant must have a decent chance of surviving, and the parents must feel that the infant is not competing with them and their older children in a struggle for survival. Throughout many centuries of European history, both of these conditions were lacking.

Another myth about the family is that it has been a static, unchanging form until recently, when it began to come apart. In reality, families have always been in flux; when the world around them changes, families have to change in response. At periods when a whole society undergoes some major transformation, family change may be especially rapid and dislocating.

In many ways, the era we are living through now resembles two earlier periods of family crisis and transformation in U.S. history (see Skolnick, 1991). The first occurred in the early nineteenth century, when the industrial era moved work out of the home (Ryan, 1981). In the older pattern, most people lived on farms. A father was not only the head of the household, but also boss of the family enterprise. The mother, children, and hired hands worked under his supervision.

When work moved out, however, so did the father and the older sons and daughters, leaving behind the mother and the younger children. These dislocations unleashed an era of personal stress and cultural confusion. Eventually, a new model of family emerged that not only reflected the new separation of work and family, but also glorified it.

The household now became idealized as "home sweet home," an emotional and spiritual shelter from the heartless world outside. Many of our culture's most basic ideas about the family and gender were formed at this time. The mother-at-home, father-out-at-work model that most people think of as "traditional" was in fact the first version of the modern family.

Historians label this nineteenth century model of the family "Victorian" because it became influential in England and Western Europe, as well as in the United States, during the reign of Queen Victoria. It reflected, in idealized form, the nineteenth-century middle-class family. The Victorian model became the prevailing cultural definition of family, but few families could live up to the ideal in all its particulars. Working-class, black, and ethnic families, for example, could not get by without the economic contributions of wives, mothers, and daughters. Even for middle-class families, the Victorian ideal prescribed a standard of perfection that was virtually impossible to fulfill (Demos, 1986).

Eventually, social change overtook the Victorian model. Beginning around the 1880s, another period of rapid economic, social, and cultural change unsettled Victorian family patterns, especially their gender arrangements. Several generations of so-called "new women" challenged Victorian notions of femininity. They became educated, pursued careers, became involved in political causes—including their own—and created the first wave of feminism. This ferment culminated in the victory of the women's suffrage movement. It was followed by the 1920s jazz-age era of flappers and flaming youth—the first, and probably the major, sexual revolution of the twentieth century.

Another cultural crisis ensued, until a new cultural blueprint emerged—the companionate model of marriage and the family. The new model was a modern, more relaxed version of the Victorian family; companionship and sexual intimacy were now defined as central to marriage.

This highly abbreviated history of family and cultural change forms the necessary backdrop for understanding the family upheavals of the late twentieth and early twenty-first centuries. As in earlier times, major changes in the economy and society have destabilized an existing model of family life and the everyday patterns and practices that have sustained it.

In the last half of the twentieth century, we experienced a triple revolution: first, the move toward a postindustrial service and information economy; second, a life course revolution brought about by reductions in mortality and fertility; and third, a psychological transformation rooted mainly in rising educational levels. Although these shifts have profound implications for everyone, women have been the pacesetters of change. Most women's lives and expectations over the past three decades, inside and outside the family, have departed drastically from those of their own mothers. Men's lives today also are different from their fathers' generation, but to a much lesser extent.

THE TRIPLE REVOLUTION

The Postindustrial Family

A service and information economy produces large numbers of jobs that, unlike factory work, seem suitable for women. Yet as Jessie Bernard (1982) once observed, the transformation of a housewife into a paid worker outside the home sends tremors through every family relationship. It blurs the sharp contrast between men's and women's roles that mark the breadwinner/housewife pattern. It also reduces women's economic dependence on men, thereby making it easier for women to leave unhappy marriages.

Beyond drawing women out of the home, shifts in the nature of work and a rapidly changing globalized economy have unsettled the lives of individuals and families at all class levels. The well-paying industrial jobs that once enabled a blue-collar worker to own a home and support a family are no longer available. The once secure jobs that sustained the "organization men" and their families in the 1950s and 1960s have been made shaky by downsizing, an unstable economy, corporate takeovers, and a rapid pace of technological change.

The new economic uncertainty has also made the transition to adulthood increasingly problematic. In the postwar years, particularly in the United States, young people entered adulthood in one giant step. They found jobs, often out of high school, married young, left home, and had children quickly. Today, few young adults can afford to marry and have children in their late teens or early twenties. In an economy where a college degree is necessary to earn a living wage, early marriage impedes education for both men and women.

Those who do not go on to college have little access to jobs that can sustain a family. Particularly in the inner cities of the United States, growing numbers of young people have come to see no future for themselves in the ordinary world of work. In middle-class families, a narrowing opportunity structure has increased anxieties about downward mobility for offspring and parents as well. Because of the new economic and social realities, a new stage of life has opened up between adolescence and adulthood. It is simply impossible for most young people in today's postindustrial societies to become financially and emotionally independent at the same ages as earlier generations did.

This new stage of life is so new it doesn't have an agreed-on name. It has been called "arrested development," "adultolescence," or "emerging adulthood." And many people assume that today's younger generations are simply slackers—unwilling to grow up, get jobs, and start their own families. But the fact is that today's economy demands more schooling than ever before, and jobs that can sustain a family are fewer and less permanent than ever before.

The Life Course Revolution

It's not just the rise of a new economy that has reshaped the stages of life. The basic facts of life and death changed drastically in the twentieth century. In 1900, average life expectancy was 47 years. Infants had the highest mortality rates, but young and middle-aged adults were often struck down by infectious diseases. Before the turn of the twentieth century, only 40 percent of women lived through all the stages of a normal life course: growing up, marrying, having children, and surviving with a spouse to the age of 50 (Uhlenberg, 1980).

Declining mortality rates have had a profound effect on women's lives. Women today are living longer and having fewer children. When infant and child mortality rates fall, women no longer have five, seven, or nine children to ensure that two or three will survive to adulthood. After rearing children, the average woman can look forward to three or four decades without maternal responsibilities.

One of the most important changes in contemporary marriage is the potential length of marriage and the number of years spent without children in the home. Our current high divorce rates may be a by-product of this shift. By the 1970s, the statistically average couple spent only 18 percent of their married lives raising young children, compared with 54 percent a century ago (Bane, 1976). As a result, marriage is becoming defined less as a union between parents raising a brood of children and more as a personal relationship between two individuals.

A Psychological Revolution

The third major transformation is a set of psychocultural changes that might be described as *psychological gentrification* (Skolnick, 1991). That is, cultural advantages once enjoyed only by the upper classes—in particular, education—have been extended to those lower down on the socioeconomic scale. Psychological gentrification also involves greater leisure time, travel, and exposure to information, as well as a general rise in the standard of living. Despite the persistence of poverty, unemployment, and economic insecurity in the industrialized world, far less of the population than in the historical past is living at the level of sheer subsistence.

Throughout Western society, rising levels of education and related changes have been linked to a complex set of shifts in personal and political attitudes. One of these is a more psychological approach to life—greater introspectiveness and a yearning for warmth and intimacy in family and other relationships (Veroff, Douvan, and Kulka, 1981). There is also evidence of an increasing preference on the part of both men and women for a more companionate ideal of marriage and a more democratic family. More broadly, these changes in attitude have been described as a shift to "postmaterialist values," emphasizing self-expression, tolerance, equality, and a concern for the quality of life (Inglehart, 1990).

The multiple social transformations of our era have brought both costs and benefits: Family relations have become both more fragile and more emotionally rich; longevity has brought us a host of problems as well as the gift of extended life. Although change has brought greater opportunities for women, persisting gender inequality means women have borne a large share of the costs of these gains. We cannot turn the clock back to the family models of the past.

Despite the upheavals of recent decades, the emotional and cultural significance of the family persists. Family remains the center of most people's lives and, as numerous surveys show, is a cherished value. Although marriage has become more fragile, the parent–child relationship—especially the mother–child relationship—remains a core attachment across the life course (Rossi and Rossi, 1990). The family, however, can be both "here to stay" and beset with difficulties.

Most European countries have recognized for some time that governments must play a role in supplying an array of supports to families, such as health care, children's allowances, and housing subsidies. Working parents are offered child care, parental leave, and shorter workdays. Services are provided for the elderly.

Each country's response to these changes, as we noted earlier, has been shaped by its own political and cultural traditions. The United States remains embroiled in a cultural war over the family; many social commentators and political leaders have promised to reverse the recent trends and restore the "traditional" family. In contrast, other Western nations, including Canada and other English-speaking countries, have responded to family change by trying to remedy the problems brought about by economic and social transformations. These countries have been spared much of the poverty and other social ills that have plagued the United States in recent decades.

Looking Ahead

The world at the beginning of the twenty-first century is vastly different from what it was at the beginning, or even the middle, of the twentieth century. Families are struggling to adapt to new realities. The countries that have been at the leading edge of family change still find themselves caught between yesterday's norms, today's new realities, and an uncertain future. As we have seen, changes in women's lives have been a pivotal factor in recent family trends. In many countries there is a considerable difference between men's and women's attitudes and expectations of one another. Even where both partners accept a more equal division of labor in the home, there is often a gap between beliefs and behavior. In no country have employers, the government, or men fully caught up to the changes in women's lives.

Families have always struggled with outside circumstances and inner conflict. Our current troubles inside and outside the family are genuine, but we should never forget that many of the most vexing issues confronting us derive from benefits of modernization few of us would be willing to give up—for example, longer, healthier lives, and the ability to choose how many children to have and when to have them.

When most people died before they reached age 50, there was no problem of a large elderly population to care for. Nor was adolescence a difficult stage of life when children worked; education was a privilege of the rich, and a person's place in society was determined by heredity rather than choice.

In short, family life is bound up with the social, economic, and cultural circumstances of particular times and places. We are no longer peasants, Puritans, pioneers, or even suburbanites in the 1950's. We face a world earlier generations could hardly imagine, and we struggle to find new ways to cope with it.

A NOTE ON *THE FAMILY*

Some family scholars have suggested that we drop the term *the family* and replace it with *families* or *family life*. The problem with *the family* is that it calls to mind the stereotyped image of the Ozzie and Harriet kind of family—two parents and their two or three minor children. But those other terms don't always work. In our own writing we use the term *the family* in much the same way we use *the economy*—a set of institutional arrangements through which particular tasks are carried out in a society. The economy deals with the production, distribution, and consumption of goods and services. The family deals with reproduction and care and support for children and adults.

References

Amato, P. R. 1994. Life span adjustment of children to their parents' divorce. *The Future of Children* 4, no. 1 (Spring).

Bane, M. J. 1976. *Here to Stay*. New York: Basic Books.

Bernard, J. 1982. *The Future of Marriage*. New York: Bantam.

Demos, J. 1986. *Past, Present, and Personal*. New York: Oxford University Press.

Emde, R. N., and R. J. Harmon, eds. 1984. *Continuities and Discontinuities in Development*. New York: Plenum Press.

Featherstone, J. 1979. Family matters. *Harvard Educational Review* 49, no. 1: 20–52.

Geertz, G. 1965. The impact of the concept of culture on the concept of man. In *New Views of the Nature of Man*, edited by J. R. Platt. Chicago: University of Chicago Press.

Harris, J. R. 1998. *The Nurture Assumption: Why Children Turn Out the Way They Do*. New York: Free Press.

Hrdy, S. B. 1999. *Mother Nature*. New York: Pantheon Books.

Inglehart, R. 1990. *Culture Shift*. Princeton, NJ: Princeton University Press.

Keller, S. 1971. Does the family have a future? *Journal of Comparative Studies*, Spring.

Macfarlane, J. W. 1964. Perspectives on personality consistency and change from the guidance study. *Vita Humana* 7: 115–126.

Mellman, A., E. Lazarus, and A. Rivlin. 1990. Family time, family values. In *Rebuilding the Nest*, edited by D. Blankenhorn, S. Bayme, and J. Elshtain. Milwaukee, WI: Family Service America.

Rossi, A. S., and P. H. Rossi. 1990. *Of Human Bonding: Parent–Child Relations across the Life Course*. Hawthorne, NY: Aldine de Gruyter.

Rubin, L. 1996. *The Transcendent Child*. New York: Basic Books.

Ryan, M. 1981. *The Cradle of the Middle Class*. New York: Cambridge University Press.

Schnaiberg, A., and S. Goldenberg. 1989. From empty nest to crowded nest: The dynamics of incompletely launched young adults. *Social Problems* 36, no. 3 (June): 251–269.

Skolnick, A. 1991. *Embattled Paradise: The American Family in an Age of Uncertainty*. New York: Basic Books.

Stephens, W. N. 1963. *The Family in Cross-Cultural Perspective*. New York: World.

Uhlenberg, P. 1980. Death and the family. *Journal of Family History* 5, no. 3: 313–320.

Veroff, J., E. Douvan, and R. A. Kulka. 1981. *The Inner American: A Self-Portrait from 1957 to 1976*. New York: Basic Books.

PART I

The Changing Family

The study of the family does not belong to any single scholarly field; genetics, physiology, archaeology, history, anthropology, sociology, psychology, and economics all touch on it. Religious and ethical authorities claim a stake in the family, and troubled individuals and families generate therapeutic demands on family scholarship. In short, the study of the family is interdisciplinary, controversial, and necessary for the formulation of social policy and practices.

Interdisciplinary subjects present characteristic problems. Each discipline has its own assumptions and views of the world, which may not directly transfer into another field. For example, some biologists and physically oriented anthropologists analyze human affairs in terms of individual motives and instincts; for them, society is a shadowy presence, serving mainly as the setting for biologically motivated individual action. Many sociologists and cultural anthropologists, in contrast, perceive the individual as an actor playing a role written by culture and society. One important school of psychology sees people neither as passive recipients of social pressures nor as creatures driven by powerful lusts, but as information processors trying to make sense of their environment. There is no easy way to reconcile such perspectives. Scientific paradigms—characteristic ways of looking at the world—determine not only what answers will be found, but also what questions will be asked. This fact has perhaps created special confusion in the study of the family.

There is the assumption that family life, so familiar a part of everyday experience, is easily understood. But familiarity may breed a sense of destiny—what we experience is transformed into the "natural."

Social scientists have been arguing for many years about how to define the family, even before the dramatic changes of the past four decades. Now the question of how to define the family has become a hot political issue. Is a mother and her child a family? A cohabiting couple? A cohabiting couple with children? A married couple without children? A grandmother who is raising her grandchildren? A gay couple? A gay couple with children?

In his article, "The Theoretical Importance of the Family," William Goode defines family as a special kind of relationship between people rather than a particular kind of household or group, such as two married parents and their children. He argues that in all known societies, and under many social conditions, people develop family-like social patterns—a "familistic package"—even when some of the traditional aspects of family are missing.

What is in this "familistic package"? Continuity is an essential element: the expectation that the relationship will continue. This makes it possible to share money and goods and offer help to the other person, knowing that in the future that person will reciprocate. Familiarity is another benefit; family members know one another and their likes and dislikes. In other words, the family is something like a mutual aid society. It helps individuals meet their multiple needs, including the need for affection and companionship, and also serves as an insurance policy in times of sickness or other troubles. Still another obstacle to understanding family life is that it is hard to see the links between the larger world outside the home and the individuals and families inside.

Several of the selections in Part One aim to show us these links. For example, Anthony Giddens argues that there is a global revolution going on in sexuality, in marriage and the family, and in how people think of themselves and their relationships. He argues that we are living through another wave of technological and economic modernization that is having a profound impact on personal life. Further, he sees a strong parallel between the ideals of a democratic society and the emerging new ideals of family relationships. For example, a good marriage is coming to be seen as a relationship between equals. Giddens recognizes that many of the changes in family life are worrisome, but we can't go back to the family patterns of an earlier time. Nor would most of us really want to. Nostalgic images of the family in earlier times typically omit the high mortality rates that prevailed before the twentieth century. Death could strike at any age, and was a constant threat to family stability.

So, how has the global revolution in marriage and family been working out in different countries? How do current American family patterns compare with those in Europe? Erikka Oinonin compares family life in Finland and Spain. She doesn't look directly at the American family, but her findings are relevant to what other researchers have found here. A major difference, however, is that other countries don't have the kind of intense political and cultural "wars" over "family values" that we have here.

Oinonin finds that Finland and Spain, like other Western European countries have experienced similar social and economic changes from the early 1960s onward. In addition, they share similar family ideologies. Both have moved from the ideal of the breadwinner-homemaker family in the early twentieth century to a more egalitarian model of marriage.

And in both countries, marriage remains "the bedrock of the family" but, at the same time it is not the only accepted form of intimate relationship. Cohabitation and same-sex partnerships, for example, are granted some legal protection in both countries, with Spain granting marriage rights to same-sex couples.

But although their family ideologies are similar, people in the two countries behave differently. For example, cohabitation rates are high in Finland and low in Spain; birth rates are higher in Finland than in other European Union countries, and have nearly "collapsed" in Spain. Oinonin offers possible explanations for these differences. She concludes that while the "traditional" male breadwinner family may be in crisis, the "new" ideal of a nuclear family in which both partners are employed most of the time is going strong.

The readings in Chapter 2 are concerned with controversies over the meaning of family in modern American society. As women increasingly participate in the paid workforce, argues Sharon Hays, they find themselves caught up in a web of cultural contradictions that remain unresolved and indeed have deepened. There is no way, she says, for contemporary women to get it "just right." Both stay-at-home and working mothers maintain an intensive commitment to motherhood, although they work it out in different ways. Women who stay at home no longer feel comfortable and fulfilled being defined by themselves and others as "mere housewives." And, working women are frequently anxious about the time away from children and the complexities of balancing parental duties with the demands of the job.

The cultural contradictions that trouble motherhood can be seen as a part of the larger "cultural war" over the family. But there are more than two sides in the family wars. Janet Z. Giele carefully draws three positions on the family: the conservative, the liberal, and the feminist. The latter, for Giele, is the most promising for developing public policies that would combine conservative and liberal perspectives. The feminist vision, she argues, appreciates both the "premodern nature of the family" with the inevitable interdependence of family and a modern, fast-changing economy.

Chapter

1

Families Past and Present

READING 1

The Theoretical Importance of the Family

William J. Goode

Through the centuries, thoughtful people have observed that the family was disintegrating. In the past several decades, this idea has become more and more common. Many analysts have reported that the family no longer performs tasks once entrusted to it—production, education, protection, for example. From these and other data we might conclude that the family is on its way out.

But almost everyone who lives out an average life span enters the married state. Most eventually have children, who will later do the same. Of the increasing number who divorce, many will hopefully or skeptically marry again. In the Western nations, a higher percentage of people marry than a century ago. Indeed, the total number of years spent within marriage by the average person is higher now than at any previous time in the history of the world. In all known societies, almost everyone lives enmeshed in a network of family rights and obligations. People are taught to accept these rules through a long period of childhood socialization. That is, people come to feel that these family patterns are both right and desirable.

At the present time, human beings appear to get as much joy and sorrow from the family as they always have, and seem as bent as ever on taking part in family life. In most of the world, the traditional family may be shaken, but the institution will probably enjoy a longer life than any nation now in existence. The family does not seem to be a powerful institution, like the military, the church, or the state, but it seems to be the most resistant to conquest, or to the efforts people make to reshape it. Any specific family may appear to be fragile or unstable, but the family system as a whole is tough and resilient.

THE FAMILY: VARIOUS VIEWS

The intense emotional meaning of family relations for almost everyone has been observed throughout history. Philosophers and social analysts have noted that any society is a structure made up of families linked together. Both travelers and anthropologists often describe the peculiarities of a given society by outlining its family relations.

The earliest moral and ethical writings of many cultures assert the significance of the family. Within those commentaries, the view is often expressed that a society loses its strength if people do not fulfill family obligations. Confucius thought that happiness and prosperity would prevail if everyone would behave "correctly" as a family member. This meant primarily that no one should fail in his filial obligations. That is, the proper relationship between ruler and subjects was like that between a father and his children. The cultural importance of the family is also emphasized in the Old Testament. The books of Exodus, Deuteronomy, Ecclesiastes, Psalms, and Proverbs, for example, proclaim the importance of obeying family rules. The earliest codified literature in India, the Rig-Veda, which dates from about the last half of the second millennium B.C., and the Law of Manu, which dates from about the beginning of the Christian era, devote much attention to the family. Poetry, plays, novels, and short stories typically seize upon family relationships as the primary focus of human passion, and their ideas and themes often grow from family conflict. Even the great epic poems of war have subthemes focusing on problems in family relations.[1]

From time to time, social analysts and philosophers have presented plans for societies that *might* be created (these are called utopias) in which new family roles (rights and obligations of individual members) are offered as solutions to traditional social problems. Plato's *Republic* is one such attempt. Plato was probably the first to urge the creation of a society in which all members, men and women alike, would have an equal opportunity to develop their talents to the utmost, and to achieve a position in society solely through merit. Since family patterns in all societies prevent selection based entirely on individual worth, to Plato's utopia the tie between parents and children would play no part, because knowledge of that link would be erased. Approved conception would take place at the same time each year at certain hymeneal festivals; children born out of season would be eliminated (along with those born defective). All children would be taken from their parents at birth and reared by specially designated people.

Experimental or utopian communities like Oneida, the Shakers, the Mormons, and modern communes have typically insisted that changes in family relations were necessary to achieve their goals. Every fundamental political upheaval since the French Revolution of 1789 has offered a program that included profound changes in family relations. Since World War II, most countries of the world have written new constitutions. In perhaps all of them, but especially in all the less developed nations, these new laws have been far more advanced than public opinion in those countries. They have aimed at creating new family patterns more in conformity with the leaders' views of equality and justice, and often antagonistic to traditional family systems. This wide range of commentary, analysis, and political action, over a period of twenty-five hundred years, suggests that throughout history we have been at least implicitly aware of the importance of family patterns as a central element in human societies.

THE CENTRAL POSITION OF THE FAMILY IN SOCIETY

In most tribal societies, kinship patterns form the major part of the whole social structure. By contrast, the family is only a small part of the social structure of modern industrial societies. It is nevertheless a key element in them, specifically linking individuals with other social institutions, such as the church, the state, or the economy. Indeed modern society, with its complex advanced technology and its highly trained bureaucracy, would collapse without the contributions of this seemingly primitive social agency. The class system, too, including its restrictions on education and opportunity, its high or low social mobility rates, and its initial social placement by birth, is founded on the family.

Most important, it is within the family that the child is first socialized to serve the needs of the society, and not only its own needs. A society will not survive unless its needs are met, such as the production and distribution of commodities, protection of the young and old or the sick and the pregnant, conformity to the law, and so on. Only if individuals are motivated to serve these needs will the society continue to operate, and the foundation for that motivation is laid by the family. Family members also participate in informal social control processes. Socialization at early ages makes most of us wish to conform, but throughout each day, both as children and as adults, we are often tempted to deviate. The formal agencies of social control (such as the police) are not enough to do more than force the extreme deviant to conform. What is needed is a set of social pressures that provide feedback to the individual whenever he or she does well or poorly and thus support internal controls as well as the controls of the formal agencies. Effectively or not, the family usually takes on this task.

The family, then, is made up of individuals, but it is also a social unit, and part of a larger social network. Families are not isolated, self-enclosed social systems; and the other institutions of society, such as the military, the church, or the school system, continually rediscover that they are not dealing with individuals, but with members of families. Even in the most industrialized and urban of societies, where it is sometimes supposed that people lead rootless and anonymous lives, most people are in continual interaction with other family members. Men and women who achieve high social position usually find that even as adults they still respond to their parents' criticisms, are still angered or hurt by a sibling's scorn. Corporations that offer substantial opportunities to rising executives often find that their proposals are turned down because of objections from family members.

So it is through the family that the society is able to elicit from the individual his or her contributions. The family, in turn, can continue to exist only if it is supported by the larger society. If these two, the smaller and the larger social system, furnish each other the conditions necessary for their survival, they must be interrelated in many important ways. Thus, the two main themes in this [reading] will be the relations among family members, and the relations between the family and the society.

PRECONCEPTIONS ABOUT THE FAMILY

The task of understanding the family presents many difficulties, and one of the greatest barriers is found in ourselves. We are likely to have strong emotions about the family. Because of our own deep involvement in family relationships, objective analysis is not easy. When we read about other types of family behavior, in other classes or societies, we are likely to feel that they are odd or improper. We are tempted to argue that this or that type of family behavior is wrong or right, rather than to analyze it. Second, although we have observed many people in some of their family behavior, usually we have had very limited experience with what goes on behind the walls of other homes. This means that our sample of observations is very narrow. It also means that for almost any generalization we create or read about, we can often find some specific experience that refutes it, or fits it. Since we feel we "already know," we may not feel motivated to look for further data against which to test generalizations.

However, many supposedly well-known beliefs about the family are not well grounded in fact. Others are only partly true and must be studied more precisely if they are to be understood. One such belief is that "children hold the family together." Despite repeated attempts to affirm it, this generalization does not seem to be very strong. A more correct view seems to be that there is a modest association between divorce and not having children, but it is mostly caused by the fact that people who do not become well adjusted, and who may for some reasons be prone to divorce, are also less likely to have children.

Another way of checking whether the findings of family sociology are obvious is to present some research findings, and ask whether it was worth the bother of discovering them since "everybody knew them all along." Consider the following set of facts. Suppose a researcher had demonstrated those facts. Was it worthwhile to carry out the study, or were the facts already known?

1. Because modern industrial society breaks down traditional family systems, one result is that the age of marriage in Western nations (which was low among farmers) has risen greatly over many generations.
2. Because of the importance of the extended family in China and India, the average size of the household has always been large, with many generations living under one roof.
3. In polygynous societies, most men have several wives, and the fertility rate is higher than in monogamous societies.

Although these statements sound plausible to many people, and impressive arguments have been presented to support them, in fact they are all false. For hundreds of years, the age at marriage among farmers in Western nations has been relatively high (25–27 years), and though it rises and falls somewhat over time, there seems to be no important trend in any particular direction. With reference to multifamily households, every survey of Chinese and Indian households has shown that even generations ago they were relatively modest in size (from four to six persons, varying by region and time period). Only under special historical circumstances will large, extended households be common. As to polygyny, the fact is that except under special circumstances, almost all men in all societies must be content with only one wife, and the fertility rate of polygynous marriages (one man married to several wives) is lower than that for monogamous marriages. Thus we see that with reference to the incorrect findings just cited, common beliefs did require testing, and they were wrong.

On the other hand, of course, many popular beliefs about how families work *are* correct. We cannot assume their correctness, however. Instead, we have to examine our observations, and make studies on our own to see how well these data fit in order to improve our understanding of the dynamics of family processes in our own or in other societies. If we emphasize the problems of obtaining facts, we should not lose sight of the central truth of any science: vast quantities of figures may be entirely meaningless, unless the search is guided by fruitful hypotheses or broad conceptions of social behavior. What we seek is organized facts, a structure of propositions, in which theory and fact illuminate one another. If we do not seek actual observation, we are engaged in blind speculation. If we seek facts without theoretical guidance, our search is random and often yields findings that have no bearing on anything. Understanding the family, then, requires the same sort of careful investigation as any other scientific endeavor.

WHY THE FAMILY IS THEORETICALLY SIGNIFICANT

Because the family is so much taken for granted, we do not often stop to consider the many traits that make it theoretically interesting. A brief consideration of certain peculiarities of the family will suggest why it is worthwhile exploring this social unit.

The family is the only social institution other than religion that is formally developed in all societies: a specific social agency is in charge of a great variety of social behaviors and activities. Some have argued that legal systems did not exist in preliterate or technologically less developed tribes or societies because there was no formally organized legislative body or judiciary. Of course, it is possible to abstract from concrete behavior the legal *aspects* of action, or the economic aspects, or the political dynamics, even when there are no explicitly labeled agencies formally in control of these areas in the society. However, kinship statuses and their responsibilities are the object of both formal and informal attention in societies at a high or a low technological level.

Family duties are the direct role responsibility of everyone in the society, with rare exceptions. Almost everyone is both born into a family and founds one of his or her own. Each individual is kin to many others. Many people, by contrast, may escape the religious duties others take for granted, or military or political burdens. Moreover, many family role responsibilities cannot usually be delegated to others, while in a work situation specialized obligations can be delegated.

Taking part in family activities has the further interesting quality that though it is not backed by the formal punishments supporting many other obligations, almost everyone takes part nonetheless. We must, for example, engage in economic or productive acts, or face starvation. We must enter the army, pay taxes, and appear before courts, or face money penalties and force. Such punishments do not usually confront the individual who does not wish to marry, or refuses to talk with his father or brother. Nevertheless, so pervasive are the social pressures, and so intertwined with indirect or direct rewards and punishments, that almost everyone conforms, or claims to conform, to family demands.

Although the family is usually thought of as an *expressive* or emotional social unit, it serves as an *instrumental* agency for the larger social structures, and all other institutions and agencies depend upon its contributions. For example, the role behavior learned within the family becomes the model or prototype for behavior required in other segments of the society. Inside the family, the content of the *socialization* process is the cultural tradition of the larger society. Families are also themselves *economic* units with respect to production and allocation. With reference to *social control*, each person's total range of behavior, and how his or her time and energies are budgeted, is more easily visible to family members than to outsiders. They can evaluate how the individual is allocating his or her time and money, and how well he or she is carrying out various duties. Consequently, the family acts as a source of pressure on the individual to adjust—to work harder and play less, or go to church less and study more. In all these ways, the family is partly an instrument or agent of the larger society. If it fails to perform adequately, the goals of the larger society may not be effectively achieved.

Perhaps more interesting theoretically is the fact that the various *tasks of the family are all separable* from one another, but in fact are not separated in almost all known family systems. We shall discuss these functions or tasks in various contexts in this book, so no great elaboration is needed at this point. Here are some of the contributions of the family to the larger society: reproduction of young, physical maintenance of family members, social placement of the child, socialization, and social control.

Let us consider how these activities could be separated. For example, the mother could send her child to be fed in a neighborhood mess hall, and of course some harassed mothers do send their children to buy lunch in a local snack bar. Those who give birth to a child need not socialize the child. They might send the child to specialists, and indeed specialists do take more responsibility for this task as the child grows older. Parents might, as some eugenicists have suggested, be selected for their breeding qualities, but these might not include any great talent for training the young. Status placement might be accomplished by random drawing of lots, by IQ tests or periodic examinations in physical and intellectual skills, or by popularity polls. This assignment of children to various social positions could be done without regard to an individual's parents, those who socialized or fed the child, or others who might supervise the child's daily behavior.

Separations of this kind have been suggested from time to time, and a few hesitant attempts have been made here and there in the world to put them into operation. However, three conclusions relevant to this kind of division can be drawn: (1) In all known societies, the *ideal* (with certain qualifications to be noted) is that the family be entrusted with all these functions. (2) When one or more family tasks are entrusted to another agency by a revolutionary or utopian society, the change can be made only with the support of much ideological fervor, and usually political pressure as well. (3) These experiments are also characterized by a gradual return to the more traditional type of family. In both the Israeli *kibbutzim* and the Russian experiments in relieving parents of child care, the ideal of completely communal living was once urged. Husband and wife were to have only a personal and emotional tie with one another: divorce would be easy. The children were to see their parents at regular intervals but look to their nursery attendants and mother surrogates for affection and direction during work hours. Each individual was to contribute his or her best skills to the cooperative unit without regard to family ties or sex status (there would be few or no "female" or "male" tasks). That ideal was attempted in a modest way, but behavior gradually dropped away from the ideal. The only other country in which the pattern has been attempted on a large scale is China. Already Chinese communes have retreated from their high ambitions, following the path of the *kibbutz* and the Russian *kolkhoz*.

Various factors contribute to these deviations from attempts to create a new type of family, and the two most important sets of pressures cannot easily be separated from each other. First is the problem, also noted by Plato, that individuals who develop their own attitudes and behaviors in the usual Western (European and European-based) family system do not easily adjust to the communal "family" even when they believe it is the right way. The second is the likelihood that when the family is radically changed, the various relations between it and the larger society are changed. New strains are created, demanding new kinds of adjustments on the part of the individuals in the society. Perhaps the planners must develop somewhat different agencies, or a different blueprint, to transform the family.

These comments have nothing to do with "capitalism" in its current political and economic argument with "communism." They merely describe the historical fact that though various experiments in separating the major functions of the family from one another have been conducted, none of these evolved from a previously existing family system. In addition, the several modern important attempts at such a separation, including the smaller communes that were created in the United States during the 1960s and 1970s, mostly exhibit a common pattern, a movement *away* from the utopian blueprint of separating the various family activities and giving each of them to a different social unit.

It is possible that some of these activities (meals) can be more easily separated than others; or that some family systems (for example, matrilineal systems) might lend themselves to such a separation more easily than others. On the other hand, we have to begin with the data that are now available. Even cautiously interpreted, they suggest that the family is a rather stable institution. On the other hand, we have not yet analyzed what this particular institution is. In the next section we discuss this question.

DEFINING THE FAMILY: A MATTER OF MORE OR LESS

Since thousands of publications have presented research findings on the family, one might suppose that there must be agreement on what this social unit is. In fact, sociologists and anthropologists have argued for decades about how to define it. Indeed, creating a clear, formal definition of any object of study is sometimes more difficult than making a study of that object. If we use a *concrete* definition, and assert that "a family is a social unit made up of father, mother, and children," then only about 35 percent of all U.S. households can be classed as a family. Much of the research on the family would have to exclude a majority of residential units. In addition, in some societies, one wife may be married to several husbands, or one husband to several wives. The definition would exclude such units. In a few societies there have been "families" in which the "husband" was a woman; and in some, certain "husbands" were not expected to live with their "wives." In the United States, millions of households contain at least one child, but only one parent. In a few communes, every adult male is married to all other adult females. That is, there are many kinds of social units that seem to be like a family, but do not fit almost any concrete definition that we might formulate.

We can escape such criticisms in part by claiming that most adults eventually go through such a *phase* of family life; that is, almost all men and women in the United States marry at some time during their lives, and most of them eventually have children. Nevertheless, analysis of the family would be much thinner if we focused only on that one kind of household. In ordinary language usage, people are most likely to agree that a social unit made up of father, mother, and child or children is a genuine family. They will begin to disagree more and more, as one or more of those persons or social roles is missing. Few people would agree that, at the other extremes, a household with only a single person in it is a family. Far more would think of a household as a family if it comprised a widow and her several children. Most people would agree that a husband-wife household is a family if they have children, even if their children are now living somewhere else. However, many would not be willing to class a childless couple as a family, especially if that couple planned never to have children. Very few people would be willing to accept a homosexual couple as a family.

What can we learn from such ordinary language usage? First, that *family* is not a single thing, to be captured by a neat verbal formula. Second, many social units can be thought of as "more or less" families, as they are more or less similar to the traditional type of family. Third, much of this graded similarity can be traced to the different kinds of role relations to be found in that traditional unit. Doubtless the following list is not comprehensive, but it includes most of those relationships: (1) At least two adult persons of opposite sex reside together. (2) They engage in some kind of division of labor; that is, they do not both perform exactly the same tasks. (3) They engage in many types of economic and social exchanges; that is, they do things for one another. (4) They share many things in common, such as food, sex, residence, and both goods and social activities. (5) The adults have parental relations with their children, as their children have filial relations with them; the parents have some authority over their children, and both share with one another, while also assuming some obligation for protection, cooperation, and nurturance. (6) There are sibling relations among the children themselves, with, once more, a range of obligations to share, protect, and help one another. When all these conditions exist, few people would deny that the unit is a family. As we consider households in which more are missing, a larger number of people would express some doubt as to whether it really is a family. Thus, if two adults live together, but do nothing for each other, few people would agree that it is a family. If they do not even live together, fewer still would call the couple a family.

Individuals create all sorts of relations with each other, but others are more or less likely to view them as a family to the extent that their continuing social relations exhibit some or all of the role patterns noted above. Most important for our understanding of the family is that in all known societies, and under a wide range of social conditions, some kinds of familistic living arrangements seem to emerge, with some or all of these traits. These arrangements can emerge in prisons (with homosexual couples as units), under the disorganized conditions of revolution, conquest, or epidemic; or even when political attempts are made to reduce the importance of the family, and instead to press people to live in a more communal fashion. That is, people create and re-create some forms of familistic social patterns even when some of those traditional elements are missing.

This raises the inevitable question: Why does this happen? Why do people continue to form familistic relations, even when they are not convinced that it is the ideal social arrangement? Why is *this* and not some *other* social pattern so widespread? Of course, this is not an argument for the *universality* of the conjugal family. Many other kinds of relations between individuals are created. Nevertheless, some approximation of these familistic relationships do continue to occur in the face of many alternative temptations and opportunities as well as counterpressures. Unless we are willing to assert that people are irrational, we must conclude that these relationships must offer some *advantages*. What are they?

ADVANTAGES OF THE "FAMILISTIC PACKAGE"

We suppose that the most fundamental set of advantages is found in the division of labor and the resulting possibility of social exchanges between husband and wife (or members of a homosexual couple), as well as between children and parents. This includes not only economic goods, but help, nurturance, protection, and affection. It is often forgotten that the modern domestic household is very much an *economic* unit even if it is no longer a farming unit. People are actually producing goods and services for one another. They are buying objects in one place, and transporting them to the household. They are transforming food into meals. They are engaged in cleaning, mowing lawns, repairing, transporting, counseling—a wide array of services that would have to be paid for in money if some member of the family did not do them.

Families of all types also enjoy some small economies of scale. When there are two or more members of the household, various kinds of activities can be done almost as easily for everyone as for a single person; it is almost as easy to prepare one meal for three or four people as it is to prepare a similar meal for one person. Thus, the cost of a meal is less per person within a family. Families can cooperate to achieve what an individual cannot, from building a mountain cabin to creating a certain style of life. Help from all members will make it much easier to achieve that goal than it would be for one person.

All the historic forms of the family that we know, including communal group marriages, are also attractive because they offer *continuity*. Thus, whatever the members produce together, they expect to be able to enjoy together later. Continuity has several implications. One is that members do not have to bear the costs of continually searching for new partners, or for new members who might be "better" at various family tasks. In addition, husband and wife, as well as children, enjoy a much longer line of social credit than they would have if they were making exchanges with people outside the family. This means that an individual can give more at one time to someone in the family, knowing that in the longer run this will not be a loss: the other person will remain long enough to reciprocate at some point, or perhaps still another member will offer help at a later time.

Next, the familistic mode of living offers several of the advantages of any informal group.[2] It exhibits, for example, a very short line of communication; everyone is close by, and members need not communicate through intermediaries. Thus they can respond quickly in case of need. A short line of communication makes cooperation much easier. Second, everyone has many idiosyncratic needs and wishes. In day to day interaction with outsiders, we need not adjust to these very much, and they may be a nuisance; others, in turn, are likely not to adjust to our own idiosyncracies. However, within the familistic mode of social interaction, people learn what each other's idiosyncratic needs are. Learning such needs can and does make life together somewhat more attractive because adjusting to them may not be a great burden, but does give pleasure to the other. These include such trivia as how strong the tea or coffee should be, how much talk there will be at meals, sleep and work schedules, levels of noise, and so on. Of course with that knowledge we can more easily make others miserable, too, if we wish to do so.

Domestic tasks typically do not require high expertise, and as a consequence most members of the family can learn to do them eventually. Because they do learn, members derive many benefits from one another, without having to go outside the family unit. Again, this makes a familistic mode of living more attractive than it would be otherwise. In addition, with reference to many such tasks, there are no outside experts anyway (throughout most of world history, there have been no experts in childrearing, taking care of small cuts or bruises, murmuring consoling words in response to some distress, and so on). That is, the tasks within a family setting are likely to be tasks at which insiders are at least as good as outsiders, and typically better.

No other social institutions offer this range of complementarities, sharing, and closely linked, interwoven advantages. The closest possible exception might be some ascribed, ritual friendships in a few societies, but even these do not offer the range of exchanges that are to be found in the familistic processes.

We have focused on advantages that the *members* of families obtain from living under this type of arrangement. However, when we survey the wide range of family patterns in hundreds of societies, we are struck by the fact that this social unit is strongly supported by *outsiders*—that is, members of the larger society.

It is supported by a structure of norms, values, laws, and a wide range of social pressures. More concretely, other members of the society believe such units are necessary, and they are concerned about how people discharge their obligations within the family. They punish members of the family who do not conform to ideal behavior, and praise those who do conform. These intrusions are not simply whimsical, or a matter of oppression. Other members of the society do in fact have a stake in how families discharge their various tasks. More broadly, it is widely believed that the collective needs of the whole society are served by some of the activities individual families carry out. In short, it is characteristic of the varieties of the family that participants on an average enjoy more, and gain more comfort, pleasure, or advantage from being in a familistic arrangement than from living alone; and *other* members of the society view that arrangement as contributing in some measure to the survival of the society itself. Members of societies have usually supposed it important for most *other* individuals to form families, to rear children, to create the next generation, to support and help each other—whether or not individual members of specific families do in fact feel they gain real advantages from living in a familistic arrangement. For example, over many centuries, people opposed legal divorces, whether or not they themselves were happily married, and with little regard for the marital happiness of others.

This view of what makes up the "familistic social package" explains several kinds of widely observable social behavior. One is that people experiment with different kinds of arrangements, often guided by a new philosophy of how people ought to live. They do so because their own needs have not been adequately fulfilled in the traditional modes of family arrangements available to them in their own society. Since other people have a stake in the kinds of familistic arrangements people make, we can also expect that when some individuals or groups attempt to change or experiment with the established system, various members of the society will object, and may even persecute them for it. We can also see why it is that even in a high-divorce society such as our own, where millions of people have been dissatisfied or hurt by their marriages and their divorces, they nevertheless move back into a marital arrangement. That is, after examining various alternatives, the familistic social package still seems to offer a broader set of personal advantages, and the outside society supports that move. And, as noted earlier, even when there are strong political pressures to create new social units that give far less support for the individual family, as in China, Russia, and the Israeli *kibbutzim*, we can expect that people will continue to drift back toward some kind of familistic arrangement.

A SOCIOLOGICAL APPROACH TO FAMILY RESEARCH

The unusual traits the family exhibits as a type of social subsystem require that some attention be paid to the analytic approach to be used in studying it. First, neither ideal nor reality can be excluded from our attention. It would, for example, be naive to suppose that because some 40 percent of all U.S. couples now marrying will eventually divorce, they do not cherish the ideal of remaining married to one person. Contemporary estimates suggest that about half of all married men engage in extramarital intercourse at some time, but public opinion surveys report that a large majority of both men and women in the

United States, even in these permissive times, approve of the ideal of faithfulness. On a more personal level, every reader of these lines has lied at some time, but nevertheless most believe in the ideal of telling the truth.

A sociologist ascertains the ideals of family systems partly because they are a rough guide to behavior. Knowing that people prefer to have their sons and daughters marry at least at the same class level, we can expect them to try to control their children's mate choices if they can do so. We can also specify some of the conditions under which they will have a greater or lesser success in reaching that goal. We also know that when a person violates the ideal, he or she is likely to conceal the violation if possible. If that is not possible, people will try to find some excuse for the violation, and are likely to be embarrassed if others find out about it.

The sociology of the family cannot confine itself only to contemporary urban (or suburban) American life. Conclusions of any substantial validity or scope must include data from other societies, whether these are past or present, industrial or nonindustrial, Asian or European. Data from the historical past, such as Periclean Athens or imperial Rome, are not often used because no sociologically adequate account of their family systems has as yet been written.[3] On the other hand, the last two decades have seen the appearance of many studies about family systems in various European cities of the last five centuries.

The study of customs and beliefs from the past yields a better understanding of the possible range of social behavior. Thereby, we are led to deny or at least to qualify a finding that might be correct if limited only to modern American life (such as the rise in divorce rates over several decades). The use of data from tribal societies of the past or present helps us in testing conclusions about family systems that are not found at all in Western society, such as matrilineal systems or polygyny. Or, an apparently simple relationship may take a different form in other societies. For example, in the United States most first marriages are based on a love relationship (whatever else they may be based on), and people are reluctant to admit that they have married someone with whom they were not in love. By contrast, though people fall in love in other societies, love may play a small or a large part in the marriage system. . . .

It is possible to study almost any phenomenon from a wide range of viewpoints. We may study the economic aspects of family behavior, or we may confine ourselves to the biological factors in family patterns. A full analysis of any concrete object is impossible. Everything can be analyzed from many vantage points, each of them yielding a somewhat different but still limited picture. Everything is infinitely complex. Each science limits its perspective to the range of processes that it considers important. Each such approach has its own justification. Here we examine the family mainly from a sociological perspective.

The sociological approach focuses on the family as a social institution, the peculiar and unique quality of family interaction as *social.* For example, family systems exhibit the characteristics of legitimacy and authority, which are not biological categories at all. The values and the prescribed behavior to be found in a family, or the rights and duties of family statuses such as father or daughter, are not psychological categories. They are peculiar to the theoretical approach of sociology. Personality theory is not very useful in explaining the particular position of the family in Chinese and Japanese social structures, although it may help us understand how individuals respond emotionally to those rights and obligations. If we use a consistently sociological approach, we will miss some important information about concrete family interaction. The possible gain when we stay on one theoretical level may be the achievement of some increased systematization, and some greater rigor.

At a minimum, however, when an analyst moves from the sociological to the psychological level of theory, he or she ought at least to be conscious of it. If the investigation turns to the impact of biological or psychological factors on the family, they should be examined with reference to their *social* meaning. For example, interracial marriage appears to be of little biological significance, but it has much social impact on those who take part in such a marriage. A sociologist who studies the family is not likely to be an expert in the *psychodynamics* of mental disease, but is interested in the effect of mental disease on the social relations in a particular family or type of family, or in the adjustment different family types make to it.

Notes

1. See in this connection Nicholas Tavuchis and William J. Goode (eds.), *The Family through Literature* (Oxford University Press, 1973).
2. For further comparisons of bureaucracy and informal groups, see Eugene Litwak, "Technical Innovation and Theoretical Functions of Primary Groups and Bureaucratic Structures," *American Journal of Sociology, 73* (1968), 468–481.
3. However, Keith Hopkins has published several specialized studies on various aspects of Roman families. See his *Conquerors and Slaves* (Cambridge University Press, 1978).

READING 2

The Global Revolution in Family and Personal Life

Anthony Giddens

Among all the changes going on today, none are more important than those happening in our personal lives—in sexuality, emotional life, marriage and the family. There is a global revolution going on in how we think of ourselves and how we form ties and connections with others. It is a revolution advancing unevenly in different regions and cultures, with many resistances.

As with other aspects of the runaway world, we don't know what the ratio of advantages and anxieties will turn out to be. In some ways, these are the most difficult and disturbing transformations of all. Most of us can tune out from larger problems for much of the time. We can't opt out, however, from the swirl of change reaching right into the heart of our emotional lives.

There are few countries in the world where there isn't intense discussion about sexual equality, the regulation of sexuality and the future of the family. And where there isn't open debate, this is mostly because it is actively repressed by authoritarian governments or fundamentalist groups. In many cases, these controversies are national or local—as are the social and political reactions to them. Politicians and pressure groups will suggest that if only family policy were modified, if only divorce were made harder or easier to get in their particular country, solutions to our problems could readily be found.

But the changes affecting the personal and emotional spheres go far beyond the borders of any particular country, even one as large as the United States. We find the same issues almost everywhere, differing only in degree and according to the cultural context in which they take place.

In China, for example, the state is considering making divorce more difficult. In the aftermath of the Cultural Revolution, very liberal marriage laws were passed. Marriage is a working contract, that can be dissolved, I quote: "when husband and wife both desire it."

Even if one partner objects, divorce can be granted when "mutual affection" has gone from the marriage. Only a two week wait is required, after which the two pay $4 and are henceforth independent. The Chinese divorce rate is still low as compared with Western countries, but it is rising rapidly—as is true in the other developing Asian societies. In Chinese cities, not only divorce, but cohabitation is becoming more frequent.

In the vast Chinese countryside, by contrast, everything is different. Marriage and the family are much more traditional—in spite of the official policy of limiting childbirth through a mixture of incentives and punishment. Marriage is an arrangement between two families, fixed by the parents rather than the individuals concerned.

A recent study in the province of Gansu, which has only a low level of economic development, found that 60% of marriages are still arranged by parents. As a Chinese saying has it: "meet once, nod your head and marry." There is a twist in the tail in modernising China. Many of those currently divorcing in the urban centres were married in the traditional manner in the country.

In China there is much talk of protecting the family. In many Western countries the debate is even more shrill. The family is a site for the struggles between tradition and modernity, but also a metaphor for them. There is perhaps more nostalgia surrounding the lost haven of the family than for any other institution with its roots in the past. Politicians and activists routinely diagnose the breakdown of family life and call for a return to the traditional family.

Now the "traditional family" is very much a catch-all category. There have been many different types of family and kinship systems in different societies and cultures. The Chinese family, for instance, was always distinct from family forms in the West. Arranged marriage was never as common in most European countries, as in China, or India. Yet the family in non-modern cultures did, and does, have some features found more or less everywhere.

The traditional family was above all an economic unit. Agricultural production normally involved the whole family group, while among the gentry and aristocracy, transmission of property was the main basis of marriage. In mediaeval Europe, marriage was not contracted on the basis of sexual love, nor was it regarded as a place where such love should flourish. As the French historian, Georges Duby, puts it, marriage in the middle ages was not to involve "frivolity, passion, or fantasy."

The inequality of men and women was intrinsic to the traditional family. I don't think one could overstate the importance of this. In Europe, women were the property of their husbands or fathers—chattels as defined in law.

In the traditional family, it wasn't only women who lacked rights—children did too. The idea of enshrining children's rights in law is in historical terms relatively recent. In premodern periods, as in traditional cultures today, children weren't reared for their own sake, or for the satisfaction of the parents. One could almost say that children weren't recognised as individuals.

It wasn't that parents didn't love their children, but they cared about them more for the contribution they made to the common economic task than for themselves. Moreover, the death rate of children was frightening. In Colonial America nearly one in four infants died in their first year. Almost 50% didn't live to age 10.

Except for certain courtly or elite groups, in the traditional family sexuality was always dominated by reproduction. This was a matter of tradition and nature combined. The absence of effective contraception meant that for most women sexuality was inevitably closely connected with childbirth. In many traditional cultures, including in Western Europe up to the threshold of the 20th Century, a woman might have 10 or more pregnancies during the course of her life.

Sexuality was regulated by the idea of female virtue. The sexual double standard is often thought of as a creation of the Victorian period. In fact, in one version or another it was central to almost all non-modern societies. It involved a dualistic view of female sexuality—a clear cut division between the virtuous woman on the one hand and the libertine on the other.

Sexual promiscuity in many cultures has been taken as a positive defining feature of masculinity. James Bond is, or was, admired for his sexual as well as his physical heroism. Sexually adventurous women, by contrast, have nearly always been beyond the pale, no matter how much influence the mistresses of some prominent figures might have achieved.

Attitudes towards homosexuality were also governed by a mix of tradition and nature. Anthropological surveys show that homosexuality—or male homosexuality at any rate—has been tolerated, or openly approved of, in more cultures than it has been outlawed.

Those societies that have been hostile to homosexuality have usually condemned it as specifically unnatural. Western attitudes have been more extreme than most; less than half a century ago homosexuality was still widely regarded as a perversion and written up as such in manuals of psychiatry.

Antagonism towards homosexuality is still widespread and the dualistic view of women continues to be held by many—of both sexes. But over the past few decades the main elements of people's sexual lives in the West have changed in an absolutely basic way. The separation of sexuality from reproduction is in principle complete. Sexuality is for the first time something to be discovered, moulded, altered. Sexuality, which used to be defined so strictly in relation to marriage and legitimacy, now has little connection to them at all. We should see the increasing acceptance of homosexuality not just as a tribute to liberal tolerance. It is a logical outcome of the severance of sexuality from reproduction. Sexuality which has no content is by definition no longer dominated by heterosexuality.

What most of its defenders in Western countries call the traditional family was in fact a late, transitional phase in family development in the 1950's. This was a time at which the proportion of women out at work was still relatively low and when it was still difficult, especially for women, to obtain divorce without stigma. On the other hand, men and women by this time were more equal than they had been previously, both in fact and in law. The family had ceased to be an economic entity and the idea of romantic love as basis for marriage had replaced marriage as an economic contract.

Since then, the family has changed much further. The details vary from society to society, but the same trends are visible almost everywhere in the industrialised world. Only a minority of people now live in what might be called the standard 1950's family—both parents living together with their children of the marriage, where the mother is a full time housewife, and the father the breadwinner. In some countries, more than a third of all births happen outside wedlock, while the proportion of people living alone has gone up steeply and looks likely to rise even more.

In most societies, like the U.S., marriage remains popular—the U.S. has aptly been called a high divorce, high marriage society. In Scandinavia, on the other hand, a large proportion of people living together, including where children are involved, remain unmarried. Moreover, up to a quarter of women aged between 18 and 35 in the U.S. and Europe say they do not intend to have children—and they appear to mean it.

Of course in all countries older family forms continue to exist. In the U.S., many people, recent immigrants particularly, still live according to traditional values. Most family life, however, has been transformed by the rise of the couple and coupledom. Marriage and the family have become what I termed in an earlier lecture shell institutions. They are still called the same, but inside their basic character has changed.

In the traditional family, the married couple was only one part, and often not the main part, of the family system. Ties with children and other relatives tended to be equally or even more important in the day to day conduct of social life. Today the couple, married or unmarried, is at the core of what the family is. The couple came to be at the centre of family life as the economic role of the family dwindled and love, or love plus sexual attraction, became the basis of forming marriage ties.

A couple once constituted has its own exclusive history, its own biography. It is a unit based upon emotional communication or intimacy. The idea of intimacy, like so many other familiar notions I've discussed in these lectures, sounds old but in fact is very new. Marriage was never in the past based upon intimacy—emotional communication. No doubt this was important to a good marriage but it was not the foundation of it. For the couple, it is. Communication is the means of establishing the tie in the first place and it is the chief rationale for its continuation.

We should recognise what a major transition this is. "Coupling" and "uncoupling" provide a more accurate description of the arena of personal life now than do "marriage and the family." A more important question for us than "are you married?" is "how good is your relationship?"

The idea of a relationship is also surprisingly recent. Only 30 or so years ago, no one spoke of "relationships." They didn't need to, nor did they need to speak in terms of intimacy and commitment. Marriage at that time was the commitment, as the existence of shotgun marriages bore witness. While statistically marriage is still the normal condition, for most people its meaning has more or less completely changed. Marriage signifies that a couple is in a stable relationship, and may indeed promote that stability, since it makes a public declaration of commitment. However, marriage is no longer the chief defining basis of coupledom.

The position of children in all this is interesting and somewhat paradoxical. Our attitudes towards children and their protection have altered radically over the past several generations. We prize children so much partly because they have become so much rarer, and partly because the decision to have a child is very different from what it was for previous generations. In the traditional family, children were an economic benefit. Today in Western countries a child, on the contrary, puts a large financial burden on the parents. Having a child is more of a distinct and specific decision than it used to be, and it is a decision guided by psychological and emotional needs. The worries we have about the effects of divorce upon children, and the existence of many fatherless families, have to be understood against the background of our much higher expectations about how children should be cared for and protected.

There are three areas in which emotional communication, and therefore intimacy, are replacing the old ties that used to bind together people's personal lives—in sexual and love relations, parent-child relations and in friendship.

To analyse these, I want to use the idea of what I call the "pure relationship." I mean by this a relationship based upon emotional communication, where the rewards derived from such communication are the main basis for the relationship to continue.

I don't mean a sexually pure relationship. Also I don't mean anything that exists in reality. I'm talking of an abstract idea that helps us understand changes going on in the world. Each of the three areas just mentioned—sexual relationships, parent-child relations and friendship—is tending to approximate to this model. Emotional communication or intimacy, in other words, are becoming the key to what they are all about.

The pure relationship has quite different dynamics from more traditional social ties. It depends upon processes of active trust—opening oneself up to the other. Self-disclosure is the basic condition of intimacy.

The pure relationship is also implicitly democratic. When I was originally working on the study of intimate relationships, I read a great deal of therapeutic and self-help literature on the subject. I was struck by something I don't believe has been widely noticed or remarked upon. If one looks at how a therapist sees a good relationship—in any of the three spheres just mentioned—it is striking how direct a parallel there is with public democracy.

A good relationship, of course, is an ideal—most ordinary relationships don't come even close. I'm not suggesting that our relations with spouses, lovers, children or friends aren't often messy, conflictful and unsatisfying. But the principles of public democracy are ideals too, that also often stand at some large distance from reality.

A good relationship is a relationship of equals, where each party has equal rights and obligations. In such a relationship, each person has respect, and wants the best, for the other. The pure relationship is based upon communication, so that understanding the other person's point of view is essential.

Talk, or dialogue, are the basis of making the relationship work. Relationships function best if people don't hide too much from each other—there has to be mutual trust. And trust has to be worked at, it can't just be taken for granted.

Finally, a good relationship is one free from arbitrary power, coercion or violence.

Every one of these qualities conforms to the values of democratic politics. In a democracy, all are in principle equal, and with equality of rights and responsibilities comes mutual respect. Open dialogue is a core property of democracy. Democratic systems substitute open discussion of issues—a public space of dialogue—for authoritarian power, or for the sedimented power of tradition. No democracy can work without trust. And democracy is undermined if it gives way to authoritarianism or violence.

When we apply these principles—as ideals, I would stress again—to relationships, we are talking of something very important—the possible emergence of what I shall call, a democracy of the emotions in everyday life. A democracy of the emotions, it seems to me, is as important as public democracy in improving the quality of our lives.

This holds as much in parent-child relations as in other areas. These can't, and shouldn't, be materially equal. Parents must have authority over children, in everyone's interests. Yet they should presume an in-principle equality. In a democratic family, the authority of parents should be based upon an implicit contract. The parent in effect says to the child: "If you were an adult, and knew what I know, you would agree that what I ask you to do is legitimate."

Children in traditional families were—and are—supposed to be seen and not heard. Many parents, perhaps despairing of their children's rebelliousness, would dearly like to resurrect that rule. But there isn't any going back to it, nor should there be. In a democracy of the emotions, children can and should be able to answer back.

An emotional democracy doesn't imply lack of discipline, or absence of authority. It simply seeks to put them on a different footing.

Something very similar happened in the public sphere, when democracy began to replace arbitrary government and the rule of force. And like public democracy the democratic family must be anchored in a stable, yet open, civil society. If I may coin a phrase—"It takes a village."

A democracy of the emotions would draw no distinctions of principle between heterosexual and same-sex relationships. Gays, rather than heterosexuals, have actually been pioneers in discovering the new world of relationships and exploring its possibilities. They have had to be, because when homosexuality came out of the closet, gays weren't able to depend upon the normal supports of traditional marriage. They have had to be innovators, often in a hostile environment.

To speak of fostering an emotional democracy doesn't mean being weak about family duties, or about public policy towards the family. Democracy, after all, means the acceptance of obligations, as well as rights sanctioned in law. The protection of children has to be the primary feature of legislation and public policy. Parents should be legally obliged to provide for their children until adulthood, no matter what living arrangements they enter into. Marriage is no longer an economic institution, yet as a ritual commitment it can help stabilise otherwise fragile relationships. If this applies to heterosexual relationships, I don't see why it shouldn't apply to homosexual ones too.

There are many questions to be asked of all this—too many to answer in a short lecture. I have concentrated mainly upon trends affecting the family in Western countries. What about areas where the traditional family remains largely intact, as in the example of China with which I began? Will the changes observed in the West become more and more global?

I think they will—indeed that they are. It isn't a question of whether existing forms of the traditional family will become modified, but when and how. I would venture even further. What I have described as an emerging democracy of the emotions is on the front line in the struggle between cosmopolitanism and fundamentalism that I described in the last lecture. Equality of the sexes, and the sexual freedom of women, which are incompatible with the traditional family, are anathema to fundamentalist groups. Opposition to them, indeed, is one of the defining features of religious fundamentalism across the world.

There is plenty to be worried about in the state of the family, in Western countries and elsewhere. It is just as mistaken to say that every family form is as good as any other, as to argue that the decline of the traditional family is a disaster.

I would turn the argument of the political and fundamentalist right on its head. The persistence of the traditional family—or aspects of it—in many parts of the world is more worrisome than its decline. For what are the most important forces promoting democracy and economic development in poorer countries? Well, they are the equality and education of women. And what must be changed to make these possible? Most importantly, what must be changed is the traditional family.

In conclusion, I should emphasise that sexual equality is not just a core principle of democracy. It is also relevant to happiness and fulfilment.

Many of the changes happening to the family are problematic and difficult. But surveys in the U.S. and Europe show that few want to go back to traditional male and female roles, much less to legally defined inequality.

If ever I were tempted to think that the traditional family might be best after all, I remember what my great aunt said. She must have had one of the longest marriages of anyone. She married young, and was with her husband for over 60 years. She once confided to me that she had been deeply unhappy with him the whole of that time. In her day there was no escape.

READING 3

Family in Finland and Spain: The Focal Findings

Erikka Oinonin

AMBIGUOUS FAMILY IDEOLOGIES

The analysis of Finnish and Spanish families demonstrates that parallel social changes have resulted in congruent family ideologies, on the one hand, and different patterns of family formation and fertility, on the other. To start with the family ideology, the basic socially shared and upheld definition of the family is analogous in Finland and Spain and it has evolved in the same direction although at different paces. In the early 20th century and before, the ideal family was based on an indissoluble marriage and the purpose of the marriage was procreation and socializing offspring. Thus marriage and family were inseparable. The family ideology endorsed the hierarchical male breadwinner/female homemaker family model, although more vigorously and longer in Spain than in Finland. In the course of the latter part of the 20th century, egalitarianism between the genders (and generations) and the notion of shared spheres became the leading principles.

Considering the present-day ideas of what the family is or ought to be, the family ideologies in both countries are ambiguous. On the one hand, the family ideology prescribed and maintained by civil and social legislation and policies is inclined towards family pluralism. Divorces are granted in both countries. In Finland, social legislation and policies treat married and non-married couples equally. In parts of Spain, heterosexual cohabiting couples have a legal status similar to that of married ones even though cohabitation is rare, and the national law grants same-sex couples the right to marry and adopt children. On the other hand, The Family composed of a heterosexual married couple and their children is still considered to be the 'normal' and 'proper' family, which is the bedrock of the society. In legal terms, marriage is the best-protected form of the couple relationship in both countries. The societal endorsement of the heterosexual conjugal nuclear family as The Family in both societies in question is reflected in the laws on registered couples, which in neither of the countries give adoption rights to same-sex couples. Furthermore, in Finland, there is no specific law in civil legislation that regulates heterosexual cohabitation even though it is common.

Something has changed, though, in the 'conservative' conception of The Family. Unlike before, marriage and family are separate institutions, as the definition of the functions and purpose of marriage has changed from procreation to the production of security, affection and emotional satisfaction. Nowadays, the couple relationship is an intrinsic value in itself. The elevation of the couple as well as the legal and social recognition of divorce, cohabitation and same-sex unions undermines the supremacy of marriage as a form of intimate relationship. But, although it is accepted to live in an intimate relationship outside marriage, being a family is still very much related to marriage; people tend to marry when having children is topical or, like often is the case in Finland, when the child is born. According to people's opinions and public discourses in both countries, children are considered the qualifiers of the family; a couple is not considered to be a complete family without a child.

MARRIAGE: THE BEDROCK OF THE FAMILY

Although marriage is no longer the only accepted form of intimate relationship, the alternatives have not necessarily debilitated its role as the bedrock of the family. The fact that no specific national law in civil legislation regulating heterosexual cohabitation exists in either of the countries may be interpreted as an implicit means of the society to encourage opposite-sex couples to contract marriage and thus to affirm the role of marriage as the foundation of the family. Furthermore, the fact that the possibility of same-sex marriage is under discussion in the first place and that in some countries, like in Spain, marriage is available for all regardless of their sexual orientation signals the enduring importance of marriage as an institution. In his study on same-sex partnerships in Europe and the United States, Yuval Merin (2002) points out that the number of registrations of same-sex unions is low compared to the number of opposite-sex marriages even in those countries that were the first to provide comprehensive legal recognition of same-sex partnerships, such as Denmark, Norway, Sweden and the Netherlands. This unpopularity indicates that registered partnership is regarded as 'second-class marriage'.

Merin (2002, p. 275) refers to a Dutch survey according to which 80 per cent of the same-sex couples who made use of the registered partnership before same-sex marriage became an option would have chosen marriage had that been an available option at the time, and a large majority said they would like to convert their registered partnership into marriage when it is possible. In fact, many Dutch same-sex partners have done so since same-sex marriage became available. This indicates that marriage is perceived as an institution with more significance and weight than a registered partnership. Although granting the marriage right to same-sex couples has its origins in human rights issues and in demands of equality between the majority and minority, it is clearly not only a question about equal rights but also of the cultural and social significance of marriage as an institution.

Even though European societies are little by little coming to terms with same-sex partnerships, registered and even married, they are not willing to grant parenting rights equal to opposite-sex couples, with the exception of married same-sex couples in Spain. The restriction of homosexuals' opportunities to form families with children reinforces the distinction between marriage or other types of intimate couple relationships and parenthood. In addition, it reflects the deeply rooted idea of 'The Family', which is composed of a man and a woman and their children.

PARALLEL CHANGES, DIFFERENT PATTERNS

The considerably similar social developments in Finland and Spain during the period from the early 1960s onwards have resulted in both parallel changes in the family and different patterns of family formation and fertility.

First, both countries have followed the trend referred to as the second demographic transition, although Spain has lagged behind the 'schedule'.* Both Finns and Spaniards postpone the first marriage and child-bearing longer than before. Marriage rates in both countries have fallen practically at the same pace, coming to an equally low level. Consequently, one would expect that cohabitation and, thus, births outside marriage must be common. The expectation holds true in the case of Finland but not in the case of Spain. The most striking difference between the countries is that fertility in Spain

*Editor's note: The "second demographic transition" is what some researchers have called the set of changes in family patterns in modern societies since the 1960's—more women in the paid workforce, later marriage and child-bearing, cohabitation, unwed motherhood, etc. The first demographic transition was the shift from high birth and high mortality rates in pre-industrial society, to the lower birth and mortality rates after industrialization.

has collapsed, whereas in Finland, the fertility rate has actually risen since the slump at the turn of the 1970s and 1980s.

Second, the analysis reveals that regardless of the congruent socio-demographic changes, the patterns of first family formation differ in the respective countries. Finns move out of their parental homes at a relatively young age and they tend to live in a cohabiting union before marrying, and they often have their first child while still cohabiting. Spaniards tend to take the more traditional route and move out of their parental homes when marrying and have a child after a few years of marriage.

INDIVIDUALIZATION THESIS CONTESTED

Individualization and the emergence of post-modern values are often taken as starting points when explaining recent changes in the family. The decline in fertility and marriage rates and the delay of marriage and childbearing are often explained by the increased availability and use of modern contraceptives, and the increase in cohabitation and in women's labour-force participation, which are seen both as causes and consequences of individualization and the value shift. However, based on this study, I would argue that these explanations are not valid in these particular cases. In Finland, the use of modern contraceptives is common, as is (premarital) cohabitation and women's labour-force participation and, yet, fertility is relatively high and the marriage rate is practically at the same level as it is in Spain. In Spain, the use of traditional methods of contraception is still common, cohabitation is exceptional and, regardless of the constant rise, female labour-force participation is low compared to most EU countries. And, yet, the marriage rate in Spain is almost as low as it is in Finland and the fertility rate is among the lowest in Europe and the Western world.

PUBLIC POLICIES AND THE LABOUR MARKET

The combination of a low female-employment rate and low fertility in Spain is often explained by the lack of public support for families, whereas the high employment rate among Finnish women and relatively high fertility are explained by the existence of family-friendly policies. But as this study attests, the correlation between the extent of family-friendly policies and female employment is not obvious. The lack of services does not prevent Spanish women from entering working life nor did it prevent Finnish women in the 1960s and 1970s. On the other hand, the cases also indicate that public policies may have either a positive or a negative effect on the family and fertility. Considering the constant increase of Spanish women's labour-force participation, the underdevelopment of benefits and services for families with children might be one of the causes of declining fertility and family size. In Finland, on the other hand, fertility rose in the course of the 1980s when 'family policy' was intensely developed and it started to fall again along with the retrenchment policies. However, in neither of the countries does the level of benefits and services determine whether people decide to have children or not but rather it most likely affects family size.

Although public policies may provide incentives to form a family and especially to increase family size, this study indicates that the labour market plays a crucial role in people's decisions about the family. Since the recession in the 1990s, women's labour-market position has not improved similar to men's in either of the countries; unemployment and sporadic employment affects women more than men. However, the Spanish labour market is more heavily masculine than the Finnish one, which makes it more difficult for Spanish women to establish themselves and to advance their careers. This and the underdevelopment of public measures to ease the reconciliation of work and family together with younger women's growing reluctance to devote themselves only to family and children are factors that might force women to choose childlessness, or to limit the size of the family and to postpone childbearing longer than in Finland. On the other hand, when the state does little to support families in their coping with professional and family obligations, two incomes are necessary to buy the services needed. Furthermore, and regardless of the type of welfare state, living expenses and the expected standard of living in Spain, Finland and European countries in general have risen and, thus, two incomes are often perceived as necessary for the family economy.

ROUGH PATH TO ADULTHOOD

Several studies, including this one, show that even though marriage and fertility rates are declining, most men and women say that having a stable partnership (mostly in marriage) and children are their aims in life. Thus, the focal question to be asked is why the young people of today 'fail' to achieve this aim more often than the previous generations (see Beck and Beck-Gernsheim, 2002). The comparative study of Finland and Spain shows that in both countries, the major reason for the changes in patterns of family formation is young people's difficulties in establishing themselves in the labour market and gaining financial independence, which is a precondition for household and family formation. According to the individualization thesis, the weakening of traditional forms of authority as directors of our biographies and the increased valuing and seeking of personal gratification has paved the way for lifestyles competing with the family and family life (see Beck and Beck-Gernsheim, 2002; Giddens, 1995, 1999). Although it is undeniable that individuals increasingly negotiate their own moral stance, their relationships and biographies, the decisions concerning one's life, such as marriage, remaining single, having children, remaining childless and becoming independent, are never totally up to an individual. They are made in particular social contexts, with significant others and with the influence of social and individual resources (see Edgar, 2004).

Prolonged studies, the instability of the labour market and low or irregular income are major factors that postpone family formation in both countries. However, owing largely to the welfare state types, differences exist between the countries. In Spain, the lack of individual public support for young adults, the lack of affordable housing and the cultural tradition of leaving home when marrying are factors that postpone gaining independence and family formation even longer than in Finland, where individual social security, the availability of publicly owned rented housing, housing allowances, student housing, the system of student loans and grants and the tradition of early emancipation make establishing one's own household and having children possible (although not desired) even without a regular income, wealth or affluent parents. It appears that public support for young people might further the formation of new families, but enhancing young people's entrance into the labour market and limiting fixed-term contracts and periodic employment might make a more substantive difference in forming new families with children.

The instability of employment and low or sporadic income creates insecurity and the inability to plan for the future, despite the measures of public support. The postponement of such commitments as family and children is not only a matter of adopting post-modern and individualistic values and attitudes but also represents a means of risk control or a strategy to cope with uncertainty. As the expectations of couple relationships increase, so does the chance of a break-up and, therefore, being dependent on a partner is a risk that fewer women, in particular, are willing to take and this emphasizes the importance of personal income. Furthermore, forming a family and having children before one has attained sufficient financial and material security is considered a major risk, especially for successful parenting and for the welfare of the children.

FAMILY: STILL A COMMUNITY OF NEED

According to Ulrich Beck and Elisabeth Beck-Gernsheim (2002), individualization—the historical process that increasingly questions and tends to break up the traditional or normal life history, paving the way to the do-it-yourself life history—is the reference point for explaining changes in the family. What counted in the pre-industrial family was not the individual person but common goals and purposes. In this respect, the family in pre-industrial times could be defined as a 'community of need' held together by an 'obligation of solidarity'. Modernization, particularly the emergence of the wage work society and the development of the welfare state, paved the way and enforced the logic of individually designed lives, first for men and later also for women. The development of the welfare state played a focal role in the process of individualization. By reducing economic dependence on the family, the state increases the scope of individual action. Thus, the contemporary family of individual times could be described as comprising elective affinities which, unlike the pre-industrial family, are based on emotional ties rather than economic and material ones (Beck-Beck-Gernsheim, 2002; see also Giddens, 1995, 1999).

This thesis is undoubtedly correct, but there are some remarks to be made on the basis of the findings of this comparative study regarding the meaning and role of the family. Although emotional 'need' is nowadays more emphasized than 'economic' need, the family may still be described as a 'community of need'. The family remains an important source of economic and material support for its members, especially when the labour market is erratic and the welfare state tightens its belt. Besides, as the Spanish case in particular demonstrates, the family is still held together not only by emotional ties but also by an 'obligation of solidarity'. Spanish legislation, like the Finnish legislation, obliges parents to be liable for providing maintenance to their minor children, but it also obliges major children to be liable for their parents' maintenance and siblings to be liable for helping each other (under certain circumstances). In Finland, this kind of broad liability between parents and their grown children and between siblings is a moral obligation rather than a legal one. Considering the definition of the family in terms of the legal maintenance liability, the Finnish family is clearly defined as a nuclear family whereas the definition of the Spanish family is broader.

In Finland, the welfare state has supported individuality and the individual's independence from the family, particularly in the case of women and young people. In Spain, there is a long history of public emphasis on the family, its role as the principal provider of welfare and on women's caretaker role within the family. Owing to this, the democratic state has, until recently, deemed the family to be a private matter. Generally speaking, the Finnish welfare state has reduced the individual's economic dependence on the family but the Spanish one has not. This difference is reflected in the possibilities for and patterns of forming new families. Paradoxically, the family-centred society makes it more difficult to establish new families than the more individualistic one. In addition to reducing the individual's dependence on the family, the welfare state also ought to reduce the individual's dependence on market forces (see Esping-Andersen, 1990, 1999, 2002). However, the recent retrenchment policies have turned the course of the Finnish welfare state in the opposite direction and brought the Spanish one to a standstill. As has become apparent, the choices of life, family lives and the well-being of both Spaniards and Finns are more dependent on the labour market and earnings than on the welfare state even if it is the type of welfare state that has policies designed to mitigate dependency on market forces, like the Finnish one.

THE FAMILY—STILL GOING STRONG

Social change not only influences the conception of the family in society but also in research. Considering the conceptual shift regarding the family in research, basically three views on the family prevail among social scientists. First, there are those who perceive a massive change in the family, even the end of the traditional family. Others criticize the talk of crisis and predict the revival of the family. The third group, positioned somewhere in between, prefers to speak of tendencies towards pluralism. All these standpoints are based on empirical data and especially on demographic statistics.

The analysis of Finnish and Spanish families indicates that the traditional or conservative idea of the family is in crisis if the family is defined as a conjugal male breadwinner/female homemaker family. It is suited neither to egalitarian values nor to the reality within which people live in contemporary societies. Nonetheless, a life-long marriage—a prerequisite of the traditional definition of the family—has remained the ideal most people hope to pursue in both countries regardless of the differences in divorce law and the frequency of divorce.

If the 'normal' family is defined as a conjugal, nuclear family in which both spouses are employed most of the time during the family cycle, then the family is going strong both in ideological and practical terms. Most Finns and Spaniards hope to live and do end up living in this sort of a family, although not always permanently and some more than once.

Family pluralism is a reality in both societies although 'alternative' family forms such as families based on cohabiting couples, single-parent families and reconstituted families are still more common in Finland than in Spain. However, the two latter ones are not usually consciously chosen from the outset but rather are consequences of failed marriages (and/or relationships). Families based on a cohabiting couple, on the other hand, often lead to a family based on a married couple. Furthermore, there are families that are based on a couple but composed of three generations living in the same household. These types of families are more common in Spain than in Finland, so far.

Chapter

2

Public Debates and Private Lives

READING 4

The Mommy Wars: Ambivalence, Ideological Work, and the Cultural Contradictions of Motherhood

Sharon Hays

I have argued that all mothers ultimately share a recognition of the ideology of intensive mothering. At the same time, all mothers live in a society where child rearing is generally devalued and the primary emphasis is placed on profit, efficiency, and "getting ahead." If you are a mother, both logics operate in your daily life.

But the story is even more complicated. Over half of American mothers participate directly in the labor market on a regular basis; the rest remain at least somewhat distant from that world as they spend most of their days in the home. One might therefore expect paid working mothers to be more committed to the ideology of competitively maximizing personal profit and stay-at-home mothers to be more committed to the ideology of intensive mothering. As it turns out, however, this is not precisely the way it works.

Modern-day mothers are facing two socially constructed cultural images of what a good mother looks like. Neither, however, includes the vision of a cold, calculating businesswoman—that title is reserved for childless career women. If you are a good mother, you *must* be an intensive one. The only "choice" involved is whether you *add* the role of paid working woman. The options, then, are as follows. On the one side there is the portrait of the "traditional mother" who stays at home with the kids and dedicates her energy to the happiness of her family. This mother cheerfully studies the latest issue of *Family Circle*, places flowers in every room, and has dinner waiting when her husband comes home. This mother, when she's not cleaning, cooking, sewing, shopping, doing the laundry, or comforting her mate, is focused on attending to the children and ensuring their proper development. On the other side is the image of the successful "supermom." Effortlessly juggling home and work, this mother can push a stroller with one hand and carry a briefcase in the other. She is always properly coiffed, her nylons have no runs, her suits are freshly pressed, and her home has seen the white tornado. Her children are immaculate and well mannered but not passive, with a strong spirit and high self-esteem.[1]

Although both the traditional mom and the supermom are generally considered socially acceptable, their coexistence represents a serious cultural ambivalence about how mothers should behave. This ambivalence comes out in the widely available indictments of the failings of both groups of women. Note, for instance, the way Mecca, a welfare mother, describes these two choices and their culturally provided critiques:

> The way my family was brought up was, like, you marry a man, he's the head of the house, he's the provider, and you're the wife, you're the provider in the house. Now these days it's not that way. Now the people that stay home are classified, quote, "lazy people," we don't "like" to work.
>
> I've seen a lot of things on TV about working mothers and nonworking mothers. People who stay home attack the other mothers 'cause they're, like, bad mothers because they left the kids behind and go to work. And, the other ones aren't working because we're lazy. But it's not lazy. It's the lifestyle in the 1990s it's, like, too much. It's a demanding world for mothers with kids.

The picture Mecca has seen on television, a picture of these two images attacking each other with ideological swords, is not an uncommon one.

It is this cultural ambivalence and the so-called choice between these paths that is the basis for what Darnton (1990) has dubbed the "mommy wars."[2] Both stay-at-home and paid working mothers, it is argued, are angry and defensive; neither group respects the other. Both make use of available cultural indictments to condemn the opposing group. Supermoms, according to this portrait, regularly describe stay-at-home mothers as lazy and boring, while traditional moms regularly accuse employed mothers of selfishly neglecting their children.

My interviews suggest, however, that this portrait of the mommy wars is both exaggerated and superficial. In fact, the majority of mothers I spoke with expressed respect for one another's need or right to choose whether to go out to work or stay at home with the kids. And, as I have argued, they also share a whole set of similar concerns regarding appropriate child rearing. These mothers have not formally enlisted in this war. Yet the rhetoric of the mommy wars draws them in as it persists in mainstream American culture, a culture that is unwilling, for various significant reasons, to unequivocally embrace either vision of motherhood, just as it remains unwilling to embrace wholeheartedly the childless career woman.[3] Thus, the charges of being lazy and bored, on the one hand, or selfish and money-grubbing, on the other, are made available for use by individual mothers and others should the need arise.

What this creates is a no-win situation for women of child-bearing years. If a woman voluntarily remains childless, some will say that she is cold, heartless, and unfulfilled as a woman. If she is a mother who works too hard at her job or career, some will accuse her of neglecting the kids. If she does not work hard enough, some will surely place her on the "mommy track" and her career advancement will be permanently slowed by the claim that her commitment to her children interferes with her workplace efficiency (Schwartz 1989). And if she stays at home with her children, some will call her unproductive and useless. A woman, in other words, can never fully do it right.

At the same time that these cultural images portray all women as somehow less than adequate, they also lead many mothers to feel somehow less than adequate in their daily lives. The stay-at-home mother is supposed to be happy and fulfilled, but how can she be when she hears so often that she is mindless and bored? The supermom is supposed to be able to juggle her two roles without missing a beat, but how can she do either job as well as she is expected if she is told she must dedicate her all in both directions? In these circumstances, it is not surprising that many supermoms feel guilty about their inability to carry out both roles to their fullest, while many traditional moms feel isolated and invisible to the larger world.

Given this scenario, both stay-at-home and employed mothers end up spending a good deal of time attempting to make sense of their current positions. Paid working mothers, for instance, are likely to argue that there are lots of good reasons for mothers to work in the paid labor force; stay-at-home mothers are likely to argue that there are lots of good reasons for mothers to stay at home with their children. These arguments are best understood not as (mere) rationalizations or (absolute) truths but rather as socially necessary "ideological work." Berger (1981) uses this notion to describe the way that all people make use of available ideologies in their "attempt to cope with the relationship between the ideas they bring to a social context and the practical pressures of day-to-day living in it" (15). People, in other words, select among the cultural logics at their disposal in order to develop some correspondence between what they believe and what they actually do.[4] For mothers, just like others, ideological work is simply a means of maintaining their sanity.

The ideological work of mothers, as I will show, follows neither a simple nor a straightforward course. First, as I have pointed out, both groups face two contradictory cultural images of appropriate mothering. Their ideological work, then, includes a recognition and response to both portraits. This duality is evident in the fact that the logic the traditional mother uses to affirm her position matches the logic that the supermom uses to express ambivalence about her situation, and the logic that the employed mother uses to affirm her position is the same logic that the stay-at-home mother uses to express ambivalence about hers. Their strategies, in other words, are mirror images, but they are also incomplete—both groups are left with some ambivalence. Thus, although the two culturally provided images of mothering help mothers to make sense of their own positions, they simultaneously sap the strength of mothers by making them feel inadequate in one way or the other. It is in coping with these feelings of inadequacy that their respective ideological strategies take an interesting turn. Rather than taking divergent paths, as one might expect, both groups attempt to resolve their feelings of inadequacy by returning to the logic of the ideology of intensive mothering.

THE FRUMPY HOUSEWIFE AND THE PUSH TOWARD THE OUTSIDE WORLD

Some employed mothers say that they go out to work for pay because they need the income.[5] But the overwhelming majority also say that they *want* to work outside the home. First, there's the problem of staying inside all day: "I decided once I started working that I need that. I need to work. Because I'll become like this big huge hermit frumpy person if I stay home." Turning into a "big huge hermit frumpy person" is connected to the feeling of being confined to the home. Many women have had that experience at one time or another and do not want to repeat it:

> When I did stay home with him, up until the time when he was ten months old, I wouldn't go out of the house for three days at a time. Ya know, I get to where I don't want to get dressed, I don't care if I take a shower. It's like, what for? I'm not going anywhere.

Not getting dressed and not going anywhere are also tied to the problem of not having a chance to interact with other adults:

> I remember thinking, "I don't even get out of my robe. And I've gotta stay home and breast-feed and the only adult I hear is on *Good Morning America*—and he's not even live!" And that was just for a couple of months. I don't even know what it would be like for a couple of years. I think it would be really difficult.

Interacting with adults, for many paid working mothers, means getting a break from the world of children and having an opportunity to use their minds:

> When I first started looking for a job, I thought we needed a second income. But then when I started working it was like, this is great! I do have a mind that's not *Sesame Street!* And I just love talking with people. It's just fun, and it's a break. It's tough, but I enjoyed it; it was a break from being with the kids.

If you don't get a break from the kids, if you don't get out of the house, if you don't interact with adults, and if you don't have a chance to use your mind beyond the *Sesame Street* level, you might end up lacking the motivation to do much at all. This argument is implied by many mothers:

> If I was stuck at home all day, and I did do that 'cause I was waiting for day care, I stayed home for four months, and I went crazy, I couldn't stand it. I mean not because I didn't want to spend any time with her, but because we'd just sit here and she'd just cry all day and I couldn't get anything done. I was at the end of the day exhausted, and feeling like shit.

Of course, it is exhausting to spend the day meeting the demands of children. But there's also a not too deeply buried sense in all these arguments that getting outside the home and using one's mind fulfill a longing to be part of the larger world and to be recognized by it. One mother made this point explicitly:

> [When you're working outside the home] you're doing something. You're using your mind a little bit differently than just trying to figure out how to make your day work with your kid. It's just challenging in a different way. So there's part of me that wants to be, like, *recognized.* I think maybe that's what work does, it gives you a little bit of a sense of recognition, that you don't feel like you get [when you stay home].

Most employed mothers, then, say that if they stay at home they'll go stir-crazy, they'll get bored, the demands of the kids will drive them nuts, they won't have an opportunity to use their brains or interact with other adults, they'll feel like they're going nowhere, and they'll lose their sense of identity in the larger world. And, for many of these mothers, all these points are connected:

> Well, I think [working outside is] positive, because I feel good about being able to do the things that I went to school for, and keep up with that, and use my brain. As they grow older, [the children are] going to get into things that they want to get into, they're going to be out with their friends and stuff, and I don't want to be in a situation where my whole life has been wrapped around the kids. That's it. Just some outside interests so that I'm not so wrapped up in how shiny my floor is. [She laughs.] Just to kind of be out and be stimulated. Gosh, I don't want this to get taken wrong, but I think I'd be a little bit bored. And the other thing I think of is, I kind of need a break, and when you're staying at home it's constant. It's a lot harder when you don't have family close by, [because] you don't get a break.

In short, paid working mothers feel a strong pull toward the outside world. They hear the world accusing stay-at-home moms of being mindless and unproductive and of lacking an identity apart from their kids, and they experience this as at least partially true.

Stay-at-home mothers also worry that the world will perceive them as lazy and bored and watching television all day as children scream in their ears and tug at their sleeves. And sometimes this is the way they feel about themselves. In other words, the same image that provides working mothers with the reasons they should go out to work accounts for the ambivalence that stay-at-home mothers feel about staying at home.

A few stay-at-home mothers seem to feel absolutely secure in their position, but most do not.[6] Many believe that they will seek paid work at some point, and almost all are made uncomfortable by the sense that the outside world does not value what they do. In all cases, their expressions of ambivalence about staying at home mimic the concerns of employed mothers. For instance, some women who stay at home also worry about becoming frumpy: "I'm not this heavy. I'm, like, twenty-seven pounds overweight. It sounds very vain of me, in my situation. It's like, I'm not used to being home all the time, I'm home twenty-four hours. I don't have that balance in my life anymore." And some stay-at-home mothers feel as if they are physically confined inside the home. This mother, for example, seems tired of meeting the children's demands and feels that she is losing her sense of self:

> There's a hard thing of being at home all the time. You have a lot of stress, because you're constantly in the house. I think having a job can relieve some of that stress and to make it a lot more enjoyable, to want to come home all the time... . My outings are [limited]. I'm

> excited when I have to go grocery shopping. Everything I pick is what they eat, everything they like, or what they should eat. Me, I'm just *there.* I'm there for them. I feel that I'm here for them.

Both of these stay-at-home mothers, like over one-third of the stay-at-home mothers in my sample, plan to go out to work as soon as they can find paid employment that offers sufficient rewards to compensate (both financially and ideologically) for sending the kids to day care. Most of the remaining mothers are committed to staying at home with the children through what they understand as formative years. The following mother shares that commitment, while also echoing many paid working mothers in her hopes that one day she will have a chance to be around adults and further her own growth:

> Well, we could do more, we'd have more money, but that's really not the biggest reason I'd go back to work. I want to do things for myself, too. I want to go back and get my master's [degree] or something. I need to grow, and be around adults, too. I don't know when, but I think in the next two years I'll go back to work. The formative years—their personality is going to develop until they're about five. It's pretty much set by then. So I think it's pretty critical that you're around them during those times.

One mother stated explicitly that she can hardly wait until the kids are through their formative years:

> At least talking to grown-ups is a little more fulfilling than ordering the kids around all day. My life right now is just all theirs. Sometimes it's a depressing thought because I think, "Where am I? I want my life back." ... I mean, they are totally selfish. It's like an ice cream. They just gobble that down and say, "Let me have the cinnamon roll now."
>
> . . . [But] I had them, and I want them to be good people. So I've dedicated myself to them right now. Later on I get my life back. They won't always be these little sponges. I don't want any deficiency—well, nobody can cover all the loopholes—but I want to be comfortable in myself to know that I did everything that I could. It's the least I can do to do the best I can by them.

Mothers, she seems to be saying, are like confections that the kids just gobble down—and then they ask for more.

Thus, many stay-at-home moms experience the exhaustion of meeting the demands of children all day long, just as employed mothers fear they might. And many stay-at-home mothers also experience a loss of self. Part of the reason they feel like they are losing their identity is that they know the outside world does not recognize a mother's work as valuable. This woman, committed to staying at home until her youngest is at least three years old, explains:

> You go through a period where you feel like you've lost all your marbles. Boy, you're not as smart as you used to be, and as sharp as you used to be, and not as respected as you used to be. And those things are really hard to swallow. But that's something I've discussed with other mothers who are willing to stay home with their kids, and we've formed a support group where we've said, "Boy, those people just don't know what they're talking about." We're like a support group for each other, which you have to have if you've decided to

> stay at home, because you have so many people almost pushing you to work, or asking "Why don't you work?" You're not somehow as good as anybody else 'cause you're staying at home; what you're doing isn't important. We have a lot of that in this society.

Another mother, this one determined to stay at home with her kids over the long haul, provides a concrete example of the subtle and not-so-subtle ways in which society pushes mothers to participate in the paid labor force, and of the discomfort such mothers experience as a result:

> As a matter of fact, somebody said to me (I guess it was a principal from one of the schools.) . . . "Well, what do you *do?* Do you have a *job?*" And it was just very funny to me that he was so uncomfortable trying to ask me what it was in our society that I did. I guess that they just assume that if you're a mom at home that it means nothing. I don't know, I just don't consider it that way. But it's kind of funny, worrying about what you're gonna say at a dinner party about what you do.

And it's not just that these mothers worry about being able to impress school principals and people at cocktail parties, of course. The following mother worries about being "interesting" to other women who do not have children:

> I find myself, now that I'm not working, not to have as much in common [with other women who don't have children]. We don't talk that much because I don't have that much to talk about. Like I feel I'm not an interesting person anymore.

In short, the world presents, and mothers experience, the image of the lazy, mindless, dull housewife—and no mother wants to be included in that image.

THE TIME-CRUNCHED CAREER WOMAN AND THE PULL TOWARD HOME

Stay-at-home mothers use a number of strategies to support their position and combat the image of the frumpy housewife. Many moms who are committed to staying at home with their kids often become part of formal or informal support groups, providing them an opportunity to interact with other mothers who have made the same commitment. Others, if they can afford the cost of transportation and child care, engage in a variety of outside activities—as volunteers for churches, temples, and community groups, for instance, or in regular leisure activities and exercise programs. They then have a chance to communicate with other adults and to experience themselves as part of a larger social world (though one in which children generally occupy a central role).

But the primary way that stay-at-home mothers cope with their ambivalence is through ideological work. Like paid working mothers, they make a list of all the good reasons they do what they do. In this case, that list includes confirming their commitment to good mothering, emphasizing the importance of putting their children's needs ahead of their own, and telling stories about the problems that families, and especially children, experience when mothers go out to work for pay.

Many stay-at-home mothers argue that kids require guidance and should have those cookies cooling on the kitchen counter when they come home from school:

> The kids are the ones that suffer. The kids need guidance and stuff. And with two parents working, sometimes there isn't even a parent home when they come home from school. And that's one thing that got me too. I want to be home and I want to have cookies on the stove when they come home from school. Now we eat meals together all the time. It's more of a homey atmosphere. It's more of a *home* atmosphere.

Providing this homey atmosphere is difficult to do if one works elsewhere all day. And providing some period of so-called quality time in the evening, these mothers tell me, is not an adequate substitute. One mother elaborates on this point in response to a question about how she would feel if she was working outside the home:

> Oh, guilty as anything. I know what I'm like after dinner, and I'm not at my best. And neither are my kids. And if that's all the time I had with them, it wouldn't be, quote, "quality time." I think it's a bunch of b.s. about quality time.

And quality time, even if it *is* of high quality, cannot make up for children's lack of a quantity of time with their mothers. This argument is often voiced in connection with the problem of paid caregiver arrangements. Most mothers, whether they work for pay or not, are concerned about the quality of day care, but stay-at-home mothers often use this concern to explain their commitment to staying at home. This mother, for example, argues that children who are shuffled off to a series of day-care providers simply will not get the love they need:

> I mean, if I'm going to have children I want to *raise* them. I feel really strongly about that. Really strongly. I wish more people did that. Myself, I think it's very underestimated the role the mother plays with the child. I really do. From zero to three [years], it's like their whole self-image. [Yet, working mothers will say,] "Well, okay, I've got a caretaker now," "Well, that nanny didn't work out." So by the time the children are three years old they've had four or five people who have supposedly said "I'll love you forever," and they're gone. I think that's really tough on the kids.[7]

Since paid caregivers lack that deep and long-lasting love, I'm told, they won't ever be as committed to ministering to the child's needs as a mom will:

> I don't think anybody can give to children what a mother can give to her own children. I think there's a level of willingness to put up with hard days, crying days, cranky days, whining days, that most mothers are going to be able to tolerate just a little bit more than a caretaker would. I think there's more of a commitment of what a mother wants to give her children in terms of love, support, values, etcetera. A caretaker isn't going to feel quite the same way.

Stay-at-home mothers imply that all these problems of kids who lack guidance, love, and support are connected to the problem of mothers who put their own interests ahead of the interests of their children. A few stay-at-home mothers will explicitly argue, as this one does, that employed mothers are allowing material and power interests to take priority over the well-being of their kids:

> People are too interested in power, they just aren't interested in what happens to their kids. You know, "Fine, put them in day care." And I just feel sad. If you're so interested in money or a career or whatever, then why have kids? Why bring them into it?

Putting such interests ahead of one's children is not only somehow immoral; it also produces children with real problems. The following mother, echoing many stories about "bad mothers" that we have heard before, had this to say about her sister:

> My sister works full-time—she's a lawyer. And her kids are the most obnoxious, whiny kids. I can't stand it. They just hang on her. She thinks she's doing okay by them because they're in an expensive private school and they have expensive music lessons and they have expensive clothes and expensive toys and expensive cars and an expensive house. I don't know. Time will tell, I guess. But I can't believe they're not going to have some insecurities. The thing that gets me is, they don't need it. I mean, he's a lawyer too. Basically, it's like, "Well, I like you guys, but I don't really want to be there all day with you, and I don't want to have to do the dirty work."

These are serious indictments indeed.

It is just these sorts of concerns that leave paid working mothers feeling inadequate and ambivalent about *their* position. Many of them wonder at times if their lives or the lives of their children might actually be better if they stayed at home with the kids. Above all, many of them feel guilty and wonder, "Am I doing it right?" or "Have I done all I can do?" These are the mothers who, we're told, have it all. It is impossible to have it all, however, when "all" includes two contradictory sets of requirements. To begin to get a deeper sense of how these supermoms do not always feel so super, two examples might be helpful.

Angela is a working-class mother who had expected to stay home with her son through his formative years. But after nine months she found herself bored, lonely, and eager to interact with other adults. She therefore went out and got a full-time job as a cashier. She begins by expressing her concern that she is not living up to the home-making suggestions she reads in *Parenting* magazine, worrying that she may not be doing it right:

> I get *Parenting* magazine and I read it. I do what is comfortable for me and what I can do. I'm not very creative. Where they have all these cooking ideas, and who has time to do that, except for a mother who stays home all day? Most of this is for a mother who has five, six hours to spend with her child doing this kind of thing. I don't have time for that.
>
> So then that's when I go back to day care. And I know that she's doing this kind of stuff with him, teaching him things. You know, a lot of the stuff that they have is on schooling kinds of things, flash cards, that kind of thing. Just things that I don't do. That makes me feel bad. Then I think, "I should be doing this" and "Am I doing the right thing?" I know I have a lot of love for him.

Although she loves her son and believes that this is probably "the most important thing," she also feels guilty that she may not be spending a sufficient amount of time with him, simply because she gets so tired:

> I think sometimes that I feel like I don't spend enough time with him and that's my biggest [concern]. And when I am with him, sometimes I'm not really up to being with him. Even though I am with him, sometimes I want him to go away because I've been working all day and I'm exhausted. And I feel sometimes I'll stick him in bed early because I just don't want to deal with him that day. And I feel really guilty because I don't spend enough time with him as it is. When I do have the chance to spend time with him, I don't want to spend time with him, because I'm so tired and I just want to be with myself and by myself.

Even though Angela likes her paid work and does not want to give it up, the problems of providing both a quantity of time and the idealized image of quality time with her child, just like the challenge of applying the creative cooking and child-rearing ideas she finds in *Parenting* magazine, haunt her and leave her feeling both inadequate and guilty.

Linda is a professional-class mother with a well-paying and challenging job that gives her a lot of satisfaction. She spent months searching for the right preschool for her son and is relieved that he is now in a place where the caregivers share her values. Still, she worries and wonders if life might be better if she had made different choices:

> I have a friend. She's a very good mom. She seems very patient, and I never heard her raise her voice. And she's also not working. She gets to stay home with her children, which is another thing I admire. I guess I sort of envy that too. There never seems to be a time where we can just spend, like, playing a lot. I think that's what really bothers me, that I don't feel like I have the time to just sit down and, in a relaxing way, play with him. I can do it, but then I'm thinking "Okay, well I can do this for five minutes." So that's always in the back of my mind. Time, time, time. So I guess that's the biggest thing.
>
> And just like your question, "How many hours a day is he at preschool and how many hours do you spend per day as the primary caregiver?" just made me think, "Oh my gosh!" I mean they're watching him grow up more than I am. They're with him more than I am. And that makes me feel guilty in a way, and it makes me feel sad in a way. I mean I can just see him, slipping, just growing up before me. Maybe it's that quality-time stuff. I don't spend a lot of time, and I don't know if the time I do spend with him is quality.
>
> [But] if I just stay at home, I'll kind of lose, I don't know if I want to say my sense of identity, but I guess I'll lose my career identity. I'm afraid of that I guess. . . . My friend who stays at home, she had a career before she had her children, but I forget what it was. So that whole part of her, I can't even identify it now.

On the one hand, Linda envies and admires stay-at-home moms and worries about not spending enough quality time with her son, or enough play time. She is also upset that her day-care provider spends more hours with her son each day than she can. On the other hand, Linda worries that if she did stay at home she'd lose her identity as a professional and a member of the larger society. "Time, time, time," she says, there's never enough time to do it all—or at least to do it all "right."

The issue of time is a primary source of paid working mothers' ambivalence about their double shift. Attempting to juggle two commitments at once is, of course, very difficult and stressful. This mother's sense of how time pressures make her feel that she is always moving too fast would be recognizable to the majority of paid working mothers:

> I can see when I get together with my sister [who doesn't have a paid job] . . . that she's so easygoing with the kids, and she takes her time, and when I'm with her, I realize how stressed out I am sometimes trying to get things done.
>
> And I notice how much faster I move when I shop. . . . She's so relaxed, and I think I kind of envy that.

The problem of moving too fast when shopping is connected to the problem of moving too fast when raising children. Many paid working mothers envy those who can do such things at a more relaxed pace.

For a few employed mothers (two out of twenty in my sample) the problems of quality and quantity time outweigh the rewards of paid work, and they intend to leave their jobs as soon as they can afford to do so. This woman is one example:

> I believe there's a more cohesive family unit with maybe the mother staying at home. Because a woman tends to be a buffer, mediator, you name it. She pulls the family together. But if she's working outside the home, sometimes there's not that opportunity anymore for her to pull everyone together. She's just as tired as the husband would be and, I don't know, maybe the children are feeling like they've been not necessarily abandoned but, well, I'm sure they accept it, especially if that's the only life they've seen. But my daughter has seen a change, even when I was only on maternity leave. I've seen a change in her and she seemed to just enjoy it and appreciate us as a family more than when I was working. So now she keeps telling me, "Mom, I miss you."

When this mother hears her daughter say "I miss you," she feels a tremendous pull toward staying at home. And when she talks about the way a family needs a mother to bring its members together, she is pointing to an idealized image of the family that, like quality and quantity time, weighs heavily in the minds of many mothers.

The following paid working mother also wishes she could stay at home with the kids and wishes she could be just like the television mom of the 1950s who bakes cookies every afternoon. But she knows she has to continue working for financial reasons:

> Yes. I want to be Donna Reed, definitely. Or maybe Beaver Cleaver's mother, Jane Wyatt. Anybody in an apron and a pretty hairdo and a beautiful house. Yes. Getting out of the television set and making the most of reality is really what I have to do. Because I'll always have to work.

But the majority of paid working mothers, as I have stated, not only feel they need to work for financial reasons but also *want* to work, as Angela and Linda do. Nonetheless, their concerns about the effects of the double shift on their children match the concerns of those employed moms who wish they could stay at home as well as mimicking those of mothers who actually do stay at home. This mother, for instance, loves her paid work and does not want to give it up, but she does feel guilty, wondering if she's depriving her kids of the love and stimulation they need, particularly since she does not earn enough to justify the time she spends away:

> Honestly, I don't make that much money. So that in itself brings a little bit of guilt, 'cause I know I work even though we don't have to. So there's some guilt associated. If kids are coming home to an empty house every day, they're not getting the intellectual stimulation [and] they're not getting the love and nurturing that other mothers are able to give their kids. So I think in the long run they're missing out on a lot of the love and the nurturing and the caring.

And this mother does not want it to seem that she is putting her child second, but she feels pressure to live up to the image of a supermom:

> I felt really torn between what I wanted to do. Like a gut-wrenching decision. Like, what's more important? Of course your kids are important, but you know, there's so many outside pressures for women to work. Every ad you see in magazines or on television shows this working woman who's coming home with a briefcase and the kids are all dressed and clean. It's such a lie. I don't know of anybody who lives like that.
>
> There's just a lot of pressure that you're not a fulfilled woman if you're not working outside of the home. But yet, it's just a real hard choice.

This feeling of being torn by a gut-wrenching decision comes up frequently:

> I'm constantly torn between what I feel I should be doing in my work and spending more time with them. . . . I think I would spend more time with them if I could. Sometimes I think it would be great not to work and be a mom and do that, and then I think, "well?"
>
> I think it's hard. Because I think you do need to have contact with your kid. You can't just see him in the morning and put him to bed at night because you work all day long. I think that's a real problem. You need to give your child guidance. You can't leave it to the schools. You can't leave it to churches. You need to be there. So, in some ways I'm really torn.

The overriding issue for this mother is guidance; seeing the children in the morning and putting them to bed at night is just not enough.

This problem, of course, is related to the problem of leaving kids with a paid caregiver all day. Paid working mothers do not like the idea of hearing their children cry when they leave them at day care any more than any other mother does. They are, as we have seen, just as concerned that their children will not get enough love, enough nurturing, enough of the right values, enough of the proper education, and enough of the right kind of discipline if they spend most of their time with a paid caregiver. To this list of concerns, paid working mothers add their feeling that when the kids are with a paid caregiver all day, it feels as if someone else is being the mother. One woman (who stayed at home until her son was two years old) elaborates:

> Well, I think it's really sad that kids have to be at day care forty hours a week. Because basically the person who's taking care of them is your day-care person. They're pretty much being the mother. It's really sad that this other person is raising your child, and it's

> basically like having this other person *adopting* your child. It's *awful* that we have to do that. I just think it's a crime basically. I wish we didn't have to do it. I wish everybody could stay home with their kids and have some kind of outlet. . . .
>
> And I think having a career is really important, but I think when it comes time to have children, you can take that time off and spend it with your kid. Because you can't go backwards, and time does fly with them. It's so sad . . . I hear people say, "Oh, my day-care lady said that so-and-so walked today or used a spoon or something." I mean it's just so devastating to hear that you didn't get to see that.

Leaving one's child with a paid caregiver for hours on end is therefore a potential problem not only because that "other mother" may not be a good mother but also because the real mother misses out on the joys that come from just being with the child and having a chance to watch him or her grow. This is a heart rending issue for many mothers who work outside the home.

Once again, the arguments used by stay-at-home mothers to affirm their commitment to staying home are mimicked by the arguments paid working mothers use to express their ambivalence about the time they spend away from their children. And again, though the reasoning of these women is grounded in their experiences, it is also drawn from a widely available cultural rhetoric regarding the proper behavior of mothers.

THE CURIOUS COINCIDENCE OF PAID WORK AND THE IDEOLOGY OF INTENSIVE MOTHERING

Both paid working moms and stay-at-home moms, then, do the ideological work of making their respective lists of the reasons they should work for pay and the reasons they should stay at home. Yet both groups also continue to experience and express some ambivalence about their current positions, feeling pushed and pulled in two directions. One would assume that they would cope with their ambivalence by simply returning to their list of good reasons for doing what they do. And stay-at-home mothers do just that: they respond to the push toward work in the paid labor force by arguing that their kids need them to be at home. But, as I will demonstrate, working mothers do not use the mirror strategy. The vast majority of these women do not respond to the pull toward staying at home by arguing that kids are a pain in the neck and that paid work is more enjoyable. Instead, they respond by creating a new list of all the reasons that they are good mothers even though they work outside the home. In other words, the ideological work meant to resolve mothers' ambivalence generally points in the direction of intensive mothering.

Most paid working mothers cope with the ambivalence by arguing that their participation in the labor force is ultimately good for their kids. They make this point in a number of ways. For instance, one mother thinks that the example she provides may help to teach her kids the work ethic. Another says that with the "outside constraints" imposed by her work schedule, she's "more organized and effective" as a mom.[8] Yet another mother suggests that her second child takes just as much time and energy away from her first child as her career does:

> I think the only negative effect [of my employment] is just [that] generally when I'm over-stressed I don't do as well as a mother. But work is only one of the things that gets me overstressed. In fact it probably stresses me less than some other things. I think I do feel guilty about working 'cause it takes time away from [my oldest daughter]. But it struck me that it's acceptable to have a second child that takes just as much time away from the other child. *That* I'm not supposed to feel guilty about. But in some ways this [pointing to the infant she is holding] takes my time away from her more than my work does. Because this is constant.

More often, however, paid working mothers share a set of more standard explanations for why their labor-force participation is actually what's best for their kids. First, just as Rachel feels that her income provides for her daughter's toys, clothing, outings, and education, and just as Jacqueline argues, "I have weeks when I don't spend enough time with them and they suffer, but those are also the weeks I bring home the biggest paychecks," many mothers point out that their paid work provides the financial resources necessary for the well-being of their children:

> How am I supposed to send her to college without saving up? And also the money that I make from working helps pay for her toys, things that she needs, clothes. I never have to say, "Oh, I'm on a budget, I can't go buy this pair of shoes." I want the best for her.

Some mothers express a related concern—namely, what would happen to the family if they did not have paying jobs and their husbands should die or divorce them? One woman expressed it this way:

> Well, my dad was a fireman, so I guess there was a little bit of fear, well, if anything happened to him, how are we gonna go on? And I always kind of wished that [my mother] had something to fall back on. I think that has a lot to do with why I continue to work after the kids. I've always just felt the need to have something to hold on to.

The second standard argument given by employed mothers is that paid caregiver arrangements can help to further children's development. With respect to other people's kids, I'm told, these arrangements can keep them from being smothered by their mothers or can temporarily remove them from bad family situations. With reference to their own children, mothers emphasize that good day care provides kids with the opportunity to interact with adults, gives them access to "new experiences" and "different activities," "encourages their independence," and allows them to play with other kids—which is very important, especially now that neighborhoods no longer provide the sort of community life they once did:

> They do say that kids in preschool these days are growing up a little more neurotic, but I don't think that my daughter would have had a better life. In fact I think her life would have been a thousand times worse if I was a low-income mother who stayed home and she only got to play with the kids at the park. Because I think that preschool is really good for them.

> Maybe not a holding tank, but a nice preschool where they play nice games with them and they have the opportunity to play with the same kids over and over again. I think that's really good for them. Back in the 1950s, everybody stayed home and there were kids all over the block to play with. It's not that way now. The neighborhoods are deserted during the week.

Third, several mothers tell me that the quality of the time they spend with their kids actually seems to increase when they have a chance to be away from them for a part of the day. Listen to these mothers:

> When I'm with them too long I tend to lose my patience and start yelling at them. This way we both get out. And we're glad to see each other when we come home.

> If women were only allowed to work maybe ten to fifteen hours a week, they would appreciate their kids more and they'd have more quality time with them, rather than having to always just scold them.

> I think I have even less patience [when I stay home with the children], because it's like, "Oh, is this all there is?" . . . Whereas when I go to work and come home, I'm glad to see him. You know, you hear people say that they're better parents when they work because they spend more quality time, all those clichés, or whatever. For me that happens to be true.

> And now when I come home from work (although I wish I could get off earlier from work), I think I'm a better mom. There you go! Because when I come home from work, I don't have *all* day, just being with the kids. It's just that when I'm working I feel like I'm competent, I'm a person!

Getting this break from the kids, a break that reinforces your feeling of competence and therefore results in more rewarding time with your children is closely connected to the final way paid working mothers commonly attempt to resolve their ambivalence. Their children's happiness, they explain, is dependent upon their *own* happiness as mothers. One hears this again and again: "Happy moms make happy children"; "If I'm happy in my work then I think I can be a better mom"; and "I have to be happy with myself in order to make the children happy." One mother explains it this way:

> In some ways working is good. It's definitely got its positive side, because I get a break. I mean, now what I'm doing [working part-time] is perfect. I go to work. I have time to myself. I get to go to the bathroom when I need to go to the bathroom. I come home and I'm very happy to see my kids again. What's good for the mother and makes the mother happy is definitely good for the kids.

In all these explanations for why their participation in the paid labor force is actually good for their kids, these mothers want to make it clear that they still consider children their primary interest. They are definitely not placing a higher value on material success or power, they say. Nor are they putting their own interests above the interests of their children. They want the children to get all they need. But part of what children need, they argue, is financial security, the material goods required for proper development, some time away from their mothers, more quality time when they are with their mothers, and mothers who are happy in what they do. In all of these statements, paid working mothers clearly recognize the ideology of intensive mothering and testify that they are committed to fulfilling its requirements.

To underline the significance of this point, let me remind the reader that these paid working mothers use methods of child rearing that are just as child-centered, expert-guided, emotionally absorbing, labor-intensive, and financially expensive as their stay-at-home counterparts; they hold the child just as sacred, and they are just as likely to consider themselves as primarily responsible for the present and future well-being of their children. These are also the very same mothers who put a tremendous amount of time and energy into finding appropriate paid caregiver arrangements. Yet for all that they do to meet the needs of their children, they still express some ambivalence about working outside the home. And they still resolve this ambivalence by returning to the logic of intensive mothering and reminding the observer that ultimately they are most interested in what is best for their kids. This is striking.

CONTINUING CONTRADICTIONS

All this ideological work is a measure of the power of the pushes and pulls experienced by American mothers today. A woman can be a stay-at-home mother and claim to follow tradition, but not without paying the price of being treated as an outsider in the larger public world of the market. Or a woman can be a paid worker who participates in that larger world, but she must then pay the price of an impossible double shift. In both cases, women are enjoined to maintain the logic of intensive mothering. These contradictory pressures mimic the contradictory logics operating in this society, and almost all mothers experience them. The complex strategies mothers use to cope with these contradictory logics highlight the emotional, cognitive, and physical toll they take on contemporary mothers.

As I have argued, these strategies also highlight something more. The ways mothers explain their decisions to stay at home or work in the paid labor force, like the pushes and pulls they feel, run in opposite directions. Yet the ways they attempt to resolve the ambivalence they experience as a result of those decisions run in the *same* direction. Stay-at-home mothers, as I have shown, reaffirm their commitment to good mothering, and employed mothers maintain that they are good mothers even though they work. Paid working mothers do not, for instance, claim that child rearing is a relatively meaningless task, that personal profit is their primary goal, and that children are more efficiently raised in child-care centers. If you are a mother, in other words, although both the logic of the workplace and the logic of mothering operate in your life, the logic of intensive mothering has a *stronger* claim.

This phenomenon is particularly curious. The fact that there is no way for either type of mother to get it right would seem all the more reason to give up the logic of intensive mothering, especially since both groups of mothers recognize that paid employment confers more status than motherhood in the larger world. Yet images of freshly baked cookies and *Leave It to Beaver* seem to haunt mothers more often than the housewives' "problem that has no name" (Friedan 1963), and far more often than the image of a corporate manager with a big office, a large staff, and lots of perks. Although these mothers do not want to be defined as "mere" housewives and do want to achieve recognition in the outside world, most would also like to be there when the kids come home from school. Mothers surely try to balance their own desires against the requirements of appropriate child rearing, but in the world of mothering, it is socially unacceptable for them (in word if not in deed) to place their own needs above the needs of their children. A good mother certainly would never simply put her child aside for her own convenience. And placing material wealth or power on a higher plane than the well-being of children is strictly forbidden. It is clear that the two groups come together in holding these values as primary, despite the social devaluation of mothering and despite the glorification of wealth and power.

The portrait of the mommy wars, then, is overdrawn. Although the ideological strategies these groups use to explain their choice of home or paid work include an implicit critique of those "on the other side," this is almost always qualified, and both groups, at least at times, discuss their envy or admiration for the others. More important, as should now be abundantly clear, both groups ultimately share the same set of beliefs and the same set of concerns. Over half the women in my sample explicitly state that the choice between home and paid work depends on the individual woman, her interests, desires, and circumstances. Nearly all the rest argue that home is more important than paid work because children are simply more important than careers or the pursuit of financial gain. The paid working women in my sample were actually twice as likely as their stay-at-home counterparts to respond that home and children are more important and rewarding than paid work.[9] Ideologically speaking, at least, home and children actually seem to become more important to a mother the more time she spends away from them.

There *are* significant differences among mothers—ranging from individual differences to more systematic differences of class, race, and employment. But in the present context, what is most significant is the commitment to the ideology of intensive mothering that women share in spite of their differences. In this, the cultural contradictions of motherhood persist.

The case of paid working mothers is particularly important in this regard, since these are the very mothers who, arguably, have the most to gain from redefining motherhood in such a way as to lighten their load on the second shift. As we have seen, however, this is not exactly what they do. It is true, as Gerson (1985) argues, that there are ways in which paid working mothers do redefine motherhood and lighten their load—for instance, by sending their kids to day care, spending less time with them than their stay-at-home counterparts, legitimating their paid labor-force participation, and engaging in any number of practical strategies to make child-rearing tasks less energy- and time-consuming.[10] But, as I have argued, this does not mean that these mothers have given up the ideology of intensive mothering. Rather, it means that, whether or not they actually do, they feel they should spend a good deal of time looking for appropriate paid caregivers, trying to make up for the lack of quantity time by focusing their energy on providing quality time, and remaining attentive to the central tenets of the ideology of intensive child rearing. It also means that many are left feeling pressed for time, a little guilty, a bit inadequate, and somewhat ambivalent about their position. These stresses and the strain toward compensatory strategies should actually be taken as a measure of the persistent strength of the ideology of intensive mothering.

To deepen the sense of paradox further, one final point should be repeated. There are reasons to expect middle-class mothers to be in the vanguard of transforming ideas about child rearing away from an intensive model. First, middle-class women were historically in the vanguard of transforming child-rearing ideologies. Second, while many poor and working-class women have had to carry a double shift of wage labor and domestic chores for generations, middle-class mothers have had little practice, historically speaking, in juggling paid work and home and therefore might be eager to avoid it. Finally, one could argue that employed mothers in the middle class have more to gain from reconstructing ideas about appropriate child rearing than any other group—not only because their higher salaries mean that more money is at stake, but also because intensive mothering potentially interferes with their career trajectories in a more damaging way than is true of less high-status occupations. But, as I have suggested, middle-class women are, in some respects, those who go about the task of child rearing with the greatest intensity.

When women's increasing participation in the labor force, the cultural ambivalence regarding paid working and stay-at-home mothers, the particular intensity of middle-class mothering, and the demanding character of the cultural model of appropriate child rearing are taken together, it becomes clear that the cultural contradictions of motherhood have been deepened rather than resolved. The history of child-rearing ideas demonstrates that the more powerful the logic of the rationalized market became, so too did its ideological opposition in the logic of intensive mothering. The words of contemporary mothers demonstrate that this trend persists in the day-to-day lives of women.

Notes

1. It seems to me that the popular-culture images of both the traditional mother and the supermom tend to be portraits of professional-class women; the life-styles of working-class and poor women are virtually ignored. Hochschild (1989) does a particularly nice job of describing the image of a professional-class supermom, an image that our society pastes on billboards and covers in full-page ads in popular magazines: "She has that working-mother look as she strides forward, briefcase in one hand, smiling child in the other. Literally and figuratively, she is moving ahead. Her hair, if long, tosses behind her; if it is short, it sweeps back at the sides, suggesting mobility and progress. There is nothing shy or passive about her. She is confident, active, 'liberated.' She wears a dark tailored suit, but with a silk bow or colorful frill that says, 'I'm really feminine underneath.' She has made it in a man's world without sacrificing her femininity. And she has done this on her own. By some personal miracle, this image suggests, she has managed to combine what 150 years of industrialization have split wide apart—child and job, frill and suit, female culture and male" (1).
2. Women's decisions to remain childless or to become stay-at-home mothers or paid working mothers are based in social-structural circumstances. Kathleen Gerson's *Hard Choices: How Women Decide about Work, Career, and Motherhood* (1985) focuses precisely on this issue.
3. For discussions of this war in its various forms, see, for instance, Berger and Berger (1983); Gerson (1985); Ginsburg (1989); Hunter (1991, 1994); Klatch (1987); and Luker (1984).
4. The fact that people use ideological work to come to terms with their social circumstances does not mean that people's ideas are purely the result of their social position. An individual's ideas may well be the reason he or she came to that position in the first place. There is, as Berger points out, a dialectical relationship between ideas and circumstances. And neither one's ideas nor one's position is a matter of completely "free" or individual choice. Both are socially shaped.
5. A full half of the paid working women in my sample were employed only part-time. Nationally, approximately 33 percent of the married mothers employed in 1992 worked part-time; the remaining 67 percent worked full-time, that is, 35 hours or more per week (Hayghe and Bianche

1994). When one adds to this reality the facts that a number of stay-at-home mothers engage in forms of temporary or hidden paid work (such as child care for others) and that all mothers tend to move in and out of the labor force over time, it becomes clear that there is actually a *continuum* rather than a sharp divide between the statuses of paid working mothers and stay-at-home mothers. Nonetheless, the mothers in my sample systematically defined themselves as either paid working mothers or stay-at-home mothers and focused on the divide rather than on the continuum, as their arguments in this chapter make clear.

6. Over one-third of the stay-at-home mothers I talked to planned to enter the paid labor force within the next five years, one-third were not sure if they would or not, and just under one-third felt sure that they would stay at home for at least another five years. These figures compare with the eighteen of twenty paid working mothers who planned to continue working outside the home; only two hoped they would at some point be able to stay at home with the kids.

   Two of the eighteen stay-at-home mothers in my sample wanted to stay home *indefinitely*. Here's how one of them explained her position: "I don't want to go to work. I enjoy being [at home]. I enjoy it. I don't mind if somebody would call me a housewife or a homemaker. It doesn't bother me. I'm not a feminist. There's no need for me to be out there. For the amount of money I made, it's not worth it." Her concluding remark is, of course, telling. But poorly paid jobs are not the only reason that mothers want to stay home. . . . It should also be recognized that many women want to work outside the home even if their jobs pay poorly.

7. This can be hard on a mother too. For instance: "[My friend] was working full-time, and she came to the baby-sitter's, and her daughter was just kind of clinging to the baby-sitter and wouldn't come to her. And that was it for her. She quit her job."

8. This same argument is also found in popular-press pieces such as "The Managerial Mother" (Schneider 1987). Since the time of these interviews a number of the middle-class employed mothers I know (nearly all of whom are academics) have made this same argument: that they are more "organized, efficient, and effective" as moms because their paid work trains them to develop those skills, just as their double shift forces them to be organized, efficient, and effective *all* the time. In fact, many of these mothers argue that the professionalism they learn as working women explains their intensive mothering. The problem with this explanation is that the ideology of intensive motherhood, as I have shown, is not confined to middle-class, paid-working mothers. Many other women argue that it is mothering itself that teaches them to be more organized, efficient, and effective as mothers and as workers.

   But there is some truth in what my paid professional women friends say. Although intensive mothering has a much broader social basis, there are reasons why middle-class mothers on the one side, and paid working women on the other, are, in some respects, more intensive in their mothering. It makes sense that women who are both middle-class and paid professionals add to this an overlay of training in organization and focused commitment to their assigned tasks. But this only explains differences in degree; it does not explain the larger social grounding for the ideology of intensive mothering.

9. My sample is too small to make any definitive comment on this, but the numbers are as follows: half of the paid working mothers in my study say that children and home are more important for a woman than work, whereas only one-quarter of the stay-at-home mothers respond in this way (with the remainder providing the "it depends" response). And, it is interesting to note, professional-class and affluent paid-working mothers are the group most likely to say that home and children are more important and rewarding than careers; nearly three-quarters of them respond this way.

10. While the historical increase in the use of day-care facilities and alternative caregivers might be seen as an attempt to lessen the cultural contradictions of motherhood, it should be recognized that, historically speaking, mothers rarely did the job of raising children alone: rural families often had live-in help and relied on older siblings to take care of the younger ones; working-class women in urban areas also relied on older children as well as on friends and neighbors; and many upper-class women depended upon servants, nannies, and nursemaids. Although there does seem to have been a period during the 1950s and 1960s when families were less able to obtain and less likely to use help in raising children, today's alternatives to exclusively maternal care are probably

in large measure a simple *substitute* for the help that was previously available. Furthermore, it is important to note that the expectations for the task are much higher today than they once were, that mothers must therefore expend much time and energy seeking out and assuring the maintenance of the proper day-care situation, and that the use of day care coexists with increased expectations for mothers to make up for the hours their children spend under the care of others.

References

Berger, Bennett. 1981. *Survival of a Counterculture.* Berkeley: University of California Press.

Berger, Brigitte, and Peter Berger. 1983. *The War over the Family: Capturing the Middle Ground.* Garden City, N.Y.: Anchor.

Darnton, Nina. 1990. "Mommy vs. Mommy." *Newsweek,* June 4.

Friedan, Betty. 1963. *The Feminine Mystique.* New York: Dell.

Gerson, Kathleen. 1985. *Hard Choices: How Women Decide about Work, Career, and Motherhood.* Berkeley: University of California Press.

Ginsburg, Faye D. 1989. *Contested Lives: The Abortion Debate in an American Community.* Berkeley: University of California Press.

Hayghe, Howard V., and Suzanne M. Bianchi. 1994. "Married Mothers' Work Patterns: The Job-Family Compromise." *Monthly Labor Review* 117 (6):24–30.

Hochschild, Arlie, with Anne Machung. 1989. *The Second Shift: Working Parents and the Revolution at Home.* New York: Viking.

Hunter, James Davison. 1991. *Culture Wars: The Struggle to Define America.* New York: Basic.

———. 1994. *Before the Shooting Begins: Searching for Democracy in America's Culture War.* New York: Free Press.

Klatch, Rebecca E. 1987. *Women of the New Right.* Philadelphia: Temple University Press.

Luker, Kristin. 1984. *Abortion and the Politics of Motherhood.* Berkeley: University of California Press.

Schneider, Phyllis. 1987. "The Managerial Mother." *Working Woman,* December, 117–26.

Schwartz, Felice. 1989. "Management Women and the New Facts of Life." *Harvard Business Review* 67 (1):65–77.

READING 5

Decline of the Family: Conservative, Liberal, and Feminist Views

Janet Z. Giele

In the 1990s the state of American families and children became a new and urgent topic. Everyone recognized that families had changed. Divorce rates had risen dramatically. More women were in the labor force. Evidence on rising teenage suicides, high rates of teen births, and disturbing levels of addiction and violence had put children at risk.

Conservatives have held that these problems can be traced to a culture of toleration and an expanding welfare state that undercut self-reliance and community standards.

They focus on the family as a caregiving institution and try to restore its strengths by changing the culture of marriage and parenthood. Liberals center on the disappearance of manual jobs that throws less educated men out of work and undercuts their status in the family as well as rising hours of work among the middle class that makes stable two-parent families more difficult to maintain. Liberals argue that structural changes are needed outside the family in the public world of employment and schools.

The feminist vision combines both the reality of human interdependence in the family and individualism of the workplace. Feminists want to protect diverse family forms that allow realization of freedom and equality while at the same time nurturing the children of the next generation.

THE CONSERVATIVE EXPLANATION: SELFISHNESS AND MORAL DECLINE

The new family advocates turn their spotlight on the breakdown in the two-parent family, saying that rising divorce, illegitimacy, and father absence have put children at greater risk of school failure, unemployment, and antisocial behavior. The remedy is to restore religious faith and family commitment as well as to cut welfare payments to unwed mothers and mother-headed families.

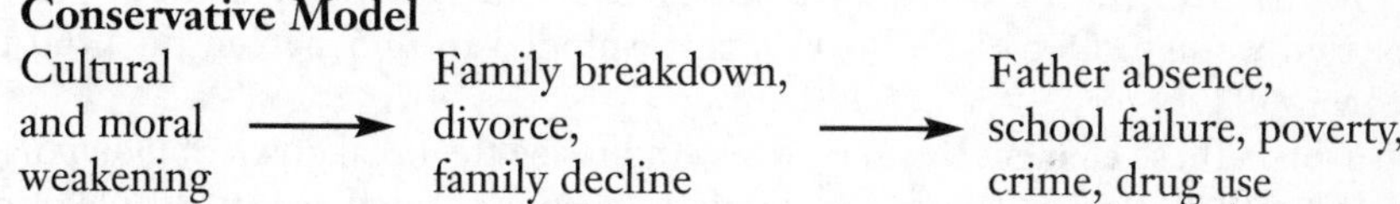

Cultural and Moral Weakening

To many conservatives, the modern secularization of religious practice and the decline of religious affiliation have undermined the norms of sexual abstinence before marriage and the prohibitions of adultery or divorce thereafter. Sanctions against illegitimacy or divorce have been made to seem narrow-minded and prejudiced. In addition, daytime television and the infamous example of Murphy Brown, a single mother having a child out of wedlock, helped to obscure simple notions of right and wrong. Barbara Dafoe Whitehead's controversial article in the *Atlantic* entitled "Dan Quayle Was Right" is an example of this argument.[1]

Gradual changes in marriage law have also diminished the hold of tradition. Restrictions against waiting periods, race dissimilarity, and varying degrees of consanguinity were gradually disappearing all over the United States and Europe.[2] While Mary Ann Glendon viewed the change cautiously but relativistically—as a process that waxed and waned across the centuries—others have interpreted these changes as a movement from status to contract (i.e., from attention to the particular individual's characteristics to reliance on the impersonal considerations of the market place).[3] The resulting transformation lessened the family's distinctive capacity to serve as a bastion of private freedom against the leveling effect and impersonality of public bureaucracy.

Erosion of the Two-Parent Family

To conservatives, one of the most visible causes of family erosion was government welfare payments, which made fatherless families a viable option. In *Losing Ground*, Charles Murray used the rise in teenage illegitimate births as proof that government-sponsored welfare programs had actually contributed to the breakdown of marriage.[4] Statistics on rising divorce and mother-headed families appeared to provide ample proof that the two-parent family was under siege. The proportion of all households headed by married couples fell from 77 percent in 1950 to 61 percent in 1980 and 55 percent in 1993.[5] Rising cohabitation, divorce rates, and births out of wedlock all contributed to the trend. The rise in single-person households was also significant, from only 12 percent of all households in 1950 to 27 percent in 1980, a trend fed by rising affluence and the undoubling of living arrangements that occurred with the expansion of the housing supply after World War II.[6]

The growth of single-parent households, however, was the most worrisome to policymakers because of their strong links to child poverty. In 1988, 50 percent of all children were found in mother-only families compared with 20 percent in 1950. The parental situation of children in poverty changed accordingly. Of all poor children in 1959, 73 percent had two parents present and 20 percent had a mother only. By 1988, only 35 percent of children in poverty lived with two parents and 57 percent lived with a mother only. These developments were fed by rising rates of divorce and out-of-wedlock births. Between 1940 and 1990, the divorce rate rose from 8.8 to 21 per thousand married women. Out-of-wedlock births exploded from 5 percent in 1960 to 26 percent in 1990.[7]

To explain these changes, conservatives emphasize the breakdown of individual and cultural commitment to marriage and the loss of stigma for divorce and illegitimacy. They understand both trends to be the result of greater emphasis on short-term gratification and on adults' personal desires rather than on what is good for children. A young woman brings a child into the world without thinking about who will support it. A husband divorces his wife and forms another household, possibly with other children, and leaves children of the earlier family behind without necessarily feeling obliged to be present in their upbringing or to provide them with financial support.

Negative Consequences for Children

To cultural conservatives there appears to be a strong connection between erosion of the two-parent family and the rise of health and social problems in children. Parental investment in children has declined—especially in the time available for supervision and companionship. Parents had roughly 10 fewer hours per week for their children in 1986 than in 1960, largely because more married women were employed (up from 24 percent in 1940 to 52 percent in 1983) and more mothers of young children (under age six) were working (up from 12 percent in 1940 to 50 percent in 1983). By the late 1980s just over half of mothers of children under a year old were in the labor force for at least part of the year.[8] At the same time fathers were increasingly absent from the family because of desertion, divorce, or failure to marry. In 1980, 15 percent of white children, 50 percent of black children, and 27 percent of children of Hispanic origin had no father present. Today 36 percent of children are living apart from their biological fathers compared with only 17 percent in 1960.[9]

Without a parent to supervise children after school, keep them from watching television all day, or prevent them from playing in dangerous neighborhoods, many more children appear to be falling by the wayside, victims of drugs, obesity, violence, suicide, or failure in school. During the 1960s and 1970s the suicide rate for persons aged fifteen to nineteen more than doubled. The proportion of obese children between the ages of six and eleven rose from 18 to 27 percent. Average SAT scores fell, and 25 percent of all high school students failed to graduate.[10] In 1995 the Council on Families in America reported, "Recent surveys have found that children from broken homes, when they become teenagers, have 2 to 3 times more behavioral and psychological problems than do children from intact homes."[11] Father absence is blamed by the fatherhood movement for the rise in violence among young males. David Blankenhorn and others reason that the lack of a positive and productive male role model has contributed to an uncertain masculine identity which then uses violence and aggression to prove itself. Every child deserves a father and "in a good society, men prove their masculinity not by killing other people, impregnating lots of women, or amassing large fortunes, but rather by being committed fathers and loving husbands."[12]

Psychologist David Elkind, in *The Hurried Child*, suggests that parents' work and time constraints have pushed down the developmental timetable to younger ages so that small children are being expected to take care of themselves and perform at levels which are robbing them of their childhood. The consequences are depression, discouragement, and a loss of joy at learning and growing into maturity.[13]

Reinvention of Marriage

According to the conservative analysis, the solution to a breakdown in family values is to revitalize and reinstitutionalize marriage. The culture should change to give higher priority to marriage and parenting. The legal code should favor marriage and encourage parental responsibility on the part of fathers as well as mothers. Government should cut back welfare programs which have supported alternate family forms.

The cultural approach to revitalizing marriage is to raise the overall priority given to family activities relative to work, material consumption, or leisure. Marriage is seen as the basic building block of civil society, which helps to hold together the fabric of volunteer activity and mutual support that underpins any democratic society.[14] Some advocates are unapologetically judgmental toward families who fall outside the two-parent mold. According to a 1995 *Newsweek* article on "The Return of Shame," David Blankenhorn believes "a stronger sense of shame about illegitimacy and divorce would do more than any tax cut or any new governmental program to maximize the life circumstances of children." But he also adds that the ultimate goal is "to move beyond stigmatizing only teenage mothers toward an understanding of the terrible message sent by all of us when we minimize the importance of fathers or contribute to the breakup of families."[15]

Another means to marriage and family revitalization is some form of taking a "pledge." Prevention programs for teenage pregnancy affirm the ideal of chastity before marriage. Athletes for Abstinence, an organization founded by a professional basketball player, preaches that young people should "save sex for marriage." A Baptist-led national program called True Love Waits has gathered an abstinence pledge from hundreds of thousands of teenagers since it was begun in the spring of 1993. More than 2,000 school districts now offer an abstinence-based sex education curriculum entitled "Sex Respect." Parents who are desperate about their children's sexual behavior are at last seeing ways that society can resist the continued sexualization of childhood.[16]

The new fatherhood movement encourages fathers to promise that they will spend more time with their children. The National Fatherhood Initiative argues that men's roles as fathers should not simply duplicate women's roles as mothers but should teach those essential qualities which are perhaps uniquely conveyed by fathers—the ability to take risks, contain emotions, and be decisive. In addition, fathers fulfill a time-honored role of providing for children as well as teaching them.[17]

Full-time mothers have likewise formed support groups to reassure themselves that not having a job and being at home full-time for their children is an honorable choice, although it is typically undervalued and perhaps even scorned by dual-earner couples and women with careers. A 1994 *Barron's* article claimed that young people in their twenties ("generation X") were turning away from the two-paycheck family and scaling down their consumption so that young mothers could stay at home. Although Labor Department statistics show no such trend but only a flattening of the upward rise of women's employment, a variety of poll data does suggest that Americans would rather spend less time at work and more time with their families.[18] Such groups as Mothers at Home (with 15,000 members) and Mothers' Home Business Network (with 6,000 members) are trying to create a sea change that reverses the priority given to paid work outside the home relative to unpaid caregiving work inside the family.[19]

Conservatives see government cutbacks as one of the major strategies for strengthening marriage and restoring family values. In the words of Lawrence Mead, we have "taxed Peter to pay Paula."[20] According to a *Wall Street Journal* editorial, the "relinquishment of personal responsibility" among people who bring children into the world without any visible means of support is at the root of educational, health, and emotional problems of children from one-parent families, their higher accident and mortality rates, and rising crime.[21]

The new congressional solution is to cut back on the benefits to young men and women who "violate social convention by having children they cannot support."[22] Sociologist Brigitte Berger notes that the increase in children and women on welfare coincided with the explosion of federal child welfare programs—family planning, prenatal and postnatal care, child nutrition, child abuse prevention and treatment, child health and guidance, day care, Head Start, and Aid to Families with Dependent Children (AFDC), Medicaid, and Food Stamps. The solution is to turn back the debilitating culture of welfare dependency by decentralizing the power of the federal government and restoring the role of intermediary community institutions such as the neighborhood and the church. The mechanism for change would be block grants to the states which would change the welfare culture from the ground up.[23] Robert Rector of the American Heritage Foundation explains that the states would use these funds for a wide variety of alternative programs to discourage illegitimate births and to care for children born out of wedlock, such as promoting adoption, closely supervised group homes for unmarried mothers and their children, and pregnancy prevention programs (except abortion).[24]

Government programs, however, are only one way to bring about cultural change. The Council on Families in America puts its hope in grassroots social movements to change the hearts and minds of religious and civil leaders, employers, human service professionals, courts, and the media and entertainment industry. The Council enunciates four ideals: marital permanence, childbearing confined to marriage, every child's right to have a father, and limitation of parents' total work time (60 hours per week) to permit adequate time with their families.[25] To restore the cultural ideal of the two-parent family, they would make all other types of family life less attractive and more difficult.

ECONOMIC RESTRUCTURING: LIBERAL ANALYSIS OF FAMILY CHANGE

Liberals agree that there are serious problems in America's social health and the condition of its children. But they pinpoint economic and structural changes that have placed new demands on the family without providing countervailing social supports. The economy has become ever more specialized with rapid technological change undercutting established occupations. More women have entered the labor force as their child-free years have increased due to a shorter childbearing period and longer lifespan. The family has lost economic functions to the urban workplace and socialization functions to the school. What is left is the intimate relationship between the marital couple, which, unbuffered by the traditional economic division of labor between men and women, is subject to even higher demands for emotional fulfillment and is thus more vulnerable to breakdown when it falls short of those demands.

Liberal Model

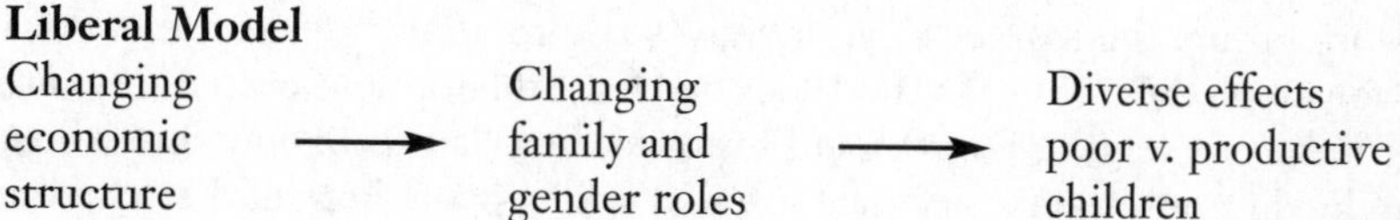

The current family crisis thus stems from structural more than cultural change—changes in the economy, a pared-down nuclear family, and less parental time at home. Market forces have led to a new ethic of individual flexibility and autonomy. More dual-earner couples and single-parent families have broadened the variety of family forms. More single-parent families and more working mothers have decreased the time available for parenting. Loss of the father's income through separation and divorce has forced many women and children into poverty with inadequate health care, poor education, and inability to save for future economic needs. The solution that most liberals espouse is a government-sponsored safety net which will facilitate women's employment, mute the effects of poverty, and help women and children to become economically secure.

Recent Changes in the Labor Market

Liberals attribute the dramatic changes in the family to the intrusion of the money economy rather than cultural and moral decline. In a capitalist society individual behavior follows the market. Adam Smith's "invisible hand" brings together buyers and sellers who maximize their satisfaction through an exchange of resources in the marketplace. Jobs are now with an employer, not with the family business or family farm as in preindustrial times. The cash economy has, in the words of Robert Bellah, "invaded" the diffuse personal relationships of trust between family and community members and transformed them into specific impersonal transactions. In an agricultural economy husbands and wives and parents and children were bound together in relationships of exchange that served each others' mutual interests. But modern society erodes this social capital of organization, trust among individuals, and mutual obligation that enhances both productivity and parenting.[26]

The market has also eroded community by encouraging maximum mobility of goods and services. Cheaper labor in the South, lower fuel prices, and deeper tax breaks attracted first textile factories, then the shoe industry, and later automobile assembly plants which had begun in the North. Eventually, many of these jobs left the country. Loss of manufacturing jobs has had dramatic consequences for employment of young men without a college education and their capacity to support a family. In the 1970s, 68 percent of male high school graduates had a full-time, year-round job compared with only 51 percent in the 1980s. Many new jobs are located in clerical work, sales, or other service occupations traditionally associated with women. The upshot is a deteriorating employment picture for less well educated male workers at the same time that there are rising opportunities for women. Not surprisingly, even more middle income men and women combine forces to construct a two-paycheck family wage.[27]

Changing Family Forms

Whereas the farm economy dictated a two-parent family and several children as the most efficient work group, the market economy gives rise to a much wider variety of family forms. A woman on the frontier in the 1800s had few other options even if she were married to a drunken, violent, or improvident husband. In today's economy this woman may have enough education to get a clerical job that will support her and her children in a small apartment where the family will be able to use public schools and other public amenities.[28]

Despite its corrosive effect on family relations, the modern economy has also been a liberating force. Women could escape patriarchal domination; the young could seek their fortune without waiting for an inheritance from their elders—all a process that a century ago was aligned with a cultural shift that Fred Weinstein and Gerald Platt termed "the wish to be free."[29] Dramatic improvements took place in the status of women as they gained the right to higher education, entry into the professions, and the elective franchise.[30] Similarly, children were released from sometimes cruel and exploitive labor and became the object of deliberate parental investment and consumption.[31] Elders gained pensions for maintenance and care that made them economically independent of their adult children. All these developments could be understood as part of what William J. Goode has referred to as the "world revolution in family patterns" which resulted in liberation and equality of formerly oppressed groups.[32]

The current assessment of change in family forms is, however, mostly negative because of the consequences for children. More parental investment in work outside the family has meant less time for children. According to liberals, parents separate or divorce or have children outside of marriage because of the economic structure, not because they have become less moral or more selfish. Young women have children out of wedlock when the young men whom they might marry have few economic prospects and when the women themselves have little hope for their own education or employment.[33] Change in the family thus begins with jobs. Advocates of current government programs therefore challenge the conservatives' assertion that welfare caused the breakup of two-parent families by supporting mothers with dependent children. According to William Julius Wilson, it is partly the lack of manual labor jobs for the would-be male breadwinner in inner-city Chicago—the scarcity of "marriageable males"—which drives up the illegitimacy rate.[34]

Among educated women, it is well known that the opportunity costs of foregone income from staying home became so high during the 1950s and 1960s that ever increasing numbers of women deserted full-time homemaking to take paid employment.[35] In the 1990s several social scientists have further noted that Richard Easterlin's prediction that women will return to the home during the 1980s never happened. Instead, women continued in the labor force because of irreversible normative changes surrounding women's equality and the need for women's income to finance children's expensive college education.[36] Moreover, in light of globalization of the economy and increasing job insecurity in the face of corporate downsizing, economists and sociologists are questioning Gary Becker's thesis that the lower waged worker in a household (typically the woman) will tend to become a full-time homemaker while the higher waged partner becomes the primary breadwinner. Data from Germany and the United States on the trend toward women's multiple roles suggests that uncertainty about the future has made women invest more strongly than ever in their own careers. They know that if they drop out for very long they will have difficulty reentering if they have to tide over the family when the main breadwinner loses his job.[37]

Consequences for Children

The ideal family in the liberal economic model, according to political philosopher Iris Young, is one which has sufficient income to support the parents and the children and "to foster in those children the emotional and intellectual capacities to acquire such well-paid, secure jobs themselves, and also sufficient to finance a retirement."[38] Dependent families do not have self-sufficient income but must rely on friends, relatives, charity, or the state to carry out their contribution to bringing up children and being good citizens.

Among liberals there is an emerging consensus that the current economic structure leads to two kinds of underinvestment in children that are implicated in their later dependency—material poverty, characteristic of the poor, and "time" poverty, characteristic of the middle class.

Thirty years ago Daniel Patrick Moynihan perceived that material poverty and job loss for a man put strain on the marriage, sometimes to the point that he would leave. His children also did less well in school.[39] Rand Conger, in his studies of Iowa families who lost their farms during the 1980s, found that economic hardship not only puts strain on the marriage but leads to harsh parenting practices and poorer outcomes for children.[40] Thus it appears possible that poverty may not just be the result of family separation, divorce, and ineffective childrearing practices; it may also be the *cause* of the irritability, quarrels, and violence which lead to marital breakdown. Material underinvestment in children is visible not just with the poor but in the changing ratio of per capita income of children and adults in U.S. society as a whole. As the proportion of households without children has doubled over the last century (from 30 to 65 percent), per capita income of children has fallen from 71 percent of adult income in 1870 to 63 percent in 1930 and 51 percent in 1983.[41]

The problem of "time" poverty used to be almost exclusively associated with mothers' employment. Numerous studies explored whether younger children did better if their mother was a full-time homemaker rather than employed outside the home but found no clear results.[42] Lately the lack of parental time for children has become much more acute because parents are working a total of twenty-one hours more per week than in 1970 and because there are more single-parent families. In 1965 the average child spent about thirty hours a week interacting with a parent, compared with seventeen hours in the 1980s.[43] Moreover, parents are less dependent on their children to provide support for them during old age, and children feel less obligated to do so. As skilled craftsmanship, the trades, and the family farms have disappeared, children's upbringing can no longer be easily or cheaply combined with what parents are already doing. So adults are no longer so invested in children's futures. The result is that where the social capital of group affiliations and mutual obligations is the lowest (in the form of continuity of neighborhoods, a two-parent family, or a parent's interest in higher education for her children), children are 20 percent more likely to drop out of high school.[44]

It is not that parents prefer their current feelings of being rushed, working too many hours, and having too little time with their families. Economist Juliet Schor reports that at least two-thirds of persons she surveyed about their desires for more family time versus more salary would take a cut in salary if it could mean more time with their families. Since this option is not realistically open to many, what parents appear to do is spend more money on their children as a substitute for spending more time with them.[45]

Fixing the Safety Net

Since liberals believe in a market economy with sufficient government regulation to assure justice and equality of opportunity, they support those measures which will eradicate the worst poverty and assure the healthy reproduction of the next generation.[46] What particularly worries them, however, is Charles Murray's observation that since 1970 the growth of government welfare programs has been associated with a *rise* in poverty among children. Payments to poor families with children, while not generous, have nevertheless enabled adults to be supported by attachment to their children.[47] Society is faced with a dilemma between addressing material poverty through further government subsidy and time poverty through policies on parental leave and working hours. It turns out that the United States is trying to do both.

Measures for addressing material poverty would stimulate various kinds of training and job opportunities. The Family Support Act of 1988 would move AFDC mothers off the welfare rolls by giving them job training and requiring them to join the labor force. Such action would bring their economic responsibility for supporting their children into line with their parental authority. A whole program of integrated supports for health insurance, job training, earned income tax credits for the working poor, child support by the noncustodial parent, and supported work is put forward by economist David Ellwood in *Poor Support*.[48] An opposite strategy is to consolidate authority over children with the state's economic responsibility for their care by encouraging group homes and adoption for children whose parents cannot support them economically.[49]

Means for addressing time poverty are evident in such legislative initiatives as the Family and Medical Leave Act of 1993. By encouraging employers to grant parental leave or other forms of flexible work time, government policy is recognizing the value of parents having more time with their children, but the beneficiaries of such change are largely middle-class families who can afford an unpaid parental leave.[50] Another tactic is to reform the tax law to discourage marital splitting. In a couple with two children in which the father earns $16,000 annually and the mother $9,000, joint tax filing gives them no special consideration. But if they file separately, each taking one child as a dependent, the woman will receive about $5,000 in Earned Income Tax Credit and an extra $2,000 in food stamps.[51] Changing the tax law to remove the incentives for splitting, establishing paternity of children born out of wedlock, and intensifying child support enforcement to recover economic support from fathers are all examples of state efforts to strengthen the kinship unit.

INTERDEPENDENCE: THE FEMINIST VISION OF WORK AND CAREGIVING

A feminist perspective has elements in common with both conservatives and liberals: a respect for the family as an institution (shared with the conservatives) and an appreciation of modernity (valued by the liberals). In addition, a feminist perspective grapples with the problem of women's traditionally subordinate status and how to improve it through both a "relational" and an "individualist" strategy while also sustaining family life and the healthy rearing of children.[52] At the same time feminists are skeptical of both conservative and liberal solutions. Traditionalists have so often relied on women as the exploited and underpaid caregivers in the family to enable men's activities in the public realm. Liberals are sometimes guilty of a "male" bias in focusing on the independent individual actor in the marketplace who does not realize that his so-called "independence," is possible only because he is actually *dependent* on all kinds of relationships that made possible his education and life in a stable social order.[53]

By articulating the value of caregiving along with the ideal of women's autonomy, feminists are in a position to examine modern capitalism critically for its effects on families and to offer alternative policies that place greater value on the quality of life and human relationships. They judge family strength not by their *form* (whether they have two-parents) but by their functioning (whether they promote human satisfaction and development) and whether both women and men are able to be family caregivers as well as productive workers. They attribute difficulties of children less to the absence of the two-parent family than to low-wage work of single mothers, inadequate child care, and inhospitable housing and neighborhoods.

Feminist Model

Lack of cooperation among community, family, and work	→	Families where adults are stressed and overburdened	→	Children lack sufficient care and attention from parents

Accordingly, feminists would work for reforms that build and maintain the social capital of volunteer groups, neighborhoods, and communities because a healthy civil society promotes the well-being of families and individuals as well as economic prosperity and a democratic state. They would also recognize greater role flexibility across the life cycle so that both men and women could engage in caregiving, and they would encourage education and employment among women as well as among men.

Disappearance of Community

From a feminist perspective, family values have become an issue because individualism has driven out the sense of collective responsibility in our national culture. American institutions and social policies have not properly implemented a concern for all citizens. Comparative research on family structure, teenage pregnancy, poverty, and child outcomes in other countries demonstrates that where support is generous to help *all* families and children, there are higher levels of health and general education and lower levels of violence and child deviance than in the United States.[54]

Liberal thinking and the focus on the free market have made it seem that citizens make their greatest contribution when they are self-sufficient, thereby keeping themselves off the public dole. But feminist theorist Iris Young argues that many of the activities that are basic to a healthy democratic society (such as cultural production, caretaking, political organizing, and charitable activities) will never be profitable in a private market. Yet many of the recipients of welfare and Social Security such as homemakers, single mothers, and retirees are doing important volunteer work caring for children and helping others in their communities. Thus the social worth of a person's contribution is not just in earning a paycheck that allows economic independence but also in making a social contribution. Such caretaking of other dependent citizens and of the body politic should be regarded as honorable, not inferior, and worthy of society's support and subsidy.[55]

In fact it appears that married women's rising labor force participation from 41 percent in 1970 to 58 percent in 1990 may have been associated with their withdrawal from unpaid work in the home and community.[56] Volunteer membership in everything from the PTA to bowling leagues declined by over 25 percent between 1969 and 1993. There is now considerable concern that the very basis that Alexis de Tocqueville thought necessary to democracy is under siege.[57] To reverse this trend, social observers suggest that it will be necessary to guard time for families and leisure that is currently being sucked into the maw of paid employment. What is needed is a reorientation of priorities to give greater value to unpaid family and community work by both men and women.

National policies should also be reoriented to give universal support to children at every economic level of society, but especially to poor children. In a comparison of countries in the Organization for Economic Cooperation and Development, the United States ranks at the top in average male wages but near the bottom in its provision for disposable income for children. In comparison with the $700 per month available to children in Norway, France, or the Netherlands in 1992, U.S. children of a single nonemployed mother received only slightly under $200.[58] The discrepancy is explained by very unequal distribution of U.S. income, with the top quintile, the "fortunate fifth," gaining 47 percent of the national income while the bottom fifth receives only 3.6 percent.[59] This sharp inequality is, in turn, explained by an ideology of individualism that justifies the disproportionate gains of the few for their innovation and productivity and the meager income of the poor for their low initiative or competence. Lack of access to jobs and the low pay accruing to many contingent service occupations simply worsen the picture.

Feminists are skeptical of explanations that ascribe higher productivity to the higher paid and more successful leading actors while ignoring the efforts and contribution of the supporting cast. They know that being an invisible helper is the situation of many women. This insight is congruent with new ideas about the importance "social capital" to the health of a society that have been put forward recently by a number of social scientists.[60] Corporations cannot be solely responsible for maintaining the web of community, although they are already being asked to serve as extended family, neighborhood support group, and national health service.

Diversity of Family Forms

Those who are concerned for strengthening the civil society immediately turn to the changing nature of the family as being a key building block. Feminists worry that seemingly sensible efforts to reverse the trend of rising divorce and single parenthood will privilege the two-parent family to the detriment of women; they propose instead that family values be understood in a broader sense as valuing the family's unique capacity for giving emotional and material support rather than implying simply a two-parent form.

The debate between conservatives, liberals, and feminists on the issue of the two-parent family has been most starkly stated by sociologist Judith Stacey and political philosopher Iris Young.[61] They regard the requirement that all women stay in a marriage as an invitation to coercion and subordination and an assault on the principles of freedom and self-determination that are at the foundation of democracy. Moreover, as Christopher Jencks and Kathryn Edin conclude from their study of several hundred welfare families, the current welfare reform rhetoric that no couple should have a child unless they can support it, does not take into account the uncertainty of life in which people who start out married or with adequate income [do] not always remain so. In the face of the worldwide dethronement of the two-parent family (approximately one-quarter to one-third of all families around the globe are headed by women), marriage should not be seen as the cure for child poverty. Mothers should not be seen as less than full citizens if they are not married or not employed (in 1989 there were only 16 million males between the ages of 25 and 34 who made over $12,000 compared with 20 million females of the same age who either had a child or wanted one).[62] National family policy should instead begin with a value on women's autonomy and self-determination that includes the right to bear children. Mother-citizens are helping to reproduce the next generation for the whole society, and in that responsibility they deserve at least partial support.

From a feminist perspective the goal of the family is not only to bring up a healthy and productive new generation; families also provide the intimate and supportive group of kin or fictive kin that foster the health and well-being of every person—young or old, male or female, heterosexual, homosexual, or celibate. Recognition as "family" should therefore not be confined to the traditional two-parent unit connected by blood, marriage, or adoption, but should be extended to include kin of a divorced spouse (as Stacey documented in her study of Silicon Valley families), same-sex partnerships, congregate households of retired persons, group living arrangements, and so on.[63] Twenty years ago economist Nancy Barrett noted that such diversity in family and household form was already present. Among all U.S. households in 1976, no one of the six major types constituted more than 15–20 percent: couples with and without children under eighteen with the wife in the labor force (15.4 and 13.3 percent respectively); couples with or without children under 18 with the wife not in the labor force (19.1 and 17.1 percent); female- or male-headed households (14.4 percent); and single persons living alone (20.6 percent).[64]

Such diversity both describes and informs contemporary "family values" in the United States. Each family type is numerous enough to have a legitimacy of its own, yet no single form is the dominant one. As a result the larger value system has evolved to encompass beliefs and rules that legitimate each type on the spectrum. The regressive alternative is "fundamentalism" that treats the two-parent family with children as the only legitimate form, single-parent families as unworthy of support, and the nontraditional forms as illegitimate. In 1995 the general population appears to have accepted diversity of family forms as normal. A Harris poll of 1,502 women and 460 men found that only 2 percent of women and 1 percent of men defined family as "being about the traditional nuclear family." One out of ten women defined family values as loving, taking care of, and supporting each other, knowing right from wrong or having good values, and nine out of ten said society should value all types of families.[65] It appears most Americans believe that an Aunt Polly single-parent type of family for a Huck Finn that provides economic support, shelter, meals, a place to sleep and to withdraw, is better than no family at all.

Amidst gradual acceptance of greater diversity in family form, the gender-role revolution is also loosening the sex-role expectations traditionally associated with breadwinning and homemaking. Feminists believe that men and women can each do both.[66] In addition, women in advanced industrial nations have by and large converged upon a new life pattern of multiple roles by which they combine work and family life. The negative outcome is an almost universal "double burden" for working women in which they spend eighty-four hours per week on paid and family work, married men spend seventy-two hours, and single persons without children spend fifty hours.[67] The positive consequence, however, appears to be improved physical and mental health for those women who, though stressed, combine work and family roles.[68] In addition, where a woman's husband helps her more with the housework, she is less likely to think of getting a divorce.[69]

The Precarious Situation of Children

The principal remedy that conservatives and liberals would apply to the problems of children is to restore the two-parent family by reducing out-of-wedlock births, increasing the presence of fathers, and encouraging couples who are having marital difficulties to avoid divorce for the sake of their children. Feminists, on the other hand, are skeptical that illegitimacy, father absence, or divorce are the principal culprits they are made out to be. Leon Eisenberg reports that over half of all births in Sweden and one-quarter of births in France are to unmarried women, but without the disastrous correlated effects observed in the United States. Arlene Skolnick and Stacey Rosencrantz cite longitudinal studies showing that most children recover from the immediate negative effects of divorce.[70]

How then, while supporting the principle that some fraction of women should be able to head families as single parents, do feminists analyze the problem of ill health, antisocial behavior, and poverty among children? Their answer focuses on the *lack of institutional supports* for the new type of dual-earner and single-parent families that are more prevalent today. Rather than attempt to force families back into the traditional mold, feminists note that divorce, lone-mother families, and women's employment are on the rise in every industrialized nation. But other countries have not seen the same devastating decline in child well-being, teen pregnancy, suicides and violent death, school failure, and a rising population of children in poverty. These other countries have four key elements of social and family policy which protect all children and their mothers: (1) work guarantees and other economic supports; (2) child care; (3) health care; and (4) housing subsidies. In the United States these benefits are scattered and uneven; those who can pay their way do so; only those who are poor or disabled receive AFDC for economic support, some help with child care, Medicaid for health care, and government-subsidized housing.

A first line of defense is to raise women's wages through raising the minimum wage, then provide them greater access to male-dominated occupations with higher wages. One-half of working women do not earn a wage adequate to support a family of four above the poverty line. Moreover, women in low-wage occupations are subject to frequent lay-offs and lack of benefits. Training to improve their human capital, provision of child care, and broadening of benefits would help raise women's capacity to support a family. Eisenberg reports that the Human Development Index of the United Nations (HDI), which ranks countries by such indicators as life expectancy, educational levels, and per capita income, places the United States fifth and Sweden sixth in the world. But when the HDI is recalculated to take into account equity of treatment of women, Sweden rises to first place and the United States falls to ninth. Therefore, one of the obvious places to begin raising children's status is to "raise the economic status and earning power of their mothers."[71]

A second major benefit which is not assured to working mothers is child care. Among school-age children up to thirteen years of age, one-eighth lack any kind of after-school child care. Children come to the factories where their mothers work and wait on the lawn or in the lobby until their mothers are finished working. If a child is sick, some mothers risk losing a job if they stay home. Others are latchkey kids or in unknown circumstances such as sleeping in their parents' cars or loitering on the streets. Although 60 percent of mothers of the 22 million preschool children are working, there are only 10 million child care places available, a shortfall of one to three million slots.[72] Lack of good quality care for her children not only distracts a mother, adds to her absences from work, and makes her less productive, it also exposes the child to a lack of attention and care that leads to violent and antisocial behavior and poor performance in school.

Lack of medical benefits is a third gaping hole for poor children and lone-parent families. Jencks and Edin analyze what happens to a Chicago-area working woman's income if she goes off welfare. Her total income, in 1993, dollars on AFDC (with food stamps, unreported earnings, help from family and friends) adds up to $12,355, in addition to which she receives Medicaid and child care. At a $6 per hour full-time job, however, without AFDC, with less than half as much from food stamps, with an Earned Income Tax Credit, and help from relatives, her total income would add to $20,853. But she would have to pay for her own medical care, bringing her effective income down to $14,745 if she found free child care, and $9,801 if she had to pay for child care herself.[73]

Some housing subsidies or low-income housing are available to low-income families. But the neighborhoods and schools are frequently of poor quality and plagued by violence. To bring up children in a setting where they cannot safely play with others introduces important risk factors that cannot simply be attributed to divorce and single parenthood. Rather than being protected and being allowed to be innocent, children must learn to be competent at a very early age. The family, rather than being child-centered, must be adult-centered, not because parents are selfish or self-centered but because the institutions of the society have changed the context of family life.[74] These demands may be too much for children, and depression, violence, teen suicide, teen pregnancy, and school failure may result. But it would be myopic to think that simply restoring the two-parent family would be enough to solve all these problems.

Constructing Institutions for the Good Society

What is to be done? Rather than try to restore the two-parent family as the conservatives suggest or change the economy to provide more jobs as recommended by the liberals, the feminists focus on the need to revise and construct institutions to accommodate the new realities of work and family life. Such an undertaking requires, however, a broader interpretation of family values, a recognition that families benefit not only their members but the public interest, and fresh thinking about how to schedule work and family demands of everyday life as well as the entire life cycle of men and women.

The understanding of family values has to be extended in two ways. First, American values should be stretched to embrace all citizens, their children and families, whether they are poor, white, or people of color, or living in a one-parent family. In 1977, Kenneth Keniston titled the report of the Carnegie Commission on Children *All Our Children*. Today many Americans still speak and act politically in ways suggesting that they *disown* other people's children as the next generation who will inherit the land and support the economy. Yet in the view of most feminists and other progressive reformers, all these children should be embraced for the long-term good of the nation.[75] By a commitment to "family values" feminists secondly intend to valorize the family as a distinctive intimate group of many forms that is needed by persons of all ages but especially children. To serve the needs of children and other dependent persons, the family must be given support and encouragement by the state to carry out its unique functions. Iris Young contends that marriage should not be used to reduce the ultimate need for the state to serve as a means to distribute needed supports to the families of those less fortunate.[76] Compare the example of the GI Bill of Rights after World War II, which provided educational benefits to those who had served their country in the military. Why should there not be a similar approach to the contribution that a parent makes in raising a healthy and productive youngster?[77]

At the community level families should be embraced by all the institutions of the civil society—schools, hospitals, churches, and employers—as the hidden but necessary complement to the bureaucratic and impersonal workings of these formal organizations. Schools rely on parents for the child's "school readiness." Hospitals send home patients who need considerable home care before becoming completely well. The work of the church is carried out and reinforced in the family; and when families fail, it is the unconditional love and intimacy of family that the church tries to replicate. Employers depend on families to give the rest, shelter, emotional support, and other maintenance of human capital that will motivate workers and make them productive. Increasingly, the professionals and managers in these formal organizations are realizing that they need to work more closely with parents and family members if they are to succeed.

Feminists would especially like to see the reintegration of work and family life that was torn apart at the time of the industrial revolution when productive work moved out of the home and into the factory. Several proposals appear repeatedly: parental leave (which now is possible through the Family and Medical Leave Act of 1993); flexible hours and part-time work shared by working parents but without loss of benefits and promotion opportunities; home-based work; child care for sick children and after-school supervision. Although some progress has been made, acceptance of these reforms has been very slow. Parental leave is still *unpaid.* The culture of the workplace discourages many persons from taking advantage of the more flexible options which do exist because they fear they will be seen as less serious and dedicated workers. In addition, most programs are aimed at mothers and at managers, although there is growing feeling that fathers and hourly workers should be included as well.[78]

Ultimately these trends may alter the shape of women's and men's life cycles. Increasingly, a new ideal for the life course is being held up as the model that society should work toward. Lotte Bailyn proposes reorganization of careers in which young couples trade off periods of intense work commitment with each other while they establish their families so that either or both can spend more time at home.[79] Right now both women and men feel they must work so intensely to establish their careers that they have too little time for their children.[80] For the poor and untrained, the problem is the opposite: childbearing and childrearing are far more satisfying and validating than a low-paying, dead-end job. The question is how to reorient educators or employers to factor in time with family as an important obligation to society (much as one would factor in military service, for example). Such institutional reorganization is necessary to give families and childrearing their proper place in the modern postindustrial society.

CONCLUSION

A review of the conservative, liberal, and feminist perspectives on the changing nature of the American family suggests that future policy should combine the distinctive contributions of all three. From the conservatives comes a critique of modernity that recognizes the important role of the family in maintaining child health and preventing child failure. Although their understanding of "family values" is too narrow, they deserve credit for raising the issue of family function and form to public debate. Liberals see clearly the overwhelming power of the economy to deny employment, make demands on parents as workers, and drive a wedge between employers' needs for competitiveness and families' needs for connection and community.

Surprising although it may seem, since feminists are often imagined to be "way out," the most comprehensive plan for restoring family to its rightful place is put forward by the feminists who appreciate both the inherently premodern nature of the family and at the same time its inevitable interdependence with a fast-changing world economy. Feminists will not turn back to the past because they know that the traditional family was often a straightjacket for women. But they also know that family cannot be turned into a formal organization or have its functions performed by government or other public institutions that are incapable of giving needed succor to children, adults, and old people which only the family can give.

The feminist synthesis accepts both the inherent particularism and emotional nature of the family and the inevitable specialization and impersonality of the modern economy. Feminists are different from conservatives in accepting diversity of the family to respond to the needs of the modern economy. They are different from the liberals in recognizing that intimate nurturing relationships such as parenting cannot all be turned into a safety net of formal care. The most promising social policies for families and children take their direction from inclusive values that confirm the good life and the well-being of every individual as the ultimate goal of the nation. The policy challenge is to adjust the partnership between the family and its surrounding institutions so that together they combine the best of private initiative with public concern.

Notes

1. Barbara Dafoe Whitehead, "Dan Quayle Was Right," *Atlantic Monthly* (April 1993): 47. Her chapter in [*Promises to Keep: Decline and Renewal of Marriage in America*, edited by D. Popenoe, J. B. Elshtain, and D. Blankenhorn] on the "Story of Marriage" continues the theme of an erosion of values for cultural diversity.
2. Mary Ann Glendon, "Marriage and the State: The Withering Away of Marriage," *Virginia Law Review* 62 (May 1976): 663–729.
3. See chapters by Milton Regan and Carl Schneider in [*Promises to Keep: Decline and Renewal of Marriage in America*, edited by D. Popenoe, J. B. Elshtain, and D. Blankenhorn].
4. Charles A. Murray, *Losing Ground: American Social Policy: 1950–1980* (New York: Basic Books,

1984). Critics point out that the rise in out-of-wedlock births continues, even though welfare payments have declined in size over the last several decades, thereby casting doubt on the perverse incentive theory of rising illegitimacy.

5. U.S. Bureau of the Census. *Statistical Abstract of the United States: 1994*, 114th ed. (Washington, DC: 1994), 59.
6. Suzanne M. Bianchi and Daphne Spain, *American Women in Transition* (New York: Russell Sage Foundation, 1986), 88.
7. Donald J. Hernandez, *America's Children: Resources from Family, Government, and the Economy* (New York: Russell Sage Foundation, 1993), 284, 70. Janet Zollinger Giele, "Woman's Role Change and Adaptation: 1920–1990," in *Women's Lives through Time: Educated American Women of the Twentieth Century*, ed. K. Hulbert and D. Schuster (San Francisco: Jossey-Bass. 1993), 40.
8. Victor Fuchs, "Are Americans Underinvesting in Children?" in *Rebuilding the Nest*, ed. David Blankenhorn, Stephen Bayme, and Jean Bethke Elshtain (Milwaukee: Family Service America, 1990), 66. Bianchi and Spain, *American Women in Transition*, 141, 201, 226. Janet Zollinger Giele, "Gender and Sex Roles," in *Handbook of Sociology*, ed. N. J. Smelser (Beverly Hills, CA: Sage Publications, 1988), 300.
9. Hernandez, *America's Children*, 130. Council on Families in America, *Marriage in America* (New York: Institute for American Values. 1995), 7.
10. Fuchs, "Are Americans Underinvesting in Children?" 61. Some would say, however, that the decline was due in part to a larger and more heterogeneous group taking the tests.
11. Council on Families in America, *Marriage in America*, 6. The report cites research by Nicholas Zill and Charlotte A. Schoenborn, "Developmental, Learning and Emotional Problems: Health of Our Nation's Children, United States, 1988." *Advance Data*, National Center for Health Statistics, Publication #120, November 1990. See also, Sara McLanahan and Gary Sandefur, *Growing Up with a Single Parent* (Cambridge, MA: Harvard University Press, 1994).
12. Edward Gilbreath, "Manhood's Great Awakening," *Christianity Today* (February 6, 1995): 27.
13. David Elkind, *The Hurried Child: Growing Up Too Fast Too Soon* (Reading, MA: Addison-Wesley, 1981).
14. Jean Bethke Elshtain, *Democracy on Trial* (New York: Basic Books, 1995).
15. Jonathan Alter and Pat Wingert, "The Return of Shame," *Newsweek* (February 6, 1995): 25.
16. Tom McNichol, "The New Sex Vow: 'I won't' until 'I do'," *USA Weekend*, March 25–27, 1994, 4 ff. Lee Smith. "The New Wave of Illegitimacy," *Fortune* (April 18, 1994): 81 ff.
17. Susan Chira, "War over Role of American Fathers," *New York Times*, June 19, 1994, 22.
18. Juliet Schor, "Consumerism and the Decline of Family and Community: Preliminary Statistics from a Survey on Time, Money, and Values." Harvard Divinity School, Seminar on Families and Family Policy, April 4, 1995.
19. Karen S. Peterson, "In Balancing Act, Scale Tips toward Family," *USA Today*, January 25, 1995.
20. Lawrence Mead, "Taxing Peter to Pay Paula," *Wall Street Journal*, November 2, 1994.
21. Tom G. Palmer, "English Lessons: Britain Rethinks the Welfare State," *Wall Street Journal*, November 2, 1994.
22. Robert Pear, "G.O.P. Affirms Plan to Stop Money for Unwed Mothers," *New York Times*, January 21, 1995, 9.
23. Brigitte Berger. "Block Grants: Changing the Welfare Culture from the Ground Up," *Dialogue* (Boston: Pioneer Institute for Public Policy Research), no. 3, March, 1995.
24. Robert Rector, "Welfare," *Issues '94: The Candidate's Briefing Book* (Washington, DC: American Heritage Foundation, 1994), chap. 13.
25. Council on Families in America, *Marriage in America*, 13–16.
26. Robert Bellah, "Invasion of the Money World," in *Rebuilding the Nest*, ed. David Blankenhorn, Steven Bayme, and Jean Bethke Elshtain (Milwaukee: Family Service America, 1990), 227–36. James Coleman, *Foundations of Social Theory* (Cambridge, MA: Harvard University Press, 1990).
27. Sylvia Nasar, "More Men in Prime of Life Spend Less Time Working," *New York Times*, December 1, 1994, Al.
28. John Scanzoni, *Power Politics in the American Marriage* (Englewood Cliffs, NJ: Prentice-Hall, 1972). Ruth A. Wallace and Alison Wolf, *Contemporary Sociological Theory* (Englewood Cliffs, NJ: Prentice-Hall, 1991), 176.

29. Fred Weinstein and Gerald M. Platt, *The Wish to Be Free: Society, Psyche, and Value Change* (Berkeley, CA: University of California Press, 1969).
30. Kingsley Davis, "Wives and Work: A Theory of the Sex-Role Revolution and Its Consequences," in *Feminism, Children, and the New Families*, ed. S. M. Dornbusch and M. H. Strober (New York: Guilford Press. 1988), 67–86. Janet Zollinger Giele, *Two Paths to Women's Equality: Temperance, Suffrage, and the Origins of American Feminism* (New York: Twayne Publishers, Macmillan, 1995).
31. Vivianna A. Zelizer, *Pricing the Priceless Child: The Changing Social Value of Children* (New York: Basic Books, 1985).
32. William J. Goode, *World Revolution in Family Patterns* (New York: The Free Press, 1963).
33. Constance Willard Williams, *Black Teenage Mothers: Pregnancy and Child Rearing from Their Perspective* (Lexington, MA: Lexington Books, 1990).
34. William Julius Wilson, *The Truly Disadvantaged: The Inner City, the Underclass, and Public Policy* (Chicago: University of Chicago Press, 1987).
35. Jacob Mincer, "Labor-Force Participation of Married Women: A Study of Labor Supply," in *Aspects of Labor Economics*, Report of the National Bureau of Economic Research (Princeton, NJ: Universities-National Bureau Committee of Economic Research, 1962). Glen G. Cain, *Married Women in the Labor Force: An Economic Analysis* (Chicago: University of Chicago Press, 1966).
36. Richard A. Easterlin, *Birth and Fortune: The Impact of Numbers on Personal Welfare* (New York: Basic Books, 1980). Valerie K. Oppenheimer, "Structural Sources of Economic Pressure for Wives to Work—Analytic Framework," *Journal of Family History* 4, no. 2 (1979): 177–99. Valerie K. Oppenheimer, *Work and the Family: A Study in Social Demography* (New York: Academic Press, 1982).
37. Janet Z. Giele and Rainer Pischner, "The Emergence of Multiple Role Patterns Among Women: A Comparison of Germany and the United States," *Vierteljahrshefte zur Wirtschaftsforschung* (Applied Economics Quarterly) (Heft 1–2, 1994). Alice S. Rossi, "The Future in the Making," *American Journal of Orthopsychiatry* 63, no. 2 (1993): 166–76. Notburga Ott, *Intrafamily Bargaining and Household Decisions* (Berlin: Springer-Verlag, 1992).
38. Iris Young, "Mothers, Citizenship and Independence: A Critique of Pure Family Values," *Ethics* 105, no. 3 (1995): 535–56. Young critiques the liberal stance of William Galston, *Liberal Purposes* (New York: Cambridge University Press, 1991).
39. Lee Rainwater and William L. Yancey, *The Moynihan Report and the Politics of Controversy* (Cambridge, MA: MIT Press, 1967).
40. Glen H. Elder, Jr., *Children of the Great Depression* (Chicago: University of Chicago Press, 1974). Rand D. Conger, Xiao-Jia Ge, and Frederick O. Lorenz, "Economic Stress and Marital Relations," in *Families in Troubled Times: Adapting to Change in Rural America*, ed. R. D. Conger and G. H. Elder, Jr. (New York: Aldine de Gruyter, 1994), 187–203.
41. Coleman, *Foundations of Social Theory*, 590.
42. Elizabeth G. Menaghan and Toby L. Parcel, "Employed Mothers and Children's Home Environments," *Journal of Marriage and the Family* 53, no. 2 (1991): 417–31. Lois Hoffman, "The Effects on Children of Maternal and Paternal Employment," in *Families and Work*, ed. Naomi Gerstel and Harriet Engel Gross (Philadelphia: Temple University Press, 1987), 362–95.
43. Juliet Schor, *The Overworked American: The Unexpected Decline of Leisure* (New York: Basic Books, 1991). Robert Haveman and Barbara Wolfe, *Succeeding Generations: On the Effects of Investments in Children* (New York: Russell Sage Foundation, 1994), 239.
44. Coleman, *Foundations of Social Theory*, 596–97.
45. Schor, "Consumerism and Decline of Family."
46. Iris Young, "Mothers, Citizenship and Independence," puts Elshtain, Etzioni, Galston, and Whitehead in this category.
47. Coleman, *Foundations of Social Theory*, 597–609.
48. Sherry Wexler, "To Work and To Mother: A Comparison of the Family Support Act and the Family and Medical Leave Act" (Ph.D. diss. draft, Brandeis University, 1995). David T. Ellwood, *Poor Support: Poverty in the American Family* (New York: Basic Books, 1988).
49. Coleman, *Foundations of Social Theory*, 300–21. Coleman, known for rational choice theory in sociology, put forward these theoretical possibilities in 1990, fully four years ahead of what in 1994 was voiced in the Republican Contract with America.

50. Wexler, "To Work and To Mother."
51. Robert Lerman, "Marketplace," National Public Radio, April 18, 1995.
52. Karen Offen, "Defining Feminism: A Comparative Historical Approach," *Signs* 14, no. 1 (1988): 119–51.
53. Young, "Mothers, Citizenship and Independence."
54. Robert N. Bellah et al., *Habits of the Heart* (Berkeley, CA: University of California Press, 1985), 250–71. Gosta Esping-Andersen, *The Three Worlds of Welfare Capitalism* (Princeton, NJ: Princeton University Press, 1990). Susan Pedersen, *Family, Dependence, and the Origins of the Welfare State: Britain and France,* 1914–1945 (New York: Cambridge University Press, 1993).
55. Young, "Mothers, Citizenship and Independence."
56. Giele, "Woman's Role Change and Adaptation" presents these historical statistics.
57. Elshtain, *Democracy on Trial.* Robert N. Bellah et al., *The Good Society* (New York: Knopf, 1991), 210. Robert D. Putnam, "Bowling Alone: America's Declining Social Capital," *Journal of Democracy* 4, no. 1 (1995): 65–78.
58. Heather McCallum, "Mind the Gap" (paper presented to the Family and Children's Policy Center colloquium, Waltham, MA, Brandeis University, March 23, 1995). The sum was markedly better for children of employed single mothers, around $700 per mother in the United States. But this figure corresponded with over $1,000 in eleven other countries, with only Greece and Portugal lower than the U.S. Concerning the high U.S. rates of teen pregnancy, see Planned Parenthood advertisement, "Let's Get Serious About Ending Teen Childbearing," *New York Times,* April 4, 1995, A25.
59. Ruth Walker, "Secretary Reich and the Disintegrating Middle Class," *Christian Science Monitor,* November 2, 1994, 19.
60. For reference to "social capital," see Coleman, *Foundations of Social Theory;* Elshtain, *Democracy on Trial;* and Putnam, "Bowling Alone." For "emotional capital," see Arlie Russell Hochschild, *The Managed Heart: The Commercialization of Human Feeling* (Berkeley, CA: University of California Press, 1983). For "cultural capital," see work by Pierre Bourdieu and Jurgen Habermas.
61. Judith Stacey, "Dan Quayle's Revenge: The New Family Values Crusaders," *The Nation,* July 25/August 1, 1994, 119–22. Iris Marion Young, "Making Single Motherhood Normal," *Dissent* (Winter 1994): 88–93.
62. Christopher Jencks and Kathryn Edin, "Do Poor Women Have a Right to Bear Children," *The American Prospect* (Winter 1995): 43–52.
63. Stacey, "Dan Quayle's Revenge." Arlene Skolnick and Stacey Rosencrantz, "The New Crusade for the Old Family," *The American Prospect* (Summer 1994): 59–65.
64. Nancy Smith Barrett, "Data Needs for Evaluating the Labor Market Status of Women," in *Census Bureau Conference on Federal Statistical Needs Relating to Women,* ed. Barbara B. Reagan (U.S. Bureau of the Census, 1979), Current Population Reports, Special Studies, Series P-23, no. 83, pp. 10–19. These figures belie the familiar but misleading statement that "only 7 percent" of all American families are of the traditional nuclear type because "traditional" is defined so narrowly—as husband and wife with two children under 18 where the wife is not employed outside the home. For more recent figures and a similar argument for more universal family ethic, see Christine Winquist Nord and Nicholas Zill, "American Households in Demographic Perspective," working paper no. 5, Institute for American Values, New York, 1991.
65. Tamar Levin, "Women Are Becoming Equal Providers," *New York Times,* May 11, 1995, A27.
66. Marianne A. Ferber and Julie A. Nelson, *Beyond Economic Man: Feminist Theory and Economics* (Chicago: University of Chicago Press, 1993).
67. Fran Sussner Rodgers and Charles Rodgers, "Business and the Facts of Family Life," *Harvard Business Review,* no. 6 (1989): 199–213, especially 206.
68. Ravenna Helson and S. Picano, "Is the Traditional Role Bad for Women?" *Journal of Personality and Social Psychology* 59 (1990): 311–20. Rosalind C. Barnett, "Home-to-Work Spillover Revisited: A Study of Full-Time Employed Women in Dual-Earner Couples," *Journal of Marriage and the Family* 56 (August 1994): 647–56.
69. Arlie Hochschild, "The Fractured Family," *The American Prospect* (Summer 1991): 106–15.
70. Leon Eisenberg, "Is the Family Obsolete?" *The Key Reporter* 60, no. 3 (1995): 1–5. Arlene Skolnick

and Stacey Rosencrantz, "The New Crusade for the Old Family," *The American Prospect* (Summer 1994): 59–65.

71. Roberta M. Spalter-Roth, Heidi I. Hartmann, and Linda M. Andrews, "Mothers, Children, and Low-Wage Work: The Ability to Earn a Family Wage," in *Sociology and the Public Agenda*, ed. W. J. Wilson (Newbury Park, CA: Sage Publications, 1993), 316–38.
72. Louis Uchitelle, "Lacking Child Care, Parents Take Their Children to Work," *New York Times*, December 23, 1994, 1.
73. Jencks and Edin, "Do Poor Women Have a Right," 50.
74. David Elkind, *Ties That Stress: The New Family in Balance* (Boston: Harvard University Press, 1994).
75. It is frequently noted that the U.S. is a much more racially diverse nation than, say, Sweden, which has a concerted family and children's policy. Symptomatic of the potential for race and class division that impedes recognition of all children as the nation's children is the book by Richard J. Herrnstein and Charles A. Murray, *The Bell Curve: Intelligence and Class Structure in American Life* (New York: The Free Press, 1994).
76. Young, "Making Single Motherhood Normal," 93.
77. If the objection is that the wrong people will have children, as Herrnstein and Murray suggest in *The Bell Curve*, then the challenge is to find ways for poor women to make money or have some other more exciting career that will offset the rewards of having children, "such as becoming the bride of Christ or the head of a Fortune 500 corporation," to quote Jencks and Edin, "Do Poor Women Have a Right," 48.
78. Beth M. Miller, "Private Welfare: The Distributive Equity of Family Benefits in America" (Ph.D. thesis, Brandeis University, 1992). Sue Shellenbarger, "Family-Friendly Firms Often Leave Fathers Out of the Picture," *Wall Street Journal*, November 2, 1994. Richard T. Gill and T. Grandon Gill, *Of Families, Children, and a Parental Bill of Rights* (New York: Institute for American Values, 1993). For gathering information on these new work-family policies, I wish to acknowledge help of students in my 1994–95 Family Policy Seminar at Brandeis University, particularly Cathleen O'Brien, Deborah Gurewich, Alissa Starr, and Pamela Swain, as well as the insights of two Ph.D. students, Mindy Fried and Sherry Wexler.
79. Lotte Bailyn, *Breaking the Mold: Women, Men and Time in the New Corporate World* (New York: The Free Press, 1994).
80. Penelope Leach, *Children First: What Our Society Must Do and Is Doing* (New York: Random House, 1994).

PART II

Sex and Gender

The United States, along with other advanced countries, has experienced both a sexual revolution and a gender revolution. The first has liberalized attitudes toward erotic behavior and expression; the second has changed the roles and status of women and men in the direction of greater equality. Both revolutions have been brought about by the rapid social changes in recent years, and both revolutions have challenged traditional conceptions of marriage.

The traditional idea of sexuality defines sex as a powerful biological drive continually struggling against restraints imposed by civilization. The notion of sexual instincts also implies a kind of innate knowledge: A person intuitively knows his or her own identity as male or female, he or she knows how to act accordingly, and he or she is attracted to the "proper" sex object—a person of the opposite gender. In other words, the view of sex as biological drive, pure and simple, implies "that sexuality has a magical ability, possessed by no other capacity, that allows biological drives to be expressed directly in psychological and social behaviors" (Gagnon & Simon, 1970, p. 24).

The whole issue of the relative importance of biological versus psychological and social factors in sexuality and sex differences has been dominated by a debate between two extreme views. On the one extreme, there are the strict biological determinists who declare that anatomy is destiny. In other words, they argue that "men are from Mars and women from Venus," or that there is a male brain and female brain. On the other extreme, there are those who argue that all aspects of gender differences are learned.

There are two essential points to be made about the nature-versus-nurture argument. First, modern genetic theory views biology and environment as interacting, not opposing, forces. Second, both biological determinists and their opponents assume that if a biological force exists, it must be overwhelmingly strong. But the most sophisticated evidence concerning both gender development *and* erotic arousal suggests that physiological forces are less than powerful. Despite all the media stories about a "gay gene" or "a gene for lung cancer," the scientific reality is more complicated. As one researcher puts it, "The scientists have identified a number of genes that may, under certain circumstances, make an individual more or less susceptible to the action of a variety of environmental agents" (as cited in Berwick, 1998, p. 4).

Many sociologists and psychologists used to take it for granted that women's roles and functions in society reflect universal physiological and temperamental traits. Since in practically every society men have been considered superior to women, inequality was interpreted as an inescapable necessity of organized social life. Such analysis suffered from the same flaw as the idea that discrimination against nonwhites implies their innate inferiority. All such explanations failed to look at the social institutions and forces producing and supporting the observed differences.

As Robert M. Jackson points out, modern economic and political institutions have been moving toward gender equality. For example, both the modern workplace and the state have increasingly come to treat people as workers or voters without regard for their gender or their family status. Educational institutions from nursery school to graduate school are open to both sexes. Whether or not men who have traditionally run these institutions were in favor of gender inequality, their actions eventually improved women's status in society. Women have not yet attained full equality, but in Jackson's view, the trend in that direction is irreversible.

In this section, Gail Collins' reading selection "What Happened?" comes from her book *When Everything Changed* and tells the story of the revolution in women's lives in the 1960s and how it came about. The changes were so sudden, and dramatic that they seemed to have happened overnight. But Collins, like Jackson, shows how women's lives had been evolving throughout the twentieth century. So why did the revolution erupt when it did? Collins argues that the civil rights movement of the 1960s was the key that set off the women's movement at the start of the 1970s. The fight against one kind of discrimination enabled women to protest against their own discrimination.

As a result of the women's movement, people born since the 1970s have grown up in a more equal society than their parents' generation. Kathleen Gerson reports on a number of findings from her interviews with 18- to 30-year-old "children of the gender revolution." She finds that young men and women share similar hopes; both would like to be able to combine work and family life in an egalitarian way. But they also recognize that in today's world, such aspirations will be hard to fulfill. Jobs require long hours, and good child care options are scarce and expensive.

In the face of such obstacles, young women and men pursue different second choices or "fall-back strategies." Men are willing to fall back on a more "traditional" arrangement where he is the main breadwinner in the family, and his partner is the main caregiver. Young women, however, find this situation much less attractive; they are wary of giving up their ability to support themselves and their children, should the need arise. Gerson concludes that the lack of institutional supports for today's young families creates tensions between partners that may undermine marriage itself.

In her article, Beth Bailey presents a historian's overview of the sexual revolution. She finds that it was composed of at least three separate strands. First, there has been a gradual increase, over the course of the twentieth century, in sexual imagery and openness about sexual matters in the media and in public life generally. Second, in the 1960s and 1970s, premarital sex, which in some form, had always been part of dating, came to include intercourse and even living together before or without marriage. Finally, the shameless sex radicals of the sixties' counterculture were the loudest but the least numerous part of the sexual revolution. Yet to most Americans, they were the cause of the whole upheaval.

Both the sexual revolution and gender revolution have reshaped the ways young men and women get together. On college campuses, the traditional "date" has been replaced by "hook up." In her reading here, Kathleen Bogle explores the similarities and differences between dating and the current hook-up culture. After interviewing students at a "faith-based" college and a state university, she finds that the main difference between then and now is how sex fits into the picture. In the past, a "date" used to mean that a man called a woman in advance to invite her out to dinner or a movie or some other event. Some amount of sexual interaction would be expected to take place after the date or a series of them. But the rules of the dating era were clear and strict, especially for women; sexual intercourse was not supposed to happen before marriage, even between a couple engaged to marry.

In the hook-up culture, some form of sexual behavior usually comes first, even in casual encounters. It may be "just kissing" or it may go "all the way." Dating may come later, if at all. Bogle finds that for most students, the hook-up scene is not as extreme and out-of-control as it has been portrayed in the media, but she finds that in some ways men benefit from the new era more than women.

In her article "Red Sex, Blue Sex," Margaret Talbot asks why do so many conservative Christian teenagers, like Sarah Palin's daughter, become pregnant? And why are their parents so accepting of these pregnancies given that they support abstinence-only sex education and denounce sex before marriage?

Talbot cites research showing that there is a cultural divide in sexual beliefs and behavior that mirrors the political divide between "red states" and "blue states." Researchers have found that there is a new and distinct morality among middle and upper middle class people who are not social conservatives. In short, there are two different versions of "family values."

The new "middle class morality" is tolerant of premarital sex, and it supports sex education. Nevertheless, it is likely to view a teenage daughter's pregnancy as a disaster. Meanwhile, social conservatives in red states believe in abstinence before marriage, but are likely to be supportive of a pregnant teenage daughter, as long as she doesn't try to get an abortion. Also, they are more likely to favor dealing with unwed pregnancy by marrying. But early marriage—that is, before age 25—is more likely to result in divorce.

These contrasting attitudes to sex reflect two different patterns of life, based on differences in education and social class. For middle-class young people, pregnancy and early marriage could derail life plans based on college and developing a career before settling down to marry and start a family. On the whole, this "blue-state" morality is firmly but quietly pro-family and has more stable marriages.

Where does cohabitation fit into the picture? Is living together going to replace marriage eventually? In their article here, Lynne M. Casper and Suzanne M. Bianchi look at the demographic evidence on cohabitation—how widespread it is, who does it, and what it means for "traditional marriage." They conclude, as have other researchers, that cohabitation will not replace marriage in the United States. In some European countries, living together has become a standard living arrangement for raising children.

In America, however, people cohabit for diverse reasons. For many couples, living together is a step on the way to a planned marriage. Some cohabit because they are uncommitted or unsure about a future together. Young couples with low incomes may live together and put off marriage because they feel they can't afford a wedding or a home.

So, what do young adults themselves say about meaning of marriage? The article by Maria Kefalas, Frank Furstenberg, and Laura Napolitano reports on the results of a MacArthur Foundation study based on over 350 men and women, in the age group of 22 to 38 years. The sample was diverse in terms of socioeconomic background, race, ethnicity, and geographic background. It included a "heartland sample" of young people from rural Iowa. Some were already married; some had children but were not married.

The major finding is that because of the longer and more complicated pathways to adulthood these days, we are living through a "post-romantic era." The researchers were surprised by a de-emphasis on love and romance among these young adults. Most of the group were "marriage planners" who believe you should be feeling settled, mature, and have already achieved educational and career goals. Marriage "naturalists" were ready to marry early in life, having finished their schooling; they saw marriage as the natural outcome of a long relationship.

The ideal marriage partner should be a friend, someone you feel comfortable with, who shares your outlook. They didn't want to be under the spell of "out-of-control love"; rather, "love" is something that keeps you together after marrying.

Looking at American marriage more broadly, Andrew J. Cherlin describes the forces, both economic and cultural, that have transformed family life in recent decades. Economic change has made women less dependent on men; it has drawn women into the workplace and deprived less-educated men of the blue-collar jobs that once enabled them to support their families. Getting married and staying married have become increasingly optional. Despite all the changes, however, Americans value marriage more than people in other developed countries, and the two-parent family remains the most common living arrangement for raising children.

Despite all the changes, marriage remains a cherished U.S. institution. The Census Bureau estimates that 90 percent of Americans will marry at some point in their lives. Very few do so expecting that the marriage will end in divorce. So what makes a marriage break down? In her article here, Arlene Skolnick shows that in recent years researchers have found out a great deal about couple relationships, and some of the findings are contrary to widespread assumptions. For example, happy families are not all alike. And every marriage contains within it two marriages—a happy one and an unhappy one.

Laurence M. Friedman shows that the "divorce revolution" of the 1970s—when many states passed no-fault divorce laws—did not spring up suddenly out of nowhere, nor was it the result of feminism or any other public protest movement. In the first half of the twentieth century, a dual system of divorce prevailed; the official law allowed divorce only on the basis of "fault"—one partner had to be proven guilty of adultery or cruelty or some other offense. But most divorces were actually "collusive"—the result of a deal between husbands and wives, who would concoct a story or act one out—to permit a divorce to be granted. Legal reformers proposed no-fault divorce to remedy what they saw as a mockery of the law.

Divorce has become a common experience for Americans. In the past decade, there has been a backlash against divorce, especially for couples with children. The media have featured dramatic stories about the devastating, life-long scars that parental divorce supposedly inflicts on children. Legislators in some states have been considering making divorce more difficult. Given the bad press divorce gets these days, Virginia Rutter asks, "Is there a case for divorce?" Are there some situations where divorce leads to better outcomes than if the couple stayed together?

Rutter observes there is often a large gap between stories about divorce that appear in the media, and what the research actually shows. She points to a number of questions anyone should ask about reports of alarming findings on divorce. For example, readers should ask, who are the children of divorce being compared to? Sometimes, there are no comparison groups. Sometimes, the comparison is with presumably happy marriages. But those are not the families that get divorced in the first place. In addition, readers should beware of what researchers call "selection effects": People who get divorced may not be a random sample of the married population; they may have pre-existing problems that lead to marital problems, and also to negative outcomes after divorce.

Because most divorced people remarry, more children will live with stepparents than in the recent past. As Mary Ann Mason points out in her article, stepfamilies are a large and growing part of American family life, but their roles in the family are not clearly defined. Moreover, stepfamilies are largely ignored by public policymakers, and they exist in a legal limbo. She suggests a number of ways to remedy the situation.

Despite all its difficulties, marriage is not likely to go out of style in the near future. Ultimately we agree with Jessie Bernard (1982), who, after a devastating critique of traditional marriage from the point of view of a sociologist, who is also a feminist, said: "The future of marriage is as assured as any social form can be. . . . For men and women will continue to want intimacy, they will continue to want to celebrate their mutuality, to experience the mystic unity which once led the church to consider marriage a sacrament. . . . There is hardly any probability such commitments will disappear or that all relationships between them will become merely casual or transient" (p. 301).

References

Bernard, Jessie. *The Future of Marriage*. New York: World Publishing, 1982.

Berwick, Robert C. 1998. The doors of perception. The Los Angeles Times Book Review, March 15.

Gagnon, J. R., and W. Simon. *The Sexual Scene*. Chicago: Aldine Transaction, 1970.

Chapter 3

Changing Gender Roles

READING 6

Destined for Equality

Robert M. Jackson

Over the past two centuries, women's long, conspicuous struggle for better treatment has masked a surprising condition. Men's social dominance was doomed from the beginning. Gender inequality could not adapt successfully to modern economic and political institutions. No one planned this. Indeed, for a long time, the impending extinction of gender inequality was hidden from all.

In the middle of the nineteenth century, few said that equality between women and men was possible or desirable. The new forms of business, government, schools, and the family seemed to fit nicely with the existing division between women's roles and men's roles. Men controlled them all, and they showed no signs of losing belief in their natural superiority. If anything, women's subordination seemed likely to grow worse as they remained attached to the household while business and politics became a separate, distinctively masculine, realm.

Nonetheless, 150 years later, seemingly against all odds, women are well on the way to becoming men's equals. Now, few say that gender equality is impossible or undesirable. Somehow our expectations have been turned upside down.

Women's rising status is an enigmatic paradox. For millennia women were subordinate to men under the most diverse economic, political, and cultural conditions. Although the specific content of gender-based roles and the degree of inequality between the sexes varied considerably across time and place, men everywhere held power and status over women. Moreover, people believed that men's dominance was a natural and unchangeable part of life. Yet over the past two centuries, gender inequality has declined across the world.

The driving force behind this transformation has been the migration of economic and political power outside households and its reorganization around business and political interests detached from gender. Women (and their male supporters) have fought against prejudice and discrimination throughout American history, but social conditions governed the intensity and effectiveness of their efforts. Behind the very visible conflicts between women and male-dominated institutions, fundamental processes concerning economic and political organization have been paving the way for women's success. Throughout these years, while many women struggled to improve their status and many men resisted those efforts, institutional changes haltingly, often imperceptibly, but persistently undermined gender inequality. Responding to the emergent imperatives of large-scale, bureaucratic organizations, men with economic or political power intermittently adopted policies that favored greater equality, often without anticipating the implications of their actions. Gradually responding to the changing demands and possibilities of households without economic activity, men acting as individuals reduced their resistance to wives and daughters extending their roles, although men rarely recognized they were doing something different from their fathers' generation.

Social theorists have long taught us that institutions have unanticipated consequences, particularly when the combined effect of many people's actions diverges from their individual aims. Adam Smith, the renowned theorist of early capitalism, proposed that capitalist markets shared a remarkable characteristic. Many people pursuing only selfish, private interests could further the good of all. Subsequently, Karl Marx, considering the capitalist economy, proposed an equally remarkable but contradictory assessment. Systems of inequality fueled by rational self-interest, he argued, inevitably produce irrational crises that threaten to destroy the social order. Both ideas have suffered many critical blows, but they still capture our imaginations by their extraordinary insight. They teach us how unanticipated effects often ensue when disparate people and organizations each follow their own short-sighted interests.

Through a similar unanticipated and uncontrolled process, the changing actions of men, women, and powerful institutions have gradually but irresistibly reduced gender inequality. Women had always resisted their constraints and inferior status. Over the past 150 years, however, their individual strivings and organized resistance became increasingly effective. Men long continued to oppose the loss of their privileged status. Nonetheless, although men and male-controlled institutions did not adopt egalitarian values, their actions changed because their interests changed. Men's resistance to women's aspirations diminished, and they found new advantages in strategies that also benefited women.

Modern economic and political organization propelled this transformation by slowly dissociating social power from its allegiance to gender inequality. The power over economic resources, legal rights, the allocation of positions, legitimating values, and setting priorities once present in families shifted into businesses and government organizations. In these organizations, profit, efficiency, political legitimacy, organizational stability, competitiveness, and similar considerations mattered more than male privileges vis-à-vis females. Men who had power because of their positions in these organizations gradually adopted policies ruled more by institutional interests than by personal prejudices. Over the long run, institutional needs and opportunities produced policies that worked against gender inequality. Simultaneously, ordinary men (those without economic or political power) resisted women's advancements less. They had fewer resources to use against the women in their lives, and less to gain from keeping women subordinate. Male politicians seeking more power, businessmen pursuing wealth and success, and ordinary men pursuing their self-interest all contributed to the gradual decline of gender inequality.

Structural developments produced ever more inconsistencies with the requirements for continued gender inequality. Both the economy and the state increasingly treated people as potential workers or voters without reference to their family status. To the disinterested, and often rationalized, authority within these institutions, sex inequality was just one more consideration with calculating strategies for profit and political advantage. For these institutions, men and women embodied similar problems of control, exploitation, and legitimation.

Seeking to further their own interests, powerful men launched institutional changes that eventually reduced the discrimination against women. Politicians passed laws giving married women property rights. Employers hired women in ever-increasing numbers. Educators opened their doors to women. These examples and many others show powerful men pursuing their interests in preserving and expanding their economic and political power, yet also improving women's social standing.

The economy and state did not systematically oppose inequality. On the contrary, each institution needed and aggressively supported some forms of inequality, such as income differentials and the legal authority of state officials, that gave them strength. Other forms of inequality received neither automatic support nor automatic opposition. Over time, the responses to other kinds of inequality depended on how well they met institutional interests and how contested they became.

When men adopted organizational policies that eventually improved women's status, they consciously sought to increase profits, end labor shortages, get more votes, and increase social order. They imposed concrete solutions to short-term economic and political problems and to conflicts associated with them. These men usually did not envision, and probably did not care, that the cumulative effect of these policies would be to curtail male dominance.

Only when they were responding to explicitly egalitarian demands from women such as suffrage did men with power consistently examine the implications of their actions for gender inequality. Even then, as when responding to women's explicit demands for legal changes, most legislators were concerned more about their political interests than the fate of gender inequality. When legislatures did pass laws responding to public pressure about women's rights, few male legislators expected the laws could dramatically alter gender inequality.

Powerful men adopted various policies that ultimately would undermine gender inequality because such policies seemed to further their private interests and to address inescapable economic, political, and organizational problems. The structure and integral logic of development within modern political and economic institutions shaped the problems, interests, and apparent solutions. Without regard to what either women or men wanted, industrial capitalism and rational legal government eroded gender inequality.

MAPPING GENDER INEQUALITY'S DECLINE

When a band of men committed to revolutionary change self-consciously designed the American institutional framework, they did not imagine or desire that it would lead toward gender equality. In 1776 a small group of men claimed equality for themselves and similar men by signing the Declaration of Independence. In throwing off British sovereignty, they inaugurated the American ideal of equality. Yet after the success of their revolution, its leaders and like-minded property-owning white men created a nation that subjugated women, enslaved blacks, and withheld suffrage from men without property.

These men understood the egalitarian ideals they espoused through the culture and experiences dictated by their own historical circumstances. Everyone then accepted that women and men were absolutely and inalterably different. Although Abigail Adams admonished her husband that they should "remember the ladies," when these "fathers" of the American nation established its most basic rights and laws, the prospect of fuller citizenship for women was not even credible enough to warrant the effort of rejection. These nation builders could not foresee that their political and economic institutions would eventually erode some forms of inequality much more emphatically than had their revolutionary vision. They could not know that the social structure would eventually extend egalitarian social relations much further than they might ever have thought desirable or possible.

By the 1830s, a half-century after the American Revolution, little had changed. In the era of Jacksonian democracy, women still could not vote or hold political office. They had to cede legal control of their inherited property and their income to their husbands. With few exceptions, they could not make legal contracts or escape a marriage through divorce. They could not enter college. Dependence on men was perpetual and inescapable. Household toil and family welfare monopolized women's time and energies. Civil society recognized women not as individuals but as adjuncts to men. Like the democracy of ancient Athens, the American democracy limited political equality to men.

Today women enjoy independent citizenship; they have the same liberty as men to control their person and property. If they choose or need to do so, women can live without a husband. They can discard an unwanted husband to seek a better alternative. Women vote and occupy political offices. They hold jobs almost as often as men do. Ever more women have managerial and professional positions. Our culture has adopted more affirmative images for women, particularly as models of such values as independence, public advocacy, economic success, and thoughtfulness. Although these changes have not removed all inequities, women now have greater resources, more choices in life, and a higher social status than in the past.

In terms of the varied events and processes that have so dramatically changed women's place in society, the past 150 years of American history can be divided into three half-century periods. The *era of separate spheres* covers roughly 1840–1890, from the era of Jacksonian democracy to the Gilded Age. The *era of egalitarian illusions*, roughly 1890–1940, extends from the Progressive Era to the beginning of World War II. The third period, the *era of assimilation*, covers the time from World War II to the present (see Table 6.1).

Over the three periods, notable changes altered women's legal, political, and economic status, women's access to higher education and to divorce, women's sexuality, and the cultural images of women and men. Most analysts agree that people's legal, political, and economic status largely define their social status, and we will focus on the changes in these. Of course, like gender, other personal characteristics such as race and age also define an individual's status, because they similarly influence legal, political, and economic rights and resources. Under most circumstances, however, women and men are not systematically differentiated by other kinds of inequality based on personal characteristics, because these other differences, such as race and age, cut across gender lines. Educational institutions have played an ever-larger role in regulating people's access to opportunities over the last

TABLE 6.1 ***The Decline of Gender Inequality in American Society***

	1840–1890 The Era of Separate Spheres	*1890–1940 The Era of Egalitarian Illusions*	*1940–1990 The Era of Assimilation*	*1990–? Residual Inequities*
Legal and political status	Formal legal equality instituted	Formal political equality instituted	Formal economic equality instituted	Women rare in high political offices
Economic opportunity	Working-class jobs for single women only	Some jobs for married women and educated women	All kinds of jobs available to all kinds of women	"Glass ceiling" and domestic duties hold women back
Higher education	A few women admitted to public universities and new women's colleges	Increasing college; little graduate or professional education	Full access at all levels	Some prestigious fields remain largely male domains
Divorce	Almost none, but available for dire circumstances	Increasingly available, but difficult	Freely available and accepted	Women typically suffer greater costs
Sexuality and reproductive control	Repressive sexuality; little reproductive control	Positive sexuality but double standard; increasing reproductive control	High sexual freedom; full reproductive control	Sexual harassment and fear of rape still widespread
Cultural image	Virtuous domesticity and subordination	Educated motherhood, capable for employment & public service	Careers, marital equality	Sexes still perceived as inherently different

century. Changes in access to divorce, women's sexuality, and cultural images of gender will not play a central role in this study. They are important indicators of women's status, but they are derivative rather than formative. They reveal inequality's burden.

The creation of separate spheres for women and men dominated the history of gender inequality during the first period, 1840–1890. The cultural doctrine of separate spheres emerged in the mid-nineteenth century. It declared emphatically that women and men belonged to different worlds. Women were identified with the household and maintenance of family life. Men were associated with income-generating employment and public life. Popular ideas attributed greater religious virtue to women but greater civic virtue to men. Women were hailed as guardians of private morality while men were regarded as the protectors of the public good. These cultural and ideological inventions were responses to a fundamental institutional transition, the movement of economic activity out of households into independent enterprises. The concept of separate spheres legitimated women's exclusion from the public realm, although it gave them some autonomy and authority within their homes.

Women's status was not stagnant in this period. The cultural wedge driven between women's and men's worlds obscured diverse and significant changes that did erode inequality. The state gave married women the right to control their property and income. Jobs became available for some, mainly single, women, giving them some economic independence and an identity apart from the household. Secondary education similar to that offered to men became available to women, and colleges began to admit some women for higher learning. Divorce became a possible, though still difficult, strategy for the first time and led social commentators to bemoan the increasing rate of marital dissolution. In short, women's opportunities moved slowly forward in diverse ways.

From 1890 to 1940 women's opportunities continued to improve, and many claimed that women had won equality. Still, the opportunities were never enough to enable women to transcend their subordinate position. The passage of the Woman Suffrage Amendment stands out as the high point of changes during this period, yet women could make little headway in government while husbands and male politicians belittled and rejected their political aspirations. Women entered the labor market in ever-increasing numbers, educated women could get white-collar positions for the first time, and employers extended hiring to married women. Still, employers rarely considered women for high-status jobs, and explicit discrimination was an accepted practice. Although women's college opportunities became more like men's, professional and advanced degree programs still excluded women. Married women gained widespread access to effective contraception. Although popular opinion expected women to pursue and enjoy sex within marriage, social mores still denied them sex outside it. While divorce became more socially acceptable and practically available, laws still restricted divorce by demanding that one spouse prove that the other was morally repugnant. Movies portrayed glamorous women as smart, sexually provocative, professionally talented, and ambitious, but even they, if they were good women, were driven by an overwhelming desire to marry, bear children, and dedicate themselves to their homes.

Writing at the end of this period, the sociologist Mirra Komarovsky captured its implications splendidly. After studying affluent college students during World War II, Komarovsky concluded that young women were beset by "serious contradictions between two roles." The first was the feminine role, with its expectations of deference to men and a future focused on familial activities. The second was the "modern" role that "partly obliterates the differentiation in sex," presumably because the emphasis on education made the universal qualities of ability and accomplishment seem the only reasonable limitations on future activities. Women who absorbed the egalitarian implications of modern education felt confused, burdened, and irritated by the contrary expectations that they display a subordinate femininity. The intrinsic contradictions between these two role expectations could only end, Komarovsky declared, when women's real adult role was redefined to make it "consistent with the socioeconomic and ideological modern society."[1]

Since 1940, many of these contradictions have been resolved. At an accelerating pace, women have continually gained greater access to the activities, positions, and statuses formerly reserved to men.

Despite the tremendous gains women have experienced, they have not achieved complete equality, nor is it imminent. The improvement of women's status has been uneven, seesawing between setbacks and advances. Women still bear the major responsibility for raising children. They suffer from lingering harassment, intimidation, and disguised discrimination. Women in the United States still get poorer jobs and lower income. They have less access to economic or political power. The higher echelons of previously male social hierarchies have assimilated women slowest and least completely. For example, in blue-collar hierarchies they find it hard to get skilled jobs or join craft unions; in white-collar hierarchies they rarely reach top management; and in politics the barriers to women's entry seem to rise with the power of the office they seek. Yet when we compare the status of American women today with their status in the past, the movement toward greater equality is striking.

While women have not gained full equality, the formal structural barriers holding them back have largely collapsed and those left are crumbling. New government policies have discouraged sex discrimination by most organizations and in most areas of life outside the family. The political and economic systems have accepted ever more women and have promoted them to positions with more influence and higher status. Education at all levels has become equally available to women. Women have gained great control over their reproductive processes, and their sexual freedom has come to resemble that of men. It has become easy and socially acceptable to end unsatisfactory marriages with divorce. Popular culture has come close to portraying women as men's legitimate equal. Television, our most dynamic communication media, regularly portrays discrimination as wrong and male abuse or male dominance as nasty. The prevailing theme of this recent period has been women's assimilation into all the activities and positions once denied them.

This book [this reading was taken from] focuses on the dominant patterns and the groups that had the most decisive and most public roles in the processes that changed women's status: middle-class whites and, secondarily, the white working class. The histories of gender inequality among racial and ethnic minorities are too diverse to address adequately here.[2] Similarly, this analysis neglects other distinctive groups, especially lesbians and heterosexual women who avoided marriage, whose changing circumstances also deserve extended study.

While these minorities all have distinctive histories, the major trends considered here have influenced all groups. Every group had to respond to the same changing political and economic structures that defined the opportunities and constraints for all people in the society. Also, whatever their particular history, the members of each group understood their gender relations against the backdrop of the white, middle-class family's cultural preeminence. Even when people in higher or lower-class positions or people in ethnic communities expressed contempt for these values, they were familiar with the middle-class ideals and thought of them as leading ideas in the society. The focus on the white middle classes is simply an analytical and practical strategy. The history of dominant groups has no greater inherent or moral worth. Still, except in cases of open, successful rebellion, the ideas and actions of dominant groups usually affect history much more than the ideas and actions of subordinate groups. This fact is an inevitable effect of inequality.

THE MEANING OF INEQUALITY AND ITS DECLINE

We will think differently about women's status under two theoretical agendas. Either we can try to evaluate how short from equality women now fall, or we can try to understand how far they have come from past deprivations.

Looking at women's place in society today from these two vantage points yields remarkably different perspectives. They accentuate different aspects of women's status by altering the background against which we compare it. Temporal and analytical differences separate these two vantage points, not distinctive moral positions, although people sometimes confuse these differences with competing moral positions.

If we want to assess and criticize women's disadvantages today, we usually compare their existing status with an imagined future when complete equality reigns. Using this ideal standard of complete equality, we would find varied shortcomings in women's status today. These shortcomings include women's absence from positions of political or economic power, men's preponderance in the better-paid and higher-status occupations, women's lower average income, women's greater family responsibilities, the higher status commonly attached to male activities, and the dearth of institutions or policies supporting dual-earner couples.

Alternatively, if we want to evaluate how women's social status has improved, we must turn in the other direction and face the past. We look back to a time when women were legal and political outcasts, working only in a few low-status jobs, and always deferring to male authority. From this perspective, women's status today seems much brighter. Compared with the nineteenth century, women now have a nearly equal legal and political status, far more women hold jobs, women can succeed at almost any occupation, women usually get paid as much as men in the same position (in the same firm), women have as much educational opportunity as men, and both sexes normally expect women to pursue jobs and careers.

As we seek to understand the decline of gender inequality, we will necessarily stress the improvements in women's status. We will always want to remember, however, that gender inequality today stands somewhere between extreme inequality and complete equality. To analyze the modern history of gender inequality fully, we must be able to look at this middle ground from both sides. It is seriously deficient when measured against full equality. It is a remarkable improvement when measured against past inequality.

Notes

1. Mirra Komarovsky, "Cultural Contradictions and Sex Roles," pp. 184, 189. Cf. Helen Hacker, "Women as a Minority Group."
2. For studies of these various groups see, e.g., Paula Giddings, *When and Where I Enter;* Alfredo Mirande and Evangelina Enriquez, *La Chicana;* Evelyn Nakana Glen, *Issei, Nisei, War Bride;* Jacqueline Jones, *Labor of Love, Labor of Sorrow.*

References

Giddings, Paula. *When and Where I Enter: The Impact of Black Women on Race and Sex in America.* New York: William Morrow, 1984.

Glen, Evelyn Nakano. *Issei, Nisei, War Bride.* Philadelphia: Temple University Press, 1986.

Hacker, Helen. "Women as a Minority Group." *Social Forces* 30 (1951): 60–69.
Jones, Jacqueline. *Labor of Love, Labor of Sorrow: Black Women, Work, and the Family from Slavery to the Present.* New York: Basic Books, 1986.
Komarovsky, Mirra. "Cultural Contradictions and Sex Roles." *American Journal of Sociology* 52 (1946): 184–189.
Mirande, Alfredo, and Evangelina Enriquez. *La Chicana.* Chicago: University of Chicago Press, 1979.

READING 7

The Ice Cracks

Gail Collins

On Election Day in 1960, women around the country celebrated the fortieth anniversary of their constitutional right to vote, and newspapers noted that for the first time in the nation's history, there were likely to be more women than men casting their ballots for president. "Women now hold the balance of power," said the assistant chair of the Republican Party, Clare B. Williams Shank. It was hard to say exactly what that meant in practical terms. The suffragists of the early twentieth century had presumed that when women got the vote, they would press for a specific pro-family agenda—things like better care for infants and pregnant women, and better schools. But it turned out that women voters made their choices much like their husbands and fathers and brothers did—on the basis of class, ethnicity, or regional loyalties. In the first national election after passage of the Nineteenth Amendment, women helped choose the utterly inept Warren Harding, who would distinguish himself for his perennial appearance on the ten-worst-presidents-of-all-time lists.

The women who were cutting the anniversary cake might also have contemplated the fact that the highest-ranking female judge in the nation served on the Customs Court and that in forty years, only two women had ever been appointed to cabinet-level posts in the federal government: Frances Perkins, during the Roosevelt administration, and Oveta Culp Hobby, who was the first secretary of the Department of Health, Education, and Welfare under Dwight Eisenhower. The record was not going to be improved under the about-to-be-elected President John Kennedy or by his immediate successors. At the end of the decade, when Richard Nixon brought the White House back under Republican control, some of his women supporters expressed hope he might follow Eisenhower's example and appoint the first female cabinet member since the 1950s. Unenthusiastically, a spokesperson pointed out that "the departments had grown" since then.

Women took part in the presidential-nominating conventions that summer, but newspaper accounts of their gatherings did not suggest deal-making in smoke-filled rooms. "The meal begins with 'Swan Canterbury,' which consists of fresh pineapple on a bed of laurel leaves surrounded by swans' heads in meringue," the *New York Times* reported in a story headlined "GOP Women Facing a Calorie-Packed Week." Meanwhile, nearly two-thirds of women ages 18 to 60 who were surveyed by George Gallup said that they didn't approve of the idea of a female president.

The Eighty-seventh Congress that was elected in 1960 included two women in the Senate and seventeen in the 435-member House, and that would turn out to be the high-water mark for the next decade. Both of the female senators and half the women in the House had gotten to their exalted positions through the same time-honored career path: marry a congressman, and succeed him when he passes away. Edna Simpson of Illinois, the ultimate congressional widow, was just finishing her first and last term in office. Simpson's congressman-husband had died just nine days before the election of 1958, and she bowed to pleas from Republican leaders and let her name go on the ballot in his place. She did not campaign, and after she was elected she never spoke on the floor of the House or—it seemed—to any of her fellow members. Her only legislative initiative was to protest when her name appeared in the *Congressional Biographical Directory* as Edna Oakes Simpson rather than as her preference: Edna (Mrs. Sid) Simpson.

Even the congresswomen who didn't succeed their husbands tended to be widows—voters were wary of female candidates with family obligations. The disasters that could befall them were vividly displayed in the case of Coya Knutson, who had managed to topple an incumbent House member in Minnesota in 1954 and win a seat in her own right. Her alcoholic husband, Andy, who was left behind to run the family hotel, torpedoed her career in 1958 by issuing a "Coya, Come Home" letter claiming his marriage was being destroyed by her political success. She became the only Democratic incumbent to lose the 1958 election. Her marriage did not last much longer than her congressional career. . . .

IT WAS LIKE—*WHAT*?

. . . It seemed that overnight everything that America had taken for granted about a woman's role was being called into question. Her place was in the home, and then—zap—she was applying to medical school or going for an MBA. She was supposed to defer to her husband as head of the house—except suddenly there she was, holding consciousness-raising meetings in the living room to discuss his failure to give her help with the baby or the right kind of orgasm. "I always felt bad for the guys who had gotten married under the old rules," said Nora Ephron wryly. "It was like—*What?*" One day coeds were in school just to earn an MRS degree, and then—whoops—there were so many qualified, competitive young women winning the best places in the best colleges that the media worried about what would become of the boys. One year little girls were learning the importance of losing gracefully, and the next they were suing for admission to the Little League. It left many people shaking their heads, wondering what propelled such extraordinary changes so rapidly.

The apparent suddenness of it all was not due to the arrival of a great leader, although some of the leaders were amazing. If the only thing women needed was a powerful voice to articulate their grievances, everything would have been worked out in the nineteenth century when Susan B. Anthony and Elizabeth Cady Stanton were around. The female colonists and pioneers, the early-twentieth-century settlement-house workers, and the World War II nurses who lived with the old gender biases were not less resourceful or insightful than the women of 1968. There was something else—or a collection of something elses—buried deep in the social fabric.

EXPERIENCE IN BUSINESS BROADENS A WOMAN'S MIND

Now that we've marveled at the rapidity of the change, we have to acknowledge that it didn't really happen overnight. Women's lives had been evolving throughout the century. They had been having fewer children, marrying later, and taking jobs outside the home more often. In a placid world, the changes might have looked like a gentle slope on a chart. But the Americans had to struggle through two world wars, with the Great Depression sandwiched in between. All of this left the charts looking less like a gentle slope and more like the peaks and valleys of an EKG for a heart-attack patient.

There was no "normal" in the twentieth century, but there was one near constant: a changing economy put a higher value on women's skills. Telephone companies started by hiring men as operators, but they found that women were better at handling customers and less likely to argue with the people on the other end of the line. American businesses found they needed fewer laborers and more customer-service representatives. At the same time, work conditions became more pleasant. Once glamorous department stores took the place of small, dingy shops, and the growing office bureaucracies needed typists, clerks, and receptionists, not-so-poor young women who would have shunned a job in a factory were tempted to think about working. And as the economy's demand for women to take these positions grew, society regarded their participation in the workforce with increasing benevolence.

This was an old pattern. Whenever the nation suddenly required a large supply of new workers—particularly literate workers for relatively low-paying jobs—the answer was women, and the nation's position on women's place adapted quickly. When the public-school system began growing after the Revolutionary War, society decided teaching was a maternal function that respectable women could perform. (And, as one nineteenth-century school superintendent in Ohio happily reported, perform at half the male teachers' wages.) When the industrial age produced far more clerical, sales and other low-paying white-collar jobs than the male population could fill, the nation readily agreed that a few years of typing or manning department-store counters was an excellent preparation for marriage. "Experience in business broadens a woman's mind and makes her views more practical," concluded *Harper's Weekly* in 1903.

During World War II, women were asked—actually the better word would be nagged—to go to work. There were more than three million jobs going begging as men left civilian work for the military, and the government propaganda machine warned housewives that if they refused to join the factory assembly line, defective weapons might go uninspected and airplanes might be improperly welded. *A soldier might die*, the stay-at-home women were told, and it would be their fault. Those who responded were celebrated for breaking out of their sexual roles and becoming streetcar conductors or welders. *("She's making history, working for victory, Rosie the Riveter...")* The Office of War Information urged newspapers and magazines to run "stories showing the advent of women in logging camps, on the railroads, riding the ranges, and showing them not as weak sisters but as coming through in manly style."

Some of the women who responded—particularly married women who had always worked but who loved the higher pay in the war-industry jobs—were dismayed to find themselves elbowed out of the way when peace broke out and the soldiers came home.

But most of the single women readily complied with society's demand that they go back home and leave the jobs for the returning veterans. They made up for lost nesting time by marrying early and having several children in rapid succession. The government generously underwrote the impulse to domesticity with cheap mortgages, college scholarships, and a huge program of public works that sent incomes shooting up.

SO THEY HIRE WOMEN

After the war, the economy didn't just improve. It exploded. Americans were producing half the world's goods in the mid-'50s, even though they made up only 6 percent of the world's population. Business was expanding by leaps and bounds, but the available workforce was relatively small. The "baby-bust" generation of men born during the Depression could not supply enough labor to fill the need. In the 1960s, as the economy was constantly creating employment, two-thirds of those new jobs went to women.

"A Good Man Is Hard to Find—So They Hire Women," announced *Time* in November 1966. That year, President Johnson urged employers to consider hiring women (along with teenagers, the handicapped, and immigrants) to fill their openings. Large firms such as IBM and Texas Instruments targeted stay-at-home moms in recruiting campaigns. So did temporary-employment agencies. "First, we must overcome the married woman's prejudice against returning to work, and this prejudice, in most cases, boils down to her conviction that a mother's place is in the home so long as there are children there," said Manpower's public-relations counsel.

The idea of married women working was indeed hard for middle-class Americans to swallow. Their benevolent attitude toward women employed in department stores or business offices was limited, in the main, to young singles. Even during World War II, very few stay-at-home wives took off their aprons and signed up to become welders or streetcar conductors. But the ones who answered the call were proud. "Darling—you are now the husband of a career woman. Just call me your Ship Yard Babe!" wrote one new defense worker to her husband in the service. And after the fighting was over, as single women left the workforce in droves to start families, many of the older married women continued on the job. They were joined by other housewives who were attracted by the pleas of employers and the rising salaries they could earn—especially for part-time white-collar jobs. These working wives and mothers still tended to be below the top of the social scale, so it was easy to underrate the trend. That was particularly true since, as we've seen, the nation preferred to ignore the fact that they were working at all.

The fact that the percentage of married women in the workforce kept quietly going up was really the key to women's liberation. The nation had to accept the idea that most women would work through their adult lives. That didn't mean, of course, that every woman had to hold down a job all the time. But as a sex, they were not going to have standing in the public world unless men saw them as having an important economic role. If young women did not expect to work after marriage, most of them would not plan for serious careers. Most schools would not want to train them. The nation might honor them for their roles as wives and mothers, but they would not be taken seriously in business, academia, the arts, or politics.

Even within the family, women who made a substantial contribution to the household's finances tended to have more power and respect. And, of course, the ability to support themselves gave them far more independence when it came to handling an unsatisfactory spouse, or filling in for one who vanished.

A DESIRE FOR ALL THE ADVANTAGES OF THE 'TWO-INCOME' FAMILY

The consultant for Manpower who was trying to figure out how to lure married women into the postwar workforce had another suggestion beyond eliminating the prejudice against working wives. "Second, we must develop a desire for all the advantages of the 'Two-Income' family," he proposed.

Business was not only offering women incentives to work; it was in overdrive when it came to wooing them to spend. American families were willing consumers, but before World War II their vision of what they should—and could—acquire was limited. A significant minority of households had no electricity to power modern conveniences. Louise Meyer of Wyoming was hardly the only housewife laundering clothes with boiled water and eliminating wrinkles with a piece of iron heated on a wood-burning stove. During the war, the nation's premier washboard manufacturer churned out more than a million boards a year for housewives who were still doing their clothes by hand. Half of American homes had no central heating, and a quarter lacked flush toilets. Even in the best times most people could remember—the boom years before the Depression—less than a third of the country had a middle-class standard of living. But after the war, thanks to the stunning economic boom and generous federal spending in the 1950s, 60 percent of American families reached the middle class. Family income, adjusted for inflation, rose 42 percent in the 1950s and 38 percent in the 1960s.

For the economy to keep growing, consumers had to keep buying. Helped along by the new, mighty voice of television, advertisers were constantly expanding family visions of what the good life entailed. The number of families living in their own homes soared, and most of those new homes were in the suburbs. Family cars, then second cars, became necessities. So did—as far as most people were concerned—second televisions and summer camp for the kids. An entire middle-class generation grew up in the postwar era taking for granted a lifestyle of three-bedroom homes, washer/dryer combos, annual family vacations, and college education for their children.

Then the economy began to slow. Fewer and fewer families could afford to buy the things they had gotten used to having on one person's salary. Over the '70s and '80s, the weekly earning of nonmanagement workers fell 19 percent. While women continued to drop in and out of the workforce, often taking time off when their children were young and working more when the kids went to school full-time, they no longer regarded their work as optional or as a matter of bringing home pin money. In the 1970s wives who worked provided, on average, a third of the family's income.

THAT DEFINED THE TWENTIETH CENTURY

Until the postwar baby boom, American women had been having fewer children for as long as the nation had been keeping population statistics. That was a rational response to the change from an agricultural to an industrial economy. An extra child on a farm was usually an unalloyed benefit—another little helper who, in relatively few years, would be available to work the fields or spin the thread or tend the chickens. But as people moved into cities and developed higher expectations for the next generation, children moved from being an economic plus to an economic drain. They had to be fed, clothed, educated, and—in a middle-class family—supported for eighteen or more years without any return on investment. Obviously, parents got their reward in other ways. But it was much easier to appreciate the pluses if there were only two or three little minuses to take care of.

The baby boom was an exception—an extraordinarily large exception—to the pattern of smaller families. The men and women who produced it had grown up in the Depression, fought World War II, and then returned home to a booming economy to have more children than any Americans since the beginning of the twentieth century, their reproductive enthusiasm rivaling countries like India. It was no wonder we called them the Greatest Generation, but their offspring had no intention of repeating the performance.

American women had always been fairly adept at limiting the size of their families when they wanted to, through means ranging from diaphragms to abstinence. However, all their strategies worked best when the goal was to reduce the odds of pregnancy rather than to prevent it entirely. A woman who wanted a family of two or three children rather than six or seven had good odds for success, but not a woman who wanted to be sexually active without reproducing.

The birth control pill was simpler and far more reliable than anything that came before. It had only a fourth the failure rate of condom use and a seventh of diaphragms. The Pill, which went on the market in 1960, not only gave women more confidence about their ability to plan a career; it gave employers more confidence that when a woman said she wasn't planning to get pregnant, she meant it. "There is, perhaps, one invention that historians a thousand years in the future will look back on and say, 'That defined the twentieth century,'" wrote *The Economist* at the end of 1999. "It is also one that a time-traveler from 1000 would find breathtaking—particularly if she were a woman. That invention is the contraceptive pill."

Young unmarried women did not have widespread access to the Pill until the early 1970s—which not coincidentally was the same time they began to apply to medical, law, dental, and business schools in large numbers. This was an enormous shift. American girls had always done better than boys in most subjects in high school, but those who went to college had been funneled into relatively low-paying careers such as nursing and teaching—professions that you could pursue for a few years before marriage, and return to when your children were grown.

Once young women had confidence that they could make it through training and the early years in their profession without getting pregnant, their attitude toward careers that required a long-term commitment changed. And the sexual revolution, which arrived at the same time as widespread Pill use, reassured them that even if they delayed marriage, they would have the same opportunities as unmarried young men for a satisfying sexual life.

JUST A HOUSEWIFE

There were other social forces at work that, while perhaps not as sweeping, were combining to make the old patterns of women's lives look less attractive. The first wave of the baby-boom generation grew up hearing their mothers describe themselves, self-deprecatingly, as "just a housewife," and in truth, the status of homemakers was dwindling. Perhaps it was due in part to complaints from magazines such as *Playboy* about men being trapped in marriage, forced to support unproductive wives. Perhaps it had to do with changes in the home-makers' jobs. Before the automated kitchen and laundry, running a house was a daunting responsibility. You needed to be a good manager and to have, particularly when it came to cooking, a lot of skill. But the postwar housewife's duties were more about driving children to multitudinous activities, microwaving quick dinners for family members on different schedules, and constantly running washing machines and dryers. Once children were out of the nest, some mothers found new challenges in volunteer work or caring for the offspring of their working daughters. But many women, still in the prime of their lives, were left with no real role at all. The attractions of marriage and motherhood didn't fade, but women felt an increasing need for a second string—a place in the working world that would provide them with a sense of identity and usefulness once the children had grown.

At the same time, the rising divorce rate was driving home the peril of trusting your future entirely to a spouse's ability and willingness to support his family. Divorce, like the tendency toward smaller families, had been on an upward trend for a long time, until the postwar period disrupted the graph. But that dip was followed by a huge surge of divorce in the 1970s, along with an increase in unmarried couples living together and never-married mothers. The message to younger women was clear: marriage was an unreliable basket in which to put all of your eggs.

THE WHOLE LAND SEEMS AROUSED

The civil rights battles of the 1960s went to the core of the nation's identity, forcing the country to grapple with the fact that it had never lived up to the standards it set for itself in the Declaration of Independence. White Americans who accepted the message of what had happened went through a moral shock, made all the worse for the realization that they and their leaders had not been all that eager to rectify the injustice when it was driven home to them. As a result, young people became more skeptical about the wisdom of traditional cultural rules. Americans grew extremely sensitive to questions of fairness, and that opened the way for other discriminated-against groups, including women, to demand their rights.

The effect of the civil rights movement was crucial for women, because their fight was unique. It was, as the sociologist Alice Rossi said, the only instance in which people being discriminated against lived in much more intimate association with the "enemy" than with other members of their own group. Women's interests were bound up with those of their fathers, husbands, brothers, and sons in every aspect of their lives. It was difficult for them to mount the kind of clear-cut fight that racial or ethnic minorities were able to make against an establishment that had discriminated against them. That was probably why the women's movement always tended to ride on the wake of other fights for justice.

Fighting slavery had been the first moral issue so grave that housebound middle-class Victorian matrons felt compelled to go into the outside world and engage in politics. "We have given great offense on account of our womanhood, which seems to be as objectionable as our abolitionism. The whole land seems aroused to discussion on the province of women, and I am glad of it," said Angelina Grimké, the abolitionist lecturer who was one of the first to consider the plight of African-Americans and find similarities to the condition of white American women. The earliest women's rights movement grew up out of antislavery actions, and in the twentieth century, the suffrage cause finally succeeded during the Progressive era, when the nation was focused on the evils of poverty and unbridled capitalism. In the 1960s women's greatest legislative victory was an amendment tacked onto the Civil Rights Act.

Many of the young women who took the lead on the radical side of women's liberation had been trained in confrontation by their involvement in the civil rights movement. All of them had learned from that struggle how injustice can run deep in a nation's laws, traditions, and customs. They did not believe that the fact that things had always been done one way made them right. To the contrary, that made them suspect. And they could see, even by the late 1960s, that history was going to celebrate the people who had the strength to stand up against popular conventions and demand justice for black Americans. They had confidence from the beginning that women, too, would win.

So there it was: the postwar economy created a demand for women workers, and the postindustrial economy created jobs that they were particularly suited to fill. The soaring expectations of the postwar boom, followed by the decline in men's paychecks in the 1970s, made wives' participation in the workforce almost a requisite for middle-class life. The birth control pill gave young women confidence that they could pursue a career without interruption by pregnancy. The civil rights movement made women conscious of the ways they had been treated like second-class citizens and made them determined that their own status was one of the things they were going to change. It was, all in all, a benevolent version of the perfect storm.

READING 8

Falling Back on Plan B: The Children of the Gender Revolution Face Uncharted Territory

Kathleen Gerson

Young adults today grew up with mothers who marched into the workplace and parents who forged innovative alternatives to traditional marriage. These "children of the gender revolution" now face a world that is far different than that of their parents or grandparents. While massive changes in work and family arrangements have expanded their options, these changes also pose new challenges to crafting a marriage, rearing children, and building a career. Members of this new generation walk a fine line between their desire to achieve egalitarian, sharing relationships that can meld with satisfying work and succumbing to the realities of gender conflict, fragile relationships, and uncertain job prospects. The choices they are able to make will shape work and family life for decades to come.

Social forecasters have reached starkly different conclusions about what these choices will be. Some proclaim that the recent upturn in "opt out" mothers foreshadows a wider return to tradition among younger women.[1] Others believe the rising number of single adults foretells a deepening "decline of commitment" that is threatening family life and the social fabric.[2] While there is little doubt that tumultuous changes have shaped the lives of a new generation, there is great disagreement about how. Does the diversification of families into two-earner, single-parent, and cohabiting forms represent a waning of family life or the growth of more flexible relationships? Will this new generation integrate family and work in new ways, or will older patterns inexorably pull them back?

To find out how members of the first generation to grow up in diversifying families look back on their childhoods and forward to their own futures, I conducted in-depth, life history interviews with a carefully selected group of young people between 18 and 32. These young women and men experienced the full range of changes that have taken place in family life, and most lived in some form of "nontraditional" arrangement at some point in their childhood.[3] My interviews reveal a generation that does not conform to prevailing media stereotypes, whether they depict declining families or a return to strict gender divisions in caretaking and breadwinning.

In contrast to popular images of twenty- and thirty-somethings who wish to return to tradition or reject family life altogether, the young women and men I interviewed are more focused on *how well* their parents met the challenges of providing economic and emotional support than on *what form* their families took. Now facing their own choices, women and men share a set of lofty aspirations. Despite their varied family experiences, most hope to blend the traditional value of lifelong commitment with the modern value of flexible sharing. In the best of all possible worlds, the majority would like to create a lasting marriage (or a "marriage like" relationship) that allows them to blend home and work in a flexible, egalitarian way.

Yet young people are also developing strategies to prepare for "second best" options in a world where time-demanding workplaces, a lack of child care, and fragile relationships may place their ideals out of reach. Concerned about the difficulty of finding a reliable and egalitarian partner to help them integrate work with family caretaking, most women see work as essential to their own and their children's survival, whether or not they marry. Worried about time-greedy workplaces, most men feel they must place work first and will need to count on a partner at home. As they prepare for second best options, the differing fallback positions of "self-reliant" women and "neo-traditional" men may point to a new gender divide. But this divide does not reflect a new generation's highest aspirations.

GROWING UP IN CHANGING FAMILIES

Even though theorists and social commentators continue to debate the merits of various family forms, my informants did not focus on their family's "structure."[4] Instead, I found large variation among children who grew up in apparently similar family types. Those who grew up in families with a homemaking mother and breadwinning father hold divided assessments. While a little more than half thought this was the best arrangement, close to a half reached a different conclusion. When domesticity appeared to undermine a mother's satisfaction, disturb the household's harmony, or threaten its economic security, the children concluded that it would have been better if their mothers had pursued a sustained commitment to work.

Many of those who grew up in a single-parent home also expressed ambivalence about their parents' breakups. Slightly more than half wished their parents had stayed together, but close to half believed that a breakup, while not ideal, was better than continuing to live in a conflict-ridden or silently unhappy home. The longer-term consequences of a breakup shaped the lessons children drew.[5] If their parents got back on their feet and created better lives, children developed surprisingly positive outlooks on the decision to separate.

Those who grew up in a dual-earner home were the least ambivalent about their parents' arrangements. More than three-fourths believed that having two work-committed parents provided increased economic resources and also promoted marriages that seemed more egalitarian and satisfying.[6] If, however, the pressures of working long hours or coping with blocked opportunities and family-unfriendly workplaces took their toll, some children concluded that having overburdened, time-stressed caretakers offset these advantages.

In short, growing up in this era of diverse families led children to focus more on how well—or poorly—parents (and other caretakers) were able to meet the twin challenges of providing economic and emotional support than on its form. Even more important, children experienced family life as a dynamic process that changed over time. Since family life is a film, not a snapshot, the key to understanding young people's views lies in charting the diverse paths their families took.

FAMILY PATHS AND GENDER FLEXIBILITY

Families can take different paths from seemingly common starting points, and similar types of families can have travel toward different destinations. When young adults reflect on their families, they focus on how their homes either came to provide stability and support or failed to do so. About a third reported growing up in a stable home, while a quarter concluded that their families grew more supportive as time passed. In contrast, just under one in ten reported living in a chronically insecure home, while a bit more than a third felt that family support eroded as they grew up. Why, then, do some children look back on families that became supportive and secure, while others experienced a decline in their family's fortunes?

Parents' strategies for organizing breadwinning and caretaking hold the key to understanding a family's pathway.[7] Flexible strategies, which allowed mothers, fathers, and other caretakers to transcend rigid gender boundaries, helped families prevail in the face of unexpected economic and interpersonal crises. Inflexible responses, in contrast, left families ill-equipped to cope with eroding supports for a strict division in mothers' and fathers' responsibilities.

RISING FAMILY FORTUNES

The sources of expanding support differed by family situation, but all reflect a flexible response to unexpected difficulties. Sometimes marriages became more equal as demoralized mothers went to work and pushed for change or helped overburdened fathers. Josh, for example, reported that his mother's decision to go to work gave her the courage to insist that his father tackle his drug addiction:[8]

> My parents fought almost constantly. Then my mom got a job. They separated about five, six, seven months. Even though I was upset, I thought it was for the best. That's when (my dad) got into some kind of program and my mom took him back. That changed the whole family dynamic. We got extremely close. A whole new relationship developed with my father.

Chris recalled how his mother's job allowed his father to quit a dead-end job and train for a more satisfying career:

> Between 7th and 8th grade, my dad had a business which didn't work. It was a dead-end thing, and he came home frustrated, so my mom got him to go to school. It was hard financially, but it was good because he was actually enjoying what he was doing. He really flourished. A lot of people say, "Wow, your mom is the breadwinner, and that's strange." It's not. It is a very joint thing.

Parental breakups that relieved domestic conflict or led to the departure of an unstable parent also helped caretaking parents get back on their feet. Connie recounted how her mother was able to create a more secure home after separating from an alcoholic husbands and finding a job that offered a steady income and a source of personal esteem:

> My father just sat in the corner and once in a while got angry at us, but (my mom)—I don't know if it was him or the money, but she didn't stand up for herself as much as I think she should. The tension with my dad never eased, and my mom had gotten sick with multiple bleeding ulcers. That was her real turning point. It was building inside of her to leave, 'cause she'd got a job and started to realize she had her own money . . . (She) became a much happier person. And because she was better, I was better. I had a weight taken off of me.

More stable and egalitarian remarriages could also give children the economic and emotional support they had not previously received. Having never known her biological father, Shauna recalled about how her stepfather became a devoted caretaker and the "real" father she always wanted:

> At first, I was feeling it was a bad change because I wanted my mom to myself. Then my mom said, "Why don't you call him daddy?" The next thing I was saying "Daddy!" I remember the look on his face and his saying "She called me daddy!" I was so happy. After that, he's always been my dad, and there's never been any question about it. . . . (He) would get home before my mom, so he would cook the dinner and clean. My dad spoiled me for any other man, because this is the model I had.

> When Isabella's parents divorced, her grandfather became a treasured caretaker: It's not like I didn't have a father, because my grandfather was always there. He was there to take me to after-school clubs and pick me up. I was sheltered—he had to take me to the library, wait till I finished all my work, take me home. I call him dad. Nobody could do better.

And when Antonio's single mother lost her job, his grandparents provided essential income that kept the family afloat:

> My mom and grandparents were the type of people that even if we didn't have (money), we was gonna get it. Their ideal is, "I want to give you all the things I couldn't have when I was young." My grandparents and my mother thought like that, so no matter how much in poverty we were living, I was getting everything I wanted.

Despite their obvious differences, the common ingredient in these narratives is the ability of parents and other caretakers to reorganize child rearing and breadwinning in a more flexible, less gender-divided way. Mothers going to work, fathers becoming more involved in child rearing, and others joining in the work of family life—all of these strategies helped families overcome unexpected difficulties and create more economically secure, emotionally stable homes. Growing flexibility in how parents met the challenges of a earning needed income and caring for children nourished parental morale, increased a home's financial security, and provided inspiring models of adult resilience. While children acknowledged the costs, they valued these second chances and gleaned lessons from watching parents find ways to create a better life. Looking back, they could conclude that "all's well that end's well."

DECLINING FAMILY FORTUNES

For some children, however, home life followed a downward slope. Here, too, the key to their experiences lies in the work and caretaking strategies of those entrusted with their care; but in this case, gender inflexibility in the face of domestic difficulties left children with less support than they had once taken for granted. Faced with a father's abandonment or a stay-at-home mother's growing frustration, children described how their parents' resistance to more flexible strategies for apportioning paid and domestic work left them struggling to meet children's economic and emotional needs. Over time, deteriorating marriages, declining parental morale, and financial insecurity shattered a once rosy picture of family stability and contentment.

When parents became stuck in a rigid division of labor, with unhappy mothers and fathers ill-equipped to support the household, traditional marriages could deteriorate. Sarah explains how her mother became increasingly depressed and "over-involved" after relinquishing a promising career to devote all of her time to child rearing:

> When my sister was born, (my mom's) job had started up, career-wise, so she wasn't happy (but) she felt she had to be home. She had a lot of conflicts about work and home and

> opted to be really committed to family, but also resented it. . . . She was the supermom, but just seemed really depressed a lot of time . . . (It came) with an edge to it—"in return, I want you to be devoted to me." If we did something separate from her, that was a major problem. So I was making distance because I felt I had to protect myself from this invasion. . . . She thought she was doing something good to sacrifice for us. . . . but it would have been better if my mother was happier working.

Megan recalls her father's mounting frustration as his income stagnated and he endured the complaints of a wife who expected to him to provide a "better lifestyle":

> My mother was always dissatisfied. She wanted my father to be more ambitious, and he wasn't an ambitious man. As long as he was supporting the family, it didn't matter if it was a bigger house or a bigger car. Forty years of being married to a woman saying, "Why don't we have more money?"—I think that does something to your self-esteem.

Unresolved power struggles in dual-earner marriages could also cause problems, as wives felt the weight of "doing it all" and fathers resisted egalitarian sharing. For Justin, juggling paid and domestic work left his mother exhausted, while a high-pressured job running a restaurant left his father with no time to attend nightly dinners or even Little League games:

> I was slightly disappointed that I could not see my father more—because I understood but also because it depends on the mood he's in. And it got worse as work (went) downhill . . . (So) I can't model my relationship on my parents. My mother wasn't very happy. There was a lot of strain on her.

Harmful breakups, where fathers abandoned their children and mothers could not find new ways to support the family or create an identity beyond wife and mother, also eroded family support. Nina remembers how her father's disappearance, combined with her mother's reluctance to seek a job and create a more independent life, triggered descent from a comfortable middle-class existence to one of abiding poverty:

> My mother ended up going on welfare. We went from a nice place to living in a really cruddy building. And she's still in the same apartment. To this day, my sister will not speak to my father because of what he's done to us.

Children (and their parents) sometimes lost the support of other caretakers. Shortly after Jasmine's father left to live with another woman and her mother fell into a deep depression, she suffered the loss of a "third parent" when her beloved grandmother died:

> It seemed like I had everything I wanted. My mom worked at a good paying job and was doing great. My dad worked at night, so he was around when I'd get home from school. I just thought of it as the way it was supposed to be. I was used to him being there, cooking dinner for us. So after he moved in with another woman and her children, it made me feel worse 'cause I felt that he was leaving me to be with other kids. I miss him, and I know he misses me.

The events that propelled families on a downward track—including rising financial instability, declining parental involvement and morale, and a dearth of other supportive caretakers—share a common element. Whether parents faced marital impasses or difficult breakups, resistance to more flexible gender arrangements left them unable to sustain an emotionally or economically secure home. Their children concluded that all did *not* end well.

In sum, sustained parental support and economic security were more important to my informants than the form their families took. Since any family type holds potential pitfalls if parents do not or cannot prevail over the difficulties that arise, conventional categories that see families as static "forms" cannot account for the ways that families change as children grow to adulthood. Instead, young women and men from diverse family backgrounds recounted how parents and other family members who transcended gender boundaries and developed flexible strategies for breadwinning and caretaking were better able to cope with marital crises, economic insecurities, and other unanticipated challenges.

A range of social trends—including the erosion of single-earner paychecks, the fragility of modern marriages, and the expanding options and pressures for women to work—require varied and versatile ways of earning and caring. These institutional shifts make gender flexibility increasingly desirable and even essential. Flexible approaches to work and parenting help families adapt, while inflexible ones leave them ill-prepared to cope with new economic and social realities.

CONVERGING IDEALS, DIVERGING FALLBACKS

How are young adults using the lessons of growing up in changing families to formulate their own plans for the future? Women and men from diverse family backgrounds share a set of lofty aspirations. Whether or not their parents stayed together, more than nine out of ten hope to rear children in the context of a satisfying lifelong bond. Far from rejecting the value of commitment, almost everyone wants to create a lasting marriage or "marriage-like" partnership. This does not, however, reflect a desire for a traditional relationship. Most also aspire to build a committed bond where both paid work and family caretaking are shared. Three-fourths of those who grew up in dual-earner homes want their spouses to share breadwinning and caretaking; but so do more that two-thirds of those from traditional homes, and close to nine-tenths of those with single parents. While four-fifths of women want an egalitarian relationship, but so do two-thirds of men. In short, most share an ideal that stresses the value of a lasting, flexible, and egalitarian partnership with considerable room for personal autonomy. Amy, an Asian American with two working parents, thus explains that:

> I want a fifty-fifty relationship, where we both have the potential of doing everything—both of us working and dealing with kids. With regard to career, if neither has flexibility, then one of us will have to sacrifice for one period, and the other for another.

And Wayne, an African American raised by a single mother, expresses the essentially same hopes when he says that:

> I don't want the '50s type of marriage, where I come home and she's cooking. I want her to have a career of her own. I want to be able to set my goals, and she can do what she wants, too.

While most of my interviewees hope to strike a flexible breadwinning and caretaking balance with an egalitarian partner, they are also skeptical about their chances of achieving this ideal. Women and men both worry that work demands, a lack of child rearing supports, and the fragility of modern relationships will undermine their desire to forge an enduring, egalitarian partnership. In the face of barriers to equality, most have concluded that they have little choice but to prepare for options that may fall substantially short of their ideals. Despite their shared aspirations, however, men and women are facing different institutional obstacles and cultural pressures, which are prompting divergent fallback strategies. If they cannot find a supportive partner, most women prefer self-reliance over economic dependence within a traditional marriage. Most men, if they cannot strike an equal balance between work and parenting, prefer a neo-traditional arrangement that allows them to put work first and rely on a partner for the lion's share of caregiving. In the event that Plan A proves unreachable, women and men are thus pursuing a different Plan B as insurance against their "worst case" fears. These divergent fallback strategies point toward the emergence of a new gender divide between young women, most of whom who see a need for self-reliance, and young men, who are more inclined to retain a modified version of traditional expectations.

WOMEN'S PLAN B

Torn between high hopes for combining work and family and worries about sustaining a lasting and satisfying partnership, young women are navigating uncertain waters. While some are falling back on domesticity, most prefer to find a more independent base than traditional marriage provides. In contrast to the media-driven message that young women are turning away from work and career in favor of domestic pursuits, the majority of my interviewees are determined to seek financial and emotional self-reliance, whether or not they also forge a committed relationship. Regardless of class, race, or ethnicity, most are reluctant to surrender their autonomy in a traditional marriage. When the bonds of marriage are so fragile, relying on a husband for economic security seems foolhardy. And if a relationship deteriorates, economic dependence on a man leaves few means of escape. Danisha, an African American who grew up in an inner-city, working-class neighborhood, and Jennifer, who was raised in a middle-class, predominantly white suburb, agree. Danisha proclaims that:

> Let's say that my marriage doesn't work. Just in case, I want to establish myself, because I don't ever want to end up, like, "What am I going to do?" I want to be able to do what I have to do and still be okay.

Jennifer agrees:

I will have to have a job and some kind of stability before considering marriage. Too many of my mother's friends went for that—"Let him provide everything"—and they're stuck in a very unhappy relationship, but can't leave because they can't provide for themselves or the children they now have. So it's either welfare or putting up with somebody else's c–p.

Hoping to avoid being trapped in an unhappy marriage or left by an unreliable partner without a way to survive, almost three-fourths of women plan to build a non-negotiable base of self-reliance and an independent identity in the world of paid work. But they do not view this strategy as incompatible with the search for a life partner. Instead, it reflects their determination to set a high standard for a worthy relationship. Economic self-reliance and personal independence make it possible to resist "settling" for anything less than a satisfying, mutually supportive bond.

Women from all backgrounds have concluded that work provides indispensable economic, social, and emotional resources. They have drawn lessons about the rewards of self-reliance and the perils of domesticity from their mothers, other women, and their own experiences growing up. When the bonds of marriage are fragile, relying on a husband for economic security seems foolhardy. They are thus seeking alternatives to traditional marriage by establishing a firm tie to paid work, by redesigning motherhood to better fit their work aspirations, and by looking to kin and friends as a support network to enlarge and, if needed, substitute, for an intimate relationship. These strategies do not preclude finding a life partner, but they reflect a determination to set a high standard for choosing one. Maria, who grew up in a two-parent home in a predominantly white, working-class suburb, declares:

I want to have this person to share [my] life with—(someone) that you're there for as much as they're there for you. But I can't settle.

And Rachel, whose Latino parents separated when she was young, shares this view:

I'm not afraid of being alone, but I am afraid of being with somebody's who's a jerk. I want to get married and have children, but it has to be under the right circumstances, with the right person.

Maria and Rachel also agree that if a worthy relationship ultimately proves out of reach, then remaining single need not mean social disconnection. Kin and friends provide a support network that enlarges and, if needed, even substitutes for an intimate relationship. Maria explains:

If I don't find (a relationship), then I cannot live in sorrow. It's not the only thing that's ultimately important. If I didn't have my family, if I didn't have a career, if I didn't have friends, I would be equally unhappy. (A relationship) is just one slice of the pie.

And Rachel concurs:

I can spend the rest of my life on my own, and as long as I have my sisters and my friends, I'm okay.

By blending support from friends and kin with financial self-sufficiency, these young women are pursuing a strategy of autonomy rather than placing their own fate or their children's in the hands of a traditional relationship.[9] Whether or not this strategy ultimately leads to marriage, it appears to offer the safest and most responsible way to prepare for the uncertainties of relationships and the barriers to men's equal sharing.

MEN'S PLAN B

Young men, in contrast, face a different dilemma: Torn between women's pressures for an egalitarian partnership and their own desire to succeed—or at least survive—in time-demanding workplaces, they are more inclined to fall back on a modified traditionalism that contrasts vividly with women's search for self-reliance. While they do not want or expect to return to a 1950s model of fathers as the only breadwinner, most men prefer a modified traditionalism that recognizes a mother's right (and need) to work, but puts his own career first. Although Andrew grew up in a consistently two-income home, he distinguished between a woman's "choice" to work and a man's "responsibility" to support his family:

> I would like to have it be equal—just from what I was exposed to and what attracts me—but I don't have a set definition for what that would be like. I would be fine if both of us were working, but if she thought, "At this point in my life, I don't want to work," then it would be fine.

Because equality may prove to be too costly to their careers, seven out of ten men are pursuing a strategy that positions them as the main breadwinner, even if it allows for two working spouses. When push comes to shove, and the demands of work collide with the needs of children, this approach allows men to resist equal caretaking, even in a two-earner context. Like women, men from a range of family, class, and ethnic backgrounds fall back on neo-traditionalism. They favor retaining a clear boundary between a breadwinning father and a caretaking mother, even when she holds a paid job. This neo-traditional strategy stresses women's primary status as mothers and defines equality as a woman's "choice" to add work onto mothering.

By making room for two earners, these strategies offer the financial cushion of a second income, acknowledge women's desire for a life beyond the home, and allow for more involved fatherhood. But this vision, which still claims separate spheres of responsibility for women and men, does not challenge a man's position as the primary earner or undermine the claim that his work prospects should come first. Although James's mother became too mentally ill to care for her children or herself, Josh plans to leave the lion's share of caretaking to his wife:

> All things being equal, it (caretaking) should be shared. It may sound sexist, but if somebody's going to be the breadwinner, it's going to be me. First of all, I make a better salary, and I feel the need to work, and I just think the child really needs the mother more than the father at a young age.

Men are thus more likely to favor a fallback arrangement that retains the gender boundary between breadwinning and caretaking, even when mothers hold paid jobs.

From young men's perspective, this modified but still gendered household offers women the chance to earn income and establish an identity at the workplace without imposing the costs of equal parenting on men. Granting a mother's "right" to work supports women's claims for independence, but does not undermine men's claim that their work prospects should come first. Acknowledging men's responsibilities at home provides for more involved fatherhood, but does not envision domestic equality. And making room for two earners provides a buffer against the difficulties of living on one income, but does not challenge men's position as the primary earner. Modified traditionalism thus appears to be a good compromise when the career costs of equality remain so high.[10] New economic insecurities, coupled with women's growing desire for equality, are creating dilemmas for men, even if they take a different form than the ones confronting women. Ultimately, however, men's desire to protect work prerogatives collides with women's growing desire for equality and need for independence.

ACROSS THE GENDER DIVIDE

In contrast to the popular images of a generation who feels neglected by working mothers, unsettled by parental breakups, and wary of equality, these life stories show strong support for working mothers, a greater concern with the quality of a relationship, and a shared desire to create lasting, flexible, and egalitarian partnerships. The good news is that most young women and men had largely positive experiences with mothers who worked and parents who strove for flexibility and equality. Those who grew up with a caring support network and sufficient economic security, whether in a single or a two-parent household, did well. Young women and men both recounted how gender flexibility in breadwinning and caretaking helped their parents (and other caretakers) overcome such increasingly prevalent family crises as the loss of a father's income or the decline of a mother's morale. By letting go of rigid patterns that once narrowly defined women's and men's "proper" places in the family and the wider world, all kinds of families were able to overcome unexpected challenges and create more financially stable and emotionally supportive homes. And most, even among those who lived in less flexible families, hope to build on the gains of their parents' generation by seeking equality and flexibility in their own lives.

The bad news, however, is that most young adults remain skeptical about their chances of achieving their ideals. Amid their shared desire to transcend gender boundaries and achieve flexibility in their own lives, however, young women and men harbor strong concerns that their aspirations will prove impossible to reach. Faced with the many barriers to egalitarian relationships and fearful that they will not find the right partner to help them integrate work with family caretaking, they are also preparing for options that may fall substantially short of their ideals. Reversing the argument that women are returning to tradition, however, these divergent fallback strategies suggest that a new divide is emerging between "self-reliant" women, who see work, an independent income, and emotional autonomy as essential to their survival, and "neo-traditional" men, who grant women's "choice" to work but also feel the need and pressure to be a primary breadwinner.

While women are developing more innovative strategies than are men, the underlying story is one of a resilient, but realistic generation that has changed far more than the institutions it has inherited. Whether they grew up in a flexible home or one with more rigid definitions of women's and men's proper places, their hard won lessons about the need for new, more egalitarian options for building relationships and caring for children are outpacing their ability to implement these aspirations.

Yet young men and women still hope to reach across the divide that separates them. Aware that traditional job ladders and traditional marriages are both waning, they are seeking more flexible ways to build careers, care for families, and integrate the two.[11] Convinced that the "organized career" is a relic of the past, most hope to craft a "personal career" that is not bound by a single employer or work organization. Most men as well as women are trying to redefine the "ideal worker" to accommodate the ebb and flow of family life, even if that means sacrificing some income for a more balanced life.[12] They hope to create a shared "work-family" career that interweaves breadwinning and caretaking.

Growing up in changing families and facing uncertainty in their own lives has left this generation weary of rigid, narrowly framed "family values" that moralize about their personal choices or those of others. They are searching for a morality without moralism that balances an ethic of tolerance and inclusiveness with the core values of behaving responsibly and caring for others. The clash between self-reliant women and neo-traditional men may signal a new divide, but it stems from intensifying work-family dilemmas, not from a decline of laudable values.

Since new social realties are forcing young adults to seek new ways to combine love and work, the best hope for bridging new gender divides lies in creating social policies that will allow 21st century Americans to pursue the flexible, egalitarian gender strategies they want rather than forcing them to fall back on less desirable—and ultimately less workable—options. Whether the goal is equal opportunity or a healthy family landscape, the best family values can only be achieved by creating the social supports for gender flexibility in our communities, homes, and workplaces.

Notes

1. Anecdotal, but high profile stories have touted an "opt out revolution," to use Lisa Belkin's term (2003), although a number of analysts have shown that "revolution" is a highly misleading and exaggerated term to describe the recent slight downturn in young mothers' labor force participation (Boushey, 2008; Williams, 2007). Most well-educated women are not leaving the workforce, and even though mothers with infants have shown a small downtown from their 1995 peak, mothers with children over the age of one are still just as likely as other women to hold a paid job. Even mothers with children under one show levels of employment that are much higher than the 1960's levels, which averaged 30 percent. Moreover, Williams (2007), Stone (2007), Bennetts (2007), and Hirshman (2006) also point out that the metaphor of "opting out" obscures the powerful ways that mothers are, in Williams words, "pushed out."
2. Recent overviews of the rise of single adults can be found in Pew (2007a and 2007b) and Roberts (2007). Prominent proponents of the "family decline" perspective include Blankenhorn (1995), Popenoe (1988,1996), Poponoe et al. (1996), and Whitehead (1997). Waite and Gallagher (2000) focus on the personal and social advantages of marriage. For rebuttals to the "family decline" perspective, see Bengston et al. (2002), Coontz (2005), Moore et al. (2002), Skolnick and Rosencrantz (1994), and Stacey (1996).
3. Randomly chosen from a broad range of city and suburban neighborhoods dispersed throughout the New York metropolitan region, the group includes 120 respondents from diverse race and

class backgrounds and all parts of the country. In all, 54 percent identified as non-Hispanic white, 21 percent as African American, 18 percent as Latino, and 7 percent as Asian. About 43 percent grew up in middle and upper-middle class homes, while 43 percent lived in homes that were solidly working class, and another 15 percent lived in or on the edge of poverty. With an average age of 24, they are evenly divided between women and men, and about 5 percent identified as either lesbian or gay. As a group, they reflect the demographic contours of young adults throughout metropolitan America. See Gerson (2006 and forthcoming) for a full description of my sample and methods.

4. Most research shows that diversity *within* family types, however defined, is as large as the differences *between* them. Acock and Demo (1994) argue that family type does not predict children's well-being. Parcel and Menaghan (1994) make the same case for different forms of parental employment.
5. In the case of one vs. two-parent homes, children living with both biological parents do appear on average to fare better, but most of the difference disappears after taking account of the family's financial resources and the degree of parental conflict prior to a break-up (Amato and Booth, 1997; Amato and Hohmann-Marriott, 2007; Booth and Amato, 2001; Furstenberg and Cherlin, 1991; Hetherington, 1999; McLanahan and Sandefur, 1994). In a recent study of the effects of divorce on children's behavior, Li (2007) shows that "while certain divorces harm children, others benefit them."
6. Decades of research have shown that children do not suffer when their mothers work outside the home. A mother's satisfaction with her situation, the quality of care a child receives, and the involvement of fathers and other caretakers are far more important factors (Galinsky, 1999; Harvey, 1999; Hoffman, 1987; Hoffman et al., 1999). Bianchi, Robinson, and Milkie (2006) report that parents are actually spending more time with their children. Recent research on the effects of daycare have found only small, temporary differences. Barnett and Rivers (1996) demonstrate a range of advantages for two-income couples, and Springer (2007) reports significant health benefits for men whose wives work.
7. Hochschild (1989) refers to dual earner couples' "gender strategies," although she focuses more on how these strategies reproduce gender divisions than on when, how, and why they might undermine gender distinctions. See Lorber (1994), Risman (1998), and West and Zimmerman (1987) for discussions of the social construction of gender. Zerubavel (1991) analyzes the social roots of mental flexibility.
8. All of the names have been changed to protect confidentiality, and some quotes have been shortened or lightly edited to remove extraneous phrases.
9. About a quarter of women concluded that if work and family collide, they would rather make a more traditional compromise. These women worried about inflexible workplaces and the difficulty finding an equal partner. Yet they still hoped to fit work into their lives. This outlook, too, reflects the dilemmas facing young women who lack the supports to share work and caretaking equally. (See Gerson, forthcoming, for a full analysis of the variation in women's fallback strategies.)
10. About three in ten men stress independence over traditional marriage, but autonomy has a different meaning for them than it does for women. Poor work prospects left them determined to remain single unless they find a partner who does not expect financial support. Unlike self-reliant women, who hoped to support themselves and their children, autonomous men worried about their ability to earn enough to support a family. (See Gerson, forthcoming, for a full analysis of men's varied strategies.)
11. See Moen and Roehling (2005).
12. See Williams (2000).

References

Acock, Alan C. and David H. Demo. 1994. *Family Diversity and Well-being.* Thousand Oaks, CA: Sage.

Amato, Paul R. and Alan Booth. 1997. *A Generation at Risk: Growing Up in an Era of Family Upheaval.*

Cambridge, Mass.: Harvard University Press. (Cited twice)

Amato, Paul R. and Bryndl Hohmann-Marriott. 2007. "A Comparison of High- and Low-Distress Marriages That End in Divorce." *Journal of Marriage and Family* 69(3): 621–638.

Barnett, Rosalind C. and Caryl Rivers. 1996. *She works/He works: How Two-income Families Are Happier, Healthier, and Better-off.* San Francisco, CA: Harper.

Belkin, Lisa. 2003. "The Opt Out Revolution." *The New York Times Magazine.*

Bengtson, Vern L., Timothy J. Biblarz and Robert E. L. Roberts. 2002. *How Families Still Matter: A Longitudinal Study of Youth in Two Generations.* New York, NY: Cambridge University Press.

Bennetts, Leslie. 2007. *The Feminine Mistake: Are We Giving Up Too Much?* New York: Voice/Hyperion.

Bianchi, Suzanne M., John P. Robinson and Melissa A. Milkie. 2006. *Changing Rhythms of American Family Life.* New York: Russell Sage Foundation.

Blankenhorn, David. 1995. *Fatherless America: Confronting Our Most Urgent Social Problem.* New York: BasicBooks.

Booth, Alan and Paul R. Amato. 2001. "Parental Predivorce Relations and Offspring Postdivorce Well-Being." *Journal of Marriage and the Family* 63(1): 197–212.

Boushey, Heather. 2008. ""Opting out"? The Effect of Children on Women's Employment in the United States." *Feminist Economics* 14(1):1–36.

Coontz, Stephanie. 2005. *Marriage, a History: From Obedience to Intimacy, or How Love Conquered Marriage.* New York: Viking.

Furstenberg, Frank F. and Andrew J. Cherlin. 1991. *Divided Families: What Happens to Children When Parents Part.* Cambridge, Mass.: Harvard University Press.

Galinsky, Ellen. 1999. *Ask the Children: What America's Children Really Think about Working Parents.* New York: William Morrow.

Gerson, Kathleen. Forthcoming. *Blurring Boundaries: How the Children of the Gender Revolution are Remaking Family and Work.* Oxford University Press: New York.

———. 2006. "Families as Trajectories: Children's Views of Family Life in Contemporary America." In *Families Between Flexibility and Dependability: Perspectives for a Life Cycle Family Policy*, edited by Hans Bertram et al. Farmington Hills, MI: Verlag Barbara Budrich.

Harvey, Lisa. 1999. "Short-Term and Long-Term Effects of Early Parental Employment on Children of the National Longitudinal Study of Youth." *Developmental Psychology* 35(2): 445–459.

Hetherington, E. M. 1999. *Coping with Divorce, Single Parenting, and Remarriage: A Risk and Resiliency Perspective.* Mahwah, NJ: Lawrence Erlbaum Associates.

Hirshman, Linda. 2006. *Get to Work.* New York, NY: Viking.

Hochschild, Arlie R. 1989. *The Second Shift: Working Parents and the Revolution at Home.* New York, NY: Viking.

Hoffman, Lois. 1987. "The Effects on Children of Maternal and Paternal Employment." Pp. 362–395 in *Families and Work*, edited by N. Gerstel and H.E. Gross. Philadelphia: Temple U. Press.

Hoffman, Lois, Norma Wladis and Lise M. Youngblade. 1999. *Mothers at Work: Effects on Children's Well-being.* New York: Cambridge University Press.

Li, Allen J. 2007. "The Kids are OK: Divorce and Children's Behavior Problems." Santa Monica, CA: Rand Working Paper WR 489.

Lorber, Judith. 1994. *Paradoxes of Gender.* New Haven: Yale University Press.

McLanahan, Sara and Gary D. Sandefur. 1994. *Growing Up with a Single Parent: What Hurts, What Helps.* Cambridge, MA: Harvard University Press.

Moen, Phyllis and Patricia Roehling. 2005. *The Career Mystique: Cracks in the American Dream.* Lanham, MD: Rowman & Littlefield Publishers.

Moore, Kristin A., Rosemary Chalk, Juliet Scarpa and Sharon Vandiverre. *Family Strengths: Often Overlooked, But Real.* Washington, D.C.: Annie E. Casey Foundation.

Parcel, Toby L. and Elizabeth G. Menaghan. 1994. *Parents' Jobs and Children's Lives.* New York: A. de Gruyter.

Pew Research Center. 2007. "As Marriage and Parenthood Drift Apart, Public Is Concerned about Social Impact." Retrieved June 19, 2008 (http://pewresearch.org/pubs/526/marriage-parenthood).

———. 2007. "How Young People View Their Lives, Futures and Politics: A Portrait of the "Generation Next"" Retrieved June 19, 2008 (http://people-press.org/reports/pdf/300.pdf).

Popenoe, David. 1996. *Life without Father: Compelling New Evidence that Fatherhood and Marriage Are Indispensable for the Good of Children and Society.* New York: Martin Kessler Books.

———. 1988. *Disturbing the Nest: Family Change and Decline in Modern Societies.* New York: A. de Gruyter.

Popenoe, David, Jean B. Elshtain and David Blankenhorn. 1996. *Promises to Keep: Decline and Renewal of Marriage in America.* Lanham, MD: Rowman & Littlefield Publishers.

Risman, Barbara J. 1998. *Gender Vertigo: American Families in Transition.* New Haven, CT: Yale University Press.

Roberts, Sam. 2007. "Fifty-one percent of Women are Now Living without Spouse." *The New York Times*, January 16.

Skolnick, Arlene and Stacy Rosencrantz. 1994. "The New Crusade for the Old Family." *The American Prospect*, pp. 59.

Springer, Kristen W. 2007. "Research or Rhetoric? A Response to Wilcox and Nock." *Sociological Forum* 22(1): 111–116.

Stacey, Judith. 1996. *In the Name of the Family: Rethinking Family Values in the Postmodern Age.* Boston: Beacon Press.

Stone, Pamela. 2007. *Opting Out? Why Women Really Quit Careers and Head Home.* Berkeley: University of California Press.

Waite, Linda J. and Maggie Gallagher. 2000. *The Case for Marriage: Why Married People Are Happier, Healthier, and Better off Financially.* New York: Doubleday.

Whitehead, Barbara D. 1997. *The Divorce Culture.* New York: Alfred A. Knopf: Distributed by Random House.

West, Candace & Don H. Zimmerman. 1987. "Doing Gender." *Gender & Society* 1(2): 125–151.

Williams, Joan. 2007. "The Opt-Out Revolution Revisited." *The American Prospect* (March): A12–A15.

———. 2000. *Unbending Gender: Why Family and Work Conflict and What to Do About It.* New York: Oxford University Press.

Zerubavel, Eviatar. 1991. *The Fine Line: Making Distinctions in Everyday Life.* Chicago: University of Chicago Press.

Chapter 4

Sexuality and Society

READING 9

Sexual Revolution(s)

Beth Bailey

In 1957 America's favorite TV couple, the safely married Ricky and Lucy Ricardo, slept in twin beds. Having beds at all was probably progressive—as late as 1962 June and Ward Cleaver did not even have a bedroom. Elvis's pelvis was censored in each of his three appearances on the *Ed Sullivan Show* in 1956, leaving his oddly disembodied upper torso and head thrashing about on the TV screen. But the sensuality in his eyes, his lips, his lyrics was unmistakable, and his genitals were all the more important in their absence. There was, likewise no mistaking, Mick Jagger's meaning when he grimaced ostentatiously and sang "Let's spend some *time* together" on *Ed Sullivan* in 1967. Much of the audience knew that the line was really "Let's spend the night together," and the rest quickly got the idea. The viewing public could see absence and hear silence—and therein lay the seeds of the sexual revolution.

What we call the sexual revolution grew from these tensions between public and private—not only from tensions manifest in public culture, but also from tensions between private behaviors and the public rules and ideologies that were meant to govern behavior. By the 1950s the gulf between private acts and public norms was often quite wide—and the distance was crucial. People had sex outside marriage, but very, very few acknowledged that publicly. A woman who married the only man with whom she had had premarital sex still worried years later: "I was afraid someone might have learned that we had intercourse before marriage and I'd be disgraced." The consequences, however, were not just psychological. Young women (and sometimes men) discovered to be having premarital sex were routinely expelled from school or college; gay men risked all for engaging in consensual sex. There were real penalties for sexual misconduct and while many deviated from the sexual orthodoxy of the day, all but a few did so furtively, careful not to get "caught."

Few episodes demonstrate the tensions between the public and private dimensions of sexuality in midcentury America better than the furor that surrounded the publication of the studies of sexual behavior collectively referred to as the "Kinsey Reports." Though a dry, social scientific report, *Sexual Behavior in the Human Male* (1948) had sold over a quarter of a million copies by 1953, when the companion volume on the human female came out. The male volume was controversial, but the female volume was, in *Look* magazine's characterization, "stronger stuff." Kinsey made it clear that he understood the social implications of his study, introducing a section on "the pre-marital coital behavior of the female sample which has been available for this study" with the following qualification: "Because of this public condemnation of pre-marital coitus, one might believe that such contacts would be rare among American females and males. But this is only the overt culture, the things that people openly confess to believe and do. Our previous report (1948) on the male has indicated how far publicly expressed attitudes may depart from the realities of behavior—the covert culture, what males actually do."

Kinsey, a biologist who had begun his career with much less controversial studies of the gall wasp, drew fire from many quarters, but throughout the criticism is evident concern about his uncomfortable juxtaposition of public and private. "What price biological science . . . to reveal intimacies of one's private sex life and to draw conclusions from inscriptions on the walls of public toilets?" said one American in a letter to the editor of *Look* magazine.

Much of the reaction to Kinsey did hinge on the distance between the "overt" and the "covert." People were shocked to learn how many men and women were doing what they were not supposed to be doing. Kinsey found that 50 percent of the women in his sample had had premarital sex (even though between 80 percent and 89 percent of his sample disapproved of premarital sex on "moral grounds"), that 61 percent of college-educated men and 84 percent of men who had completed only high school had had pre-marital sex, that over one-third of the married women in the sample had "engaged in petting" with more than ten different men, that approximately half of the married couples had engaged in "oral stimulation" of both male and female genitalia, and that at least 17 percent of American men had had "some homosexual experience" during their lifetimes.

By pulling the sheets back, so to speak, Kinsey had publicized the private. Many people must have been reassured by the knowledge that they were not alone, that their sexual behaviors were not individual deviant acts but part of widespread social trends. But others saw danger in what Kinsey had done. By demonstrating the distance between the overt and the covert cultures, Kinsey had further undermined what was manifestly a beleaguered set of rules. *Time* magazine warned its readers against the attitude that "there is morality in numbers," the *Chicago Tribune* called Kinsey a "menace to society," and the *Ladies' Home Journal* ran an article with the disclaimer: "The facts of behavior reported . . . are not to be interpreted as moral or social justification for individual acts."

Looking back to the century's midpoint, it is clear that the coherence of (to use Kinsey's terms) covert and overt sexual cultures was strained beyond repair. The sexual revolution of the 1960s emerged from these tensions, and to that extent it was not revolutionary, but evolutionary. As much as anything else, we see the overt coming to terms with the covert. But the revision of revolution to evolution would miss a crucial point. It is not historians who have labeled these changes "sexual revolution"—it was people at the time, those who participated and those who watched. And they called it that before much of what we would see as revolutionary really emerged—before gay liberation and the women's movement and Alex Comfort's *The Joy of Sex* (1972) and "promiscuity" and singles' bars. The term was in general use by 1963—earlier than one might expect.

To make any sense of the sexual revolution, we have to pay attention to the label people gave it. Revolutions, for good or ill, are moments of danger. It matters that a metaphor of revolution gave structure to the myriad changes taking place in American society. The changes in sexual mores and behaviors could as easily have been cast as evolutionary—but they were not.

Looking back, the question of whether or not the sexual revolution was revolutionary is not easy to answer; it depends partly on one's political (defined broadly) position. Part of the trouble, though, is that the sexual revolution was not one movement. It was instead a set of movements, movements that were closely linked, even intertwined, but which often made uneasy bedfellows. Here I hope to do some untangling, laying out three of the most important strands of the sexual revolution and showing their historical origins, continuities, and disruptions.

The first strand, which transcended youth, might be cast as both evolutionary and revolutionary. Throughout the twentieth century, picking up speed in the 1920s, the 1940s and the 1960s, we have seen a sexualization of America's culture. Sexual images have become more and more a part of public life, and sex—or more accurately, the representation of sex—is used to great effect in a marketplace that offers Americans fulfillment through consumption. Although the blatancy of today's sexual images would be shocking to someone transported from an earlier era, such representations developed gradually and generally did not challenge more "traditional" understandings of sex and of men's and women's respective roles in sex or in society.

The second strand was the most modest in aspect but perhaps the most revolutionary in implication. In the 1960s and early 1970s an increasing number of young people began to live together "without benefit of matrimony," as the phrase went at the time. While sex was usually a part of the relationship (and probably a more important part than most people acknowledged), few called on concepts of "free love" or "pleasure" but instead used words like "honesty," "commitment," and "family." Many of the young people who lived together could have passed for young marrieds and in that sense were pursuing fairly traditional arrangements. At the same time, self-consciously or not, they challenged the tattered remnants of a Victorian epistemological and ideological system that still, in the early 1960s, fundamentally structured the public sexual mores of the American middle class.

The third strand was more self-consciously revolutionary, as sex was *actively claimed* by young people and used not only for pleasure, but also for power in a new form of cultural politics that shook the nation. As those who threw themselves into the "youth revolution" (a label that did not stick) knew so well, the struggle for America's future would take place not in the structure of electoral politics, but on the battlefield of cultural meaning. Sex was an incendiary tool of a revolution that was more than political. But not even the cultural revolutionaries agreed on goals, or on the role and meaning of sex in the revolution.

These last two strands had to do primarily with young people, and that is significant. The changes that took place in America's sexual mores and behaviors in the sixties were *experienced* and *defined* as revolutionary in large part because they were so closely tied to youth. The nation's young, according to common wisdom and the mass media, were in revolt. Of course, the sexual revolution was not limited to youth, and sex was only one part of the revolutionary claims of youth. Still it was the intersection of sex and youth that signaled danger. And the fact that these were often middle-class youths, the ones reared in a culture of respectability (told that a single sexual misstep could jeopardize their bright futures), made their frontal challenges to sexual mores all the more inexplicable and alarming.

Each of these strands is complex, and I make no pretense to be exhaustive. Thus, rather than attempting to provide a complete picture of changes in behaviors or ideologies, I will examine several manifestations of seemingly larger trends. The sexualization of culture (the first strand) is illustrated by the emergence of *Playboy* and *Cosmo* magazines. For the "modest revolutionaries" (the second strand), I look to the national scandal over a Barnard College junior's "arrangement" in 1968 and the efforts of University of Kansas students to establish a coed dormitory. Finally, the cultural radicals (the third strand) are represented by the writings of a few counterculture figures.

By focusing on the 1960s, we lose much of the "sexual revolution." In many ways, the most important decade of that revolution was the 1970s, when the "strands" of the 1960s joined with gay liberation, the women's movement, and powerful assertions of the importance of cultural differences in America. Yet, by concentrating on the early years of the sexual revolution, we see its tangled roots—the sexual ideologies and behaviors that gave it birth. We can also understand how little had been resolved—even begun—by the end of the 1960s.

BEFORE THE REVOLUTION: YOUTH AND SEX

Like many of the protest movements that challenged American tranquility in the sixties, the sexual revolution developed within the protected space and intensified atmosphere of the college campus. An American historian recalls returning to Harvard University in 1966 after a year of postgraduate study in England. Off balance from culture shock and travel fatigue, he entered Harvard Yard and knew with absolute certainty that he had "missed the sexual revolution." One can imagine a single symbolic act of copulation signaling the beginning of the revolution (it has a nicely ironic echo of "the shot heard round the world"). The single act and the revolution complete in 1966 are fanciful constructions; not everything began or ended at Harvard even in those glory years. But events there and at other elite colleges and universities, if only because of the national attention they received, provide a way into the public intersections of sex, youth and cultural politics.

Harvard had set a precedent in student freedom in 1952, when girls (the contemporary term) were allowed to visit in Harvard men's rooms. The freedom offered was not supposed to be sexual—or at least not flagrantly so. But by 1963 Dean Jon Monro complained that he was "badly shaken up by some severe violations," for a once "pleasant privilege" had come to be "considered a license to use the college rooms for wild parties or sexual intercourse." The controversy went public with the aid of *Time* magazine, which fanned the flames by quoting a senior's statement that "morality is a relative concept projecting certain mythologies associated with magico-religious beliefs." The Parietals Committee of the Harvard Council for Undergraduate Affairs, according to the *Boston Herald,* concluded that "if these deep emotional commitments and ties occasionally lead to sexual intercourse, surely even that is more healthy than the situation a generation ago when 'nice girls' were dated under largely artificial circumstances and sexual needs were gratified at a brothel." Both justifications seemed fundamentally troubling in different ways, but at least the controversy focused on men. The sexual double standard was strong. When the spotlight turned on women, the stakes seemed even higher.

The media had a field day when the president of Vassar College, Sarah Blanding, said unequivocally that if a student wished to engage in premarital sex she must withdraw from the college. The oft-quoted student reply to her dictum chilled the hearts of middle-class parents throughout the country: "If Vassar is to become the Poughkeepsie Victorian Seminary for young Virgins, then the change of policy had better be made explicit in admissions catalogs."

Such challenges to authority and to conventional morality were reported to eager audiences around the nation. None of this, of course, was new. National audiences had been scandalized by the panty raid epidemic of the early 1950s, the antics and petting parties of college youth had provided sensational fodder for hungry journalists in the 1920s. The parents—and grandparents—of these young people had chipped away at the system of sexual controls themselves. But they had not directly and publicly denied the very foundations of sexual morality. With few exceptions, they had evaded the controls and circumvented the rules, climbing into dorm rooms through open windows, signing out to the library and going to motels, carefully maintaining virginity in the technical sense while engaging in every caress known to married couples. The evasions often succeeded, but that does not mean that the controls had no effect. On the contrary, they had a great impact on the ways people experienced sex.

There were, in fact, two major systems of sexual control, one structural and one ideological. These systems worked to reinforce one another, but they affected the lives of those they touched differently.

The structural system was the more practical of the two but probably the less successful. It worked by limiting opportunities for the unmarried to have intercourse. Parents of teenagers set curfews and promoted double dating, hoping that by preventing privacy they would limit sexual exploration. Colleges, acting in loco parentis, used several tactics: visitation hours, parietals, security patrols, and restrictions on students' use of cars. When Oberlin students mounted a protest against the college's policy on cars in 1963, one male student observed that the issue was not transportation but privacy: "We wouldn't care if the cars had no wheels, just so long as they had doors."

The rules governing hours applied only to women and, to some extent, were meant to guarantee women's safety by keeping track of their comings and goings. But the larger rationale clearly had to do with sexual conduct. Men were not allowed in women's rooms but were received in lounges or "date rooms," where privacy was never assured. By setting curfew hours and requiring women to sign out from their dormitories, indicating who they were with and where they were going, college authorities meant to limit possibilities for privacy. Rules for men were not deemed necessary—because of a sexual double standard, because men's safety and well-being seemed less threatened in general, and because the colleges and universities were primarily concerned with controlling their own populations. If women were supervised or chaperoned and in by 11:00 P.M., the men would not have partners—at least, not partners drawn from the population that mattered.

Throughout the 1950s, the structural controls became increasingly complex; by the early 1960s they were so elaborate as to be ludicrous. At the University of Michigan in 1962, the student handbook devoted nine of its fifteen pages to rules for women. Curfews varied by the night of the week, by the student's year in college, and even, in some places, by her grade point average. Students could claim Automatic Late Permissions (ALPs) but only under certain conditions. Penalties at Michigan (an institutional version of "grounding") began when a student had eleven "late minutes"—but the late minutes could be acquired one at a time throughout the semester. At the University of Kansas in the late 1950s, one sorority asked the new dean of women to discipline two women who had flagrantly disregarded curfew. The dean, investigating, discovered that the women in question had been between one and three minutes late signing in on three occasions.

The myriad of rules, as anyone who lived through this period well knows, did not prevent sexual relations between students so much as they structured the times and places and ways that students could have sexual contact. Students said good-nights on the porches of houses, they petted in dormitory lounges while struggling to keep three feet on the floor and clothing in some semblance of order, and they had intercourse in cars, keeping an eye out for police patrols. What could be done after eleven could be done before eleven, and sex need not occur behind a closed door and in a bed—but this set of rules had a profound impact on the *ways* college students and many young people, living in their parents' homes *experienced sex*.

The overelaboration of rules, in itself, offers evidence that the controls were beleaguered. Nonetheless, the rules were rarely challenged frontally and thus they offered some illusion of control. This system of rules, in all its inconsistency, arbitrariness, and blindness, helped to preserve the distinction between public and private, the coexistence of overt and covert, that defines midcentury American sexuality.

The ideological system of controls was more pervasive than the structured system and probably more effective. This system centered on ideas of difference: men and women were fundamentally different creatures, with different roles and interests in sex. Whether one adopted a psychoanalytic or an essentialist approach, whether one looked to scholarly or popular analysis, the final conclusion pointed to *difference*. In sex (as in life), women were the limit setters and men the aggressors.

The proper limits naturally depended on one's marital status, but even within marriage sex was to be structured along lines of difference rather than of commonality. Marital advice books since the 1920s had the importance of female orgasm, insisting that men must satisfy their wives, but even these calls for orgasm equality posited male and female pleasure as competing interests. The language of difference in postwar America, which was often quite extreme, can be seen as a defensive reaction to changing gender roles in American society.

One influential psychoanalytic study, provocatively titled *Modern Woman: The Lost Sex*, condemned women who tried to be men and argued the natural difference between men and women by comparing their roles in sexual intercourse. The woman's role is "passive," the authors asserted. "[Sex] is not as easy as rolling off a log for her. It is easier. It is as easy as being the log itself. She cannot fail to deliver a masterly performance, by doing nothing whatever except being duly appreciative and allowing nature to take its course." For the man, in contrast, sexuality is "overt, apparent and urgent, outward and ever-present," fostered by psychological and physiological pressures toward orgasm. Men might experiment sexually with few or no consequences and no diminution of pleasure. Women, on the other hand, could not: "The strong desire for children or lack of it in a woman has a crucial bearing on how much enjoyment she derives from the sexual act. . . . Women cannot make . . . pleasure an end in itself without inducing a decline in the pleasure."

These experts argued from a psychoanalytic framework, but much less theoretical work also insisted on the fundamental difference between men and women, and on their fundamentally different interests in sex. Texts used in marriage courses in American high schools and college typically included chapters on the difference between men and women—and these difference were not limited to their reproductive systems.

Women did in fact have a different and more imperative interest in controlling sex than men, for women could become pregnant. Few doctors would fit an unmarried woman with a diaphragm, though one might get by in the anonymity of a city with a cheap "gold" ring from a drugstore or by pretending to be preparing for an impending honeymoon. Relying on the ubiquitous condom in the wallet was risky and douching (Coca-Cola had a short-lived popularity) even more so. Abortion was illegal, and though many abortions took place, they were dangerous, expensive, and usually frightening and degrading experiences. Dependable and *available* birth control might have made a difference (many could later attribute "the sexual revolution" to the "pill"), but sexual behaviors and sexual mores were not based simply on the threat of illegitimate pregnancy. Kinsey found that only 44 percent of the women in his sample said that they restricted their pre-marital coitus "because of fear of pregnancy," whereas 80 percent cited "moral reasons." Interestingly, 44 percent of the sample also noted their "fear of public opinion."

Women who were too "free" with sexual favors could lose value and even threaten their marriageability. In this society, a woman's future socioeconomic status depended primarily on her husband's occupation and earning power. While a girl was expected to "pet to be popular," girls and women who went "too far" risked their futures. Advice books and columns from the 1940s and 1950s linked girls' and women's "value" to their "virtue," arguing in explicitly economic terms that "free" kisses destroyed a woman's value in the dating system: "The boys find her easy to afford. She doesn't put a high value on herself." The exchange was even clearer in the marriage market. In chilling language, a teen adviser asked: "Who wants second hand goods?"

It was not only the advisers and experts who equated virtue and value. Fifty percent of the male respondents in Kinsey's study wanted to marry a virgin. Even though a relatively high percentage of women had intercourse before marriage, and a greater number engaged in "petting," most of these women at least *expected* to marry the man, and many did. Still, there might be consequences. Elaine Tyler May, who analyzed responses to a large, ongoing psychological study of married couples in the postwar era, found that many couples struggled with the psychological burdens of premarital intimacy for much of their married lives. In the context of a social/cultural system that insisted that "nice girls don't," many reported a legacy of guilt or mistrust. One woman wrote of her husband: "I think he felt that because we had been intimate before marriage that I could be as easily interested in any man that came along."

Of course, sexual mores and behaviors were highly conditioned by the sexual double standard. Lip service was paid to the ideal of male premarital chastity, but that ideal was usually obviated by the notion, strong in peer culture and implicity acknowledged in the larger culture, that sexual intercourse was a male rite of passage. Middle-class boys pushed at the limits set by middle-class girls but they generally looked elsewhere for "experience." A man who went to high school in the early 1960s (and did not lose his virginity until his first year of college) recalls the system with a kind of horror: "You slept with one kind of woman, and dated another kind, and the women you slept with, you didn't have much respect for, generally."

The distinction was often based on class—middle-class boys and men had sex with girls and women of the lower classes, or even with prostitutes. They did not really expect to have intercourse with a woman of their own class unless they were to be married. Samuel Hynes, in his memoir of coming of age as a navy flier during World War II, describes that certain knowledge: "There were nice girls in our lives, too. Being middle-class is more than a social station, it's kind of destiny. A middle-class boy from Minneapolis will seek out nice middle-class girls, in Memphis or anywhere else, will take them out on middle-class dates and try to put their hand inside their middle-class underpants. And he will fail. It was all a story that had already been written."

Dating, for middle-class youth, was a process of sexual negotiation. "Good girls" had to keep their virginity yet still contend with their own sexual desires or with boys who expected at least some petting as a "return" on the cost of the date. Petting was virtually universal in the world of heterosexual dating. A 1959 *Atlantic* article, "Sex and the College Girl," described the ideal as having "done every possible kind of petting without actually having intercourse."

For most middle-class youth in the postwar era, sex involved a series of skirmishes that centered around lines and boundaries: kissing, necking, petting above the waist, petting below the waist, petting through clothes, petting under clothes, mild petting, heavy petting. The progression of sexual intimacy had emerged as a highly ordered system. Each act constituted a stage, ordered in a strict hierarchy (first base, second base, and so forth), with vaginal penetration as the ultimate step. But in their attempts to preserve technical virginity, many young people engaged in sexual behaviors that, in the sexual hierarchy of the larger culture, should have been more forbidden than vaginal intercourse. One woman remembers: "We went pretty far, very far; everything but intercourse. But it was very frustrating. . . . Sex was out of the question. I had it in mind that I was going to be a virgin. So I came up with oral sex. . . . I thought I invented it."

Many young men and women acted in defiance of the rules, but that does not make the rules irrelevant. The same physical act can have very different meanings depending on its emotional and social/cultural contexts. For America's large middle class and for all those who aspired to "respectability" in the pre-revolutionary twentieth century, sex was overwhelmingly secret or furtive. Sex was a set of acts with high stakes and possibly serious consequences, acts that emphasized and reinforced the different roles of men and women in American society. We do not know how each person felt about his or her private acts, but we do know that few were willing or able to publicly reject the system of sexual controls.

The members of the generation that would be labeled "the sixties" were revolutionary in that they called fundamental principles of sexual morality and control into question. The system of controls they had been inherited and lived within was based on a set of presumptions rooted in the previous century. In an evolving set of arguments and actions (which never became thoroughly coherent or unified), they rejected a system of sexual controls organized around concepts of difference and hierarchy.

Both systems of control—the structural and the ideological—were firmly rooted in a Victorian epistemology that had, in most areas of life, broken down by the early twentieth century. This system was based on a belief in absolute truth and a passion for order and control. Victorian thought, as Joseph Singal has argued persuasively, insisted on "preserving absolute standards based on a radical dichotomy between that which was deemed 'human' and that regarded as 'animal.'" On the "human" side were all forces of civilization; on the "animal," all instincts, passions, and desires that threatened order and self-control. Sex clearly fell into the latter category. But the Victorian romance was not restricted to human versus animal, civilized versus savage. The moral dichotomy "fostered a tendency to see the world in polar terms." Thus we find rigid dichotomous pairs not only of good and evil, but of men and women, body and soul, home and world, public and private.

Victorian epistemology, with its remarkably comfortable and comforting certainties and its stifling absolutes, was shaken by the rise of a new science that looked to "dynamic process" and "relativism" instead of the rigid dichotomies of Victorian thought. It was challenged from within by those children of Victorianism who "yearned to smash the glass and breathe freely," as Jackson Lears argued in his study of antimodernism. And most fundamentally, it was undermined by the realities of an urban industrial society. American Victorian culture was, as much as anything, a strategy of the emerging middle classes. Overwhelmed by the chaos of the social order that had produced them and that they sought to manage, the middling classes had attempted to separate themselves from disorder and corruption. This separation, finally, was untenable.

The Victorian order was overthrown and replaced by a self-consciously "modern culture." One place we point to demonstrate the decline of Victorianism is the change in sexual "manners and mores" in the early twentieth century. Nonetheless, sex may be the place that Victorian thought least relinquished its hold. This is not to say that prudishness reigned—the continuity is more subtle and more fundamental. Skirts rose above the knee, couples dated and petted, sexologists and psychologists acknowledged that women were not naturally "passionless," and the good judge Ben Lindsey called for the "companionate marriage." But the systems of control that regulated and structured sex were Victorian at their core, with science replacing religion to authorize absolute truth, and with inflexible bipolar constructions somewhat reformulated but intact. The system of public controls over premarital sex was based on rigid dichotomous pairings: men and women, public and private. This distinction would be rejected—or at least recast—in the cultural and sexual struggles of the sixties.

REVOLUTIONARIES

All those who rejected the sexual mores of the postwar era did not reject the fundamental premises that gave them shape. *Playboy* magazine played an enormously important (if symbolic) role in the sexual revolution, or at least in preparing the ground for the sexual revolution. *Playboy* was a men's magazine in the tradition of *Esquire* (for which its founder had worked briefly) but laid claim to a revolutionary stance partly by replacing *Esquire's* airbrushed drawings with airbrushed flesh.

Begun by Hugh Hefner in 1953 with an initial print run of 70,000, *Playboy* passed the one million circulation mark in three years. By the mid-1960s Hefner had amassed a fortune of $100 million, including a lasciviously appointed forty-eight-room mansion staffed by thirty Playboy "bunnies" ("fuck like bunnies" is a phrase we have largely left behind, but most people at the time caught the allusion). Playboy clubs, also staffed by large-breasted and long-legged women in bunny ears and cottontails, flourished throughout the country. Though *Playboy* offered quality writing and advice for those aspiring to sophistication, the greatest selling point of the magazine was undoubtedly its illustrations.

Playboy, however, offered more than masturbatory opportunities. Between the pages of coyly arranged female bodies—more, inscribed in the coyly arranged female bodies—flourished a strong and relatively coherent ideology. Hefner called it a philosophy and wrote quite a few articles expounding it (a philosophy professor in North Carolina took it seriously enough to describe his course as "philosophy from Socrates to Hefner").

Hefner saw his naked women as "a symbol of disobedience, a triumph of sexuality, an end of Puritanism." He saw his magazines as an attack on "our ferocious anti-sexuality, our dark antieroticism." But his thrust toward pleasure and light was not to be undertaken in partnership. The Playboy philosophy according to Hefner, had less to do with sex and more to do with sex roles. American society increasingly "blurred distinctions between the sexes . . . not only in business, but in such diverse realms as household chores, leisure activities, smoking and drinking habits, clothing styles, upswinging homosexuality and the sex-obliterating aspects of togetherness," concluded the "Playboy Panel" in June 1962. In Part 19 of his extended essay on the Playboy philosophy, Hefner wrote: "PLAYBOY stresses a strongly heterosexual concept of society—in which the separate roles of men and women are clearly defined and compatible."

Read without context, Hefner's call does not necessarily preclude sex as a common interest between men and women. He is certainly advocating heterosexual sex. But the models of sex offered are not partnerships. Ever innovative in marketing and design, *Playboy* offered in one issue a special "coloring book" section. A page featuring three excessively voluptuous women was captioned "Make one of the girls a blonde. Make one of the girls a brunette. Make one of the girls a redhead. It does not matter which is which. The girls' haircolors are interchangeable. So are the girls."

Sex, in the Playboy mode, was a contest—not of wills, in the model of the male seducer and the virtuous female, but of exploitative intent, as in the playboy and the would-be wife. In *Playboy's* world, women were out to ensnare men, to entangle them in a web of responsibility and obligation (not the least of which was financial). Barbara Ehrenreich has convincingly argued that *Playboy* was an integral part of a male-initiated revolution in sex roles, for it advocated that men reject burdensome responsibility (mainly in the shape of wives) for lives of pleasure through consumption. Sex, of course, was part of this pleasurable universe. In *Playboy*, sex was located in the realm of consumption, and women were interchangeable objects, mute, making no demands, each air-brushed beauty supplanted by the next month's model.

It was not only to men that sexual freedom was sold through exploitative visions. When Helen Gurley Brown revitalized the traditional women's magazine that was *Cosmopolitan* in 1965, she compared her magazine to *Playboy*—and *Cosmo* did celebrate the pleasures of single womanhood and "sexual and material consumerism." But before Brown ran *Cosmo*, she had made her contribution to the sexual revolution with *Sex and the Single Girl*, published in May 1962. By April 1963, 150,000 hard-cover copies had been sold, garnering Brown much media attention and a syndicated newspaper column, "Woman Alone."

The claim of *Sex and the Single Girl* was, quite simply, "nice, single girls *do*." Brown's radical message to a society in which twenty-three-year-olds were called old maids was that singleness is good. Marriage, she insisted, should not be an immediate goal. The Single Girl sounds like the Playboy's dream, but she was more likely a nightmare revisited. Marriage, Brown advised, is "insurance for the worst years of your life. During the best years you don't need a husband." But she quickly amended that statement: "You do need a man every step of the way, and they are often cheaper emotionally and more fun by the dozen." That fun explicitly included sex, and on the woman's terms. But Brown's celebration of the joys of single life still posed men and women as adversaries. "She need never be bored with one man per lifetime," she enthused. "Her choice of partners is endless and they seek *her* . . . Her married friends refer to her pursuers as wolves, but actually many of them turn out to be lambs—to be shorn and worn by her."

Brown's celebration of the single "girl" actually began with a success story—her own. "I married for the first time at thirty-seven. I got the man I wanted," begins *Sex and the Single Girl.* Brown's description of that union is instructive: "David is a motion picture producer, forty-four, brainy, charming and sexy. He was sought after by many a Hollywood starlet as well as some less flamboyant but more deadly types. And I got him! We have two Mercedes-Benzes, one hundred acres of virgin forest near San Francisco, a Mediterranean house overlooking the Pacific, a full-time maid and a good life."

While Brown believes "her body wants to" is a sufficient reason for a man to have an "affair," she is not positing identical interests of men and women in sex. Instead, she asserts the validity of women's interests—interests that include Mercedes-Benzes, full-time maids, lunch ("Anyone can take you to lunch. How bored can you be for an hour?"), vacations, and vicuna coats. But by offering a female version of the Playboy ethic, she greatly strengthened its message.

Unlike the youths who called for honesty, who sought to blur the boundaries between male and female, *Playboy* and *Cosmo* offered a vision of sexual freedom based on difference and deceit, but within a shared universe of an intensely competitive market economy. They were revolutionary in their claiming of sex as a legitimate pleasure and in the directness they brought to portraying sex as an arena for struggle and exploitation that could be enjoined by men and women alike (though in different ways and to different ends). Without this strand, the sexual revolution would have looked very different. In many ways *Playboy* was a necessary condition for "revolution," for it linked sex to the emerging culture of consumption and the rites of the marketplace. As it fed into the sexual reconfigurations of the sixties, *Playboy* helped make sex more—or less—than a rite of youth.

In the revolutionary spring of 1968, *Life* magazine looked from the student protests at Columbia across the street to Barnard College: "A sexual anthropologist of some future century, analyzing the pill, the drive-in, the works of Harold Robbins, the Tween-Bra and all the other artifacts of the American Sexual Revolution, may consider the case of Linda LeClair and her boyfriend, Peter Behr, as a moment in which the morality of an era changed."

The LeClair affair, as it was heralded in newspaper headlines and syndicated columns around the country, was indeed such a moment. Linda LeClair and Peter Behr were accidental revolutionaries, but as *Life* not so kindly noted "history will often have its little joke. And so it was this spring when it found as its symbol of the revolution a champion as staunch, as bold and as unalluring as Linda LeClair." The significance of the moment is not to be found in the actions of LeClair and Behr, who certainly lacked revolutionary glamour despite all the headlines about "Free Love," but in the contest over the meaning of those actions.

The facts of the case were simple. On 4 March 1968 the *New York Times* ran an article called "An Arrangement: Living Together for Convenience, Security, Sex." (The piece ran full-page width; below it appeared articles on "How to Duck the Hemline Issue" and "A Cook's Guide to the Shallot.") An "arrangement," the author informs us, was one of the current euphemisms for what was otherwise known as "shacking up" or, more innocuously, "living together." The article, which offers a fairly sympathetic portrait of several unmarried student couples who lived together in New York City, features an interview with Barnard sophomore, "Susan," who lived with her boyfriend "Peter" in an off campus apartment. Though Barnard had strict housing regulations and parietals (the curfew was midnight on weekends and ten o'clock on weeknights, and students were meant to live either at home or in Barnard housing), Susan had received permission to live off campus by accepting a job listed through Barnard's employment office as a "live-in maid." The job had, in fact, been listed by a young married woman who was a good friend of "Susan's."

Not surprisingly, the feature article caught the attention of Barnard administrators, who had little trouble identifying "Susan" as Linda LeClair. LeClair was brought before the Judiciary Council—not for her sexual conduct, but for lying to Barnard about her housing arrangements. Her choice of roommate was certainly an issue; if she had been found to be living alone or, as one Barnard student confessed to the *Times*, with a female cat, she would not have been headline-worthy.

Linda, however, was versed in campus politics, and she and Peter owned a mimeograph machine. She played it both ways, appearing for her hearings in a demure, knee-length pastel dress and churning out pamphlets on what she and Peter called "A

Victorian Drama." She and Peter distributed a survey on campus, garnering three hundred replies, most of which admitted to some violation of Barnard's parietals or housing regulations. Sixty women were willing to go public and signed forms that read: "I am a student of Barnard College and I have violated the Barnard Housing Regulations. . . . In the interest of fairness I request that an investigation be made of my disobedience."

Linda LeClair had not done anything especially unusual, as several letters from alumnae to Barnard's president, Martha Peterson, testified. But her case was a symbol of change, and it tells us much about how people understood the incident. The president's office received over two hundred telephone calls (most demanding LeClair's expulsion) and over one hundred letters; editorials ran in newspapers, large and small, throughout the country. Some of the letters were vehement in their condemnation of LeClair and of the college. Francis Beamen of Needham, Massachusetts, suggested that Barnard should be renamed "BARNYARD"; Charles Orsinger wrote (on good quality letterhead), "If you let Linda stay in college, I can finally prove to my wife with a front page news story about that bunch of glorified whores going to eastern colleges." An unsigned letter began: "SUBJECT: Barnard College—and the kow-tow to female students who practice prostitution, PUBLICLY!"

Though the term "alley cat" cropped up more than once, a majority of the letters were thoughtful attempts to come to terms with the changing morality of America's youth. Many were from parents who understood the symbolic import of the case. Overwhelmingly, those who did not simply rant about "whoredom" structured their comments around concepts of public and private. The word *flaunt* appeared over and over in the letters to President Peterson. Linda was "flaunting her sneering attitude"; Linda and Peter were "openly flaunting their disregard of moral codes"; they were "openly flaunting rules of civilized society." Mrs. Bruce Bromley, Jr., wrote her first such letter on a public issue to recommend, "Do not let Miss LeClair attend Barnard as long as she flaunts immorality in your face." David Abrahamson, M.D., identifying himself as a former Columbia faculty member, offered "any help in this difficult case." He advised President Peterson, "Undoubtedly the girl's behavior must be regarded as exhibitionism, as her tendency is to be in the limelight which clearly indicates some emotional disturbance or upset."

The public-private question *was* the issue in this case—the letter writers were correct. Most were willing to acknowledge that "mistakes" can happen; many were willing to allow for some "discreet" sex among the unmarried young. But Linda LeClair *claimed* the right to determine her own "private" life; she rejected the private—public dichotomy *as it was framed around sex*, casting her case as an issue of individual right versus institutional authority.

But public response to the case is interesting in another way. When a woman wrote President Peterson that "it is time for these young people to put sex back in its proper place, instead of something to be flaunted" and William F. Buckley condemned the "delinquency of this pathetic little girl, so gluttonous for sex and publicity," they were not listening. Sex was not what Linda and Peter talked about. Sex was not mentioned. Security was, and "family." "Peter is my family," said Linda. "It's a very united married type of relationship—it's the most important one in each of our lives. And our lives are very much intertwined."

Of course they had sex. They were young and in love, and their peer culture accepted sex within such relationships. But what they claimed was partnership—a partnership that obviated the larger culture's insistence on the difference between men and women. The letters suggesting that young women would "welcome a strong rule against living with men to protect them against doing that" made no sense in LeClair's universe. When she claimed that Barnard's rules were discriminatory because Columbia men had no such rules, that "Barnard College was founded on the principle of equality between women and men," and asked, "If women are able, intelligent people, why must we be supervised and curfewed?" she was denying that men and women had different interests and needs. Just as the private-public dichotomy was a cornerstone of sexual control in the postwar era, the much-touted differences between men and women were a crucial part of the system.

Many people in the 1960s and 1970s struggled with questions of equality and difference in sophisticated and hard-thought ways. Neither Peter Behr nor Linda LeClair was especially gifted in that respect. What they argued was commonplace to them—a natural language and set of assumptions that nonetheless had revolutionary implications. It is when a set of assumptions becomes natural and unself-conscious, when a language appears in the private comments of a wide variety or people that it is worth taking seriously. The unity of interests that Behr and LeClair called upon as they obviated the male-female dichotomy was not restricted to students in the progressive institutions on either coast.

In 1969 the administration at the University of Kansas (KU), a state institution dependent on a conservative, though populist, legislature for its funding, attempted to establish a coed dormitory for some of its scholarship students. KU had tried coed living as an experiment in the 1964 summer session and found students well satisfied, though some complained that it was awkward to go downstairs to the candy machines with one's hair in curlers. Curlers were out of fashion by 1969, and the administration moved forward with caution.

A survey on attitudes toward coed housing was given to those who lived in the scholarship halls, and the answers of the men survive. The results of the survey go against conventional wisdom about the provinces. Only one man (of the 124 responses recorded) said his parents objected to the arrangement ("Pending further discussion," he noted). But what is most striking is the language in which the men supported and opposed the plan. "As a stereotypical answer," one man wrote, "I already am able to do all the role-playing socially I need, and see communication now as an ultimate goal." A sophomore who listed his classification as both "soph." and "4-F I hope" responded: "I believe that the segregation of the sexes is unnatural. I would like to associate with women on a basis other than dating roles. This tradition of segregation is discriminatory and promotes inequality of mankind." One man thought coed living would make the hall "more homey." Another said it would be "more humane." Many used the word "natural." The most eloquent of the sophomores wrote: "[It would] allow them to meet and interact with one another in a situation relatively free of sexual overtones; that is, the participating individuals would be free to encounter one another as human beings, rather than having to play the traditional stereotyped male and female roles. I feel that coed living is the only feasible way to allow people to escape this stereotypical role behavior."

The student-generated proposal that went forward in December 1970 stressed these (as they defined them) "philosophical" justifications. The system would NOT be an arrangement for increased boy-meets-girl contact or for "convenience in finding dates," the committee insisted. Instead, coed living would "contribute to the development of each resident as a full human being." Through "interpersonal relationships based on friendship and cooperative efforts rather than on the male/female roles we usually play in dating situations" students would try to develop "a human concern that transcends membership in one or the other sex."

While the students disavowed "'boy-meets-girl' contact" as motivation, no one seriously believed that sex was going to disappear. The most cogently stated argument against the plan came from a young man who insisted: "[You] can't ignore the sexual overtones involved in coed living, after all, sex is the basic motivation for your plan. (I didn't say lust, I said sex)." Yet the language in which they framed their proposal was significant: they called for relationships (including sexual) based on a common humanity.

Like Peter Behr and Linda LeClair, these students at the University of Kansas were attempting to redefine both sex and sex roles. Sex should not be negotiated through the dichotomous pairings of male and female, public and private. Instead, they attempted to formulate and articulate a new standard that looked to a model of "togetherness" undreamed of and likely undesired by their parents. The *Life* magazine issue with which this essay began characterized the "sexual revolution" as "dull." "Love still makes the world go square," the author concluded, for the revolutionaries he interviewed subscribed to a philosophy "less indebted to *Playboy* than Peanuts, in which sex is not so much a pleasure as a warm puppy." To his amusement, one "California girl" told him: "Besides being my lover, Bob is my best friend in all the world," and a young man insisted, "We are not sleeping together, we are living together."

For those to whom *Playboy* promised revolution, this attitude was undoubtedly tame. And in the context of the cultural revolution taking place among America's youth, and documented in titillating detail by magazines such as *Life*, these were modest revolutionaries indeed, seeming almost already out of step with their generation. But the issue, to these "dull" revolutionaries, as to their more flamboyant brothers and sisters, was larger than sex. They understood that the line between public and private had utility; that the personal was political.

In 1967, The Summer of Love

It was a "holy pilgrimage," according to the Council for a Summer of Love. In the streets of Haight-Ashbury, thousands and thousands of "pilgrims" acted out a street theater of costumed fantasy, drugs and music and sex that was unimaginable in the neat suburban streets of their earlier youth. Visionaries and revolutionaries had preceded the deluge; few of them drowned. Others did. But the tide flowed in the vague countercultural yearnings, drawn by the pop hit "San Francisco (Be Sure to Wear Flowers in Your Hair)" and its promise of a "love-in," by the pictures in *Life* magazine or in *Look* magazine or in *Time* magazine, by the proclamations of the underground press that San Francisco would be "the love-guerilla training school for drop-outs from mainstream America . . . where the new world, a human world of the 21st century is being constructed." Here sexual freedom would be explored; not cohabitation, not "arrangements," not "living together" in ways that looked a lot like marriage except for the lack of a piece of paper that symbolized the sanction of the state. Sex in the Haight was revolutionary.

In neat suburban houses on neat suburban streets, people came to imagine this new world, helped by television and by the color pictures in glossy-paper magazines (a joke in the Haight told of "bead-wearing *Look* reporters interviewing bead-wearing *Life* reporters"). Everyone knew that these pilgrims represented a tiny fraction of America's young, but the images reverberated. America felt itself in revolution.

Todd Gitlin, in his soul-searching memoir of the sixties, argues the cultural significance of the few:

> Youth culture seemed a counterculture. There were many more weekend dope-smokers than hard-core "heads"; many more readers of the *Oracle* than writers for it; many more co-habitors than orgiasts; many more turners-on than droppers-out. Thanks to the sheer number and concentration of youth, the torrent of drugs, the sexual revolution, the traumatic war, the general stampede away from authority, and the trend-spotting media, it was easy to assume that all the styles of revolt and disaffection were spilling together tributaries into a common torrent of youth and euphoria, life against death, joy over sacrifice, now over later, remaking the whole bleeding world.

Youth culture and counterculture, as Gitlin argues so well, were not synonymous, and for many the culture itself was more a matter of lifestyle than revolutionary intent. But the strands flowed together in the chaos of the age, and the few and the marginal provided archetypes that were read into the youth culture by an American public that did not see the lines of division. "Hippies, yippies, flippies," said Mayor Richard Daley of Chicago. "Free Love," screamed the headlines about Barnard's Linda LeClair.

But even the truly revolutionary youths were not unified, no more on the subject of sex than on anything else. Members of the New Left, revolutionary but rarely countercultural, had sex but did not talk about it all the time. They consigned sex to a relatively "private" sphere. Denizens of Haight-Ashbury lived a Dionysian sexuality, most looking nowhere but to immediate pleasure. Some political-cultural revolutionaries, however, claimed sex and used it for the revolution. They capitalized on the sexual chaos and fears of the nation, attempting to use sex to politicize youth and to challenge "Amerika."

In March 1968 the *Sun*, a Detroit people's paper put out by a "community of artists and lovers" (most notably John Sinclair of the rock group MC5), declared a "Total Assault on the Culture." Sinclair, in his "editorial statement," disavowed any prescriptive intent but informed his readers: "We *have* found that there are three essential human activities of the greatest importance to all persons, and that people are well and healthy in proportion to their involvement in these activities: rock and roll, dope, and fucking in the streets. . . . We suggest the three in combination, all the time."

He meant it. He meant it partly because it was outrageous, but there was more to it. "Fucking" helps you "escape the hangups that are drilled into us in this weirdo country"—it negates "private lives," "feels good," and so destroys an economy of pain and scarcity. Lapsing into inappropriately programmatic language, Sinclair argued:

> Our position is that all people must be free to fuck freely, whenever and wherever they want to, or not to fuck if they don't wanna—in bed, on the floor, in the chair, on the streets, in the parks and fields, "back seat boogie for the high school kids" sing the Fugs who brought it all out in the open on stage and on records, fuck whoever wants to fuck you and everybody else do the same. America's silly sexual "mores" are the end-product of thousands of years of deprivation and sickness, of marriage and companionship based on the ridiculous misconception that one person can "belong" to another person, that "love" is something that has to do with being "hurt," sacrificing, holding out, "teardrops on your pillow," and all that shit.

Sinclair was not alone in his paean to copulation. Other countercultural seekers believed that they had to remake love and reclaim sex to create community. These few struggled, with varying degrees of honesty and sincerity, over the significance of sex in the beloved community.

For others, sex was less a philosophy than a weapon. In the spring of 1968, the revolutionary potential of sex also suffused the claims of the Yippies as they struggled to stage a "Festival of Life" to counter the "Death Convention" in Chicago. "How can you separate politics and sex?" Jerry Rubin asked with indignation after the fact. Yippies lived by that creed. Sex was a double-edged sword, to be played two ways. Sex was a lure to youth; it was part of their attempt to tap the youth market, to "sell a revolutionary consciousness." It was also a challenge, "flaunted in the face" (as it were) of America.

The first Yippie manifesto, released in January 1968, summoned the tribes of Chicago. It played well in the underground press, with its promise of "50,000 of us dancing in the streets, throbbing with amplifiers and harmony . . . making love in the parks." Sex was a politics of pleasure, a politics of abundance that made sense to young middle-class whites who had been raised in the world without limits that was postwar America.

Sex was also incendiary, and the Yippies knew that well. It guaranteed attention. Thus the "top secret" plans for the convention that Abbie Hoffman mimeographed and distributed to the press promised a barbecue and lovemaking by the lake, followed by "Pin the Tail on the Donkey," "Pin the Rubber on the Pope," and "other normal and healthy games." Grandstanding before a crowd of Chicago reporters, the Yippies presented a city official with an official document wrapped in a *Playboy* centerfold inscribed, "To Dick with love, the Yippies." The *Playboy* centerfold in the Yippies' hands was an awkward nexus between the old and the new sexuality. As a symbolic act, it did not proffer freedom so much as challenge authority. It was a sign of disrespect—to Mayor Richard Daley and to straight America.

While America was full of young people sporting long hair and beads, the committed revolutionaries (of cultural stripe) were few in number and marginal at best. It is telling that the LeClair affair could still be a scandal in a nation that had weathered the Summer of Love. But the lines were blurred in sixties America. One might ask with Todd Gitlin, "What was marginal anymore, where was the mainstream anyway?" when the Beatles were singing, "Why Don't We Do It in the Road?"

CONCLUSION

The battles of the sexual revolution were hard fought, its victories ambiguous, its outcome still unclear. What we call the sexual revolution was an amalgam of movements that flowed together in an unsettled era. They were often at odds with one another, rarely well thought out, and usually without a clear agenda.

The sexual revolution was built on equal measures of hypocrisy and honesty, equality and exploitation. Indeed, the individual strands contain mixed motivations and ideological charges. Even the most heartfelt or best intentions did not always work out for the good when put into practice by mere humans with physical and psychological frailties. As we struggle over the meaning of the "revolution" and ask ourselves who, in fact, *won*, it helps to untangle the threads and reject the conflation of radically different impulses into a singular revolution.

READING 10

Hooking Up and Dating: A Comparison

Kathleen A. Bogle

SEX

The most notable difference in the shift from the dating script to the hookup script is how sexual behavior fits into the equation. But it would be a mistake to assume that men and women in the dating era were any less interested in sexual interaction than those in today's hookup culture. In some cases, a man asking a woman on a date was a thinly veiled attempt to see how much she would "put out" sexually. Therefore, one of the primary objectives of a date was the same as that of a hookup (i.e., that something sexual would happen). Although men and women in both the hooking-up and dating eras had sexual objectives, the timing has changed. With traditional dating, sexual interaction occurred after the two parties had gone on a date or series of dates. With hooking up, the sexual interaction comes first; going on a date comes later, or not at all for those who never make it to the point of "going out" or at least "hanging out." Marie, a senior at State University, discussed what typically happens after an initial hookup. "Most [girls] who hook up initially get a lot of bullshit, like a lot of guys will be like: 'Yeah, I'll call you,' but they don't. You know, so it might take them a while to see you out and then hook up with you more before they really, you know, want to like call and hang out."

Some college women I interviewed said they would prefer to "get to know someone" before engaging in sexually intimate acts. The hookup script does not preclude getting to know someone prior to the first hookup; however, it does not require it, either. The dating script did require it.

The content of what can fall under the rubric of a "sexual encounter" has also changed with the shift to the hookup script. Most college students during the dating era restricted their sexual experimentation on dates to so-called "necking" and "petting." Oral sex was not a part of the sexual script for the majority of people during the dating era. The sexual possibilities are much greater for the contemporary hookup script. According to the college students I spoke with, hooking up can mean "just kissing," "fooling around" (i.e., petting), "oral sex," or "sex-sex" (i.e., sexual intercourse). Although "going all the way" was not unheard of during the dating era, it was not the norm. There is evidence that many women had sexual intercourse prior to marriage, but most did so only with the man they would eventually marry. In the hookup era, intercourse is not limited to exclusive, marriage-bound relationships. The hookup script includes the potential for a wide array of sexual behavior, including intercourse, even in the most casual encounters. This represents a significant departure from what the dating script allowed.

THE RULES

In the dating era the rules were clear: young people, especially women, were not supposed to have sexual intercourse prior to marriage. Religious leaders played a primary role in communicating this standard to the American public. Since the sexual revolution, Americans largely rebuffed religious reasons for delaying sexual intimacy, and attitudes toward premarital sex became more lax. For example, most approve of sexual intercourse prior to marriage, but only in the context of an ongoing, exclusive relationship. Most of the college men and women I interviewed indicated that neither their religious affiliation nor their religious beliefs had a major effect on their participation in the hookup culture. Adrienne, a senior at Faith University, considered herself a practicing Catholic. She also indicated that her religious beliefs affected her day-to-day behavior; however, these beliefs did not prevent her from hooking up or engaging in premarital sex with her boyfriend.

KB: Do you think that [Faith University] is any different because it's a Catholic school with regard to male-female stuff?

ADRIENNE: Not really. I don't think so . . .well, obviously they don't like hand out condoms. And I don't think you'd be able, like I don't even know if you had a problem with your birth control or anything, I don't even know if you could like say anything to the health people. I think that might make people a little more like apprehensive to go [to the campus health center]. I mean you might have [some people who] come here that want to wait until marriage [to have sex] and stuff like that. . . . Once a year you might see a poster or something [that says] like: "Wait until marriage" or something. But it's not like anything else [is different than any other school]. Like [I said before] there's not condoms in the bathroom or anything like that. But

> I think the girls and the guys, they pretty much hook up, they just hook up the same [whether they are at a Catholic college or not]. Because I think you can still be like religious, like I said before, I'm religious, but I still engage in like premarital sex. But I don't think that's wrong necessarily. So I think that's where a lot of people are right now.

The change in the script for sexual behavior on the college campus is part of a larger trend toward increased premarital sexual experience throughout our culture. In one of the most comprehensive studies on sexual behavior of men and women in the United States, Laumann et al. found that the median age at first sexual intercourse decreased throughout the twentieth century, particularly for white women. In the latest birth cohort, the median age at first intercourse was approximately 17 for white men and women. This change coupled with the increased age at first marriage, has led those who came of age in more recent years to accumulate more sexual partners than those in the pre-sexual-revolution dating era. Changing times and circumstances have led to a change in society's standards regarding premarital sex. In the dating era, "waiting for marriage" meant delaying intercourse for a relatively short period of time. In the hookup era, men and women spend more time being single adults, so delaying intercourse for marriage has become an increasingly difficult standard to achieve. Therefore, in the hookup era, society does not strictly dictate that men and women wait for marriage, and any religious regulations to that effect are not staunchly followed.

Although the contemporary ideal may be for intercourse to occur only in committed relationships, on the college campus many students were willing to have sex under other circumstances when the ideal was not available or, in the case of some college men, when the ideal was not desired. The increased sexual possibilities with the hookup script may seem to create more options for college students. In other words, while those in the dating era were not supposed to engage in sexual intercourse on dates, those in the hookup era can choose to have sexual intercourse or choose to abstain (until they are in an exclusive relationship or married). However, increased choice has also brought about a sense of normlessness.

The fact that there are no clear standards has led to confusion for students trying to decide when sex is appropriate. Many students believe that having sex is simply a matter of personal choice. The problem is that students' "personal" choices are affected by what they perceive "everybody else" is doing sexually. Unfortunately, students' perceptions are often distorted. For example, if students perceive other students as being highly sexually active under a wide array of circumstances via the hookup scene, they may not want to be left behind. This helps explain how virginity, at least for women, went from a "treasure to be safeguarded" (in the dating era) to a "problem to be solved" (in the post-sexual-revolution hooking-up era). In fact, some college students spoke of virginity as something to "get rid of" to avoid being "known as a virgin."

KB: Do you know any people that are virgins?
LARRY: Very few. Very few.
KB: How is that viewed? Is it males or females that you know that are virgins?
LARRY: I'd say I know both and it's very shady. People that are virgins I've found, I

find out that they are virgins because they won't come out and tell you. They kind of seem a little shameful of it. They haven't "done it" yet, if you want to put it that way.

KB: Guys are embarrassed about it or girls are embarrassed about it too?

LARRY: Both.

KB: Okay. Is that something people would get teased about?

LARRY: Sure. Sometimes [people will say] like: "You haven't done it yet, what are you waiting for?" I've seen that before. [Senior, Faith University]

REBECCA: I know a lot of people who just want to get the sex thing, well one person, who just wanted to get the sex thing over with. She didn't need it really to mean a lot, she just needed it to be over, so she could have her virginity gone, you know [laughing]. [But losing your virginity is] supposed to be a special moment kind of thing. [Sophomore, State University]

The lack of a clear standard in the hookup era has also led to some problematic behavior. For those students who believe "anything goes," college social life can take the form of excessive drinking and exploitive sexual encounters. In 2006, the media spotlight turned to Duke University when rape allegations were made against three members of their lacrosse team. Although this scandal held the attention of the public for a variety of reasons, it underscored the problem many college campuses face with regard to the extremes of the hookup culture. Regardless of the outcome of the criminal investigation, it was clear that members of this team were engaging in heavy alcohol consumption and creating a sex-charged atmosphere by hiring two exotic dancers. It is this type of behavior that has concerned many scholars who have studied binge drinking, fraternity life, and rape.

Students define normal sexual behavior relative to their peers. Those who get caught up with certain groups on campus, who define their college experience as the characters did in the movie *Animal House*, might have trouble distinguishing the behavior of their friends from that of a typical college student. With no firm guidelines decreeing when, where, and with whom sex is appropriate, some students can engage in lewd behavior and think it's permissible because there are no rules saying otherwise.

WHAT'S LOVE GOT TO DO WITH IT?

Along with the rule forbidding premarital sex, the conventions of the dating script pertaining to the emotional side of relationships also wavered in the shift to hooking up. In the dating era, the script offered an opportunity for men and women to learn about their dating partners. While there may have been plenty of cross-sex interaction generally, going on a date represented a distinct time where the pair could get to know each other. While the dating script dictated that men and women spend "quality time" together, hooking up does not. Although the hookup script does not preclude two people from getting to know each other (aside from sexually), it does not require it, either. Liz, a freshman at Faith University, began hooking up with someone she met in the first weeks of school. Although hooking up continued for months and eventually led to sexual intercourse, it never became a romantic relationship. When Liz's partner began to show less interest in frequent hookup encounters and the sexual aspect of the relationship fizzled, she found that there was not much of a foundation for a relationship. Even building a close friendship was a struggle.

> KB: If you could paint an ideal scenario of how you would meet and get together with someone, how would it be?
>
> LIZ: Well, I guess . . . seeing them at a party or something and having a nice conversation, realizing that we have something in common or that we seem to hit it off. And then, um, like maybe he would get my number and then we'd talk or I would see him on campus or something. And then we would hang out the next weekend and see where it went from there. I don't like jumping into things because that always ends up bad, I feel like.
>
> KB: Why do you think it does?
>
> LIZ: Because you don't give it a chance to become friends with someone or you don't really know someone [if you hook up with him right away]. I think that's what happened to me in the beginning [of this year] because we just jumped into it so fast and . . . we're just starting now to like become like real friends. . . . Of course we were friends before, but it was more on like a physical level and now that it's backed off [and we don't hook up as often anymore] it's kind of like upsetting. Like I feel bad for myself, you know, that I let that happen. . . .

Men and women in the hookup scene seem to have to work harder to build a relationship of any kind. Thus, to the extent that relationship formation is a goal, dating offered a better script for doing this. This point was emphasized by many recent graduates. After college, the men and women I interviewed became increasingly focused on finding a boyfriend/girlfriend, and in order to do so, most virtually abandoned hooking up in favor of traditional dating.

Getting to know someone, via the dating script, was also a way for men and women to ascertain whether or not they had romantic feelings toward their dating partner. Presumably, if feelings got stronger as the couple continued dating, sexual intimacy would also increase. Thus, in the dating era, there was some expectation that the degree of sexual intimacy would match the degree of emotional intimacy. In other words, two people would become increasingly sexually intimate as they grew "closer." In fact, during the dating era there was a level of sexual intimacy deemed appropriate for each stage of the dating process. Ideally, young men and women would initially limit their sexual interaction to kissing. Within an ongoing dating relationship, necking and petting were hallmarks of the dating experience. Sexual intercourse was supposed to be reserved for marriage, but often took place with dating couples once marriage was imminent. These rules were not always followed, but there was a standard sense of appropriate behavior for each stage of the dating script, and love or a strong romantic attachment was a part of the equation.

Sexual intimacy in the hookup era is no longer as symbolic of relationship status as it was in the dating era. There is still a sequential pattern for relationships: hooking up, seeing each other, and going out, but it is not altogether clear what the corresponding sexual behavior is for each stage. Sexual intercourse is expected in many of the "going out" relationships; however, it is less clear what one should do sexually in the other contexts. The students I spoke with were vague in response to questions about when certain degrees of sexual intimacy were appropriate. Some suggested one should wait (at least for sexual intercourse) until "it feels right" or "until you can trust someone." Interestingly none of the men and women mentioned love as a prerequisite for sex.

It is safe to say that in the hookup era the degree of sexual intimacy is often unrelated to the level of commitment to the relationship. In fact, many of the college students, particularly women, indicated that they were more likely to "go farther" sexually with someone during a hookup if they did not like the person that much or believed there was no relationship potential. This is not to say that romantic feelings are absent among hookup partners, but that the hookup script does not dictate an emotional attachment.

THE GROUP

Perhaps the decreasing importance of emotional attachment between sexual partners in college derives from the increasing importance of friendship groups among students. In the shift from the dating era to the hooking up era, the focus went from the pair to group-oriented socializing. The dating script called for a couple to go out together and the man and woman would each play a strict gender role. According to advice books from that era, men and women were supposed to play opposite but "complementary" roles in the dating script. Men were expected to initiate the date and "take the lead" throughout the evening; men were also responsible for any expenses incurred on the date. Women, on the other hand, were supposed to wait to be asked out on a date, let the man determine the plan for the date, and so on. The dating script did not allow much room for altering the roles played by men and women. In the hooking-up era, college students are more focused on groups of friends going out together. Of course, those who end up engaging in a hookup encounter pair off at the end of the night, but the evening's socializing is done among a gathering of classmates.

The shift to group socializing also means that no one is forced out of the social scene. Although there may have been some "mixers" where singles could go to socialize in the dating era, weekends were often reserved for "date nights." There also may have been occasions where a person would go "stag," but socializing was done primarily in dating pairs. The hookup script does not dictate that one must hook up in order to socialize in places where hooking up is possible. On any given night there are many more students out partying or bar hopping than will actually hook up. In fact, many of the men and women I interviewed who were in exclusive relationships still went to campus parties and bars with their friends at least some of the time. Thus, although the dating script left many students sitting at home while their classmates went out on "hot dates," the hookup scene promotes a form of interaction where, at least theoretically, anyone can join the party. To be sure, there are men and women, in the hookup scene who are more sought after than others (just as there were in the dating era). The difference is that the men and women who do not rate high on the desirability scale are less likely to be shut out from being a part of the social scene altogether.

Group socializing is also central to men and women after college. Although alumni switch primarily to a dating script, the dating pair is not at the center of social life as it was in the dating era. As a result, the men and women I interviewed revealed that they primarily intermingle among friends at parties and bars, with dating an outgrowth of the way they socialize in general.

UNDER THE INFLUENCE

As group partying became increasingly central to the lives of students, so did the significance of alcohol to the sexual script. During the dating era, drinking was not a major focus of the typical date. It is well documented that many contemporary college students consume a great deal of alcohol. Many of the students I spoke with, including Liz, a freshman from Faith University, indicated that drinking and hooking up went hand-in-hand because hookup encounters generally occur after a night of partying.

> KB: If somebody was interested in someone else, how would they have something happen with them? How do you get from A to B?
>
> LIZ: Probably alcohol would be a big factor and like the parties and stuff. Like it's just, like if something's going to happen it will be like at the party or things will evolve [from there and] you'll hang out with them one on one [later].

The hookup culture and the alcohol culture on campus are so inextricably linked that students who choose to forgo the party and bar scene are also excluding themselves from the hookup scene. Since hooking up is the primary means for finding potential sexual and romantic partners, those who do not participate struggle to form relationships.

> KB: So what do people do then . . . if most hooking up happens when you're drinking and you don't really drink much, then how can people like you have something going [relationship-wise] . . . or would it be really difficult?
>
> KIM: I kind of feel like in college it's more difficult just because that's what everybody does . . . that's been my experience. I mean, it's fine; it's not hard to meet people through classes and through organizations and stuff. But, I really feel like a lot of relationships do start at parties and stuff. So . . . maybe I am missing out on that right now. [Sophomore, Faith University]

The connection between hooking up and alcohol-centered socializing on campus is not insignificant. Researchers have demonstrated that alcohol consumption is correlated with the decision to have sexual intercourse as well as engaging in so-called risky sexual behavior, such as having casual sex. Many college students I interviewed recognized that, at times, alcohol "made them do things" that they would not otherwise do, particularly with regard to hooking up. Brian, a sophomore at Faith University, said, "Usually when you're hooking up . . . [both parties have] probably been drinking. You know, it's just like: 'Oh we're doing this cause we're both drunk and we're both kind of horny,' to be honest with you."

Although alcohol consumption may lead to hooking up, the link could also be reversed; that is, perhaps the hookup script requires alcohol. In other words, alcohol appears to be a desirable social lubricant to aid the hookup process. Although hooking up is often a desired outcome for students after an evening at a party or bar, for the most part it is not clear who is going to hook up with whom. During the dating era, it was clear to everyone who someone's date was for the evening. If a sexual advance was going to be made, the person, generally the man, knew who would be the target: his date. The hookup scene carries a lot more uncertainty. Students must utilize many nonverbal cues in order to indicate interest to a potential hookup partner; however, there is a great deal of trepidation about getting one's signals crossed. As Robert, a sophomore at Faith University, put it:

> The likelihood of [hooking up] happening when you are totally sober is very unlikely, I would say. It is only when people start loosening up by drinking, I call it liquid courage. Most guys are shy about going up to pretty girls, [so that is why] I call it liquid courage. They got enough courage up to go up and talk to the girl. And if she was the same status regarding alcohol consumption, then the two people that are attracted to each other will just go ahead and [hook up].

Drinking alcohol makes navigating this difficult system easier for the participants. If one person indicates interest in another and the feeling is not mutual, the party of the first part can easily claim, "I was drunk, I didn't know what I was doing," rather than admitting, "I was rejected." This also holds true for a regrettable hookup encounter. Thus, the awkwardness and uncertainty of the hookup script may encourage participants to use alcohol in a way that the dating script did not. Indeed, the alumni I spoke with dramatically reduced drinking when they went on formal dates because it was defined as "inappropriate" for the postcollege dating script.

UNDER COVER

Alcohol use may be one strategy employed by students trying to cope with the hooking-up system, which has made male-female interaction more covert. In the dating era, many aspects of a date were out in the open. It was socially acceptable for a man to ask a woman out on a date anywhere and at any time (i.e., a grocery store in the afternoon), and the invitation for a date was direct and verbal. The man had to ask the woman if she would like to go out with him and risk that she might say "no." If she accepted the invitation, the man had to put some thought into where he would take the woman, how they would get to their destination, and so forth. The date itself would take place somewhere in public, such as at a restaurant or theater. Regardless of the precise location, the woman was the man's date (and vice versa) for the evening, something that was readily apparent to onlookers. Thus, the public nature of the date, coupled with the "work" the man had to put in to make the date happen, insured that the dating partners could not easily disclaim any affiliation with each other.

The hookup era allows for much more private and spur-of-the-moment interaction. For example, the advent of Web sites such as MySpace and Facebook, where students can create personal profiles and converse with others by posting messages on their Web page, has revolutionized the way young people interact. Although these profiles are often accessible to anyone (and therefore far from private), the internet has made connecting with the opposite sex more anonymous and secretive. Contemporary college students can be "socializing" with others while sitting alone in their dorm rooms or apartments. Other technological advances, such as cell phones, have also made waiting at home for a suitor's phone call a thing of the past. There is no longer a need for advance plans when today's students can call or "text" each other to make last-minute arrangements to get together to "hang out."

Additionally, unlike a date, a hookup encounter typically begins at the end of the night with nonverbal cues between two people who have been drinking. If one party is not proud of their hookup partner (due to appearance or some other reason), he or she can act like it never happened. A number of men I interviewed said they were careful about admitting whom they hooked up with for fear of being teased or getting their "balls busted" by their friends. Moreover, both men and women who are immersed in the hookup scene occasionally use alcohol as an excuse for having engaged in a hookup with someone they later considered undesirable. Thus, the public nature of dating made it a less anonymous way of getting together. Someone of the opposite sex was your date for the evening, he or she was the person "on your arm," and there was no easy way to pretend otherwise.

Outward signs of romance also accompanied the dating script. Traditional symbols of wooing a partner, like flowers and candy, are no longer part of the early stages of a romantic relationship in college. In the hookup era, these types of gestures are reserved for special occasions, such as Valentine's Day, among men and women who are already a couple. Thus, those who participate in the hookup script do not use the customary trappings of courtship that, in the dating era, were public signs of affection among romantic/sexual partners.

MONEY, STATUS, AND WORTH

Gestures such as flowers and candy may also have become passé as money became less significant as a status symbol in the hookup script. In the dating era, the script called for the dating pair to go out together, which often involved men paying for entertainment of some kind. However, it was not just a matter of men needing money to date; rather, with dating, men and women began to determine what the other was "worth." A woman could determine a man's worth by what kind of car he drove, by his family name, and by what kinds of dates he could afford or was willing to "spring for." A man determined how much a woman was "worth" by considering the "assets" she had that would make it worth it to take her on an expensive date. In many cases, a woman's worth was determined less by intrinsic or individual qualities than by her popularity or reputation as a sought-after date. Indeed, the discourse surrounding dating indicated that women, in particular, were treated as commodities. This point is clearly demonstrated by the comparison often made between women and cars during the dating era. According to social historian Beth Bailey: "The equation of women and cars was common in mid-century American culture. Both were property, both expensive; cars and women came in different styles or models, and both could be judged on performance. The woman he escorted, just as the car he drove, publicly defined both a man's taste and his means."

Since hooking up does not involve a pair going out together, there is no reason to directly spend money. Although financial costs are still associated with collegiate social activities, they no longer consist of men spending money on their dates the way they did during the dating era. According to the college students I interviewed, both men and women generally "pay their own way" for admission into an event, such as a party that has a cover charge to gain entrance. Thus, women are no longer subject to being evaluated in terms of how much they are "worth" as they were during the dating era, and men are less often judged by the size of their wallet (or their family's bank account). The fact that finances have been taken out of the equation for the hookup script in college creates an atmosphere that is less money focused. Jake, a 28-year-old alumnus of State University, discussed the difference in money and status during college and after.

KB: You mentioned that sorority girls only seemed to want to be involved with fraternity guys. Why do you think it worked like that?

JAKE: Because that's the way it always is. Girls want the football guys. They want the jocks or whatever. That's the way it has always been, probably always will be.

KB: So they just want people with high status and certain people have high status?

JAKE: Exactly. If you are not in, you're out. Just like in the real world there are certain things that girls want, if you don't have it, you are out.

KB: Okay. Do you have it?

JAKE: [Laughs] Do I have it? Now I do. Back then [in college] I didn't.

KB: So you weren't an athlete or fraternity member [during college]? What do you have now?

JAKE: See what happens is, and this is from everybody I hear, and this definitely includes myself, when you're out in the working world for a few years and you start making a few bucks, you start learning how to dress, you get better friends, you get a nice car, you start to put things together. You figure out who you are, in college you don't have a clue. . . .

POSTPONING ADULTHOOD

In Jake's observation on the difference between students and alumni, he mentions college students' dependence on parents. Since most college students are of legal age upon entering college (a traditional marker of the beginning of adulthood), it raises the question: Do contemporary college students see themselves as adults? In the dating era, most considered marriage as the most important factor in the transition to adulthood. With the average age at first marriage in the 1950s dating era 20 for women and 22 for men, students were likely to be considered by society, and to think of themselves, as adults during their college years. In recent decades, men and women have been postponing marriage and many other role transitions (such as parenthood and home ownership) and college students have become less likely to think of themselves as adults.

In the hookup era, students tend to view their college years as a last chance to "live it up" before settling down into their postcollege career. The men and women I spoke with defined college as a time to have fun and referred to graduation as a time when "real life" and adult responsibilities began. This mentality greatly affects their attitude and behavior in the realm of sex and relationships during their college years, allowing contemporary college students more freedom to experiment and "play the field."

BATTLE OF THE SEXES

Although there are many differences between the dating and hooking-up scripts, there are also important similarities. One thing that has not changed with the shift to hooking up is that men continue to hold most of the power, as they did in the dating era. . . . abandoned in favor of dating, there was a shift in power from women to men. In the calling era, [the era before dating, which began in the 1920's–A.S.] young women and their mothers had the power to invite men to call (i.e., come to their home for a visit). If a man was interested in a woman, he had to hope for this invitation. However, when dating became the dominant script, only men could initiate a date. Men were responsible for paying for the date, so the decision was in the hands of the man to figure out what he could afford and then ask a woman of interest to accompany him for the evening. This often left women waiting by the phone for a man's invitation.

With the hookup script, the power to initiate is less gendered; both men and women can signal interest in hooking up. So, with regard to initiation, women in the hookup era may have more power than women had in the dating era. However, in the hookup era, it is not the power to initiate, but the ability to ultimately get what they want that demonstrates men's continuing dominance. Many of the women I interviewed indicated that they wanted "something more" than just a one-night hookup encounter. Women do not necessarily object to hooking up per se; rather, they object to how often hooking up fails to evolve into some semblance of a relationship. Moreover, women feel that men have the power to decide whether a hookup turns into "seeing each other" or "going out." Thus, women have a great deal of difficulty obtaining what they want via the hookup script. This is not the case for men. Many of the men I interviewed indicated that they could choose to be in a relationship if they wanted to; however, they often preferred to hook up with no strings attached. . . .

Although Tony did "go out" with someone for part of his college years, he often terminated relationships before they got to the point of being serious or exclusive. Many of the men I interviewed, like Tony, were active members of the hookup scene, but were not utilizing it for the purpose of finding a relationship. They were able to have satisfying sexual encounters via the hookup script without offering commitment in return.

During the dating era, a man often had to spend a great deal of time with a woman before she was willing to become sexual with him. Moreover, the man often had to ask a woman to marry him before he could hope to have sexual intercourse. This is no longer the case in the college hookup scene. Although this is a difference between the hookup and the dating scripts, the commonality is that men have a greater share of power in both eras. During the dating era, men held the power because only they could initiate dates, while women played a more passive role. During the hookup era, both men and women can initiate hookup encounters, but it is men who still have the power to control the intensity of the relationship.

As in the dating script, as described in Waller's study of Perm State University students in the 1930s, relationships today are governed by the "principle of least interest." This means that the person with the least interest in continuing the relationship holds all of the power or has the upper hand. In the dating era, this could be either the man or the woman. In the college hookup scene, men typically are the ones with the least interest in a continuing relationship. The college men I interviewed talked about the feeling of having many women to choose from, so there was no need to hold on to a particular woman. Most of the college women I spoke to, on the other hand, were interested in turning hookup partners into boyfriends. Violet, a junior at State University, relayed an example from her own experience.

KB: Have you ever had a situation where you wanted a hookup to turn into something more and they didn't want it, or vice versa?

VIOLET: Yeah. I had a friend of mine who I hooked up [with] one night and it was the kind of scenario where we were friends and I wanted something more out of it and he didn't.

KB: And how did he know you wanted more and how did you know he didn't?

VIOLET: Well, like I called him after we hooked up and he was like: "Hey, what is going on?" And I was like: "If you want to go out sometime give me a call." And he was like: "Yeah, okay." And he never called me. And we would see each other [sometimes] . . . and he'd just be like: "Hey." And it never came to anything; [it was] just that one time.

Both in college and after, women were interested in pursuing relationships with marriage potential sooner than men were interested in doing so. The idea that a woman's "clock is ticking" while a man has "all the time in the world" fundamentally affects who holds the power. Thus, the hookup era's power dynamic carries over postcollege. Many of the alumni women I spoke with discussed the challenge they face in trying to get the men in whom they were interested to commit to them.

KB: How did you know you were together [in a relationship]? Did you verbalize it?

Raquel: I had been calling him my boyfriend from the very beginning . . . but he's very handsome and . . . he had a bunch of women he was juggling in the beginning and they fell by the wayside and I was the one still standing . . . he would not call me his girlfriend until one day in August when we went

> out to dinner and ran into somebody and he introduced me as his girlfriend. That was the first time I ever heard those words, and I was like: "Thank God . . ."

Many of the women I interviewed had a story similar to Raquel's: a woman who was involved, sexually and otherwise, with a man often wanted that man to be in an exclusive relationship with her. When the two parties were not on the same page, women struggled with whether to keep "hanging on" with the hope of a happy ending or to "move on" and start searching for a new partner. These women found it very difficult to end a relationship, even when they were not satisfied with its quality. For college women this sometimes came in the form of booty-call relationships or repeat hookup relationships with a man they were hoping would eventually agree to a committed relationship (i.e., "seeing each other" or "going out"). Unfortunately, these women were often disappointed when hooking up failed to evolve into something more than that. This difficulty became amplified for alumni women who were looking for a boyfriend and ultimately a potential lifelong mate. Despite women's interest in finding boyfriends, many reported that the men they were interested in pursuing a relationship with were hesitant to be in an exclusive relationship. Several alumni women indicated that this problem led to an "on again, off again" relationship while the tug-of-war over commitment was fought.

One can clearly see that Waller's "principle of least interest" is still (60-some years after he coined the phrase) largely dictating who holds the power among young singles. Given the relationship struggles that many women go through, it is obvious why advice books, such as *He's Just Not That Into You*, end up being best-sellers.

WALKING THE LINE

Men's greater control has led to the sexual exploitation of women in both the dating and hooking-up eras. According to Waller's study of the dating era, exploitation occurred when one party was more interested in a continuing relationship than the other and thereby she or he was willing to give in to the other's demands. Among dating partners during this time, women might exploit men by "gold digging," while men could exploit women for sexual favors or "thrills." Therefore, in a case where a woman had stronger feelings toward a man and was trying to secure him, she might offer more sexual favors. In the hookup era, sexual exploitation continues to be an issue for women. Since hooking up does not involve men spending money on women, college men have no fear of gold digging. Women, on the other hand, must be cautious about being used. Many of the college men I spoke with were aware that women were desirous of more committed relationships, yet men were often able to keep a woman as just a hookup partner.

Exploitation was an issue not just for women in some version of a relationship, but for those seeking relationships, too. Throughout the dating era, women who had a reputation for "putting out" might be asked on dates by a variety of men, each having the purpose of seeing how much he could get sexually. Certain women might be sought after for dates because they were defined as being sexually available merely due to their social class or occupation. For example, student nurses were stereotyped as a "good time" by college men. Thus, college men sought dates with student nurses in order to "get a little" sexually. Some college men in the hookup era who are interested in accumulating various hookup partners do so by going after certain women, as men did in the dating era. For example, several college students mentioned that freshman males have a great deal of difficulty getting into campus parties unless they know one of the hosts personally, while freshman women are granted free admission. This practice increases the likelihood of upperclassmen being able to hook up with freshman women who are a target because they are naive about the unwritten rules of the hookup scene.

Like women of the dating era, college women in the hookup culture must walk a fine line between being exploited and being excluded. Those who choose to take part in the script not only risk being used for sex, but also risk their reputations. There are a host of norms to which contemporary college women must adhere in order to avoid being labeled a "slut." College women can be negatively labeled if they hook up too often or with too many different partners. Indeed, women must be careful not even to appear to be conducting themselves in an overtly provocative manner or they will be perceived as "easy." Kyle, a senior at State University, summarized it this way: "One night can screw up a girl's reputation."

Another pitfall for women is going "too far" sexually during a hookup. Many of the students I spoke with took for granted that it is a woman's responsibility to decide "how far" a sexual encounter will go. Lee, a freshman at Faith University, explained this attitude: "Because I think guys will always try to make [sexual] advances and it's up to the girl to go along with that or not. And I think girls are scared to say no and to say that they are not into doing that because they don't want to look stupid. . . . But I think ultimately it is up to the girl."

In the hookup culture, college women's reputations can be affected not only by their own behavior, but even by whom they associate with on campus. For example, certain sororities on the campuses I studied were given nicknames having a sexual connotation. Similarly, an article in *Rolling Stone* magazine about Duke University quotes an anonymous blog entry entitled "How-to Guide to Banging a Sorority Girl," which ranks the women of the "Core Four" sororities on campus in terms of their attractiveness. The blogger contends: "I would include a ranking for sluttiness, but in general all four are equally slutty." The blogger goes on to say it may be difficult to have sex with women in one of the "hottest" sororities, "unless you are part of the lucky group of dudes that pass these bitches around." Although this blogger's point of view may be more extreme than that of most students on campus, it demonstrates how college women exist in a fishbowl, for others to watch and judge.

In the dating era, women's sexual behavior was also scrutinized. Women were permitted to allow some necking and petting, but were absolutely supposed to maintain their virginity. Advice books were filled with suggestions for women on how to conduct themselves in sexual matters. These books suggested that women were responsible for playing the "gatekeeper" role during sexual interaction on dates. The 1958 advice book *The Art of Dating* warned young women about what men really think about girls who go "all the way." It suggested that if a girl allows a guy to go all the way, afterwards he is haunted by the question: "If she went all the way with me, how can I be sure there have not been others?" It continues by saying that men do not want to get "stuck with a tramp" for a long-term relationship.

Although the dating script and the hookup script differ with regard to specific sexual norms, women's sexual conduct continues to be scrutinized in a way that men's behavior is not. Thus, the sexual double standard, which prevailed during the dating era, is still very much a part of the hookup scene. This scrutiny makes navigating sex and relationships in the hookup era difficult for women. Women want "romantic" interaction with men, but there are many pitfalls for them in doing so. The catch is that a woman needs to hook up in order to find someone with whom to have a potential relationship, yet her very participation in hooking up can mean that she is not taken seriously as a potential girlfriend, is exploited for sex, and/or is labeled a slut. Women of the dating era faced the same dilemma. For example, student nurses found themselves in a difficult situation because of the stereotype that they were promiscuous.

> If she is not cooperative and does not meet the college boys' expectations of sexual permissiveness, she is likely to be dropped immediately and have no further dates. If she is cooperative, she easily builds a reputation and becomes fair game for her current dating partner and later his friends and fraternity brothers. The authors suspect that more girls than not choose to solve the dilemma by being more permissive than they normally would, just in order to keep dating.

Despite this dilemma, women actively participate in hooking up, as they did in dating. Why? Because the prevailing script in any era is seen as the only way, or at least the most likely way, to get together with men and feel a part of the social scene of their peers.

CONCLUSION

In the final analysis, much has changed since the dating era. Some of the changes can be seen as an improvement, and others can be viewed as negative. One of the most interesting things to examine about the shift from dating to hooking up is its impact on women. Since the emergence of hooking up can be traced back to the sexual revolution period, it begs the question: Have the goals of the women's liberation movement been met? If the objective of women's rights activists was for women to be able to have sexual experiences without having to barter exclusive sexual access in exchange for a wedding ring, there is evidence that it has been realized. Women's sexual behavior has changed more than men's since the 1960s, and on several key indicators women are reaching "parity" with men. For example, historically men had their first experience of sexual intercourse earlier than women; today, it is roughly equal. Historically, men also had a higher number of sexual partners than women; however, in more recent decades gender differences are less pronounced. These changes were precisely what many architects of the women's liberation movement had in mind.

However, even as similarities between men and women increased, the double standard remains. On the campuses I studied, contemporary college women may be permitted to engage in a wider variety of sexual behaviors under a wider array of circumstances than their dating-era counterparts, but there are no clear rules guiding what they should do and under what conditions. The ostensible lack of rules in the hookup script may seem to be liberating, and perhaps it can be, but it is also problematic because there are many unwritten rules that women must learn as they go along. These unwritten rules continue to limit the options available to women who are interested in pursuing sexual relationships.

Despite the double standard, women do have more sexual freedom today than they did in the dating era. But, it was not only women who gained sexual freedom since the sexual revolution; men did also. Since "respectable" women were not supposed to have premarital sex in the dating era, men who wanted to engage in sexual intercourse (while society looked the other way) had to do so with women of ill repute. In the hooking-up era, men have many more women to choose from for potential sexual encounters. For better or worse, men also do not have to put forth the amount of effort (e.g., phone calls, flowers, expensive dates, etc.) that their grandfathers did for sexual interaction to take place. Men today also do not have to propose marriage or walk down the aisle in order to have regular access to sexual intercourse. Indeed, men can have sex without entering into a relationship at all. Thus, hooking up is a system whereby men can engage in sexual encounters without the pretext of a relationship and where no guarantee of an ongoing or future bond with the woman is required. In a sense, it can be argued that men are the ones who really benefited from the sexual revolution. Robert, a sophomore at Faith University, opined:

ROBERT: It almost seems like [the hookup scene] is a guy's paradise. No real commitment, no real feelings involved, this is like a guy's paradise. This age [era] that we are in I guess.

KB: So you think guys are pretty happy with the [hookup] system?

ROBERT: Yeah! I mean this is what guys have been wanting for many, many years. And women have always resisted, but now they are going along with it. It just seems like that is the trend.

Clearly, women's rights activists who called for sexual equality with men did not intend to promote a form of interaction that would be considered a "guy's paradise."

Despite the increase in sexual freedom since the dating era, the hookup culture is not as out of control as some observers (and college students) believe. Hooking up is dominant on campus, but it represents a wide range in terms of level of participation and sexual behavior. There are many students who do not take part in hooking up at all and others who, for various reasons (e.g., they are in a relationship), have only hooked up a few times. For those students who have engaged in hooking up, many encounters involved nothing more than kissing. Although a hookup can involve casual sex between two parties who just met that evening, a hookup could also mean two people kissing after having a crush on each other for a year. Likewise, a hookup encounter may happen only once or evolve into repeatedly hooking up or even become a relationship. The point is that hooking up can mean different things, and it is too often assumed, by scholars and commentators alike, that it refers to only the most promiscuous scenarios.

This is not to say that extreme behavior is not happening in the hookup culture. For some students, college life can become an endless spring break. These are the same students who consume a disproportionate amount of alcohol on campus and hook up with different partners on a weekly basis. This behavior raises a variety of health concerns, particularly with regard to the level of binge drinking and the potential for STD transmission or rape. It is students caught up in the extremes of the hookup culture who, to the exclusion of their more moderate classmates, have captured the attention of critics. Although this behavior needs attention, it can also distort the reality of life on campus for the student body as a whole.

Acknowledging the variation in the hookup culture is important not only for students generally, but also for understanding differences between genders. Although I chose to highlight the differences between men and women throughout the preceding chapters, there is, no doubt, as much variation within gender as there is across it. Just as not all students fit the mold of the most raucous partiers, not *all* men want sex and not *all* women want relationships. I spoke with some men who preferred being in a relationship over hookup encounters with new partners. I also spoke to some women who enjoyed the freedom and experimentation of the hookup scene (at least during freshman year). Therefore, it would be unfair to oversimplify the behavior of the sexes. However, I found that women's interest in hookup encounters evolving into some semblance of a relationship and men's interest in "playing the held" was a theme that fundamentally affects the dynamic between men and women in the hookup culture.

Given that there is a wide range of possibilities available to men and women coming of age in the hookup era, it would seem that there is an almost endless array of choices an individual can make. For example, if a student wants to go to parties and hook up every weekend, he or she can choose to do so. Likewise, if a student wants to be part of the hookup scene, but as a more moderate participant, he or she can do that too. However, in many ways, the hookup system creates an illusion of choice. Although students have many options about how they conduct themselves within the hookup culture, they cannot change the fact that hooking up is the dominant script on campus. An individual student may decide to abstain from hooking up altogether, but they are more or less on their own to figure out an alternative. In other words, no other script exists side-by-side with hooking up that students can opt to use instead. Emily, a sophomore at Faith University, put it this way: "If [hooking up] is not what you're looking for, then I guess it is hard to escape it."

Students who would prefer to go out on traditional dates every weekend cannot change the fact that they did not enter college during a time when that was the "in" thing to do. Thus, students can use their own moral compass to make personal decisions on how to use the hookup script, but their decisions are constrained by their environment and the time period. The modern college campus is conducive to hooking up, and no individual can change that.

Notes

1. Coontz 1992.
2. For example, see Glenn and Marquardt (2001).
3. Although Whyte (1990), in his quantitative study of women in Detroit, examined changes and continuities in dating throughout most of the twentieth century, he did not consider the contemporary hookup scene on the college campus.

4. Skipper and Nass 1966.
5. Bailey 1988.
6. Gagnon and Simon 1987.
7. This finding confirms what previous researchers have found (see Glenn and Marquardt 2001; Paul, McManus, and Hayes 2000; Williams 1998).
8. Whyte 1990. See also Kinsey 1953.
9. In fact, Paul, McManus, and Hayes (2000) found that 30.4 percent of the college students in their study had engaged in at least one hookup that culminated in sexual intercourse. This finding is particularly interesting when one considers that the definition of hooking up employed by Paul, McManus, and Hayes referred to encounters with a stranger or brief acquaintance (or what interviewees in my sample referred to as "random' hookups).
10. Rubin 1990.
11. Carpenter 2005.
12. Reiss 1997; Harding and Jencks 2003.
13. Laumann et al. 1994.
14. Those born between 1933 and 1942 had their first experience of intercourse at approximately 18, while the age for those born 20 to 30 years later decreased by six months (Laumann et al. 1994).
15. Laumann et al. 1994.
16. See Hollander (1997) for a discussion of how different religious affiliations (i.e., Catholics and "mainstream" Protestants versus conservative or fundamentalist Christians) affect attitudes on premarital sex.
17. Rubin 1990, 46.
18. See Carpenter (2005) for more on how many people view virginity as stigma.
19. See Martin and Hummer 1989; Boswell and Spade 1996; Sanday 1992.
20. Bailey 1988; Whyte 1990. See also Thornton (1990).
21. See King and Christensen (1983) for a discussion of the stages in dating relationships.
22. Women were advised to avoid kissing on the first date (Duvall 1958).
23. Bailey 1988.
24. Goffman 1977.
25. Despite the fact that sexual intercourse is expected in exclusive relationships, some research indicates that a sizable percentage of college couples are not having intercourse. Specifically, Glenn and Marquardt (2001) found that 24 percent of the college women they surveyed had a boyfriend but had never had sexual intercourse.
26. Horowitz 1987; Moffatt 1989, Strouse 1987.
27. Duvall 1958.
28. The expectation that the man is responsible for paying for the date is tied, in part, to the relative economic positions of men and women during the 1920s, when dating became the dominant script for young heterosexual interactions throughout the United States.
29. There is no doubt that some college students feel more welcome than others at campus parties and nearby bars. Recall from Chapter 4 that minority students as well as gay and lesbian students were far less involved with the alcohol-centered hookup scene on campus.
30. In Waller's (1937) classic study of the dating script at Penn State University, he found that fraternity men dominated the dating scene, while freshman men were generally blocked from dating co-eds. This restriction was not placed on freshman males by the administration; rather, upperclassmen attempted to combat their institution's unfavorable sex ratio (six men for every woman) by excluding some of the "competition" from participating at all. Although women, at least those at Penn State, had a much more favorable sex ratio on their side, there were other issues that might prevent them from participating in the dating scene. For instance, a woman who did not meet the standard of feminine beauty might find herself "waiting for the phone to ring" while her more attractive classmates were being treated to an evening of socializing.
31. Waller 1937; Bailey 1988.
32. See Wechsler 2003.
33. Cooper 2002; Dermen, Cooper, and Agocha 1998.

34. See Peralta (2001) for a discussion of the effects of drinking on the college culture.
35. See MacAndrew and Edgerton (1969) for a discussion of cross-cultural variation in how alcohol affects members of a society. Interestingly, there are some cultures that use alcohol but do not connect it to sexual activity.
36. See Williams (1998) for more on the connection between alcohol and sexual behavior among college women.
37. A couple of male students from State University told me that if a man hooks up with a woman his peers deem "fat," he can neutralize any teasing he might receive the morning after by proclaiming that he "went hoggin'." However, when I asked students directly during interviews if they knew what this term meant, most did not.
38. See also Williams 1998.
39. Bailey 1988.
40. Waller 1937.
41. Bailey 1988.
42. Waller 1937.
43. Bailey 1988.
44. Bailey 1988, 70.
45. US. Bureau of the Census, Current Population Reports, 1998.
46. See Arnett (2004) for a thorough discussion of "emerging adults" and what factors they believe are most important in making the transition to adulthood. See Arnett (1994) for a discussion of the transition to adulthood specifically among college students.
47. Bailey 1988.
48. Bailey 1988.
49. See Sarch for a discussion of how contemporary single women use the telephone to "exert control and power" in their relationships with men, while being "confined by the cultural belief that a woman ought to have a man without pursuing one aggressively" (1993, 128).
50. Virtually any sociology textbook defines power as the ability to impose one's will on others (e.g., see Andersen 2003).
51. This is consistent with Glenn and Marquardt's (2001) finding that the burden is on college women to initiate "the talk" in order to see if a series of hookups with the same partner can evolve into a relationship. Women ask, men decide.
52. Goffman 1977.
53. Waller 1937.
54. Behrendt and Tuccillo 2004.
55. Waller 1937.
56. Although none of the college men in my sample were afraid that women might exploit them financially, many feared women "clinging onto them" by trying to form an unwanted serious relationship.
57. Rubin 1990.
58. Rubin 1990; Skipper and Nass 1966.
59. Skipper and Nass 1966, 417.
60. Reitman 2006.
61. Rubin 1990.
62. See Duvall 1958.
63. See Holland and Eisenhart (1990) for a discussion of gender roles, sexual intimacy, and the cultural model of romance.
64. Duvall 1958, 205.
65. Skipper and Nass 1966, 417.
66. Laumann et al. 1994.
67. Laumann et al. 1994.
68. Rubin 1990.
69. Paul et al. (2000) found in their quantitative study of a large university in the northeastern United States that approximately 22 percent of undergraduate students had never engaged in a hookup.

References

Andersen, Margaret L. 2003. *Thinking about Women: Sociological Perspectives on Sex and Gender.* Boston: Allyn & Bacon.

Arnett, Jeffrey Jensen. 2004. *Emerging Adulthood: The Winding Road from the Late Teens through the Twenties.* Oxford: Oxford University Press.

Bailey, Beth L. 1988. *From Front Porch to Back Seat: Courtship in Twentieth Century America.* Baltimore: Johns Hopkins University Press.

Behrendt, Greg, and Liz Tuccillo. 2004. *He's Just Not That Into You: The No-Excuses Truth to Understanding Guys.* New York: Simon Spotlight Entertainment.

Boswell, A. Ayres, and Joan Z. Spade. 1996. Fraternities and Collegiate Rape Culture: Why Are Some Fraternities More Dangerous Places for Women? *Gender & Society* 10:133–147.

Carpenter, Laura M. 2005. *Virginity Lost: An Intimate Portrait of First Sexual Experiences.* New York: New York University Press.

Coontz, Stephanie. 1992. *The Way We Never Were: American Families and the Nostalgia Trap.* New York: Basic Books.

Cooper, M. Lynne. 2002. Alcohol Use and Risky Sexual Behavior among College Students and Youth: Evaluating the Evidence. *Journal of Studies on Alcohol* 63: 101–117.

Dermen, Kurt H., M. Lynne Cooper, and V. Bede Agocha. 1998. Sex-Related Expectancies as Moderators between Alcohol Use and Risky Sex in Adolescents. *Journal of Studies on Alcohol* 59: 71–77.

Duvall, Evelyn R. M. 1958. *The Art of Dating.* New York: Association Press.

Gagnon, John H., and William Simon. 1987. The Sexual Scripting of Oral Genital Contacts *Archives of Sexual Behavior* 16: 1–25.

Glenn, Norval, and Elizabeth Marquardt. 2001. *Hooking Up, Hanging Out and Hoping for Mr. Right: College Women on Dating and Mating Today.* An Institute for American Values Report to the Independent Women's Forum.

Goffman, Erving. 1977. The Arrangement between the Sexes. *Theory and Society* 4: 301–331.

Holland, Dorothy C., and Margaret A. Eisenhart. 1990. *Educated in Romance: Women, Achievement, and College Culture.* Chicago: University of Chicago Press.

Hollander, Dore. 1997. Times They Are A-Changin', Mostly. *Family Planning Perspectives* 29: 151.

Horowitz, Helen L. 1987. *Campus Life: Undergraduate Cultures from the End of the Eighteenth Century to the Present.* New York: Alfred A. Knopf.

Paul, Elizabeth L., Brian McManus, and Allison Hayes. 2000. Hookups: Characteristics and Correlates of College Students' Spontaneous and Anonymous Sexual Experiences. *Journal of Sex Research* 37: 76–88.

Peralta, Robert. 2001. Getting Trashed in College: Doing Alcohol, Doing Gender, Doing Violence. Unpublished dissertation, University of Delaware.

Reiss, Ira. 1997. *Solving America's Sexual Crises.* Amherst, NY: Prometheus Books.

Reitman, Janet. 2006. Sex and Scandal at Duke. *Rolling Stone*, June 1.

Rubin, Lillian. 1990. *Erotic Wars: What Happened to the Sexual Revolution?* New York: Farrar, Straus, Giroux.

Sarch, Amy. 1993. Making the Connection: Single Women's Use of the Telephone in Dating Relationships with Men. *Journal of Communication* 43: 128–144.

Skipper, James K., and Gilbert Nass. 1966. Dating Behavior: A Framework for Analysis and an Illustration. *Journal of Marriage and the Family* 28: 412–420.

Strouse, Jeremiah S. 1987. College Bars as Social Settings for Heterosexual Contacts. *Joumal of Sex Research* 23: 374–382.

King, Charles E., and Andrew Christensen. 1983. The Relationship Event Scale: A Guttman Scaling of Progress in Courtship. *Journal of Marriage and the Family* 45: 671–678.

Kinsey, Alfred C., Wardell B. Pomeroy, Clyde E. Martin, and Paul Gebhard. 1953. *Sexual Behavior in the Human Female.* Philadelphia: W. B. Saunders.

Laumann, Edward, John H. Gagnon, Robert T. Michael, and Stuart Michaels. 1994. *The Social Organization of Sexuality: Sexual Practices in the United States.* Chicago: University of Chicago Press.

MacAndrew, Craig, and Robert B. Edgerton. 1969. *Drunken Comportment: A Social Explanation.* Chicago: Aldine.
Martin, Patricia Y., and Robert Hummer. 1989. "Fraternities and Rape on Campus." *Gender & Society* 3(4): 457–473.
Moffatt, Michael. 1989. *Coming of Age in New Jersey: College and American Culture.* New Brunswick, NJ: Rutgers University Press.
Thornton, Arland. 1990. The Courtship Process and Adolescent Sexuality. *Journal of Family Issues* 11: 239–273.
U.S. Bureau of the Census, Current Population Reports. *Marital Status and Living Arrangements,* 1998.
Waller, Willard W. 1938. *The Family.* New York: Cordon Company.
Waller, Willard W. 1937. The Rating and Dating Complex. *American Sociological Review* 2: 727–734.
Wechsler, Henry, and Bernice Wuethrich. 2003. *Dying to Drink: Confronting Binge Drinking on College Campuses.* New York: St. Martin's Press.
Whyte, Martin K. 1990. *Dating, Mating, and Marriage.* New York: Aldine de Gruyter.
Williams, Kimberly M. 1998. *Learning Limits: College Women, Drugs, and Relationships.* Westport, CT: Bergin & Garvey.

READING 11

Red Sex, Blue Sex

Margaret Talbot

In early September, when Sarah Palin, the Republican candidate for Vice-President, announced that her unwed seventeen-year-old daughter, Bristol, was pregnant, many liberals were shocked, not by the revelation but by the reaction to it. They expected the news to dismay the evangelical voters that John McCain was courting with his choice of Palin. Yet reports from the floor of the Republican Convention, in St. Paul, quoted dozens of delegates who seemed unfazed, or even buoyed, by the news. A delegate from Louisiana told CBS News, "Like so many other American families who are in the same situation, I think it's great that she instilled in her daughter the values to have the child and not to sneak off someplace and have an abortion." A Mississippi delegate claimed that "even though young children are making that decision to become pregnant, they've also decided to take responsibility for their actions and decided to follow up with that and get married and raise this child." Palin's family drama, delegates said, was similar to the experience of many socially conservative Christian families. As Marlys Popma, the head of evangelical outreach for the McCain campaign, told *National Review,* "There hasn't been one evangelical family that hasn't gone through some sort of situation." In fact, it was Popma's own "crisis pregnancy" that had brought her into the movement in the first place.

During the campaign, the media has largely respected calls to treat Bristol Palin's pregnancy as a private matter. But the reactions to it have exposed a cultural rift that mirrors

America's dominant political divide. Social liberals in the country's "blue states" tend to support sex education and are not particularly troubled by the idea that many teen-agers have sex before marriage, but would regard a teen-age daughter's pregnancy as devastating news. And the social conservatives in "red states" generally advocate abstinence-only education and denounce sex before marriage, but are relatively unruffled if a teen-ager becomes pregnant, as long as she doesn't choose to have an abortion.

A handful of social scientists and family-law scholars have recently begun looking closely at this split. Last year, Mark Regnerus, a sociologist at the University of Texas at Austin, published a startling book called "Forbidden Fruit: Sex and Religion in the Lives of American Teenagers," and he is working on a follow-up that includes a section titled "Red Sex, Blue Sex." His findings are drawn from a national survey that Regnerus and his colleagues conducted of some thirty-four hundred thirteen-to-seventeen-year-olds, and from a comprehensive government study of adolescent health known as Add Health. Regnerus argues that religion is a good indicator of attitudes toward sex, but a poor one of sexual behavior, and that this gap is especially wide among teenagers who identify themselves as evangelical. The vast majority of white evangelical adolescents—seventy-four per cent—say that they believe in abstaining from sex before marriage. (Only half of mainline Protestants, and a quarter of Jews, say that they believe in abstinence.) Moreover, among the major religious groups, evangelical virgins are the least likely to anticipate that sex will be pleasurable, and the most likely to believe that having sex will cause their partners to lose respect for them. (Jews most often cite pleasure as a reason to have sex, and say that an unplanned pregnancy would be an embarrassment.) But, according to Add Health data, evangelical teen-agers are more sexually active than Mormons, mainline Protestants, and Jews. On average, white evangelical Protestants make their "sexual debut"—to use the festive term of social-science researchers—shortly after turning sixteen. Among major religious groups, only black Protestants begin having sex earlier.

Another key difference in behavior, Regnerus reports, is that evangelical Protestant teen-agers are significantly less likely than other groups to use contraception. This could be because evangelicals are also among the most likely to believe that using contraception will send the message that they are looking for sex. It could also be because many evangelicals are steeped in the abstinence movement's warnings that condoms won't actually protect them from pregnancy or venereal disease. More provocatively, Regnerus found that only half of sexually active teen-agers who say that they seek guidance from God or the Scriptures when making a tough decision report using contraception every time. By contrast, sixty-nine per cent of sexually active youth who say that they most often follow the counsel of a parent or another trusted adult consistently use protection.

The gulf between sexual belief and sexual behavior becomes apparent, too, when you look at the outcomes of abstinence-pledge movements. Nationwide, according to a 2001 estimate, some two and a half million people have taken a pledge to remain celibate until marriage. Usually, they do so under the auspices of movements such as True Love Waits or the Silver Ring Thing. Sometimes, they make their vows at big rallies featuring Christian pop stars and laser light shows, or at purity balls, where girls in frothy dresses exchange rings with their fathers, who vow to help them remain virgins until the day they marry. More than half of those who take such pledges—which, unlike abstinence-only classes in public schools, are explicitly Christian—end up having sex before marriage, and not usually with their future spouse. The movement is not the complete washout its critics portray it as: pledgers delay sex eighteen months longer than non-pledgers, and have fewer partners. Yet, according to the sociologists Peter Bearman, of Columbia University, and Hannah Brückner, of Yale, communities with high rates of pledging also have high rates of S.T.D.s. This could be because more teens pledge in communities where they perceive more danger from sex (in which case the pledge is doing some good); or it could be because fewer people in these communities use condoms when they break the pledge.

Bearman and Brückner have also identified a peculiar dilemma: in some schools, if too many teens pledge, the effort basically collapses. Pledgers apparently gather strength from the sense that they are an embattled minority, once their numbers exceed thirty per cent, and proclaimed chastity becomes the norm, that special identity is lost. With such a fragile formula, it's hard to imagine how educators can ever get it right: once the self-proclaimed virgin clique hits the thirty-one-per-cent mark, suddenly it's Sodom and Gomorrah.

Religious belief apparently does make a potent difference in behavior for one group of evangelical teenagers: those who score highest on measures of religiosity—such as how often they go to church, or how often they pray at home. But many Americans who identify themselves as evangelicals, and who hold socially conservative beliefs, aren't deeply observant.

Even more important than religious conviction, Regnerus argues, is how "embedded" a teen-ager is in a network of friends, family, and institutions that reinforce his or her goal of delaying sex, and that offer a plausible alternative to America's sexed-up consumer culture. A church, of course, isn't the only way to provide a cohesive sense of community. Close-knit families make a difference. Teen-agers who live with both biological parents are more likely to be virgins than those who do not. And adolescents who say that their families understand them, pay attention to their concerns, and have fun with them are more likely to delay intercourse, regardless of religiosity.

A terrific 2005 documentary, "The Education of Shelby Knox," tells the story of a teen-ager from a Southern Baptist family in Lubbock, Texas, who has taken a True Love Waits pledge. To the chagrin of her youth pastor, and many of her neighbors, Knox eventually becomes an activist for comprehensive sex education. At her high school, kids receive abstinence-only education, but, Knox says, "maybe twice a week I see a girl walking down the hall pregnant." In the film, Knox seems successful at remaining chaste, but less because she took a pledge than because she has a fearlessly independent mind and the kind of parents who—despite their own conservative leanings—admire her outspokenness. Devout Republicans, her parents end up driving her around town to make speeches that would have curled their hair before their daughter started making them. Her mother even comes to take pride in Shelby's efforts, because while abstinence pledges are lovely in the abstract, they don't acknowledge "reality."

Like other American teens, young evangelicals live in a world of Internet porn, celebrity sex scandals, and raunchy reality TV, and they have the same hormonal urges that their peers have. Yet they come from families and communities in which sexual life is supposed to be forestalled until the first night of a transcendent honeymoon. Regnerus writes, "In such an atmosphere, attitudes about sex *may formally* remain unchanged (and restrictive) while sexual activity becomes increasingly common. This clash of cultures and norms is felt most poignantly in the so-called Bible Belt." Symbolic commitment to the institution of marriage remains strong there, and politically motivating—hence the drive to outlaw gay marriage—but the actual practice of it is scattershot.

Among blue-state social liberals, commitment to the institution of marriage tends to be unspoken or discreet, but marriage in practice typically works pretty well. Two family-law scholars, Naomi Cahn, of George Washington University, and June Carbone, of the University of Missouri at Kansas City, are writing a book on the subject, and they argue that "red families" and "blue families" are "living different lives, with different moral imperatives." (They emphasize that the Republican-Democrat divide is less important than the higher concentration of "moral-values voters" in red states.) In 2004, the states with the highest divorce rates were Nevada, Arkansas, Wyoming, Idaho, and West Virginia (all red states in the 2004 election); those with the lowest were Illinois, Massachusetts, Iowa, Minnesota, and New Jersey. The highest teen-pregnancy rates were in Nevada, Arizona, Mississippi, New Mexico, and Texas (all red); the lowest were in North Dakota, Vermont, New Hampshire, Minnesota, and Maine (blue except for North Dakota). "The 'blue states' of the Northeast and Mid-Atlantic have lower teen birthrates, higher use of abortion, and lower percentages of teen births within marriage," Cahn and Carbone observe. They also note that people start families earlier in red states—in part because they are more inclined to deal with an unplanned pregnancy by marrying rather than by seeking an abortion.

Of all variables, the age at marriage may be the pivotal difference between red and blue families. The five states with the lowest median age at marriage are Utah, Oklahoma, Idaho, Arkansas, and Kentucky, all red states, while those with the highest are all blue: Massachusetts, New York, Rhode Island, Connecticut, and New Jersey. The red-state model puts couples at greater risk for divorce; women who marry before their mid-twenties are significantly more likely to divorce than those who marry later. And younger couples are more likely to be contending with two of the biggest stressors on a marriage: financial struggles and the birth of a baby before, or soon after, the wedding.

There are, of course, plenty of exceptions to these rules—messily divorcing professional couples in Boston, high-school sweethearts who stay sweetly together in rural Idaho. Still, Cahn and Carbone conclude, "the paradigmatic red-state couple enters marriage not long after the woman becomes sexually active, has two children by her mid-twenties, and reaches the critical period of marriage at the high point in the life cycle for risk-taking and experimentation. The paradigmatic blue-state couple is more likely to experiment with multiple partners, postpone marriage until after they reach emotional and financial maturity, and have their children (if they have them at all) as their lives are stabilizing."

Some of these differences in sexual behavior come down to class and education. Regnerus and Carbone and Cahn all see a new and distinct "middle-class morality" taking shape among economically and socially advantaged families who are not social conservatives. In Regnerus's survey, the teen-agers who espouse this new morality are tolerant of premarital sex (and of contraception and abortion) but are themselves cautious about pursuing it. Regnerus writes, "They are interested in remaining free from the burden of teenage pregnancy and the sorrows and embarrassments of sexually transmitted diseases. They perceive a bright future for themselves, one with college, advanced degrees, a career, and a family. Simply put, too much seems at stake. Sexual intercourse is not worth the risks." These are the kids who tend to score high on measures of "strategic orientation"—how analytical, methodical, and fact-seeking they are when making decisions. Because these teenagers see abstinence as unrealistic, they are not opposed in principle to sex before marriage—just careful about it. Accordingly, they might delay intercourse in favor of oral sex, not because they cherish the idea of remaining "technical virgins" but because they assess it as a safer option. "Solidly middle- or upper-middle- class adolescents have considerable socioeconomic and educational expectations, courtesy of their parents and their communities' lifestyles," Regnerus writes. "They are happy with their direction, generally not rebellious, tend to get along with their parents, and have few moral qualms about expressing their nascent sexuality." They might have loved Ellen Page in "Juno," but in real life they'd see having a baby at the wrong time as a tragic derailment of their life plans. For this group, Regnerus says, unprotected sex has become "a moral issue like smoking or driving a car without a seat-belt. It's not just unwise anymore; it's wrong."

Each of these models of sexual behavior has drawbacks—in the blue-state scheme, people may postpone child-bearing to the point where infertility becomes an issue. And delaying child-bearing is better suited to the more affluent, for whom it yields economic benefits, in the form of educational opportunities and career advancement. But Carbone and Cahn argue that the red-state model is clearly failing on its own terms—producing high rates of teen pregnancy, divorce, sexually transmitted disease, and other dysfunctional outcomes that social conservatives say they abhor. In "Forbidden Fruit," Regnerus offers an "unscientific postscript," in which he advises social conservatives that if they really want to maintain their commitment to chastity and to marriage, they'll need to do more to help young couples stay married longer. As the Reverend Rick Marks, a Southern Baptist minister, recently pointed out in a Florida newspaper, "Evangelicals are fighting gay marriage, saying it will break down traditional marriage, when divorce has already broken it down." Conservatives may need to start talking as much about saving marriages as they do about, say, saving oneself for marriage.

"Having to wait until age twenty-five or thirty to have sex *is* unreasonable," Regnerus writes. He argues that religious organizations that advocate chastity should "work more creatively to support younger marriages. This is not the 1950s (for which I am glad), where one could bank on social norms, extended (and larger) families, and clear gender roles to negotiate and sustain early family formation."

Evangelicals could start, perhaps, by trying to untangle the contradictory portrayals of sex that they offer to teenagers. In the Shelby Knox documentary, a youth pastor, addressing an assembly of teens, defines intercourse as "what two dogs do out on the street corner— they just bump and grind awhile, *boom boom boom*." Yet a typical evangelical text aimed at young people, "Every Young Woman's Battle," by Shannon Ethridge and Stephen Arterburn, portrays sex between two virgins as an ethereal communion of innocent souls: "physical, mental, emotional, and spiritual pleasure beyond description." Neither is the most realistic or helpful view for a young person to take into marriage, as a few advocates of abstinence acknowledge. The savvy young Christian writer Lauren

Winner, in her book "Real Sex: The Naked Truth About Chastity," writes, "Rather than spending our unmarried years stewarding and disciplining our desires, we have become ashamed of them. We persuade ourselves that the desires themselves are horrible. This can have real consequences if we do get married." Teenagers and single adults are "told over and over not to have sex, but no one ever encourages" them "to be bodily or sensual in some appropriate way"—getting to know and appreciate what their bodies can do through sports, especially for girls, or even thinking sensually about something like food. Winner goes on, "This doesn't mean, of course, that if only the church sponsored more softball leagues, everyone would stay on the chaste straight and narrow. But it does mean that the church ought to cultivate ways of teaching Christians to live in their bodies well—so that unmarried folks can still be bodily people, even though they're not having sex, and so that married people can give themselves to sex freely."

Too often, though, evangelical literature directed at teen-agers forbids all forms of sexual behavior, even masturbation. "Every Young Woman's Battle," for example, tells teen-agers that "the momentary relief of "self-gratification" can lead to "shame, low self-esteem, and fear of what others might think or that something is wrong with you." And it won't slake sexual desire: "Once you begin feeding baby monsters, their appetites grow bigger and they want MORE! It's better not to feed such a monster in the first place."

Shelby Knox, who spoke at a congressional hearing on sex education earlier this year, occupies a middle ground. She testified that it's possible to "believe in abstinence in a religious sense," but still understand that abstinence-only education is dangerous "for students who simply are not abstaining." As Knox's approach makes clear, you don't need to break out the sex toys to teach sex ed—you can encourage teen-agers to postpone sex for all kinds of practical, emotional, and moral reasons. A new "abstinence-plus" curriculum, now growing in popularity, urges abstinence while providing accurate information about contraception and reproduction for those who have sex anyway. "Abstinence works," Knox said at the hearing. "Abstinence-only-until-marriage does not."

It might help, too, not to present virginity as the cornerstone of a virtuous life. In certain evangelical circles, the concept is so emphasized that a girl who regrets having been sexually active is encouraged to declare herself a "secondary" or "born-again" virgin. That's not an idea, surely, that helps teen-agers postpone sex or have it responsibly.

The "pro-family" efforts of social conservatives—the campaigns against gay marriage and abortion—do nothing to instill the emotional discipline or the psychological smarts that forsaking all others often involves. Evangelicals are very good at articulating their sexual ideals, but they have little practical advice for their young followers. Social liberals, meanwhile, are not very good at articulating values on marriage and teen sexuality—indeed, they may feel that it's unseemly or judgmental to do so. But in fact the new middle-class morality is squarely pro-family. Maybe these choices weren't originally about values—maybe they were about maximizing education and careers—yet the result is a more stable family system. Not only do couples who marry later stay married longer; children born to older couples fare better on a variety of measures, including educational attainment, regardless of their parents' economic circumstances. The new middle-class culture of intensive parenting has ridiculous aspects, but it's pretty successful at turning out productive, emotionally resilient young adults. And its intensity may be one reason that teen-agers from close families see child-rearing as a project for which they're not yet ready. For too long, the conventional wisdom has been that social conservatives are the upholders of family values, whereas liberals are the proponents of a polymorphous selfishness. This isn't true, and, every once in a while, liberals might point that out.

Some evangelical Christians are starting to reckon with the failings of the preaching-and-pledging approach. In "The Education of Shelby Knox," for example, Shelby's father is uncomfortable, at first, with his daughter's campaign. Lubbock, after all, is a town so conservative that its local youth pastor tells Shelby, "You ask me sometimes why I look at you a little funny. It's because I hear you speak and I hear tolerance." But as her father listens to her arguments he realizes that the no-tolerance ethic simply hasn't worked in their deeply Christian community. Too many girls in town are having sex, and having babies that they can't support. As Shelby's father declares toward the end of the film, teen-age pregnancy "is a problem—a major, major problem that everybody's just shoving under the rug."

Chapter 5

Courtship and Marriage

READING 12

Cohabitation

Lynne M. Casper and Suzanne M. Bianchi

Shacking up. Living in sin. Living together. Persons of the opposite sex sharing living quarters. Doubling up. Sleeping together. All of these expressions have been used to describe the living arrangement that demographers refer to as cohabitation. Some of these terms are more value laden than others, and the one an individual chooses to describe this living arrangement can say a great deal about how he or she views unmarried sexual partners. Although *cohabitation* can refer to same-sex couples, most of the demographic research conducted to date has been concerned with opposite-sex partners.

The increase in heterosexual cohabitation that has accompanied the delay in marriage and increase in divorce is one of the most significant changes in family life to take place in the latter half of the 20th century (Seltzer 2000; Smock 2000). Some observers believe that the increase in cohabitation has eroded commitment to marriage and "traditional" family life (e.g., Waite and Gallagher 2000). One of the best examples of this view is presented in a report titled *Should We Live Together? What Young Adults Need to Know About Cohabitation Before Marriage*, published by the National Marriage Project (Popenoe and Whitehead 1999). This controversial report paints an overwhelmingly negative picture of cohabitation, asserting that "cohabiting unions tend to weaken the institution of marriage and pose clear and present dangers to women and children."

Most adults in the United States eventually marry: 91 percent of women ages 45 to 54 in 1998 had been married at least once (Bianchi and Casper 2000:15), and an estimated 88 percent of women in younger cohorts are likely to marry eventually (Raley 2000). But the meaning and permanence of marriage may be changing as cohabitation increases.

Marriage used to be the demographic event that almost exclusively marked the formation of a new household, the beginning of sexual relations, and the birth of a child. Marriage also typically implied that each partner had one sexual partner and identified the two individuals who would parent any child born of the union. The increasing social acceptance of cohabitation outside marriage has meant that these linkages can no longer be assumed. Also, what it means to be "married" or "single" is changing as the personal lives of unmarried couples come to resemble those of their married counterparts in some ways but not in others (Seltzer 2000; Smock 2000).

Cohabiting and marital relationships have much in common: coresidence; emotional, psychological, and sexual intimacy; and some degree of economic interdependence. But the two relationships differ in other important ways. Marriage is a relationship between two people of opposite sexes that adheres to legal, moral, and social rules, a social institution that rests upon common values and shared expectations for appropriate behavior within the partnership (Nock 1998). Society upholds and enforces appropriate marital behavior both formally and informally. In contrast, there is no widely recognized social blueprint or script for the appropriate behavior of cohabitors, or for the behavior of the friends, families, and other individuals and institutions with whom they interact. There is no common term in use for referring to one's nonmarital live-in lover, whereas the terms *spouse*, *husband*, and *wife* are institutionalized. Most important, there is far greater societal acceptance of marriage—and far more ambivalence about cohabitation—as a desirable adult relationship for the rearing of children.

We begin this chapter with the intriguing story of the growth in cohabitation in the latter decades of the 20th century. Tracking trends in cohabitation has been difficult because until recently there was no direct measurement of the numbers of unmarried partners living together. Until the late 1980s, when national surveys began the routine collection of information on cohabitation, researchers relied on indirect estimates to document the increase in cohabitation. The 1987–88 National Survey of Families and Households (NSFH) collected the first cohabitation histories. The 1990 Census was the first census enumeration that included "unmarried partner" among a list of categories from which a respondent could choose in identifying his or her household relationship. Beginning in 1995, the Current Population Survey (CPS) also included the category "unmarried partner" as a possible response to the household relationship question, and the National Survey of Family Growth began to obtain detailed data on cohabitation.

In the discussion that follows, we use CPS data and indirect estimates to examine the growth in cohabitation since the late 1970s. In an effort to understand more about the meaning of cohabitation, we review relevant research on this topic, compare cohabitors with married and single people, and examine how cohabitors view themselves. We also investigate whether cohabitors are becoming more like married people over time as cohabitation becomes a more common experience and gains wider social acceptance. We describe the linkages between cohabitation and other demographic events and the potential positive and negative consequences they engender. We conclude the chapter with a discussion of what demographers know about cohabitation and what this implies for the future of marriage and family life in the United States.

WHO COHABITS AND HOW HAS THIS CHANGED OVER TIME?

Unmarried heterosexual cohabitation began to capture national attention during and after the period of well-publicized student unrest on college campuses in the late 1960s and early 1970s. The image of the time was of sexually promiscuous college students experimenting with new family forms by living with their boyfriends or girlfriends rather than marrying, often trying to keep their arrangements secret from their disapproving parents. In the 1970s, Paul Glick and Arthur Norton (1977) of the U.S. Census Bureau were the first to use information on household composition from the decennial census and CPS to define cohabitors as "persons of the opposite sex sharing living quarters," or POSSLQs for short.

Figure 12.1 shows changes in cohabitation using a modified version of the indirect POSSLQ measure (Casper and Cohen 2000). The proportion of unmarried women who were cohabiting tripled, from 3 percent to 9 percent, between 1978 and 1998. Increases were similar among unmarried men—from 5 percent to nearly 12 percent—with men more likely than women to cohabit, both in 1978 and in 1998.

These estimates of cohabitation may seem low, especially considering the heightened concern of some observers that cohabitation is eroding commitment to marriage and family life. The rates are low, in part, because they represent only those who are

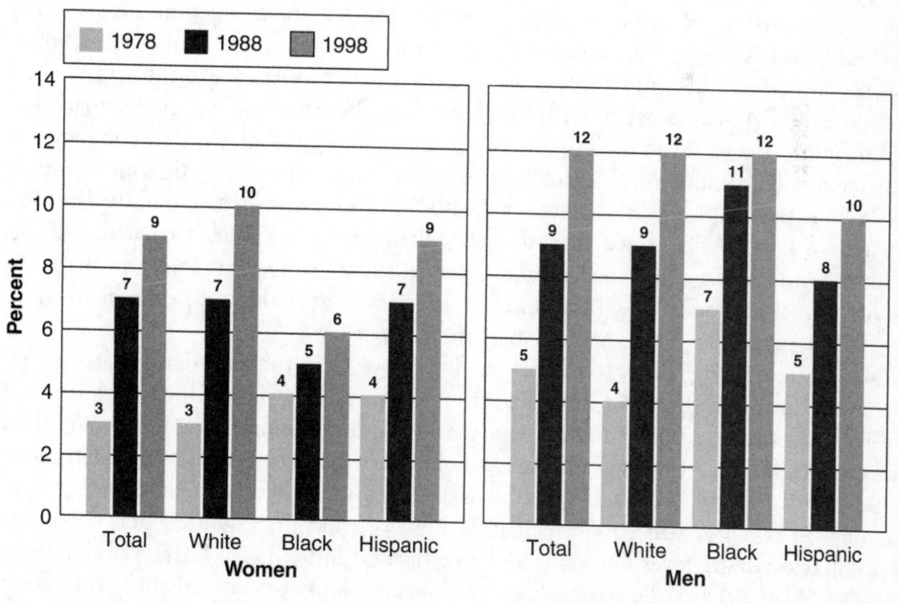

FIGURE 12.1 ***Percentages of Unmarried Men and Women Cohabiting, by Race and Gender: 1978–1998***

Race/ethnicity categories are white, non-Hispanic; black, non-Hispanic; and Hispanic.

Source: Current Population Survey, March supplements, 1978, 1988, 1998.

co-habiting at a given point in time. A much larger proportion of people have ever cohabited, and the likelihood of cohabiting appears to be increasing over time. Only 8 percent of first marriages in the late 1960s were preceded by cohabitation, compared with 49 percent in 1985–86 (Bumpass 1990) and 56 percent by the early to mid-1990s (Bumpass and Lu 2000). Thus, young couples today are more likely to begin their coresidential relationships in cohabitation than in marriage.

Why has cohabitation increased so much? A number of factors, including increased uncertainty about the stability of marriage, the erosion of norms against cohabitation and sexual relations outside of marriage, the availability of reliable birth control, and the weakening of religious and other normative constraints on individuals' family decisions, seem to be ending the taboo against living together without marrying. For example, by the mid-1990s, a majority of high school seniors thought that living together prior to marriage was a good idea (Axinn and Thornton 2000).

Some argue that cohabitation reduces the costs of partnering, especially if one is uncertain about a potential mate, and allows a couple to experience the benefits of an intimate relationship without committing to marriage (Willis and Michael 1994). If a cohabiting relationship is not successful, one can simply move out; if a marriage is not successful, one suffers through a sometimes lengthy and messy divorce.

Meanwhile, the development of effective contraceptives has given childbearing-age couples greater freedom to engage in sexual intercourse without the risk of unwanted pregnancy. The availability of reliable birth control has increased the prevalence of premarital sex. As premarital sex has become more common, it has become more widely accepted, and so has living with a partner before marriage (Bumpass and Sweet 1989a). Widespread availability of contraception also makes it easier to avoid unwanted pregnancy if one chooses to live with a partner after separation or divorce from a previous marriage.

Shifting norms mean that adults today are more likely to believe that cohabitation and divorce are acceptable and less likely to believe that marriage is a lifelong commitment than was true in the past (Thornton 1989; Thornton and Freedman 1983). Thus the normative barrier that once discouraged cohabitation has begun to wither away. Increasingly, American values have shifted from those favoring family commitment and self-sacrifice to those favoring self-fulfillment, individual growth, and personal freedom (Lasch 1979; Lesthaeghe 1995; McLanahan and Casper 1995).

Early estimates suggested that college students were in the vanguard of attitudinal and behavior changes that fostered the growth in cohabitation. Glick and Norton (1977:34), for example, highlighted the fact that a greater proportion of unmarried than married couples (8 percent versus 5 percent) included two partners who were college students and that, in 1970, one-fourth of unmarried couples had at least one partner who was enrolled in college. Subsequent research, however, has documented that cohabitation is a behavior that is prevalent among less educated individuals. Larry Bumpass and James Sweet (1989b), in discussing the first direct estimates of cohabitation, note: "Contrary to a common view of cohabitation as college student behavior, education is strongly and negatively related to rates of cohabitation before first marriage. The highest rates are found among the least educated" (p. 622).

CPS trends, based on indirect estimates, indicate that about 16 percent of men who cohabit are college graduates; this figure has remained quite stable over time (see

TABLE 12.1 ***Presence of Children, Age, and Marital Status among Unmarried Couples: 1978–1998 (in percentages)***

	All Couples		
	1978	*1988*	*1998*
Age			
Men			
Total	100.0	100.0	100.0
15–24	21.2	18.2	15.1
25–34	40.3	40.5	37.2
35+	38.5	41.3	47.7
Women			
Total	100.0	100.0	100.0
15–24	35.5	25.8	21.8
25–34	29.9	39.4	34.4
35+	34.6	34.8	43.8
Marital status			
Men			
Total	100.0	100.0	100.0
Separated/divorced	46.9	45.3	42.2
Widowed	6.5	3.3	3.2
Never married	46.7	51.4	54.6
Women			
Total	100.0	100.0	100.0
Separated/divorced	39.3	44.2	44.9
Widowed	15.1	8.0	5.7
Never married	45.7	47.9	49.4
Children in the household	27.6	33.8	37.1
College graduates			
Men	15.8	16.0	16.3
Women	13.4	13.3	17.1

Unmarried partners estimated with adjusted POSSLQ measure (see Casper and Cohen 2000).

Source: Current Population Survey, March supplements, 1978, 1988, 1998.

Table 12.1). Among women, the estimate in 1998 was 17 percent, up from 13 percent in 1978 and 1988. Other estimates of the likelihood that an individual will ever cohabit suggest that increases in the rates of cohabitation continue to be greater for those with only a high school education than for those with a college education (Bumpass and Lu 2000).

Who cohabits defies stereotypes in other ways as well. For example, increasingly, cohabitation is not a phenomenon confined to early adulthood. Although more than 60 percent of cohabiting men and almost two-thirds of women in unmarried partnerships were under age 35 in 1978, these proportions have declined. In 1998, a relatively high percentage of cohabitors were in their mid-30s or older (almost 50 percent of men and more than 40 percent of women in 1998). As age at first marriage increases, the average

age of cohabitors also appears to be increasing. In addition, living together without marrying is common after first marriages end as well as before they begin. In 1998, 45 percent of the men and 51 percent of the women in heterosexual unmarried couples had been previously married, with the vast majority either separated or divorced.

One of the biggest compositional shifts that is occurring among unmarried couples is the increase in the presence of children in these households, either children born to the couple or those that one of the partners has from a prior relationship. In 1978, about 28 percent of cohabitor households included children under age 18 (see Table 12.1). By 1998, the proportion had increased to 37 percent. About two-fifths of all children spend at least some years during their childhoods living with a parent and the parent's unmarried partner, according to recent estimates by Bumpass and Lu (2000:35). This percentage is high both because of the popularity of cohabitation after separation and divorce, where children from a prior marriage may be present, and because more births outside marriage are to mothers who are living with their partners.

The proportion of births to unmarried mothers who are actually living with their partners (often their children's fathers) increased from 29 percent in the mid-1980s to near 40 percent in the mid-1990s (Bumpass and Lu 2000:35). In some European countries, most notably Scandinavian countries, cohabitation increasingly seems to function as a substitute for marriage, with couples unlikely to marry before the birth of their children. In the United States, the likelihood of marriage with the birth of a child is declining but seems to be a far smaller component of the increase in children in cohabiting unions than in Europe.

As more women spend time in cohabiting relationships, the time "at risk" of a pregnancy while a women is living with an unmarried partner goes up. Most of the increase in births to cohabitors (as much as 70 percent) is due to this factor (Raley 2001). Cohabiting women who become pregnant have become a little less likely to marry before the birth, and single women who become pregnant have become more likely to move in with the father of the child rather than remain single or marry. Yet these two changes in behavior—staying in a cohabiting arrangement rather than marrying if one becomes pregnant or moving in with a partner rather than marrying if one becomes pregnant while single—account for only about 10 percent of the increase in births to cohabiting women (Raley 2001:66).

The increased recognition that many unmarried couples are raising children is leading to greater attention to the ways in which children's lives may be affected by the marital status of their parents. For example, children born to unmarried couples have a higher risk of experiencing their parents' separation than do children born to married couples (Bumpass, Raley, and Sweet 1995). The ties that bind fathers to their children may also be weaker in cohabiting than in marital relationships: After parents separate, children whose parents never married see their fathers less often and are less likely to be financially supported by their fathers than are children born to married parents (Cooksey and Craig 1998; Seltzer 2000). . . .

COHABITATION AND MARRIAGE

Much of the demographic research on cohabitation has been oriented around one question: How similar is (heterosexual) cohabitation to marriage? Economic theorists often view marriage as an institution in which individual goals are replaced by altruism and the subordination of self-interest in favor of goals that benefit the family (e.g., Becker 1991). Married couples supposedly maximize benefits for their families by specializing in different activities—wives tend to specialize in homemaking and husbands tend to specialize in breadwinning. This gender role difference has meant that women tend to seek spouses with higher education and earnings than themselves—men who would be good breadwinners. Men, by contrast, tend to look for women who will be good mothers and homemakers.

Evidence suggests that cohabitation may attract individuals who value more egalitarian, less specialized, gender roles. Gender-differentiated roles are not absent from cohabiting unions; for example, cohabiting couples with higher-earning male (but not female) partners are the ones that proceed more quickly to marriage (Sanchez, Manning, and Smock 1998). Yet research has found that cohabiting relationships endure longer when partners' employment patterns and earnings are more similar than different (Brines and Joyner 1999). Cohabiting couples also tend to divide housework in a more egalitarian fashion than do married couples (South and Spitze 1994), and cohabitors are less likely to espouse traditional gender roles (Clarkberg, Stolzenberg, and Waite 1995; Lesthaeghe and Surkyn 1988).

Cohabitation may also be especially attractive to those with more individualistic, more materialistic, and less family-oriented outlooks on life. Cohabitors are more likely than others to believe that individual freedom is important in a marriage (Thomson and Colella 1992). Men and women are more likely to choose cohabitation as their first union if it is important to them to have "lots of money" in life (Clarkberg et al. 1995). Women who value their careers are more likely than other women to cohabit for their first union, whereas those who think that finding the right person to marry and having a happy family life is important are more likely than others to begin their first union with marriage (Clarkberg et al. 1995).

Cohabitors are also more accepting of divorce. They are less likely than married persons to disapprove of divorce (Lesthaeghe and Surkyn 1988), with those who disapprove of divorce more likely to begin their first union with marriage (Axinn and Thornton 1992). Children of divorced parents are more likely to cohabit than are children of married parents (Cherlin, Kiernan, and Chase-Lansdale 1995), in part because people whose mothers divorced tend to hold attitudes that are more approving of cohabitation (Axinn and Thornton 1996).

To the extent that cohabitation is an "incomplete institution" lacking clear normative standards (Nock 1995), it may provide a more comfortable setting than marriage for less conventional couples. Perhaps the strongest indicator of this is the higher percentage of cohabiting than married couples who cross the racial divide in their partnerships (see Table 12.2). Cohabiting couples are more than twice as likely to be of different races than married couples—13 percent compared with 5 percent. About half of interracial cohabiting couples are made up of a white woman and a man of another race (data not shown).

Schoen and Weinick (1993) argue that because cohabiting relationships tend to be short-term relationships, cohabiting partners are less concerned with the ascribed characteristics of their partners than are the partners in married couples. Half of all cohabitations last a year or less; only about one-sixth of cohabitations last at least 3 years, and only one-tenth last 5 years or more (Bumpass and Lu 2000). Thus an individual's choosing a partner of the same age, race, and religion as him- or herself is not as important in cohabitation as it is in marriage, because cohabitation does not necessarily entail a long-term commitment or the accompanying normative standards such a relationship implies.

TABLE 12.2 ***Characteristics of Cohabiting and Married Couples: 1998***

	Cohabiting	*Married*
Total number of couples (thousands)	3,142	54,317
% of couples in which		
Woman is of different race/ethnicity than man	13	5
Woman is at least 2 years older than man	24	12
Woman has more education than man	21	16
Both man and woman worked for pay	77	60
Woman worked more hours[a]	24	16
Woman's contribution to couple's 1997 income (% of total income)[b]	41	37

[a]Woman worked more hours than her partner in the preceding year.

[b]Calculated for couples in which both partners were employed.

A cohabiting couple is defined as an unmarried couple who maintains a household together. Race/ethnicity categories are white, non-Hispanic; black, non-Hispanic; and Hispanic.

Source: Current Population Survey, March supplement, 1998.

It is much more common in cohabiting than in marital relationships for the female partner to be older and better educated than her male partner (see Table 12.2). Women are more than 2 years older than their partners in 24 percent of unmarried couples but in only 12 percent of married couples, and women have a higher educational level in 21 percent of cohabiting couples compared with only 16 percent of married couples.

The data displayed in Table 12.2 support the notion that cohabiting couples are more egalitarian in terms of their labor force participation and earnings. Almost four out of five cohabiting couples have both partners employed, compared with only three in five married couples. Men tend to work more hours than their partners in cohabiting and marital relationships, but women's hours of employment exceed their partners' hours in a greater percentage of cohabiting (24 percent) than married (16 percent) couples. When employed, women and men have earnings that are closer to equality in cohabiting than in married couples; women in cohabiting couples contribute 41 percent of the couple's annual earnings, compared with 37 percent, on average, for married women.

Some of the differences shown in Table 12.2 reflect the fact that unmarried couples tend to be younger, on average, than married couples, and younger generations have more egalitarian attitudes toward the labor force roles of men and women and are more likely to choose partners with different racial backgrounds. However, the evidence in Table 12.2, combined with the attitudinal and family background differences between unmarried and married couples noted in other research, suggests that cohabitation provides a living arrangement that suits couples who may be somewhat uncertain about whether their partnerships can be sustained over the long term. These may be couples who must work out issues that surround partnering across racial lines, couples who defy patterns that are considered "normal" in the larger society (such as when an "older" woman partners with a "younger" man or a more educated woman partners with a less educated mate), or couples for whom an equal economic partnership is a priority and who may be concerned that marriage will propel them into a gendered division of labor that will make it difficult to sustain their egalitarianism. . . .

CONCLUSION

Cohabitation has increased dramatically over a relatively short period of time, raising concerns about the effects of this new family form on the institutions of marriage and the family in the United States. Currently, the majority of individuals live with partners before they marry. Hence the lines that differentiate marriage from being single have faded over time. The effects of cohabitation on the institution of marriage are likely to vary according to how cohabitors view their relationships. Some cohabitors have definite plans to marry their partners and end up doing so, whereas others live together in relationships of convenience with low levels of commitment—these couples often separate.

Not only is cohabitation increasing among people who have not entered a first marriage, it is also slowing the rate of remarriage after divorce or separation. Almost one-half of those cohabiting at any given point in time are doing so after rather than before a first marriage. In part due to the role cohabitation is playing after marriages end, the characteristics of cohabitors are changing. Compared with 20 years ago, more of them are older than age 35 and more cohabiting households include children. And, although cohabitation was initially linked to experimentation among college students, its increase has been widespread and its popularity today is as great or greater among those with less education.

As cohabitation continues to increase and to become more normative, will it replace marriage as the preferred living arrangement for raising children in the United States, as it seems to have done in some countries, most notably Sweden? The answer still seems to be no. Although unmarried partners do not necessarily rush to marry if the woman becomes pregnant, and single women who become pregnant may move in with their partners rather than marry them, these behaviors are still not widespread in the United States, at least not among the majority white population. And only 1 in 10 cohabitors believes that the cohabiting relationship is a substitute for marriage. The largest factor explaining why more births occur in cohabiting relationships today than two decades ago is merely that so many more people cohabit before and after marriage. What this means, however, is that a significant percentage of the babies born to unmarried mothers—perhaps as large a proportion as 40 percent—actually begin life residing with both parents, who live together but are not married.

Demographers are only beginning to study the heterogeneity of cohabiting relationships. New estimates suggest that about 4 percent of cohabiting couples are in same-sex relationships. One-fifth of lesbian-couple and about 5 percent of gay-couple households include children, often from one partner's previous heterosexual union. Heterosexual cohabitation is on the rise among all racial groups, although estimates of the prevalence among different groups vary by whether the percentages are calculated for all adults, unmarried adults, or all unions. Blacks have a high portion of all unions that are unmarried partnerships, but black unmarried women have relatively low rates of living with partners. The gender gap in rates of cohabitation is greatest for blacks because black unmarried men have rates of partnering as great as or greater than other racial groups. Also, more unmarried than married heterosexual couples are mixed-race couples.

Cohabiting couples defy gender stereotypes more often than do married couples: Women's and men's labor force roles are more similar and the woman's age, education, and hours of market work more often exceed the man's in cohabiting than in marital unions. Partly this is because cohabitors are younger than married couples and younger cohorts have more gender-egalitarian attitudes. Yet cohabitation also seems to be chosen as a first relationship more often by women who value career goals than by other women and by couples who either value an equal economic partnership or defy gender stereotypes in other ways (such as having a female partner who is older than the male partner).

Although researchers have been preoccupied with comparisons of cohabitation to marriage (or, in some cases, to singlehood), the reality is that cohabitation is serving a diverse set of couples with an array of reasons for living together rather than marrying. About one-half of cohabitors indicate strong intentions to marry their partners, and 1 in 10 claims that the unmarried partnership is a substitute for marrying. The remainder seem uncertain about their compatibility with their current partners, their future plans, and/or marriage as an institution. Not surprisingly, whether cohabitors marry, break up, or continue living together as unmarried couples varies by how they see their relationships. And partners often disagree on the quality of the relationship, with the partnership more likely to dissolve if the woman is unhappy and more likely to continue as a cohabitation but not proceed to marriage if the man is unhappy.

Finally, although one might think that couples' living together before or instead of marrying should make marriages more stable, because partners can discover irreconcilable differences before they tie the knot, one of the strongest findings is that those who cohabit prior to marriage divorce more often than those who do not. The debate is over whether living together makes such couples more "irreverent" toward the institution of marriage or whether they have characteristics and attitudes that are more accepting of divorce in the first place. The evidence to date suggests it is more the latter than the former, and the question is whether cohabitation will become less selective of certain types of individuals. If living together is increasingly "what one does" before marrying or remarrying, and as marital partnerships change as well, those who cohabit may become less distinct from those who marry. On economic dimensions such as labor force participation and earnings, married and unmarried partners seem less differentiated today than they were 20 years ago. Still, among whites, educational attainment may be diverging between the two groups. How cohabitation alters the future of marriage will ultimately rest on whether unmarried cohabiting couples are increasingly a distinct group of persons who doubt the possibility of long-term commitment or are merely couples captured at different points in their relationships than those who have married, but who nonetheless continue to aspire to the goal of committed family life.

References

Axinn, William G. and Arland T. Thornton. 1992. "The Relationship between Cohabitation and Divorce: Selectivity or Causal Influence?" *Demography* 29:357–74.

———. 1996. "The Influence of Parents' Marital Dissolutions on Children's Attitudes toward Family Formation." *Demography* 33:66–81.

Becker, Gary S. 1991. *A Treatise on the Family*. Rev. ed. Cambridge, MA: Harvard University Press.

Bianchi, Suzanne M. and Lynne M. Casper. 2000. "American Families." *Population Bulletin* 55(4):3–42.
Brines, Julie and Kara Joyner. 1999. "The Ties That Bind: Principles of Cohesion in Cohabitation and Marriage." *American Sociological Review* 64:333–55.
Brown, Eleanor and Alison P. Hagy. 1997. "The Demand for Multiple Child Care Arrangements." Center for Economic Studies, U.S. Bureau of the Census. Unpublished manuscript.
Brown, Susan L. 2000. "Union Transitions among Cohabiters: The Significance of Relationship Assessment and Expectations." *Journal of Marriage and Family* 62:833–46.
Brown, Susan L. and Alan Booth. 1996. "Cohabitation versus Marriage: A Comparison of Relationship Quality." *Journal of Marriage and Family* 58:668–78.
Bryant, W. Keith. 1996. "A Comparison of the Household Work of Married Females: The Mid-1920s and the Late 1960s." *Family and Consumer Sciences Research Journal* 24:358–84.
Bryant, W. Keith and Cathleen D. Zick. 1996a. "Are We Investing Less in the Next Generation? Historical Trends in Time Spent Caring for Children." *Journal of Family and Economic Issues* 17:365–91.
———. 1996b. "An Examination of Parent-Child Shared Time." *Journal of Marriage and Family* 58:227–37.
Bryson, Ken and Lynne M. Casper. 1998. *Household and Family Characteristics: March 1997.* Current Population Reports, Series P-20, No. 509. Washington, DC: Government Printing Office.
———. 1999. *Co-resident Grandparents and Their Grandchildren.* Current Population Reports, Series P-23, No. 198. Washington, DC: Government Printing Office.
Bumpass, Larry L. 1990. "What's Happening to the Family? Interactions between Demographic and Institutional Change." *Demography* 27:483–93.
Bumpass, Larry L. and Hsien-Hen Lu. 2000. "Trends in Cohabitation and Implications for Children's Family Contexts in the United States." *Population Studies* 54:29–41.
Bumpass, Larry L., R. Kelly Raley, and James A. Sweet. 1995. "The Changing Character of Stepfamilies: Implications of Cohabitation and Nonmarital Childbearing." *Demography* 32:425–36.
Bumpass, Larry L. and James A. Sweet. 1989a. "Children's Experience in Single-Parent Families: Implications of Cohabitation and Marital Transitions." *Family Planning Perspectives* 21:256–60.
———. 1989b. "National Estimates of Cohabitation." *Demography* 26:615–25.
Casper, Lynne M. and Philip N. Cohen. 2000. "How Does POSSLQ Measure Up? Historical Estimates of Cohabitation." *Demography* 37:237–45.
Cherlin, Andrew J., Kathleen E. Kiernan, and P. Lindsay Chase-Lansdale. 1995. "Parental Divorce in Childhood and Demographic Outcomes in Young Adulthood." *Demography* 32:299–318.
Clarkberg, Marin, Ross M. Stolzenberg, and Linda J. Waite. 1995. "Attitudes, Values, and Entrance into Cohabitational versus Marital Unions." *Social Forces* 74:609–34.
Cooksey, Elizabeth C. and Patricia H. Craig. 1998. "Parenting from a Distance: The Effects of Paternal Characteristics on Contact between Nonresidential Fathers and Their Children." *Demography* 35:187–200.
Glick, Paul C. and Arthur J. Norton. 1977. "Marrying, Divorcing, and Living Together in the U.S. Today." *Population Bulletin* 32(1):3–41.
Lasch, Christopher. 1979. *The Culture of Narcissism: American Life in an Age of Diminishing Expectations.* New York: W. W. Norton.
Lesthaeghe, Ron. 1995. "The Second Demographic Transition in Western Countries: An Interpretation." Pp. 17–62 in *Gender and Family Change in Industrialized Countries,* edited by Karen Oppenheim Mason and An-Magritt Jensen. Oxford: Clarendon.
Lesthaeghe, Ron and John Surkyn. 1988. "Cultural Dynamics and Economic Theories of Fertility Change." *Population and Development Review* 14:1–45.
McLanahan, Sara S. and Lynne M. Casper. 1995. "Growing Diversity and Inequality in the American Family." Pp. 1–45 in *State of the Union: America in the 1990s,* vol. 2, *Social Trends,* edited by Reynolds Farley. New York: Russell Sage Foundation.
Nock, Steven L. 1995. "A Comparison of Marriages and Cohabiting Relationships." *Journal of Family Issues* 16:53–76.
———. 1998. *Marriage in Men's Lives.* New York: Oxford University Press.
Popenoe, David and Barbara Dafoe Whitehead. 1999. *Should We Live Together? What Young Adults Need to Know about Cohabitation before Marriage.* New Brunswick, NJ: National Marriage Project.

Raley, R. Kelly. 2000. "Recent Trends and Differentials in Marriage and Cohabitation: The United States." Pp. 19–39 in *The Ties That Bind: Perspectives on Marriage and Cohabitation*, edited by Linda J. Waite, Christine A. Bachrach, Michelle Hinden, Elizabeth Thomson, and Arland T. Thornton. New York: Aldine de Gruyter.

———. 2001. "Increasing Fertility in Cohabiting Unions: Evidence for the Second Demographic Transition in the United States?" *Demography* 38:59–66.

Sanchez, Laura, Wendy D. Manning, and Pamela J. Smock. 1998. "Sex-Specialized or Collaborative Mate Selection: Union Transitions among Cohabiting Couples." *Social Science Research* 27:280–304.

Schoen, Robert and Robin M. Weinick. 1993. "Partner Choice in Marriages and Cohabitations." *Journal of Marriage and Family* 55:408–14.

Seltzer, Judith A. 2000. "Families Formed outside Marriage." *Journal of Marriage and Family* 62:1247–68.

Smock, Pamela J. 2000. "Cohabitation in the United States: An Appraisal of Research Themes, Findings and Implications." *Annual Review of Sociology* 26:1–20.

South, Scott J. and Glenna Spitze. 1994. "Housework in Marital and Non-marital Households." *American Sociological Review* 59:327–47.

Thomson, Elizabeth and Ugo Colella. 1992. "Cohabitation and Marital Stability: Quality or Commitment?" *Journal of Marriage and Family* 54:259–67.

Thornton, Arland T. 1989. "Changing Attitudes toward Family Issues in the United States." *Journal of Marriage and Family* 51:873–93.

Thornton, Arland T. and Deborah Freedman. 1983. "The Changing American Family." *Population Bulletin* 38(4).

Waite, Linda J. and Maggie Gallagher. 2000. *The Case for Marriage: Why Married People Are Happier, Healthier and Better Off Financially*. Garden City, NY: Doubleday.

Willis, Robert J. and Robert T. Michael. 1994. "Innovation in Family Formation: Evidence on Cohabitation in the U.S." Pp. 9–45 in *The Family, the Market, and the State in Aging Societies*, edited by John Ermisch and Naohiro Ogawa. Oxford: Clarendon.

READING 13

Marriage Is More Than Being Together: The Meaning of Marriage among Young Adults in the United States

Maria Kefalas, Frank Furstenberg, and Laura Napolitano

Is marriage in trouble? Over the past four decades, public handwriting over marriage has grown more intense (Popenoe and Whitehead 2001, Waite and Gallagher 2000, Wilson 2002). Even though marital instability, single parenthood and nonmarital childbearing tend to be concentrated among the most economically disadvantaged, urban populations (Edin and Kefalas 2005, Furstenberg 2001, Jencks and Ellwood 2001, MacLaughlin and Lichter 1997, McLanahan 2004, Wilson 1987), there is growing concern that these trends are spreading to other segments of American society (Jencks and

Ellwood 2002). Marriage pessimists point to rising divorce rates, increased levels of cohabitation, the advent of gay marriage, nonmarital childbearing, and the fact that Americans spend fewer of their adult years married (Popenoe and Whitehead 2001, Waite and Gallagher 2000, Wilson 2002) as evidence of the steady and seemingly inexorable decline of marriage as a social institution.

Not everyone agrees with this bleak assessment. Some family experts counter that these changes reflect a shift in the meaning and function of marriage (Edin and Kefalas 2005, Edin, Kefalas, and Reed 2004; Cherlin 2004, Coontz 2005). Marriage is not disappearing, so much as being transformed by a host of contemporary conditions, not only in the U.S. but also in virtually all industrialized countries throughout the world (Cherlin 2004, Coontz 2005). The vast majority of Americans still hold on both to the ideal and the practice of matrimony (Goldstein and Kenney 2001, Thornton and Young-DeMarco 2001). They cite the fact that demographers project that at least four out of five of today's young people will marry, hardly a sign that marriage is in retreat.

Family scholars have identified a number of conditions that have reshaped young people's notions of marriage. The extension of schooling beyond the teen years, the liberalization of sexual behavior, the availability of reliable methods of contraception, changing gender roles, the threat of divorce, and the option to remain single are but a few of the significant influences affecting the timing and attractiveness of marriage. To be sure, young people have a great deal more discretion about whether or not to marry; yet the proportion opting for marriage is hardly different from it was at the beginning of the last century (Fussell and Furstenberg 2004). Increasingly, young people whom we refer to as "marriage planners" are inclined to regard marriage as developmental process which progresses over time and is tested by real-life circumstances. A small minority, whom we label "marriage drifters," continue to think of marriage as inevitable and a natural outcome of an early and untested relationship. The drifters are inclined to regard marriage as a "promise" of future commitment, the planners see marriage as the celebration of a commitment that is already established and time tested.

Undoubtedly for many educated middle- and upper-class young men and women, delaying marriage until personal and professional goals are achieved is a rational response given the reality of what is currently required to qualify for a well-paying and stable job (Axinn and Thornton 2000). For those in the bottom two thirds of society, getting married has surely become more problematic, especially for those with very limited education and earnings (Edin and Kefalas 2005, Gibson, Edin, and MacLanahan forthcoming; MacLanahan 2004). Couples appear to be more discerning about whether marriage will indeed improve their economic and social fortunes. Accordingly, they have resorted to delay and temporary unions until their prospects are clarified (Smock 2000, Smock 2004, Smock, Manning and Porter 2005). And, to be sure, a minority will probably never make the transition to formal marriage at all.

Does this mean that commitment to marriage is weakening or merely shifting to a later point in the life course? Of course, answering this question involves projecting current behaviors into the future, always a problematic exercise. In doing so, it is useful to probe in more depth about the way that young adults of marriageable age are thinking about the reasons for and against marriage. This paper goes beyond the confines of census and survey data to explore the way that young adults are thinking about marriage. It draws evidence from a large, qualitative study sponsored by the MacArthur Network on Adult Transitions, a diverse population of several hundred men and women in their twenties and early thirties who are currently navigating the passage to adulthood. We examine the ways that social class, community context, ethnic background, and gender are linked to how young adults construct their hopes and expectations for relationships, whether marriage is a likely prospect in their future, and, if so, the conditions under which they foresee entering into matrimony. Within a social world where young people do not have to marry if they want to engage in engage in sexual relations, cohabit, or bear children: what purpose does it now serve?

SAMPLE AND METHODS

The data used for this paper comes from a national qualitative study sponsored by the MacArthur Foundation's Network on Adult Transitions. From 2001-2002, researchers in four sites: New York City, San Diego, St. Paul, and Iowa conducted in-depth 2 to 4 hour interviews with a socioeconomically, racially, and ethnically diverse group of young people ranging in ages from 22 to 38 years old. The majority of respondents were selected from larger, random samples of pre-existing studies.[1] The on-going youth studies in Minnesota, New York, and San Diego were selected to provide the broadest diversity in terms of experience, socioeconomic background and geographical location. While all of the young people in the sample were born in the United States, nearly half are the children of immigrants. Though the Minnesota site targeted TANF recipients, New York, Iowa, and San Diego researchers interviewed young people from a range of socioeconomic conditions that reflected cross-sections of the communities and/or the larger random samples where the respondents were drawn.

Each respondent was asked a series of open-ended questions about various facets of the transition to adulthood, and this paper uses data from the relationship and marriage section of the questionnaire. In San Diego, the largest site (n = 136) researchers used a similar approach to interview a slightly younger group of children of immigrants (specifically Mexican, Laotian, Vietnamese, Dominicans, South Asian, Hmong, Thai, Filipino, and Cambodian) as part of the (Children of Immigrant Longitudinal Study) CILS project. In New York City site, the second largest sample (n = 130), researchers conducted in-depth interviews with second-generation Americans (Russian Jews, Puerto Ricans, Dominicans, Columbians, Ecquadorian, Peruvian, West Indians, and Chinese). For the Heartland Study, the third largest sample (n = 104), and the only one that was created exclusively for the purpose of this study: we surveyed 275[2] young people who entered the Ellis Community High School between 1986 and 1988 and between 1991 and 1993. We then followed up with 104 in-depth interviews when they were aged 22–31. This group had no children of immigrants and only two respondents (siblings) were of mixed racial ancestry. Finally, the Minnesota sample (n = 54) targeted native born whites, African Americans, and a small sample of Hmong.[3] The Minnesota sample was overwhelmingly female, partly because, in an effort to create an economically diverse sample, interviewers targeted past and present TANF recipients. All of the in-depth interviews covered a set range of topics in a mutually agreed upon questionnaire. . . .

RELATIONSHIPS IN THE POST-ROMANTIC ERA

A half century ago, family texts and professional advice touted the advantages of marriage. The dominant model of marriage was the companionate marriage that deemed, in matrimony, two people would merge their fortunes and their selves into a single identity to which their personal interests and needs would be subordinated (Cherlin 2004). Many such unions occurred and were celebrated at anniversaries and funerals. However, the demands of a companionate marriage were high and the rewards and obligations were not always equally shared in arrangements that required a relatively strict division of labor. The implicit understanding that men ruled the roost created a hierarchy within marriage that is no longer widely shared by most of the young people whom we interviewed.

We sense that many young people have modified essential elements of the companionate marriage. Whether they adhere to the ideal or not, they recognize that the traditional hierarchy based on a sharp, gender-based division of labor is no longer viable. Moreover, the young adults that we spoke with acknowledged that a successful marriage must allow for greater space for individual lives within and outside the union, what Andrew Cherlin has described as the *individualized marriage* (Cherlin 2004:852). Today's young people take a highly choreographed view of relationships. The idealized couple dynamic is something akin to a pair of figure skaters. Each partner moves on the ice separately, and yet, each one must always be aware of their partner and somehow manage to move in tandem.

Even though many of the tenants of companionate marriage remain intact, especially the strong emphasis on friendship and compatibility, we heard little talk of romantic love, especially among the older youth in our sample. For this single, 28-year-old woman college graduate living in New York, there is no time for romance's volatility and passion's unpredictability now that she is more mature and, like so many other twenty and thirty something adults we spoke to, she has a child of her own to raise. She explains, "When you're younger you [go out] and you have boyfriends. . . . you don't see people in the same way as you get older . . . If he's not someone you're gonna be with [for the long haul], you might as well just let them go ahead because it's not worth the time. And you know that now [when you get older], but back then, it's like, 'Oh my God, he's the world,' you know. But now it is like you don't have the time to waste. And I have a daughter and I don't, you know, you don't want this one and that one in and out of her life."

Giordorno, Manning, and Longmore (forthcoming) offer a useful typology for distinguishing between friendship and romantic relationships. Friendships, they observe, are "cooperatively constructed" while romances must contend with the concept of "exclusivity." Communication in romances can be awkward while the communication between friends is "relaxed" and marked by "social ease." Romances suffer from "heightened emotionality" and power "asymmetries" while friendships are settled and characterized by "balanced reciprocity."

Love, in the words of a 27-year-old New York man with some post secondary education, "is the best and worst thing" about his relationship with his serious girlfriend. "It's good that we love each other so much but at the same time, because maybe she loves me so much and I love her, she knows that it's her advantage and my advantage too. But there's certain things that you can say to a person, and you can *hurt* them, and you know that you're gonna hurt them because they love you . . . there's like a saying in Spanish 'ambos' it means, it goes both ways- it could be good and it could be bad."

Couples fight; friends get along. Friends accept you at face value; romantic partners can be needy and demanding. A 26-year old New Yorker currently enrolled in a four year college says that she and her longtime boyfriend have moved to a more secure phase in their relationship now that they are not "lovey-dovey" and more like friends "who get along." She explains, "Like I know he's there for me, in my hard moments. . . . You know, we're not like calling each other every minute, like a lot of people we know. My friends are always on the cell phone [with the people they are seeing]. Let's say I was going to the library and I changed plans and I was going out to eat . . . I would have to call my boyfriend and tell him. Maybe [we just] have a more mature relationship."

Comfort in knowing one another, a defining characteristic of "grown-up" relationships, is one of the most valued features of a successful marriage. A marriage partner should allow you to be yourself and accept you fully. According to a 29-year-old Minnesota man currently enrolled in a four year college and working full time, being friends with his future wife for several years made it possible for them to know what they were "dealing with" within their relationship. He continues "I mean we get along well and part of that, I think, what helped was that we were friends for three, four years, and so I knew exactly who she was because there was nothing for her to change who she was and what she was all about. I got to see the true side of her during that time period. It was the same for me. We knew exactly what we were dealing with."

When young people do talk about love and marriage, they do not want to be under the spell of "out-of-control romantic love." Their notion of love within marriage gives partners the means to sublimate personal desire and self-interest for the collective good of a relationship. While a marriage ideally offers partners space and freedom to follow their own paths, even the most flexible arrangements will call on a partner to make sacrifices. In these moments, love is the resource couples invoke as they try to see beyond their own preferences. A 33-year-old New York woman with a vocational certificate talks about love when she recounts her struggles with her husband. "He loves me to death, I mean, we've been up and down with lots of stuff. I guess all marriages are like mat. You have to grow into each other, you know what I mean, and everybody's changing. Everybody changes. You've been through different changes throughout your life. As you get older, you're able to cope with it, you know."

According to a 30-year-old New York woman with a bachelor's degree, "I never realized how hard marriage could be. I love him dearly. I did marry him cause he's my best friend; he's also a pain in the ass. . . . It was just hard. I never imagined it would be so hard. I think we fought for 11 months and it just magically went away. It was miserable. And it was really weird. Now we're just in love, we do argue, but it's good. I don't know. It's a trip." Finally, a 34-year-old New Yorker with a high school diploma says love "isn't romance and stars and what TV [perceives] it to be. It's a decision. Either you decide to love somebody or you don't. And that's all there is to it." Another New Yorker, a 23-year-old woman about to begin a Master's degree program, believes "love comes after marriage." She explains, "Like in the beginning you don't even know what it is, it's just attraction, but real love grows over time and over giving to that person and love keeps growing. You don't fall out of love in a marriage. You work really hard at a marriage." Love is not spell-binding but it is a binding force nonetheless.

The ideal marriage partner should "share a similar outlook" and make you feel "grounded" and "centered." A 29-year-old Minnesota woman with a bachelor's degree who hopes to marry her boyfriend soon sees her current relationship as "a place that's comfortable, exciting, empowering and centering." She continues, "All the pieces come together and I like who I am in the relationship. I don't need to change anything about myself to be better in this. That feels really good."

WHAT IT TAKES TO GET MARRIED: THE STAGES OF DEVELOPMENT

We found little evidence that young people reject marriage outright, it is just that the complex nature of early adulthood in the 21st century combined with young people's high expectations for marriage place many obstacles on the way of young people's pursuit of marriage. Marriage, once the master status from which all the other milestones of adulthood were achieved, is now something young people are only prepared to do once they feel settled into adult roles (Furstenberg 1978, Furstenberg and Cherlin 1991). In years past, being married meant you were an adult, today you have to be an adult to be married. Young people in rural Iowa feel ready for marriage more quickly than their counterparts in suburban Minneapolis, New York, and San Diego (McLaughlin, Lichter, and Johnston 1993).

For a group we call the *marriage planners*, marriage remains a life goal, but it is just one of many options that can command young people's immediate attention. While those who view marriage as a natural outcome of a relationship that has endured over a period of time are *marriage drifters [naturalists]*. Iowans speedy transitions through work and school combined with a social context where marriage occurs at an earlier age feeds into this more traditional timing and orientation towards marriage consistent with *marriage drifters [naturalists]*. A 24-year-old Iowa woman with an associate's degree who married her high school sweetheart at the age of 21 epitomizes such a view, "I was ready. I mean we had been together forever. It seemed like it was just, you know, it's either now or never." A 24-year-old single Iowan and in the final stages of law school, explains how his sense of the right time for marriage has altered since he left his small hometown. He has shifted from being a *marriage drifter [naturalist]* to a *marriage planner.* "I always thought growing up, oh 22 or 23 years old [is the time to get married] and now it's like there's so much more that I want to do. I think that's something about Ellis; people that stick around there tend to get married a lot quicker, a lot more quickly and we were just talking about this last night. We have a friend who came down to see us. She's got it in her mind that she needs to be married now, or engaged because all her friends are. I'm just like, you came down here to go to school and with women getting more education now and everything, it's not 20 year olds getting married anymore."

No one speaks specifically of courtships, but in fact there is a distinct notion that relationships must develop over time, be tested, and ultimately move to "absolute commitment." The hurdles that slow young people's progress on the way towards marriage offer revealing insights into what marriage means today. *Marriage planners* talk a great deal about being ready (or not ready) for marriage. Being ready means feeling settled, mature and having achieved personal, educational, and career goals. Within the high-pressured lives so prevalent among the urban young people, focus on work, school, and children become incompatible with the emotional labor required for serious, committed relationships. The fast pace of modern life, the high cost of housing, the demands on completing one's education, the challenges of the labor market, and not to mention a social context which makes it relatively easy for young people to enjoy the benefits of marriage without its obligations, makes the transition to marriage for young people in metropolitan areas more tumultuous and uncertain.

As a single 24-year-old San Diego man with a bachelor's degree in engineering tells us, his life "is too hard" for a serious relationship. "This living situation I have right now . . . I only work part time but it feels like I have very little time." When a 23-year-old New York man's girlfriend pressures him for an engagement ring his response is: "'Talk to law school!' cause I can't make a commitment until I have a career." For a single, 25-year-old San Diego man with an associate's degree in auto mechanics, marriage will happen sometime in the distant future. Right now, "I'd rather concentrate on work and stuff like that . . ." There is no time for time even for dating because he is such a "workaholic." He explains, "I think I'd prefer to marry one of these days. Like every other guy I say 'I'm not getting married.' [laughing] but somehow it ends up happening."

According to a 23-year-old New York man going into his third year of law school, balancing the demands of school has put stress on his serious relationship. "We tend to get along pretty well but it seems that once law school came into the picture it put a little space between us, but we tend to get along pretty well . . . . I spend more time in law school than I do in my own house. I mean, before law school we'd see each other almost every day. After law school, at most we see each other on weekends." A 30-year old New York woman with a bachelor's degree recounts the story of her long distance relationship. Her account chronicles how the complexity of contemporary couple dynamics means that she and her boyfriend live their separate and "entrenched" lives. Her views capture the essence of being a *marriage planner*, because even though the young woman wants a marriage, neither she nor her boyfriend seems willing to alter their individual lives and goals.

> We've talked about marriage and living together but it's hard when we don't have a chance to see each other. It's not like, 'Hey, what are you doing? I want to come over.' It's very strategic, like it's very planned. I've just closed on a condo [in New York] and he's closed on one in Boston. Don't ask me what we're doing, because my grandmother says to me, 'You guys aren't even working . . . to get closer together.' *It's like we're being entrenched in our current situations. . .* We haven't really said that in a year from now [let's reevaluate our plans] because we don't want to put any pressure on ourselves.

Economic, work, and educational considerations aside, twenty and thirty somethings also insist that personal growth and maturity should come before marriage. A single 24-year-old San Diego man with some post-secondary education tells us that a successful relationship is impossible if the romantic partners are not settled and mature before they commit. He uses his experiences in a recent relationship to illustrate the point: "I had my money issue, and [my ex-girlfriend] had her future issue. Like goals, she didn't have any. She was lazy. She didn't go to school. So we were always fighting with each other about money and school or stuff like that." Even though this 24-year-old New York woman with a bachelor's degree believes her boyfriend "is the one for her," she insists both she and her boyfriend need to mature *on their own* before they can move to a higher level of commitment. "I feel like I have growing up to do individually and together before we're able to get married or have children." Finally, a single 25-year-old woman New Yorker, enrolled in a four year college and working full-time, declares you can only be ready for marriage after you achieve "personal goals" and are "satisfied as a person" and "stable." The young woman goes on to list what she needs, besides a fiance, before walking down the aisle. "I'm hoping that in five years, I will have completed my Bachelor's degree and my Master's. I'm hoping to be employed as a teacher . . . happy and satisfied in [my profession]. I'm hoping that I will have my house, if not one of my own, one with my mother. I'm hoping that if I'm not married, that I will at least be with somebody that I care about and with plans of marriage, but I don't necessarily have to be married. But, number one, the education goals and then two, I hope to be financially stable and content."

THE MARRIAGE MENTALITY

There is no doubt that today's young people expect to have completed personal and professional goals before they marry, but making partner and buying a home do not guarantee that the next step will be walking down the aisle. The personal and professional prerequisites for marriage must come in conjunction with the marriage mentality. The marriage mentality includes accepting the norm of exclusivity for marital relationship and embracing life-altering responsibilities the status of wife or husband demands. Within a social context where marriage is a natural part of early adulthood, as is the case for the *marriage drifters [naturalists]*, marriage flows inevitably from a relationship of a certain duration, that is, when the couple has been time tested.

In Iowa, young people marry because they have been together for a while and this is what is expected. Iowans do not seem to require the marriage mentality. When a 24-year-old Iowan with a bachelor's degree recounts how he decided to get married, he tells a typical account for his peers. "I guess [marriage] just seemed like the next step. We had been dating 7 or 8 years, all throughout high school and college, so it pretty much just felt natural. It was the next thing to do I guess you know I pretty much knew that she was the person that I wanted to spend the rest of my life with so I guess that was the next step that's the last step you can take."

In contrast, a 27-year-old New Yorker with a vocational certificate who now feels ready for marriage, describes the transformation as an internal change she recognizes in herself. "I want to be married. Lately, I've been thinking, 'Oh, I want to get married.' I never used to think about that. You know what it is, I've changed my mentality. It's family, you know, before it used to be, 'I don't care if I leave my boyfriend, that's fine.' Whatever. Now it's changed. I want to have a family. I want to have kids. I want that. I want to get married, like in a church."

According to a single 25-year-old New Yorker enrolled in a four year college, who says he would like to marry if he "finds the right person," the major obstacle to more serious relationships and ultimately marriage is that he does not "see himself old" and settled. He insists, "I want to enjoy life. There's people I know that are married. They don't really feel happy because when you're married you can't do that much."

Others say they put off marriage because it is such a momentous and permanent choice. In the words of a single 27-year-old New York professional "You can't rush into marriage." He continues, "I'm a little older and things are different, but financially, I'm not ready. And mentally, there's days when I feel like I could and days when I feel like I'd rather be single. . . . Not in the sense that I want to go out and play around and stuff. I feel like I don't want to come home to a wife."

Here a 25-year-old San Diego woman with a GED and some Naval experience, describes the pitfalls of getting married before each partner is truly ready. This young wife and mother recounts how she and her husband recently separated because while she has embraced the marriage mentality, her husband has not.

> I was 21 and he was 18 [when we got married], so he's still very immature. . . . Yeah, and like I said, [for] my first pregnancy I was alone, so I expected him [to be different and] to be there 24/7, you know. You see in the TV and all the movies, [the men] are always there, so that's what I expected, and he wasn't [. . .] And he played a lot, and he's admitted it now. He was really into his sports. He was really into basketball, and doing the single guy thing still, which is what he did a lot. . . . I was in that marriage mentality. I already had been a mother for three years. I wanted a husband. I wanted to be settled. I was tired of dating and going from guy to guy, you know, I wanted a father for my daughter. So, the fact that it wasn't like that it was a very very rocky. We actually have only been living together [...] since October cause he moved out.

The willingness to make such a commitment is forged by a process of individual development and interpersonal change that produces a readiness for the sacrifices required for marriage and family building. This attitude comes slowly to young adults in New York and perhaps especially to men.

Two elements of relationships couples struggle to come to terms with are exclusivity and the balance of power. Men complain about women who will not allow them to indulge in the occasional night out or who force them to stop spending money on things for themselves. When men explain their ambivalence towards relationships, they frame their uncertainty in an unwillingness to give up the self-centered ways of bachelordom and settle down. A 23-year-old, college educated New York man tells us that the pressure he feels from his girlfriend is the age-old battle between the sexes.

> That's how [. . .] most women operate. They need to settle down and a man needs to run around. I don't have an issue settling down -well, I do . . . I wish that [. . . .] she didn't have her biological clock ticking and 'cause she and I understand [...] that it's not good to

> have children after thirty . . . but I don't want children before thirty, but probably, you know, if I'm going to stay with her, it's going to have to be a decision that I'm gonna have to make. . . . So it's hard, and it's something that needs to work itself out in the next couple of years, if we are to be together. There's obviously pressure for marriage. . . . She says there's no pressure for marriage, but there will be . . .

For this 23-year-old New Yorker in law school there is growing tension between him and his longtime girlfriend over the way he spends his free time. "There's a lot of issues regarding female friends I have at law school and stuff of that nature. It's quite understandable, I mean, I see where she's coming from." A 25-year-old New York man enrolled in a four year college blames a recent break up on the fact that his girlfriend was too demanding of his time. "The kind of person I am, I'm kind of independent. She kind of wanted to see me all the time. It's like smothering, I guess, is the way I feel. I want to have my own freedom; I want to have my own time." A 26-year-old newlywed in San Diego, who works as an auto technician, echoes this view when he describes his struggle to adjust to married life. "[When I got married], I lost my privacy that I used to have before. It's not always about me no more. You know, it's not. I just can't think only about myself now, you know, I can't be selfish no more. I have to think of her."

For women though, they fight against a sense that they will lose themselves in marriage. A 26-year-old high school graduate from San Diego blames the problems in her relationship on her estranged husband's controlling behavior. "You know, I mean I had a rough time with him. I mean, he's very overprotective and possessive. He wouldn't let me do whatever I want. He's just like my dad when I was a teenager living at home. He'd give me curfew, you know, check the time when I was coming home. Just calling me constantly. He don't trust me. Even when I come home to visit my mom and dad, he would call there. . . . I didn't like that."

For a 29-year-old teacher's assistant and single mother in Minnesota, the problem in her current relationship with her youngest child's father is that he expects her to be "cave womanish." "I have my place and duties and he has his, he truly believes he's supposed to be the breadwinner and I shouldn't work. I don't know why men do that, but it seems like it's a possessive thing. He's not that bad but he's not that good either. He could work on it a little more." A married 29-year-old white housewife from Minnesota remembers how her former boyfriend's despotic behavior destroyed their relationship. "I could not even go to the bathroom without him at the door. . . . I was physically abused by him, I went through hell and back because of him." She continues, "When you are trapped in a relationship 24-7, and they have that control and that power over you, you don't know who you are, you are what they want you to become. And until you've had enough or until you've had that glimmer of hope that there is that hope out there again, you can't do anything. You're literally frozen in here. I know what it's like to be frozen in here, and I hate it."

Even though men and women worry about power dynamics within marriage, women frame their anxieties of power in terms of being dominated and men worry about not being allowed to be "selfish." Thus, young couples are trying to achieve the delicate balance between a commitment to the collectivity and a hard earned struggle to preserve an individual identity that will be respected and preserved in the union. Cherlin refers to the increasing importance of self within modern American marriage as the *individualized marriage* (Cherlin 2004: 852). In this respect, the ideal marriage does not embody the old formula of "one plus one equals one" but a new model that could be described as "one plus one equals three: you, me, and us."

MAKING A COMMITMENT

Another element of the *marriage planner* view is the way today's young adults understand making a commitment as an on-going effort in which romantic partners come to think of one another as us, rather than simply you and me. It must be achieved by gaining intimate knowledge of one's partner, experiencing decisions and setbacks together, learning to communicate and develop a sense of mutual trust, and, acquiring a sense that their relationship has a kind of inevitability, that is they are the "right person" for one another. Given that relationships gradually evolve over an extended period of time; in our interviews young people describe cohabitation, not as a marriage-substitute but rather an intermediate phase—a dress rehearsal of sorts—for couples working towards a marriage's absolute commitment.[4]

A cohabitating 23-year-old college graduate from San Diego describes the changes in a relationship that seems to be inching in the direction of marriage. Even though the practical concerns of saving time and money pushed this couple to cohabit, the young woman says the pair moved in together because they were "ready" for what she regards as a new phase in the relationship. Indeed, she ranks this relationship as the most marriage-worthy precisely because "He's probably the person I've been with the longest." Even though there are no specific plans to wed at this juncture, the woman insists this is only because she and her boyfriend do not want to get married "at this point."

This 30-year-old college educated New York woman also feels ready to live with, but not marry, her current boyfriend. Though she describes marriage as a label, it is a label, she says, she wants for herself at some point in the future. She explains, "I wouldn't know how to be married or not, it's like a label to me. It's something I want to do, but I don't necessarily know if it would make our relationship stronger or better. At this point, I would just like to live together, then we could spend more time together and that would be the best thing. I think I'd be terrified about getting married at this point. [But] I want to be married and this is the closest I would say I've ever been to wanting to be married."

The most striking examples of how *marriage planners* see commitment as an evolving process may be among the unmarried parents we interviewed. During the 1950s, only one in 20 children were born to single parents, today the number is one in three. Unmarried parents' slow and difficult march towards marriage brings to life the unique challenge such couples face (Edin 2000; Edin, Kefalas, and Reed 2004, Edin and Kefalas 2005). When childbearing occurs outside of marriage, young people recognize that parents ought to want to stay together for the sake of a child (Edin, Kefalas, and Reed 2004; Edin and Kefalas 2005). But, changing norms—specifically the fear of divorce and the declining stigmatization of nonmarital childbearing—have made the shotgun wedding a thing of the past.

For this 24-year-old high school graduate from San Diego, there is a growing sense that he and the mother of his children should be married, and yet, he tells us he still does not feel ready, even though it is the children who are pressuring their parents to wed.

> [Marriage], it's somewhat important . . . it's somewhat important [because] now the children want to know why [we're] not married. And explaining to them, and making sure that you plant that right seed in your child's mind that they can understand why, it's more challenging, more and more complicated. And it's also somewhat important. Because again, you want to show them that I love your mom this much. That we need to be married. So that when they grow up, they understand that that was important, as well. And not grow up living with the person that they're living with or having relationships, that their relationships, and that they're actually having something solid, and something more, more pure. More, I don't know. Just something that just means more than just being together. . . . I've gone through these many years and not been married. And you know, it hasn't been all that important. But, you know, there comes a time and a point where, you know, that decision has to be made.

When he says how marriage "hasn't been all that important," his words demonstrate the widespread sense that marriage's practical significance has declined. At the same, its symbolic role has expanded, even among the most marriage wary, marriage "is more than just being together." (Cherlin 2004, Edin and Kefalas 2005)

To a 23-year-old first generation immigrant living in San Diego and attending a four year college while working full-time who is also living with the mother of his child, there is no need to rush into a marriage for the sake of appearances. He says, "Marriage is something you earn. . . . If [she] graduates and [I] graduate, you can start working and we can afford [a wedding] and that's when you get married. It's not just cause we have a child and all of a sudden we need to go out and do it." Even though this single 22-year-old New York man enrolled in a four year college sees himself getting married in the future, he does not believe marriage is necessary for being a responsible parent "I can't see myself at the church with a suit and all that. But I can see myself with some person for life, you know. I don't think you have to [be married] to be parents cause marriage, nowadays, it's just a piece of paper."

For a cohabitating 25-year-old New York woman with an associate's degree, who has been with the father of her child for five years, marriage will only come once the couple has some economic security. "Actually, from my family, I was getting pressure [to get married], but I just didn't like feed into it 'cause we weren't ready, even though we had a child, but, we weren't ready to get married. Financially we couldn't deal with it 'cause we were still living at my mother's house when we had our son, so, I just couldn't see the need for anybody to approach us to get married, we are planning on doing it, so whenever we're ready, we'll do it. RT: How long have you been engaged for, like officially? R: Five years, (laugh)."

A 24-year-old woman enrolled in community college in San Diego who has been living with her boyfriend for seven years wants to get married. She and her boyfriend, who have a daughter, have broken up, reconciled, gotten engaged, and yet there is still no wedding date. As the years wear on, she insists the pair will only wed when she is truly confident that they are ready to make a lasting commitment.

> I'm hoping [we get married]. I don't know. It depends on how everything turns out. I don't know, I don't know where we're going. I mean like we, I had pretty much almost broken it off with him last year. I mean, we were, I mean like I had him out of the house and everything. It's like, I mean, we've been together seven years in January . . . January 29th. And I mean, it was just like to the point where I don't know what he's doing, I don't know where he wants us to go. You know? And I'm thinking about it and stuff like that. And I think about it a lot. It's like, I don't know if he's just afraid that he's going to be all alone. . . . It's just like some days I feel like [a proposal] was forced out of him, you know? Kind of like I [made him do it]. So I haven't decided yet . . . I just want to make sure that like, you know, he really means it. That it's something he really wants to do. Or if was just like something to keep me from going away, you know?

A 24-year-old San Diego woman, with some post secondary experience and a six year old son describes the reasons she chose not to become engaged to her child's father. Although she was with the father of her child for two years, his proposals—which never included a ring–made her uncertain about his intentions. To her way of thinking, it is not enough to "just ask" for a woman's hand. His casual attitude towards an engagement, failure to purchase a ring, and penchant for the bachelor lifestyle gives her pause.

> He'[d] asked me twice, but I thought it was a joke. Because you just don't ask. [And anyway], my son's father, he still liked hanging out with his friends. He still liked the girls' attention. And I just never trusted him. So that's why I never married him. I just thought it was a joke [when he proposed]. . . . He didn't do no kind of romantic thing. He just asked me. And I just said no and I guess later on that night, I guess his cousin told his mom that he was crying cause I said no. [But] he showed me no ring or nothing. You know, when someone serious, they would do it right. You just don't ask . . . so I didn't take it seriously. . . . He's like 'How could I ask?' I was like, Well, that's not the right way to ask.' . . . That's why I'm kind of iffy on seeing someone new cause like I don't want to mess that up. But then, we both need to feel the same way. It's just that right now, we have a lot of working to do on ourselves. And, you know, of course, we want a family for our son.

To her way of thinking, she is wary about walking down the aisle, not because she trivializes marriage, but because she cherishes it. Even in cases of a shared child, today's young people demand a great deal of prospective marriage partner.

There can be little doubt that fifty years ago, the social prohibitions against nonmarital childbearing would have led a young woman with a baby (or expecting one) to accept a man's marriage proposal (whether or not a ring was offered or how she was asked). The ambivalence that many young people exhibit comes, in part, from a combination of myriad alternatives to not marrying, an abiding apprehension that many marriages do not work out, an excessively high set of standards for what a successful marriage (and proposal) is and the perceived need for attaining personal maturity and having the resources to settle down and form a family.

FINDINGS: THE NEW MARRIAGE NORMS

When young adults discuss their apprehensions about marriage, their reservations rarely reveal that they reject marriage as a socially relevant institution; rather their doubts arise over whether they will be able to find the right partner establish a viable and rewarding relationship, or satisfy the economic conditions for a permanent union. Even among the most marriage wary—there was a sense that marriage could still be a possibility if the right partner and circumstances arise. Most young people hold a *marriage planner* view: they would like to do at some point in their lives, even if they are not clear if they will meet the right partner or when they will ever be prepared to make such a commitment. In other words, the high demands associated with building a successful marriage and the tremendous pressures on young people to create a degree of economic independence and establish themselves in their labor market are formidable barriers to getting married early in life.

We also find that young people have modified the ideal form of marriage, what family sociologists called the companionate model, in order to adjust to the growing reality that young people must pursue individual paths within the framework of a conjugal marriage relationship. Over and over again, young people report that they are looking for partners who fit into their lifestyles and complement their personal goals and individual interests.

While young people also insist educational attainment, economic security, maturity, and personal development must come before marriage, the achievement of these goals, however, does not guarantee that a young man or women is ready to wed. Another distinguishing feature of the *marriage planners* is that they must acquire the "marriage mentality." The "marriage mentality" refers to a young person's self-definition. With the marriage mentality, a young adult decides they are emotionally and psychically ready to take on life-altering responsibilities of becoming a husband or wife. No one who is unwilling to give up the carefree, youthful ways of the single life, we were told, has any business making the lifetime commitment required of a marriage unless, of course, they are willing to risk divorce. The more traditional external, institutional pressures to wed from the state or religious institutions that define *marriage drifters [naturalists]* have been replaced by a profoundly internal mechanism which is self-directed and contingent on other life circumstances. Of course, acquiring the marriage mentality, no doubt, also is dependent on cues provided by the decisions of friends and peers who are also struggling with similar decisions and signaling when marriage and whether marriage is an appropriate life-choice.

One of the more striking findings was the surprising de-emphasis on love and romance.[5] While young people may spend their adolescence integrating romantic relationships into friendship ones, when young adults approach the time of life when they want to wed, it is the more predictable and stable dynamics of friendship that they value in finding a partner for the lifetime commitment. Most of the young adults whom we spoke to never mentioned love or stated explicitly how they were wary about using love as a compelling reason for marriage.

CLASS, RACIAL, AND ETHNIC DIFFERENCES IN THE MEANING OF MARRIAGE

Quantitative analysis of our national samples reveals that higher levels of education delay the timing of marriage (Lichter, McLaughlin, Kephart and Landry 1992; Oppenheimer, Blossfield and Wackerow 1995; Quian and Preston 1993, Sweeney 2002, Turcotte and Goldscheider 1998). The most striking socioeconomic difference we noted in our data was the way unmarried parents discussed the role of children in their romantic relationships. While the college educated delay marriage and childbearing, less-educated young adults put off marriage, but not always children (Edin and Kefalas 2005, Furstenberg 2001, Wilson 1987). Among the parents we interviewed, the existence of shared children is not a strong incentive to get married. Even though the shotgun wedding is a thing of the past, children are not wholly irrelevant to marital decisions since a couple's ability to come together and raise their children together represents one of the most important ways couples assess their readiness for marriage (Edin, Kefalas, and Reed 2004; Edin and Kefalas 2005). Less-educated and less-affluent young people often have children in informal unions or enter cohabitation when they become pregnant in what might be called a "shotgun cohabitation," but do not typically choose marriage merely because of a pregnancy. The informal union only is converted into marriage when it is time-tested and a couple has achieved economic security (Smock, Manning, and Porter 2004; Edin and Kefalas 2005).

While the quantitative data revealed different rates of marriage among ethnic groups, the qualitative analysis failed to uncover systematic racial and ethnic variations within young people's orientations to marriage, perhaps because our ethnic sub-samples were simply too small to detect variation. We can say that most young people see marriage as a desirable goal and very few young people from any group saying they see no reason to marry.[6] For the most part, marriage is something young people would like to do at some point in their lives, even if they are not clear if they will meet the right partner or when they will feel prepared to make such a commitment.

REGIONAL DIFFERENCES: MARRIAGE DRIFTERS VERSUS MARRIAGE PLANNERS

The strongest differences in young people's expectations for marriage were by region (See McLaughlin, Lichter, and Johnston 1993). Among the overwhelmingly urban and suburban *marriage planners*, marriage must compete for a young person's time and interest. To *marriage planners*, marriage remains a life goal, but it is just one of many options that can command young people's immediate attention. The portion of the sample who grew up in rural Iowa were *marriage drifters [naturalists]* who continue to view marriage as a natural outcome of relationship that has endured over a period of time, *marriage planners*, in contrast, were far more circumspect and deliberate about their marital plans. Strong social pressures supporting young people's desire to wed during their early twenties still exist for the *marriage drifters [naturalists]* in rural Iowa.

Such regional differences originate in the way metropolitan young people's lives are filled with a complex array of activities that makes marriage just one of many things that competes for a young person's time and interest (Grazian 2005). There are also greater numbers of potential partners and less social pressure to view marriage as a necessary part of adulthood in diverse urban settings. While marriage remains a strong life objective, it is just one of many options that can command young people's immediate attention in urban, suburban settings. It is possible that marriage trends among rural youth could be attributed to their lower levels of educational attainment. However, urban and suburban working- and lower-class young people were far more likely to express views consistent with *marriage planners*, not *marriage drifters [naturalists]*, irregardless of their educational level.

CONCLUSION

Our framework for understanding these differences is consistent with survey data showing deep social class and regional differences in the timing of marriage. It is also bolstered by results of public opinion data showing that many adults no longer regard marriage as an event that needs to occur during the transition to adulthood. Instead, a growing number of young people and even adults in their parents and grandparents generation think of marriage as something that takes place after other transitions have occurred. This is markedly different from the way that adulthood was constructed at the middle of the last century when marriage was the mainspring of adult transitions and occurred, at least for most women and many men, at the time that they left the natal household (Furstenberg et. al. 2004, Fussell and Furstenberg 2004). The careful and meticulous testing and planning young people endure on their way to today's marriages could be seen as evidence of this generation's reverence for, not rejection of, marriage's significance (Edin and Kefalas 2005). In the words of a 29-year-old Minnesota woman with a bachelor's degree and four children "The moment we got married it changed. It changed because now it was like we knew it was a serious thing, a serious commitment and to just walk away was something you should not do quickly . . . I pretty much believe in sticking something out."

Notes

1. The Iowa Heartland Sample was created by the Network to have a rural sample for comparison. While the sample is quite diverse, it is not based on a pre-existing longitudinal youth study.
2. The survey response rate was 81 percent of students who had entered the high school as freshman. We did not seek interviews with young people who moved away and completed high school in another community or visiting foreign exchange students. We did, however, complete surveys with young people who dropped out of high and completed GEDs.
3. The Hmong were not included in our analysis because of they have a "cultural marriage" which is distinctive from state recognized unions. We have excluded such unions because they do not fall within in the bounds of conventional state marriages. Because of the varying levels of recognition for gay marriage, we have also excluded discussions of marriage among young people who identified themselves as homosexuals.

4. Kathleen **Kiernan** (2002) refers to a society that sees cohabitation as a rehearsal, but not yet a substitute for marriage as "stage two." In Smock and Gupta (2002) the authors analyze marriage rates among cohabiting couples and contend that the declining rates of marriage among these partnerships demonstrates how American society is somewhere in between Kiernan's stage two and stage three, a society in which cohabitation is a socially recognized alternative to marriage. Stage Three societies include The Netherlands, Denmark, and Sweden.
5. It is interesting to note that Coontz finds that contemporary marriage places a very high degree of emphasis on romantic love, but in this sample of younger people (many of whom have yet to wed), there was a striking caution about the role of love in marriage.
6. The strongest rejections of marriage came from a handful of African Americans in the New York sample.

Bibliography

Anderson, Elijah. 1999. *Code of the Street: Decency, Violence, and the Moral Life of the Inner City.* New York: W.W. Norton.

Axinn, William and Arland Thornton. 2000. "The Transformation in the Meaning of Marriage." In *The Ties that Bind: Perspectives on Marriage and Cohabitation*, ed. Linda Waite, 147-65. New York: Aldine de Gruyter.

Burgess, Ernest and Howard Locke. 1945. *The Family: From Institution to Companionship.* New York: American Book.

Cherlin, Andrew. 2004. "The Deinstutionalization of Marriage." *Journal of Marriage and the Family.* Volume 66 (4), November 2004.

Coontz, Stephanie. 2005. *Marriage, a History: From Obedience to Intimacy, or How Love Conquered Marriage.* New York: Viking.

Edin, Kathryn and Maria Kefalas. 2005. *Promises I Can Keep: Why Poor Women Put Motherhood Before Marriage.* Berkeley and Los Angeles: University of California Press.

Edin, Kathryn, Maria Kefalas, and Joanna Reed, "A Peek Inside the Black Box: What Marriage Means to Low-Income Unmarried Parents," Symposium on the Future of Marriage and Cohabitation, *Journal of Marriage and Family*, Volume 66 (4), November 2004.

Ellwood, David and Christopher Jencks. 2001. "The Spread of Single-Parent Families in the United States since 1960." Cambridge, MA: John F. Kennedy School of Government, Harvard University.

——. 2002. "The Growing Differences in Family Structure: What do We Know? Where Do We Look For Answers?" Cambridge, MA: John F. Kennedy School of Government, Harvard University.

Furstenberg, Frank. 2001. *The Fading Dream: Prospects for Marriage in the Inner City. In Problem of the Century: Racial Stratification in the United States*, Eds. Elijah Anderson and Douglas Massey, 224-246. New York: Russell Sage Foundation.

Furstenberg, Frank and Andrew Cherlin. 1991. *Divided Families: What Happens to Children When Parents Part.* Cambridge, MA: Harvard University Press.

Furstenberg, Frank, John Modell and Douglas Strong. 1978. "The timing of marriage in the transition to adulthood: Continuity and change, 1860-1975." *The American Journal of Sociology*, 84:Suppl:S120-150.

Fussell, Elizabeth and Frank Furstenberg. 2004. "Race, Nativity, and Gender Differences in the Transition to Adulthood in the 20th Century." In *On the Frontier of Adulthood: Theory, Research, and Public Policy.* Eds. Richard Settersten, Frank Furstenberg, and Ruben Rumbaut. Chicago: University of Chicago Press.

Gibson, Christina, Kathryn Edin, and Sara McLanahan. "High Hopes, but Even Higher Expectations: The Retreat from Marriage Among Low-Income Couples." *Journal of Marriage and Family.*

Giordano, Peggy, Wendy Manning, and Monica Longmore. Forthcoming. The Impact of Adolescents' Romantic and Sexual Relationships on Early Adulthood, Eds. Crouter, Ann C. and Alan Booth. *Romance and Sex in Adolescence and Emerging Adulthood: Risks and Opportunities.* Mahwah, NJ: Earlbaum Associates.

Goldstein, J.R. and C. T. Kenney. 2001. "Marriage Delayed or Forgone? New Cohort Forecasts of First Marriage for U.S. Women," *American Sociological Review*, 66, 505-519.

Grazian, David. 2005. "Women at Night: Gender, Emerging Adulthood, and the Experience of Urban Nightlife," Unpublished Manuscript, Presented at MacArthur Network on Adult Transitions, August 5, 2004, Philadelphia, PA.

Harknett, Kristen and Sara McLanahan. "Forsaking All Others: The Role of Marriage Market Characteristics in Explaining Race/Ethnic differences in Marriage, *American Sociological Review*. 69: 790-811.

Kiernan, Kathleen. 2002. "Cohabitation in Western Europe: Trends, Issues and Implications." Eds. Ann Crouter and Allan Booth. *Just Living Together: Implications of Cohabitation on Families, Children and Social Policy*. Mahwah, NJ: Earlbaum: 3-31.

Lichter, Daniel T., Diane K. McLaughlin, George Kephart and David J. Landry. 1992. "Race and the Retreat from Marriage: A Shortage of Marriageable Men?" *American Sociological Review* 57:781-99.

Manning, Wendy and Pamela Smock. 1995. "Why Marry? Race and the Transition to Marriage among Cohabitors." *Demography* 32: 509-20.

McLauglin, Diane K. and Daniel Lichter. 1997. "Poverty and the Marital Behavior of Young Women." *Journal of the Marriage and the Family* 59: 582-94.

McLauglin, Diane K., Daniel Lichter and G.M. Johnston (1993). "Some Women Marry Young: Transitions to First Marriage in Metropolitan and Nonmetropolitan Areas." *Journal of Marriage and the Family* 55(4):827-838.

McLanahan, Sara. "Diverging Destinies: How Children Fare Under the Second Demographic Transition." *Demography*. 41 (4): 607-627.

Maclanahan, Sara and Gary Sandefur. 1994. *Growing Up With a Single Parent: What Helps, What Hurts*. Cambridge, MA: Harvard University Press.

Oppenheimer, Valerie, Hans Peter. Blossfield, and A. Wackerow. 1995. United States of America. Ed. Hans Peter. Blossfield. *The New Role of Women: Family Formation in Modern Societies*. Boulder, CO: Westview Press: 150-179.

Popenoe, David and Barbara Dafoe Whitehead. 2001. "Who Wants to Marry a Soul Mate?" In *The State of Our Unions: 2001* (National Marriage Project pp 6-16) (http://marriage.rutgers.edu/Publications/SOOU /NMPAR2001.pdf)

Quian, Zhenchao and Samuel Preston. 1993. Changes in the American Family, 1972-1987: Availability and Forces of Attraction by Age and Education, *American Sociological Review* 58: 482-495.

Roussel, L. 1989. *La Famille Incertaine*. Paris: Editions Odile Jacob.

Smock, Pamela. 2000. "Cohabitation in the United State: An Appraisal of Research Themes, Findings and Implications." *Annual Review of Sociology* 26: 1-20.

——. 2004. The Wax and Wane of Marriage: Prospects for Marriage in the 21st Century. *Journal of Family and Marriage* 66: 966-979.

Smock, Pamela, Wendy Manning, and Meredith Porter. 2005. "Everything's There Except the Money: How Money Shapes Decisions to Marry Among Cohabitors." *Journal of Marriage and Family* 67:

Smock, Pamela and S. Gupta. 2002. "Cohabitation in Contemporary North America." In *"Just Living Together": Implications of Cohabitation on Families, Children, and Social Policy*. Eds. Allan Booth and Ann Crouter. Mahwah, NJ: Erlbaum: 53-84.

Sweeney, Megan. M. 2002. "Two Decades of Family Change: The Shifting Economic Foundations of Marriage." *American Sociological Review* 67:132-47.

Thornton, Arland, and Linda Young DeMarco. 2001. "Four Decades of Attitudes toward Family Issues in the United States: The 1960s through the 1990s." *Journal of Marriage and the Family* 64: 100.

Waller, Maureen and Sara McLanahan. "'His' and 'Her' Marriage Expectations: Determinants and Consequences." *Journal of Marriage and the Family*. 67: 53-67.

Waite, Linda and Maggie Gallagher. 2000. *The Case for Marriage: Why Married People are Happier, Healthier, and Better off Financially*. New York: Doubleday.

Wilson, James Q. 2002. *The Marriage Problem: How Our Culture Has Weakened Families*. New York: Harper Collins.

Wilson, William J. 1987. *The Truly Disadvantaged: The Inner City, The Underclass, and Public Policy*. Chicago: The University of Chicago Press.

READING 14

American Marriage in the Early Twenty-First Century

Andrew J. Cherlin

The decline of American marriage has been a favorite theme of social commentators, politicians, and academics over the past few decades. Clearly the nation has seen vast changes in its family system—in marriage and divorce rates, cohabitation, childbearing, sexual behavior, and women's work outside the home. Marriage is less dominant as a social institution in the United States than at any time in history. Alternative pathways through adulthood—childbearing outside of marriage, living with a partner without ever marrying, living apart but having intimate relationships—are more acceptable and feasible than ever before. But as the new century begins, it is also clear that despite the jeremiads, marriage has not faded away. In fact, given the many alternatives to marriage now available, what may be more remarkable is not the decline in marriage but its persistence. What is surprising is not that fewer people marry, but rather that so *many* still marry and that the desire to marry remains widespread. Although marriage has been transformed, it is still meaningful. In this [reading] I review the changes in American marriage, discuss their causes, compare marriage in the United States with marriage in the rest of the developed world, and comment on how the transformation of marriage is likely to affect American children in the early twenty-first century.

CHANGES IN THE LIFE COURSE

To illuminate what has happened to American marriage, I begin by reviewing the great demographic changes of the past century, including changes in age at marriage, the share of Americans ever marrying, cohabitation, nonmarital births, and divorce.

Recent Trends

Figure 14.1 shows the median age at marriage—the age by which half of all marriages occur—for men and women from 1890 to 2002. In 1890 the median age was relatively high, about twenty-six for men and twenty-two for women. During the first half of the twentieth century the typical age at marriage dropped—gradually at first, and then precipitously after World War II. By the 1950s it had reached historic lows: roughly twenty-three for men and twenty for women. Many people still think of the 1950s as the standard by which to compare today's families, but as Figure 14.1 shows, the 1950s were the anomaly: during that decade young adults married earlier than ever before or since. Moreover, nearly all young adults—about 95 percent of whites and 88 percent of African Americans—eventually married.[1] During the 1960s, however, the median age at marriage

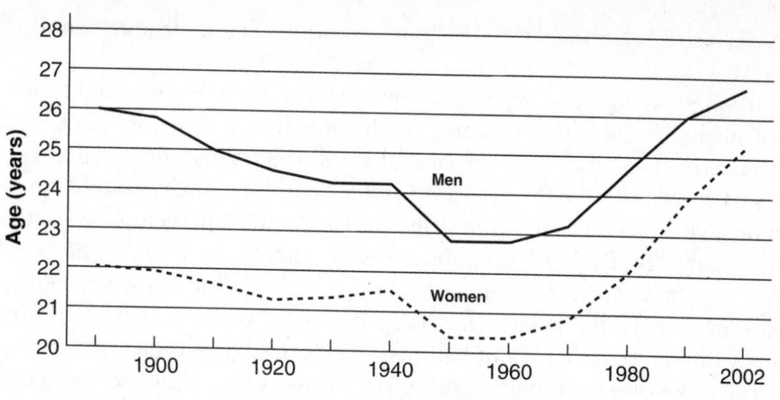

FIGURE 14.1 ***Median Age at Marriage, 1890–2002***

Source: U.S. Bureau of the Census, "Estimated Median Age at First Marriage, by Sex: 1890 to Present," 2003, www.census.gov/population/socdemo/hh-fam/tabMS-2.pdf (accessed July 23, 2004).

began to climb, returning to and then exceeding that prevalent at the start of the twentieth century. Women, in particular, are marrying substantially later today than they have at any time for which data are available.

What is more, unmarried young adults are leading very different lives today than their earlier counterparts once did. The late-marrying young women and men of the early 1900s typically lived at home before marriage or paid for room and board in someone else's home. Even when they were courting, they lived apart from their romantic interests and, at least among women, the majority abstained from sexual intercourse until they were engaged or married. They were usually employed, and they often turned over much of their paycheck to their parents to help rear younger siblings. Few went to college; most had not even graduated from high school. As recently as 1940, only about one-third of adults in their late twenties had graduated from high school and just one in sixteen had graduated from college.[2]

Today's unmarried young adults are much more likely to be living independently, in their own apartments. Five out of six young adults graduate from high school, and about one-third complete college.[3] They are more likely than their predecessors to spend their wages on themselves. Their sexual and intimate lives are also very different from those of earlier generations. The vast majority of unmarried young adults have had sexual intercourse. In fact, most women who married during the 1990s first had intercourse five years or more before marrying.[4]

About half of young adults live with a partner before marrying. Cohabitation is far more common today than it was at any time in the early- or mid-twentieth century (although it was not unknown among the poor and has been a part of the European family system in past centuries). Cohabitation today is a diverse, evolving phenomenon. For some people, it is a prelude to marriage or a trial marriage. For others, a series of cohabiting relationships may be a long-term substitute for marriage. (Thirty-nine percent of cohabiters in 1995 lived with children of one of the partners.) It is still rare in the

United States for cohabiting relationships to last long—about half end, through marriage or a breakup, within a year.[5]

Despite the drop in marriage and the rise in cohabitation, there has been no explosion of nonmarital births in the United States. Birth rates have fallen for unmarried women of all reproductive ages and types of marital status, including adolescents. But because birth rates have fallen faster for married women than for unmarried women, a larger share of women who give birth are unmarried. In 1950, only 4 percent of all births took place outside of marriage. By 1970, the figure was 11 percent; by 1990, 28 percent; and by 2003, 35 percent. In recent years, then, about one-third of all births have been to unmarried women—and that is the statistic that has generated the most debate.[6] Of further concern to many observers is that about half of all unmarried first-time mothers are adolescents. Academics, policymakers, and private citizens alike express unease about the negative consequences of adolescent childbearing, both for the parents and for the children, although whether those consequences are due more to poverty or to teen childbearing per se remains controversial.

When people think of nonmarital or "out-of-wedlock" childbearing, they picture a single parent. Increasingly, however, nonmarital births are occurring to cohabiting couples—about 40 percent according to the latest estimate.[7] One study of unmarried women giving birth in urban hospitals found that about half were living with the fathers of their children. Couples in these "fragile families," however, rarely marry. One year after the birth of the child, only 15 percent had married, while 26 percent had broken up.[8]

Marriage was not an option for lesbians and gay men in any U.S. jurisdiction until Massachusetts legalized same-sex marriage in 2004. Cohabitation, however, is common in this group. In a 1992 national survey of sexual behavior, 44 percent of women and 28 percent of men who said they had engaged in homosexual sex in the previous year reported that they were cohabiting.[9] The Census Bureau, which began collecting statistics on same-sex partnerships in 1990, does not directly ask whether a person is in a romantic same-sex relationship; rather, it gives people the option of saying that a housemate is an "unmarried partner" without specifying the nature of the partnership. Because some people may not wish to openly report a same-sex relationship to the Census Bureau, it is hard to determine how reliable these figures are. The bureau reports, however, that in 2000, 600,000 households were maintained by same-sex partners. A substantial share—33 percent of female partnerships and 22 percent of male partnerships—reported the presence of children of one or both of the partners.[10]

As rates of entry into marriage were declining in the last half of the twentieth century, rates of exit via divorce were increasing—as they have been at least since the Civil War era. At the beginning of the twentieth century, about 10 percent of all marriages ended in divorce, and the figure rose to about one-third for marriages begun in 1950.[11] But the rise was particularly sharp during the 1960s and 1970s, when the likelihood that a married couple would divorce increased substantially. Since the 1980s the divorce rate has remained the same or declined slightly. According to the best estimate, 48 percent of American marriages, at current rates, would be expected to end in divorce within twenty years.[12] A few percent more would undoubtedly end in divorce after that. So it is accurate to say that unless divorce risks change, about half of all marriages today

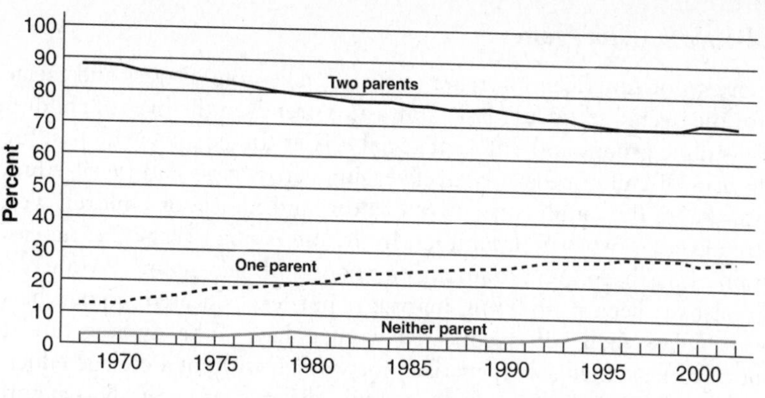

FIGURE 14.2 ***Living Arrangements of U.S. Children, 1968–2002***
Source: U.S. Bureau of the Census, "Living Arrangements of U.S. Children under 18 Years Old: 1960 to Present," 2003, www.census.gov/population/socdemo/hh-fam/tabCH-1.pdf (accessed July 23, 2004).

would end in divorce. (There are important class and racial-ethnic differences, which I will discuss below.)

The combination of more divorce and a greater share of births to unmarried women has increased the proportion of children who are not living with two parents. Figure 14.2 tracks the share of children living, respectively, with two parents, with one parent, and with neither parent between 1968 and 2002. It shows a steady decline in the two-parent share and a corresponding increase in the one-parent share. In 2002, 69 percent of children were living with two parents, including families where one biological (or adoptive) parent had remarried. Not counting step- or adoptive families, 62 percent, according to the most recent estimate in 1996, were living with two biological parents.[13] Twenty-seven percent of American children were living with one parent; another 4 percent, with neither parent.[14] Most in the latter group were living with relatives, such as grandparents.

Where do all these changes leave U.S. marriage patterns and children's living arrangements in the early twenty-first century? As demographers have noted, many of the above trends have slowed over the past decade, suggesting a "quieting" of family change.[15] Marriage remains the most common living arrangement for raising children. At any one time, most American children are being raised by two parents. Marriage, however, is less dominant in parents' and children's lives than it once was. Children are more likely to experience life in a single-parent family, either because they are born to unmarried mothers or because their parents divorce. And children are more likely to experience instability in their living arrangements as parents form and dissolve marriages and partnerships. Although children are less likely to lose a parent through death today than they once were, the rise in nonmarital births and in divorce has more than compensated for the decline in parental death.[16] From the adult perspective, the overall drop in birth rates and the increases in nonmarital childbearing and divorce mean that, at any one time, fewer adults are raising children than in the past.

Class and Racial-Ethnic Divergence

To complete this portrait of American marriage one must take note of class and racial-ethnic variations, for the overall statistics mask contrasting trends in the lives of children from different racial-ethnic groups and different social classes. In fact, over the past few decades, the family lives of children have been diverging across class and racial-ethnic lines.[17] A half-century ago, the family structures of poor and non-poor children were similar: most children lived in two-parent families. In the intervening years, the increase in single-parent families has been greater among the poor and near-poor.[18] Women at all levels of education have been postponing marriage, but less-educated women have postponed childbearing less than better-educated women have. The divorce rate in recent decades appears to have held steady or risen for women without a college education but fallen for college-educated women.[19] As a result, differences in family structure according to social class are much more pronounced than they were fifty years ago.

Consider the share of mothers who are unmarried. Throughout the past half-century, single motherhood has been more common among women with less education than among well-educated women. But the gap has grown over time. In 1960, 14 percent of mothers in the bottom quarter of the educational distribution were unmarried, as against 4.5 percent of mothers in the top quarter—a difference of 9.5 percentage points. By 2000, the corresponding figures were 43 percent for the less-educated mothers and 7 percent for the more educated—a gap of 36 percentage points.[20] Sara McLanahan argues that societal changes such as greater opportunities for women in the labor market, a resurgence of feminist ideology, and the advent of effective birth control have encouraged women to invest in education and careers. Those who make these investments tend to delay childbearing and marriage, and they are more attractive in the marriage market.[21] Put another way, women at the top and bottom of the educational distribution may be evolving different reproductive strategies. Among the less educated, early childbearing outside of marriage has become more common, as the ideal of finding a stable marriage and then having children has weakened, whereas among the better educated, the strategy is to delay childbearing and marriage until after investing in schooling and careers.

One result of these developments has been growth in better-educated, dual-earner married-couple families. Since the 1970s these families have enjoyed much greater income growth than have breadwinner-homemaker families or single-parent families. What we see today, then, is a growing group of more fortunate children who tend to live with two parents whose incomes are adequate or ample and a growing group of less fortunate children who live with financially pressed single parents. Indeed, both groups at the extremes—the most and the least fortunate children—have been expanding over the past few decades, while the group of children in the middle has been shrinking.[22]

The family lives of African American children have also been diverging from those of white non-Hispanic children and, to a lesser extent, Hispanic children. African American family patterns were influenced by the institution of slavery, in which marriage was not legal, and perhaps by African cultural traditions, in which extended families had more influence and power compared with married couples. As a result, the proportion of African American children living with single parents has been greater than that of white children for a century or more.[23] Nevertheless, African American women married at an earlier age than did white women through the first half of the twentieth century.[24]

But since the 1960s, the decline of marriage as a social institution has been more pronounced among African Americans than among whites. The best recent estimates suggest that at current rates only about two-thirds of African American women would be expected ever to marry.[25] Correspondingly, the share of African American children born outside of marriage has risen to 69 percent.[26] In fact, about three-fifths of African American children may never live in a married-couple family while growing up, as against one-fifth of white children.[27] The greater role of extended kin in African American families may compensate for some of this difference, but the figures do suggest a strikingly reduced role of marriage among African Americans.

The family patterns of the Hispanic population are quite diverse. Mexican Americans have higher birth rates than all other major ethnic groups, and a greater share of Mexican American births than of African American births is to married women.[28] Moreover, Mexican American families are more likely to include extended kin.[29] Consequently, Mexican Americans have more marriage-based, multigenerational households than do African Americans. Puerto Ricans, the second largest Hispanic ethnic group and the most economically disadvantaged, have rates of nonmarital childbearing second only to African Americans.[30] But Puerto Ricans, like many Latin Americans, have a tradition of consensual unions, in which a man and woman live together as married but without approval of the church or a license from the state. So it is likely that more Puerto Rican "single" mothers than African American single mothers are living with partners.

EXPLAINING THE TRENDS

Most analysts would agree that both economic and cultural forces have been driving the changes in American family life over the past half-century. Analysts disagree about the relative weight of the two, but I will assume that both have been important.

Economic Influences

Two changes in the U.S. labor market have had major implications for families.[31] First, demand for workers increased in the service sector, where women had gained a foothold earlier in the century while they were shut out of manufacturing jobs. The rising demand encouraged women to get more education and drew married women into the workforce—initially, those whose children were school-aged, and later, those with younger children. Single mothers had long worked, but in 1996 major welfare reform legislation further encouraged work by setting limits on how long a parent could receive public assistance. The increase in women's paid work, in turn, increased demand for child care services and greatly increased the number of children cared for outside their homes.

The second work-related development was the decline, starting in the 1970s, in job opportunities for men without a college education. The flip side of the growth of the service sector was the decline in manufacturing. As factory jobs moved overseas and industrial productivity increased through automated equipment and computer-based controls, demand fell for blue-collar jobs that high school–educated men once took in hopes of supporting their families. As a result, average wages in these jobs fell. Even during the prosperous 1990s, the wages of men without a college degree hardly rose.[32] The decline in job opportunities had two effects. It decreased the attractiveness of non-college-educated men on the marriage market—made them less "marriageable" in William Julius Wilson's terms—and thus helped drive marriage rates down among the less well educated.[33] It also undermined the single-earner "family wage system" that had been the ideal in the first half of the twentieth century and increased the incentive for wives to take paying jobs.

Cultural Developments

But economic forces, important as they were, could not have caused all the changes in family life noted above. Declines in the availability of marriageable men, for example, were not large enough to account, alone, for falling marriage rates among African Americans.[34] Accompanying the economic changes was a broad cultural shift among Americans that eroded the norms both of marriage before childbearing and of stable, lifelong bonds after marriage.

Culturally, American marriage went through two broad transitions during the twentieth century. The first was described famously by sociologist Ernest Burgess as a change "from institution to companionship."[35] In institutional marriage, the family was held together by the forces of law, tradition, and religious belief. The husband was the unquestioned head of the household. Until the late nineteenth century, husband and wife became one legal person when they married—and that person was the husband. A wife could not sue in her own name, and her husband could dispose of her property as he wished. Until 1920 women could not vote; rather, it was assumed that almost all women would marry and that their husbands' votes would represent their views. But as the forces of law and tradition weakened in the early decades of the twentieth century, the newer, companionate marriage arose. It was founded on the importance of the emotional ties between wife and husband—their companionship, friendship, and romantic love. Spouses drew satisfaction from performing the social roles of breadwinner, homemaker, and parent. After World War II, the spouses in companionate marriages, much to everyone's surprise, produced the baby boom: they had more children per family than any other generation in the twentieth century. The typical age at marriage fell to its lowest point since at least the late nineteenth century, and the share of all people who ever married rose. The decade of the 1950s was the high point of the breadwinner-homemaker, two-, three-, or even four-child family.

Starting around 1960, marriage went through a second transition. The typical age at marriage returned to, and then exceeded, the high levels of the early 1900s. Many young adults stayed single into their mid- to late twenties or even their thirties, some completing college educations and starting careers. Most women continued working for pay after they married. Cohabitation outside marriage became much more acceptable. Childbearing outside marriage became less stigmatized. The birth rate resumed its long decline and sank to an all-time low. Divorce rates rose to unprecedented levels. Same-sex partnerships found greater acceptance as well.

During this transition, companionate marriage waned as a cultural ideal. On the rise were forms of family life that Burgess had not foreseen, particularly marriages in which both husband and wife worked outside the home and single-parent families that came into being through divorce or through childbearing outside marriage. The roles of wives and husbands became more flexible and open to negotiation. And a more individualistic perspective on the rewards of marriage took root. When people evaluated how satisfied they were with their marriages, they began to think more in terms of developing their own sense of self and less in terms of gaining satisfaction through building a family and playing the roles of spouse and parent. The result was a transition from the companionate marriage to what we might call the individualized marriage.[36]

THE CURRENT CONTEXT OF MARRIAGE

To be sure, the "companionate marriage" and the "individualized marriage" are what sociologists refer to as ideal types. In reality, the distinctions between the two are less sharp than I have drawn them. Many marriages, for example, still follow the companionate ideal. Nevertheless, as a result of the economic and cultural trends noted above, marriage now exists in a very different context than it did in the past. Today it is but one among many options available to adults choosing how to shape their personal lives. More forms of marriage and more alternatives to it are socially acceptable. One may fit marriage into life in many ways: by first living with a partner, or sequentially with several partners, without explicitly considering whether to marry; by having children with one's eventual spouse or with someone else before marrying; by (in some jurisdictions) marrying someone of the same gender and building a shared marital world with few guidelines to rely on. Within marriage, roles are more flexible and negotiable, although women still do more of the household work and childrearing.

The rewards that people seek through marriage and other close relationships have also shifted. Individuals aim for personal growth and deeper intimacy through more open communication and mutually shared disclosures about feelings with their partners. They may insist on changes in a relationship that no longer provides them with individualized rewards. They are less likely than in the past to focus on the rewards gained by fulfilling socially valued roles such as the good parent or the loyal and supportive spouse. As a result of this changing context, social norms about family and personal life count for less than they did during the heyday of companionate marriage and far less than during the era of institutional marriage. Instead, personal choice and self-development loom large in people's construction of their marital careers.

But if marriage is now optional, it remains highly valued. As the practical importance of marriage has declined, its symbolic importance has remained high and may even have increased.[37] At its height as an institution in the mid-twentieth century, marriage was almost required of anyone wishing to be considered a respectable adult. Having children outside marriage was stigmatized, and a person who remained single through adulthood was suspect. But as other lifestyle options became more feasible and acceptable, the need to be married diminished. Nevertheless, marriage remains the preferred option for most people. Now, however, it is not a step taken lightly or early in young adulthood. Being "ready" to marry may mean that a couple has lived together to test their compatibility, saved for a down payment on a house, or possibly had children to judge how well they parent together. Once the foundation of adult family life, marriage is now often the capstone.

Although some observers believe that a "culture of poverty" has diminished the value of marriage among poor Americans, research suggests that the poor, the near-poor, and the middle class conceive of marriage in similar terms. Although marriage rates are lower among the poor than among the middle class, marriage as an ideal remains strong for both groups. Ethnographic studies show that many low-income individuals subscribe to the capstone view of marriage. In a study of low-income families that I carried out with several collaborators, a twenty-seven-year-old mother told an ethnographer:[38]

> I was poor all my life and so was Reginald. When I got pregnant, we agreed we would marry some day in the future because we loved each other and wanted to raise our child together. But we would not get married until we could afford to get a house and pay all the utility bills on time. I have this thing about utility bills. Our gas and electric got turned off all the time when we were growing up and we wanted to make sure that would not happen when we got married. That was our biggest worry. . . . We worked together and built up savings and then we got married. It's forever for us.

The poor, the near-poor, and the middle class also seem to view the emotional rewards of marriage in similar terms. Women of all classes value companionship in marriage: shared lives, joint childrearing, friendship, romantic love, respect, and fair treatment. For example, in a survey conducted in twenty-one cities, African Americans were as likely as non-Hispanic whites to rate highly the emotional benefits of marriage, such as friendship, sex life, leisure time, and a sense of security; and Hispanics rated these benefits somewhat higher than either group.[39] Moreover, in the "fragile families" study of unmarried low- and moderate-income couples who had just had a child together, Marcia Carlson, Sara McLanahan, and Paula England found that mothers and fathers who scored higher on a scale of relationship supportiveness were substantially more likely to be married one year later.[40] Among the items in the scale were whether the partner "is fair and willing to compromise" during a disagreement, "expresses affection or love," "encourages or helps," and does not insult or criticize. In a 2001 national survey of young adults aged twenty to twenty-nine conducted by the Gallup Organization for the National Marriage Project, 94 percent of never-married respondents agreed that "when you marry, you want your spouse to be your soul mate, first and foremost." Only 16 percent agreed that "the main purpose of marriage these days is to have children."[41]

As debates over same-sex marriage illustrate, marriage is also highly valued by lesbians and gay men. In 2003 the Massachusetts Supreme Court struck down a state law limiting marriage to opposite-sex couples, and same-sex marriage became legal in May 2004 (although opponents may eventually succeed in prohibiting it through a state constitutional amendment). Advocates for same-sex marriage argued that gay and lesbian couples should be entitled to marry so that they can benefit from the legal rights and protections that marriage brings. But the Massachusetts debate also showed the symbolic value of marriage. In response to the court's decision, the state legislature crafted a plan to enact civil unions for same-sex couples. These legally recognized unions would have given same-sex couples most of the legal benefits of marriage but would have withheld the status of being married. The court rejected this remedy, arguing that allowing civil unions but not marriage would create a "stigma of exclusion," because it would deny to same-sex couples "a status that is specially recognized in society and has significant social and other advantages." That the legislature was willing to provide legal benefits was not sufficient for the judges, nor for gay and lesbian activists, who rejected civil unions as second-class citizenship. Nor would it be enough for mainstream Americans, most of whom are still attached to marriage as a specially recognized status.

PUTTING U.S. MARRIAGE IN INTERNATIONAL PERSPECTIVE

How does the place of marriage in the family system in the United States compare with its place in the family systems of other developed nations? It turns out that marriage in the United States is quite distinctive.

A Greater Attachment to Marriage

Marriage is more prevalent in the United States than in nearly all other developed Western nations. Figure 14.3 shows the total first marriage rate for women in the United States and in six other developed nations in 1990. (Shortly after 1990, the U.S. govern-

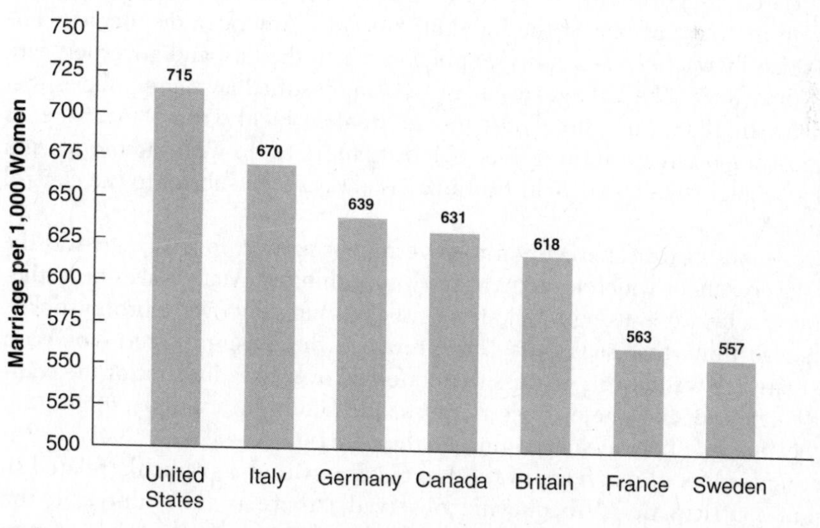

FIGURE 14.3 ***Total First Marriage Rates of Women, Selected European and English-Speaking Countries, 1990***

Sources: Alain Monnier and Catherine de Guibert-Lantoine, "The Demographic Situation of Europe and Developed Countries Overseas: An Annual Report," *Population; An English Selection* 8 (1996): 235–50; U.S. National Center for Health Statistics, "Advance Report of Final Marriage Statistics, 1989 and 1990," *Monthly Vital Statistics Report* 43, no. 12, supp. (Government Printing Office, 1995).

ment stopped collecting all the information necessary to calculate this rate.) The total first marriage rate provides an estimate of the proportion of women who will ever marry.[42] It must be interpreted carefully because it yields estimates that are too low if calculated at a time when women are postponing marriage until older ages, as they were in 1990 in most countries. Thus, all the estimates in Figure 14.3 are probably too low. Nevertheless, the total first marriage rate is useful in comparing countries at a given time point, and I have selected the nations in Figure 14.3 to illustrate the variation in this rate in the developed world. The value of 715 for the United States—the highest of any country—implies that 715 out of 1,000 women were expected to marry. Italy had a relatively high value, while France and Sweden had the lowest. In between were Britain, Canada, and Germany.

Not only is marriage stronger demographically in the United States than in other developed countries, it also seems stronger as an ideal. In the World Values Surveys conducted between 1999 and 2001, one question asked of adults was whether they agreed with the statement, "Marriage is an outdated institution." Only 10 percent of Americans agreed—a lower share than in any developed nation except Iceland. Twenty-two percent of Canadians agreed, as did 26 percent of the British, and 36 percent of the French.[43] Americans seem more attached to marriage as a norm than do citizens in other developed countries.

This greater attachment to marriage has a long history. As Alexis de Tocqueville wrote in the 1830s, "There is certainly no country in the world where the tie of marriage is more respected than in America or where conjugal happiness is more highly or worthily appreciated."[44] Historian Nancy Cott has argued that the nation's founders viewed Christian marriage as one of the building blocks of American democracy. The marriage-based family was seen as a mini-republic in which the husband governed with the consent of the wife.[45] The U.S. government has long justified laws and policies that support marriage. In 1888, Supreme Court justice Stephen Field wrote, "marriage, as creating the most important relation in life, as having more to do with the morals and civilization of a people than any other institution, has always been subject to the control of the legislature."[46]

The conspicuous historical exception to government support for marriage was the institution of slavery, under which legal marriage was prohibited. Many slaves nevertheless married informally, often using public rituals such as jumping over a broomstick.[47] Some scholars also think that slaves may have retained the kinship patterns of West Africa, where marriage was more a process that unfolded over time in front of the community than a single event.[48] The prospective husband's family, for example, might wait until the prospective wife bore a child to finalize the marriage.

The distinctiveness of marriage in the United States is also probably related to greater religious participation. Tocqueville observed, "there is no country in the world where the Christian religion retains a greater influence over the souls of men than in America."[49] That statement is still true with respect to the developed nations today: religious vitality is greatest in the United States.[50] For instance, in the World Values Surveys, 60 percent of Americans reported attending religious services at least monthly, as against 36 percent of Canadians, 19 percent of the British, and 12 percent of the French.[51] Americans look to religious institutions for guidance on marriage and family life more than do the citizens of most Western countries. Sixty-one percent of Americans agreed with the statement, "Generally speaking, do you think that the churches in your country are giving adequate answers to the problems of family life?" Only 48 percent of Canadians, 30 percent of the British, and 28 percent of the French agreed.[52]

Moreover, family policies in many European nations have long promoted births, whereas American policies generally have not. This emphasis on pronatalism has been especially prominent in France, where the birth rate began to decline in the 1830s, decades before it did in most other European nations.[53] Since then, the French government has been concerned about losing ground in population size to potential adversaries such as Germany.[54] (The Germans felt a similar concern, which peaked in the Nazis' pronatalist policies of the 1930s and early 1940s.)[55] As a result, argues one historian, French family policy has followed a "parental logic" that places a high priority on supporting parents with young children—even working wives and single parents.[56] These policies have included family allowances prorated by the number of children, maternity insurance, and maternity leave with partial wage replacement. In contrast, policies in Britain and the United States followed a "male breadwinner logic" of supporting married couples in which the husband worked outside the home and the wife did not.[57] Pronatalist pressure has never been strong in the United States, even though the decline in the U.S. birth rate started in the early 1800s, because of the nation's openness to increasing its population through immigration.

More Transitions Into and Out of Marriage

In addition to its high rate of marriage, the United States has one of the highest rates of divorce of any developed nation. Figure 14.4 displays the total divorce rate in 1990 for the countries shown in Figure 14.3. The total divorce rate, which provides an estimate of the number of marriages that would end in divorce, has limits similar to those of the total marriage rate but is likewise useful in international comparisons.[58] Figure 14.4 shows that the United States had a total divorce rate of 517 divorces per 1,000 marriages, with just over half of all marriages ending in divorce. Sweden had the second highest total divorce rate, and other Scandinavian countries had similar levels. The English-speaking countries of Britain and Canada were next, followed by France and Germany. Italy had a very low level of predicted divorce.

Both entry into and exit from marriage are indicators of what Robert Schoen has called a country's "marriage metabolism": the number of marriage- and divorce-related transitions that adults and their children undergo.[59] Figure 14.5, which presents the sum of the total first marriage rate and the total divorce rate, shows that the United States has by far the highest marriage metabolism of any of the developed countries in question.[60] Italy, despite its high marriage rate, has the lowest metabolism because of its very low divorce rate. Sweden, despite its high divorce rate, has a lower metabolism than the United States because of its lower marriage rate. In other words, what makes the United States most distinctive is the combination of high marriage and high divorce rates—which implies that Americans typically experience more transitions into and out of marriages than do people in other countries.

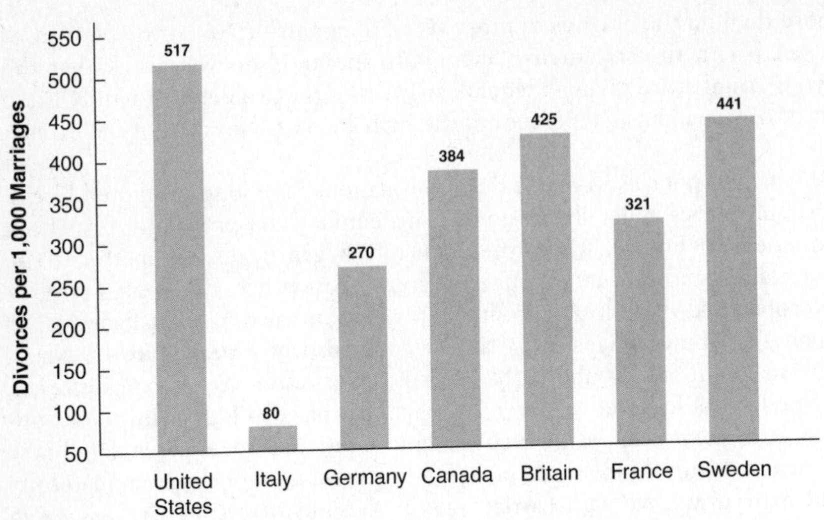

FIGURE 14.4 ***Total Divorce Rates, Selected European and English-Speaking Countries, 1990***

Sources: Monnier and de Guibert-Lantoine, "The Demographic Situation of Europe and the Developed Countries Overseas" (see Figure 14.3); U.S. National Center for Health Statistics, "Advance Report of Final Divorce Statistics, 1989 and 1990," *Monthly Vital Statistics Report* 43, no. 9, supp. (Government Printing Office, 1995).

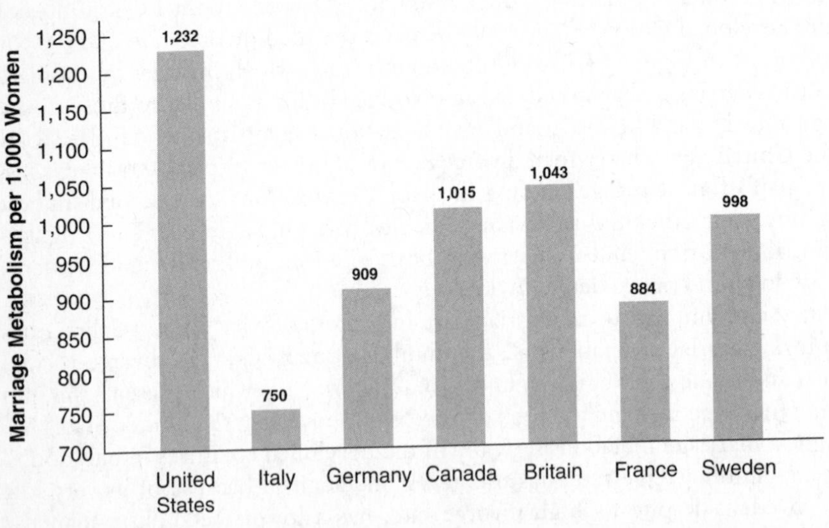

FIGURE 14.5 ***Marriage Metabolism, Selected European and English-Speaking Countries, 1990***

Sources: See Figures 14.3 and 14.4.

A similar trend is evident in movement into and out of cohabiting unions. Whether in marriage or cohabitation, Americans appear to have far more transitions in their live-in relationships. According to surveys from the mid-1990s, 5 percent of women in Sweden had experienced three or more unions (marriages or cohabiting relationships) by age thirty-five. In the rest of Europe, the comparable figure was 1 to 3 percent.[61] But in the United States, according to a 1995 survey, 9 percent of women aged thirty-five had experienced three or more unions, nearly double the Swedish figure and far higher than that of other European nations.[62] By 2002, the U.S. figure had climbed to 12 percent.[63] No other comparable nation has such a high level of multiple marital and cohabiting unions.

American children are thus more likely to experience multiple transitions in living arrangements than are children in Europe. Another study using the same comparative data from the mid-1990s reported that 12 percent of American children had lived in three or more parental partnerships by age fifteen, as against 3 percent of children in Sweden, which has the next highest figure.[64] As transitions out of partnerships occur, children experience a period of living in a single-parent family. And although American children, in general, are more likely to live in a single-parent family while growing up than are children elsewhere, the trend differs by social class. As Sara McLanahan shows in a comparison of children whose mothers have low or moderate levels of education, American children are much more likely than those in several European nations to have lived with a single mother by age fifteen. The cross-national difference is less pronounced among children whose mothers are highly educated.[65]

Also contributing to the prevalence of single-parent families in the United States is the relatively large share of births to unmarried, noncohabiting women—about one in five.[66] In most other developed nations with numerous nonmarital births, a greater share of unmarried mothers lives with the fathers of their children. In fact, the increases in nonmarital births in Europe in recent decades largely reflect births to cohabiting couples rather than births to single parents.[67] As noted, the United States is seeing a similar trend toward births to cohabiting couples, but the practice is still less prevalent in the United States than in many European nations.

Greater Economic Inequality

Children in the United States experience greater inequality of economic well-being than children in most other developed nations. One recent study reported that the gap between the cash incomes of children's families in the lowest and highest 10 percent was larger in the United States than in twelve other developed countries.[68] The low ranking of the United States is attributable both to the higher share of births to single parents and to the higher share of divorce. But even when the comparison is restricted to children living in single-parent families, children in the United States have the lowest relative standard of living. For example, one comparative study reported that 60 percent of single-mother households in the United States were poor, as against 45 percent in Canada, 40 percent in the United Kingdom, 25 percent in France, 20 percent in Italy, and 5 percent in Sweden.[69] The differences are caused by variations both in the income earned by single parents and in the generosity of government cash transfers. In other words, having a high share of single-parent families predisposes the United States to have a higher poverty rate, but other countries compensate better for single parenthood through a combination of social welfare spending and supports for employed parents, such as child care.

More Controversy over Gay and Lesbian Partnerships

Other developed countries tend to be more open to gay and lesbian partnerships than is the United States. Two European nations, Belgium and the Netherlands, have legalized same-sex marriage. By 2005, courts in seven Canadian provinces had ruled that laws restricting marriage to opposite-sex couples were discriminatory, and the Canadian federal government had introduced a bill to legalize gay marriage nationwide. Many other developed nations, including all the Scandinavian countries and Germany, have amended their family laws to include legal recognition of same-sex partnerships.[70]

France enacted its somewhat different form of domestic partnership, the *pacte civil de solidarité* (PACS), in 1999. Originally conceived in response to the burden placed on gay couples by the AIDS epidemic, the 1999 legislation was not restricted to same-sex partnerships.[71] In fact, it is likely that more opposite-sex partners than same-sex partners have chosen this option.[72] The PACS does not provide all the legal benefits of marriage. It is a privately negotiated contract between two persons who are treated legally as individuals unless they have children. Even when they have children, the contract does not require one partner to support the other after a dissolution, and judges are reluctant to award joint custody. Moreover, individuals in a same-sex PACS do not have the right to adopt children or to use reproductive technology such as in vitro fertilization.

For the most part, the issue of marriage has been less prominent in European than in North American debates about same-sex partnerships. To this point, no serious movement for same-sex marriage has appeared in Britain.[73] The French debate, consistent with the nation's child-oriented social policies, has focused more on the kinship rights and relationships of the children of the partners than on whether the legal form of partnership should include marriage.[74] In 2004, the mayor of Bogles, France, created a furor—similar to that seen in the United States following the granting of marriage licenses in San Francisco—by marrying a gay couple. But marriage remains less central to the politics of same-sex partnerships in France and elsewhere in Europe than it is in North America.

MARRIAGE TRANSFORMED

Marriage remains an important part of the American family system, even if its dominance has diminished. Sentiment in favor of marriage appears to be stronger in the United States than elsewhere in the developed world, and the share of adults who are likely to marry is higher—as is, however, their propensity to get divorced. Increasingly, gay and lesbian activists are arguing, with some success, that they, too, should be allowed to marry. Even poor and near-poor Americans, who are statistically less likely to marry, hold to marriage as an ideal. But the contemporary ideal differs from that of the past in two important ways.

The Contemporary Ideal

First, marriage is now more optional in the United States than it has ever been. Until recently, family formation rarely occurred outside of marriage. Now, to a greater extent than ever before, one can choose whether to have children on one's own, in a cohabiting relationship, or in a marriage. Poor and working-class Americans have radically separated the timing of childbearing and marriage, with many young adults having children many years before marrying. At current rates, perhaps one-third of African Americans will never marry. To be sure, some of the increase in seemingly single-parent families reflects a rise in the number of cohabiting couples who are having children, but these cohabiting relationships often prove unstable. How frequently the option of marriage becomes a reality depends heavily on one's race, ethnicity, or social class. African Americans and less well-educated Americans, for example, still value marriage highly but attain it less frequently than whites and better-educated Americans.

Second, the rewards of marriage today are more individualized. Being married is less a required adult role and more an individual achievement—a symbol of successful self-development. And couples are more prone to dissolve a marriage if their individualized rewards seem inadequate. Conversely, marriage is less centered on children. Today, married couples in the United States are having fewer children than couples have had at any time in the nation's history except during the Great Depression.

The changes in marriage, however, have not been solely cultural in origin. It is still the norm that a man must be able to provide a steady income to be seen as a good prospect for marriage. He no longer need earn all the family's income, but he must make a substantial, stable contribution. As the labor market position of young men without a college education has eroded, their attractiveness in the marriage market has declined. Many of their potential partners have chosen to have children outside marriage early in adulthood rather than to wait for the elusive promise of finding a spouse. Moreover, the introduction of the birth control pill and the legalization of abortion have allowed young women and men to become sexually active long before they think about marriage.

When the American family system is viewed in international perspective, it is most distinctive for the many transitions into and out of marital and cohabiting unions. Americans are more likely to experience multiple unions over the course of their lives than are Europeans. Moreover, cohabiting relationships in the United States still tend to be rather short, with a median duration (until either marriage or dissolution) of about one year. The median duration of cohabiting unions is about four years in Sweden and France and two or more years in most other European nations.[75] All this means that American children probably face greater instability in their living arrangements than children anywhere else in the developed world. Recent research has suggested that changes in family structure, regardless of the beginning and ending configurations, may cause problems for children.[76] Some of these apparent problems may reflect preexisting family difficulties, but some cause-and-effect association between instability and children's difficulties probably exists. If so, the increase in instability over the past decades is a worrisome trend that may not be receiving the attention it deserves.

Positive Developments

This is not to suggest that all the trends in marriage in America have been harmful to children. Those who live with two parents or with one well-educated parent may be doing better than comparable children a few decades ago. As noted, income growth has been greater in dual-career families, and divorce rates may have fallen among the college educated. In addition, the time spent with their parents by children in two-parent families has gone up, not down, and the comparable time spent by children with single parents has not changed, even though mothers' work outside the home has increased.[77] Working mothers appear to compensate for time spent outside the home by cutting back on housework and leisure—and, for those who are married, relying on modest but noticeable increases in husbands' housework—to preserve time with children.[78]

Meanwhile, the decline in fertility means that there are fewer children in the home to compete for their parents' attention. Middle-class parents engage in an intensive childrearing style that sociologist Annette Lareau calls "concerted cultivation": days filled with organized activities and parent-child discussions designed to enhance their children's talents, opinions, and skills.[79] While some social critics decry this parenting style, middle-class children gain skills that will be valuable to them in higher education and in the labor market. They learn how to communicate with professionals and other adults in positions of authority. They develop a confident style of interaction that Lareau calls "an emerging sense of entitlement," compared with "an emerging sense of constraint" among working-class and lower-class youth.

MARRIAGE AND PUBLIC POLICY

Because marriage has been, and continues to be, stronger in the United States than in much of Europe, American social welfare policies have focused more on marriage than have those of many European countries. That emphasis continues. George W. Bush's administration advocates marriage-promotion programs as the most promising way to assist families. No European country has pursued a comparable policy initiative. Moreover, the issue of gay marriage has received more attention in the United States than in most of Europe. This greater emphasis on marriage in public policy reflects the history and culture of the United States. Policies that build on and support marriage are likely to be popular with American voters because they resonate with American values. Europe's more generous public spending on children, regardless of their parents' marital status, is rooted in concerns about low population growth that have never been strong in the United States. Such public spending on single-parent families also reflects the lesser influence of religion in Europe. So it is understandable that American policymakers wishing to generate support for new family policy initiatives might turn to marriage-based programs.

Yet the relatively high value placed on marriage in the United States coexists with an unmatched level of family instability and large numbers of single-parent families. This, too, is part of the American cultural heritage. The divorce rate appears to have been higher in the United States than in most of Europe since the mid-nineteenth century.[80]

This emblematic American pattern of high marriage and divorce rates, cohabiting unions of short duration, and childbearing among unpartnered women and men makes it unrealistic to think that policymakers will be able to reduce rates of multiple unions and of single parenthood in the United States to typical European levels. Consequently, a family policy that relies too heavily on marriage will not help the many children destined to live in single-parent and cohabiting-parent families—many of them economically disadvantaged—for some or all of their formative years. Only assistance directed to needy families, regardless of their household structure, will reach them. Such policies are less popular in the United States, as the widespread disdain for cash welfare and the popularity of the 1996 welfare reform legislation demonstrate. Moreover, some American policymakers worry that programs that support all parents without regard to partnership status may decrease people's incentive to marry.[81] The dilemma for policymakers is how to make the trade-off between marriage-based and marriage-neutral programs. A careful balance of both is needed to provide adequate support to American children.

Notes

1. W. C. Rodgers and A. Thornton, "Changing Patterns of First Marriage in the United States," *Demography* 22 (1985): 265–79; Joshua R. Goldstein and Catherine T. Kenney, "Marriage Delayed or Marriage Forgone? New Cohort Forecasts of First Marriage for U.S. Women," *American - Sociological Review* 66 (2001): 506–19.
2. U.S. Bureau of the Census, "Percent of People 25 Years Old and Over Who Have Completed High School or College, by Race, Hispanic Origin and Sex: Selected Years 1940 to 2002," 2003, table A-2, www.census.gov/population/socdemo/education/tabA-2.pdf (accessed June 24, 2004).
3. Ibid.
4. U.S. National Center for Health Statistics, "Fertility, Family Planning, and Women's Health: New Data from the 1995 National Survey of Family Growth," *Vital and Health Statistics* 23, no. 19 (1997), available at www.cdc.gov/nchs/data/series/sr_23/sr23_019.pdf (accessed July 13, 2004).
5. Larry L. Bumpass and Hsien-Hen Lu, "Trends in Cohabitation and Implications for Children's Family Contexts in the United States," *Population Studies* 54 (2000): 29–41. They note that 49 percent of women aged thirty to thirty-four years old in the 1995 National Survey of Family Growth reported ever cohabiting.
6. U.S. National Center for Health Statistics, "Number and Percent of Births to Unmarried Women, by Race and Hispanic Origin: United States, 1940–99," *Vital Statistics of the United States, 1999*, vol. 1, *Natality*, table 1-17 (available at www.cdc.gov/nehs/data/statab/t99lxl7.pdf [accessed January 12, 2005]); and U.S. National Center for Health Statistics, "Births: Preliminary Data for 2002," *National Vital Statistics Report* 53, no. 9, www.cdc.gov/nchs/data/nvsr/nvsr53/nvsr53_09.pdf (accessed January 12, 2005). For 2003, the figures were 34.6 percent overall, 23.5 percent for non-Hispanic whites, 68.5 percent for non-Hispanic blacks, and 45 percent for Hispanics.
7. Ibid.
8. Marcia Carlson, Sara McLanahan, and Paula England, "Union Formation in Fragile Families," *Demography* 41 (2004): 237–61.
9. Dan Black and others, "Demographics of the Gay and Lesbian Population in the United States: Evidence from Available Systematic Data," *Demography* 37 (2000): 139–54.
10. U.S. Bureau of the Census, "Married-Couple and Unmarried-Partner Households: 2000" (Government Printing Office, 2003).

11. Andrew Cherlin, *Marriage, Divorce, Remarriage* (Harvard University Press, 1992).
12. Matthew Bramlett and William D. Mosher, *Cohabitation, Marriage, Divorce and Remarriage in the United States*, series 22, no. 2 (U.S. National Center for Health Statistics, Vital and Health Statistics, 2002), available at www.cdc.gov/nchs/data/series/sr_23/sr23_022.pdf (accessed June 2003).
13. U.S. Bureau of the Census. "Detailed Living Arrangements of Children by Race and Hispanic Origin, 1996," 2001, www.census.gov/population/socdemo/child/p70-74/tab0l.pdf (accessed June 28, 2004). The data are from the 1996 Survey of Income and Program Participation, wave 2.
14. Some of the one-parent families contain an unmarried cohabiting partner, whom the Census Bureau normally does not count as a "parent." According to the 1996 estimates cited in the previous note, about 2.5 percent of children live with a biological or adoptive parent who is cohabiting.
15. Lynne Casper and Suzanne M. Bianchi, *Continuity and Change in the American Family* (Thousand Oaks, Calif.: Sage, 2002).
16. David Ellwood and Christopher Jencks, "The Uneven Spread of Single-Parent Families: What Do We Know? Where Do We Look for Answers?" in *Social Inequality*, edited by Kathryn M. Neckerman (New York: Russell Sage Foundation, 2004), pp. 3–118.
17. Sara McLanahan, "Diverging Destinies: How Children Are Faring under the Second Demographic Transition," *Demography* 41 (2004): 607–27.
18. Ellwood and Jencks, "The Uneven Spread of Single-Parent Families" (see note 16).
19. Steven P. Martin, "Growing Evidence for a 'Divorce Divide'? Education and Marital Dissolution Rates in the U.S. since the 1970s," Working Paper on Social Dimensions of Inequality (New York: Russell Sage Foundation, 2004).
20. McLanahan, "Diverging Destinies" (see note 17).
21. Ibid.
22. Isabel Sawhill and Laura Chadwick, *Children in Cities: Uncertain Futures* (Brookings, 1999); and Donald J. Hernandez, *America's Children: Resources from Family, Government, and Economy* (New York: Russell Sage Foundation, 1993).
23. S. Philip Morgan and others, "Racial Differences in Household and Family Structure at the Turn of the Century," *American Journal of Sociology* 98 (1993): 798–828.
24. Cherlin, *Marriage, Divorce, Remarriage* (see note 11).
25. Goldstein and Kenney, "Marriage Delayed or Marriage Forgone?" (see note 1).
26. U.S. National Center for Health Statistics, "Births: Preliminary Data" (see note 6).
27. Bumpass and Lu, "Trends in Cohabitation" (see note 5).
28. U.S. National Center for Health Statistics, "Revised Birth and Fertility Rates for the 1990s and New Rates for the Hispanic Populations, 2000 and 2001: United States," *National Vital Statistics Reports* 51, no. 12 (Government Printing Office, 2003); and U.S. National Center for Health Statistics, "Births: Final Data for 2000," *National Vital Statistics Report* 50, no. 5 (Government Printing Office, 2002).
29. Frank D. Bean and Marta Tienda, *The Hispanic Population of the United States* (New York: Russell Sage Foundation, 1987).
30. U.S. National Center for Health Statistics, "Births: Final Data for 2000" (see note 28).
31. McLanahan, "Diverging Destinies" (see note 17).
32. Elise Richer and others, *Boom Times a Bust: Declining Employment among Less-Educated Young Men* (Washington: Center for Law and Social Policy, 2003); available at www.clasp.org/DMS/Documents/1058362464.08/Boom_Times.pdf (accessed July 13, 2004).
33. William J. Wilson, *The Truly Disadvantaged: The Inner City, the Underclass, and Public Policy* (University of Chicago Press, 1987).
34. Robert D. Mare and Christopher Winship, "Socioeconomic Change and the Decline in Marriage for Blacks and Whites," in *The Urban Underclass*, edited by Christopher Jencks and Paul Peterson (Brookings, 1991), pp. 175–202; and Daniel T. Lichter, Diane K. McLaughlin, and David C. Ribar, "Economic Restructuring and the Retreat from Marriage," *Social Science Research* 31 (2002): 230–56.
35. Ernest W. Burgess and Harvey J. Locke, *The Family: From Institution to Companionship* (New York: American Book Company, 1945).

36. Andrew J. Cherlin, "The Deinstitutionalization of American Marriage," *Journal of Marriage and the Family* 66 (2004): 848–61.
37. Ibid.
38. Linda Burton of Pennsylvania State University directed the ethnographic component of the study. For a general description, see Pamela Winston and others, "Welfare, Children, and Families: A Three-City Study Overview and Design," 1999, www.jhu.edu\~welfare\overviewanddesign.pdf (accessed July 10, 2004).
39. M. Belinda Tucker, "Marital Values and Expectations in Context: Results from a 21-City Survey," in *The Ties That Bind: Perspectives on Marriage and Cohabitation*, edited by Linda J. Waite (New York: Aldine de Gruyter, 2000), pp. 166–87.
40. Carlson, McLanahan, and England, "Union Formation" (see note 8).
41. Barbara Dafoe Whitehead and David Popenoe, "Who Wants to Marry a Soul Mate?" in *The State of Our Unions, 2001*, The National Marriage Project, Rutgers University, pp. 6–16, 2001, available at marriage.rutgers.edu/Publications/SOOU/NMPAR200l.pdf (accessed February 12, 2004).
42. The estimate assumes that the age-specific marriage rates in the year of calculation (in this case, 1990) will remain unchanged in future years. Since this assumption is unrealistic, the total marriage rate is unlikely to predict the future accurately. But it does demonstrate the rate of marriage implied by current trends.
43. Ronald Inglehart and others, *Human Beliefs and Values: A Cross-Cultural Soureebook Based on the 1999–2002 Values Surveys* (Mexico City: Siglo Veintiuno Editores, 2004).
44. Alexis de Tocqueville, *Democracy in America*, vol. 1 (New York: Knopf, Everyman's Library, 1994), p. 304.
45. Nancy Cott, *Public Vows: A History of Marriage and the Nation* (Harvard University Press, 2000).
46. Quoted in ibid., pp. 102–03.
47. Herbert G. Gutman, *The Black Family in Slavery and Freedom, 1750–1925* (New York: Pantheon, 1976).
48. Jacqueline Jones, *Labor of Love, Labor of Sorrow: Black Women and the Family from Slavery to the Present* (New York: Basic Books, 1985).
49. Tocqueville, *Democracy in America* (see note 44), p. 303.
50. Grace Davie, "Patterns of Religion in Western Europe: An Exceptional Case," in *The Blackwell Companion to the Sociology of Religion*, edited by Richard K. Fenn (Oxford: Blackwell, 2001), pp. 264–78; and Seymour Martin Lipset, "American Exceptionalism Reaffirmed," *Tocqueville Review* 10 (1990): 3–35.
51. Inglehart and others, *Human Beliefs and Values* (see note 43).
52. Ibid.
53. See the discussion in Ron J. Lesthaeghe, *The Decline of Belgian Fertility, 1800–1970* (Princeton University Press, 1977), p. 304.
54. Alisa Klaus, "Depopulation and Race Suicide: Maternalism and Pronatalist Ideologies in France and the United States," in *Mothers of a New World: Maternalist Politics and the Origins of the Welfare State*, edited by Seth Koven and Sonya Michel (New York: Routledge, 1993), pp. 188–212.
55. Paul Ginsborg, "The Family Politics of the Great Dictators," in *Family Life in the Twentieth Century*, edited by David I. Kertzer and Marzio Barbagli (Yale University Press, 2003), pp. 188–97.
56. Susan Pedersen, *Family, Dependence, and the Origins of the Welfare State: Britain and France, 1914–1945* (Cambridge University Press, 1993).
57. Ibid.
58. The total divorce rate is formed by summing duration-specific divorce rates prevalent in the year of observation—in this case, 1990. It therefore assumes that the duration-specific rates of 1990 will remain the same in future years. It shares the limits of the total marriage rate (see note 42).
59. Robert Schoen and Robin M. Weinick, "The Slowing Metabolism of Marriage: Figures from 1988 U.S. Marital Status Life Tables," *Demography* 39 (1993): 737–46. Schoen and Weinick used life table calculations to establish the marriage and divorce probabilities for American men and women. Unfortunately, only total marriage rates and total divorce rates are available for other

countries. Consequently, I calculated a total divorce rate for the United States from published duration-specific divorce rates for 1990. I then summed the total first marriage rate and total divorce rate for the United States and the other countries displayed in Figure 14.4. Although this procedure is not as accurate as using rates generated by life tables, the difference is unlikely to alter the relative positions of the countries in the figure.

60. Strictly speaking, I should use the total divorce rate for people in first marriages (as opposed to including people in remarriages), but the available data do not allow for that level of precision.
61. Alexia Fürnkranz-Prskawetz and others, "Pathways to Stepfamily Formation in Europe: Results from the FFS," *Demographic Research* 8 (2003): 107–49.
62. Author's calculation from the 1995 National Survey of Family Growth microdata file.
63. Author's calculation from the 2002 National Survey of Family Growth microdata file.
64. Patrick Heuveline, Jeffrey M. Timberlake, and Frank F. Furstenberg Jr., "Shifting Childrearing to Single Mothers: Results from 17 Western Countries," *Population and Development Review* 29 (2003): 47–71. The figures quoted appear in note 6.
65. McLanahan, "Diverging Destinies" (see note 17).
66. About one-third of all births are to unmarried mothers, and Bumpass and Lu report that about 60 percent of unmarried mothers in 1995 were not cohabiting ($0.33 \times 0.60 = 0.198$). Bumpass and Lu, "Trends in Cohabitation" (see note 5).
67. Kathleen Kiernan, "European Perspectives on Nonmarital Childbearing," in *Out of Wedlock: Causes and Consequences of Nonmarital Fertility*, edited by Lawrence L. Wu and Barbara Wolfe (New York: Russell Sage Foundation, 2001), pp. 77–108.
68. Lars Osberg, Timothy M. Smeeding, and Jonathan Schwabish, "Income Distribution and Public Social Expenditure: Theories, Effects, and Evidence," in *Social Inequality*, edited by Kathryn M. Neckerman (New York: Russell Sage Foundation, 2004), pp. 821–59.
69. Poverty was defined as having a family income of less than half of the median income for all families. Bruce Bradbury and Markus Jäntti, "Child-Poverty across the Industrialized World: Evidence from the Luxembourg Income Study," in *Child Well-Being, Child Poverty and Child Policy in Modern Nations: What Do We Know?* edited by Koen Vleminckx and Timothy M. Smeeding (Bristol, England: Policy Press, 2000), pp. 11–32.
70. Marzio Barbagli and David I. Kertzer, "Introduction," and Paulo Ronfani, "Family Law in Europe," in *Family Life in the Twentieth Century*, edited by David I. Kertzer and Marzio Barbagli (Yale University Press, 2003), respectively, pp. xi–xliv and 114–51.
71. Claude Martin and Irène Théry, "The Pacs and Marriage and Cohabitation in France," *International Journal of Law, Policy and the Family* 15 (2001): 135–58.
72. Patrick Festy, "The 'Civil Solidarity Pact' (PACS) in France: An Impossible Evaluation," *Population et Sociétés*, no. 369 (2001): 1–4.
73. John Eekelaar, "The End of an Era?" *Journal of Family History* 28 (2003): 108–22.
74. Eric Fassin, "Same Sex, Different Politics: 'Gay Marriage' Debates in France and the United States," *Popular Culture* 13 (2001): 215–32.
75. Kathleen Kiernan, "Cohabitation in Western Europe," *Population Trends* 96 (Summer 1999): 25–32.
76. See, for example, Lawrence L. Wu and Brian C. Martinson, "Family Structure and the Risk of Premarital Birth," *American Sociological Review* 59 (1993): 210–32, Jake M. Najman and others, "Impact of Family Type and Family Quality on Child Behavior Problems: A Longitudinal Study," *Journal of the American Academy of Child and Adolescent Psychiatry* 36 (1997): 1357–65.
77. John F. Sandberg and Sandra D. Hofferth, "Changes in Children's Time with Parents, U.S. 1981–1997," *Demography* 38 (2001): 423–36.
78. Suzanne M. Bianchi, "Maternal Employment and Time with Children: Dramatic Change or Surprising Continuity?" *Demography* 37 (2000): 401–14.
79. Annette Lareau, *Unequal Childhoods: Class, Race, and Family Life* (University of California Press, 2003).
80. Gören Therborn, *Between Sex and Power: Family in the World, 1900–2000* (London: Routledge, 2004).
81. This proposition is similar to what David Ellwood has called the "assistance-family structure conundrum." David T. Ellwood, *Poor Support: Poverty and the American Family* (New York: Basic Books, 1988).

READING 15

Grounds for Marriage: How Relationships Succeed or Fail

Arlene Skolnick

> The home made by one man and one woman bound together "until death do ye part" has in large measure given way to trial marriage.
>
> —*Chauncy J. Hawkins (1907)*

> Marriage has universally fallen into awful disrepute.
>
> —*Martin Luther (1522)*

On June 2, 1986, *Newsweek* magazine featured a cover story that proclaimed that a woman over 40 had a greater chance of being "killed by a terrorist" than of getting married. The story, based on one study, set off a media blitz, along with a wave of alarm and anxiety among single women. Eventually, however, after the furor died down, other researchers pointed to serious flaws in the study *Newsweek* had relied on for the story. The study had relied on trends in earlier generations of women to make predictions about the future of unmarried women today.

In the summer of 1999, another report about the alarming state of marriage was released (National Marriage Project Report, 1999). Exhibit A was a finding that, between 1960 and 1990, the marriage rate among young adults had gone down 23 percent. Again a widely publicized "finding" had to be corrected. The problem this time was including teenagers as young as 15 as "young adults" in 1960 and 1996. Teenagers were far more likely to get married in the 1950s than the 1990s or at any previous time in American history.

The death of marriage has been proclaimed many times in American history, but in the first years of the twenty-first century, the institution is still alive. Despite today's high divorce rates, the rise in one-parent families, and other trends, the United States today has the highest marriage rate among the advanced industrial countries. The Census Bureau estimates that about 90 percent of Americans will eventually marry.

The combination of both high marriage and high divorce rates seems paradoxical, but actually represents two sides of the same coin: the importance of the emotional relationship between the partners. Marriage for love was not unknown in earlier eras, but other, more practical considerations usually came first—economic security, status, and the interests of parents and kin.

Even in the 1950s, the heyday of the marital "togetherness" ideal, researchers found that so-called "empty shell" or "disengaged" marriages were widespread. Such couples lived under one roof, but seemed to have little or no emotional connection to one another. Some of these spouses considered themselves happily married, but others, particularly women, lived in quiet desperation.

Couples today have much higher expectations. Between the 1950s and the 1970s, American attitudes toward marriage changed dramatically as part of what has been called a "psychological revolution"—a transformation in the way people look at marriage, parenthood, and their lives in general (Veroff, Donvan, and Kulka, 1981). In 1957, people judged themselves and their partners in terms of how well the partners fulfilled their social roles in marriage. Is he a good provider? Is she a good homemaker?

By the 1970s, people had become more psychologically oriented, seeking emotional warmth and intimacy in marriage. Why the change? The shift is linked to higher educational levels. In the 1950s, the psychological approach to relationships was found among the relatively few Americans who had been to college. By the 1970s the psychological approach to marriage and family life had become, as the authors put it, "common coin."

In an era when divorce has lost its stigma and remaining married has become as much a choice as getting married in first place, it's not surprising that a loving and rewarding relationship has become the gold standard for marital success. Although they know the statistics, few if any couples go to the altar expecting that their own relationship will break down. How do relationships become unhappy? What is the process that transforms happy newlyweds into emotional strangers? In the rest of this paper, I discuss my own research on marriage in the context of what others have been learning in answer to these questions.

THE STUDY OF MARRIAGE PAST AND PRESENT

In recent years, there have been great advances in the study of couple relationships. Until the 1970s there were many studies of what was called marital "adjustment," "happiness," "success," or "satisfaction." This research was usually based on large surveys in which people's ratings of their own marital happiness were correlated with other characteristics. The best-established correlates were demographic factors, such as occupation, education, income, age at marriage, religious participation, and the like. There was little theorizing about why these links might exist.

The use of self-reported ratings to study marriage came under a lot of criticism. Some researchers argued that the concept of marital happiness was hopelessly vague; others questioned the validity of simply asking people to rate their own marriages. But there were deeper problems with these earlier studies. Even the best self-report measure can hardly capture what goes on in the private psychosocial theater of married life.

In the 1970s, a new wave of marital research began to breach the wall of marital privacy. Psychologists, clinicians, and social scientists began to observe families interacting with one another in laboratories and clinics, usually through one-way mirrors. The new technology of videotaping made it possible to preserve these interactions for later analysis. Behavioral therapists and researchers began to produce a literature describing the behavior of happy and unhappy couples. At the same time, social psychologists began to study close relationships of various kinds.

During this period I began my own research into marriage, using couples who had taken part in the longitudinal studies carried out at the Institute of Human Development

(IHD) at the University of California at Berkeley. One member of the couple had been part of the study since childhood, and had been born either in 1921 or 1928. Each spouse had been interviewed in depth in 1958, when the study members were 30 or 37 years old. They were interviewed again in 1970 and 1982.

Despite the richness of the longitudinal data, it did not include observations of the spouses interacting with one another, a method of research that did not come on the scene until the study was decades old. On the other hand, few of the new observational studies of marriage have included the kind of in-depth material on the couples' lives as did the longitudinal study. It seemed to me that the ideal study of marriage, assuming cost was not an issue, would include both observational and interview data as well as a sort of ethnography of the couples' lives at home. A few years ago, I was offered the opportunity to be involved in a small version of such a project in a study of the marriages of police officers. I will discuss this study later on.

The new wave of research has revealed a great deal about the complex emotional dynamics of marriage, and perhaps most usefully, revealed that some widespread beliefs about couple relations are incorrect. But there is still a great deal more to learn. There is as yet no grand theory of marriage, no one royal road to understanding marriage, no one size fits all prescriptions for marital success. But we have gained some important insights to marital (and marriage-like) relationships. And there seems to be a striking convergence of findings emerging from different approaches to studying couples. Here are some of these insights.

For Better and For Worse

The sociologist Jesse Bernard argued that every marriage contains two marriages, the husband's and the wife's (1972), and that his is better than hers. Bernard's claims have been controversial, but in general, her idea that husbands and wives have different perspectives on their marriage has held up over time.

But apart from gender differences, marital relationships also seem to divide in two another way: every marriage contains within it both a good marriage and bad marriage. Early studies of marital quality assumed that all marriages could be lined up along a single dimension of satisfaction, adjustment or happiness—happy couples would be at one end of the scale, unhappy ones at the other, and most couples would fall somewhere in between.

More recently, marriage researchers have found that that you need two separate dimensions to capture the quality of a relationship, a positive dimension and a negative one. The key to marital happiness is the balance between the good marriage and the bad one. The finding emerges in different ways in studies using different methods.

In my own research, I came across this same "good marriage-bad marriage" phenomenon among the Berkeley longitudinal couples (Skolnick, 1981). First, we identified couples ranging from high and low in marital satisfaction based on ratings of the marriage each spouse had made, combined with ratings made by clinical interviewers who had seen each separately. Later we examined transcripts of the clinical interviews to see how people who had scored high or low on measures of marital quality described their marriages. In the course of the interview, each person was asked about his or her satisfactions and dissatisfactions in the relationship.

Surprisingly, looking only at statements about dissatisfaction, it was hard to tell the happily married from their unhappy counterparts. None of the happy spouses were without some complaints or irritations. One husband went on at length at what a terrible homemaker his wife was. The wife in one of the most highly rated marriages reported having "silent arguments"—periods of not speaking to one another—which lasted about a week. "People always say you should talk over your differences," the wife said, "but it doesn't work in our family."

Only in descriptions of the satisfactions of the marriage did the contrast emerge. The happy couples described close, affectionate, and often romantic relationships. One man remarked after almost 30 years of marriage, "I still have stars in my eyes." A woman said, "I just can't wait for him to get home every night; just having him around is terrific."

The most systematic evidence for this good marriage/bad marriage model emerges from the extensive program of studies of marital interaction carried out by Gottman, Levenson, and associates (1992, 1998). Their research is based on videotaped observations of couple discussions in a laboratory setting. These intensive studies not only record facial expressions, gestures, and tone of voice, but also monitor heart rates and other physiological indicators of stress.

Surprisingly, these studies do not confirm the widespread notion that anger is the great destroyer of marital relationships. Among the indicators that do predict marital distress and eventual divorce are high levels of physiological arousal, that is stress, as couples interact with one another, a tendency for quarrels to escalate in intensity, and a tendency to keep the argument going even after the other person has tried to "make up" and end it.

As noted earlier, the key factor in the success of a marriage is not the amount of anger or other negative emotion in the relationship—no marriage always runs smoothly and cheerfully—but the balance between positive and negative feelings and actions. Indeed, Gottman gives a precise estimate of this ratio in successful marriages—five to one. In other words, the "good" marriage has to be five times better than the "bad" marriage is bad.

It seems as if the "good" marriage acts like a reservoir of positive feelings that can keep arguments from escalating out of control. In virtually every marriage and family, "emotional brushfires" are constantly breaking out. Whether these flare-ups develop into major bonfires depends on the balance between the good marriage and the bad one.

Gottman identifies a set of four behavioral patterns, that he calls "the four horsemen of the apocalypse;" they constitute a series of escalating signs of marital breakdown. These include: criticism (not just complaining about a specific act, but denouncing the spouse's whole character); contempt (insults, name calling, mockery); then defensiveness (each spouse feeling hurt, mistreated and misunderstood by the other); and finally, stonewalling (one or both partners withdraws into silence and avoidance).

Tolstoy Was Wrong: Happy Marriages Are Not All Alike

The most common approach to understanding marriage, as we have seen, is to correlate ratings of marital happiness with other variables. But focusing on *variables* masks an enormous amount of *individual* variation. Some studies over the years, however, have looked at differences among marriages at a given level of satisfaction. Among the first was a widely cited study published in 1965. John Cuber and Peggy Harroff interviewed 437 successful upper-middle-class men and women about their lives and marriages. These people had been married for at least 15 years to their original spouses, and reported themselves as being satisfied with their marriages. Yet the authors found enormous variation in marital style among these stable, contented upscale couples.

Only one out of six marriages in the sample conformed to the image of what marriage is supposed to be—that is, a relationship based on strong emotional bonds of love and friendship. The majority of others, however, did not fit the ideal model. Some couples were "conflict habituated," the bickering, battling spouses often portrayed in plays, movies, and television. Yet they were content with their marriages and did not define their fighting as a problem.

A second group of couples were in "devitalized" marriages; starting out in close, loving relationships, they had drifted apart over the years. In the third "passive congenial" type of relationship, the partners were never in love or emotionally close in the first place. Marriage for these couples was a comfortable and convenient lifestyle, leaving them free to devote their energy to their careers or other interests.

The most recent studies of marital types come from the research of John Gottman and his colleagues, described earlier. Along with identifying early warning signs of later marital trouble and divorce, Gottman also observed that happy, successful marriages were not all alike. Moreover, he also found that much of the conventional wisdom about marriage is misguided.

For example, marital counselors and popular writings on marriage often advocate what Gottman calls a "validation" or "active-listening" model. They recommend that when couples have a disagreement, they should speak to one another as a therapist speaks to a client. For example, a wife is supposed to state her complaints directly to the husband, in the form of "I" statements, for example, "I feel you're not doing your share of the housework." Then he is supposed to calmly respond by paraphrasing what she has said, and empathize with her feelings, "Sounds like you're upset about this."

To their surprise, Gottman and his colleagues found that very few couples actually fit this therapeutically approved, "validating" model of marriage. Like Cuber and Harroff, they found that people can be happily married even if they fight a lot; Gottman calls these "volatile" marriages. At the opposite extreme, were "avoidant" couples, who did not argue or even talk about their conflicts. These happily married couples also defied conventional wisdom about the importance of "communication" in marriage.

In my own study, I too found a great deal of variation among the longitudinal couples. Apart from the deep friendship that typified all the happy couples they differed in many other ways. Some spent virtually 24 hours a day together, others went their own ways, going off to parties or weekends alone. Some were very traditional in their gender patterns, others egalitarian. Some were emotionally close to their relatives, some were distant. Some had a wide circle of friends, some were virtual hermits.

They could come from happy or unhappy families. The wife in one of the happiest marriages had a very difficult relationship with her father; she grew up "hating men" and planned never to marry. Her husband also grew up in an unhappy home where the parents eventually divorced. In short, if the emotional core of marriage is good, it seems to matter very little what kind of lifestyle the couple chooses to follow.

Marriage Is a Movie, Not a Snapshot

The ancient Greek philosopher Heroclitis once said that you can never step into the same river twice, because it is always moving. The same is true of marriage. A variety of studies show that over a relatively short period of time, marriages and families can change in the ways they interact and in their emotional atmosphere. In studies of police officer couples, to be described in more detail below, the same marriage could look very different from one laboratory session to the next, depending on how much stress the officer had experienced on each day.

The IHD longitudinal studies made it possible to follow the same couples over several decades. Consider the following examples, based on the first two adult follow-ups around 1960 and the early 1970s (Skolnick, 1981).

Seen in 1960, when they were in their early 30s, the marriage of Jack and Ellen did not look promising. Jack was an aloof husband and uninvolved father. Ellen was overwhelmed by caring for three small children. She had a variety of physical ailments, and needed a steady dose of tranquilizers to calm her anxieties. Ten years later, however, she was in good health and enjoying life. She and Jack had become a warm, loving couple.

Martin and Julia were a happily married couple in 1960. They had two children they adored, an active social life, and were fixing up a new home they had bought. Martin was looking forward to a new business venture. A decade later, Martin had developed a severe drinking problem that had disrupted every aspect of their relationship. Thinking seriously about divorce, Julia said it all had started when the business had started to fail and ultimately went bankrupt.

Perhaps the most striking impression from following these marriages through long periods of time is the great potential for change in intimate relationships. Those early interviews suggest that many couples had what would today be called "dysfunctional" marriages. At the time, it seemed to the spouses, as well as to the interviewers, that the source of the trouble was psychological problems in the husband or wife or both, or else that they were incompatible.

For some couples, such explanations were valid: at later interviews the same emotional or personality difficulties were clear. Some people, however, had divorced and married again to people with whom they were a better fit. One man who had seemed emotionally immature all his life finally found happiness in his third marriage. He married a younger woman who was both nurturing to him and yet a "psychological age mate," as he put it.

Although close to a third of the IHD marriages eventually did end in divorce, all the IHD couples were married years before the divorce revolution of the 1970s made divorce legally easier to obtain, as well as more common and socially acceptable. Many unhappy couples remained married long enough to outgrow their earlier difficulties, or advance past the circumstances that were causing the difficulties in the first place. Viewed from a later time, marital distress at one period or stage in life seemed to be rooted in situational factors: problems at work, trouble with in-laws or money, bad housing, or too many babies too close together. In the midst of these strains, however, it was easy to blame problems on a husband's or a wife's basic character. Only later, when the situation had changed, did it seem that there was nothing inherently wrong with the couple's relationship.

The Critical Events of a Marriage May Not Be inside the Marriage

The longitudinal data, as noted above, revealed a striking amount of change for better or worse depending on a large variety of life circumstances. While the impact of such external factors remains a relatively understudied source of marital distress, there has been growing interest in the impact of work and working conditions—especially job stress—on family life. One of the most stressful occupations, police work, also suffers from very high rates of divorce, domestic violence, and alcoholism. In 1997, Robert Levenson and I took part in collaboration between the University of California and a West Coast urban police department (Levenson, Roberts, and Bellows, 1998; Skolnick, 1998). We focused on job stress and marriage. This was a small, exploratory study, using too few couples—eleven—for statistical analysis, but it yielded some striking preliminary findings.

Briefly, Levenson's part of the study looked at the impact of stress on couple interaction in the laboratory. His procedures called for each spouse to keep a stress diary every day for 30 days. Once a week for four weeks, the couples came to the laboratory at the end of the work day, after eight hours of being apart. Their interaction was videotaped, and physiological responses of each spouse were monitored continuously.

In my part of the project, we used an adaptation of the IHD clinical interview with officers and their wives in their homes. (The sample did not include female officers or police couples.) The aim was to examine their perceptions of police work and its impact on their marriages, their general life circumstances, and the sources of stress and support in their lives. I discovered that these officers and their wives were making heroic efforts to do well in their work and family lives against enormous odds. The obvious dangers and disasters police must deal with are only part of the story; sleep deprivation, frustration with the department bureaucracy, and inadequate equipment were some of the other factors adding up to an enormous stress.

In spite of their difficult lives, these couples seemed to have good, well-functioning marriages, at home and in the laboratory, except on high stress days. Levenson's study was able to examine the direct effects of different levels of stress on the face-to-face interaction of these couples—something that had not been done before. The findings were striking. Variations in the husband's work stress had a marked impact on both couple interaction and the physiological indicators of emotional arousal.

More surprising, it was not just the police officer who showed evidence of stress, but the partner as well. Even before either partner had said a word, while they were just sitting quietly, both the officer and the spouse showed signs of physiological arousal. In particular, there was a kind of "paralysis of the positive emotion system" in both partners (Levenson, Roberts, and Bellows, 1998). Looking at the videotapes, you didn't need the physiological measures to see what was going on. The husband's restless agitation was clear, as was the wife's tense and wary response to it. The wives seemed frozen in their seats, barely able to move. In fact, just watching the couples on videotape is enough to make a viewer also feel tense and uneasy.

Recall that these couples did not look or act this way on the days they were not under high job stress. However, on high stress days, the couples were showing the same warning signs that Gottman and Levenson had found in their earlier studies to be predictors of divorce. The "paralysis of the positive emotion system" means that the "good" aspects of the marriage were unavailable just when they were most needed. Repeated often enough, such moments can strain even a good marriage; they create an emotional climate where tempers can easily flare, hurtful things may be said, and problems go unsolved. Police work may be an extreme example of a high-pressure occupation, but it is far from the only one. "What's the difference between a stressed-out business executive and a stressed-out police officer?" asked a New York columnist not long ago, after a terrible case of domestic violence in a police family. "The officer," he went on, "brings home a loaded gun."

CAN MARRIAGE BE SAVED?

The notion that marriage is a dying institution is remarkably persistent among the American public. Politicians and social critics, particularly conservative ones, insist that divorce, cohabitation, single parenthood, and other recent trends signal moral decline and the unraveling of the social fabric. Some family scholars agree with these pessimistic conclusions. Others argue that marriage and the family are not collapsing but simply becoming more diverse.

A third possibility is that American families are passing through a cultural lag, a difficult in-between period, as they adapt to new social and economic conditions. While a rapidly changing world outside the home has moved towards greater gender equality, the roles of men and women inside the home have changed relatively little. Across the twentieth century, schools, businesses, the professions, and other institutions have become increasingly neutral about gender. Moreover, legal and political trends in modern democracies have undermined the legitimacy of gender and other forms of caste-like inequality, at least in principle.

To be sure, we have not yet achieved full equality. But we have become used to seeing women in the workplace, even in such formerly all-male institutions as the police, the military, the Congress, and the Supreme Court. The family remains the one institution still based on separate and distinct roles for men and women. Despite the vast social and economic changes that have transformed our daily lives, the old gender roles remain deeply rooted in our cultural assumptions and definitions of masculinity and femininity. At the same time, a more equal or "symmetrical" model of marriage is struggling to be born. Surveys show that most Americans, especially young people, favor equal rather than traditional marriage.

But the transition to such a model has been difficult, even for those committed to the idea of equal partnerships. The difficulties of raising children, and men's continuing advantages in the workplace, make it hard for all but the most dedicated couples to live up to their own ideals.

Adding to the difficulties are the economic shifts of recent years—growing economic inequality, the demise of the well-paying blue-collar job, and the end of the stable career of the 1950s "organization man." The long hours and working weeks that have replaced the nine-to-five corporate workplace take their toll on relationships.

Traditionally, marriage has always been linked to economic opportunity—a young man had to be able to support a wife to be considered eligible to marry. The high rates of marriage in the 1950s were sustained in part by rising wages and a relatively low cost of living; the average 30-year-old man could afford to buy an average-priced house for less than 20 percent of his salary. Today, marriage is becoming something of a "luxury item," a form of "having" available mainly to those already enjoying economic advantages (Furstenberg, 1996). The vast majority of low income men and women would like the "luxury" model, but feel they can't afford it.

Inside marriage, conflicts stemming from gender issues have become the leading cause of divorce (Nock, 1999). Studies of couples married since the 1970s reveal the dynamics of these conflicts. Arlie Hochchild, for example, has found that the happiest marriages are those where the husband does his share of the "second shift," the care of home and children. Another recent study shows that today's women also expect their husbands to do their share of the emotional work of marriage—monitoring and talking about the relationship itself; this "marital work ethic" has emerged in middle class couples married since the 1970s, in response to easy and widespread divorce (Hackstaff, 2000).

Dominance is another sore point in many of today's marriages. Gottman and his colleagues (1998) have found that a key factor in predicting marital happiness and divorce is a husband's willingness to accept influence from his wife; but to many men, the loss of dominance in marriage doesn't feel like equality, it feels more like a shift in power that leaves their wives dominant over them. Studies of battered women show that domestic violence may be the extreme form of this common problem—the man's attempt to assert what he sees as his prerogative to dominate and control his partner.

Still, change is happening, even while men lag behind in the gender revolution. Today's men no longer expect to be waited on in the home the way their grandfathers were by their grandmothers. Middle class norms demand a more involved kind of father than those of a generation ago. The sight of a man with a baby in his arms or on his back is no longer unusual.

In sum, marriage today is passing through a difficult transition to a new economy and a new ordering of gender relations. Those who sermonize about "family values" need to recall that the family is also about "bread and butter" issues and back up their words with resources. And while some people believe that equality and stable marriage are incompatible, the evidence seems so far to show the opposite. As one therapist and writer puts it:

> The feminist revolution of this century has provided the most powerful challenge to traditional patterns of marriage. Yet paradoxically, it may have strengthened the institution by giving greater freedom to both partners, and by allowing men to accept some of traditionally female values (Rubenstein, 1990).

References

Bernard, J. 1972. *The Future of Marriage*. New York: Bantam Books.

Furstenberg, F. 1996. The future of marriage. *American Demographics* (June): 34–40.

Gottman, J. M. and R. W. Levenson. 1992. Marital processes predictive of later dissolution: behavior, physiology and health. *Journal of Personality and Social Psychology* 63:221–33.

Gottman, J. M., J. Coan, S. Carrere, and C. Swanson. 1998. Predicting marital happiness and stability from newlywed interactions. *Journal of Marriage and the Family* 60:5–22.

Hackstaff, K. 2000. *Marriage in a Culture of Divorce*. Boston: Beacon Press.

Levenson, R. W., N. Roberts, and S. Bellows. 1998. Report on police marriage and work stress study. Unpublished paper, University of California, Berkeley.

National Marriage Project. 1999. *Report on Marriage*. Rutgers University.

Nock, S. L. 1999. The problem with marriage. *Society* 36, No. 5 (July/August).

Rubinstein, H. 1990. *The Oxford Book of Marriage*. New York: Oxford University Press.

Skolnick, A. 1981. Married lives: longitudinal perspectives on marriage. In *Present and Past in Middle Life*, edited by D. H. Eichorn, J. A. Clausen, N. Haan, M. P. Honzik, and P. H. Mussen, 269–298. New York: Academic Press.

———. 1993. His and her marriage in longitudinal perspective. In *Feminine/Masculine: Gender and Social Change*. Compendium of Research Summaries. New York: The Rockefeller Foundation.

———. 1998. Sources and processes of police marital stress. Paper presented at National Conference on Community Policing. November. Arlington, Va.

Veroff, J. G., E. Douvan, and R. A. Kulka. 1981. *The Inner American: A Self-Portrait from 1957–1976*. New York: Basic Books.

Chapter

6

Divorce and Remarriage

READING 16

Divorce: The "Silent Revolution"

Lawrence M. Friedman

In the first half of the twentieth century . . . [t]he vast majority of divorces were in fact collusive; they resulted from a deal between husband and wife. (Whether the deal was really "consensual"—that is, a bargain between equals, between two people who both wanted a divorce—is . . . another question.) Collusive divorces were, strictly speaking, illegal. . . . But the official law was a living lie. In Illinois, for example, if the court found that the parties colluded, "no divorce shall be decreed," according to the statute. This was . . . standard doctrine. But according to a study published in the 1950s, almost all divorce cases in Illinois were actually collusive—they came about as a result of "agreement by the parties to the divorce as such." The "testimony" in these cases was usually cut and dried. The typical plaintiff complained of cruelty: her husband beat her, slapped her, abused her. As the author of the study remarked sarcastically, the "number of cruel spouses in Chicago . . . who strike their marriage partners in the face exactly twice . . . is remarkable." To back up her story, the plaintiff almost always brought along her mother or a sister or brother.[1]

Deep into the twentieth century, the formal law, stubbornly insisted that an agreement "between husband and wife that suit shall be brought and no defense entered" was unacceptable; and such a case had to be dismissed. The "policy of our law favors marriage, and disfavors divorce," as a New Jersey judge put it in 1910.[2] In Indiana as late as the 1950s, according to the law, if the defendant failed to make an appearance, the judge was supposed to notify the prosecutor, and the duty of the prosecutor was to enter and defend the case; this was also to happen if the judge suspected any sort of collusion. But these were empty strictures. In practice, almost all cases in Indiana were still uncontested, no defense was made by anybody, the prosecutor never intervened, and plaintiffs could have their divorce virtually "for the asking."[3] In New York, where adultery was the only practical grounds for divorce, a bizarre form of collusion was commonplace. The husband would check into a hotel. A woman hired to play his lover would join him in the room. Both of them would take off some or all of their clothes. A study of 500 divorce cases conducted in the 1930s actually counted how often the man was nude (23), in a nightgown (8), in "B.V.D. or underwear (119)" or in pajamas (227). The woman was nude more often (55 times); in a nightgown 126 times; in a "kimono" 68 times. At this point of undress, a maid would arrive with towels, or a bellboy with a telegram. Suddenly, a photographer would burst into the room and take pictures. Then the man would pay the woman; she then thanked him and left. The photographs would be shown in court as "evidence" of adultery.[4] In England, too, adultery was the only grounds for divorce before 1938; and, as in New York, hotel evidence of this phony type was used in many cases.[5] There were occasional scandals and crackdowns, but the system always went back to normal, after some decent interval.

In the nineteenth century, the British government had been less complacent about collusion than the states. Divorce was socially unacceptable, especially for the lower orders. In 1860, only three years after the divorce law was passed, a new statute created the office of the Queen's Proctor. This officer had the duty of sniffing out collusion and protecting the interests of society in divorce cases. The point was to prevent consensual divorce. On the whole, the experiment did not succeed.[6] The rigid class system of the British did provide some support for a tough regime of divorce; but slowly, the same forces that overwhelmed American divorce overwhelmed the British system as well.

What seems clear is that everywhere in the developed world there was a tremendous, pent-up demand for divorce—a powerful force that simply had to find an outlet. Change or reform remained difficult, if not impossible; respectable society (and legislatures frightened of some of their voters) simply did not permit "easy" divorce. The result was the dual system—collusion and migratory divorce. Another outlet for the divorce demand, at least in New York state, was annulment. In New York, the law, as we have seen, was unusually severe, allowing divorce only for adultery. As a result, New York became the annulment capital of the United States. An annulled marriage, legally speaking, never existed. It was dead from the start because of some grave impediment or fraud. In most states, annulments were much less common than divorces. They were used mostly by Roman Catholics, whose church did not recognize divorce. In San Mateo County, California, in the 1950s, 12 percent of the petitions to end a marriage were petitions for annulment; in the period 1890–1910, only 1 or 2 percent of such petitions in Alameda County, California, were petitions for annulment.[7]

But in New York the situation was entirely different. Annulments were exceedingly common. The New York statute allowed annulment of a marriage if the "consent" of one party was "obtained by force, duress, or fraud" or if "one of the parties was physically incapable of entering into the marriage state" or was a "lunatic."[8] There was nothing unusual about this statute. But in most states, the courts interpreted annulment laws rather strictly. Fraud was not easy to prove. Joel Bishop, writing in the late nineteenth century, found annulment cases "inherently" embarrassing (and "not numerous").[9] It is one thing to want to get rid of a spouse, quite another to accuse that spouse of fraud (or even worse, of total impotence or frigidity). In New York, however, the courts stretched the concept of "fraud" almost beyond recognition, and in general they opened up the legal grounds of annulment to an astonishing degree. By 1950, in ten counties in New York, there were more annulments than divorces; for the state as a whole, there were two-thirds as many annulments as decrees of divorce.[10] To be sure, the appellate courts were not always willing to grant annulments in dubious cases. The case law was quite involute and complex.[11] Loretta Coiley Pawloski failed to get an annulment for fraud against her husband, Alex John; she claimed he lied about his name and told her he was "German" when in fact he was Polish. Loretta "did not care much for Polish people." They had been married over twenty years. This "fraud," even if proven, did not "go to the essence" of the marriage contract, said the court.[12]

Still, it says something that Loretta even *thought* she had a chance at annulment. In most states, her claim would have gotten exactly nowhere. And in many other cases, the New York appellate courts were more willing to discover "fraud" and other impediments. In a 1923 case, James Truiano told Florence Booth, a schoolteacher, that he was a U.S. citizen; in fact he was not. The court granted an annulment.[13] And a young man was able to get an annulment in 1935, when he claimed that his (foreign) wife married him only to get his money, as part of a "scheme" of European "nobility" to "inveigle" wealthy Americans into marriage. The man, said the court, was "unaccustomed to dealing with the workings of a shrewd and cunning European mind"; he had been "deceived and defrauded." The marriage was duly wiped off the books.[14] Most annulment cases, one must remember, were never appealed. They began and ended in the trial courts. They were just as consensual as the thousands of divorces in other states. The New York annulment statistics speak for themselves on this point.

Contemporary Chile is another jurisdiction where annulments have been terrifically and abnormally common. Chile, until 2004, was the only major Western country that still did not recognize absolute divorce. (In that year, the legislature finally enacted such a law.)[15] Annulment was an obvious escape hatch. People used all sorts of tricks and stratagems . . . in their quest for an annulment. In both Chile and New York state, the official law said one thing, and the ordinary lower-level courts did something quite different. Both jurisdictions were trapped in a situation of historic stalemate.

The stalemate, however, came to an end in New York, and in the United States in general, in the second half of the twentieth century. Up to that point, official reform was slow and difficult. But underneath, the dual system was simply rotting away. Divorce became more and more common. Its stigma slowly evaporated. As a judge in Chicago put it around 1950, most people thought divorce was nobody's business, except that of the man and woman in question. Getting a divorce was, or should be, like getting a marriage license: a couple was "entitled to a marriage license for a certain fee" and a blood test, and nothing else. Why not make getting a divorce equally easy? This judge thought "Hollywood" was to blame for the change in attitudes, for the loss of "scandal and shame."[16] This was surely giving Hollywood too much credit (or blame). Movie stars got divorces, of course, but the movies themselves were quite skittish on the subject; indeed, for a while in the 1930s and 1940s they almost never dealt with divorce at all.[17] The judge might even have been somewhat off base in his reading of general public opinion. But there is no doubt that the winds were shifting; even the official law began to evolve, though in a rather gingerly way. New Mexico was bolder than most states: from 1933 on, its divorce statute specifically listed "incompatibility" as grounds for divorce.[18]

"Incompatibility" means basically that two people do not and cannot get along. As far as traditional divorce law was concerned, this was rank heresy.

New Mexico was unusual. But in a fair number of states, the law began to ease the path to divorce in a different way. Divorce became available, even without "grounds," if the couple had been separated for a specific number of years—from two to ten, depending on the state. By 1950, about twenty states had a provision of this sort. In Arizona, Idaho, Kentucky, and Wisconsin, the period was five years; in Rhode Island, it was ten; in Arkansas and Nevada, it was three years; in Louisiana and North Carolina, two years.[19] These statutes, too, were heretical. They plainly recognized that some marriages were dead and gone. It was only decent to give them a proper burial and let people get on with their lives. In fact, in many of these states few couples took advantage of this device. Why wait two, five or ten years when a few harmless lies could bring about a divorce right away?[20]

In many states, a spouse was entitled to a divorce if the other spouse had become "incurably insane" or the like. Sometimes the statute required actual confinement in an insane asylum—for five years in Vermont and Kansas.[21] A spouse also commonly had the right to a divorce if the other spouse was in prison on a felony charge. These seem fairly obvious grounds; but in fact they contradicted the theory of traditional marriage—the promise to cleave together in sickness and in health; in good times and in bad. Cancer or heart disease were never grounds for divorce. Why then insanity? or imprisonment, for a crime not committed against the spouse? Neither of these was technically desertion. But from the standpoint of the sane spouse, or the spouse not in prison, the marriage was a hollow shell and a daily frustration.

There were a few cracks in the armor at the level of appellate courts. In California, a 1952 case, *De Burgh v. De Burgh*,[22] was an important sign of oncoming change. Daisy and Albert De Burgh were suffering through what was obviously a rotten marriage. Albert beat her, bragged about his other women, was often drunk, was lavish with waiters but stingy with Daisy. This was her story. His story was different. He claimed she was spreading lies about him; she was trying to ruin him in business and wreck his reputation, sending letters to partners and associates, accusing him of "dishonesty and homosexuality." Under standard legal doctrine, if both parties were cruel or otherwise at fault, there could be no divorce. The Superior Court, accordingly, denied the divorce and dismissed the case. The California Supreme Court reversed. The family, wrote Justice Roger Traynor, "is the core of our society," and the state should "foster and preserve marriage." But when a marriage "has failed, and the family has ceased to be a unit," the couple should be able to end it through divorce. The evidence in the case showed a "total and irremedial breakdown of the marriage." Traynor sent the case back to trial; the trial judge was instructed to "determine whether the legitimate objects of matrimony have been destroyed" and whether the marriage could be "saved." Theoretically, the judge had the power to deny the divorce; but Traynor's words made that very unlikely.

In the last third of the twentieth century, what Herbert Jacob has called a "silent revolution" finally destroyed the dual system.[23] The "silent revolution" refers to the passage of no-fault divorce laws. Jacob called this revolution a "silent" one because, though it seemed like a radical change, it was accomplished with little discussion and even less controversy. It was as if no-fault crept into the law like a thief in the night. Technocrats drafted the laws, and they were adopted almost without serious debate. A system that had lasted a century vanished in the twinkling of an eye.

Socially, if not legally, the old system had simply rotted away. In the age of individualism and the sexual revolution, in the age of the enthronement of choice, people felt there was no point saving marriages that no longer satisfied either husband or wife or both. They had a right to a divorce whenever the marriage "just didn't work out." Demand for recognition of this social fact finally overwhelmed the forces that held traditional views. And, of course, nobody ever really liked the collusive system. It was corrupt, dirty, and expensive. It demeaned everybody involved in the process—lawyers, judges, and the parties to the divorce themselves.

What came out of California was the so-called no-fault divorce. No-fault divorce is not consensual divorce; it goes far beyond that. It is really unilateral divorce, divorce at will, divorce when either partner, husband or wife, wants a divorce and asks for it. Under a no-fault system, there are absolutely no defenses to an action for divorce. There are no longer any "grounds" for divorce. No-fault reconstructs divorce in the image of marriage; marriage and divorce become parallel, legally speaking. For a marriage to take place, two people have to agree to get married. Breach of promise has been abolished. Both the man and the woman have a veto, then; each one has a right to back out of marriage, up to the very moment when someone pronounces them man and wife. In movie after movie—*The Graduate* is one of the best known—somebody in fact does pull out in the very shadow of the altar. Under no-fault, this veto power continues after marriage. Either partner can decide if the marriage goes on or comes to an end. Either one can break the marriage off, at any time, for any reason—or for no reason at all. This is the practical meaning of a no-fault system—the way it actually operates.

The first no-fault divorce law took effect in California in 1970. The old "grounds" for divorce were eliminated, except for two: total insanity, and "irreconcilable differences, which have caused the irremediable breakdown of the marriage."[24] Interestingly, the experts and jurists who wrote the reports and drafted the law never intended a no-fault system. They wanted to get rid of the old dual system; they wanted to clean house, eliminate hypocrisy and fraud, end the dirty business of collusion, and allow consensual divorce—divorce by mutual agreement. This was already the living law, and they wanted to make it official. They never intended to make divorce easy or automatic, and certainly not unilateral. Marriages were a good thing, they felt; and if at all possible, marriages should be saved. They wanted, for example, a system of marriage counseling. They wanted the courts to mend sick marriages and, if possible, cure them. Their notion was to give more power and resources to family courts; couples in trouble could find help, advice, and perhaps a certain amount of therapy.[25] Herma Hill Kay, a scholar and expert in family law active in the reform movement, suggested remodeling family court in the image of juvenile court. Husband and wife would meet with a counselor; they would explore together whether the marriage could be saved. An important role would be played by "professional caseworkers," psychiatrists, and "experienced supervisors." There would be no "coercion." Ultimately, the court would decide whether "the legitimate objects of matrimony have been destroyed."[26] None of Kay's proposals, as it turned out, would actually stir into life.

Still, the original California law, taken literally, contemplated something other than what actually happened. The law asked a question of fact: are there "irreconcilable differences," and has the marriage completely broken down? Presumably, it would be up to a judge to decide this factual question. But almost immediately the law came to mean something radically different. It took on a life of its own. Divorce became simply automatic.

Judges never inquired into reasons; they never actually asked whether a marriage had "irretrievably broken down," or broken down at all. They merely signed the papers. What is more, the no-fault "revolution" swept the country. State after state adopted a no-fault statute—or, more accurately, a statute that turned out to mean no-fault. The details varied from state to state, but almost everywhere no-fault made its mark on the statute book. Some states, like California, were "pure" no-fault states—in Rhode Island, for example, divorce was to be "decreed, irrespective of the fault of either party, on the ground of irreconcilable differences which have caused the irremediable breakdown of the marriage."[27] In some states, the legislature simply added no-fault to the list of "grounds," even though this was in a way illogical, since no-fault meant that the grounds were no longer important.[28] Utah and Tennessee, for example, added "irreconcilable differences" to their list. In Ohio, what was added was "incompatibility, unless denied by either party."[29] But in most states, divorce became automatic, just as in California. Either party could end the marriage. Judges never did any looking, questioning, or counseling. They became a rubber stamp, nothing more.

To be sure, tough issues of property rights and custody of children remained to plague family law. Many hotly contested cases turned on these issues. They provide plenty of business for divorce lawyers. But the divorce itself was no longer something to fight and contest. No-fault is the epitome of what used to be called "easy" divorce. In fact, divorce is almost never easy, psychologically speaking. But no-fault made the legal part of it much less painful—and cheaper, too. This is especially true if the duration of the marriage was short, no children were born, and there either was no money to divide or no argument about how to divide it. Divorce can even be, for some people, a do-it-yourself project. Nowadays one can buy books that tell readers how to get rid of a spouse in ten easy lessons, without paying for the time and services of a lawyer.

Changes in sexual mores, in the social meaning of marriage and divorce, and in the relationship of men and women underlay the no-fault movement. These factors were more or less common to all developed countries. All of them have moved in the same direction. Some countries in Europe and Latin America—those that are strongly Catholic by tradition—resisted divorce altogether. Italy, Spain, and Ireland for a long time had no laws allowing absolute divorce at all (they did recognize legal separation, however). Gordon Ireland and Jesus de Galindez surveyed divorce laws in the countries of the Western hemisphere just after the end of the Second World War.[30] At that time, there was still no such thing as absolute divorce in Argentina, Brazil, Chile, Colombia, and Paraguay. Divorce had had a long history in some of the republics of Latin America; in others it had come only later—in Uruguay, for example, in 1907, and in Bolivia only in 1932. With the exception of Chile (where absolute divorce, as we saw, was not legally available until 2004), every Latin American country by 2000 had provisions for breaking the bonds of matrimony. Brazil adopted a divorce law in 1977. Strongly Catholic countries in Europe, too, eventually came to adopt divorce laws, though often in the teeth of furious opposition. Italy began to allow divorce in 1970; Spain did so in 1981, after the end of the Franco regime. Divorce is now available in Ireland as well.

Moreover, many countries have modified their laws along paths roughly similar to that of the United States. Brazil, as mentioned, had no divorce at all until 1977; and its first divorce law was quite restrictive (for example, no one was allowed to get divorced twice). In 1992, however, a more modern, consensual divorce law was enacted.[31] In some countries—France, for example—divorce by mutual consent has become available, along with a no-fault system (if the couple had a long-time separation). Germany in the late 1970s adopted a no-fault system; divorce is available whenever the marriage has simply broken down. Sweden, too, has a no-fault system.[32] Most countries have not gone to the same extreme as the United States. But even so conservative a state as Switzerland has liberalized its divorce laws. A new law, in force as of 2000, allowed for divorce by mutual agreement of the parties; and either party can ask for divorce after four years of separation. The law in Austria is quite similar: a couple can get a divorce after six months of separation, if both declare that their marriage has broken down.[33] In England, despite waves of reform, it is still the law as of 2003 that a divorce is allowed only if a marriage has "irretrievably" broken down. In practice, however, as Stephen Cretney has put it, "divorce is readily and quickly available if both parties agree"; and even if one does not, the marriage is basically over. After all, there is no point "denying that the marriage has broken down if one party firmly asserts that it has."[34] Divorce rates have also risen in almost all Western countries. The ropes that bind married people together have gotten weaker; for millions, they are altogether gone.

Notes

1. Maxine B. Virtue, *Family Cases in Court* (1956), pp. 90–91.
2. The case is Sheehan v. Sheehen, 77, N. J. Eq. 411, 77 A. 1063 (Ct. of Chancery of N. J., 1910).
3. Virtue, *Family Cases*, pp. 118, 140.
4. The study is reported in a note, "Collusive and Consensual Divorce and the New York Anomaly," *Col. L. Rev.* 36:1121, 1131 (1936); see Lawrence M. Friedman, "A Dead Language: Divorce Law and Practice before No-Fault," *Va. L. Rev.* 86:1497, 1512–1513 (2000).
5. Colin S. Gibson, *Dissolving Wedlock* (1994), pp. 96–97.
6. On the Queen's Proctor, see Wendie Ellen Schneider, "Secrets and Lies: The Queen's Proctor and Judicial Investigation of Party-Controlled Narratives," *Law and Social Inquiry* 27:449 (2002). The situation in Canada in the first part of the twentieth century was also complex. There was probably plenty of collusion, but the courts were less willing to close their eyes to it. As in England, the "king's proctor" was an official who acted on behalf of the state in divorce cases, snooping about to see if there was conniving or colluding. In Nova Scotia, this official was called a "watching counsel." These busybodies appear to have been at least somewhat effective. See James G. Snell, *In the Shadow of the Law: Divorce in Canada, 1900–1939* (1991), pp. 104–106.
7. I am indebted to Albert Lopez for the figures on San Mateo County. For Alameda County, see Joanna Grossman and Chris Guthrie, "The Road Less Taken: Annulment at the Turn of the Century," *Am. J. of Legal History* 40:307 (1996).
8. *Thompson's Laws of New York* (1939), Part 2, N.Y. Civil Practice Act, sec. 1137, 1139, 1141.
9. Bishop, *New Commentaries*, vol. 1, p. 193.
10. Paul H. Jacobson, *American Marriage and Divorce* (1959), p. 113.
11. See William E. Nelson, *The Legalist Reformation: Law, Politics, and Ideology in New York, 1920–1980* (2001), pp. 51–54, 231–236.
12. Pawloski v. Pawloski, 65 N.Y.S. 2d 413 (Sup. Ct., Cayuga County, 1946).
13. Truiano v. Truiano, 121 Misc. Rep. 635, 201 N.Y.S. 573 (Sup. Ct., Special Term, Warren County, 1923). In fairness to Florence, it has to be said that under a federal statute at the time of the marriage, she would have lost her citizenship (and taken on her husband's citizenship). This would have cost her job. After the couple separated, the law was changed, in 1922, under the Married Women's Citizenship Act, 42 Stat. 1021 (act of Sept. 12, 1922). This was in effect at the time of the Truiano annulment case; but this fact, said the court, "cannot relieve defendant of the fraud, or cause denial to the plaintiff of the relief which she asks," since she would not have married James had she known of his blemish.
14. Ryan v. Ryan, 156 Misc. 251, 281 N.Y.S. 709 (Sup. Ct., Spec. Term, N.Y. County, 1935).

15. Jen Ross, "Separate Ways: Divorce to Become Legal," *Washington Post*, Mar. 30, 2004, p. C1. Malta apparently still does not allow absolute divorce.
16. Cited in Virtue, *Family Cases*, pp. 145–146.
17. Michael Asimow, "Divorce in the Movies: From the Hays Code to *Kramer vs. Kramer*," *Legal Studies Forum* 24:221 (2000).
18. Act of March 3, 1933, ch. 62, sec. 1.
19. J. Herbie DiFonzo, *Beneath the Fault Line: The Popular and Legal Culture of Divorce in Twentieth-Century America* (1997), pp. 78–79.
20. Friedman, "A Dead Language," p. 1497.
21. Vt. Laws 1933, ch. 140, sec. 3117; Gen'l Stats. Kansas 1935, sec. 60–1501 (11).
22. 39 Cal. 2d 858, 250 P 2d 598 (1952).
23. Herbert Jacob, *Silent Revolution: The Transformation of Divorce Law in the United States* (1988).
24. Cal. Civ. Code, sec. 4506.
25. See DiFonzo, *Beneath the Fault Line*, pp. 112–137.
26. Herma Hill Kay, "A Family Court: The California Proposal," *Cal. L. Rev.* 56:1205, 1230 (1968).
27. Rhode Island Rev. Stats., sec. 15-5-3.1.
28. Jacob, *Silent Revolution*, p. 102.
29. Utah Code Ann. (1998), sec. 30-3-1; Tenn. Code sec. 36-4-101. Ohio Rev. Code (2000), sec. 3105.01.
30. Gordon Ireland and Jesus de Galindez, *Divorce in the Americas* (1947).
31. I am indebted to Eliane B. Junqueiro for this information about Brazil. See also Eliane B. Junqueiro, "Brazil: The Road of Conflict Bound for Total Justice," in Lawrence M. Friedman and Rogelio Perez-Perdomo, eds., *Legal Culture in the Age of Globalization: Latin America and Latin Europe* (2003), pp. 64, 74–75.
32. Mary Ann Glendon, *Abortion and Divorce in Western Law. American Failures, European Challenges* (1987), pp. 71–76.
33. For Switzerland, see Andrea Büchler, "Family Law in Switzerland: Recent Reforms and Future Issues—an Overview," *European J. of Law Reform* 3:275, 279 (2001); for Austria, see Monika Hinteregger, "The Austrian Matrimonial Law—a Patchwork Pattern of History," *European J. of Law Reform* 3:199, 212 (2001).
34. Stephen Cretney, *Family Law in the Twentieth Century: A History* (2003), p. 391.

READING 17

Divorce in Research vs. Divorce in Media

Virginia E. Rutter

The U.S. divorce rate did not start increasing in the 1960s. Our divorce statistics began to be recorded in 1880, and starting then, our rate of divorce increased steadily for the next 80 years (Ruggles 1997). It then doubled between 1960 and 1980. By the end of that period, about half of marriages ended in divorce. Since 1980, our 50 percent divorce rate has leveled off, and we haven't seen much change (Goldstein 1999).

Divorce, then, is a fixture in family life—and a 'problem' to be understood, interpreted, analyzed, and fixed (Coltrane & Adams 2003). But what exactly is the problem? A better understanding of divorce—and divorce research—clarifies the reasoning behind making a 'case for divorce'. By extension, this understanding informs us about the realities faced by contemporary families. Some perceptions of divorce as a problem emerge because research fails to ask a simple question: Divorce is a problem, but compared to what?

Put another way, the case for divorce asks: Are there some cases where divorce is a *better* outcome than remaining married? Using research developments from three distinct time periods, this paper demonstrates that research on the impact on adults and children points to yes. These three episodes also provide an opportunity to understand *why* 'a case for divorce' is being made. Each of these three episodes involves paired research results. Studies that include a comparison group (that analytically represents that divorce is a choice made most often in already bad circumstances) are paired in each of three cases with studies that do not provide a comparison. The discussion of the three episodes includes description of media coverage of the work.

A second, related question is: Do we have reasons why we value divorce, as part of our liberal democracy? The history of divorce goes hand in hand with our history of individual rights that have improved the status of women, minorities, workers, and people without property throughout our history. Since the shift in divorce laws in the 1960s and 1970s to allow unilateral divorce ('no-fault divorce') in the United States, the rate of suicide among wives, domestic violence, and spousal homicide have declined (Stevenson & Wolfers 2006). Meanwhile, part and parcel with declining fertility rates in the United States, the number of children involved in any given divorce has gone from 1.34 children to less than 1 child per divorce (Cowen 2007). Hence, there is a decline in the impact of any given divorce on children. These data do suggest that divorce is associated with outcomes that we value in a liberal democracy.

DIVORCE RESEARCH: TWO THEMES

In research and public conversations, researchers and journalists have earnestly parsed the causes and consequences of divorce in light of the hastened growth of divorce between 1960 and 1980. Researchers find that divorce's impact depends on what the comparison is: compared to a happy marriage, divorce is associated with many disadvantages for the divorced couple and their children; compared to a harsh marriage, however, the research generally shows that divorce has benefits. Meanwhile, policy makers and general audiences alike get their information about divorce research via the news media, where the negative consequences of divorce tend to be exaggerated, especially when comparisons are neglected. At least some of the time, this neglect is advanced by special interest groups seeking to promote a conservative family agenda. Over the past 20 years, U.S. news coverage of divorce illustrates two key intertwined topics: moral entrepreneurship using divorce as an issue and divorce research using (or not) careful methods of comparison. Three cases discussed below (in 1988–1989, 2002–2004, and 2008) make the case.

Moral entrepreneurs

What information about divorce enters into popular awareness? Over the years, when research results produce apparently conflicting results, the more alarming (and simpler) results consistently get more ink. In the context of divorce research, sociologists Scott Coltrane and Michele Adams (2003) have argued that *moral entrepreneurs* act to heighten collective anxiety in order to promote 'family values' and their more traditional gender norms.

Moral entrepreneurs (Becker 1973) seek to adopt or maintain a norm or tradition. Enterprising opinion leaders seek to shape public awareness about the 'case against divorce' by making *knowledge claims* grounded in a version of social science that, especially in the most conservative cases, reinforces traditional, two-parent, in-tact, biologically related families. A knowledge claim is a statement that we know something is a *fact*. Where research shows that divorce harms children or women or the economy, the case *seems* to be clear. In the cases presented here, the claims against divorce are made based on research that fails to make reasonable comparisons or to provide representative samples.

Organizations–ranging from the more moderate Institute for American Values to the more conservative Heritage Foundation—have skillfully spread the word about research—the kind that supports their concerns about the way they believe that divorce has contributed to the decay of American family life. From the perspective of moral entrepreneurship, worry is good for business—and consistent with a moral agenda that questions changes in family organization. Family historian Steven Mintz (2004) describes case after case of Americans' fondness for the story of decay, and the penchant for worry about divorce is like hand wringing about teen sexuality, delinquency, the corrupting force of television, the problem of working mothers, the problem of mothers not working, etc. Indeed, worry about divorce is not new. As Mintz describes, moral entrepreneurs raved about the scourge of divorce, for example, from 1890 to 1920.

Research methods: Look for comparison groups

Scientists reviewing research will always ask whether or not it makes a logical and reasonable comparison. When researchers examine, 'divorce compared to what?' they are searching for *selection bias* or preceding factors that may explain a given set of results. People who end up divorcing may be different from people who remain married and it may be these pre-marriage differences between the two groups—and not divorce itself—that explain differences in health and mental health outcomes after divorce. This type of selection bias may influence results and the interpretation of results. In diverse studies, several factors suggest that the divorced group is, indeed, already different from the stably married group. For example, divorced couples are younger in age at first marriage, more likely to be living in poverty, and less likely to have a college degree. Researchers must also answer the question about how whether and, if so, how, divorce *causes* problems for adults or their children?

1988–2008: DUELING DIVORCE COVERAGE

Three episodes of divorce research in the news—in 1988–1989, 2002–2004, and 2008—exemplify themes of *moral entrepreneurship* and *research issues with* they were civil. Hetherington was able to analyze the well-being of children in extremely distressed married families versus children of divorce and children in harmonious, married families. By adding comparisons about the level of distress in all the families, she observed that children in harmonious, married families fared better than children in divorced families, *and* in distressed married families. By making comparisons based on the quality of the intact marriages in her study, she was able to make an important distinction: The worst kind of family for a child to be raised in, in terms of mental health and behavior, was a *distressed, married* family (Hetherington 1999).

Several key pieces of research extended Hetherington's results by using comparison groups and a prospective design. In 1991, demographer Andrew Cherlin and colleagues wrote about longitudinal studies in Great Britain and the United States in the journal *Science.* The studies included data from parents, children, and teachers over time. At the first time point, age 7, all the children's parents were married. Over the study period, some went on to divorce, and some did not. Cherlin confirmed Hetherington's findings: while about 10 percent of children overall were at risk for adjustment and mental health problems, children of divorce were at 20–25 percent at risk for problems.

Cherlin also found that the difference between the children of divorce versus stable marriages existed *prior* to the divorce. These were *predisruption effects,* a term that highlights that parents who end up divorcing (but are not yet divorced) are different from parents who don't end up divorcing. They relate to each other differently, they relate to their children differently, and their children relate to them differently. Cherlin had identified selection bias, or a case of selection into divorce.

In 1998, Cherlin and colleagues offered an update on their continuing research, which modified his conclusions. Respondents analyzed in the 1991 study had gotten older, so he had more information. While the 1991 paper highlighted predisruption effects, this one reported that in addition, there were *postdisruption* effects (negative effects after the divorce) that accumulated and made life more difficult for children of divorce. Financial hardship and the loss of paternal involvement were key culprits. He called this phenomenon the 'cascade of negative life events', and emphasized, as he had back in 1991, the importance of social and institutional supports for children in disrupted and remarried families.

Starting with Hetherington in the 1980s, and following through Cherlin's parallel work in the 1990s, research designs that included comparison groups helped bring to light three points: first, using a population-based rather than a clinical sample provided a rate of distress among children of divorce that exemplified their *resilience:* approximately 80 percent were doing well, versus 90 percent of children in the general population. Second, difficulties—*pre-disruption effects*—found in longitudinal, prospective studies, meant that children in families where their parents were headed for divorce were having troubles prior to the break-up. *Postdisruption effects*—and the cascade of negative life events—also played a role and suggested that institutions and communities can do more to support these families. Third, severely distressed marriages were more damaging to children than divorces. This last point foreshadowed the results in the studies of adults that I describe in the next section.

At the same time, the 'adult child of divorce' research remained popular in mainstream reporting. This trope showed the robustness of uncertainty about the impact of divorce and the extensiveness of anxiety about changes to family life, of which divorce was a part. (It also helped to create it.) Above all, such discourse represented a missed opportunity for people to know in greater detail where the hazards of divorce actually lie.

DOES DIVORCE MAKE YOU HAPPY?

The question of well-being among adults who divorce provides additional evidence for the case for divorce—and the case for research methods.

In 2002, the Institute for American Values released a paper by Linda Waite, a demographer at the University of Chicago, and several of her colleagues. The paper was titled, 'Does Divorce Make You Happy?' Around that time, other, similar research, 'The Case for Divorce: Under What Conditions Is Divorce Beneficial and for Whom?' (Rutter 2004), also sought to examine emotional consequences of divorcing versus staying married.

Both researchers asked: how does people's level of well-being change when they divorce (versus when they stay married)? Both projects relied on the same data set; they both used a longitudinal design where all subjects were married at the first time point, and some of them went on to divorce by the second time point. The results, however, were divergent. According to Rutter, adults who exited unhappy marriages were less depressed than those who stayed. According to Waite, there were no differences in happiness between those who stayed married and those who divorced.

In order to understand the divergence of these results, we can examine the research methods. The overarching research question is: 'divorce, compared to what?' (Or: is there a *selection bias?)* Were divorced individuals compared to people staying in a happy marriage? Were the divorced compared to those staying in a stressed-out marriage? One difference between Rutter's and Waite's studies was that Rutter used a more stringent measure of marital distress that was more likely to identify which couples were more likely candidates for divorce. Rutter also took severe domestic violence into account and measured depression rather than 'happiness'.

These distinctions—whether the marriage is in serious distress, whether respondents have debilitating emotional problems—made a difference.[1] When comparing how people in a truly distressed marriage fare compared to divorced people, the divorced were better off (less depressed). Rutter's additional statistical tests (which accounted for 'fixed effects', discussed below) confirmed that marital distress, not other factors, accounted for the differences in depression between the married and divorced groups.

More recent research has examined how the accumulation of marital transitions—a divorce, a cohabitation, a break up, perhaps a remarriage—may be an additional important way to examine the impact of divorce on adults. The approach is to examine 'relationship trajectories'. Meadows and colleagues (2008) examined the consequence of such transitions for women who started as single mothers, and found that women who face continuous instability—rather than a single transition—have worse health. Such research allows for even more complexity, and requires that we compare higher levels of disruption with lower levels of disruption, including divorce, in parents' and children's life stories.

Why marital quality matters

Why does marital quality make a difference? The benefits of marriage accrue only to people in happy and well-functioning marriages. For example, studies on the 'psychophysiology of marriage' show that when men and women are in distressed marriages—with, for example, contempt, criticism, defensiveness, stonewalling—their immune systems decline over time (Gottman 1994; Kiekolt-Glaser et al. 1988; Robles & Kiekolt-Glaser 2003). These people are less healthy and less happy. Troubled marriages have immediate costs; they also have downstream health costs.

When researchers measure marital distress in terms of level of conflict, or they use multiple measures of distress, they find that divorce is a relief to those couples. This parallels what Hetherington found for children: that divorce is better than living in a high-conflict family. It is easy enough to ask, 'how was marital distress measured?' in order to learn whether a measure of general sentiment that captures more transient feelings of satisfaction was used, or whether a measure of serious distress or conflict, which tends to tell us which couples would be 'candidates' for divorce if they considered divorce an option, was used.

On happiness

The Waite and Rutter studies had in common looking at the personal costs of divorcing. While Waite measured 'happiness', Rutter's outcome measure was 'depression'. Does it matter how we specify 'personal well-being'? In brief, the answer is yes. While happiness and depression are correlated (van Hemert et al. 2002), there is a difference. Out of hundreds of correlational studies catalogued in the World Database of Happiness (Veenhoven 2004), there are scarcely any gender differences in happiness. Nor does happiness have the major correlates to race or poverty that have been well established for depression.

All these differences suggest that 'happiness' is measuring something psychologically different from 'distress' or 'depression'. The societal implications are quite different between these two measures: unhappy people are not usually functionally impaired; depression, however, involves costs in terms of lost wages, productivity, and negative impact on children (Greenberg et al. 1993a, b).

For media, Waite's study had sufficient scientific authority. Reporters, such as those at *USA Today* and the Today Show, covered the results. The news coverage 'punchline': divorce isn't going to make you any happier, so stay married! But other studies showed that the case for divorce is more complex. Such coverage helps sustain public 'uncertainty' related to any case for divorce.

WHERE'S THE COMPARISON GROUP? REDUX

In April 2008, the questions about the impact of divorce and its costs continued to be alive and well: Two studies were released the very same week on the topic. What, these studies asked, is the impact of divorce? A research brief from the researchers' think-tank

Council on Contemporary Families (2008)[2] was based on demographer Allen Li's Rand Corporation working paper (Li 2007). The other paper by economist Ben Scafidi was released by the Institute for American Values (Scafidi 2008). Li's paper pertained to the emotional impact of divorce on children, while Scafidi's paper addressed the economic impact of divorce across America. Comparing these papers, we can examine the sponsors, the media coverage, and the research content of the work.

The results were completely divergent. Li asked, what is the impact of divorce on children? He found that divorce itself does not explain the difference we see between children with divorced versus married parents. Yes, he found differences between the two groups (on average)—just as researchers had been finding since the 1980s. With increasingly refined research techniques, however, Li was able to show that *selection bias* accounts for the difference.

The technique included testing for 'fixed effects'. 'Fixed effects' refers to time-invariant characteristics of individuals that may be correlated with both the outcomes of interest (psychological-well-being, for example) and explanatory variables in the statistical model (divorce, for example) producing biased results. Longitudinal data—multiple observations on the same individual over time—can allow researchers to control for these effects. Fixed-effects models test whether there are aspects of the individuals that are not measured explicitly but that can account for results. This method helped to reveal that the children in Li's study whose parents ended up divorcing were getting a different kind of parenting all along the way than the children whose parents stayed married.

Meanwhile, Scafidi asked, what does divorce cost the general public? By his calculations, divorce—plus single parenthood—cost taxpayers 112 billion dollars. To calculate this, he assumed that divorce and single parenthood *cause* poverty. In other words, he neglected the notion that selection bias could play a role in who ends up as a single parent or divorced. But, in a 2002 report, economist Nancy Folbre and historian Stephanie Coontz were among many who examined the problems with making this assumption (Folbre and Coontz 2002). While there is a correlation between single parenthood and poverty, they explained, the correlation does not imply that single parenthood *causes* poverty. *Causation* is complex and challenging to establish, but the evidence for causality going in the other direction—that poverty *causes* or precedes single parenthood is to many minds a lot stronger. As Stevenson and Wolfers (in Li 2008) point out, Scafidi neglected comparisons in another way as well: while some women end up losing financially following divorce, others actually *gain*. According to Ananat and Michael 2008 (cited by Stevenson & Wolfers), the gains actually *exceed* the losses. Scafidi did not include these economic gains in his calculations.

Li's and Scafidi's results were divergent because of their fundamental differences in thinking about 'what causes what?' While Li's article asks, divorce, *compared to what*?, Scafidi did not assess the costs of divorce relative to, for example, remaining in a distressed, tumultuous, or violent family situation. Scafidi didn't test the assumption that divorce (and single parenthood) cause economic problems. He assumed that.

Li's results were not isolated. Like Li, other researchers continue to find selection bias accounts for some if not all of the differences between children whose parents divorce and those who don't. For example, Fomby and Cherlin (2007) found that selection effects—the characteristics of the mother that precede the divorce—helped explain the reduced cognitive outcomes for children of divorce. They also found that the divorce itself, rather than just selection bias or pre-disruption effects, was associated with behavioral problems sometimes seen in children of divorce. Just as research on relationship trajectories may help us understand in finer detail how and when divorce is difficult on adults, this same promising line of research can further examine the postdisruption effects of divorce on children: children exposed to multiple transitions—a divorce, then a cohabitation and break up, then perhaps another marriage—may be at elevated risk relative to children exposed only to one transition. In a study that focuses on single parents, Osborne and McLanahan (2007) found that the accumulation of mother's relationship transitions adds to children's troubles.[3]

How were the Li and Scafidi articles covered? Both studies were reported in *USA Today*. While Scafidi received more coverage (such as the *Associated Press*, *Newsweek*, the *Washington Times*, the *Wall Street Journal*) than Li did, still a review of the coverage shows us that news coverage may be turning a bit.

Another change over the past 20 years of discussing results of divorce research also looks promising: when searching the blogosphere on the most recent divorce research, many researchers, scientists, and citizens commented on the problematic research methods of Scafidi and the case of 'advocacy science' (or 'moral entrepreneurship'). Granted, the blogosphere also included many discussions applauding Scafidi, and others castigating Li. Thus, the Internet offers much opportunity for people to speak out and have a dialogue about moral entrepreneurship and science on the one hand, and research methods on the other. While popular dialogue on the Internet is promising for telling a more complicated story of the case for divorce, now more than ever we need citizens who can ask whether they are reading a case of moral entrepreneurship and who have a good understanding of the basics of research design—including selection bias.

LESSONS LEARNED

Students of sociology have learned that knowledge is socially constructed—social forces such as our modern interest in individual psychology (Illouz 2008), technological breakthroughs in data collection that ease longitudinal and prospective studies, and policy interest in family structure that has followed the increases in divorces between 1960 and 1980, all play a role in what we learn about families.

Sociologists, like good contextualists (Pepper 1942), recognize that just because knowledge is socially constructed, this does not pre-empt our capacity to judge science on its merits. We can still evaluate research in terms of best practices. What the story of divorce research shows is that the tools of science can help us to read the research and assess where we *really* stand on the impact of divorce.

IN SUM: WHAT IS A CASE FOR DIVORCE, AND WHY MAKE IT?

What is the impact of divorce on children? There is no arguing that the lives of children of divorce are different from the lives of children whose parents remain married. But in order to understand what happens to children (and adults), one must consider their situation relative to the alternatives available to them. This article details the process of discovery by social scientists over time—through the application of new research methods—that has given us an increasingly fine-grained understanding of divorce. The plot culminates in current research that examines how parents' relationship careers may help us understand the details of when, where, and under what conditions divorce is stressful to children.

This case for divorce involves a review of research over time and a recognition of its complexity. While researchers who use comparisons, and control for selection bias, who measure marital adjustment carefully, and who take domestic violence into account, will disagree about exactly how children of divorce differ from children of married parents (are 20 percent affected? are 25 percent affected?), there is agreement about the resilience of children of divorce. Researchers may disagree about whether the impact of divorce is neutral, as Allen Li contends, or whether some of the impact of divorce is due to pre-existing factors, but that some of the impact of divorce can still be attributed to post-disruption factors, as Andrew Cherlin argues; or that relationship trajectory research will yield more finely grained knowledge. Still, scientists agree that comparing married families to divorced families without taking selection bias into account is a case of comparing apples to oranges, and will get us nowhere in terms of helping families. As Rutter, Hawkins and Booth, and Hetherington show, failing to take the quality of the marriages seriously limits our capacity to understand the linkages between the experience of marriage and the experience of divorce. The distressed marriage is where most people considering divorce start.

Finally, *why* a 'case' for divorce? The phrase itself refers back to Waite and Gallagher's *The Case for Marriage* (2000); this in turn is reminiscent of William Eskridge's *The Case for Same-Sex Marriage* (1996). In one sense, only *The Case for Same-Sex Marriage* had a 'case' to make, given the status of same-sex marriage in the United States at the time of its publication. Yet, as these three examples from 1988 to 2008 highlight, popular understanding of divorce's impact remains contested and uncertain. In another sense, both *The Case for Marriage* and 'The Case for Divorce' draw upon this trope to conduct a literature review for the purposes of focusing attention on social institutions that are currently in flux both demographically and symbolically.

The Case for Marriage was not written because the legal rights of heterosexual people to access marriage or the fondness of Americans for marriage was under threat (though it had been declining). The book was an effort to re-organize common understanding of marriage as beneficial for men, women, children, and communities by drawing our attention to the wealth of social scientific research on the health and economic benefits associated with marriage. In a time of perceived uncertainty, *The Case for Marriage* was associated with drawing policy makers' attention to their opportunity to use the authors' data-based understanding of marriage in order to create policies shaped by the compassionate insight that marriage is associated with a good life for many. *The Case for Marriage* was also associated with a related *cultural* mission of compassion, to help refocus attention on the benefits of marriage that can make lives better. Similarly 'The Case for Divorce' seeks to re-focus common understanding of divorce by reporting on and drawing parallels across diverse times and types of divorce research, and to guide readers through the uncertainty that persists simultaneously in the understanding of the data and in the culture. This too is a mission of compassion.

SHORT BIOGRAPHY

Virginia E. Rutter's work focuses on research questions that are responsive to public concerns about social problems. As a survey researcher, she studies family, gender, and sexuality. At the same time, she has worked translating social science work in these areas to general audiences via the media. She is an assistant professor of sociology at the Framingham State College in Framingham, MA. Previously, she was a research scientist at the Battelle Centers for Public Health Research and Evaluation in Seattle and Arlington, VA, where she was a co-investigator in the NIH-funded National Couples Survey. Her most recent work is titled 'The Case for Divorce: Under What Conditions Is Divorce Beneficial and for Whom?' She is co-author of two books, *The Gender of Sexuality* and *The Love Test*, several academic book chapters, and numerous articles for general audiences. She is a board member of the Council on Contemporary Families and a columnist for *Girl w/Pen*.

Notes

* Correspondence address: Department of Sociology, Framingham State College, 100 State Street, Framingham, MA 01701, USA. Email: vrutter@framingham.edu.

1. Other longitudinal studies, including Hawkins and Booth (2005), found similar results: the more carefully marital distress is measured, the more pronounced are the psychological advantages of leaving over staying.
2. The Council on Contemporary Families is a non-partisan, non-profit organization of family scholars and clinicians whose mission is to disseminate the latest research and best-practice findings on the changing experiences and needs of today's diverse families. Authors of briefing reports receive no funding, in-kind support, or reimbursement for contributions.
3. A July 2008 briefing report (D'Onofrio 2008) at the website for the Institute for American Values offers a discussion of research on the impact of divorce on children.

References

Ananat, E. and G. Michaels 2008. 'The Effect of Marital Breakup on the Income Distribution of Women and Children.' *Journal of Human Resources*. Forthcoming, url: http://eprints.lse.ac.uk/4643/ Retrieved online June 24, 2008.

Becker, Howard S. 1973. *Outsiders: Studies in the Sociology of Deviance*. New York, NY: The Free Press, pp. 147–153.

Cherlin, A. J., Furstenberg, F. F., Chase-Lansdale, P. L. et al. 1991. 'Longitudinal Studies of Effects of Divorce on Children in Great Britain and the U.S.' *Science* **252:** 1386–89.

Cherlin, A. J., Chase-Lansdale, P. Lindsay and Christine McRae 1998. 'Effects of Parental Divorce on Mental Health through the Life Course,' *American Sociological Review* **63**, pp. 239–249.

Coltrane, Scott and Michele Adams 2003. 'The Social Construction of the Divorce "Problem": Morality, Child Victims, and the Politics of Gender.' *Family Relations* **52:** 363–372.

Cowen, Tyler 2007. 'Matrimony Has Its Benefits, and Divorce Has a Lot to do With That.' *The New York Times* April 19. url: http://www.nytimes.com/2007/04/19/business/19scene.html?emc=eta1 Retrieved online on June 20, 2008.

D'Onofrio, Brian 2008. 'Divorce, Dads, and the Well-Being of Children: Answers to Common Research Questions.' Research Brief #12, July. Washington, D.C.: Institute for American Values, url: http://center.americanvalues.org/?p=76 Retrieved online December 22, 2008.

Eskridge, William 1996. *The Case for Same-Sex Marriage: From Sexual Liberty to Civilized Commitment.* New York, NY: Free Press

Folbre, N. and S. Coontz 2002. 'Marriage, Poverty, and Public Policy.' A briefing paper from the Council on Contemporary Families, url: http://www.contemporaryfamilies.org/public/briefing.html (April). Retrieved online on June 24, 2008.

Fomby, Paula and Andrew Cherlin 2007. 'Family Instability and Child Well-Being.' *American Sociological Review* **72:** 181–204.

Goldstein, J. R. 1999. The Leveling of Divorce in the United States,' *Demography*, **36:** 409–414.

Gottman, J. M. 1994. *What Predicts Divorce?* Erlbaum: New Jersey.

Greenberg, P. E., Stiglin, L. E., Finkelstein, S. N. and E. R. Berndt 1993a. 'Depression: A Neglected Major Illness.' *Journal of Clinical Psychiatry* **54:** 419–424.

Greenberg, P. E., Stiglin, L. E., Finkelstein, S. N. and E. R. Berndt 1993b. 'The Economic Burden of Depression in 1990.' *Journal of Clinical Psychiatry* 54: 405–418.

Hawkins, Daniel N. and Alan Booth 2005. 'Unhappily Ever After: Effects of Long-Term, Low-Quality Marriages on Well-Being.' *Social Forces* **84:** 451–471.

Hetherington, E. Mavis 1988. 'The Impact of Divorce.' *Keynote Address at the Annual Conference of American Association for Marriage and Family Therapy.* New Orleans, LA: October.

Hetherington, E. M. and John Kelly 2002. *For Better or For Worse: Divorce Reconsidered.* New York, NY: W.W. Norton.

Hetherington, E. M. 1999. 'Should We Stay Together for the Sake of the Children?' Pp. 93–116 in *Coping with Divorce, Single Parenting, and Remarriage: A Risk and Resiliency Perspective*, edited by E. Mavis Hetherington. Mahwah, NJ: Lawrence Erlbaum Associates.

Hetherington, E. M. and P. Stanley-Hagan 1997. 'Divorce and the Adjustment of Children: A risk and resiliency perspective.' *Journal of Child Psychology & Psychiatry* **40:** 129–140.

Illouz, E. 2008. *Saving the modern Soul: Therapy, Emotions, and the Culture of Self-Help.* Berkeley, CA: University of California Press.

Kiekolt-Glaser, J. K., Kennedy, S., Malkoff, S., Fisher, L., Speicher, C. E. and R. Glaser 1988. 'Marital Discord and Immunity in Males.' *Psychosomatic Medicine* **50:** 213–299.

Li, Jui-Chung Allen 2007. 'The Kids Are OK: Divorce and Children's Behavior Problems.' RAND Labor and Population Working Paper No. WR-489. RAND, Santa Monica, CA.

Li, Jui-Chung Allen 2008. 'New findings on an old question: Does divorce cause children's behavior problems?' *A Briefing Paper from the Council on Contemporary Families*, url: http://www.contemporaryfamilies.org/public/briefing.html (April 24). Retrieved online June 24, 2008.

Meadows, S. O., McLanahan, S. and J. Brooks-Gunn 2008. 'Stability and Change in Family Structure and Maternal Health Trajectories.' *American Sociological Review* **73:** 314–334.

Mintz, Steve 2004. *Huck's Raft: A History of American Childhood.* Cambridge, MA: Harvard University Press.

Osborne, C. and S. McLanahan 2007. 'Partnership Instability and Child Well-Being.' *Journal of Marriage and Family* **69:** 1065–1083.

Pepper, Stephen C. 1942. *World Hypotheses: A Study in Evidence.* Berkeley, CA: University of California Press.

Robles, T. F. and J. K. Kiekolt-Glaser 2003. 'The Physiology of Marriage: Pathways to Health.' *Physiology and Behavior* **79:** 409–16.

Ruggles, Steven 1997. 'The Rise of Divorce and Separation in the United States 1880–1990. *Demography* **34**(4): 455–466.

Rutter, Virginia E. 2004. *The Case for Divorce: Under What conditions is divorce beneficial and for whom?* PhD thesis, University of Washington.

Scafidi, B. 2008. *The Taxpayer Costs of Divorce: First-Ever Estimates for the Nation and all Fifty States.* New York, NY: Institute for American Values.

Stevenson, B. and J. Wolfers 2006. 'Bargaining in the Shadow of Divorce Laws and Family Distress.' *Quarterly Journal of Economics* **121:** 267–288.

van Hemert, Dianne A., Vijver, F. J. R. vande and Ype H. Poortinga 2002. 'The Beck Depression Inventory as a Measure of Subjective Well-Being: A Cross-National Study.' *Journal of Happiness Studies* **3**(3): 257–286.

Veenhoven, Ruut 2004. *World Database of Happiness: Continuous register of scientific research on subjective appreciation of life.* Rotterdam, The Netherlands: Erasmus University, url: http://www2.eur.nl/fsw/research/happiness/.

Waite, Linda J. and Margie Gallagher 2000. *The Case for Marriage: Why Married People Are Happier, Healthier and Better Off Financially.* New York, NY: Doubleday.

Waite, Linda J., Browning, Don, Doherty, William J., Gallagher, Maggie, Luo, Ye and Scott M. Stanley 2002. *Does Divorce Make People Happy? Findings From a Study of Unhappy Marriages.* New York, NY: Institute for American Values.

Wallerstein, J. 1989. 'Children after Divorce.' *The New York Times* January 22. url: http://query.nytimes.com/gst/fullpage.html?res=950DE2DF123BF931A15752C0A96F948260&sec=&spon=. Retrieved online June 20, 2008.

Wallerstein, J. and Sandra Blakeslee 1988. *Second Chances: Men, Women, and Children a Decade after Divorce: Who Wins, Who Loses, and Why.* New York, NY: Ticknor & Fields.

READING 18

The Modern American Stepfamily: Problems and Possibilities

Mary Ann Mason

Cinderella had one, so did Snow White and Hansel and Gretel. Our traditional cultural myths are filled with the presence of evil stepmothers. We learn from the stories read to us as children that stepparents, particularly stepmothers, are not to be trusted. They may pretend to love us in front of our biological parent, but the moment our real parent is out of sight they will treat us cruelly and shower their own children with kindnesses. Few modern children's tales paint stepparents so harshly, still the negative image of stepparents lingers in public policy. While the rights and obligations of biological parents, wed or unwed, have been greatly strengthened in recent times, stepparents have been virtually ignored. At best it is fair to say that as a society we have a poorly formed concept of the role of stepparents and a reluctance to clarify that role.

Indeed, the contrast between the legal status of stepparents and the presumptive rights and obligations of natural parents is remarkable. Child support obligations, custody rights, and inheritance rights exist between children and their natural parents by virtue of a biological tie alone, regardless of the quality of social or emotional bonds between parent and child, and regardless of whether the parents are married. In recent years policy changes have extended the rights and obligations of natural parents, particularly in regard to unwed and divorced parents, but have not advanced with regard to stepparents. Stepparents in most states have no obligation during the marriage to support their step-children, nor do they enjoy any right of custody or control. Consistent with this pattern, if the marriage terminates through divorce or death, they usually have no rights to custody or even visitation, however longstanding their relationship with their stepchildren. Conversely, stepparents have no obligation to pay child support following divorce, even if their stepchildren have depended on their income for many years. In turn, stepchildren have no right of inheritance in the event of the stepparent's death (they are, however, eligible for Social Security benefits in most cases).[1]

Policymakers who spend a great deal of time worrying about the economic and psychological effects of divorce on children rarely consider the fact that about 70 percent of mothers are remarried within six years. More over, about 28 percent of children are born to unwed mothers, many of whom eventually marry someone who is not the father of their child. In a study including all children, not just children of divorce, it was estimated that one-fourth of the children born in the United States in the early 1980s will live with a stepparent before they reach adulthood.[2] These numbers are likely to increase in the future, at least as long as the number of single-parent families continues to grow. In light of these demographic trends, federal and state policies affecting families and children, as well as policies governing private-sector employee benefits, insurance, and other critical areas of everyday life, may need to be adapted to address the concerns of modern stepfamilies.

In recent years stepfamilies have received fresh attention from the psychological and social sciences but little from legal and policy scholars. We now know a good deal about who modern stepfamilies are and how they function, but there have been few attempts to apply this knowledge to policy. This [reading] first of all reviews the recent findings on the everyday social and economic functioning of today's stepfamilies, and then examines current state and federal policies, or lack of them in this arena. Finally, the sparse set of current policy recommendations, including my own, are presented. These proposals range from active discouragement of stepfamilies[3] to a consideration of stepparents as de facto parents, with all the rights and responsibilities of biological parents during marriage, and a limited extension of these rights and responsibilities following the breakup of marriage or the death of the stepparent.[4]

THE MODERN STEPFAMILY

The modern stepfamily is different and more complex than Cinderella's or Snow White's in several important ways. First, the stepparent who lives with the children is far more likely to be a stepfather than a stepmother, and in most cases the children's biological father is still alive and a presence, in varying degrees, in their lives. Today it is divorce, rather than death, which usually serves as the background event for the formation of the stepfamily, and it is the custodial mother who remarries (86 percent of stepchildren live primarily with a custodial mother and stepfather),[5] initiating a new legal arrangement with a stepfather.[6]

Let us take the case of the Jones-Hutchins family. Sara was eight and Josh five when their mother and father, Martha and Ray Jones divorced. Three years later Martha married Sam Hutchins, who had no children. They bought a house together and the children received health and other benefits from Sam's job, since Martha was working part time at a job with no benefits.

Theoretically, this new parental arrangement was a triangle, since Ray was still on the scene and initially saw the children every other weekend. In most stepfamilies the noncustodial parent, usually the father, is still alive (only in 25 percent of cases is the noncustodial parent dead, or his whereabouts unknown). This creates the phenomenon of more than two parents, a situation that conventional policymakers are not well equipped to address. However, according to the National Survey of Families and Households (NSFH), a nationally representative sample of families, contact between stepchildren and their absent natural fathers is not that frequent. Contact falls into four broad patterns: roughly one-quarter of all stepchildren have no association at all with their fathers and receive no child support; one-quarter see their fathers only once a year or less often and receive no child support; one-quarter have intermittent contact or receive some child support; and one-quarter may or may not receive child support but have fairly regular contact, seeing their fathers once a month or more. Using these data as guides to the quality and intensity of the father-child relationship, it appears that relatively few stepchildren are close to their natural fathers or have enough contact with them to permit the fathers to play a prominent role in the children's upbringing. Still, at least half of natural fathers do figure in their children's lives to some degree.[7] The presence of the noncustodial parent usually precludes the option of stepparent adoption, a solution that would solve the legal ambiguities, at least, of the stepparent's role.

In size, according to the National Survey of Families and Households, modern residential stepfamilies resemble modern nondivorced families and single-parent families, with an average of two children per family. Only families with two stepparents (the rarest type of stepfamily, in which both parents had children from previous relationships, and both are the custodial parents) are larger, with an average of 3.4 children per household. In part because divorce and remarriage take time, children are older. In the NSFH households, the youngest stepchildren in families are, on average, aged eleven, while the youngest children in nondivorced families are six and a half.[8]

There are also, of course, nonresidential stepparents (the spouses of noncustodial parents), usually stepmothers. In our case, Ray married again, the year after Martha married Sam. Ray's new wife, Leslie, was the custodial parent of Audrey, age twelve. This marriage complicated the weekend visits. The Jones children were resentful of their new stepmother, Leslie, and her daughter, Audrey Ray found it easier to see them alone, and his visits became less frequent.

Some children may spend a good deal of time with nonresidential stepparents, and they may become significant figures in the children's lives, unlike Leslie in our example. But for our purpose of reassessing the parental rights and obligations of stepparents, we will focus only on residental stepparents, since they are more likely to be involved in the everyday support and care of their stepchildren. Moreover, the wide variety of benefits available to dependent children, like Social Security and health insurance, are usually attached only to a residential stepparent.

The modern stepfamily, like those of Cinderella and Snow White, also has stresses and strains. This was certainly true for the Jones-Hutchins family. Sara was eleven and Josh seven when their mother married Sam. At first Sara refused to talk to Sam and turned her face away when he addressed her. Josh was easier. He did not say much, but was willing to play catch or go an on errand with Sam if encouraged by Sam to do so.

Sara grew only slightly more polite as she developed into adolescence. She spoke to Sam only if she needed something. But, as her mother pointed out to Sam, she hardly spoke to her either. Josh continued to be pleasant, if a little distant, as he grew older. He clearly preferred his mother's attention.

The classic longitudinal studies by Heatherington and colleagues,[9] spanning the past two decades, provide a rich source of information on how stepfamilies function. Heatherington emphasizes that stepchildren are children who have experienced several marital transitions. They have usually already experienced the divorce of their parents (although the number whose mothers have never before wed is increasing) and a period of life in a single-parent family before the formation of the stepfamily. In the early stages of all marital transitions, including divorce and remarriage, child-parent relations are often disrupted and parenting is less authoritative than in nondivorced families. These early periods, however, usually give way to a parenting situation more similar to nuclear families.[10]

The Heatherington studies found that stepfathers vary in how enthusiastically and effectively they parent their stepchildren, and stepchildren also vary in how willingly they permit a parental relationship to develop. Indeed, many stepfather-stepchild relationships are not emotionally close. Overall, stepfathers in these studies are most often disengaged and less authoritative as compared with nondivorced fathers. The small class of residential stepmothers exhibits a similar style.[11] Conversely, adolescent children tend to perceive their stepfathers negatively in the early stages of remarriage, but over time, they too become disengaged. In an interesting twist on fairy tale lore, adolescent children in stepfamilies experience less conflict with their residential stepmothers than do children in nondivorced families with their own mothers.[12]

The age and gender of the child at the time of stepfamily formation are critical in his or her adjustment. Early adolescence is a difficult time in which to have remarriage occur, with more sustained difficulties in stepfather-stepchild relations than in remarriages where the children are younger. Young (preadolescent) stepsons, but not necessarily stepdaughters, develop a closer relationship to their stepfathers after a period of time; this is not as likely with older children.[13]

Other researchers have found that in their lives outside the family, stepchildren do not perform as well as children from nondivorced families, and look more like the children from single-parent families. It seems that divorce and remarriage (or some factors associated with divorce and remarriage) increase the risk of poor academic, behavioral, and psychological outcomes.[14]

The difficulties of the stepfamily relationship are evident in the high divorce rate of such families. About one-quarter of all remarrying women separate from their new spouses within five years of the second marriage, and the figure is higher for women with children from prior relationships. A conservative estimate is that between 20 percent and 30 percent of stepchildren will, before they turn eighteen, see their custodial parent and stepparent divorce.[15] This is yet another disruptive marital transition for children, most of whom have already undergone at least one divorce.

Other researchers look at the stepfamily more positively. Amato and Keith analyzed data comparing intact, two-parent families with stepfamilies and found that while children from two-parent families performed significantly better on a multifactored measure of well-being and development, there was a significant overlap. A substantial number of children in stepfamilies actually perform as well or better than children in intact two-parent families. As Amato comments, "Some children grow up in well-functioning intact families in which they encounter abuse, neglect, poverty, parental mental illness, and parental substance abuse. Other children grow up in well-functioning stepfamilies and have caring stepparents who provide affection, effective control and economic support."[16] Still other researchers suggest that it may be the painful transitions of divorce and economically deprived single-parenthood which usually precede the formation of the stepfamily that explain the poor performance of stepchildren.[17]

Perhaps a fairer comparison of stepchildren's well-being is against single-parent families. Indeed, if there were no remarriage (or first marriage, in the case of unmarried birth mothers), these children would remain a part of a single-parent household. On most psychological measures of behavior and achievement, stepchildren look more like children from single-parent families than children from never-divorced families, but on economic measures it is a different story. The National Survey of Families and Households (NSFH) data show that stepparents have slightly lower incomes and slightly less education than parents in nuclear families, but that incomes of all types of married families with children are three to four times greater than the incomes of single mothers. Custodial mothers in stepfamilies have similar incomes to single mothers (about $12,000 in 1987). If, as seems plausible, their personal incomes are about the same before they married as after, then marriage has increased their household incomes more than threefold. Stepfathers' incomes are, on average, more than twice as great as their wives', and account for nearly three-fourths of the family's income.[18]

In contrast to residential stepparents, absent biological parents only rarely provide much financial or other help to their children. Some do not because they are dead or cannot be found; about 26 percent of custodial, remarried mothers and 28 percent of single mothers report that their child's father is deceased or of unknown whereabouts. Yet even in the three-quarters of families where the noncustodial parent's whereabouts are known, only about one-third of all custodial mothers (single and remarried) receive child support or alimony from former spouses, and the amounts involved are small compared to the cost of raising children. According to NSFH data, remarried women with awards receive on average $1780 per year, while single mothers receive $1383. Clearly, former spouses cannot be relied on to lift custodial mothers and their children out of poverty.[19]

The picture is still more complex, as is true with all issues relating to stepfamilies. Some noncustodial fathers, like Ray Jones in our scenario, have remarried and have stepchildren themselves. These relationships, too, are evident in the NSFH data. Nearly one-quarter (23 percent) of residential stepfathers have minor children from former relationships living elsewhere. Two-thirds of those report paying child support for their children.[20] In our case, Ray Jones did continue his child support payments, but he felt squeezed by the economic obligation of contributing to two households. This is a growing class of fathers who frequently feel resentful about the heavy burden of supporting two households, particularly when their first wife has remarried.

In sum, although we have no data that precisely examine the distribution of resources within a stepfamily, it is fair to assume that stepfathers' substantial contributions to family income improve their stepchildren's material well-being by helping to cover basic living costs. For many formerly single-parent families, stepfathers' incomes provided by remarriage are essential in preventing or ending poverty among custodial mothers and their children. (The data are less clear for the much smaller class of residential stepmothers.)

While legal dependency usually ends at eighteen, the economic resources available to a stepchild through remarriage could continue to be an important factor past childhood. College education and young adulthood are especially demanding economic events. The life-course studies undertaken by some researchers substantiate the interpersonal trends seen in stepfamilies before the stepchildren leave home. White reports that viewed from either the parent's or the child's perspective, relationships over the life-course between stepchildren and stepparents are substantially weaker than those between biological parents and children. These relationships are not monolithic, however; the best occur when the stepparent is a male, there are no stepsiblings, the stepparent has no children of his own, and the marriage between the biological parent and the stepparent is intact.[21] On the other end, support relationships are nearly always cut off if the stepparent relationship is terminated because of divorce or the death of the natural parent.

The Jones children were fortunate. Martha and Sam enjoyed a good marriage, in spite of the stress of stepparenting, and Sam was glad to help them with college expenses. Their biological father, Ray, felt he had his own family to support; his stepdaughter, Audrey, also needed money for college. As Sara grew older she grew more accepting of Sam. And after her first child was born, she seemed happy to accept Sam as a grandfather for her child. Josh continued on good terms with Sam.

Again, one might ask to compare these findings to single-parent households where there are no stepparents to provide additional support. The data here are less available. While we do know that stepchildren leave home earlier and are less likely to attend college than children from intact families, the comparison with single-parent families is not clear.[22] One study of perceived normative obligation to stepparents and stepchildren suggests that people in stepfamilies have weaker, but still important, family ties than do biological kin.[23] In terms of economic and other forms of adult support, even weak ties cannot be discounted. They might, instead, become the focus of public policy initiatives.

STEPFAMILIES IN LAW AND PUBLIC POLICY

Both state and federal law set policies that affect stepfamilies. Overall, these policies do not reflect a coherent policy toward stepparents and stepchildren. Two competing models are roughly evident. One, a "stranger" model, followed by most states, treats the residential stepparent as if he or she were a legal stranger to the children, with no rights and no responsibilities. The other, a "dependency" model, most often followed by federal policymakers, assumes the residential stepfather is, in fact, supporting the stepchildren and provides benefits accordingly. But there is inconsistency in both state and federal policy. Some states lean at times toward a dependency model and require support in some instances, and the federal government sometimes treats the stepparent as if he or she were a stranger to the stepchildren, and ignores them in calculating benefits.

State law governs the traditional family matters of marriage, divorce, adoption, and inheritance, while federal law covers a wide range of programs and policies that touch on the lives of most Americans, including stepfamilies. As the provider of benefits through such programs as Temporary Aid for Needy Families (TANF) and Social Security, the federal government sets eligibility standards that affect the economic well-being of many stepfamilies. In addition, as the employer of the armed forces and civil servants, the federal government establishes employee benefits guidelines for vast numbers of American families. And in its regulatory role, the federal government defines the status of stepfamilies for many purposes ranging from immigration eligibility to tax liability.

Not covered in this [reading] or, to my knowledge, yet systematically investigated are the wide range of private employee benefit programs, from medical and life insurance through educational benefits. These programs mostly take their lead from state or federal law. Therefore, it is fair to guess that they suffer from similar inconsistencies.

State Policies

State laws generally give little recognition to the dependency needs of children who reside with their stepparent; they are most likely to treat the stepparent as a stranger to the children, with no rights or obligations. In contrast to the numerous state laws obligating parents to support natural children born out of wedlock or within a previous marriage, only a few states have enacted statutes which specifically impose an affirmative duty on stepparents. The Utah stepparent support statute, for example, provides simply that, "A stepparent shall support a stepchild to the same extent that a natural or adoptive parent is required to support a child."[24] This duty of support ends upon the termination of the marriage. Most states are silent on the obligation to support stepchildren.[25]

A few states rely on common law, the legal tradition stemming from our English roots. The common law tradition leans more toward a dependency model. It dictates that a stepparent can acquire the rights and duties of a parent if he or she acts *in loco parentis* (in the place of a parent). Acquisition of this status is not automatic; it is determined by the stepparent's intent. A stepparent need not explicitly state the intention to act as a parent; he or she can "manifest the requisite intent to assume responsibility by actually providing financial support or by taking over the custodial duties."[26] Courts, however, have been reluctant to grant *in loco* parental rights or to attach obligations to unwilling stepparents. In the words of one Wisconsin court, "A good Samaritan should not be saddled with the legal obligations of another and we think the law should not with alacrity conclude that a stepparent assumes parental relationships to a child."[27]

At the extreme, once the status of *in loco parentis* is achieved, the stepparent "stands in the place of the natural parent, and the reciprocal rights, duties, and obligations of parent and child subsist." These rights, duties, and obligations include the duty to provide financial support, the right to custody and control of the child, immunity from suit by the stepchild, and, in some cases, visitation rights after the dissolution of the marriage by death or divorce.

Yet stepparents who qualify as *in loco parentis* are not always required to provide support in all circumstances. A subset of states imposes obligation only if the stepchild is in danger of becoming dependent on public assistance. For example, Hawaii provides that:

> A stepparent who acts in loco parentis is bound to provide, maintain, and support the stepparent's stepchild during the residence of the child with the stepparent if the legal parents desert the child or are unable to support the child, thereby reducing the child to destitute and necessitous circumstances.[28]

Just as states do not regularly require stepparents to support their stepchildren, they do not offer stepparents the parental authority of custody and control within the marriage. A residential stepparent generally has fewer rights than a legal guardian or a foster parent. According to one commentator, a stepparent "has no authority to make decisions about the child—no authority to approve emergency medical treatment or even to sign a permission slip for a field trip to the fire station."[29]

Both common law and state statutes almost uniformly terminate the stepparent relationship upon divorce or the death of the custodial parent. This means that the support obligations, if there were any, cease, and that the stepparent has no rights to visitation or custody. State courts have sometimes found individual exceptions to this role, but they have not created any clear precedents. Currently only a few states authorize stepparents to seek visitation rights, and custody is almost always granted to a biological parent upon divorce. In the event of the death of the stepparent's spouse, the noncustodial, biological parent is usually granted custody even when the stepparent has, in fact, raised the child. In one such recent Michigan case, *Henrickson v. Gable*,[30] the children, aged nine and ten when their mother died, had lived with their stepfather since infancy and had rarely seen their biological father. In the ensuing custody dispute, the trial court left the children with their stepfather, but an appellate court, relying upon a state law that created a strong preference for biological parents, reversed this decision and turned the children over to their biological father.

Following the stranger model, state inheritance laws, with a few complex exceptions, do not recognize the existence of stepchildren. Under existing state laws, even a dependent stepchild whose stepparent has supported and raised the child for many years is not eligible to inherit from the stepparent if there is no will. California provides the most liberal rule for stepchild recovery when there is no will, but only if the stepchild meets relatively onerous qualifications. Stepchildren may inherit as the children of a deceased stepparent only if "it is established by clear and convincing evidence that the stepparent would have adopted the person but for a legal barrier."[31] Very few stepchildren have been able to pass this test. Similarly a stepchild cannot bring a negligence suit for the accidental death of a stepparent. In most instances, then, only a biological child will inherit or receive legal compensation when a stepparent dies.

Federal Policies

The federal policies that concern us here are of two types: federal benefit programs given to families in need, including TANF and Supplemental Security Income (SSI), and general programs not based on need, including Social Security as well as civil service and military personnel employee benefits. Most of these programs follow the dependency model. They go further than do most states in recognizing or promoting the actual family relationship of residential stepfamilies. Many of them (although not all) assume that residential stepparents support their stepchildren and accordingly make these children eligible for benefits equivalent to those afforded to other children of the family.

Despite the fact that federal law generally recognizes the dependency of residential stepchildren, it remains wanting in many respects. There is a great deal of inconsistency in how the numerous federal programs and policies treat the stepparent-stepchild relationship, and the very definitions of what constitutes a stepchild are often quite different across programs. Most of the programs strive for a dependency-based definition, such as living with or receiving 50 percent of support from a stepparent. However, some invoke the vague definition, "actual family relationship," and some do not attempt any definition at all, thus potentially including nonresidential stepchildren among the beneficiaries. In some programs the category of stepchild is entirely absent or specifically excluded from the list of beneficiaries for some programs.

Even where program rules permit benefits for dependent stepchildren as for natural children, the benefits to stepchildren are typically severed by death or divorce.[32] While Social Security does cover dependent stepchildren in the event of death, several programs specifically exclude stepchildren from eligibility for certain death benefits. Under the Federal Employees' Retirement System, stepchildren are explicitly excluded from the definition of children in determining the default beneficiary, without concern for the stepchild's possible dependency. All stepchildren are similarly excluded from eligibility for lump-sum payments under the Foreign Service Retirement and Disability System and the CIA Retirement and Disability program.[33]

Stepchildren are even more vulnerable in the event of divorce. Here the stranger model is turned to. As with state law, any legally recognized relationship is immediately severed upon divorce in nearly all federal programs. The children and their stepparents become as strangers. Social Security does not provide any cushion for stepchildren if the deceased stepparent is divorced from the custodial parent. Under Social Security law, the stepparent-stepchild relationship is terminated immediately upon divorce and the stepchild is no longer eligible for benefits even if the child has in fact been dependent on the insured stepparent for the duration of a very long marriage.[34] If the divorce were finalized the day before the stepparent's death the child would receive no benefits.

In sum, current federal policy goes part way toward defining the role of the stepparent by assuming a dependency model in most programs, even when state law does not, and providing benefits to stepchildren based on this assumption of stepparent support. However, as described, existing federal stepparent policy falls short in several critical areas. And state laws and policies fall far short of federal policies in their consideration of stepfamilies, for the most part treating stepparents as strangers with regard to their stepchildren.

NEW POLICY PROPOSALS

Proposals for policy reform regarding stepfamilies are scant in number and, so far, largely unheard by policymakers. Most of the proposals come from legal scholars, a few from social scientists. Stepparents have not been organized to demand reform, nor have child advocates. All the reforms have some disagreements with the existing stranger and dependency models, but few offer a completely new model.

All of the proposals I review base their arguments to a greater or lesser degree on social science data, although not always the same data. The proposers may roughly be divided into three camps. The first, and perhaps smallest camp, I call *negativists.* These are scholars who view stepfamilies from a sociobiological perspective, and find them a troublesome aberration to be actively discouraged. The second, and by far largest group of scholars, I term *voluntarists.* This group acknowledges both the complexity and the often distant nature of stepparent relationships, and largely believes that law and policy should leave stepfamilies alone, as it does now. If stepparents wish to take a greater role in their stepchildren's lives, they should be encouraged to do so, by adoption or some other means. The third camp recognizes the growing presence of stepfamilies as an alternate family form and believes they should be recognized and strengthened in some important ways. This group, I call them *reformists,* believes the law should take the lead in providing more rights or obligations to stepparents. The few policy initiatives from this group range from small specific reforms regarding such issues as inheritance and visitation to my own proposal for a full-scale redefinition of stepparents' rights and obligations.

The negativist viewpoint on stepparenting, most prominently represented by sociologist David Popenoe, relies on a sociobiological theory of reproduction. According to this theory, human beings will give unstintingly to their own biological children, in order to promote their own genes, but will be far less generous to others. The recent rise in divorce and out-of-wedlock births, according to Popenoe, has created a pattern of essentially fatherless households that cannot compete with the two-biological-parent families.

Popenoe believes the pattern of stepparent disengagement revealed by many researchers is largely based on this biological stinginess.

> If the argument . . . is correct, and the family is fundamentally rooted in biology and at least partly activated by the "genetically selfish" activities of human beings, childbearing by non relatives is inherently problematic. It is not that unrelated individuals are unable to do the job of parenting, it is just that they are not as likely to do the job well. Stepfamily problems, in short, may be so intractable that the best strategy for dealing with them is to do everything possible to minimize their occurrence.

Moreover, Popenoe cites researchers on the greatly increased incidence of child abuse by stepfathers over natural fathers, who suggest that "stepchildren are not merely 'disadvantaged' but imperiled."[35] This argument is not so farfetched, he claims, in fact it is the stuff of our folk wisdom. Snow White and Hansel and Gretel had it right; stepparents are not merely uncaring, they may be dangerous.

Popenoe goes beyond the stranger model, which is neutral as to state activity, and suggests an active discouragement of stepparent families. He believes the best way to obstruct stepfamilies is to encourage married biological two-parent families. Premarital and marital counseling, a longer waiting period for divorce, and a redesign of the current welfare system so that marriage and family are empowered rather than denigrated are among his policy recommendations. He is heartened by what he calls the "new familism," a growing recognition of the need for strong social bonds, which he believes can best be found in the biological two-parent family.[36]

The second group of scholars, whom I call voluntarists, generally believe that the stepparent relationship is essentially voluntary and private and the stranger model most clearly reflects this. The legal bond formed by remarriage is between man and wife—stepchildren are incidental; they are legal strangers. Stepparents may choose, or not choose, to become more involved with everyday economic and emotional support of their stepchildren; but the law should not mandate this relationship, it should simply reflect it. These scholars recognize the growth of stepfamilies as a factor of modern life and neither condone nor condemn this configuration. Family law scholar David Chambers probably speaks for most scholars in this large camp when he says,

> In most regards, this state of the law nicely complements the state of stepparent relationships in the United States. Recall the inescapable diversity of such relationships—residential and non-residential, beginning when the children are infants and when they are teenagers, leading to comfortable relationships in some cases and awkward relationships in others, lasting a few years and lasting many. In this context it seems sensible to permit those relationships to rest largely on the voluntary arrangements among stepparents and biologic parents. The current state of the law also amply recognizes our nation's continuing absorption with the biologic relationship, especially as it informs our sensibilities about enduring financial obligations.[37]

Chambers is not enthusiastic about imposing support obligations on stepparents, either during or following the termination of a marriage, but is interested in promoting voluntary adoption. He would, however, approve some middle ground where biological parents are not completely cut off in the adoption process.

Other voluntarists are attracted by the new English model of parenting, as enacted in the Children Act of 1989. Of great attraction to American voluntarists is the fact that under this model a stepparent who has been married at least two years to the biological parent may voluntarily petition for a residence order for his or her spouse's child. With a residence order the stepparent has parental responsibility toward the child until the age of sixteen. But this order does not extinguish the parental responsibility of the noncustodial parent.[38] In accordance with the Children Act of 1989, parents, biological or otherwise, no longer have parental rights, they have only parental responsibilities, and these cannot be extinguished upon the divorce of the biological parents. In England, therefore, it is possible for three adults to claim parental responsibility. Unlike biological parental responsibility, however, stepparent responsibility does not usually extend following divorce. The stepparent is not normally financially responsible following divorce, but he or she may apply for a visitation order.

The third group, whom I call reformists, believe that voluntary acts on the part of stepparents are not always adequate, and that it is necessary to reform the law in some way to more clearly define the rights and responsibilities of stepparents. The American Bar Association Family Law Section has been working for some years on a proposed Model Act to suggest legislative reforms regarding stepparents' obligations to provide child support and rights to discipline, visitation, and custody. A Model Act is not binding anywhere; it is simply a model for all states to consider. Traditionally, however, Model Acts have been very influential in guiding state legislative reform. In its current form, the ABA Model Act would require stepparents to assume a duty of support during the duration of the remarriage only if the child is not adequately supported by the custodial and noncustodial parent. The issue is ultimately left to the discretion of the family court, but the Model Act does not require that the stepparent would need to have a close relationship with a stepchild before a support duty is imposed. The Model Act, however, does not describe what the rule should be if the stepparent and the custodial parent divorce.

The proposed statute is rather more complete in its discussion of stepparent visitation or custody rights following divorce. It takes a two-tiered approach, first asking if the stepparent has standing (a legal basis) to seek visitation and then asking if the visitation would be in the best interests of the child. The standing question is to be resolved with reference to five factors, which essentially examine the role of the stepparent in the child's life (almost an *in loco parentis* question), the financial support offered by the stepparent, and the detriment to the child from denying visitation. The court, if it finds standing, then completes the analysis with the best interests standard of the jurisdiction. The Model Act's section on physical custody also requires a two-tiered test, requiring standing and increasing the burden on the stepparent to present clear and convincing proof that he or she is the better custodial parent.

The ABA Model Act is a worthwhile start, in my opinion, but it is little more than that. At most it moves away from a stranger model and provides a limited concept of mandatory stepparent support during a marriage, acknowledging that stepchildren are at least sometimes dependent. It also gives a stepparent a fighting chance for visitation or custody following a divorce. It fails to clarify stepparents' rights during the marriage, however, and does not deal with the issue of economic support at the period of maximum vulnerability, the termination of the marriage through death and divorce. Moreover, the Model Act, and, indeed, all the existing reform proposals, deal only with traditional legal concepts of parenthood defined by each state and do not consider the vast range of federal programs, or other public and private programs, that define the stepparent-stepchild relationship for purposes of benefits, insurance, or other purposes.

I propose, instead, a new conceptualization of stepparent rights and responsibilities, a de facto parent model, that will cover all aspects of the stepparent-stepchild relationship and will extend to federal and private policy as well. My first concern in proposing a new framework is the welfare of the stepchildren, which is not adequately dealt with in either the stranger or the dependency model. The failure of state and, to a lesser extent, federal policy to address coherently the financial interdependencies of step relationships, described earlier in this [reading], means that children dependent upon a residential stepparent may not receive adequate support or benefits from that parent during the marriage, and they may not be protected economically in the event of divorce or parental death.

The longitudinal studies of families described earlier in this [reading] suggest that the most difficult periods for children are those of marital transition, for example, divorce and remarriage. Families with a residential stepfather have a much higher family income than mother-headed single families; indeed, their household incomes look much like nuclear families.[39] However, research demonstrates that stepfamilies are fragile and are more likely to terminate in divorce than biological families. The event of divorce can quite suddenly pull the resources available for the children back to the single-parent level. Currently children are at least financially cushioned by child support following the divorce of their biological parents, but have no protective support following the breakup of their stepfamily. Nor are they protected in the event of the death of the stepparent, which is certainly another period of vulnerability (as discussed earlier, only a small minority continue to receive support from noncustodial parents).

A second reason for proposing a new framework is to strengthen the relationship of the stepparent and stepchildren. While research generally finds that stepparents are less engaged in parenting than natural parents, research studies do not explain the causes; others must do so. In addition to the sociobiologists' claim for stingy, genetically driven behavior, sociologists have posited the explanation of "incomplete institutionalization."[40] This theory is based on the belief that, by and large, people act as they are expected to act by society. In the case of stepfamilies, there are unclear or absent societal norms and standards for how to define the remarried family, especially the role of the stepparent in relation to the stepchild.

Briefly, my new model requires, first of all, dividing stepparents into two subclasses: those who are de facto parents and those who are not. De facto parents would be defined as "those stepparents legally married to a natural parent who primarily reside with their stepchildren, or who provide at least 50 percent of the stepchild's financial support." Stepparents who do not meet the de facto parent requirements would, in all important respects, disappear from policy.

For the purposes of federal and state policy, under this scheme, a de facto parent would be treated virtually the same as a natural parent during the marriage. The same rights, obligations, and presumptions would attach vis-à-vis their stepchildren, including the obligation of support. These rights and duties would continue in some form, based on the length of the marriage, following the custodial parent's death or divorce from the stepparent, or the death of the stepparent. In the event of divorce the stepparent would have standing to seek custody or visitation but the stepparent could also be obligated for child support of a limited duration. Upon the death of a stepparent, a minor stepchild would be treated for purposes of inheritance and benefits as would a natural child.

So far this proposal resembles the common law doctrine of *in loco parentis*, described earlier, where the stepparent is treated for most purposes (except inheritance) as a parent on the condition that he or she voluntarily agrees to support the child. In the de facto model, however, support is mandatory, not voluntary, on the grounds both that it is not fair to stepchildren to be treated by the law in an unequal or arbitrary manner, and that child welfare considerations are best met by uniform support of stepchildren. Furthermore, in the traditional common law *in loco parentis* scenario, the noncustodial parent had died, and was not a factor to be reckoned with. Under this scheme, creating a de facto parent category for stepparents would not invalidate the existing rights and obligations of a noncustodial biological parent. Rather, this proposal would empower a stepparent as an additional parent.

Multiple parenting and the rights and obligations of the stepparent and children following divorce or death are controversial and difficult policy matters that require more detailed attention than the brief exposition that can be offered here. Multiple parenting is the barrier upon which many family law reform schemes, especially in custody and adoption, have foundered. It is also one of the reasons that there has been no consistent effort to reformulate the role of stepparents. Working out the details is critical. For instance, mandating stepparent support raises a central issue of fairness. If the stepparent is indeed required to support the child, there is a question about the support obligations of the noncustodial parent. Traditionally, most states have not recognized the stepparent contribution as an offset to child support.[41] While this policy promotes administrative efficiency, and may benefit some children, it may not be fair to the noncustodial parent. An important advance in recognizing the existence of multiple parents in the nonlinear family is to recognize multiple support obligations. The few states that require stepparent obligation have given limited attention to apportionment of child support obligations, offering no clear guidelines. I propose that state statutory requirements for stepparent obligation as de facto parents also include clear guidelines for apportionment of child support between the noncustodial natural parent and the stepparent.

Critics of this proposal may say that if the custodial parent's support is reduced, the child will have fewer resources. For some children, this may be true, but as discussed earlier in this [reading], only about 25 percent of all stepchildren receive child support and the average amount is less than $2000 per year.[42] Therefore, a reduction of this small amount of support to a minority of stepchildren would not have a large overall effect compared with the increased resources of living with a stepparent that most stepchildren enjoy. And, certainly, the additional safety net of protection in the event of the death of the stepparent or divorce from the custodial parent would benefit all stepchildren. In addition, under the de facto scheme, the reduction of the support payment for the noncustodial parent may help to sweeten the multiple parenting relationship.

Let us apply this model to the Jones-Hutchins family introduced earlier. If Ray Jones, the noncustodial parent, were paying $6000 a year support for his two children (on the high end for noncustodial parents according to the National Survey for Children and Families), his payments could be reduced by as much as half, since Sam Hutchins's income is $50,000 per year and he has no other dependents. It should be emphasized, however, that in most stepfamilies there would be no reduction in support, because the noncustodial parent is paying no support. In the Jones-Hutchins family the $3000 relief would certainly be welcome to Ray, who is also now living with and helping to support his new wife's child. The relief would likely make him somewhat friendlier toward Sam, or at least more accepting of his role in his children's lives. It also might make him more likely to continue support past eighteen, since he would not feel as financially pinched over the years. More important, while the children would lose some support, they would have the security that if Sam died they would be legal heirs and default beneficiaries to his life insurance. They could also ask for damages if his death were caused by negligence or work-related events. And if he and their mother divorced, they could continue for a time to be considered dependents on his health and other benefits and to receive support from him.

Another facet of multiple parenting is legal authority. If stepparents are required to accept parental support obligations, equal protection and fairness concerns dictate that they must also be given parental rights. Currently, state laws, as noted earlier, recognize only natural or adoptive parents; a stepparent currently has no legal authority over a stepchild, even to authorize a field trip. If stepparents had full parental rights, in some cases, as when the parents have shared legal custody, the law would be recognizing the parental rights of three parents, rather than two. While this sounds unusual, it is an accurate reflection of how many families now raise their children. Most often, however, it would be only the custodial parent and his or her spouse, the de facto parent, who would have authority to make decisions for the children in their home.

In the Jones-Hutchins family this policy would give Sam more recognition as a parent. Schools, camps, hospitals, and other institutions that require parental consent or involvement would now automatically include him in their consideration of the children's interests. Since Sam is the more day-to-day parent, their biological father, Ray, may not mind at all. If he did mind, the three of them would have to work it out (or in an extreme event, take it to mediation or family court). In fact, since only a minority of noncustodial dads see their children on a regular basis, three-parent decision making would be unusual.

Critics of this scheme may argue that adoption, not the creation of the legal status of de facto parent, is the appropriate vehicle for granting a stepparent full parental rights and responsibilities.[43] If, as discussed earlier, nearly three-quarters of stepchildren are not being supported by their noncustodial parents, policy initiatives could be directed to terminating the nonpaying parents' rights and promoting stepparent adoption. Adoption is not possible, however, unless the parental rights of the absent natural parent have been terminated—a difficult procedure against a reluctant parent. Normally, the rights of a parent who maintains contact with his or her child cannot be terminated even if that parent is not contributing child support. And when parental rights are terminated, visitation rights are terminated as well in most states. It is by no means clear that it is in the best interests of children to terminate contact with a natural parent, even if the parent is not meeting his or her obligation to support.[44] As discussed earlier, a large percentage (another 25 percent or so), of noncustodial parents continue some contact with their children, even when not paying support.[45] And while stepparent adoption should be strongly encouraged when it is possible, this solution will not resolve the problem of defining the role of stepparents who have not adopted.

Extending, in some form, the rights and obligations following the termination of the marriage by divorce or death is equally problematical. Currently, only a few courts have ruled in favor of support payments following divorce, and these have been decided on an individual basis. Only one state, Missouri, statutorily continues stepparent support obligations following divorce.[46] It would clearly be in the best interests of the child to experience continued support, since a significant number of children may sink below the poverty line upon the dissolution of their stepfamily.[47]

Since the de facto model is based on dependency, not blood, a fair basis for support following divorce or the death of the custodial parent might be to require that a stepparent who qualified as a de facto parent for at least one year must contribute child support for half the number of years of dependency until the child reached majority. If a child resided with the stepparent for four years, the stepparent would be liable for support for two years. If the biological noncustodial parent were still paying support payments, the amount could be apportioned. While it may be said that this policy would discourage people from becoming stepparents by marrying, it could also be said to discourage divorce once one has become a stepparent. Stepparents might consider working harder at maintaining a marriage if divorce had some real costs.

Conversely, stepparents should have rights as well as responsibilities following divorce or the death of the custodial parent. Divorced or widowed stepparents should be able to pursue visitation or custody if they have lived with and supported the child for at least one year. Once again, multiple parent claims might sometimes be an issue, but these could be resolved, as they are now, under a primary caretaker, or a best interest standard.

The death of a stepparent is a particular period of vulnerability for stepchildren for which they are unprotected by inheritance law. While Social Security and other federal survivor benefits are based on the premise that a stepchild relies on the support of the residential stepparent and will suffer the same hardship as natural children if the stepparent dies, state inheritance laws, notoriously archaic, decree that only biology, not dependency, counts. State laws should assume that a de facto parent would wish to have all his dependents receive a share of his estate if he died without a will. If the step-children are no longer dependent, that assumption would not necessarily prevail. The same assumption should prevail for insurance policies and compensation claims following an accidental death. A dependent stepchild, just as a natural child, should have the right to sue for loss of support.

On the federal front, a clear definition of stepparents as de facto parents would eliminate the inconsistencies regarding stepparents which plague current federal policies and would clarify the role of the residential stepparent. For the duration of the marriage, a stepchild would be treated as a natural child for purposes of support and the receipt of federal benefits. This treatment would persist in the event of the death of the stepparent. The stepchild would receive all the survivor and death benefits that would accrue to a natural child.[48]

In the case of divorce, the issue of federal benefits is more complicated. Stepchildren and natural children should not have identical coverage for federal benefits following divorce, again, but neither is it good policy to summarily cut off children who have been dependent, sometimes for many years, on the de facto parent. A better policy is to extend federal benefits for a period following divorce, based on a formula that matches half the number of years of dependency, as earlier suggested for child support. For instance, if the stepparent resided with the stepchild for four years, the child would be covered by Social Security survivor benefits and other federal benefits, including federal employee benefits, for a period of two years following the divorce. This solution would serve children by at least providing a transitional cushion. It would also be relatively easy to administer. In the case of the death of the biological custodial parent, benefits could be similarly extended, or continued indefinitely if the child remains in the custody of the stepparent.

All other private benefits programs would similarly gain from the application of a clear definition of the rights and obligations of residential stepparents. While these non-governmental programs, ranging from eligibility for private health and life insurance and annuities to access to employee child care, are not reviewed in this [reading], they almost surely reflect the same inconsistencies or silences evident in federal and state policies.

Ultimately, state law defines most of these stepfamily relationships, and it is difficult, if not impossible to achieve uniform reform on a state-by-state basis. In England it is possible to pass a single piece of national legislation, such as the Children Act of 1989, which completely redefines parental roles. In America, the process of reform is slower and less sure. Probably the first step in promoting a new policy would be for the federal government to insist all states pass stepparent general support obligation laws requiring stepparents acting as de facto parents (by my definition) to support their stepchildren as they do their natural children. This goal could be accomplished by making stepparent general support obligation laws a prerequisite for receiving federal welfare grants. Federal policy already assumes this support in figuring eligibility in many programs, but it has not insisted that states change their laws. Precedent for this strategy has been set by the Family Support Acts of 1988 in which the federal government mandated that states set up strict child support enforcement laws for divorced parents and unwed fathers at TANF levels in order to secure AFDC funding.[49] The second, larger step would be to require limited stepparent support following divorce, as described previously. Once the basic obligations were asserted, an articulation of basic rights would presumably follow.

CONCLUSION

Stepfamilies compose a large and growing sector of American families that is largely ignored by public policy. Social scientists tell us that these families have problems. Stepparent-stepchildren relationships, poorly defined by law and social norms, are not as strong or nurturing as those in nondivorced families, and stepchildren do not do as well in school and in other outside settings. Still, stepfamily relationships are important in lifting single-parent families out of poverty. When single or divorced mothers marry, the household income increases by more than threefold, rising to roughly the same level as nuclear families. A substantial portion of these families experiences divorce, however, placing the stepchildren at risk of falling back into poverty. It makes good public policy sense then, both to strengthen these stepfamily relationships and to cushion the transition for stepchildren should the relationship end.

Notes

1. Mary Ann Mason and David Simon, "The Ambiguous Stepparent: Federal Legislation in Search of a Model," *Family Law Quarterly* 29:446–448, 1995.
2. E. Mavis Heatherington and Kathleen M. Jodl, "Stepfamilies as Settings for Child Development," in Alan Booth and Judy Dunn (eds.), *Stepfamilies: Who Benefits? Who Does Not?* (Hillsdale, N.J.: L. Erlbaum 1994), 55; E. Mavis Heatherington, "An Overview of the Virginia Longitudinal Study of Divorce and Remarriage: A Focus on Early Adolescence," *Journal of Family Psychology* 7:39–56, 1993.
3. David Popenoe, "Evolution of Marriage and Stepfamily Problems," in Booth and Dunn (eds.), *Stepfamilies*, 3–28.
4. Mason and Simon, "The Ambiguous Stepparent," 467–482; Mary Ann Mason and Jane Mauldon, "The New Stepfamily Needs a New Public Policy," *Journal of Social Issues* 52(3), Fall 1996.
5. U.S. Bureau of Census, 1989.
6. Divorce is not always the background event. An increasing, but still relatively small number of custodial mothers have not previously wed.
7. Mason and Mauldon, "The New Stepfamily," 5.
8. Ibid., 6.
9. Heatherington and Jodl, "Stepfamilies," 55–81.
10. Ibid., 76.
11. E. Mavis Heatherington and William Clingempeel, "Coping with Marital Transitions: A Family Systems Perspective," *Monographs of the Society for Research in Child Development* 57:2–3, Serial

No. 227, New York: 1992; E. Thomson, Sara McLanahan, and R. B. Curtin, "Family Structure, Gender, and Parental Socialization," *Journal of Marriage and the Family* 54:368–378, 1992.

12. Heatherington and Jodl, "Stepfamilies," 69.
13. Ibid., 64–65.
14. Thomson, McLanahan, and Curtin, "Family Structure," 368–378.
15. L. Bumpass and J. Sweet, *American Families and Households* (New York: Russell Sage Foundation, 1987), 23.
16. Paul Amato, "The Implications of Research Findings on Children in Stepfamilies," in Booth and Dunn (eds.), *Stepfamilies*, 84.
17. Nicholas Zill, "Understanding Why Children in Stepfamilies Have More Learning and Behavior Problems Than Children in Nuclear Families," in Booth and Dunn (eds.), *Stepfamilies*, 89–97.
18. Mason and Mauldon, "The New Stepfamily Needs a New Public Policy," 7.
19. Ibid., 8.
20. Ibid.
21. Lynn White, "Stepfamilies over the Lifecourse: Social Support," in Booth and Dunn (eds.), *Stepfamilies*, 109–139.
22. Ibid., 130.
23. A. S. Rossi and P. H. Rossi, *Of Human Bonding: Parent-Child Relations Across the Life Course* (New York: A. de Gruyter, 1990).
24. Utah Code Ann. 78-45-4.1.
25. Margaret Mahoney, *Stepfamilies and the Law* (Ann Arbor: University of Michigan Press, 1994), 13–47.
26. Miller v. United States, 123 F.2d 715, 717 (8th Cir, 1941).
27. Niesen v. Niesen, 157 N. W.2d 660 664(Wis. 1968).
28. Hawaii Revised Stat. Ann., Title 31, Sec. 577–4.
29. David Chambers, "Stepparents, Biologic Parents, and the Law's Perceptions of 'Family' after Divorce," in S. Sugarman and H. H. Kay (eds.), *Divorce Reform at the Crossroads* (New Haven: Yale University Press, 1990), 102–129.
30. Henrickson v. Gable.
31. Cal. Prob. Code, Sec. 6408.
32. Mason and Simon, "The Ambiguous Stepparent: Federal Legislation in Search of a Model," 449.
33. Ibid., p. 460–466.
34. 42 U.S.C. sec. 416(e), 1994.
35. M. Daly and M. Wilson, *Homicide* (New York: Aldine de Gruyter, 1988), 230.
36. Barbara Whitehead, "A New Familism?" *Family Affairs*, Summer, 1992.
37. Chambers, "Stepparents, Biologic Parents, and the Law's Perceptions of 'Family' after Divorce," 26.
38. Mark A. Fine, "Social Policy Pertaining to Stepfamilies: Should Stepparents and Stepchildren Have the Option of Establishing a Legal Relationship?" in Booth and Dunn (eds.), *Stepfamilies*, 199.
39. Mason and Mauldon, "The New Stepfamily," 5.
40. Andrew Cherlin, "Remarriage as an Incomplete Institution," *American Journal of Sociology* 84: 634–649, 1978.
41. S. Ramsey and J. Masson, "Stepparent Support of Stepchildren: A Comparative Analysis of Policies and Problems in the American and British Experience," *Syracuse Law Review* 36:649–666, 1985.
42. Mason and Mauldon, "The New Stepfamily," 7.
43. Joan Hollinger (ed.) et al., *Adoption Law and Practice* (New York: Matthew Bender, 1988).
44. Katherine Bartlett, "Re-thinking Parenthood as an Exclusive Status: The Need for Alternatives When the Premise of the Nuclear Family Has Failed," *Virginia Law Review* 70:879–903, 1984.
45. Mason and Mauldon, "The New Stepfamily," 5.
46. Vernon's Ann. Missouri Stats. 453.400, 1994.
47. Mason and Mauldon, "The New Stepfamily," 5.
48. Mason and Simon, "The Ambiguous Stepparent," 471.
49. 100 P.L. 485; 102 Stat. 2343 (1988).

PART 

Parents and Children

No aspect of family life seems more natural, universal, and changeless than the relationship between parents and children. Yet historical and cross-cultural evidence reveal major changes in conceptions of childhood and adulthood and in the psychological relationships between children and parents. For example, the shift from an agrarian to an industrial and then a post-industrial society over the past 200 years has revolutionized parent-child relations and the conditions of child development.

Among the changes associated with this transformation of childhood are: the decline of farming as a way of life, the elimination of child labor, the fall in infant death rates, the spread of literacy and mass schooling, and a focus on childhood as a distinct and valuable stage of life. As a result of these changes, modern parents bear fewer children, make greater emotional and economic investments in them, and expect less in return than their agrarian counterparts. Agrarian parents and children were bound together by economic necessity: Children were an essential source of labor in the family economy and a source of support in an old age. Today, almost all children are economic liabilities. In addition, children now have deep emotional significance. Parents hope offspring will provide intimacy, even a kind of immortality. Although today's children have become economically worthless, they have become emotionally "priceless" (Zelizer, 1985).

No matter how eagerly an emotionally priceless child is awaited, becoming a parent is usually experienced as one of life's major "normal" crises. In a classic article, Alice Rossi (1968) was one of the first to point out that the transition to parenthood is often one of life's difficult passages. Since Rossi's article first appeared more than three decades ago, a large body of research literature has developed, most of which supports her view that the early years of parenting can be a period of stress and change as well as joy.

Parenthood itself has changed since Rossi wrote. As Philip and Carolyn Cowan observe, in their article here, becoming a parent may be more difficult now than it used to be. The Cowans studied couples before and after the births of their first children. Because of the rapid and dramatic social changes of the past decades, young parents today are like pioneers in a new, uncharted territory. For example, the vast majority of today's couples come to parenthood with both husband and wife in the workforce, and most have expectations of a more egalitarian relationship than their own parents had. But the balance in their lives and their relationship has to shift dramatically after the baby is born. Most couples cannot afford the traditional pattern of the wife staying home full-time, nor is this arrangement free of strain for those who try it. Young families thus face more burdens than in the past, yet they lack the supportive services for new parents, such as visiting nurses, paid parental leave, and other family policies widely available in other countries. The Cowans suggest some newly developed ways to assist couples through this difficult transition.

In recent years, the role of fathers in children's lives—especially their absence—has become a hot-button political issue. What are the everyday realities of life with a father in today's families? Of course, there is enormous diversity among fathers and families—in income, ethnicity, education, personality, and so on.

In his reading here, William Marsiglio examines an important aspect of fatherhood that is rarely discussed—a father's influence on his children's emotional and physical health. Many are poor role models. For example, one out of three American men is obese and one in ten will be an alcoholic. Men are more likely than women to engage in dangerous activities, such as drink and drive, use guns, and ignore seat belts. But financial struggles and social pressures limit men's choices.

Marsiglio shows how a theory of "constrained choice" suggests that men's opportunities to pursue healthy options are shaped by diverse social forces. These include ideals of manliness that emphasize fearlessness, ignoring pain, fast driving, hard drinking, fighting, and the fear of being called names like "fag" if they don't do these risky things.

Much of the worry about family life today is about children. Usually we compare troubling images of children now with rosy images of children growing up in past times. But as historian Steven Mintz explains, public thinking about the history of American childhood is clouded by a series of myths. One is the myth of a carefree childhood. We cling to a fantasy that once upon a time childhood and youth were years of carefree adventure; however, for most children in the past, growing up was anything but easy. Disease, family disruption, and entering into the world of work at an early age were typical aspects of family life.

The notion of a long, secure childhood, devoted to education and free from adult-like responsibilities, is a very recent invention—one that only became a reality for a majority of children during the period of relative prosperity that followed World War II. During the last quarter of the twentieth century, however, poverty and inequality grew. In addition, social mobility—the ability of a poor child to rise into the middle class—declined. Annette Lareau began her intensive study of children's everyday lives to learn how inequality is passed on from one generation to the next. Her research focused on childrearing practices among racially diverse families from poor, working-class, and middle-class families. Her major finding was that parenting styles varied more by class than by race. That is, while race is important in many ways, middle-class black and white parents behaved in similar ways toward their children. Middle-class parents used a parenting style Lareau calls "concerted cultivation." Like gardeners raising prize plants, these parents watched carefully over their children's development. They actively organized daily life to foster their children's talents and skills, and involved themselves in their children's school experiences. In contrast, working-class and poor parents used a style Lareau calls "natural growth." They work hard to get through the day and keep their children safe, but they expect their children to find their own recreation. In addition, they tend to feel alienated from and distrustful of their children's schools. Lareau argues that while each style has advantages and drawbacks, middle-class children develop a sense of "entitlement" that helps them navigate through the educational system from grade school through college and beyond.

In his article, Frank F. Furstenberg Jr. looks in more detail at how social class differences shape a child's development in the course of growing up. By early adulthood, he finds there are huge gaps between children growing up in advantaged and disadvantaged families. These realities go against the "rags to riches" idea that anyone can rise from the bottom to the top of the social ladder. Furstenberg argues that the nation has never lived up to its billing as the land of opportunity, but Americans have tended to ignore class differences. Even social scientists now emphasize gender race and ethnicity.

Furstenberg shows how social class begins to influence development even before a child is born; for example, it affects the diet and medical care of the mother-to-be and then the health care the new baby receives. Then the emotional and financial resources of the parents affect the skills the child learns and his or her readiness for school. These differences matter now more than ever because young people need more education than in past generations, and they need help from their parents for a longer time.

Indeed, in today's post-industrial society a whole new stage of life has emerged after adolescence ends. Instead of settling down into jobs, marriage, and parenthood in their early twenties, young adults move into a lengthened period of transition that may last through the twenties and thirties and beyond. This new and uncertain road to adulthood is a byproduct of globalization and the information age. In different countries around the world, these large scale shifts have reduced labor market opportunities for young adults, increased the need and demand for education, and driven up the costs of housing.

Katherine S. Newman shows that the result in many countries is "delayed adulthood"—young adults moving back into their parents' homes—or not leaving in the first place. But different countries have different cultural interpretations of delayed adulthood—or "failure to launch." Also, public policies have an effect on young people's options.

Young people in the Nordic countries, where there are strong welfare states, can choose to live on their own, but still feel the effects of delayed adulthood. Young adults in southern Europe and Japan have been hit the hardest. Parents' reactions also differ; in Italy, delayed adulthood is not considered a problem, while in Japan it's considered a catastrophe.

Chapter

7

Parenthood

READING 19

New Families: Modern Couples as New Pioneers

Philip Cowan and Carolyn Pape Cowan

Mark and Abby met when they went to work for a young, ambitious candidate who was campaigning in a presidential primary. Over the course of an exhilarating summer, they debated endlessly about values and tactics. At summer's end they parted, returned to college, and proceeded to forge their individual academic and work careers. When they met again several years later at a political function, Mark was employed in the public relations department of a large company and Abby was about to graduate from law school. Their argumentative, passionate discussions about the need for political and social change gradually expanded to the more personal, intimate discussions that lovers have.

They began to plan a future together. Mark moved into Abby's apartment. Abby secured a job in a small law firm. Excited about their jobs and their flourishing relationship, they talked about making a long-term commitment and soon decided to marry. After the wedding, although their future plans were based on a strong desire to have children, they were uncertain about when to start a family. Mark raised the issue tentatively, but felt he did not have enough job security to take the big step. Abby was fearful of not being taken seriously if she became a mother too soon after joining her law firm.

Several years passed. Mark was now eager to have children. Abby, struggling with competing desires to have a baby *and* to move ahead in her professional life, was still hesitant. Their conversations about having a baby seemed to go nowhere but were dramatically interrupted when they suddenly discovered that their birth control method had failed: Abby was unmistakably pregnant. Somewhat surprised by their own reactions, Mark and Abby found that they were relieved to have the timing decision taken out of their hands. Feeling readier than they anticipated, they became increasingly excited as they shared the news with their parents, friends, and coworkers.

Most chapters [in the book from which this reading is taken] focus on high-risk families, a category in which some observers include all families that deviate from the traditional two-parent, nonteenage, father-at-work-mother-at-home "norm." The increasing prevalence of these families has been cited by David Popenoe, David Blankenhorn, and others[1] as strong evidence that American families are currently in a state of decline. In the debate over the state of contemporary family life, the family decline theorists imply that traditional families are faring well. This view ignores clear evidence of the pervasive stresses and vulnerabilities that are affecting most families these days—even those with two mature, relatively advantaged parents.

In the absence of this evidence, it appears as if children and parents in traditional two-parent families do not face the kinds of problems that require the attention of family policymakers. We will show that Abby and Mark's life, along with those of many modern couples forming new families, is less ideal and more subject to distress than family observers and policymakers realize. Using data from our own and others' studies of partners becoming parents, we will illustrate how the normal process of becoming a family *in this culture, at this time* sets in motion a chain of potential stressors that function as risks that stimulate moderate to severe distress for a substantial number of parents. Results of a number of recent longitudinal studies make clear that if the parents' distress is not addressed, the quality of their marriages and their relationships with their children are more likely to be compromised. In turn, conflictful or disengaged family relationships during the family's formative years foreshadow later problems for the children when they reach the preschool and elementary school years. This means that substantial numbers of new two-parent families in the United States do not fit the picture of the ideal family portrayed in the family decline debate.

In what follows we: (1) summarize the changing historical context that makes life for many modern parents more difficult than it used to be; (2) explore the premises underlying the current debate about family decline; (3) describe how conditions associated with the transition to parenthood create risks that increase the probability of individual, marital, and family distress; and (4) discuss the implications of this family strain for American family policy. We argue that systematic information about the early years of family life is critical to social policy debates in two ways: first, to show how existing laws and regulations can be harmful to young families, and second, to provide information about promising interventions with the potential to strengthen family relationships during the early childrearing years.

HISTORICAL CONTEXT: CHANGING FAMILIES IN A CHANGING WORLD

From the historical perspective of the past two centuries, couples like Mark and Abby are unprecedented. They are a modern, middle-class couple attempting to create a different kind of family than those of their parents and grandparents. Strained economic conditions and the shifting ideology about appropriate roles for mothers and fathers pose new challenges for these new pioneers whose journey will lead them through unfamiliar terrain. With no maps to pinpoint the risks and hardships, contemporary men and women must forge new trails on their own.

Based on our work with couples starting families over the past twenty years, we believe that the process of becoming a family is more difficult now than it used to be. Because of the dearth of systematic study of these issues, it is impossible to locate hard evidence that modern parents face more challenges than parents of the past. Nonetheless, a brief survey of the changing context of family life in North America suggests that the transition to parenthood presents different and more confusing challenges for modern couples creating families than it did for parents in earlier times.

Less Support = More Isolation

While 75 percent of American families lived in rural settings in 1850, 80 percent were living in urban or suburban environments in the year 2000. Increasingly, new families are created far from grandparents, kin, and friends with babies the same age, leaving parents without the support of those who could share their experiences of the ups and downs of parenthood. Most modern parents bring babies home to isolated dwellings where their neighbors are strangers. Many women who stay home to care for their babies find themselves virtually alone in the neighborhood during this major transition, a time when we know that inadequate social support poses a risk to their own and their babies' well-being.[2]

More Choice = More Ambiguity

Compared with the experiences of their parents and grandparents, couples today have more choice about whether and when to bring children into their lives. In addition to the fact that about 4.5 percent of women now voluntarily remain forever childless (up from 2.2 percent in 1980), partners who do become parents are older and have smaller families—only one or two children, compared to the average of three, forty years ago. The reduction in family size tends to make each child seem especially precious, and the decision about whether and when to become parents even more momentous. Modern birth control methods give couples more control over the timing of a pregnancy, in spite of the fact that many methods fail with some regularity, as they did for Mark and Abby. Although the legal and moral issues surrounding abortion are hotly debated, modern couples have a choice about whether to become parents, even after conception begins.

Once the baby is born, there are more choices for modern couples. Will the mother return to work or school, which most were involved in before giving birth, and if so, how soon and for how many hours? Whereas only 18 percent of women with a child under six were employed outside the home in 1960, according to the 2000 census, approximately 55 percent of women with a child *under one* now work at least part time. Will the father take an active role in daily child care, and if so, how much? Although having these new choices is regarded by many as a benefit of modern life, choosing from among alternatives with such far-reaching consequences creates confusion and uncertainty for both men and women—which itself can lead to tension within the couple.

New Expectations for Marriage = New Emotional Burdens

Mark and Abby, like many other modern couples, have different expectations for marriage than their forebears. In earlier decades, couples expected marriage to be a working partnership in which men and women played unequal but clearly defined roles in terms of family and work, especially once they had children. Many modern couples are trying to create more egalitarian relationships in which men and women have more similar and often interchangeable family and work roles.

The dramatic increase of women in the labor force has challenged old definitions of what men and women are expected to do inside and outside the family. As women have taken on a major role of contributing to family income, there has been a shift in *ideology* about fathers' greater participation in housework and child care, although the *realities* of men's and women's division of family labor have lagged behind. Despite the fact that modern fathers are a little more involved in daily family activities than their fathers were, studies in every industrialized country reveal that women continue to carry the major share of the burden of family work and care of the children, even when both partners are employed full time.[3] In a detailed qualitative study, Arlie Hochschild notes that working mothers come home to a "second shift." She describes vividly couples' struggle with contradictions between the values of egalitarianism and traditionalism, and between egalitarian ideology and the constraints of modern family life.

As husbands and wives struggle with these issues, they often become adversaries. At the same time, they expect their partners to be their major suppliers of emotional warmth and support.[4] These demanding expectations for marriage as a haven from the stresses of the larger world come naturally to modern partners, but this comfort zone is difficult to create, given current economic and psychological realities and the absence of helpful models from the past. The difficulty of the task is further compounded by the fact that when contemporary couples feel stressed by trying to work and nurture their children, they feel torn by what they hear from advocates of a "simpler," more traditional version of family life. In sum, we see Abby and Mark as new pioneers because they are creating a new version of family life in an era of greater challenges and fewer supports, increased and confusing choices about work and family arrangements, ambiguities about men's and women's proper roles, and demanding expectations of themselves to be both knowledgeable and nurturing partners and parents.

POLITICAL CONTEXT: DOES FAMILY CHANGE MEAN FAMILY DECLINE?

A number of writers have concluded that the historical family changes we described have weakened the institution of the family. One of the main spokespersons for this point of view, David Popenoe,[5] interprets the trends as documenting a "retreat from the traditional nuclear family in terms of a lifelong, sexually exclusive unit, with a separate-sphere division of labor between husbands and wives." He asserts, "Nuclear units are losing ground to single-parent families, serial and stepfamilies, and unmarried and homosexual couples."[6] The main problem in contemporary family life, he argues, is a shift in which familism as a cultural value has lost ground to other values such as individualism, self-focus, and egalitarianism.[7]

Family decline theorists are especially critical of single-parent families whether created by divorce or out-of-wedlock childbirth.[8] They assume that two-parent families of the past functioned with a central concern for children that led to putting children's needs first. They characterize parents who have children under other arrangements as putting themselves first, and they claim that children are suffering as a result.

The primary index for evaluating the family decline is the well-being of children. Family decline theorists repeatedly cite statistics suggesting that fewer children are being born, and that a higher proportion of them are living with permissive, disengaged, self-focused parents who ignore their physical and emotional needs. Increasing numbers of children show signs of mental illness, behavior problems, and social deviance. The remedy suggested? A social movement and social policies to promote "family values" that emphasize nuclear families with two married, monogamous parents who want to have children and are willing to devote themselves to caring for them. These are the families we have been studying.

Based on the work of following couples starting families over the past twenty years, we suggest that there is a serious problem with the suggested remedy, which ignores the extent of distress and dysfunction in this idealized family form. We will show that in a surprisingly high proportion of couples, the arrival of the first child is accompanied by increased levels of tension, conflict, distress, and divorce, not because the parents are self-centered but because it is inherently difficult in today's world to juggle the economic and emotional needs of all family members, even for couples in relatively "low-risk" circumstances. The need to pay more attention to the underside of the traditional family myth is heightened by the fact that we can now (1) identify in advance those couples most likely to have problems as they make the transition to parenthood, and (2) intervene to reduce the prevalence and intensity of these problems. Our concern with the state of contemporary families leads us to suggest remedies that would involve active support to enable parents to provide nurturance and stability for their children, rather than exhortations that they change their values about family life.

REAL LIFE CONTEXT: NORMAL RISKS ASSOCIATED WITH BECOMING A FAMILY

To illustrate the short-term impact of becoming parents, let us take a brief look at Mark and Abby four days after they bring their daughter, Lizzie, home from the hospital.

> It is 3 A.M. Lizzie is crying lustily. Mark had promised that he would get up and bring the baby to Abby when she woke, but he hasn't stirred. After nudging him several times, Abby gives up and pads across the room to Lizzie's cradle. She carries her daughter to a rocking chair and starts to feed her. Abby's nipples are sore and she hasn't yet been able to relax while nursing. Lizzie soon stops sucking and falls asleep. Abby broods silently, the quiet broken only by the rhythmic squeak of the rocker. She is angry at Mark for objecting to

her suggestion that her parents come to help. She fumes, thinking about his romantic image of the three of them as a cozy family. "Well, Lizzie and I are cozy all right, but where is Mr. Romantic now?" Abby is also preoccupied with worry. She is intrigued and drawn to Lizzie but because she hasn't experienced the "powerful surge of love" that she thinks "all mothers" feel, she worries that something is wrong with her. She is also anxious because she told her boss that she'd be back to work shortly, but she simply doesn't know how she will manage. She considers talking to her best friend, Adrienne, but Adrienne probably wouldn't understand because she doesn't have a child.

Hearing what he interprets as Abby's angry rocking, Mark groggily prepares his defense about why he failed to wake up when the baby did. Rather than engaging in conversation, recalling that Abby "barked" at him when he hadn't remembered to stop at the market and pharmacy on the way home from work, he pretends to be asleep. He becomes preoccupied with thoughts about the pile of work he will face at the office in the morning.

We can see how two well-meaning, thoughtful people have been caught up in changes and reactions that neither has anticipated or feels able to control. Based on our experience with many new parent couples, we imagine that, if asked, Abby and Mark would say that these issues arousing their resentment are minor; in fact, they feel foolish about being so upset about them. Yet studies of new parents suggest that the stage is set for a snowball effect in which these minor discontents can grow into more troubling distress in the next year or two. What are the consequences of this early disenchantment? Will Mark and Abby be able to prevent it from triggering more serious negative outcomes for them or for the baby?

To answer these questions about the millions of couples who become first-time parents each year, we draw on the results of our own longitudinal study of the transition to parenthood and those of several other investigators who also followed men and women from late pregnancy into the early years of life with a first child.[9] The samples in these studies were remarkably similar: the average age of first-time expectant fathers was about thirty years, of expectant mothers approximately one year younger. Most investigators studied urban couples, but a few included rural families. Although the participants' economic level varied from study to study, most fell on the continuum from working class, through lower-middle, to upper-middle class. In 1995 we reviewed more than twenty longitudinal studies of this period of family life; we included two in Germany by Engfer and Schneewind[10] and one in England by Clulow,[11] and found that results in all but two reveal an elevated risk for the marriages of couples becoming parents.[12] A more recent study and review comes to the same conclusion.[13]

We talk about this major normative transition in the life of a couple in terms of risk, conflict, and distress for the relationship because we find that the effects of the transition to parenthood create disequilibrium in each of five major domains of family life: (1) the parents' sense of self; (2) parent-grandparent relationships; (3) the parent-child relationships; (4) relationships with friends and work; and (5) the state of the marriage. We find that "fault lines" in any of these domains before the baby arrives amplify marital tensions during the transition to parenthood. Although it is difficult to determine precisely when the transition to parenthood begins and ends, our findings suggest that it encompasses a period of more than three years, from before conception until at least two years after the first child is born. Since different couples experience the transition in different ways, we rely here not only on Mark and Abby but also on a number of other couples in our study to illustrate what happens in each domain when partners become parents.

Parents' Sense of Self

> Henry, aged 32, was doing well in his job at a large computer store. Along with Mei-Lin, his wife of four years, he was looking forward to the birth of his first child. Indeed, the first week or two found Henry lost in a euphoric haze. But as he came out of the clouds and went back to work, Henry began to be distracted by new worries. As his coworkers kept reminding him, he's a father now. He certainly feels like a different person, though he's not quite sure what a new father is supposed to be doing. Rather hesitantly, he confessed his sense of confusion to Mei-Lin, who appeared visibly relieved. "I've been feeling so fragmented," she told him. "It's been difficult to hold on to my sense of *me*. I'm a wife, a daughter, a friend, and a teacher, but the Mother part seems to have taken over my whole being."

Having a child forces a redistribution of the energy directed to various aspects of parents' identity. We asked expectant parents to describe themselves by making a list of the main aspects of themselves, such as son, daughter, friend, worker, and to divide a circle we called *The Pie* into pieces representing how large each aspect of self feels. Men and women filled out *The Pie* again six and eighteen months after their babies were born. As partners became parents, the size of the slice labeled *parent* increased markedly until it occupied almost one-third of the identity of mothers of eighteen-month-olds. Although men's *parent* slice also expanded, their sense of self as father occupied only one-third the "space" of their wives'. For both women and men, the *partner* or *lover* part of their identities got "squeezed" as the *parent* aspect of self expanded.

It is curious that in the early writing about the transition to parenthood, which E. E. LeMasters claimed constituted a crisis for a couple,[14] none of the investigators gathered or cited data on postpartum depression—diagnosed when disabling symptoms of depression occur within the first few months after giving birth. Accurate epidemiological estimates of risk for postpartum depression are difficult to come by. Claims about the incidence in women range from .01 percent for serious postpartum psychosis to 50 percent for the "baby blues." Results of a study by Campbell and her colleagues suggest that approximately 10 percent of new mothers develop serious clinical depressions that interfere with their daily functioning in the postpartum period.[15] There are no epidemiological estimates of the incidence of postpartum depression in new fathers. In our study of 100 couples, one new mother and one new father required medical treatment for disabling postpartum depression. What we know, then, is that many new parents like Henry and Mei-Lin experience a profound change in their view of themselves after they have a baby, and some feel so inadequate and critical of themselves that their predominant mood can be described as depressed.

Relationships with Parents and In-Laws

> Sandra, one of the younger mothers in our study, talked with us about her fear of repeating the pattern from her mother's life. Her mother gave birth at sixteen, and told her

children repeatedly that she was too young to raise a family. "Here I am with a beautiful little girl, and I'm worrying about whether I'm really grown up enough to raise her." At the same time, Sandra's husband, Daryl, who was beaten by his stepfather, is having flashbacks about how helpless he felt at those times: "I'm trying to maintain the confidence I felt when Sandra and I decided to start our family, but sometimes I get scared that I'm not going to be able to avoid being the kind of father I grew up with."

Psychoanalytically oriented writers[16] focusing on the transition to parenthood emphasize the potential disequilibration that is stimulated by a reawakening of intrapsychic conflicts from new parents' earlier relationships. There is considerable evidence that having a baby stimulates men's and women's feelings of vulnerability and loss associated with their own childhoods, and that these issues play a role in their emerging sense of self as parents. There is also evidence that negative relationship patterns tend to be repeated across the generations, despite parents' efforts to avoid them;[17] so Sandra and Daryl have good reason to be concerned. However, studies showing that a strong, positive couple relationship can provide a buffer against negative parent-child interactions suggest that the repetition of negative cycles is not inevitable.[18]

We found that the birth of a first child increases the likelihood of contact between the generations, often with unanticipated consequences. Occasionally, renewed contact allows the expectant parents to put years of estrangement behind them if their parents are receptive to renewed contact. More often, increased contact between the generations stimulates old and new conflicts—within each partner, between the partners, and between the generations. To take one example: Abby wants her mother to come once the baby is born but Mark has a picture of beginning family life on their own. Tensions between them around this issue can escalate regardless of which decision they make. If Abby's parents do visit, Mark may have difficulty establishing his place with the baby. Even if Abby's parents come to help, she and Mark may find that the grandparents need looking after too. It may be weeks before Mark and Abby have a private conversation. If the grandparents do not respond or are not invited, painful feelings between the generations are likely to ensue.

The Parent-Child Relationship

Few parents have had adequate experience in looking after children to feel confident immediately about coping with the needs of a first baby.

> Tyson and Martha have been arguing, it seems, for days. Eddie, their six-month-old, has long crying spells every day and into the night. As soon as she hears him, Martha moves to pick him up. When he is home, Tyson objects, reasoning that this just spoils Eddie and doesn't let him learn how to soothe himself. Martha responds that Eddie wouldn't be crying if something weren't wrong, but she worries that Tyson may be right; after all, she's never looked after a six-month-old for more than an evening of baby-sitting. Although Tyson continues to voice his objections, he worries that if Martha is right, *his* plan may not be the best for his son either.

To make matters more complicated, just as couples develop strategies that seem effective, their baby enters a new developmental phase that calls for new reactions and routines.

What makes these new challenges difficult to resolve is that each parent has a set of ideas and expectations about how parents should respond to a child, most based on experience in their families of origin. Meshing both parents' views of how to resolve basic questions about child rearing proves to be a more complex and emotionally draining task than most couples had anticipated.

Work and Friends

Dilemmas about partners' work outside the home are particularly salient during a couple's transition to parenthood.

> Both Hector and Isabel have decided that Isabel should stay home for at least the first year after having the baby. One morning, as Isabel is washing out José's diapers and hoping the phone will ring, she breaks into tears. Life is not as she imagined it. She misses her friends at work. She misses Hector, who is working harder now to provide for his family than he was before José was born. She misses her parents and sisters who live far away in Mexico. She feels strongly that she wants to be with her child full time, and that she should be grateful that Hector's income makes this possible, but she feels so unhappy right now. This feeling adds to her realization that she has always contributed half of their family income, but now she has to ask Hector for household money, which leaves her feeling vulnerable and dependent.
>
> Maria is highly invested in her budding career as an investment counselor, making more money than her husband, Emilio. One morning, as she faces the mountain of unread files on her desk and thinks of Lara at the child care center almost ready to take her first steps, Maria bursts into tears. She feels confident that she and Emilio have found excellent child care for Lara, and reminds herself that research has suggested that when mothers work outside the home, their daughters develop more competence than daughters of mothers who stay home. Nevertheless, she feels bereft, missing milestones that happen only once in a child's life.

We have focused on the women in both families because, given current societal arrangements, the initial impact of the struggle to balance work and family falls more heavily on mothers. If the couple decides that one parent will stay home to be the primary caretaker of the child, it is almost always the mother who does so. As we have noted, in contemporary America, about 50 percent of mothers of very young children remain at home after having a baby and more than half return to work within the first year. Both alternatives have some costs and some benefits. If mothers like Isabel want to be home with their young children, and the family can afford this arrangement, they have the opportunity to participate fully in the early day-to-day life of their children. This usually has benefits for parents and children. Nevertheless, most mothers who stay home face limited opportunities to accomplish work that leads them to feel competent, and staying home deprives them of emotional support that coworkers and friends can provide, the kinds of support that play a significant role in how parents fare in the early postpartum years. This leaves women like Isabel at risk for feeling lonely and isolated from friends and family.[19] By contrast, women like Maria who return to work are able to maintain a network of adults to work with and talk with. They may feel better about themselves and "on track" as far as their work is concerned, but many become preoccupied with worry about their children's well-being, particularly in this age of costly but less than ideal child care. Furthermore, once they get home, they enter a "second shift" in which they do the bulk of the housework and child care.[20]

We do not mean to imply that all the work-family conflicts surrounding the transition to parenthood are experienced by women. Many modern fathers feel torn about how to juggle work and family life, move ahead on the job, and be more involved with their children than their fathers were with them. Rather than receive a reduction in workload, men tend to work longer hours once they become fathers, mainly because they take their role as provider even more seriously now that they have a child.[21] In talking to more than 100 fathers in our ongoing studies, we have become convinced that the common picture of men as resisting the responsibilities and workload involved in family life is seriously in error. We have become painfully aware of the formidable obstacles that bar men from assuming more active roles as fathers and husbands.

First, parents, bosses, and friends often discourage men's active involvement in the care of their children ("How come you're home in the middle of the day?" "Are you really serious about your work here?" "She's got you baby-sitting again, huh?"). Second, the economic realities in which men's pay exceeds women's, make it less viable for men to take family time off. Third, by virtue of the way males and females are socialized, men rarely get practice in looking after children and are given very little support for learning by trial and error with their new babies.

> In the groups that we conducted for expectant and new parents, to which parents brought their babies after they were born, we saw and heard many versions of the following: we are discussing wives' tendency to reach for the baby, on the assumption that their husbands will not respond. Cindi describes an incident last week when little Samantha began to cry. Cindi waited. Her husband, Martin, picked up Samantha gingerly, groped for a bottle, and awkwardly started to feed her. Then, according to Martin, within about sixty seconds, Cindi suggested that Martin give Samantha's head more support and prop the bottle in a different way so that the milk would flow without creating air bubbles. Martin quickly decided to hand the baby back to "the expert" and slipped into the next room "to get some work done."

The challenge to juggle the demands of work, family, and friendship presents different kinds of stressors for men and women, which propels the spouses even farther into separate worlds. When wives stay at home, they wait eagerly for their husbands to return, hoping the men will go "on duty" with the child, especially on difficult days. This leaves tired husbands who need to unwind facing tired wives who long to talk to an adult who will respond intelligibly to them. When both parents work outside the family, they must coordinate schedules, arrange child care, and decide how to manage when their child is ill. Parents' stress from these dilemmas about child care and lack of rest often spill over into the workday—and their work stress, in turn, gets carried back into the family atmosphere.[22]

The Marriage

It should be clearer now why we say that the normal changes associated with becoming a family increase the risk that husbands and wives will experience increased marital dissatisfaction and strain after they become parents. Mark and Abby, and the other couples we have described briefly, have been through changes in their sense of themselves and in their relationships with their parents. They have struggled with uncertainties and disagreements about how to provide the best care for their child. Regardless of whether one parent stays home full or part time or both work full days outside the home, they have limited time and energy to meet conflicting demands from their parents, bosses, friends, child, and each other, and little support from outside the family to guide them on this complex journey into uncharted territory. In almost every published study of the transition conducted over the last four decades, men's and women's marital satisfaction declined. Belsky and Rovine found that from 30 percent to 59 percent of the participants in their Pennsylvania study showed a decline between pregnancy and nine months postpartum, depending on which measure of the marriage they examined.[23] In our study of California parents, 45 percent of the men and 58 percent of the women showed declining satisfaction with marriage between pregnancy and eighteen months postpartum. The scores of approximately 15 percent of the new parents moved from below to above the clinical cutoff that indicates serious marital problems, whereas only 4 percent moved from above to below the cutoff.

Why should this optimistic time of life pose so many challenges for couples? One key issue for couples becoming parents has been treated as a surefire formula for humor in situation comedies—husband-wife battles over the "who does what?" of housework, child care, and decision making. Our own study shows clearly that, regardless of how equally family work is divided before having a baby, or of how equally husbands and wives *expect* to divide the care of the baby, the roles men and women assume tend to be gender-linked, with wives doing more family work than they had done before becoming a parent and substantially more housework and baby care than their husbands do. Furthermore, the greater the discrepancy between women's predicted and actual division of family tasks with their spouses, the more symptoms of depression they report. The more traditional the arrangements—that is, the less husbands are responsible for family work—the greater fathers' *and* mothers' postpartum dissatisfaction with their overall marriage.

Although theories of life stress generally assume that *any* change is stressful, we found no correlation between sheer *amount* of change in the five aspects of family life and parents' difficulties adapting to parenthood. In general, parenthood was followed by increasing discrepancies between husbands' and wives' perceptions of family life and their descriptions of their actual family and work roles. Couples in which the partners showed the greatest increase in those discrepancies—more often those with increasingly traditional role arrangements—described increasing conflict as a couple and greater declines in marital satisfaction.

These findings suggest that whereas family decline theorists are looking at statistics about contemporary families through 1950 lenses, actual families are responding to the realities of life in the twenty-first century. Given historical shifts in men's and women's ideas about family roles and present economic realities, it is not realistic to expect them to simply reverse trends by adopting more traditional values and practices. Contemporary families in which the parents' arrangements are at the more traditional end of the spectrum are *less* satisfied with themselves, with their relationships as couples, and with their role as parents, than those at the more egalitarian end.

DO WE KNOW WHICH FAMILIES WILL BE AT RISK?

The message for policymakers from research on the transition to parenthood is not only that it is a time of stress and change. We and others have found that there is predictability to couples' patterns of change: this means that it is possible to know whether a couple is at risk for more serious problems before they have a baby and whether their child will be at risk for compromised development. This information is also essential for purposes of designing *preventive* intervention. Couples most at risk for difficulties and troubling outcomes in the early postpartum years are those who were in the greatest individual and marital distress before they became parents. Children most at risk are those whose parents are having the most difficulty maintaining a positive, rewarding relationship as a couple.

The "Baby-Maybe" Decision

Interviews with expectant parents about their process of making the decision to have a baby provide one source of information about continuity of adaptation in the family-making period. By analyzing partners' responses to the question, "How did the two of you come to be having a baby at this time?" we found four fairly distinct types of decision making in our sample of lower-middle- to upper-middle-class couples, none of whom had identified themselves as having serious relationship difficulties during pregnancy: (1) The *Planners*—50 percent of the couples—agreed about whether and when to have a baby. The other 50 percent were roughly evenly divided into three patterns: (2) The *Acceptance of fate couples*—15 percent—had unplanned conceptions but were pleased to learn that they were about to become parents; (3) The *Ambivalent couples*—another 15 percent—continually went back and forth about their readiness to have a baby, even late in pregnancy; and (4) The *Yes-No couples*—the remaining 15 percent—claimed not to be having relationship difficulties but nonetheless had strong disagreements about whether to complete their unplanned pregnancy.

> Alice, thirty-four, became pregnant when she and Andy, twenty-seven, had been living together only four months. She was determined to have a child, regardless of whether Andy stayed in the picture. He did not feel ready to become a father, and though he dearly loved Alice, he was struggling to come to terms with the pregnancy. "It was the hardest thing I ever had to deal with," he said. "I had this idea that I wasn't even going to have to think about being a father until I was over thirty, but here it was, and I had to decide now. I was concerned about my soul. I didn't want, under any circumstances, to compromise myself, but I knew it would be very hard on Alice if I took action that would result in her being a single parent. It would've meant that I'm the kind of person who turns his back on someone I care about, and that would destroy me as well as her." And so he stayed.[24]

The *Planners* and *Acceptance of fate couples* experienced minimal decline in marital satisfaction, whereas the *Ambivalent couples* tended to have lower satisfaction to begin with and to decline even further between pregnancy and two years later. The greatest risk was for couples who had serious disagreement—more than ambivalence—about having a first baby. In these cases, one partner gave in to the other's wishes in order to remain in the relationship. The startling outcome provides a strong statement about the wisdom of this strategy: all of the *Yes-No couples* like Alice and Andy were divorced by the time their first child entered kindergarten, and the two *Yes-No couples* in which the wife was the reluctant partner reported severe marital distress at every postpartum assessment. This finding suggests that partners' unresolved conflict in making the decision to have a child is mirrored by their inability to cope with conflict to both partners' satisfaction once they become parents. Couples' styles of making this far-reaching decision seem to be a telling indicator of whether their overall relationship is at risk for instability, a finding that contradicts the folk wisdom that having a baby will mend serious marital rifts.

Additional Risk Factors for Couples

Not surprisingly, when couples reported high levels of outside-the-family life stress during pregnancy, they are more likely to be unhappy in their marriages and stressed in their parenting roles during the early years of parenthood. When there are serious problems in the relationships between new parents and their own parents the couples are more likely to experience more postpartum distress.[25] Belsky and colleagues showed that new parents who recalled strained relationships with their own parents were more likely to experience more marital distress in the first year of parenthood.[26] In our study, parents who reported early childhoods clouded by their parents' problem drinking had a more stressful time on every indicator of adjustment in the first two years of parenthood—more conflict, less effective problem solving, less effective parenting styles, and greater parenting stress.[27] Although the transmission of maladaptive patterns across generations is not inevitable, these data suggest that without intervention, troubled relationships in the family of origin constitute a risk factor for relationships in the next generation.

Although it is never possible to make perfect predictions for purposes of creating family policies to help reduce the risks associated with family formation, we have been able to identify expectant parents at risk for later individual, marital, and parenting difficulties based on information they provided during pregnancy. Recall that the participants in the studies we are describing are the two-parent intact families portrayed as ideal in the family decline debate. The problems they face have little to do with their family values. The difficulties appear to stem from the fact that the visible fault lines in couple relationships leave their marriages more vulnerable to the shake-up of the transition-to-parenthood process.

Risks for Children

We are concerned about the impact of the transition to parenthood not only because it increases the risk of distress in marriage but also because the parents' early distress can have far-reaching consequences for their children. Longitudinal studies make it clear that parents' early difficulties affect their children's later intellectual and social adjustment. For example, parents' well-being or distress as individuals and as couples during pregnancy predicts the quality of their relationships with their children in the preschool period.[28] In turn, the quality of both parent-child relationships in the preschool years is related to the child's academic and social competence during the early elementary school years.[29] Preschoolers whose mothers and fathers had more responsive, effective parenting styles had higher scores on academic achievement and fewer acting out, aggressive, or withdrawn behavior problems with peers in kindergarten and Grade 1.[30] When we receive teachers' reports, we see that overall, five-year-olds whose parents reported making the most positive adaptations to parenthood were the ones with the most successful adjustments to elementary school.

Alexander and Entwisle[31] suggested that in kindergarten and first grade, children are "launched into achievement trajectories that they follow the rest of their school years." Longitudinal studies of children's academic and social competence[32] support this hypothesis about the importance of students' early adaptation to school: children who are socially rejected by peers in the early elementary grades are more likely to have academic problems or drop out of school, to develop antisocial and delinquent behaviors, and to have difficulty in intimate relationships with partners in late adolescence and early adulthood. Without support or intervention early in a family's development, the children with early academic, emotional, and social problems are at greater risk for later, even more serious problems.

POLICY IMPLICATIONS

What social scientists have learned about families during the transition to parenthood is relevant to policy discussions about how families with young children can be strengthened.

We return briefly to the family values debate to examine the policy implications of promoting traditional family arrangements, of altering workplace policies, and of providing preventive interventions to strengthen families during the early childrearing years.

The Potential Consequences of Promoting Traditional Family Arrangements

What are the implications of the argument that families and children would benefit by a return to traditional family arrangements? We are aware that existing data are not adequate to provide a full test of the family values argument, but we believe that some systematic information on this point is better than none. At first glance, it may seem as if studies support the arguments of those proposing that "the family" is in decline. We have documented the fact that a substantial number of new two-parent families are experiencing problems of adjustment—parents' depression, troubled marriages, intergenerational strain, and stress in juggling the demands of work and family. Nevertheless, there is little in the transition to parenthood research to support the idea that parents' distress is attributable to a decline in their family-oriented *values*. First, the populations studied here are two-parent, married, nonteenage, lower-middle- to upper-middle-class families, who do not represent the "variants" in family form that most writers associate with declining quality of family life.

Second, threaded throughout the writings on family decline is the erroneous assumption that because these changes in the family have been occurring at the same time as increases in negative outcomes for children, the changes are the *cause* of the problems. These claims are not buttressed by systematic data establishing the direction of causal influence. For example, it is well accepted (but still debated) that children's adaptation is poorer in the period after their parents' divorce.[33] Nevertheless, some studies suggest that it is the unresolved conflict between parents prior to and after the divorce, rather than the divorce itself, that accounts for most of the debilitating effects on the children.[34]

Third, we find the attack on family egalitarianism puzzling when the fact is that, despite the increase in egalitarian ideology, modern couples move toward more traditional family role arrangements as they become parents—despite their intention to do otherwise. Our key point here is that traditional family and work roles in families of the last three decades tend to be associated with *more* individual and marital distress for parents. Furthermore, we find that when fathers have little involvement in household and child care tasks, both parents are less responsive and less able to provide the structure necessary for their children to accomplish new and challenging tasks in our project playroom. Finally, when we ask teachers how all of the children in their classrooms are faring at school, it is the children of these parents who are less academically competent and more socially isolated. There is, then, a body of evidence suggesting that a return to strictly traditional family arrangements may not have the positive consequences that the proponents of "family values" claim they will.

Family and Workplace Policy

Current discussions about policies for reducing the tensions experienced by parents of young children tend to be polarized around two alternatives: (1) Encourage more mothers to stay home and thereby reduce their stress in juggling family and work; (2) Make the workplace more flexible and "family friendly" for both parents through parental leave policies, flextime, and child care provided or subsidized by the workplace. There is no body of systematic empirical research that supports the conclusion that when mothers work outside the home, their children or husbands suffer negative consequences.[35] In fact, our own data and others' suggest that (1) children, especially girls, benefit from the model their working mothers provide as productive workers, and (2) mothers of young children who return to work are less depressed than mothers who stay home full time. Thus it is not at all clear that a policy designed to persuade contemporary mothers of young children to stay at home would have the desired effects, particularly given the potential for depression and the loss of one parent's wages in single paycheck families. Unless governments are prepared, as they are in Sweden and Germany, for example, to hold parents' jobs and provide *paid* leave to replace lost wages, a stay-at-home *policy* seems too costly for the family on both economic and psychological grounds.

We believe that the issue should not be framed in terms of policies to support single-worker *or* dual-worker families, but rather in terms of support for the well-being of all family members. This goal could entail financial support for families with very young children so that parents could choose to do full-time or substantial part-time child care themselves *or* to have support to return to work.

What about the alternative of increasing workplace flexibility? Studies of families making the transition to parenthood suggest that this alternative may be especially attractive and helpful when children are young, if it is accompanied by substantial increases in the availability of high-quality child care to reduce the stress of locating adequate care or making do with less than ideal caretakers. Adults and children tend to adapt well when both parents work *if both parents support that alternative.* Therefore, policies that support paid family leave along with flexible work arrangements could enable families to choose arrangements that make most sense for their particular situation.

Preventive Services to Address Family Risk Points

According to our analysis of the risks associated with the formation of new families, many two-parent families are having difficulty coping on their own with the normal challenges of becoming a family. If a priority in our society is to strengthen new families, it seems reasonable to consider offering preventive programs to reduce risks and distress and enhance the potential for healthy and satisfying family relationships, which we know lead to more optimal levels of adjustment in children. What we are advocating is analogous to the concept of Lamaze and other forms of childbirth preparation, which are now commonly sought by many expectant parents. A logical context for these programs would be existing public and private health and mental health delivery systems in which services could be provided for families who wish assistance or are already in difficulty. We recognize that there is skepticism in a substantial segment of the population about psychological services in general, and about services provided for families by government in particular. Nonetheless, the fact is that many modern families are finding parenthood unexpectedly stressful and they typically have no access to assistance. Evidence from intervention trials suggests that when preventive programs help parents move their family relationships in more positive directions, their children have fewer academic, behavioral, and emotional problems in their first years of schooling.[36]

Parent-Focused Interventions. Elsewhere, we reviewed the literature on interventions designed to improve parenting skills and parent-child relationship quality in families at different points on the spectrum from low-risk to high-distress.[37] For parents of children already identified as having serious problems, home visiting programs and preschool and early school interventions, some of which include a broader family focus, have demonstrated positive effects on parents' behavior and self-esteem and on children's academic and social competence, particularly when the intervention staff are health or mental health professionals. However, with the exception of occasional classes, books, or tapes for parents, there are few resources for parents who need to learn more about how to manage small problems before they spiral out of their control.

Couple-Focused Interventions. Our conceptual model of family transitions and results of studies of partners who become parents suggest that family-based interventions might go beyond enhancing parent-child relationships to strengthen the relationship *between* the parents. We have seen that the couple relationship is vulnerable in its own right around the decision to have a baby and increasingly after the birth of a child. We know of only one pilot program that provided couples an opportunity to explore mixed feelings about the "Baby-Maybe" decision.[38] Surely, services designed to help couples resolve their conflict about whether and when to become a family—especially "Yes-No" couples—might reduce the risks of later marital and family distress, just as genetic counseling helps couples make decisions when they are facing the risk of serious genetic problems.

In our own work, we have been systematically evaluating two preventive interventions for couples who have not been identified as being in a high-risk category. Both projects involved work with small groups of couples who met weekly over many months, in one case expectant couples, in the other, couples whose first child is about to make the transition to elementary school.[39] In both studies, staff couples who are mental health professionals worked with *both parents* in small groups of four or five couples. Ongoing discussion over the months of regular meetings addressed participants' individual, marital, parenting, and three-generational dilemmas and problems. In both cases we found promising results when we compared adjustment in families with and without the intervention.

By two years after the Becoming a Family project intervention, new parents had avoided the typical declines in role satisfaction and the increases in marital disenchantment reported in almost every longitudinal study of new parents. There were no separations or divorces in couples who participated in the intervention for the first three years of parenthood, whereas 15 percent of comparable couples with no intervention had already divorced. The positive impact of this intervention was still apparent five years after it had ended.

In the Schoolchildren and Their Families project intervention, professional staff engaged couples in group discussions of marital, parenting, and three-generational problems and dilemmas during their first child's transition to school. Two years after the intervention ended, fathers and mothers showed fewer symptoms of depression and less conflict in front of their child, and fathers were more effective in helping their children with difficult tasks than comparable parents with no intervention. These positive effects on the parents' lives and relationships had benefits for the children as well: children of parents who worked with the professionals in an ongoing couples group showed greater academic improvement and fewer emotional and behavior problems in the first five years of elementary school than children whose parents had no group intervention.[40]

These results suggest that preventive interventions in which clinically trained staff work with "low-risk" couples have the potential to buffer some of the parents' strain, slow down or stop the spillover of negative and unrewarding patterns from one relationship to another, enhance fathers' responsiveness to their children, and foster the children's ability both to concentrate on their school work and to develop more rewarding relationships with their peers. The findings suggest that *without intervention*, there is increased risk of spillover from parents' distress to the quality of the parent-child relationships. This means that preventive services to help parents cope more effectively with their problems have the potential to enhance their responsiveness to their children *and* to their partners, which, in turn, optimizes their children's chances of making more successful adjustments to school. Such programs have the potential to reduce the long-term negative consequences of children's early school difficulties by setting them on more positive developmental trajectories as they face the challenges of middle childhood.

CONCLUSION

The transition to parenthood has been made by men and women for centuries. In the past three decades, the notion that this transition poses risks for the well-being of adults and, thus, potentially for their children's development, has been greeted by some with surprise, disbelief, or skepticism. Our goal has been to bring recent social science findings about the processes involved in becoming a family to the attention of social scientists, family policymakers, and parents themselves. We have shown that this often-joyous time is normally accompanied by changes and stressors that increase risks of relationship difficulty and compromise the ability of men and women to create the kinds of families they dream of when they set out on their journey to parenthood. We conclude that there is cause for concern about the health of "the family"—even those considered advantaged by virtue of their material and psychological resources.

Most chapters in this book focus on policies for families in more high-risk situations. We have argued that contemporary couples and their children in two-parent lower- to upper-middle-class families deserve the attention of policymakers as well. We view these couples as new pioneers, because, despite the fact that partners have been having babies for millennia, contemporary parents are journeying into uncharted terrain, which appears to hold unexpected risks to their own and their children's development.

Like writers describing "family decline," we are concerned about the strength and hardiness of two-parent families. Unlike those who advocate that parents adopt more traditional family values, we recommend that policies to address family health and well-being allow for the creation of programs and services for families in diverse family arrangements, with the goal of enhancing the development and well-being of all children. We recognize that with economic resources already stretched very thin, this is not an auspicious time to recommend additional collective funding of family services. Yet research suggests that without intervention, there is a risk that the vulnerabilities and problems of the parents will spill over into the lives of their children, thus increasing the probability of the transmission of the kinds of intergenerational problems that erode the quality of family life and compromise children's chances of optimal development. This will be very costly in the long run.

We left Mark and Abby, and a number of other couples, in a state of animated suspension. Many of them were feeling somewhat irritable and disappointed, though not ready to give up on their dreams of creating nurturing families. These couples provide a challenge—that the information they have offered through their participation in scores of systematic family studies in many locales will be taken seriously, and that their voices will play a role in helping our society decide how to allocate limited economic and social resources for the families that need them.

Notes

1. D. Blankenhorn, S. Bayme, and J. B. Elshtain (eds.), *Rebuilding the Nest: A New Commitment to the American Family* (Milwaukee, WI: Family Service America, 1990), 3–26; D. Popenoe, "American Family Decline, 1960–1990," *Journal of Marriage and the Family* 55:527–541, 1993.
2. S. B. Crockenberg, "Infant Irritability, Mother Responsiveness, and Social Support Influences on Security of Infant-Mother Attachment," *Child Development* 52:857–865, 1981; C. Cutrona,

"Non-psychotic Postpartum Depression: A Review of Recent Research," *Clinical Psychology Review* 2: 487–503, 1982.

3. A. Hochschild, *The Second Shift: Working Parents and the Revolution at Home* (New York: Viking Penguin, 1989); J. H. Pleck, "Fathers and Infant Care Leave," in E. F. Zigler and M. Frank (eds.), *The Parental Leave Crisis: Toward a National Policy* (New Haven, CT: Yale University Press, 1988).
4. A. Skolnick, *Embattled Paradise: The American Family in an Age of Uncertainty* (New York: Basic Books, 1991).
5. D. Popenoe, *Disturbing the Nest: Family Change and Decline in Modern Societies* (New York: Aldine de Gruyter, 1988); Popenoe, "American Family Decline."
6. Popenoe, "American Family Decline." 41–42. Smaller two-parent families and larger one-parent families are both attributed to the same mechanism: parental self-focus and selfishness.
7. D. Blankenhorn, "American Family Dilemmas," in D. Blankenhorn, S. Bayme, and J. B. Elshtain (eds.), *Rebuilding the Nest. A New Commitment to the American Family* (Milwaukee, WI: Family Service America, 1990), 3–26.
8. Although the proportion of single-parent families is increasing, the concern about departure from the two-parent form may be overstated. Approximately 70 percent of American babies born in the 1990s come home to two parents who are married. If we include couples with long-term commitments who are not legally married, the proportion of modern families that *begins* with two parents is even higher. The prevalence of two-parent families has declined since 1956, when 94 percent of newborns had married parents, but, by far, the predominant family form in the nonteenage population continues to be two parents and a baby.
9. J. Belsky, M. Lang, and M. Rovine, "Stability and Change across the Transition to Parenthood: A Second Study," *Journal of Personality and Social Psychology* 50:517–522, 1985; C. P. Cowan, P. A. Cowan, G. Heming, E. Garrett, W. S. Coysh, H. Curtis-Boles, and A. J. Boles, "Transitions to Parenthood: His, Hers, and Theirs," *Journal of Family Issues* 6:451–481, 1985; M. J. Cox, M. T. Owen, J. M. Lewis, and V. K. Henderson, "Marriage, Adult Adjustment, and Early Parenting," *Child Development* 60:1015–1024, 1989; F. Grossman, L. Eiehler, and S. Winickoff, *Pregnancy, Birth, and Parenthood* (San Francisco: Jossey-Bass, 1980); C. M. Heinicke, S. D. Diskin, D. M. Ramsay-Klee, and D. S. Oates, "Pre- and Postbirth Antecedents of 2-year-old Attention, Capacity for Relationships and Verbal Expressiveness," *Developmental Psychology* 22:777–787, 1986; R. Levy-Shiff, "Individual and Contextual Correlates of Marital Change Across the Transition to Parenthood," *Developmental Psychology* 30:591–601, 1994.
10. A. Engfer, "The Interrelatedness of Marriage and the Mother-Child Relationship," in R. A. Hinde and J. Stevenson-Hinde (eds.), *Relationships within Families: Mutual Influences* (Cambridge UK: Cambridge University Press, 1988), 104–118; K. A. Schneewind, "Konsequenzen der Erstelternschaft" [Consequences of the Transition to Parenthood: An Overview], *Psychologie in Erziehung and Unterricht* 30:161–172, 1983.
11. C. F. Clulow, *To Have and to Hold: Marriage, the First Baby and Preparing Couples for Parenthood* (Aberdeen, Scotland: Aberdeen University Press, 1982).
12. C. P. Cowan and P. A. Cowan, "Interventions to Ease the Transition to Parenthood: Why They Are Needed and What They Can Do," *Family Relations* 44:412–423, 1995.
13. A. F. Shapiro, J. M. Gottman, and S. Carrere, "The Baby and the Marriage. Identifying Factors that Buffer against Decline in Marital Satisfaction after the First Baby Arrives. *Journal of Family Psychology*, 14:59–70, 2000.
14. E. E. LeMasters, "Parenthood as Crisis," *Marriage and Family Living* 19:352–365, 1957.
15. S. B. Campbell, J. F. Cohn, C. Flanagan, S. Popper, and T. Myers, "Course and Correlates of Postpartum Depression during the Transition to Parenthood," *Development and Psychopathology* 4:29–48, 1992.
16. T. Benedek, "Parenthood during the Life Cycle," in E. J. Anthony and T. Benedek (eds.), *Parenthood: Its Psychology and Psychopathology* (Boston: Little, Brown, 1970); J. D. Osofsky and H. J. Osofsky, "Psychological and Developmental Perspectives on Expectant and New Parenthood," in R. D. Parke (ed.), *Review of Child Development Research 7: The Family* (Chicago: University of Chicago Press, 1984), 372–397.
17. A. Caspi and G. H. Elder, Jr. "Emergent Family Patterns: The Intergenerational Construction of Problem Behavior and Relationships," in R. A. Hinde and J. Stevenson-Hinde (eds.), *Relationships*

Within Families: Mutual Influences (Oxford: Clarendon Press, 1988), 218–241; M. H. van Ijzendoorn, F. Juffer, M. G. Duyvesteyn, "Breaking the Intergenerational Cycle of Insecure Attachment: A Review of the Effects of Attachment-based Interventions on Maternal Sensitivity and Infant Security," *Journal of Child Psychology & Psychiatry & Allied Disciplines* 36:225–248, 1995.

18. D. A. Cohn, P. A. Cowan, C. P. Cowan, and J. Pearson, "Mothers' and Fathers' Working Models of Childhood Attachment Relationships, Parenting Styles, and Child Behavior," *Development and Psychopathology* 4:417–431, 1992.
19. Crockenberg, "Infant Irritability."
20. Hochsehild, *The Second Shift.*
21. C. P. Cowan and P. A. Cowan, *When Partners Become Parents: The Big Life Change for Couples* (Mahwah, NJ: Lawrence Erlbaum, 2000).
22. M. S. Schulz, "Coping with Negative Emotional Arousal: The Daily Spillover of Work Stress into Marital Interactions," Unpublished doctoral dissertation. University of California, Berkeley, 1994; R. Repetti and J. Wood, "Effects of Daily Stress at Work on Mothers' Interactions with Preschoolers," *Journal of Family Psychology*, 11:90–108, 1997.
23. J. Belsky and M. Rovine, "Patterns of Marital Change across the Transition to Parenthood," *Journal of Marriage and the Family* 52:109–123, 1990.
24. We interviewed the couples in the mid-to-late stages of pregnancy. We were not, therefore, privy to the early phases of decision making of these couples, whether wives became pregnant on purpose, or whether husbands were coercive about the baby decision. What we saw in the Yes-No couples, in contrast with the Ambivalent couples, was that the decision to go ahead with the pregnancy, an accomplished fact, was still an unresolved emotional struggle.
25. M. Kline, P. A. Cowan, and C. P. Cowan, "The Origins of Parenting Stress during the Transition to Parenthood: A New Family Model," *Early Education and Development* 2:287–305, 1991.
26. J. Belsky and R. A. Isabella, "Marital and Parent-Child Relationships in Family of Origin and Marital Change Following the Birth of a Baby: A Retrospective Analysis," *Child Development* 56:342–349, 1985; C. P. Cowan, P. A. Cowan, and G. Heming, "Adult Children of Alcoholics: Adaptation during the Transition to Parenthood." Paper presented to the National Council on Family Relations, 1988.
27. Cowan, Cowan, and Heming; "Adult Children of Alcoholics."
28. Belsky, Lang, and Rovine, "Stability and Change across the Transition to Parenthood"; Cowan and Cowan, *When Partners Become Parents;* Cox, Owen, Lewis, and Henderson, "Marriage, Adult Adjustment, and Early Parenting"; Heinicke, Diskin, Ramsay-Klee, and Oates, "Pre- and Postbirth Antecedents of 2-Year-Old Attention, Capacity for Relationships and Verbal Expressiveness."
29. D. Baumrind, "The Development of Instrumental Competence through Socialization," in A. D. Pick (ed.), *Minnesota Symposia on Child Psychology*, vol. 7 (Minneapolis: University of Minnesota Press, 1979); J. H. Block and J. Block, "The Role of Ego-Control and Ego-Resiliency in the Organization of Behavior," in W. A. Collins (ed.), *Minnesota Symposia on Child Psychology*, vol. 13 (Hillsdale, NJ: Erlbaum, 1980).
30. P. A. Cowan, C. P. Cowan, M. Schulz, and G. Heming, "Prebirth to Preschool Family Factors Predicting Children's Adaptation to Kindergarten," in R. Parke and S. Kellam (eds.), *Exploring Family Relationships with Other Social Contexts: Advances in Family Research*, vol. 4 (Hillsdale, NJ: Erlbaum, 1994), 75–114.
31. K. L. Alexander and D. Entwisle, "Achievement in the First 2 Years of School: Patterns and Processes," *Monographs of the Society for Research in Child Development* 53:2, Serial No. 218, 1988.
32. S. Asher and J. D. Coie (eds.), *Peer Rejection in Childhood* (Cambridge: Cambridge University Press, 1990); S. G. Kellam, M. B. Simon, and M. E. Ensminger, "Antecedents in First Grade of Teenage Drug Use and Psychological Well-Being: A Ten-Year Community-wide Prospective Study," in D. Ricks and B. Dohrenwend (eds.), *Origins of Psychopathology: Research and Public Policy* (New York: Cambridge, 1982); N. Lambert, "Adolescent Outcomes for Hyperactive Children: Perspectives on General and Specific Patterns of Childhood Risk for Adolescent Educational, Social, and Mental Health Problems," *American Psychologist* 43:786–799, 1988; E. A. Carlson, L. A. Sroufe et al. "Early Environment Support and Elementary School Adjustment as Predictors of School Adjustment in Middle Adolescence," *Journal of Adolescent Research* 14:72–94, 1999.

33. E. M. Hetherington and J. Kelly, *For Better or for Worse: Divorce Reconsidered* (New York: W. W. Norton, 2002); J. Wallerstein and J. Kelly, *Surviving the Breakup* (New York: Basic Books, 1980).
34. E. M. Cummings and P. T. Davies, *Children and Marital Conflict: The Impact of Family Dispute and Resolution* (New York: Guilford Press, 1994).
35. M. Moorehouse, "Work and Family Dynamics," in P. A. Cowan, D. Field, D. A. Hansen, A. Skolnick, and G. E. Swanson (eds.), *Family, Self, and Society: Toward a New Agenda for Family Research* (Hillsdale, NJ: Erlbaum, 1993).
36. P. A. Cowan and C. P. Cowan, "What an Intervention Design Reveals about How Parents Affect Their Children's Academic Achievement and Behavior Problems," in J. G. Borkowski, S. Ramey, and M. Bristol-Power (eds.), *Parenting and the Child's World: Influences on Intellectual, Academic, and Social-Emotional Development* (Mahwah, NJ: Lawrence Erlbaum, 2002).
37. P. A. Cowan, D. Powell, and C. P. Cowan, "Parenting Interventions: A Family Systems View of Enhancing Children's Development," in I. E. Sigel and K. A. Renninger (eds.), *Handbook of Child Psychology,* 5th ed. vol. 4: *Child Psychology in Practice* (New York: Wiley, 1997).
38. L. Potts, "Considering Parenthood: Group Support for a Critical Life Decision," *American Journal of Orthopsychiatry* 50:629–638, 1980.
39. P. A. Cowan, C. P. Cowan, and T. Heming. "Two Variations of a Preventive Intervention for Couples: Effects on Parents and Children during the Transition to Elementary School," in P. A. Cowan, C. P. Cowan, J. Ablow, V. K. Johnson, and J. Measelle (eds.), *The Family Context of Parenting in Children's Adaptation to Elementary School* (Mahwah, NJ: Lawrence Erlbaum Associates, in press).
40. Ibid.

READING 20

Healthy Dads, Healthy Kids

William Marsiglio

Far too many babies and children in the United States today struggle with myriad conditions that negatively affect their emotional, mental, and physical health. We initially see this tragedy in the high rates of infant mortality and low birth weight babies and then in the discouragingly high numbers of youth who are obese, get pregnant, contract a sexually transmitted infection, smoke, binge drink, abuse drugs, develop an eating disorder, or attempt suicide. Sadly, when young people look at adult men they often find poor role models who are ill-equipped to help them avoid or correct unhealthy behaviors.

One third of American men are obese and one in 10 will become an alcoholic in his lifetime. Men are more likely than women to smoke, eat fatty foods, drink and drive, use guns, play violent sports, and not get enough sleep, and they're less likely to use seatbelts. Men are also less likely than women to seek medical attention for either routine physicals or when more serious problems occur.

Many factors contribute to children's poor health, but one we hear little about is how fathers act and what they do and don't say about health. Indeed, what men say and do can help prevent or minimize some of their children's health problems and effectively manage the adverse effects when problems do arise.

However, social pressures and financial struggles limit the choices men can make to prioritize health for themselves and their children. Understanding how fathers make decisions, as well as their social networks and diverse experiences over their lifetimes, is essential for cultivating a more engaged, health-conscious style of fathering that will, in turn, positively affect their children's health.

The theory of "constrained choice," developed by health policy experts Chloe Bird and Patricia Rieker, can guide efforts to help fathers do a better job in this regard. Touted as a "platform for prevention," the theory suggests that individuals' opportunities to pursue healthy options are shaped by decision-making processes at multiple levels: nation/state, community, workplace, family, and individual. By paying attention to gender-based health disparities, this framework also highlights the diverse social forces that organize men's and women's lives differently. These conditions, along with biological processes and other social realities like socioeconomic status, expose men and women to specific stresses, burdens, and health risks. Consequently, men in general, and fathers in particular, face unique challenges to assert themselves as more positive role models for healthy behavior.

We're entering a propitious moment in history to foster real changes in how fathers perceive, practice, and promote health. President Barack Obama's commitment to reforming health care on multiple levels while promoting preventative care and wellness resonates with Bird's and Rieker's idea that individuals' health experiences are shaped by a multilayered social context and their call for prevention strategies. Indeed, as an outspoken public advocate of getting men to step up and become more involved fathers, Obama and his administration are poised to spearhead cultural, policy, and programmatic changes that could link health promotion with good fathering.

CONNECTING FATHERS' AND CHILDREN'S HEALTH

Since the 1980s scholars have explored extensively how fathers from all kinds of families are involved with their children and how that involvement affects their children. Currently, a nascent and promising multidisciplinary research agenda (involving sociologists, nurses, pediatric psychologists, and public health experts) considers how fathers' health consciousness, practices, and outcomes relate to their children's quality of health and care. Attention has even been given to how men's actions prior to a child's conception or birth can influence that child's health.

Political scientist Cynthia Daniels argues that men's behaviors can indeed make a difference. Prevailing cultural conceptions of how masculinity is related to reproduction, she observes, have compromised scientific assessments of how sperm damaged from toxicity at work and at war, as well as from men's smoking, drinking, and drug habits, produces negative outcomes for fetuses and infants. She also notes that scientists and funding agencies apply a higher level of scrutiny when reviewing reproductive studies of male sperm compared to those examining female reproductive issues. Such scientific bias has perpetuated the public's disproportionate interest in how women's allegedly bad behavior increases fetal health risks while largely ignoring how men's preconception experiences can negatively contribute to fetal and children's health. Indeed, Daniels argues that many have resisted human and animal research that suggests connections between males and both birth defects and childhood diseases, in part because it "places men closer and closer to culpability for the health problems of their children."

In addition to direct biological influences, various studies show that fathers may indirectly affect children's health outcomes by influencing the mother's prenatal and early postnatal behavior and stress levels. Researchers can't say definitively whether and how men make a difference, but as sociologist Rachel Kimbro's work from the Fragile Families and Child Well-being study indicates, women in more stable and supportive relationships do exhibit more positive prenatal health behaviors. They're more apt to receive prenatal care and less likely to smoke, drink, or abuse drugs during pregnancy. Women with partners who have completed at least some college have lower odds of smoking and using drugs during pregnancy. (On the other hand, these women have higher odds of drinking occasionally during pregnancy and, surprisingly, fathers' education is not related to the women's inadequate prenatal care.)

Health policy researcher Laurie Martin and colleagues also show that fathers with at least a high school education, first-time fathers, and those who want a pregnancy are more likely to be involved prenatally. And, health researchers Manoj Sharma and Rick Petosa argue that partners' views consistently play a major role in whether mothers start and sustain breastfeeding. Finally, Craig Garfield, a pediatrician at the Evanston Northwestern Healthcare Research Institute, confirms that fathers' poor postnatal mental health brings on negative consequences for both children's developmental outcomes and maternal mental health.

Resident and nonresident fathers have many opportunities to affect their children's health beliefs and practices after the infant and toddler years as well. Though relatively few studies have explored these possible links, sociologist Chadwick Menning's longitudinal research with a national sample suggests that nonresident fathers' greater involvement with their adolescent children reduces the likelihood the children will begin smoking regularly. This outcome changes with fathers' level of involvement. Furthermore, children are more likely to smoke when their fathers smoke.

Menning's earlier research with family demographer Susan Stewart paints a similar portrait of resident and nonresident fathers' contributions to their children's obesity. Children are more likely to be obese if their fathers (or mothers) are obese, they found. Among nonresident fathers, those more highly educated and more involved with their children tend to have children at lower risk for obesity. Similar trends are evident among white, rural families in Iowa, where fathers' lack of exercise, poor eating, excessive drinking, and smoking predicts the same behaviors among adolescents. Lower family social status, as measured by education, increases fathers' chances of exhibiting health-risk lifestyles, partly explaining the path of intergenerational transmission of poor health behaviors from fathers to adolescents.

Fathering may also have significant health consequences for fathers themselves. For example, Garfield, the Northwestern pediatrician, describes how stressful experiences associated with fathering can accumulate and debilitate fathers' health over time. Presumably, fathers at risk of experiencing this pattern include those frustrated by their inability to fulfill their breadwinning role because of low wages or job loss, as well as those working stressful, high-risk jobs for the money.

MASCULINE BODY IMAGES, CAREGIVING IDEALS

How men see their own bodies and their role as caregivers shapes the role fathers play in influencing their kids' health. Boys and men are regularly exposed to media, family, peers, and other sources that transmit messages about health. How they think about gender and social class, for example, affects how they construct images of manliness, perceive their own and others' bodies, manage friendships, and approach fathering.

Discussions about health are influenced by how males think about gender and their individual exposure to stress and risk, factors themselves that are affected by various social processes and limited—constrained—choices, be they cultural, structural, or interpersonal. For example, the messages permeating organized sports, friendships, and workplaces often encourage males to assert a stoic, risk-taking, and "hard" image that rejects expressions of vulnerability and femininity.

Sociologist Michael Messner asserts that contrary to popular wisdom, boys' and men's sports activity often breeds "unhealthy practices, drug and alcohol abuse, pain, injury, and (in some sports) low life expectancy." Referencing the "pain principle," Messner observes that if boys don't learn to '"shake it off,' ignore their own pain, and treat their bodies as instruments to be used—and used up—to get a job done ... [then] they may lose their position on the team, or they may be labeled as 'women,' 'fags,' or 'pussies' for not being manly enough to play hurt."

The masculine ideology that perpetuates bodily harm extends well beyond the sports world, whether it's excessive drinking, drug use, fast driving, fighting, or some other display of a potentially self-destructive behavior. Much of this is tied to and supported by males having friends and acquaintances who take unnecessary risks.

For example, in his recent book *Guyland*, gender scholar Michael Kimmel discusses the disturbing way peer pressure fuels hazing rituals. In fraternities, young men seduced by the masculine status that flows from belonging to a tightly knit, all-male group, subject themselves to humiliation and sometimes untold health risks. A 2008 study of hazing in more than 50 schools found drinking was involved in the hazing of 31 percent of the men, and 17 percent "drank until they passed out."

Consistent with sociologist Erving Goffman's view that "men must be prepared to put up their lives to save their faces," men who work dangerous jobs as loggers, miners, construction workers, police officers, firefighters, EMTs, and the like are engulfed in an atmosphere that defines the drama of manhood as physical, fearless, and full of risk. Granted recent studies, such as the compelling ethnography of wildland firefighters by sociologist Matthew Desmond, suggest a much more complex picture, where the skills and dispositions children and adolescents acquire from their blue-collar upbringing prepare them to view as unthreatening the high-risk work many will perform as young men. What's fascinating, Desmond and others have observed, is that men don't avoid, but instead actively pursue, jobs that threaten their bodies and health.

In recent decades, diverse tactics have been used to persuade adult men to adopt a more attentive self-care philosophy. Men have been encouraged to become more body conscious, embrace healthier life practices, and develop closer ties with the health-care community. Magazines launched since the late 1980s like *Men's Health* found a niche among an expanding segment of professional men eager to learn the latest developments in nutrition, fitness training, and body care. Increasingly, too, a range of books, newsletters, magazines, websites, and other media outlets have driven the boom industries to educate men about a host of issues including prostate, colon, and heart care; testosterone therapy; hair replacement and surgical implants; and, of course, erectile dysfunction therapies.

Just as men's health advocates try to transform negative perceptions of self-care as feminine, they must wrestle with the notion that providing care for the ill or disabled is women's "work." Women are more likely than men to practice caregiving, but as social worker Betty Kramer and sociologist Edward Thompson illustrate in their edited volume *Men as Caregivers*, many men are effective caregivers. Estimates indicate that between 14 percent and 18 percent of men informally provide various forms of caregiving for needy friends and family.

Yet, mainstream cultural messages downplay fathers' caregiving capacity and ability to address children's health-care needs. Parenting magazines and books are commonly tailored to informing moms more so than dads about the newest and best ways to care for and protect their children. This gender bias has been so engrained in the public's mind that a book published in 2004, *From Boys to Men: A Woman's Guide to the Health of Husbands, Partners, Sons, Fathers, and Brothers*, seems intuitively marketable whereas serious doubts would accompany its hypothetical counterpart, *From Girls to Women: A Man's Guide to the Health of Wives, Partners, Daughters, Mothers, and Sisters.* Whether it's wiping noses in a childcare facility or wiping bottoms in a nursing home, societal images depict women as best suited for these positions, and the social networking patterns that shape fathers' everyday lives reinforce these stereotypes.

In her book *Do Men Mother?* sociologist Andrea Doucet interviewed Canadian primary caregiving fathers, most of whom were single fathers or stay-at-home dads. She reports that even highly motivated fathers find it difficult to feel comfortable at young children's playgroups, which they perceive as dominated by suspicious, unwelcoming mothers. Men's less intimate and more competitive friendship styles may also curtail fathers' willingness to discuss with other men their insecurities about fathering or focus on children's needs. Although Doucet doesn't emphasize typical health issues, her findings (and those of others) suggest fathers are more likely to be excluded from parental networks in which social support and children's health and childcare information are meaningfully shared. Moreover, fathers are less apt than mothers to take on the "community responsibility" tasks of engaging with adults involved with caring for children. Notably, some of these adults monitor children's physical, emotional, and mental health.

PROMOTING HEALTH-CONSCIOUS FATHERING

For far too long, many men have been ignorant of or ignored how their poor health habits jeopardize their children's well-being. With the U.S. Department of Health and Human Services report *Healthy People 2020* on the horizon, now is the time to challenge men to foster positive health outcomes for their children. So what can be done to improve these patterns?

Generally speaking, men engage in more unhealthy behaviors and are less attentive to their self-care than women. The emerging evidence tells us, too, that men's exposure to health risks prior to their children's conception can contribute to prenatal problems. Moreover, men's poor health habits are related to children being more likely to smoke, abuse drugs, and eat poorly as well as be overweight and experience other negative health outcomes.

To understand and alter these patterns we must fully grasp fathers' lives as men and the diverse decisions affecting them. In other words, as the constrained choice theory implies, choices and priorities about health exist as part of a larger context and compete with other decisions about income, work, housing, partner/family, and personal image. Thus, we must commit to a multilevel approach to promoting social change that incorporates national and state policies, community-based strategies, workplace agendas, family support, and individual commitments.

Various social circumstances make it difficult for boys and men, some more than others, to forge and sustain healthy lifestyles and transmit similar values and benefits to their children. Constraints come in many forms, including conventional masculine discussion and business cultures that glorify stereotypes of the macho athlete or worker, inner-city and rural planning that limits recreational facilities for youth and adults alike, inadequate supports to educate men about reproductive health care and the consequences of paternity, workplace conditions and economic realities that expose men—especially those from economically disadvantaged backgrounds—to work-related health hazards, and peer pressure that extols a masculinity grounded in body toughness and risk-taking. Unfortunately, too many boys and men navigate their social networks, leisure, and work lives in ways that reinforce this less-than-ideal approach toward health.

Despite the constraints, men do have choices. Some recent research suggests, in fact, that men are capable of looking out for their own health and caring for others effectively if they put their minds to it. Ideally, as feminist values promoting gender equity inside the home gain wider appeal, and research accumulates to document the connections between fathers' and children's health, definitions of "good fathering" will summon fathers to pursue a healthier lifestyle while cultivating the same for their children.

Getting large numbers of men to adopt such a mindset requires broad public support and will require an intense public health service campaign—one that an Obama administration might be well-suited to launch. Realistically, though, concrete progress in altering individual commitments and choices will come when men regularly encourage each other to be more attentive to their own and their children's health. The seeds for this shift can be sewn most visibly in places that traditionally have been instrumental in discouraging health consciousness: locker rooms, fraternities, many work sites, and other places where male respect holds sway. Of course, these efforts also need to be augmented by men's partners.

The harsh reality for some men is that their chances to perceive and pursue healthy choices for themselves and their children hinge on politically sponsored national and state initiatives. In other words, for many men living in poor inner-cities and rural areas, structural and legislative changes are needed to improve access to fresh food markets, healthcare facilities and substance abuse programs, recreation sites, and organized sports so that more fathers and their children have viable, healthy options. It makes sense to expand Head Start programs by providing poor fathers with information, screenings, and referrals for a broad range of father-child health matters.

A less direct but critical step is to have schools, other youth-oriented organizations, and public health programs do a better job of providing teenage and young adult males comprehensive instruction on reproductive health. Because men have the capacity to influence fetal and infant life directly via their sperm quality and indirectly by how they treat the mother, they need to be educated at a young age about how their smoking, drinking, and drug use as well as their readiness to become fathers can affect their offspring's health. Although all males deserve these services, those living in poor neighborhoods are most vulnerable because they typically are the least prepared to assume many of the responsibilities associated with providing and caring for children.

Work sites are another place where men can be afforded opportunities to make better decisions about eating, exercise, stress management, and substance use, and receive medical check-ups and education about how these experiences matter for their children's health. Workplace policies, reinforced by more father-friendly corporate cultures, can ensure fathers have increased access to flexible schedules and nonstigmatized family-leave time. These benefits can make it easier for fathers to accompany their children to medical visits as well as provide hands-on care for their sick children.

Health-care institutions, in addition to educating men, can promote men's greater participation by providing more convenient evening and weekend hours while making their operations more male-friendly. Like the decisive trend beginning in the 1970s that saw fathers participating in childbirth preparation classes and being present when their children were born, the medical community must find innovative ways to integrate more fathers into their children's pediatric care. Today's creative childbirth preparation classes might produce promising results by coordinating new fatherhood programs with interventions to curb smoking, drinking, and drug use.

Ultimately, fathers must answer the call to communicate proactively with their children and monitor their well-being in consultation with healthcare providers and others who have a vested interest. Perhaps most importantly, if men adopt healthier behaviors for themselves and reduce their stress, they can more readily model such behaviors and authentically encourage their children to do the same.

Recommended Resources

C.E. Bird and P.P. Rieker. *Gender and health: The effects of constrained choices and social policies* (Cambridge University Press, 2008). An overview of how diverse layers of social life are interconnected, contributing to health disparities between men and women.

W.H. Courtenay. "Constructions of masculinity and their influence on men's well-being: A theory of gender and health," *Social Science & Medicine* (2000) 50: 1385–1401. A critical review of how various conditions shape the kind of masculinity men construct and how those practices contribute to differential health risks.

A. Doucet. *Do men mother? Fathering, care and domestic responsibility* (Toronto University Press, 2006). Grounded in qualitative data, this book highlights fathers' opportunities to be more nurturing and engaged parents.

C. Garfield, E. Clark-Kauffman, and M.M. Davis. "Fatherhood as a component of men's health," *Journal of the American Medical Association* (2006) 296: 2365–2368. A thoughtful interdisciplinary essay that conceptualizes the relationship between fatherhood and men's health.

C.L. Menning and S.D. Stewart. "Nonresident father involvement, social class, and adolescent weight," *Journal of Family Issues* (2008) 29: 1673–1700. Provides a quantitative analysis of two waves of the well-respected National Longitudinal Study of Adolescent Health survey.

Chapter

8

Childhood and Youth

READING 21

Beyond Sentimentality: American Childhood as a Social and Cultural Construct

Steven Mintz

Nowhere is it easier to romanticize childhood than in Mark Twain's hometown of Hannibal, Missouri. In this small Mississippi riverfront town, where Mark Twain lived, off and on, from the age of four until he was seventeen, many enduring American fantasies about childhood come to life. There is a historical marker next to a fence like the one that Tom's friends paid him for the privilege of whitewashing. There is another marker pointing to the spot where Huck's cabin supposedly stood. There is also the window where Huck hurled pebbles to wake the sleeping Tom. Gazing out across the raging waters of the Mississippi, now unfortunately hidden behind a floodwall, one can easily imagine the raft excursion that Huck and Jim took seeking freedom and adventure.

Hannibal occupies a special place in our collective imagination as the setting of two of fiction's most famous depictions of childhood. Our cherished myth about childhood as a bucolic time of freedom, untainted innocence, and self-discovery comes to life in this river town. But beyond the accounts of youthful wonder and small-town innocence, Twain's novels teem with grim and unsettling details about childhood's underside. Huck's father Pap was an abusive drunkard who beat his son for learning how to read. When we idealize Mark Twain's Hannibal and its eternally youthful residents, we suppress his novels' more sinister aspects.[1]

Twain's real-life mid-nineteenth-century Hannibal was anything but a haven of stability and security. It was a place where a quarter of the children died before their first birthday, half before they reached the age of twenty-one. Twain himself experienced the death of two siblings. Although he was not physically abused like the fictional Huck, his father was emotionally cold and aloof. There were few open displays of affection in his boyhood home. Only once did he remember seeing his father and mother kiss, and that was at the deathbed of his brother Ben. Nor was his home a haven of economic security. His boyhood ended before his twelfth birthday when his father's death forced him to take up a series of odd jobs. Before he left home permanently at seventeen, he had already worked as a printer's apprentice; clerked in a grocery store, a bookshop, and a drug store; tried his hand at blacksmithing; and delivered newspapers. Childhood ended early in Twain's hometown, though full adulthood came no more quickly than it does today.[2]

A series of myths cloud public thinking about the history of American childhood. One is the myth of a carefree childhood. We cling to a fantasy that once upon a time childhood and youth were years of carefree adventure, despite the fact that for most children in the past, growing up was anything but easy. Disease, family disruption, and early entry into the world of work were integral parts of family life. The notion of a long childhood devoted to education and free from adult-like responsibilities is a very recent invention, a product of the past century and a half, and one that only became a reality for a majority of children after World War II.

Another myth is that of the home as a haven and bastion of stability in an ever-changing world. Throughout American history, family stability has been the exception, not the norm. At the beginning of the twentieth century, fully a third of all American children spent at least a portion of their childhood in a single-parent home, and as recently as 1940, one child in ten did not live with either parent—compared to one in twenty-five today.[3]

A third myth is that childhood is the same for all children, a status transcending class, ethnicity, and gender. In fact, every aspect of childhood is shaped by class—as well as by ethnicity, gender, geography, religion, and historical era. We may think of childhood as a biological phenomenon, but it is better understood as a life stage whose contours are shaped by a particular time and place. Childrearing practices, schooling, and the age at which young people leave home are all the products of particular social and cultural circumstances.

A fourth myth is that the United States is a peculiarly child-friendly society when, in actuality, Americans are deeply ambivalent about children. Adults envy young people their youth, vitality, and physical attractiveness, but they also resent children's intrusions on their time and resources and frequently fear their passions and drives. Many of the reforms that nominally have been designed to protect and assist the young were also instituted to insulate adults from children.

Lastly, the myth that is perhaps the most difficult to overcome is the myth of progress and its inverse, the myth of decline. There is a tendency to conceive of the history of childhood as a story of steps forward over time: of parental engagement replacing emotional distance, of kindness and leniency supplanting strict and stern punishment, of scientific enlightenment superceding superstition and misguided moralism. This progressivism is sometimes seen in reverse, that is, that childhood is disappearing: children are growing up too quickly and wildly and losing their innocence, playfulness, and malleability.

Various myths and misconceptions have contributed to this undue pessimism about the young. There has never been a golden age of childhood when the overwhelming majority of American children were well cared for and their experiences were idyllic. Nor has childhood ever been an age of innocence, at least not for the overwhelming majority of children. Childhood has never been insulated from the pressures and demands of the surrounding society and each generation of children has had to wrestle with the particular social, political, and economic constraints of its own historical period. In our own time, the young have had to struggle with high rates of family instability, a deepening disconnection from adults, and the expectation that all children should pursue the same academic path at the same pace, even as the attainment of full adulthood recedes ever further into the future.

THE SOCIAL AND CULTURAL CONSTRUCTION OF CHILDHOOD

The history of children is often treated as a marginal subject, and there is no question that the history of children is especially difficult to write. Children are rarely obvious historical actors. Compared to adults, they leave fewer historical sources, and their powerlessness makes them less visible than other social groups. Nevertheless, the history of childhood is inextricably bound up with the broader political and social events in the life of the nation—including colonization, revolution, slavery, industrialization, urbanization, immigration, and war—and children's experience embodies many of the key themes in American history, such as the rise of modern bureaucratic institutions, the growth of a consumer economy, and the elaboration of a welfare state. Equally important, childhood's history underscores certain long-term transformations in American life, such as an intensifying consciousness about age, a clearer delineation of distinct life stages, and the increasing tendency to organize institutions by age.

Childhood is not an unchanging, biological stage of life, and children are not just "grow'd," like Topsy in Harriet Beecher Stowe's *Uncle Tom's Cabin.* Rather, childhood is a social and cultural construct. Every aspect of childhood—including children's relationships with their parents and peers, their proportion of the population, and their paths through childhood to adulthood—has changed dramatically over the past four centuries. Methods of child rearing, the duration of schooling, the nature of children's play, young people's participation in work, and the points of demarcation between childhood, adolescence, and adulthood are products of culture, class, and historical era.[4]

Childhood in the past was experienced and conceived of in quite a different way than today. Just two centuries ago, there was far less age segregation than there is today and less concern with organizing experience by chronological age. There was also far less sentimentalization of children as special beings who were more innocent and vulnerable than adults. This does not mean that adults failed to recognize childhood as a stage of life, with its own special needs and characteristics, nor does it imply that parents were unconcerned about their children and failed to love them and mourn their deaths. Rather, it means that the experience of young people was organized and valued very differently than it is today.

Language itself illustrates shifts in the construction of childhood. Two hundred years ago, the words used to describe childhood were far less precise than those we use today. The word *infancy* referred not to the months after birth, but to the period in which children were under their mother's control, typically from birth to the age of 5 or 6. The word *childhood* might refer to someone as young as the age of 5 or 6 or as old as the late teens or early twenties. Instead of using our term adolescent or teenager, Americans two centuries ago used a broader and more expansive term *youth*, which stretched from the pre-teen years until the early or mid-20s. The vagueness of this term reflected the amorphousness of the life stages; chronological age was less important than physical strength, size, and maturity. A young person did not achieve full adult status until marriage and establishment of an independent farm or entrance into a full-time trade or profession. Full adulthood might be attained as early as the mid- or late teens, but usually did not occur until the late twenties or early thirties.[5]

How, then, has childhood changed over the past two hundred years? The transformations that have taken place might be grouped into three broad categories. The first involves shifts in the timing, sequence, and stages of growing up. Over the past two centuries, the stages of childhood have grown much more precise, uniform, and prescriptive. Before the Civil War, children and teens moved sporadically in and out of the parental home, schools, and jobs, in an irregular, episodic pattern that the historian Joseph F. Kett termed "semi-dependence.". . .

Beginning in the mid-nineteenth century, however, there were growing efforts to regularize and systematize childhood experiences. Unable to transmit their status position directly to their children, through bequests of family lands, transmission of craft skills, or selection of a marriage partner, middle-class parents adopted new strategies to assist their children, emphasizing birth control, maternal nurture, and prolonged schooling. Less formal methods of childrearing and education were replaced by intensive forms of childrearing and prescribed curricula in schools. Unstructured contacts with adults were supplanted by carefully age-graded institutions. Activities organized by young people themselves were succeeded by adult sponsored, adult-organized organization. Lying behind these developments was a belief that childhood should be devoted to education, play, and character-building activities; that children needed time to mature inside a loving home and segregated from adult affairs; and that precocious behavior needed to be suppressed.[6]

Demography is a second force for change. A sharp reduction in the birth rate substantially reduced the proportion of children in the general population, from half the population in the mid-nineteenth century to a third by 1900. A declining birth rate divided families into more distinct generations and allowed parents to lavish more time, attention, and resources on each child; it also made society less dependent on children's labor and allowed adult society to impose new institutional structures on young peoples' lives reflecting shifting notions about children's proper chronological development.

The third category is attitudinal. Adult conceptions of childhood have shifted profoundly over time, from the seventeenth-century Puritan image of the child as a depraved being who needed to be restrained; to the Enlightened notion of children as blank slates who could be shaped by environmental influences; to the Romantic conception of children as creatures with innocent souls and redeemable, docile wills; to the

Darwinian emphasis on highly differentiated stages of children's cognitive, physiological, and emotional development; to the Freudian conception of children as seething cauldrons of instinctual drives; and to the contemporary notions that emphasize children's competence and capacity for early learning.

The history of childhood might be conceptualized in terms of three overlapping phases. The first, pre-modern childhood, which roughly coincides with the colonial era, was a period in which the young were viewed as adults in training. Religious and secular authorities regarded childhood as a time of deficiency and incompleteness, and adults rarely referred to their childhood with nostalgia or fondness. Infants were viewed as unformed and even animalistic due to their inability to speak or stand upright. A parent's duty was to hurry a child toward adult status, especially through early engagement in work responsibilities, both inside the parental home and outside it, as servants and apprentices.

The middle of the eighteenth century saw the emergence of a new set of attitudes, which came to define modern childhood. A growing number of parents began to regard children as innocent, malleable, and fragile creatures who needed to be sheltered from contamination. Childhood was increasingly viewed as a separate stage of life that required special care and institutions to protect it. During the nineteenth century, the growing acceptance of this new ideal among the middle class was evident in prolonged residence of young people within the parental home; longer periods of formal schooling; and an increasing consciousness about the stages of young peoples' development, culminating in the "discovery" (or, more accurately, the invention) of adolescence around the turn of the twentieth century.

Universalizing the modern ideal of a sheltered childhood was a highly uneven process and one that has never encompassed all American children. Indeed, it was not until the 1950s that the norms of modern childhood defined the modal experience of young people in the United States. But developments were already under way that would bring modern childhood to an end and replace it with something quite different, a new phase that might be called postmodern childhood. This term refers to the breakdown of dominant norms about the family, gender roles, age, and even reproduction, as they were subjected to radical change and revision. Age norms that many considered "natural" were thrown into question. Even the bedrock biological process of sexual maturation accelerated. Today's children are much more likely than the Baby Boomers to experience their parents' divorce; to have a working mother; to spend significant amounts of time unsupervised by adults; to grow up without siblings; and to hold a job during high school. Adolescent girls are much more likely to have sexual relations during their mid-teens.[7]

Superficially, postmodern childhood resembles premodern childhood. As in the seventeenth century, children are no longer regarded as the binary opposites of adults, nor are they considered naïve and innocent creatures. Today, adults quite rightly assume that even preadolescents are knowledgeable about the realities of the adult world. But unlike premodern children, postmodern children are independent consumers and participants in a separate, semi-autonomous youth culture. We still assume that the young are fundamentally different from adults; that they should spend their first eighteen years in the parents' home; and devote their time to education in age-graded schools. But it is also clear that basic aspects of the ideal of a protected childhood, in which the young are kept isolated from adult realities, have broken down.[8]

DIVERSITY

Diversity has always been the hallmark of American childhood. In seventeenth-century America, demographic, economic, religious, and social factors made geographical subcultures the most important markers of diversity in children's experience. In the early period of settlement, colonial childhood took profoundly different forms in New England, the Middle Colonies, and the Chesapeake and southernmost colonies. In seventeenth century New England, hierarchical, patriarchal Calvinist families shaped children's experiences. In the Chesapeake colonies of Maryland and Virginia, in contrast, families were highly unstable and indentured servitude shaped children's experience. Only in the Middle Colonies, from New York to Delaware, did a childhood emphasizing maternal nurture and an acceptance of early autonomy emerge, yet even here, large numbers of children experienced various forms of dependence, as household and indentured servants, apprentices, or slaves.[9]

In the nineteenth century, a highly uneven process of capitalist expansion made social class, gender, and race more salient contributors to childhood diversity. The children of the urban middle class, prosperous commercial farmers, and southern planters enjoyed increasingly longer childhoods, free from major household or work responsibilities until their late teens or twenties, whereas the offspring of urban workers, frontier farmers, and blacks, both slave and free, had briefer childhoods and became involved in work inside or outside the home before they reached their teens. Many urban working-class children contributed to the family economy through scavenging in the streets, vacant lots, or back alleys, collecting coal, wood, and other items that could be used at home or sold. Others took part in the street trades, selling gum, peanuts, and crackers. In industrial towns, young people under the age of 15 contributed on average about 20 percent of their family's income. In mining areas, boys as young as 10 or 12 worked as breakers, separating coal from pieces of slate and wood, before becoming miners in their mid- or late teens. On farms, children as young as 5 or 6 might pull weeds or chase birds and cattle away from crops. By the time they reached the age of 8, many tended livestock, and as they grew older they milked cows, churned butter, fed chickens, collected eggs, hauled water, scrubbed laundry, and harvested crops. A blurring of gender roles among children and youth was especially common on frontier farms. Schooling varied as widely as did work routines. In the rural North, the Midwest, and the Far West, most mid- and late-nineteenth-century students attended one-room schools for 3 to 6 months a year. In contrast, city children attended age-graded classes taught by professional teachers 9 months a year. In both rural and urban areas, girls tended to receive more schooling than boys.[10]

Late in the nineteenth century, self-described child-savers launched a concerted campaign to overcome diversity and universalize a middle-class childhood. This was a slow and bitterly resisted process. Not until the 1930s was child labor finally outlawed and not until the 1950s did high school attendance become a universal experience. Yet for all the success in advancing this middle-class ideal, even today, social class remains a primary determinant of children's well-being.[11]

In recent years, social conservatives have tended to fixate on family structure as a source of diversity in children's well-being, while political liberals have tended to focus on ethnicity, race, and gender. In fact, it is poverty that is the most powerful predictor of children's welfare. Economic stress contributes to family instability, inadequate health care, high degrees of mobility, poor parenting, and elevated levels of stress and depression. As in the nineteenth century, social class significantly differentiates contemporary American childhoods. There is a vast difference between the highly pressured, hyper-organized, fast-track childhoods of affluent children and the highly stressed childhoods of the one-third of children who live in poverty at some point before the age of eighteen. In many affluent families, the boundaries between work and family life have diminished, and parents manage by tightly organizing their children's lives. Yet, contradictorily, most affluent children have their own television and computer and therefore unmediated access to information and are unsupervised by their parents for large portions of the day. In many affluent families there are drastic swings between parental distance from children and parental indulgence, when fathers and mothers try to compensate for parenting too little. Yet at the same time, one-sixth of all children live in poverty at any one time, including 36 percent of black children and 34 percent of Hispanic children. This generally entails limited adult supervision, inferior schooling, and a lack of easy access to productive diversions and activities.

THE POLITICS OF CHILDHOOD

In recent years, two contrasting visions of childhood have collided. One is a vision of a protected childhood, in which children are to be sheltered from adult realities, especially from sex, obscenity, and death. The opposing vision is of a prepared childhood, of children who are exposed from a relatively early age to the realities of contemporary society, such as sexuality and diverse family patterns. Proponents of a prepared childhood argue that in a violent, highly commercialized, and hypersexualized society, a naïve child is a vulnerable child.

Clashes between conflicting conceptions of childhood are not new. For four hundred years, childhood has been a highly contested category. The late twentieth-century culture war—pitting advocates of a "protected" childhood, who sought to shield children from adult realities, against proponents of a "prepared" childhood—was only the most recent in a long series of conflicts over the definition of a proper childhood. In the seventeenth century, there were bitter struggles between Puritans who regarded even newborn infants as sinful, humanistic educators who emphasized children's malleability, and Anglican traditionalists who considered children as symbols of values (including the value of deference and respect for social hierarchy) that were breaking down as England underwent the wrenching economic transformations that accompanied the rise of modern capitalist enterprise. In the late eighteenth century, battles raged over infant depravity and patriarchal authority, conflicts that gave added resonance to the American revolutionaries' struggle against royal authority. At the turn of the twentieth century, conflict erupted between the proponents of a useful childhood, which expected children to reciprocate for their parents' sacrifices, and advocates of a sheltered childhood, free from labor and devoted to play and education.[12]

PARENTING

Anxiety is the hallmark of modern parenthood. Today's parents agonize incessantly about their children's physical health, personality development, psychological well-being, and academic performance. From birth, parenthood is colored by apprehension. Contemporary parents worry about sudden infant death syndrome, stranger abductions, and physical and sexual abuse, as well as more mundane problems, such as sleep disorders and hyperactivity.

Parental anxiety about children's well-being is not a new development, but parents' concerns have taken dramatically different forms over time. Until the mid-nineteenth century, parents were primarily concerned about their children's health, religious piety, and moral development. In the late nineteenth century, parents became increasingly attentive to their children's emotional and psychological well-being, and during the twentieth century, parental anxieties dwelt on children's personality development, gender identity, and their ability to interact with peers. Today, much more than in the past, guilt-ridden, uncertain parents worry that their children not suffer from boredom, low self-esteem, or excessive school pressures. [13]

Today, we consider early childhood life's formative stage and believe that children's experiences during the first two or three years of life mold their personality, lay the foundation for future cognitive and psychological development, and leave a lasting imprint on their emotional life. We also assume that children's development proceeds through a series of physiological, psychological, social, and cognitive stages; that even very young children have a capacity to learn; that play serves valuable developmental functions; and that growing up requires children to separate emotionally and psychologically from their parents. These assumptions differ markedly from those held three centuries ago. Before the mid-eighteenth century, most adults betrayed surprisingly little interest in the very first years of life and autobiographies revealed little nostalgia for childhood. Also, adults tended to dismiss children's play as trivial and insignificant.

Parenting has evolved through a series of successive and overlapping phases, from a seventeenth-century view of children as "adults-in-training" to the early nineteenth-century emphasis on character formation; the late-nineteenth century notion of scientific childrearing, stressing regularity and systematization; the mid-twentieth century emphasis on fulfilling children's emotional and psychological needs; and the late twentieth century stress on maximizing children's intellectual and social development. Seventeenth-century colonists recognized that children differed from adults in their mental, moral, and physical capabilities and drew a distinction between childhood, an intermediate stage they called youth, and adulthood. But they did not rigidly segregate children by age. Parents wanted children to speak, read, reason, and contribute to their family's economic well-being as soon as possible. Infancy was regarded as a state of deficiency. Unable to speak or stand, infants lacked two essential attributes of full humanity. Parents discouraged infants from crawling and placed them in "walking stools," similar to today's walkers. To ensure proper adult posture, young girls wore leather corsets and parents placed rods along the spines of very young children of both sexes.

During the eighteenth century, a shift in parental attitudes took place. Fewer parents expected children to bow or doff their hats in their presence or stand during meals. Instead of addressing parents as "sir" and "madam," children called them "papa" and "mama." By the end of the eighteenth century, furniture specifically designed for children, painted in pastel colors and decorated with pictures of animals or figures from nursery rhymes, began to be widely produced, reflecting the popular notion of childhood as a time of innocence and playfulness. There was a growing stress on implanting virtue and a capacity for self-government.

By the early nineteenth century, mothers in the rapidly expanding Northeastern middle class increasingly embraced an amalgam of earlier childrearing ideas. From John Locke, they absorbed the notion that children were highly malleable creatures and that a republican form of government required parents to instill a capacity for self-government in their children. From Jean-Jacques Rousseau and the Romantic poets, middle-class parents acquired the idea of childhood as a special stage of life, intimately connected with nature and purer and morally superior to adulthood. From the evangelicals, the middle class adopted the idea that the primary task of parenthood was to implant proper moral character in children and to insulate children from the corruptions of the adult world.

Toward the end of the nineteenth century, middle-class parents began to embrace the idea that childrearing needed to become more scientific. The Child Study movement, through which teachers and mothers under the direction of psychologists identified a series of stages of childhood development, culminating with the "discovery" of adolescence as a psychologically turbulent period that followed puberty. The belief that scientific principles had not been properly applied to childrearing produced new kinds of childrearing manuals, of which the most influential was Dr. Luther Emmett Holt's *The Care and Feeding of Children*, first published in 1894. Holt emphasized rigid scheduling of feeding, bathing, sleeping, and bowel movements and advised mothers to guard vigilantly against germs and undue stimulation of infants. At a time when a well-adjusted adult was viewed as a creature of habit and self-control, he stressed the importance of imposing regular habits on infants. He discouraged mothers from kissing their babies and told them to ignore their crying and to break such habits as thumb-sucking.[14]

During the 1920s and 1930s, the field of child psychology exerted a growing influence on middle-class parenting. It provided a new language to describe children's emotional problems, such as sibling rivalry, phobias, maladjustment, and inferiority and Oedipus complexes; it also offered new insights into forms of parenting (based on such variables as demandingness or permissiveness), the stages and milestones of children's development, and the characteristics of children at particular ages (such as the "terrible twos," which was identified by Arnold Gesell, Frances L. Ilg, and Louise Bates Ames). The growing prosperity of the 1920s made the earlier emphasis on regularity and rigid self-control seem outmoded. A well-adjusted adult was now regarded as a more easy-going figure, capable of enjoying leisure. Rejecting the mechanistic and behaviorist notion that children's behavior could be molded by scientific control, popular dispensers of advice favored a more relaxed approach to childrearing, emphasizing the importance of meeting babies' emotional needs. The title of a 1936 book by pediatrician C. Anderson Aldrich—*Babies Are Human Beings*—summed up the new attitude.[15]

The Great Depression of the 1930s and World War II greatly intensified parental anxieties about childrearing. During the postwar era, there was an intense fear that faulty mothering caused lasting psychological problems in children. Leading psychologists such as Theodore Lidz, Irving Bieber, and Erik Erikson linked schizophrenia, homosexuality, and identity diffusion to mothers who displaced their frustrations and needs for independence onto their children. A major concern was that many boys, raised almost exclusively by women, failed to develop an appropriate sex role identity. In retrospect, it seems clear that an underlying source of anxiety lay in the fact that mothers were raising their children with an exclusivity and in an isolation unparalleled in American history.[16]

Since the early 1970s, parental anxieties have greatly increased both in scope and intensity. Many parents sought to protect children from every imaginable harm by baby-proofing their homes, using car seats, and requiring bicycle helmets. Meanwhile, as more mothers joined the labor force, parents arranged more structured, supervised activities for their children. A variety of factors contributed to a surge in anxiety. As parents had fewer children, they invested more emotion in each child. An increase in professional expertise about children, coupled with a proliferation of research and advocacy organizations, media outlets, and government agencies responsible for children's health and safety made parents increasingly aware of threats to children's well-being and of ways to maximize their children's physical, social, and intellectual development. Unlike postwar parents, who wanted to produce normal children who fit in, middle-class parents now wanted to give their child a competitive edge. For many middle-class parents, fears of downward mobility and anxiety that they would not be able to pass on their status and class to their children, made them worry that their offspring would underperform academically, athletically, or socially. . . .

MORAL PANICS OVER CHILDREN'S WELL-BEING

Americans are great believers in progress in all areas but one. For more than three centuries, Americans have feared that the younger generation is going to hell in a handbasket. Today, many adults mistakenly believe that compared to their predecessors, kids today are less respectful and knowledgeable, and more alienated, sexually promiscuous, and violent. They fear that contemporary children are growing up too fast and losing their sense of innocent wonder at too young an age. Prematurely exposed to the pressures, stresses, and responsibilities of adult life, they fear that the young mimic adult sophistication, dress inappropriately, and experiment with alcohol, drugs, sex, and tobacco before they are emotionally and psychologically ready.

A belief in the decline of the younger generation is one of this country's oldest convictions. In 1657, a Puritan minister, Ezekiel Rogers, admitted: "I find the greatest trouble and grief about the rising generation. . . . Much ado I have with my own family . . . the young breed doth much afflict me." For more than three centuries, American adults have worried that children are growing ever more disobedient and disrespectful. But wistfulness about a golden age of childhood is invariably misleading. Nostalgia almost always represents a yearning not for the past as it really was but rather for fantasies about the past. In 1820, children constituted about half of the workers in early factories. As recently as the 1940s, one child in ten lived apart from both parents and fewer than half of all high school students graduated. We forget that over the past century, the introduction of every new form of entertainment has generated intense controversy over its impact on children, and that the anxiety over video games and the Internet are only the latest in a long line of supposed threats to children that includes movies, radio, and even comic books. The danger of nostalgia is that it creates unrealistic expectations, guilt, and anger.[17]

Ever since the Pilgrims departed for Plymouth in 1620, fearful that "their posterity would be in danger to degenerate and be corrupted" in the Old World, Americans have experienced repeated panics over the younger generation. Sometimes these panics were indeed about children, such as the worries over polio in the early 1950s. More often, however, children stand in for some other issue, and the panics are more metaphorical than representational, such as the panic over teenage pregnancy, youth violence, and declining academic achievement in the late 1970s and 1980s, which reflected pervasive fears about family breakdown, crime, drugs, and America's declining competitiveness in the world.[18]

ABUSE OF CHILDREN

Concern about the abuse of children has waxed and waned over the course of American history. The seventeenth-century Puritans were the first people in the Western world to make the physical abuse of a children a criminal offense, though their concern with family privacy and patriarchal authority meant that these statutes were rarely enforced. During the pre-Civil War decades, temperance reformers argued that curbs on alcohol would reduce wife beating and child abuse. The first organizations to combat child abuse, which appeared in the 1870s, were especially concerned about abuse in immigrant, destitute, and foster families.[19]

Over half a century ago, Alfred Kinsey's studies found rates of sexual abuse similar to those reported today. His interviews indicated that exhibitionists had exposed themselves in front of 12 percent of preadolescent girls and that 9 percent of the girls had had their genitals fondled. But it was his findings about premarital and extramarital sex that grabbed the public's attention, not the sexual abuse of its children. Not until the publication of an influential article on "The Battered Child Syndrome" in 1962 was child abuse finally identified as a social problem demanding a significant governmental response. Even in succeeding years, however, public consciousness about abuse has fluctuated widely. In 1986, nearly a third of adults identified abuse as one of the most serious problems facing children and youth; in a survey a decade later abuse went unmentioned.[20]

We quite rightly focus on the way that young people are physically at risk, whether through physical or sexual abuse, neglect, or economic vulnerability. But across American history, some of the gravest threats to the young have involved their psychological vulnerability. Even worse than the physical sufferings under slavery were the psychological scars enslavement left. Worse than toiling in factories was the hidden curriculum that working class children were inferior to their supposed social betters, suited for little more than routine, repetitious labor. As the historian Daniel Kline has persuasively argued, contemporary American society subjects the young to three forms of psychological violence that we tend to ignore. First, there is the violence of expectations in which children are pushed beyond their social, physical, and academic capabilities, largely as an expression of their parents' needs. Then there is the violence of labeling that diagnoses normal childish behavior (for example, normal childhood exuberance or interest in sex) as pathological. Further, there is the violence of representation, the exploitation of children and adolescents by advertisers, marketers, purveyors of popular culture, and politicians, who exploit parental anxieties as well as young peoples' desire to be stylish, independent, and defiant, and eroticize teenage and preadolescent girls.

There is a fourth form of psychological abuse that is perhaps the most unsettling of all: the objectification of childhood. This involves viewing children as objects to be shaped and molded for their own good. Compared to its predecessors, contemporary American society is much more controlling in an institutional and ideological sense. We expect children to conform to standards that few adults could meet. Meanwhile, as the baby boom generation ages, we inhabit an increasingly adult-oriented society, a society that has fewer "free" spaces for the young, a society that values youth primarily as service workers and consumers and gawks at them as sex objects.

For more than three centuries, America has considered itself to be a particularly child-centered society despite massive evidence to the contrary. Today, no other advanced country allows as many young people to grow up in poverty or without health care, nor does any other western society make so poor a provision for child care or for paid parental leave. Still, Americans think of themselves as a child-centered nation. This paradox is not new. Beginning in the early nineteenth century, the United States developed a host of institutions for the young, ranging from the common school to the Sunday school, the orphanage, the house of refuge, and the reformatory, and eventually expanding to include the children's hospital, the juvenile court, and a wide variety of youth organizations. It was assumed that these institutions served children's interests, that they were caring, developmental, and educational. In practice, however, these institutions frequently proved to be primarily custodial and disciplinary. Indeed, many of the reforms that were supposed to help children were adopted partly because they served the adults' needs, interests, and convenience. The abolition of child labor removed competition from an overcrowded labor market. Age-grading not only made it much easier to control children within schools, it also divided the young into convenient market segments. One of the most serious challenges American society faces is to act on behalf of children's welfare rather than adults'.

The most important lesson that grows out of an understanding of the history of childhood is the simplest. While many fear that American society has changed too much, the sad fact is that it has changed too little. Americans have failed to adapt social institutions to the fact that the young mature more rapidly than they did in the past; that most mothers of preschoolers now participate in the paid workforce; and that a near majority of children will spend substantial parts of their childhood in a single-parent, cohabitating-parent, or stepparent household. How can we provide better care for the young, especially the one-sixth who are growing up in poverty? How can we better connect the worlds of adults and the young? How can we give the young more ways to demonstrate their growing competence and maturity? How can we tame a violence-laced, sex-saturated popular culture without undercutting a commitment to freedom and a respect for the free-floating world of fantasy? These are the questions we must confront as we navigate a new century of childhood.

Notes

1. Ron Powers, *Dangerous Water: A Biography of the Boy Who Became Mark Twain* (New York: Da Capo Press, 1999); Powers, *Tom and Huck Don't Live Here Anymore: Childhood and Murder in the Heart of America* (New York: St. Martin's Press, 2001), 2, 32–34, 40, 131; Shelley Fisher Fishkin, *Lighting Out for the Territories: Reflections on Mark Twain and American Culture* (New York: Oxford University Press, 1997).
2. Powers, *Dangerous Water*, 26, 84, 167; Powers, *Tom and Huck Don't Live Here Anymore*, 78.
3. Richard Weissbourd, *The Vulnerable Child: What Really Hurts America's Children and What We Can Do About It* (Reading, MA: Addison-Wesley, 1996), 48.
4. Colin Heywood, *A History of Childhood: Children and Childhood in the West from Medieval to Modern Times* (Cambridge, UK: Polity, 2001); Joseph Illick, *American Childhood* (Philadelphia: University of Pennsylvania Press, 2002); James A. Schultz, *The Knowledge of Childhood in the German Middle Ages, 1100–1350* (Philadelphia: University of Pennsylvania Press, 1995), 11.
5. Howard P. Chudacoff, *How Old Are You? Age Consciousness in American Society* (Princeton: Princeton University Press, 1989); Joseph F. Kett, *Rites of Passage: Adolescence in America* (New York: Basic, 1977).
6. Kett, *Rites of Passage, passim.*
7. On changes in the onset of sexual maturation, see Marcia E. Herman-Giddens and others, "Secondary Sexual Characteristics and Menses in Young Girls Seen in Office Practice: A Study from the Pediatric Research in Office Settings Network," *Pediatrics*, Vol. 99, No. 4 (April 1997), 505–512. In 1890, the average age of menarche in the United States was estimated to be 14.8 years; by the 1990s, the average age had fallen to 12.5 (12.1 for African American girls and 12.8 for girls of northern European ancestry). According to the study, which tracked 17,000 girls to find out when they hit different markers of puberty, 15 percent of white girls and 48 percent of African American girls showed signs of breast development or pubic hair by age 8. For conflicting views on whether the age of menarche has fallen, see Lisa Belkin, "The Making of an 8-Year-Old Woman," *New York Times*, December 24, 2000; Gina Kolata, "Doubters Fault Theory Finding Earlier Puberty, *New York Times*," February 20, 2001; and "2 Endocrinology Groups Raise Doubt on Earlier Onset of Girls' Puberty," *New York Times*, March 3, 2001.
8. Stephen Robertson, "The Disappearance of Childhood," http://teaching.arts.usyd.edu.au/history/2044/.
9. Gerald F. Moran, "Colonial America, Adolescence in," *Encyclopedia of Adolescence*, edited by Richard Lerner, Anne C. Petersen, Jeanne Brooks-Gunn (New York: Garland Pub., 1991), I, 159–167.
10. Priscilla Clement, *Growing Pains: Children in the Industrial Age* (New York: Twayne, 1997); David Nasaw, *Children in the City: At Work and at Play* (Garden City, NY: Anchor Press/Doubleday, 1985); Christine Stansell, *City of Women: Sex and Class in New York, 1789–1860* (New York: Knopf, 1986).
11. David I. Macleod, *The Age of the Child: Children in America, 1890–1912* (New York: Twayne, 1998).
12. Viviana Zelizer, *Pricing the Priceless Child: The Changing Social Value of Children* (Princeton: Princeton University Press).
13. Peter N. Stearns, *Anxious Parents: A History of Modern Childrearing in America* (New York: New York University Press, 2002).
14. Ann Hulbert, *Raising America: Experts, Parents, and a Century of Advice about Children* (New York: Knopf, 2003); Julia Grant, *Raising Baby by the Book: The Education of American Mothers* (New Haven: Yale University Press, 1998).
15. Kathleen W. Jones, *Taming the Troublesome Child* (Cambridge, MA: Harvard University Press, 1999).
16. Steven Mintz and Susan Kellogg, *Domestic Revolutions: A Social History of American Family Life* (New York: Free Press, 1988), 189.

17. Rogers quoted in James Axtell, *School Upon a Hill: Education and Society in Colonial New England* (New Haven: Yale University Press, 1974), 28. Hard as it is to believe, in 1951 a leading television critic decried the quality of children's television. Jack Gould, radio and TV critic for *The New York Times* from the late 1940s to 1972, complained that there was "nothing on science, seldom anything on the country's cultural heritage, no introduction to fine books, scant emphasis on the people of other lands, and little concern over hobbies and other things for children to do themselves besides watch television." *Chicago Sun Times*, Aug. 9, 1998, 35; Phil Scraton, ed., *Childhood in "Crisis"* (London; Bristol, Penn.: UCL Press, 1997), 161, 164.
18. William Bradford, *Of Plymouth Plantation*, edited by Samuel Elliot Morrison (New York: Modern Library, 1952), 25; Moran, "Colonial America, Adolescence in," 159.
19. Linda Gordon, *Heroes of Their Own Lives: The Politics and History of Family Violence* (New York: Viking, 1988); Elizabeth Pleck, *Domestic Tyranny: the Making of Social Policy against Family Violence from Colonial Times to the Present* (New York: Oxford University Press, 1987).
20. William Feldman et al., "Is Childhood Sexual Abuse Really Increasing in Prevalence? An Analysis of the Evidence," *Pediatrics*, July 1991, Vol. 88, Issue 1, 29–34; Males, *Framing Youth*, 257. In 1998, government agencies substantiated over a million cases of child maltreatment, including approximately 101,000 cases of sexual abuse. About 51 percent of lifetime rapes occur prior to age 18 and 29 percent of lifetime rapes occur prior to age 12. Coordinating Council on Juvenile Justice and Delinquency Prevention, *Combating Violence and Delinquency: The National Juvenile Justice Action Plan: Report* (Washington DC: Coordinating Council on Juvenile Justice and Delinquency Prevention, 1996), 75; National Criminal Justice Reference Service, www.ncjrs.org/html/ojjdp/action_plan_2001_10/page1.html. The 1994 Sex in America study of the sex lives of 3,400 men and women reported that 17 percent of the women and 12 percent of the men reported childhood sexual abuse. See Males, *Scapegoat Generation*, 74.

READING 22

Unequal Childhoods: Class, Race, and Family Life

Annette Lareau

There are many studies that tell us of the detrimental effects of poverty on children's lives, but it is less clear what the mechanisms are for the transmission of class advantage across generations.

I suggest that social class has an important impact on the cultural logic of childrearing (see Lareau 2003 for details). Middle-class parents, both white *and* black, appear to follow a cultural logic of childrearing that I call "concerted cultivation." They enroll their children in numerous age-specific organized activities that come to dominate family life and create enormous labor, particularly for mothers. Parents see these activities as transmitting important life skills to children. Middle-class parents also stress language use and the development of reasoning. Talking plays a crucial role in the disciplinary strategies of middle-class parents. This "cultivation" approach results in a frenetic pace for parents, creates a cult of individualism within the family, and emphasizes children's performance.

Among white and black working-class and poor families, childrearing strategies emphasize the "accomplishment of natural growth." These parents believe that as long as they provide love, food, and safety, their children will grow and thrive. They do not focus on developing the special talents of their individual children. Working-class and poor children have more free time and deeper and richer ties within their extended families than the middle-class children. Some participate in organized activities, but they do so for different reasons than their middle-class counterparts. Working-class and poor parents issue many more directives to their children and, in some households, place more emphasis on physical discipline than do middle-class parents.

The pattern of concerted cultivation, with its stress on individual repertoires of activities, reasoning, and questioning, encourages an *emerging sense of entitlement* in children. Of course, not all parents and children are equally assertive, but the pattern of questioning and intervening among the white and black middle-class parents in the study contrasts sharply with the definitions of how to be helpful and effective observed among the white and black working-class and poor families. The pattern of the accomplishment of natural growth, with its emphasis on child-initiated play, autonomy from adults, and directives, encourages an *emerging sense of constraint* [Table 22.1]. Members of these families, adults as well as children, tend to be deferential and outwardly accepting (with sporadic moments of resistance) in their interactions with professionals such as doctors and educators. At the same time, however, compared to their middle-class counterparts, the

TABLE 22.1 ***Argument of Unequal Childhoods: Class Differences in Childrearing***

	Childrearing Approach	
	Concerted Cultivation	***Accomplishment of Natural Growth***
Key Elements	Parent actively fosters and assesses child's talents, opinions, and skills	Parent cares for child and allows child to grow
Organization of Daily Life	*multiple child leisure activities orchestrated by adults	*child "hangs out" particularly with kin
Language Use	*reasoning/directives *child contestation of adult statements *extended negotiations between parents and child	*directives *rare for child to question or challenge adults *general acceptance by child of directives
Interventions in Institutions	*criticisms and interventions on behalf of child *training of child to take on this role	*dependence on institutions *sense of powerlessness and frustrations *conflict between childrearing practices at home and at school
Consequences	Emerging sense of entitlement on the part of the child	Emerging sense of constraint on the part of the child

white and black working-class and poor families are more distrustful of professionals in institutions. These are differences with long-term consequences. In a historical moment where the dominant society privileges active, informed, assertive clients of health and educational services, the various strategies employed by children and parents are not equally valuable. In sum, differences in family life lie not only in the advantages parents are able to obtain for their children, but also in the skills being transmitted to children for negotiating their own life paths.

METHODOLOGY

Study Participants

The study is based on interviews and observations of children eight to ten years of age and their families. A team of graduate research assistants and I collected the data. The first phase involved observations in third-grade public school classrooms, mainly in a metropolitan area in the Northeast. The schools serve neighborhoods in a white suburban area and two urban locales—one a white working-class neighborhood and the other a nearby poor black neighborhood. About one-half of the children are white and about one-half are black. One child is interracial. The research assistants and I carried out individual interviews (averaging two hours each) with all of the mothers and most of the fathers (or guardians) of 88 children, for a total of 137 interviews. We also observed children as they took part in organized activities in the communities surrounding the schools. The most intensive part of the research, however, involved home observations of 12 children and their families. Nine of the 12 families came from the classrooms I observed, but the boy and girl from the two black middle-class families and the boy from the poor white family came from other sites. Most observations and interviews took place between 1993 and 1995, but interviews were done as early as 1990 and as late as 1997. This chapter focuses primarily on the findings from the observations of these 12 families since the key themes discussed here surfaced during this part of the field-work. I do include some information from the larger study to provide a context for understanding the family observations. All names are pseudonyms.

Intensive Family Observations

The research assistants and I took turns visiting the participating families daily, for a total of about 20 visits in each home, often in the space of one month. The observations were not limited to the home. Fieldworkers followed children and parents as they took part in school activities, church services and events, organized play, kin visits, and medical appointments. Most field observations lasted about three hours; sometimes, depending on the event (e.g., an out-of-town funeral, a special extended family event, or a long shopping trip), they lasted much longer. In most cases, there was one overnight visit. We often carried tape recorders with us and used the audiotapes for reference in writing up field notes. Families were paid $350, usually at the end of the visits, for their participation.

A Note on Class

My purpose in undertaking the field observations was to develop an *intensive*, realistic portrait of family life. Although I deliberately focused on only 12 families, I wanted to compare children across gender and race lines. Adopting the fine-grained differentiation of categories characteristic of current neo-Marxist and neo-Weberian empirical studies was not tenable. My choice of class categories was further limited by the school populations at the sites I had selected. Very few of the students were children of employers or of self-employed workers. I decided to concentrate exclusively on those whose parents were employees. Various criteria have been proposed to differentiate within this heterogeneous group, but authority in the workplace and "credential barriers" are the two most commonly used. I assigned the families in the study to a working-class or middle-class category based on discussions with each of the employed adults. They provided extensive information about the work they did, the nature of the organization that employed them, and their educational credentials. I added a third category: families not involved in the labor market (a population traditionally excluded from social class groupings) because in the first school I studied, a substantial number of children were from households supported by public assistance. To ignore them would have restricted the scope of the study arbitrarily. The final sub-sample contained 4 middle-class, 4 working-class, and 4 poor families.

CHILDREN'S TIME USE

In our interviews and observations of white and black middle-class children, it was striking how busy they were with organized activities. Indeed, one of the hallmarks of middle-class children's daily lives is a set of adult-run organized activities. Many children have three and four activities per week. In some families, every few days activities conflict, particularly when one season is ending and one is beginning. For example in the white middle-class family of the Tallingers, Garrett is on multiple soccer teams—the "A" traveling team of the private Forest soccer club and the Intercounty soccer team—he also has swim lessons, saxophone lessons at school, private piano lessons at home, and baseball and basketball. These organized activities provided a framework for children's lives; other activities were sandwiched between them.

These activities create labor for parents. Indeed, the impact of children's activities takes its toll on parents' patience as well as their time. For example, on a June afternoon at the beginning of summer vacation, in a white-middle-class family, Mr. Tallinger comes home from work to take Garrett to his soccer game. Garrett is not ready to go, and his lackadaisical approach to getting ready irks his father:

> Don says, "Get your soccer stuff—you're going to a soccer game!" Garrett comes into the den with white short leggings on underneath a long green soccer shirt; he's number 16. He sits on an armchair catty-corner from the television and languidly watches the World Cup game. He slowly, abstractedly, pulls on shin guards, then long socks. His eyes are riveted to the TV screen. Don comes in: "Go get your other stuff." Garrett says he can't find his shorts. Don: "Did you look in your drawer?" Garrett nods. . . . He gets up to look for his shorts, comes back into the den a few minutes later. I ask, "Any luck yet?" Garrett shakes his head. Don is rustling around elsewhere in the house. Don comes in, says to

> Garrett, "Well, Garrett, aren't you wearing shoes?" (Don leaves and returns a short time later): "Garrett, we HAVE to go! Move! We're late!" He says this shortly, abruptly. He comes back in a minute and drops Garrett's shiny green shorts on his lap without a word.

This pressured search for a pair of shiny green soccer shorts is a typical event in the Tallinger household. Also typical is the solution—a parent ultimately finds the missing object, while continuing to prod the child to hurry. The fact that today's frenzied schedule will be matched or exceeded by the next day's is also par:

> Don: (describing their day on Saturday) Tomorrow is really nuts. We have a soccer game, then a baseball game, then another soccer game.

This steady schedule of activity—that none of the middle-class parents reported having when they were a similar age—was not universal. Indeed, while we searched for a middle-class child who did not have a single organized activity we could not find one, but in working-class and poor homes, organized activities were much less common and there were many children who did not have any. Many children "hung out." Television and video games are a major source of entertainment but outdoor play can trump either of these. No advanced planning, no telephone calls, no consultations between mothers, no drop-offs or pickups—no particular effort at all—is required to launch an activity. For instance, one afternoon, in a black working-class family, Shannon (in 7th grade) and Tyrec (in 4th grade) walk out their front door to the curb of the small, narrow street their house faces. Shannon begins playing a game with a ball; she soon has company:

> (Two boys from the neighborhood walk up.) Shannon is throwing the small ball against the side of the row house. Tyrec joins in the game with her. As they throw the ball against the wall, they say things they must do with the ball. It went something like this: Johnny Crow wanted to know. . . . (bounces ball against the wall), touch your knee (bounce), touch your toe (bounce), touch the ground (bounce), under the knee (bounce), turn around (bounce). Shannon and Tyrec played about four rounds.
>
> Unexpected events produce hilarity:
>
> At one point Shannon accidentally threw the ball and it bounced off of Tyrec's head. All the kids laughed; then Tyrec, who had the ball, went chasing after Shannon. It was a close, fun moment—lots of laughter, eye contact, giggling, chasing.

Soon a different game evolves. Tyrec is on restriction. He is supposed to remain inside the house all day. So, when he thinks he has taught a glimpse of his mom returning home from work, he dashes inside. He reappears as soon as he realizes that it was a false alarm. The neighborhood children begin an informal game of baiting him:

> The kids keep teasing Tyrec that his mom's coming—which sends him scurrying just inside the door, peering out of the screen door. This game is enacted about six times. Tyrec also chases Shannon around the street, trying to get the ball from her. A few times Shannon tells Tyrec that he'd better "get inside"; he ignores her. Then, at 6:50 [P.M.] Ken (a friend of Tyrec's) says, "There's your mom!" Tyrec scoots inside, then, says, "Oh, man. You were serious this time."

Informal, impromptu outdoor play is common in Tyrec's neighborhood. A group of boys approximately his age, regularly numbering four or five but sometimes reaching as many as ten, play ball games together on the street, walk to the store to get treats, watch television at each other's homes, and generally hang out together.

LANGUAGE USE

In addition to differences by social class in time use, we also observed differences in language use in the home. As others have noted (Bernstein, 1971; Heath, 1983) middle-class parents used more reasoning in their speech with children while working-class and poor parents used more directives. For example, in observations of the African American home of Alex Williams, whose father was a trial lawyer and mother was a high level corporate executive, we found that the Williamses and other middle-class parents use language frequently, pleasurably, and instrumentally. Their children do likewise. For example, one January evening, Alexander is stumped by a homework assignment to write five riddles. He sits at the dinner table in the kitchen with his mother and a fieldworker. Mr. Williams is at the sink, washing the dinner dishes. He has his back to the group at the dinner table. Without turning around, he says to Alex, "Why don't you go upstairs to the third floor and get one those books and see if there is a riddle in there?"

> Alex [says] smiling, "Yeah. That's a good idea! I'll go upstairs and copy one from out of the book." Terry turns around with a dish in hand, "That was a joke—not a valid suggestion. That is not an option." He smiled as he turned back around to the sink. Christina says, looking at Alex: "There is a word for that you know, plagiarism." Terry says (not turning around), "Someone can sue you for plagiarizing. Did you know that?" Alex: "That's only if it is copyrighted." They all begin talking at once.

Here we see Alex cheerfully (though gently) goading his father by pretending to misunderstand the verbal instruction to consult a book for help. Mr. Williams dutifully rises to the bait. Ms. Williams reshapes this movement of lightheartedness by introducing a new word into Alexander's vocabulary. Mr. Williams goes one step further by connecting the new word to a legal consequence. Alex upstages them both. He demonstrates that he is already familiar with the general idea of plagiarism and that he understands the concept of copyright, as well.

In marked contrast to working-class and poor parents, however, even when the Williamses issue directives, they often include explanations for their orders. Here, Ms. Williams is reminding her son to pay attention to his teacher:

> I want you to play close attention to Mrs. Scott when you are developing your film. Those chemicals are very dangerous. Don't play around in the classroom. You could get that stuff in someone's eye. And if you swallow it, you could die.

Alex chooses to ignore the directive in favor of instructing his misinformed mother:

> Alex corrects her, "Mrs. Scott told us that we wouldn't die if we swallowed it. But we would get very sick and would have to get our stomach pumped." Christina does not follow the argument any further. She simply reiterates that he should be careful.

Possibly because the issue is safety, Ms. Williams does not encourage Alex to elaborate here, as she would be likely to do if the topic were less charged. Instead, she restates her directive and thus underscores her expectation that Alex will do as she asks.

Although Mr. and Ms. Williams disagreed on elements of how training in race relations should be implemented, they both recognized that their racial and ethnic identity profoundly shaped their and their son's everyday experiences. They were well aware of the potential for Alexander to be exposed to racial injustice, and they went to great lengths to try to protect their son from racial insults and other forms of discrimination. Nevertheless, race did not appear to shape the dominant cultural logic of childrearing in Alexander's family or in other families in the study. All of the middle-class families engaged in extensive reasoning with their children, asking questions, probing assertions, and listening to answers. Similar patterns appeared in interviews and observations with other African American middle-class families.

A different pattern appeared in working-class and poor homes where there was simply less verbal speech than we observed in middle-class homes. There was also less speech between parents and children, a finding noted by other observational studies (Hart and Risley, 1995). Moreover, interspersed with intermittent talk are adult-issued directives. Children are told to do certain things (e.g., shower, take out the garbage) and not to do others (e.g., curse, talk back). In an African American home of a family living on public assistance in public housing, Ms. McAllister uses one-word directives to coordinate the use of the single bathroom. There are almost always at least four children in the apartment and often seven, plus Ms. McAllister and other adults. Ms. McAllister sends the children to wash up by pointing to a child, saying, "Bathroom," and handing him or her a washcloth. Wordlessly, the designated child gets up and goes to the bathroom to take a shower.

Children usually do what adults ask of them. We did not observe whining or protests, even when adults assign time-consuming tasks, such as the hour-long process of hair-braiding Lori McAllister is told to do for the four-year-old daughter of Aunt Dara's friend Charmaine:

> Someone tells Lori, "Go do [Tyneshia's] hair for camp." Without saying anything, Lori gets up and goes inside and takes the little girl with her. They head for the couch near the television; Lori sits on the couch and the girl sits on the floor. [Tyneshia] sits quietly for about an hour, with her head tilted, while Lori carefully does a multitude of braids.

Lori's silent obedience is typical. Generally, children perform requests without comment. For example, at dinner one night, after Harold McAllister complains he doesn't like spinach, his mother directs him to finish it anyway:

> Mom yells (loudly) at him to eat: "EAT! FINISH THE SPINACH!" (No response. Harold is at the table, dawdling.) Guion and Runako and Alexis finish eating and leave. I finish with Harold; he eats his spinach. He leaves all his yams.

The verbal world of Harold McAllister and other poor and working-class children offers some important advantages as well as costs. Compared to middle-class children we observed, Harold is more respectful towards adults in his family. In this setting, there are clear boundaries between adults and children. Adults feel comfortable issuing directives to children, which children comply with immediately. Some of the directives that adults issue center on obligations of children to others in the family ("don't beat on Guion" or "go do [her] hair for camp"). One consequence of this is that Harold, despite occasional tiffs, is much nicer to his sister (and his cousins) than the siblings we observed in middle-class homes. The use of directives and the pattern of silent compliance are not universal in Harold's life. In his interactions with peers, for example on the basketball "court," Harold's verbal displays are distinctively different than inside the household, with elaborated and embellished discourse. Nevertheless, there is a striking difference in linguistic interaction between adults and children in poor and working-class families when compared to that observed in the home of Alexander Williams. Ms. McAllister has the benefit of being able to issue directives without having to justify their decisions at every moment. This can make childrearing somewhat less tiring.

Another advantage is that Harold has more autonomy than middle-class children in making important decisions in daily life. As a child, he controls his leisure schedule. His basketball games are impromptu and allow him to develop important skills and talents. He is resourceful. He appears less exhausted than ten-year-old Alexander. In addition, he has important social competencies, including his deftness in negotiating the "code of the street."[1] His mother has stressed these skills in her upbringing, as she impresses upon her children the importance of "not paying no mind" to others, including drunks and drug dealers who hang out in the neighborhoods which Harold and Alexis negotiate.

Still, in the world of schools, health care facilities, and other institutional settings, these valuable skills do not translate into the same advantages as the reasoning skills emphasized in the home of Alexander Williams and other middle-class children. Compared to Alexander Williams, Harold does not gain the development of a large vocabulary, an increase of his knowledge of science and politics, a set of tools to customize situations outside the home to maximize his advantage, and instruction in how to defend his argument with evidence. His knowledge of words, which might appear, for example, on future SAT tests, is not continually stressed at home.

In these areas, the lack of advantage is *not* connected to the intrinsic value of the McAllister family life or the use of directives at home. Indeed, one can argue raising children who are polite and respectful children and do not whine, needle, or badger their parents is a highly laudable childrearing goal. Deep and abiding ties with kinship groups are also, one might further argue, important. Rather, it is the specific ways that institutions function that ends up conveying advantages to middle-class children. In their standards, these institutions also permit, and even demand, active parent involvement. In this way as well, middle-class children often gain an advantage.

INTERVENTION IN INSTITUTIONS

Children do not live their lives inside of the home. Instead, they are legally required to go to school, they go to the doctor, and many are involved in church and other adult-organized activities. In children's institutional lives, we found differences by social class in how mothers monitored children's institutional experiences. While in working-class and poor families children are granted autonomy to make their own way in organizations, in the middle-class homes, most aspects of the children's lives are subject to their mother's *ongoing* scrutiny.

For example in an African American middle-class home, where both parents are college graduates and Ms. Marshall is a computer worker and her husband a civil servant, their two daughters have a hectic schedule of organized activities including gymnastics for Stacey and basketball for Fern. When Ms. Marshall becomes aware of a problem, she moves quickly, drawing on her work and professional skills and experiences. She displays tremendous assertiveness, doggedness, and, in some cases, effectiveness in pressing institutions to recognize her daughters' individualized needs. Stacey's mother's proactive stance reflects her belief that she has a duty to intervene in situations where she perceives that her daughter's needs are not being met. This perceived responsibility applies across all areas of her children's lives. She is no more (or less) diligent with regard to Stacey and Fern's leisure activities than she is with regard to their experiences in school or church or the doctor's office. This is clear in the way she handles Stacey's transition from her township gymnastics classes to the private classes at an elite private gymnastic program at Wright's.

Ms. Marshall describes Stacey's first session at the club as rocky:

> The girls were not warm. And these were little . . . eight and nine year old kids. You know, they weren't welcoming her the first night. It was kinda like eyeing each other, to see, you know, "Can you do this? Can you do that?"

More importantly, Ms. Marshall reported that the instructor is brusque, critical and not friendly toward Stacey. Ms. Marshall cannot hear what was being said, but she could see the interactions through a window. A key problem is that because her previous instructor had not used the professional jargon for gymnastic moves, Stacey does not know these terms. When the class ends and she walks out, she is visibly upset. Her mother's reaction is a common one among middle-class parents: She does not remind her daughter that in life one has to adjust, that she will need to work even harder, or that there is nothing to be done. Instead, Ms. Marshall focuses on Tina, the instructor, as the source of the problem:

> We sat in the car for a minute and I said, "Look, Stac," I said. She said, "I-I," and she started crying. I said, "You wait here." The instructor had come to the door, Tina. So I went to her and I said, "Look." I said, "Is there a problem?" She said, "Aww . . . she'll be fine. She just needs to work on certain things." Blah-blah-blah. And I said, "She's really upset. She said you-you-you [were] pretty much correcting just about everything." And [Tina] said, "Well, she's got—she's gotta learn the terminology."

Ms. Marshall acknowledges that Stacey isn't familiar with specialized and technical gymnastics terms. Nonetheless, she continues to defend her daughter:

> I do remember, I said to her, I said, "Look, maybe it's not all the student." You know, I just left it like that. That, you know, sometimes teaching, learning and teaching, is a two-

> way proposition as far as I'm concerned. And sometimes teachers have to learn how to, you know, meet the needs of the kid. Her style, her immediate style was not accommodating to—to Stacey.

Here Ms. Marshall is asserting the legitimacy of an individualized approach to instruction. She frames her opening remark as a question ("Is there a problem?"). Her purpose, however, is to alert the instructor to the negative impact she has had on Stacey ("She's really upset."). Although her criticism is indirect ("Maybe it's not all the student . . ."), Ms. Marshall makes it clear that she expects her daughter to be treated differently in the future. In this case, Stacey does not hear what her mother says, but she knows that her wishes and feelings are being transmitted to the instructor in a way that she could not do herself.

Although parents were equally concerned about their children's happiness, in working-class and poor homes we observed different patterns of oversight for children's institutional activities. For example in the white working-class home of Wendy Driver. Wendy's mother does not nurture her daughter's language development like Alexander Williams' mother does her son's. She does not attempt to draw Wendy out or follow up on new information when Wendy introduces the term mortal sin while the family is sitting around watching television. But, just like Ms. Williams, Ms. Driver cares very much about her child and just like middle-class parents she wants to help her daughter succeed. Ms. Driver keeps a close and careful eye on her Wendy's schooling. She knows that Wendy is having problems in school. Ms. Driver immediately signs and returns each form Wendy brings home from school and reminds her to turn the papers in to her teacher.

Wendy is "being tested" as part of an ongoing effort to determine why she has difficulties with spelling, reading, and related language-based activities. Her mother welcomes these official efforts but she did not request them. Unlike the middle-class mothers we observed, who asked teachers for detailed information about every aspect of their children's classroom performance and relentlessly pursued information and assessments outside of school as well, Ms. Driver seems content with only a vague notion of her daughter's learning disabilities. This attitude contrasts starkly with that of Stacey Marshall's mother, for example. In discussing Stacey's classroom experiences with fieldworkers, Ms. Marshall routinely described her daughter's academic strengths and weaknesses in detail. Ms. Driver never mentions that Wendy is doing grade-level work in math but is reading at a level a full three years below her grade. Her description is vague:

> She's having problems. . . . They had a special teacher come in and see if they could find out what the problem is. She has a reading problem, but they haven't put their finger on it yet, so she's been through all kinds of special teachers and testing and everything. She goes to Special Ed, I think it's two classes a day . . . I'm not one hundred percent sure—for her reading. It's very difficult for her to read what's on paper. But then—she can remember things. But not everything. It's like she has a puzzle up there. And we've tried, well, they've tried a lot of things. They just haven't put their finger on it yet.

Wendy's teachers uniformly praise her mother as "supportive" and describe her as "very loving," but they are disappointed in Ms. Driver's failure to take a more active, interventionist role in Wendy's education, especially given the formidable nature of her daughter's learning problems. From Ms. Driver's perspective, however, being actively supportive means doing whatever the teachers tell her to do.

> Whatever they would suggest, I would do. They suggested she go to the eye doctor, so I did that. And they checked her and said there was nothing wrong there.

Similarly, she monitors Wendy's homework and supports her efforts to read:

> We listen to her read. We help her with her homework. So she has more attention here in a smaller household than it was when I lived with my parents. So, we're trying to help her out more, which I think is helping. And with the two [special education] classes a day at the school, instead of one like last year, she's learning a lot from that. So, we're just hoping it takes time and that she'll just snap out of it.

But Ms. Driver clearly does not have an *independent* understanding of the nature or degree of Wendy's limitations, perhaps because she is unfamiliar with the kind of terms the educators use to describe her daughter's needs (e.g., a limited "sight vocabulary," underdeveloped "language arts skills"). Perhaps, too, her confidence in the school staff makes it easier for her to leave "the details" to them: "Ms. Morton, she's great. She's worked with us for different testing and stuff." Ms. Driver depends on the school staff's expertise to assess the situation and then share the information with her:

> I think they just want to keep it in the school till now. And when they get to a point where they can't figure out what it is, and then I guess they'll send me somewhere else. . . .

Her mother is not alarmed, because "the school" has told her not to worry about Wendy's grades:

> Her report card—as long as it's not spelling and reading—spelling and reading are like F's. And they keep telling me not to worry, because she's in the Special Ed class. But besides that, she does good. I have no behavior problems with her at all.

Ms. Driver wants the best possible outcome for her daughter and she does not know how to achieve that goal without relying heavily on Wendy's teachers:

> I wouldn't even know where to start going. On the radio there was something for children having problems reading and this and that, call. And I suggested it to a couple different people, and they were like, wait a second, it's only to get you there and you'll end up paying an arm and a leg. So I said to my mom, "No, I'm going to wait until the first report card and go up and talk to them up there."

Thus, in looking for the source of Ms. Driver's deference toward educators, the answers don't seem to lie in her having either a shy personality or underdeveloped mothering skills. To understand why Wendy's mother is accepting where Stacey Marshall's mother would be aggressive, it is more useful to focus on social class position, both in terms of how class shapes worldviews and how class affects economic and educational resources. Ms. Driver understands her role in her daughter's education as involving a different set of responsibilities from those perceived by middle-class mothers. She responds to contacts from the school—such as invitations to the two annual parent-teacher conferences—but she does not initiate them. She views Wendy's school life as a separate realm, and one in which she, as a parent, is only an infrequent visitor. Ms. Driver expects that the teachers will teach and her daughter will learn and that, under normal circumstances, neither requires any additional help from her as a parent. If problems arise, she presumes that Wendy will tell her; or, if the issue is serious, the school will contact her. But what Ms. Driver fails to understand, is that the educators expect her to take on a pattern of "concerted cultivation" where she actively monitors and intervenes in her child's schooling. The teachers asked for a complicated mixture of deference and engagement from parents; they were disappointed when they did not get it.

CONCLUSIONS

I have stressed how social class dynamics are woven into the texture and rhythm of children and parents' daily lives. Class position influences critical aspects of family life: time use, language use, and kin ties. Working-class and middle-class mothers may express beliefs that reflect a similar notion of "intensive mothering," but their behavior is quite different. For that reason, I have described sets of paired beliefs and actions as a "cultural logic" of childrearing. When children and parents move outside the home into the world of social institutions, they find that these cultural practices are not given equal value. There are signs that middle-class children benefit, in ways that are invisible to them and to their parents, from the degree of similarity between the cultural repertoires in the home and those standards adopted by institutions.

Notes

1. Elijah Anderson, *Code of the Street,* New York: W. W. Norton (1999).

References

Anderson, Elijah. 1999. *Code of the Street.* New York, NY: W. W. Norton.

Bernstein, Basil. 1971. *Class, Codes, and Control: Theoretical Studies Towards a Sociology of Language.* New York, NY: Schocken.

Hart, Betty and Todd R. Risley. 1995. *Meaningful Differences in the Everyday Experiences of Young American Children.* New Haven: Yale University Press.

Heath, Shirley Brice. 1983. *Ways with Words: Language, Life, and Work in Communities and Classrooms.* Cambridge: Cambridge University Press.

Lareau, Annette. 2003. *Unequal Childhoods: Class, Race, and Family Life.* Berkeley, CA: University of California Press.

READING 23

Diverging Development: The Not-So-Invisible Hand of Social Class in the United States

Frank Furstenberg

INTRODUCTION

America has never been a class conscientious society by the standards of the rest of the world. The notion that social class determines a person's life chances has always been an anathema in this country, flying in the face of our democratic ideology. Centuries ago, some of the earliest observers of American society, most notably Alexis de Tocqueville (1945) remarked upon the disdain for class distinctions in our early history compared to France or the rest of Europe. To be sure, social class was far more prominent and salient in the U.S. at the time of Tocqueville's visit to this country in the 1830s than today; however, the seemingly boundless possibilities of land ownership and the ideology of upward mobility softened the contours of class distinctions in this country from its very inception (Wood 2004). The idea that any hardworking American by dint of good character and hard work could rise up the social ladder has long been celebrated in the great American myth of Horatio Alger who rose from "rags to riches" providing a fictional example instructing young men—and it was men—of what they needed to do to make their fortunes in 19th Century America.

Curiously, the United States, long regarded as the land of opportunity, has never entirely lived up to its billing. Comparative studies on social mobility between the U.S. and our Western counterparts have failed to demonstrate that social mobility is especially higher here than in other industrialized nations (Bendix and Lipset 1966, Goldthorpe and Erickson 1993). Yet, Americans seem as oblivious to class gradations today as they have ever been. Most of us declare that we are middle-class and finer distinctions such as working-class and upper-middle class have all but vanished in the popular vernacular and even in social science research. While the salience of social class has declined in American society during the past several decades, we have witnessed a huge rise in economic inequality (Danziger and Gottschalk 1997; Levy 1999; Wolff 2002, 2004).

When I was entering academic sociology more than four decades ago, the social world was described very differently than it is today. Even while recognizing the muted notions of social class held by most Americans, social scientists were keenly attentive to, if not obsessed with, distinctions in values, life-style, and social practices inculcated in the family that were linked to social mobility (Hollingshead 1949, Lynd and Lynd 1929, Warner 1949). Indeed, the idea that parents in different social strata deliberately or unintentionally shaped their children's ambitions, goals, and habits, affecting the chances of moving up the social ladder was widely accepted, supported by a large body of literature in psychology, sociology, and economics showing how families situated at different rungs on the social ladder held distinctive world views and adhered to different ideas of development (Bernstein and Henderson 1960; Gans 1962; Kamarovsky 1987; Miller and Swanson 1958). Most of all, social scientists believed that life chances were highly constrained by values and skills acquired in the family and structures of opportunity in the child's immediate environment that shaped his (and it usually was his) chances of economic success. Fine gradations of social class could be linked to virtually everything from toilet training to marriage practices (Blood and Wolfe 1960; Mead and Wolfenstein 1955).

Social class, not so long ago the most powerful analytic category in the researcher's conceptual toolbox has now been largely eclipsed by an emphasis on gender, race, and ethnicity. Socio-economic status has been reduced to a variable, mostly one that is often statistically controlled, to permit researchers to focus on the effect of determinants other than social class. We have stopped measuring altogether the finer grade distinctions of growing up with differential resources. True, we continue to look at poverty and economic disadvantage with no less interest than we ever have, and we certainly understand that affluence and education make a huge difference. Yet, most developmentalists view economic status as a continuum that defies qualitatively finer breakdowns. Consequently, working-class, lower-middle class families or even families in the middle of the income distribution are concealed rather than revealed in combinations of income, education, and occupation. (For exceptions, see Kefalas 2003 and Lareau 2003). In short, the idea of social class has largely been collapsed into rich and poor marked by education and earnings—above and below the poverty line. Think of the way we currently treat "single-parent families" as an example. They have become almost a proxy for poverty rather than a differentiated category of families that experiences life as differently as their two-parent counterparts.

The contention that contemporary developmental research downplays the influence of social class in no way is meant to imply that professional attention to gender or race/ethnicity is unwarranted or should be diminished. Without a firm grasp of social class differences in contemporary America, however, much of the current research on gender and ethnicity ignores class differences within the analytic categories of gender or ethnicity, blunting an understanding of how they shape social reality and social opportunities among men and women and across different racial and ethnic categories. Just as we have come to recognize the hazards of lumping together all Hispanics or Asians, I would suggest that we need a more nuanced understanding of what differences it makes to possess certain levels of education, occupation, income, and indeed a world view and life patterns attached to these constituent elements of socio-economic stratification.

Beyond a call to action, I want to outline a research agenda for examining social class in greater detail. Beginning with a brief discussion of developmental theories, I allude to some of the methodological obstacles to studying social class that must be attended to, and then turn to developmental processes that expose research questions I believe warrant greater attention by our society of scholars. My work nicely parallels observations recently put forth by Sara McLanahan (2004) in her Presidential Address to the Population Association of America on inequality and children's development though my attention is devoted more to the operation of stratification than to its implications for public policy. My central aim is to expose a series of developmental processes that work in tandem to fashion a stratification system operating from birth to maturity in this country that is pervasive, persistent, and far more powerful than we generally like to admit.

SOCIAL CLASS: A PROBLEMATIC CONSTRUCT

One reason why attention to social class has faded may be traced to the academic controversies surrounding the very idea that social classes exist in this country. If what is meant by social class is a closed set of life chances which people recognize and even affiliate with, then surely most would agree that America is a classless society. However, social class has been used in a different way to mark the structure of economic and social opportunities affecting individuals' behaviors and beliefs, networks and associations, and, ultimately, knowledge about and access to social institutions such as the family, education, and the labor market.

Viewed in this way, social classes are not tightly bounded categories; they are fuzzy sets created by experience and exposure to learning opportunities and selective social contacts that derive from resources that can be marshaled by individuals and their kinship networks. In this respect, the fuzzy nature of social class appears to differ from gender or ethnicity though both of these constructs have been appropriately critiqued when viewed as "naturally unambiguous" rather than "socially constructed" statuses. Still, there are no certain markers that identify individuals as belonging to one class or another; social class is probabilistically constructed and measured by particular constellations of socio-economic statuses. Thus, we might say that someone who has low education, works at a menial job which pays poorly is lower-class, a term that admittedly has become virtually taboo in the U.S. Nonetheless, we easily recognize that those possessing these attributes are socially isolated, often excluded from mainstream institutions, and limited in their access to mobility. Whether we refer to them as lower-class, poor, disadvantaged, or socially excluded, it really doesn't change their opportunities or their ability to confer opportunities to their children.

I will dodge the question in this paper of whether it makes sense to identify a particular number of social strata such as was common in social science a generation ago, designating four, five, or seven classes that possessed different family practices, values and beliefs, or lifestyles and cultural habits (Hollingshead 1949; Warner 1949). Instead, I merely want to observe how neglect of social class has created a void in attention by developmentalists in how stratification structures the first decades of the life course. Toward the end of this paper, I will reflect on what I and my colleagues on the MacArthur Network on Adult Transitions are learning about how social class shapes the transition to adulthood in myriad ways that have profound implications for the future of American society.

A DEVELOPMENTAL THEORY OF SOCIAL CLASS

Human development involves an ongoing interaction between individual level biological potentials and social processes shaped by children's multiple and changing social environments. Sometimes developmentalists make distinctions between maturation, regulated in part by biology, and socially arranged learning, the process that we generally refer to as socialization. One of the important legacies of late 20th Century developmental science was to put an end the useless debate between nature and nurture. Researchers initiated a theoretical re-orientation designed to explore ongoing interactions from birth to maturity in a nest of varying contexts—families, childcare settings, schools, communities, and the like to investigate how social context afforded or denied opportunities for optimal development, understanding that optimal development can vary according to children's innate abilities and their exposure to learning environments.

No one understood this scheme better or promoted it with more vigor than Urie Bronfenbrenner (1979), who, as it happens, was one of the pioneers in psychology in examining class differences in development. Bronfenbrenner's theory of development located the individual in an embedded set of contexts that extended from the intimate and direct to distant and indirect as they socially impinged and shaped the course of human development over the life span. Bronfenbrenner's ideas culled from the legacy of 19th and 20th century psychology closely parallel a tradition of sociological theory stemming from the work of George Herbert Mead (1934) and Charles Cooley (1902) that has come to be known as symbolic interaction. Like Bronfenbrenner, Mead and Cooley conceptualized human development as an ongoing process of engagement and response to social others—social exchange guided by feedback from the surrounding social system. As sociologists applied these ideas in practice, they quickly realized how differently it was possible to grow up in varying contexts and cultures, a lesson that is closely aligned with Bronfenbrenner's theory.

It was and, I believe still is, just a short step from this general theory of human development which features the ongoing interaction of children in local environments to seeing the pervasive influence of social class in shaping the course of development. That step involves a careful appraisal of how learning environments themselves are arranged to promote movement from one to the next. These more distal social arrangements are carefully regulated in all modern societies by gatekeepers who exercise presumably meritocratic standards based on a combination of talent, performance, and sponsorship (Buchman 1989; Heinz and Marshall 2003). In all developed societies, parents cede direct control of their children's fates at an increasingly early age to others who become instrumental in guiding children through an age-graded system of opportunities. Parents train and coach their children, select and direct choices in this system, advocate when problems arise, and try to arrange for remediation when their children are not following an optimal path. So, as I have argued elsewhere (Furstenberg, et al. 1999), parents' managerial skills have become increasingly important in how well children navigate the institutional arrangements that affect their opportunities in later life.

Of course, parents themselves are embedded in very different opportunity systems; specifically they are more or less privileged in the knowledge, skills, and resources that they can provide to their children. Expressed in currently fashionable terms, they have different levels of human, social, cultural and psychological capital to invest in their children. Of course, parents are not the only agents that matter. By virtue of their social position at birth and during childhood, children have differential access to kin, friends, neighbors, teachers, and peers that can and do promote or diminish their chances of socio-economic attainment. So while differences in exposure to class-related opportunities might be relatively small, nonetheless they cumulate if they consistently favor or disadvantage children's life chances. Life chances are compounded positively or negatively as opportunities or their absence play out over time.

A century ago, Max Weber used a powerful metaphor for how history operates. Weber (1949) argued that it is like a pair of loaded dice that are weighted with each throw by the result of the previous one; constraints increase with repeated tosses of the dice, leading to a more and more skewed outcome. Social class can be conceptualized as just such a mechanism, establishing a set of life chances that become more sharply pronounced as they play out over time. Micro-interactions cumulate in a patterned and successively more consequential pattern, etching a probabilistically pre-ordained trajectory of success.

To be sure, when it comes to human development, an actor, let's say a child growing up in the U.S. today, exercises a certain level of discretion or influence by dint of his or her own abilities, talents, or needs facing contexts that may be tilted toward advantage or disadvantage. The outcome is always affected by how the child comes to interpret and act in these contexts. This might be an operational definition of resiliency or vulnerability as psychologists such as Rutter (2000; 1985), Garmezy (1993; 1991), and Werner (1995) have employed, the idea that some children are able to defy the odds. Interestingly, developmentalists in recent years have given at least as much, if not more, attention to research on beating the odds as on developing a careful understanding of how the structure of opportunities operates to create systematic advantage or disadvantage over time—or we might say why and how growing up in a certain social location establishes strong and long odds of departing from an expected pattern of success.

I suspect that most of us know just how strong the odds are for rising or falling substantially from the position at birth. Based on retrospective data that understates the amount of social mobility, current estimates suggest that 42 percent of children born into the bottom fifth of the income distribution will remain there as adults. Only 7 percent will make it into the top fifth of the income distribution. For those born into the top fifth of the income distribution, 40 percent remain there while just 6 percent fall into the lowest quintile (Hertz, 2005).

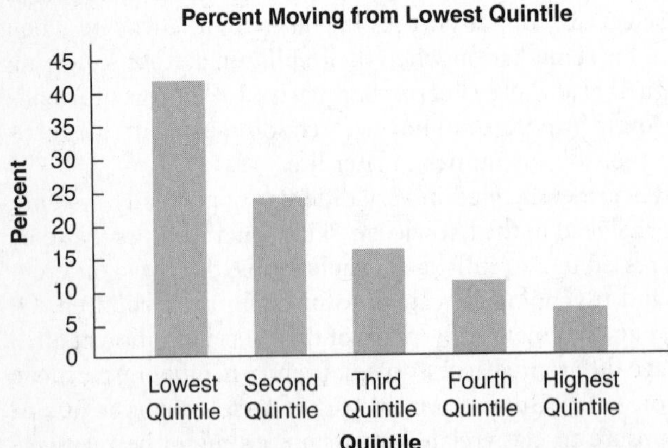

METHODOLOGICAL OBSTACLES TO STUDY

Until very recently, we lacked the data and the methods to observe how social stratification shapes the course of human development. Longitudinal research really only became widely available in the latter decades of the last century though pioneering studies were done on relatively small samples such as Glen Elder's (1974, 1999) now classic work on the Berkeley and Oakland samples. Not until the introduction of the computer could we ever imagine more than cursory treatment of large-scale samples that might provide the kind of variation over time that permit us to examine the array of experiences that children have in the course of development that necessarily calls for merging of different waves of data collection, administrative records, blood samples, and the like that permit us to understand the numerous contingencies that make up children's lives.

Disciplinary rationale sometimes have steered us away from attention to social class as well. Psychologists have been actively discouraged from working on large existing data sets and instructed to collect their own data, thus restricting the range of problems that could be examined. Sociologists, beginning in the 1960s, turned away from studying children, ceding much work on socialization to psychologists. Disciplines have been organized to encourage work on specific life periods and younger researchers have been encouraged to become specialists in infancy, early or middle-childhood, or adolescence. To be sure, exceptions abound and I would be remiss if I did not acknowledge those researchers such as Eleanor Maccoby, John Clausen, Doris Entwisle, or Emmy Werner and others who broke out of the mold or, one might say, beat the odds of doing research in disciplines that discouraged such efforts.

Added to the problems stemming from data availability and disciplinary constraints are the methods, themselves, that are required to examine how trajectories of development unfold over time. Anyone who is familiar with my work will immediately know that I am probably the last person to discuss the new methodological frontiers in developmental science. However, even a methodological simpleton like me has become familiar with a host of novel techniques for analyzing and interpreting longitudinal data such as growth curves that are now available in our packaged software. No doubt, many more will be coming in the future as new and more powerful ways of understanding career contingencies, transitions, and the evolution of trajectories of development are invented and refined. The tools are now available to describe and explain how advantage and disadvantage along many dimensions configure and crystallize the developmental pathways from birth to maturity. In fact, I would contend that data availability and methods have outpaced our theoretical and substantive understanding of how social class influences human development.

THE ORIGIN OF SOCIAL CLASS DIFFERENCES

More sensitive analytic techniques will have to take account of several features that we already know about the influence of social class on development. *First and foremost, early patterns of development may be difficult to surmount once set in place for several different and perhaps overlapping reasons.* At this stage, we know relatively little about the way that brain development during infancy and early childhood takes place, but it is entirely possible that the architecture of early development could well preclude or, at least, compromise subsequent patterns of development. There is growing evidence that cognitive and emotional capacities that form early in life are foundational, providing a template or structure for later advances (Duncan and Brooks-Gunn 2000; Danziger and Waldfogel 2000; Haggerty, et al. 1994).

Exposure to these developmental influences begins before the child is born and is shaped in no small way by parents' prenatal experiences: their exposure to toxins, their diet, the quality of health care received during pregnancy and the neonatal health provided to them. Most children experience a normal delivery and are born in good health, but steep differences exist across social classes in all of these factors. The probability of pre-natal and neo-natal health problems are sharply structured by socio-economic status. Thus, children enter the world endowed unequally even if we discount any genetic variation by social class.

The families into which they are born provide vastly different opportunities to build on that endowment. Whether children are planned or unplanned, whether they must compete for limited family resources or have enough, and whether they will receive steady and sufficient attention from parent figures are but a few of the contingencies known to vary by social class (AG1 on planning, etc.). What is less well understood is how these early influences combine and cumulate creating developmental divides with lasting effects on children's prospects in later lives. Most of the work on the consequences of social attachment, for example, has not been traced for long enough periods to understand whether or how much it affects later transitions in adolescence and early adulthood.

The remarkable research on institutional care of children in Romania under the Communist regime by Charles Nelson and his colleagues provides evidence that something like a critical period exists for emotional development that, if breached, can lead to permanent impairment. Children raised in a collective setting with little or no opportunity to develop attachments with stable emotional figures were emotionally incapacitated. Nelson and his colleagues discovered that if placed in families with emotionally engaging surrogate parents by certain ages, the pattern of emotional disfigurement could be repaired, and perhaps even reversed if the placement occurred early in life. Now, an interesting question, relevant to the discussion here, is whether stimulation and human interaction in early childhood is dichotomous or multitiered, that is whether and how much early interaction sets the parameters for later growth by establishing a critical level or in a more graduated fashion that may still fall below the optimal amount. Few children in American society are impaired by lack of stimulation, but there seems little doubt that many children get less stimulation or fewer opportunities for emotional engagement than is optimal.

A series of experiments in neuropsychology conducted on barriers to reading reveal fascinating and perhaps parallel findings on brain development. It seems that middle-class and working-class children with reading difficulties may exhibit different neural responses when faced with a task of decoding words. The researchers making this discovery hypothesize that the amount of exposure to reading and remediation could account for the differences by social class, suggesting that the causes for reading problems could differ and the remedies might vary for children by social class.

Both these studies bring to mind the impressive qualitative study by Hart and Risley (1995). Home observation of family interactions among children and their families revealed gigantic variations in the range of words, expressions, and interaction styles creating, in effect, a continuous and mounting difference in verbal environments that appeared to be linked to the vocabularies that children acquired in the early years of life (Bernstein 1971; Bernstein and Henderson 1969; Farkas and Beron, 2004). These varying cognitive contexts were later linked to reading skills and accordingly school success.

This study leads to a second observation relevant to developmental trajectories of children in different social classes. *Small differences, if persistent, become larger and more consequential over time. A process of psychological and social accretion operates both at an internal and external level as children develop self concepts, styles of thought, and habits that shape their motivation and social interactions in ways that harden over time.* If, for example, children are exposed to very modest differences in, let us say, language, reading practices, or interaction styles over long periods of time, the cumulative effects could be quite striking and large. Thus, if on average, years of education are linked to small differences in parental skills or practices, they could create significant effects on average in children's acquisition of cognitive and emotional skills. These psychological and social styles create impressions on others that are reinforced and reified in informal and formal social settings. To answer this question, we need both stable measures of social patterns established inside the home that are taken with sufficient frequency to permit us to examine growth curves of emotional and cognitive development that extend beyond the early years of childhood into middle childhood, adolescence, and early adulthood.

These styles that emerge in the home and are shaped to a great degree by class differences in childrearing practices in the family establish what sociologists used to refer as "anticipatory socialization," advanced training for social roles outside the home, especially entrance into pre-school programs that foreshadow and initiate social tracking within the school system. Modest or perhaps not so modest differences that occur within families are unlikely to be offset or compensated for by learning that takes place outside the home. To the contrary, it is easy to demonstrate that they are greatly amplified by differences in parents' capacities to locate, gain access to, and monitor settings outside the home and by institutional practices that selectively recruit children from families that have the resources and children who appear to exhibit the capabilities to perform well.

Parents, in all social strata, are well aware that beginning at an early age children require and benefit from experiences outside the home that offer opportunities for learning offsetting or reinforcing patterns established in the family. We have rightly given a good deal of attention to childcare settings (Chaudry 2004; Magnuson and Waldfogel 2005), but we have a lot less information on the impact of peer interactions or encounters with skill enhancing agencies such as recreational centers, libraries, museums and the like. However, the likelihood of receiving a steady and stable exposure to these sorts of social institutions vary tremendously by social class (Medrich et al. 1982). Qualitative studies have demonstrated large differences by social class in children's exposure both to the amount and quality of these settings. The reasons why are pretty obvious. Parents with better education are both more knowledgeable and therefore usually more discriminating in locating high quality settings. Second, they have greater resources to gain access to those settings such as time, transportation, and money to pay the cost of admission.

Finally, they have the ability to organize and implement on their children's behalf and to monitor ongoing engagements whether they be with the right kind of peers, better classes, or high quality teachers, coaches or caregivers.

The other side of the coin of what happens to young children as a result of the social class into which they are born is no less influential in channeling children from different social classes into more or less favorable settings. *Settings find and recruit children from families of different social classes with varying levels of energy and enthusiasm.* In many instances, settings regulate their clientele by the cost of services: the least affordable for parents attract mostly or exclusively children from affluent families whether we are talking about prenatal health programs, childcare facilities, after school programs, summer camps or Ivy League colleges. The availability of resources establishes to a large extent the social class distribution of families who participate in social institutions in American society. Those that can pay the cost of admission typically purchase better teachers and peers who are more motivated and prepared. We have relatively little research on the social class networks of children that emerge over time, but it is certainly a plausible hypothesis that most children in the U.S. grow up with little or no exposure to peers outside their social class. Thus, their opportunities to acquire cultural and social capital are tremendously influenced the social class composition of kinship and peer networks. And, we have every reason to believe that money and education are playing an ever larger role in regulating the level of cross-class exposure and the composition of children's social networks.

THE IMPORTANCE OF PLACE

Most parents are well aware of this fact: this is why the primary mechanism of managing opportunities for children is choice of residence. Interestingly, we have all too little information on social class and residential decision making. Since schooling is generally determined by neighborhood, parents with more knowledge and resources can select neighborhoods that package together access to better schools, better peers, and, often, better recreational facilities. In the study that my colleagues and I did in Philadelphia on how families manage risk and opportunity, we discovered that parents were acutely aware of the opportunities attached to choice of neighborhood though their awareness of its importance often did not necessarily mean that they were able to exercise much discretion in where to live.

Most working-class families in Philadelphia could not afford to live in affluent sections of the city much less move to the suburbs where they knew that they would find better schools and more desirable peers. They often resorted to the second-best option, sending their children to parochial schools where children were monitored more closely, had a longer school day with more after-school activities, and attended school with like-minded peers.

Schools in turn were able to select families that enabled them to produce higher test-scores and hence greater academic success. A good portion of these outcomes were predetermined by the selection of parents and their children though clearly more able, prepared, and motivated students may help schools to recruit higher quality teachers and administrative staff. As I sometimes like to say, economists want to rule out selection as a methodological nuisance while sociologists regard selection as a fundamental social process that must be studied as a central feature of how things happen. In any event, social life is created by multiple and interacting influences that generally come in packages rather than operate as particular or singular influences as they are studied in experimental designs.

This is one of the larger lessons learned from the extensive experimental work on Moving to Opportunity, the government research study, that has followed families who participated in a random assignment experiment of public housing recipients who were given the opportunity to move to lower-poverty neighborhoods. Moving to lower poverty neighborhoods was not an event, as the researchers tended to regard it from the onset, but a succession of adaptations and interpretations that influenced its impact on particular family members differently depending on experiences prior to moving, new and old social networks, and demographic and unmeasured psychological characteristics of the movers and stayers. The net effects—important to policy makers—conceal a huge range of varied responses that unfortunately are only dimly understood.

SOCIAL REDUNDANCY IN MULTIPLE CONTEXTS

Perhaps, what I have written thus far might lead to the impression that opportunities at the family, school, and neighborhood levels are strongly correlated. However, important work by Tom Cook and his colleagues in their study of families in Prince Georges County reveals that, at an individual level, most children experience something of a mixture of social opportunities (Cook et al. 2002). There is only a modest correlation between the quality of parental resources, school resources, and neighborhood resources—surely the opposite conclusion from the idea that children grow up in an environment of class congruent settings.

However, the research by Cook and his colleagues also reveals that at the population level—when family characteristics, school, and neighborhood quality are considered in the aggregate—there is a much more powerful correlation among these arenas of social stratification. On average, children from better endowed families are very likely to attend better schools and live in better neighborhoods. It is as if the playing field for families is tilted in ways that are barely visible to the naked eye. Another way of looking at the stratification of social space is to imagine that families with more resources are able to arrange the world so that their children will have to be only ordinarily motivated and talented to succeed. Those with fewer resources are called upon to make more effort or have greater talent to succeed. Those with limited or meager resources must be highly gifted and super-motivated to achieve at a comparable levels. Developmentalists have often implicitly acknowledged the way the world works by valorizing the families and children that do manage to swim against the current, but we should be measuring the current as well as the swimmer's efforts, especially because there is every reason to believe that the current has become stronger in recent years.

Opportunity structures, made up of multiple and overlapping environments shaped by social position, are not accurately apprehended by individuals from different vantage points in the social system. They can only be understood by examining simultaneously what families see and respond to in their familiar settings, what they do not see but can be seen by other observers, and—most difficult of all—seeing what is *not* there. Take, for example, how much parents or children know about colleges and how they work. Most children in affluent families know more about this topic at age twelve, I would guess, than children in working class families when they are ready to enter college. Cultural capital—knowledge of how the world works—is acquired like vocabulary and speech practices in the family, schools, and from peers in the community (Bourdieu 1973, 1986; Lamont 2000; Laureau 1989, 2003). Class differences result from a process of social redundancy that exposes children to information, ideas, expectations, and navigational tools leading some children to know what they must do to get ahead and others merely to think that they know what to do. Cultural knowledge of the way the world works has surely been studied by developmentalists but we have a long way to go before we have a good map of what is and is not known by parents and children about the stratification system and how this knowledge changes over time as young people's impressions of how things work run up against how they actually work. With relatively few exceptions (Edin and Kefalas 2005; Newman 1993; Burton and Stack 1993), we lack the kinds of cultural studies that peered inside the family, looking at the culture of families, that were far more common among past generations of social researchers.

THE SOCIAL CLASS DISTRIBUTION OF OBSTACLES

Social class position not only structures variations in opportunities for advancement, it also greatly influences the probability of untoward events and circumstances in the lives of children and their families. The likelihood of bad things happening to people varies enormously by social class though we know this more from inference and anecdote than we do from systematic studies of children's experiences in the course of growing up. Take, for example, the inventory of life events associated with sources of psychological stressors including mortality, serious morbidity, accidents, family dissolution, residential changes, job loss, and so on. Virtually all of these events occur much more frequently in highly disadvantaged than moderately advantaged families and least of all among the most privileged. Problems are more likely to happen to families who lack the educational, cultural, and social capital that 1 mentioned earlier. Lower-income families are more vulnerable than higher income-families to a host of troubles from credit loss, health problems, transportation breakdown, criminal victimization, divorce, mental health problems, and the list goes on. They also have fewer resources to prevent problems from happening in the first place by anticipating them or nipping them in the bud (preventive and ameliorative interventions). And, when they do occur, social class affects a family's ability to cushion their blow.

Anyone who has studied low-income households, as I have for so many decades, cannot help but notice that there is a steady stream of these events which constantly unsettle family functioning, requiring time, energy, and resources that often are in short supply or altogether unavailable. Life is simply harder and more brutish at the bottom, and, I suspect, it is more precarious in the middle than we ordinarily image. As developmentalists, I don't think that we have done a very good job in evaluating how such events affect the lives and life chances of children. They create wear and tear on families and often ignite a succession of subsequent difficulties. The problems may begin with job loss, which in turn results in marital strife or dissolution, and finally settle into long-term mental illness or substance abuse. Or this chain of events can just as easily be reversed. The point is that in the ordinary course of life, children at different social strata face vastly different probabilities of bad things happening to them and their parents and these events not infrequently spiral out of control.

Having spent part of my career examining the impact of marital disruption on children, I know all too well the difficulties of studying even single negative events if only because they are usually preceded and followed by other adversities. It clearly behooves us to give greater attention to the ways that these events are distributed and clustered in the lives of children and families. Social scientists are accustomed to describing these behaviors as "non-normative" events, but they may only be "non-normative"—at least in the statistical sense—in the lives of affluent families.

CLASS DIFFERENCES IN PROBLEM PREVENTION AND REMEDIATION

The distribution of obstacles, as I have suggested above, is negatively correlated with social class just as the distribution of means to prevent and remediate troubles is negatively related to class. Affluent families have access to a tremendous range of strategies for prevention. They purchase and practice preventive healthcare, they situate themselves in environments free of toxins, and their homes and streets are safer; when and if their children experience problems in school, they can exercise a range of actions from changing schools to procuring help in the form of tutoring, assessments, therapy, medication and so on. If their children happen to get in trouble in the community, they have means to minimize the trouble using informal contacts or legal interventions. We know a lot about the employment of these preventive and remedial strategies, but we have yet to put together a comprehensive picture of how troubles are avoided and deflected for children in different social classes. If we examined a sample of problem behaviors among adolescents, what would be the likelihood of adverse outcomes occurring from a series of incidents?

The criminological literature provides ample evidence that class (and race/ethnicity as well) accounts for a huge amount of the variation in outcomes of delinquency, for example. It is not that adolescents from affluent families do not commit delinquent acts, use drugs and alcohol, and engage in risky sex. Indeed, the evidence suggests that so-called problem behaviors are fairly evenly distributed by social class. However, the consequences of similar actions differ greatly by the capacities that families have to avert the negative sanctions that may follow or to avoid their adverse consequences. Families with greater assets and social connections can minimize the significance of troubles even when they occur, especially the more extreme sanctions such as going to court and being sentenced to incarceration.

Social class then provides a form of cover from negative events when they do occur. It provides a social airbrush for the privileged concealing mistakes and missteps that invariably occur in the course of growing up. The management of problem behavior by families, their access and use of professional delegates (doctors, lawyers, tutors, social service workers) across different social classes represents a neglected topic in adolescent development.

SOCIAL CLASS, SOCIAL CAPITAL AND SPONSORSHIP

We would miss a lot about the use of professional and non-professional agents in children's lives among different social classes were we to confine our attention to their role in problem intervention and remediation. This topic represents a broader exercise of what has come to be called social capital, the social resources that can be brought to bear by families, to promote positive development as well as prevent or correct negative courses of action. Recently, there has been considerable interest in mentoring and the roles that mentors play in children's development, especially in helping children who have limited access to positive role models, advisors, supporters and advocates, and sponsors.

Sponsors, of course, can be family members, but we generally think of them as agents outside the family who act on the behalf of children. They can be gatekeepers in institutions that allocate resources and access to programs, services and opportunities. More often, they are individuals who have connections to a range of different gatekeepers. Students of child and adolescent development know a lot less about how sponsorship operates in every day life than we should because it undoubtedly plays an important part in channeling children into successful pathways.

We know only a little bit about how various adults help to cultivate skills, talents, and special abilities such as art, music, theater, sports, and so on, but much less how sponsors operate to promote children's chances of getting ahead by non-academic means or in combination with formal schooling. This topic merits greater attention because, as I've said, sponsors can play an important role in facilitating social mobility. Less visible but perhaps equally prominent is the role that sponsors have in helping to guarantee that children in the more affluent classes retain their privileged position.

Some research exists on how young people enter the world of work and the role that families play in using contacts and connections to place adolescents in training, service, and work opportunities. Privileged parents understand that their children need to build portfolios of experience—resumes—in order to get ahead. Our research in Philadelphia on the less advantaged and the disadvantaged suggests much less understanding on the part of parents in how to connect their children to select institutions. Usually, it appears that children from less advantaged families are identified by sponsors by dint of their good efforts in school or perhaps community organizations. However, affluent parents do not simply rely on their children to attract sponsors.

They actively recruit them or place their children in organizations, programs, and social arenas where sponsors are present and looking for motivated and talented prospects. Schools with well developed extra-curricular programs, after-school classes and activities, summer camps and educational courses are part of the stock and trade of growing up well off. Children in affluent families become practiced in relating to adults and in appreciating what adult sponsors, mentors, and coaches can do for them in middle childhood and adolescence. Increasingly, I would argue, the role of sponsors figures prominently in young people's ability to navigate successfully as they move from adolescence into early adulthood.

EARLY ADULTHOOD: THE EXTENSION OF INVESTMENT

Early adulthood, the period of life when youth enter adult roles and assume adult responsibilities—entering the labor force and becoming economically self-sufficient and forming families—has in recent decades become a less orderly and more protracted process than it was a half century ago. The driving force in the extension of the passage to adulthood has been the perceived need for a college education and, for the more privileged, an advanced degree often accompanied by a lengthy apprenticeship in a professional career. Related to this trend but not wholly because of it, young people put off more permanent relationship commitments and, generally, parenthood as well. Commitments to marriage and children, public opinion tells us, have become almost a second stage of the adult transition, often put off until education has been completed and some measure of job security is attained (Furstenberg et al. 1999; Settersten, Furstenberg, and Rumbaut 2005). Social class differences are no less prominent in this new stage of life than they are during childhood or adolescence. The current demands on young adults to attain more skills, be better prepared to enter the labor force, and postpone family formation play out quite differently in advantaged, middle-class, and disadvantaged families.

Let's begin with the obvious: the costs of higher education have become less and less affordable as grants and loans have not kept pace with college tuitions, much less the cost of professional education. Among families at the bottom of the income distribution, the debt taken on by parents and young adults can be crippling even though the long-term payoff theoretically makes borrowing for education economically rational (Rouse 2004). Add to the economic problems the academic liabilities that many, if not most, youth from disadvantaged families have accumulated in school brings us to the obvious fact that a very small proportion are academically, much less financially prepared to endure a lengthy period of working and attending school (usually beginning with community college) as they work their way through college. It happens, but relatively rarely. Other events intrude: attachment to college is difficult in most community institutions because they lack the supportive staff and assistance offered by four-year institutions; financial crises arise siphoning off needed resources, parents cannot or will not offer aid or require support themselves, and so on.

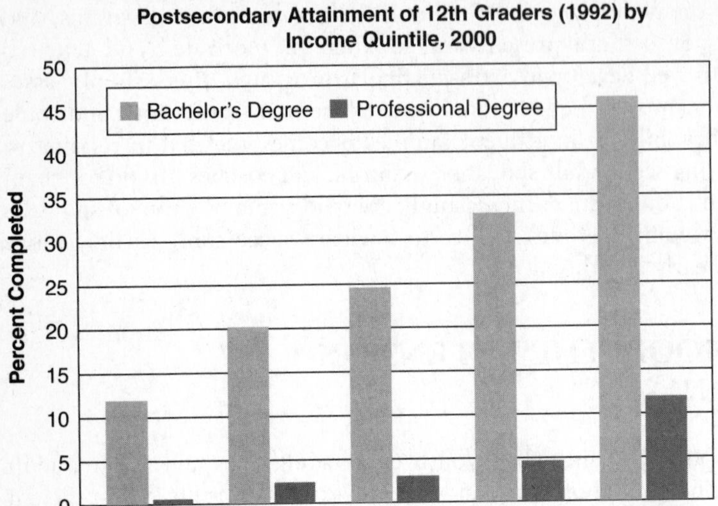

Income Quintile	*Bachelor's Degree*	*Professional Degree*
Lowest Quintile	11.9	0.6
Second Quintile	20.2	2.4
Third Quintile	24.6	3.0
Fourth Quintile	33.0	4.6
Highest Quintile	46.2	11.9

From Table 1, Postsecondary Attainment, Attendance, Curriculum and Performance: Selected Results from the NELS:88/2000 Postsecondary Education Transcript Study (PETS), 2000 (NCES 2003-394)

Basically, among 12th graders likely to go to college, about 1 in 8 of those from families in the lowest quintile completed college compared to nearly 1 in 2 of those from families in the highest quintile. Only 1 in 4 of those in the middle quintile completed college.

Among middle-class families—let's say the third income quintile that ranges from $43,400 to $65,832 in 2004 (Census Historical Income Tables, Table F-1) few young adults can afford higher education without paying for it by working at the same time. Balancing school and work commitments in early adulthood is not an easy task, leading to high rates of school stop out and dropout. Thus, even when preparation for college is adequate and grants and loans can be managed, the process can be arduous and lengthy, partially accounting for the exceptionally high rates of some college—persons attending but not completing their college education—in the U.S. Many young people who enter college settle for, willingly or not, what amounts to post-secondary, technical training, often restricting mobility in their adult years.

The situation of the affluent families permits much greater latitude for families to help out during a longer and longer period of training. The prospect of attaining a high income job in the future, along with assistance offered by parents, sustains young adults through college and into professional careers. No doubt, too, young adults from affluent families who are generally better prepared academically are far more likely to qualify for financial aid packages that require taking on less debt.

Of course, this class-based profile is stereotypical to some degree. Talented individuals do rise from the bottom and untalented youth drift down. However, the social class mechanisms that I have described in this paper continue to play out during this period. The accumulation of deficits, the likelihood of problematic events, the availability of social capital and sponsorship continue to tilt the playing field as youth enter institutions with different levels of selectivity or work situations that permit or thwart opportunities for attaining further human capital.

I cannot leave the topic of early adulthood without mentioning how social class exposure in childhood, adolescence, and early adulthood affects partnerships and family formation. We have always known that social class is linked to the quality and stability of marriage though there was a time when divorce (not separation or marital unhappiness) occurred more frequently among the better off. This has not been true for some decades. Lower human capital is related to lower social, cultural, and psychological capital—the skills, knowledge of the world, social networks, and sponsorship all of which play some part in the ability to manage and sustain emotional relationships. Striking differences emerge in the occurrence of marriage, its stability, and in the incidence of non-marital childbearing by social class (Ellwood and Jencks, 2001; Goldstein and Kenney 2001; Wu and Wolfe 2001).

These family patterns, so closely linked to class-related experiences in growing up, figure prominently in public discussions about the retreat from marriage among Americans. Curiously, the retreat has not occurred at all among the privileged and less so in the middle-class. Marriage, as I've written elsewhere, is increasingly a luxury good attainable only by those with the social, psychological, and material goods that make it happen and make it work.

References

Bendix, Reinhard, and Seymour Martin Lipset. 1966. *Class, Status, and Power.* New York: The Free Press.

Bernstein, Basil and Dorothy Henderson. 1969. "Social Class Differences and the Relevance of Language to Socialization. *Sociology.* 3(1): 1–20.

Bernstein, Basil. 1971. *Class, Codes and Control: Theoretical Studies towards a Sociology of Language, Volume 1.* London: Routledge & Kegan Paul.

Blood, R. O., and D. Wolfe. 1960. *Husbands and Wives: The Dynamics of Married Living.* New York: The Free Press.

Bourdieu, Pierre. 1973. "Cultural Reproduction and Social Reproduction." In R. Brown (ed.), *Knowledge, Education, and Cultural Change.* London: Tavistock.

_____. 1986. "The Forms of Capital." In J. C. Richardson (ed.), *Handbook of Theory and Research for the Sociology of Education.* New York: Greenwood.

Bronfenbrenner, Uri. 1979. *The Ecology of Human Development: Experiments by Nature and Design.* Cambridge, MA: Harvard University Press.

Buchmann, Marlis. 1989. *The Script of Life in Modern Society: Entry into Adulthood in a Changing World.* Chicago: University of Chicago Press.

Burton, Linda and Carol Stack. 1993. "Conscripting kin: Reflections on family, generation, and culture." In *Family, self, and society: Toward a new agenda for family research.* Cowan, Philip A.; Dorothy Field; Donald A. Hansen; Arlene Skolnick; and Guy E. Swanson (Eds). Hillsdale, NJ: Lawrence Erlbaum Associates.

Chaudry, Ajay. 2004. *Putting Children First: How Low-Income Working Mothers Manage Child Care.* New York: Russell Sage Foundation.

Cook, T.D., M. Herman, M. Phillips, and R.J. Setterson, Jr. 2002. "Some ways in which neighborhoods, nuclear families, friendship groups, and schools jointly affect changes in early adolescent development." *Child Development* 73(4): 1283–1309.

Cooley, Charles H. 1902. *Human nature and the social order.* New York: Scribners and Company.

Danziger, Sheldon H. and Peter Gottschalk. 1995. *America Unequal.* New York: Russell Sage Foundation.

Danziger, Sheldon H. and Jane Waldfogel. 2000. *Securing the Future: Investing in Children from Birth to College.* New York: Russell Sage Foundation.

Duncan, Greg J., W. Jean Yeung, Jeanne Brooks-Gunn and Judith R. Smith. 1998. "How much does childhood poverty affect the life chances of children?" *American Sociological Review.* 63(3): 406–423.

Duncan, Greg and Jeanne Brooks-Gunn. 2000. *From Neurons to Neighborhoods: The Science of Early Childhood Development.* Washington, DC: National Academy Press.

Edin, Kathryn J. and Maria Kefalas. 2005. *Promises I Can Keep: Why Low-Income Women Put Motherhood Before Marriage* (Berkeley, CA: University of California Press)

Elder, Glen H., Jr. 1974. *Children of the Great Depression: Social change in life experience.* Chicago: University of Chicago Press. (Reissued as 25th Anniversary Edition, Boulder, CO: Westview Press, 1999).

Elwood, David T. and Christopher Jencks. 2001. "The Spread of Single-Parent Families in the United States since 1960." Cambridge, MA: John F, Kennedy School of Government, Harvard University.

Farkas, George and Kurt Beron. 2004. "The detailed age trajectory of oral vocabulary knowledge: differences by class and race." *Social Science Research* 33(3): 464–497.

Furstenberg, Jr., Frank F., Thomas D. Cook, Jacquelynne Eccles, Glen H. Edler, Jr., 1999. *Managing to Make It: Urban Families and Adolescent Outcomes.* (The John D. and Catherine T. MacArthur Foundation Series on Mental Health and Development). Chicago: University of Chicago Press.

Gans, Herbert J. 1962. *The Urban Villagers. New York: The Free Press.*

Garmezy, Norman. 1991. "Resilience and Vulnerability to adverse developmental outcomes associated with poverty." *American Behavioral Scientist.* 34(4): 416–430.

Garmezy, Norman. 1993. "Vulnerability and Resilience." In *Studying Lives through Time: Personality and Development.* David C. Funder; Ross D. Parke; Carol Tomlinson-Keasey; Keith Widaman (eds). Washington, DC: American Psychological Association, pp. 377–398.

Goldstein, Joshua R. and Catherine T. Kenney. 2001. "Marriage Delayed or Marriage Forgone? New Cohort Forecasts of First Marriage for U.S. Women." *American Sociological Review.* 66(4): 506–519.

Goldthorpe, J. and R. Erickson. 1993. *The constant flux: a study of class mobility in industrial societies.* Oxford: Oxford University Press.

Haggerty, R. J., L. R. Sherrod, N. Garmezy, and M. Rutter. 1994. *Stress, Risk, and Resilience in Children and Adolescents.* New York: Cambridge University Press.

Hart, Betty and Todd R. Risley. 1995. *Meaningful Differences in the everyday experiences of young American Children.* Baltimore, MD: Paul H. Brookes Publishing.

Heath, Shirley B. 1983. *Ways with Words: Language, Life and Work in Communities and Classrooms.* New York: Cambridge University Press.

Heinz, Walter R. and Victor W. Marshall (eds). 2003. *Social Dynamics of the Life Course: Transitions, Institutions and Interrelations.* Hawthorne, NY: Aldine De Gruyter.

Hertz, Tom. 2005. "Rags, Riches and Race: The Intergenerational Economic Mobility of Black and White Families in the United States." In Samuel Bowles, Herbert Gintis and Melissa Osborne Groves (eds.) *Unequal Chances: Family Background and Economic Success.* Princeton, NJ: Princeton University Press.

Hollingshead, A. de B. 1949. *Elmtown's Youth: The Impact of Social Classes on Adolescents.* New York: Wiley.

Komarovsky, Mira. 1987. *Blue-Collar Marriage.* 2nd. ed. New Haven, CT: Yale University Press.

Kefalas, Maria. 2003. *Working Class Heroes: Protecting Home, Community and Nation in a Chicago Neighborhood.* Berkeley, CA: University of California Press.

Kohn, Melvin L. 1977. *Class and Conformity: A Study in Values (with a reassessment).* 2nd edition. Chicago: University of Chicago Press.

Lamont, Michele. 2000. *The Dignity of Working Men: Morality and the Boundaries of Race, Class and Immigration.* Cambridge, MA: Harvard University Press.

Lareau, Annette. 1989. Home Advantage: Social Class and Parental Intervention in Elementary Education. New York: Falmer Press. (2nd Edition, 2000. Lanham, MD: Rowman and Littlefield Press).

Lareau, Annette. 2003. Unequal Childhoods: Race, Class and Family Life. Berkeley, CA: University of California Press.

Levy, Frank. 1999. *The New Dollars and Dreams.* New York: Russell Sage Foundation.

Lynd, Robert S. and Helen M. Lynd. 1929. *Middletown: A Study in Contemporary American Culture.* New York: Harcourt Brace & Company.

McLanahan, Sara. 2004. "Diverging Destinies: How Children Fare Under the Second Demographic Transition." *Demography* 41(4):607–627.

READING 24

Ties that Bind: Cultural Interpretations of Delayed Adulthood in Western Europe and Japan

Katherine S. Newman

INTRODUCTION

On a warm spring day in 2003, I settled into a long lunch at a lovely restaurant in Madrid. I was in the company of faculty and administrators of a social science research center that was considering membership in an international network of scholars devoted to the study of inequality. As a complete newcomer to the Spanish research scene, this was my one opportunity to establish an intellectual connection and enough of a personal tie to smooth the way for our graduate students to "apprentice" at the institute. Our conversation moved easily back and forth from our work to our lives. They talked about the long reach of Franco's regime into Spanish universities and the important role autonomous institutions like theirs had played in keeping social science alive during the fascist regime. I talked about my research on the working poor in U.S. inner cities.

After the third glass of wine, the table talk migrated to family. The elegant administrator sitting next to me, a woman in her late 50s, spoke affectionately of her 33-year-old son who lived with her while working a full-time job in the center of Madrid. Like most other mothers of her generation, she maintained full responsibility for running the household, including tending to her son's meals and his laundry, among other mundane needs. Her Spanish colleagues nodded in recognition and seemed to think the arrangement was business as usual. Taken aback by the idea of a child of such advanced age living with his parents, I asked as casually as I could what it was like to have her son at home. "Why would he ever want to leave me?" she asked in reply.

A month later, I was seated next to a beautiful canal in the center of Aarhus, the second largest city in Denmark. My dinner partner was a lawyer and part-time judge, the older brother of a good friend from my graduate school years. I had come to Aarhus to engage colleagues in political science and economics with the same network, but took the evening off to visit with this distant connection. We, too, talked about our work, but migrated naturally to the topic of our children. My youngest was in middle school with six years to go before he would leave home for college; my companion's youngest son no longer lived at home because he decided he wanted to pursue a special certificate offered at a high school located in another city, too far from Aarhus to commute. His son packed up, moved to the city to enroll in his new high school, applied for a government stipend to meet his living needs, and found a roof over his head with the help of the municipal housing office: all at age 16.

As Figure 24.1 makes clear, a sharp divergence has emerged between the northern and southern European countries with respect to the residential choices of young adults. Indeed, today over 50% of the working men age 24–29 in Spain, Italy, and most of the other southern European countries still live in their natal homes. Clearly, my Spanish dinner partners were not unusual. Neither was the Danish lawyer.

These two extremes—delayed departure and early independence—are coming to define a set of trends in the formation of households that has caught the attention of

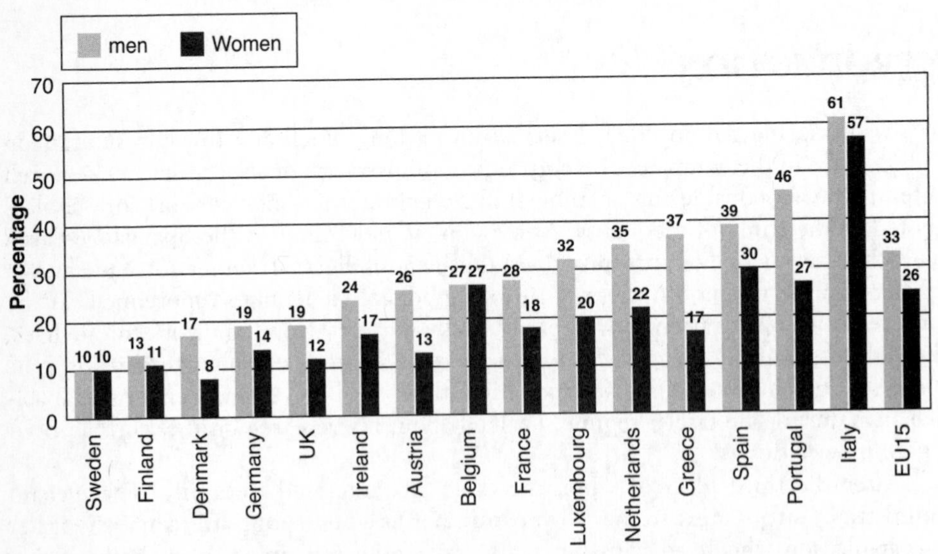

FIGURE 24.1 ***Percentage of young people (18–34) living with parents without partner or children.***

demographers and sociologists (Aassve *et al.*, 2001; Billari, 2004; Cherlin *et al.*, 1997; Cook and Furstenberg, 2002). Increasingly in the advanced, postindustrial world, we are seeing a prolonged stay in the family home become the norm in countries with weak welfare states, high housing costs, and increasingly rocky pathways into the labor market for "young" people. At the other end of the universe, mainly in the social democracies, we see state-subsidized experiments in independence, modern-day continuations of home leaving that have been the hallmark of northern European countries as far back as the Middle Ages, when unmarried youth left their homes to work as servants in the homes of the wealthy.

Perhaps the most extreme example of delayed departure is to be found in Japan. Among unmarried men age 30–34, over 60% live with their parents; 70% of unmarried women in this age group live at home as well. The proportions are even higher for unmarrieds in younger age groups (e.g., 25–29, where the number rises to 80% of women and 64% of men).[1] In many cultures, including Japan, the custom is for young men and women to remain with their parents until they marry. In the Japanese case, though, the age of marriage has been rising steadily. In 2006, the mean age at marriage was 28 for women and 30 for men (Ministry of International Affairs and Communication, 2007), the highest in the developed world.

Why have these divergent patterns developed and what do they mean for citizens, young and old, in Europe and Japan? The first question is fairly easily answered by a quick review of the changing economic context of adulthood in southern Europe and Japan. The second is more complex and requires a comparative, qualitative approach designed to uncover the emergent subjective, culturally inflected understandings of autonomy and independence, of the appropriate forms of support—material and moral—that define the relationship between parents and their adult children.

THE "PRICE OF INDEPENDENCE"[2]

Several interconnected economic trends have conspired to limit the residential options of young adults in southern Europe and Japan. Foremost among them are deleterious labor market conditions. Unemployment has always been higher in southern Europe than in the north. But starting in the 1980s, the toll of globalization began to make itself felt more strongly, prompting governments in Spain, Japan, and elsewhere to loosen the controls that had long encouraged life-time employment. This gave firms the flexibility (for the first time) to employ workers on part-time or temporary contracts (Golsch, 2003; Kosugi, 2004). Older workers with a strong foothold in the labor market were largely able to avoid the consequences, but younger workers and job seekers quickly found themselves in an unfamiliar world. Today, for example, over one-third of Spanish workers overall are governed by short-term agreements, but well over 50% of Spanish male workers 25–29 years of age are subject to these less desirable work arrangements.

In Japan, a similar trend has emerged and has been popularly recognized by the term "freeters," denoting individuals between the ages of 15–34 who "neither go on to higher education nor become full time employees. They are most likely to work as part time employees under short or temporary employment contracts" (Katsumata, 2003:17). The category emerged on the national scene in the late 1980s when the "bubble economy"

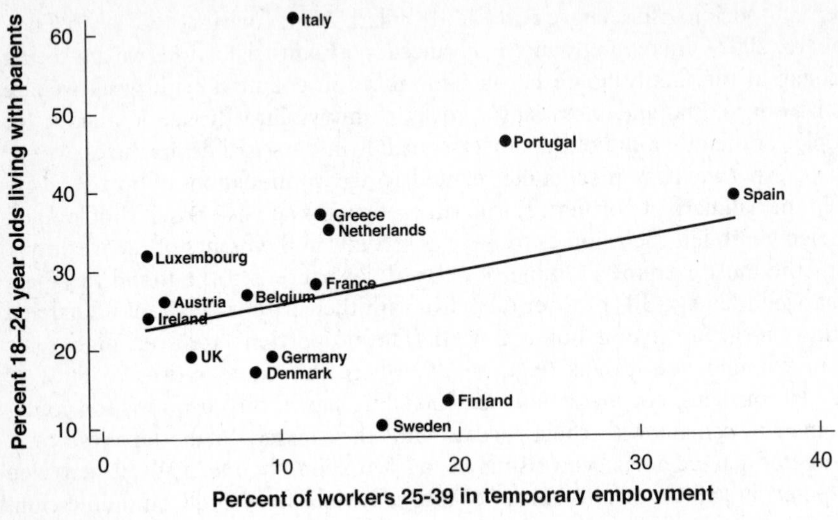

FIGURE 24.2 ***Proportion of 18–34-year-olds living with parents by proportion of young workers (aged 25–39) in temporary employment. Linear fit without Italy, R = .35.***
Source: Eurostat, Statistical Office of the European Communities (2003).

burst and, as in Spain, the government responded by liberalizing the terms of labor agreements (Kosugi, 2004). In 1982, there were an estimated 0.5 million freeters in Japan. By 2002, there were 2 million and rising (Ministry of Health, Labor and Welfare, 2003, cited in Honda, 2005:1).

Temporary employment is strongly associated with co-residence of young people with their parents. As Figure 24.2 suggests, even without including Italy (which is an extreme outlier), the $R = .35$. This would not be the case everywhere in the world, for in some countries (notably the United States), youth in a weak labor market position could elect a variety of residential options besides co-residence with their natal families. They could live with roommates, pool their income with romantic partners, or seek out rental housing in marginal neighborhoods. Remaining with Mom and Dad is hardly the only option. It is, however, for young people living in countries with very high levels of owner-occupied housing. As Figure 24.3 makes clear, the southern countries of Europe are heavily invested in owner-occupied housing. Over 85% of the population in Spain lives in owner-occupied housing, and Greece and Portugal are not far behind.

Home ownership in the Nordic countries, on the other hand, falls between 60–65% and the difference is made up by a large rental sector, much of it public housing regulated by the government. Rental stock is critical for young people striking out on their own without the savings necessary to buy their own homes. Banks are skeptical of their earning power, now sharply curtailed by temporary employment, and will not

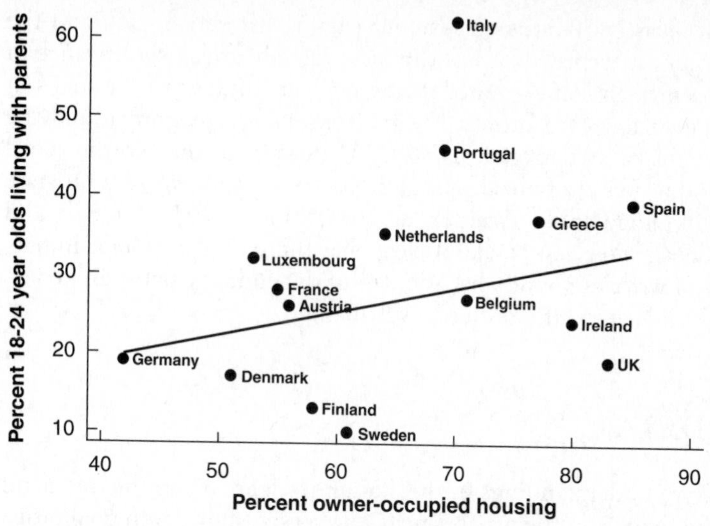

FIGURE 24.3 ***Proportion of 18–34-year-olds living with parents by percentage of owner-occupied housing. Linear fit without Italy, R = .37.***
Source: OECD Economic Review No. 38 2004/1.

lend them mortgage money. And compared to the United States where, until the subprime lending implosion of 2008, banks routinely agreed to lend 80–90% of the value of a home, European banks typically expect to lend only 50%, thus raising the stakes required for new entrants to the housing market.

These structural conditions are common to the southern European countries in Figure 24.1 and, taken together, it is hardly surprising that they produce a rising tendency for adults under the age of 40 to stick closer to home. The combination of labor market reforms that disadvantaged new entrants to the world of work (Golsch, 2003) and high levels of owner-occupied housing is toxic for young people desirous of residential independence (Holdsworth, 2000; Holdsworth and Solda, 2002).

We might expect this situation to produce a great deal of frustration as adults come to feel infantilized by their residential dependence or tension in households that have one too many adults for the social space available. Newman and Aptekar (2008) show that prolonged residence in the natal home does indeed produce dissatisfaction. Yet the more common the pattern, the less powerful the stigma. Indeed, as it becomes normative for adults in their 30s to live with their parents, the sense of being out of step with others of the same age recedes and some of the "silver lining" of co-residence becomes more salient. Indeed, survey data on life satisfaction indicates that southern Europeans see the bright side of "delayed departure" (Jurado Guerrero, 2001), even as governments go into overdrive trying to reverse the most troubling outcome: low fertility.

But there are significant variations across countries in life satisfaction and the differences reflect divergent interpretations of the meaning and social significance of prolonged quasi-adolescence. In some countries, these silver linings are the focus of attention when the issue surfaces. In others, the frustrations are magnified and the problem achieves the status of a "national disaster." Moreover, in the Nordic social welfare states, where young people typically leave home at 18 and can rely on state support to facilitate independence (Mulder and Manting, 1994; Mulder and Hooimeijer, 2002), in-depth interviews make it clear that there are "problems in paradise," an emergent set of worries about what the *lack* of dependency between generations means for social solidarity and emotional well-being.

COMPARATIVE DATA

To explore these subjective understandings of the "failure to launch" on the one hand and "accelerated independence" on the other, I turn now to set of in-depth qualitative interviews gathered by my research team[3] across four European countries and Japan in the summer of 2006.[4] With a total of 250 interviews across five countries, we cannot claim that these samples are representative in any definitive way. Yet considerable effort was made to draw the sample from different geographical regions (e.g., northern, southern, and central Italy, capital cities such as Madrid and Tokyo, rural regions in northern Spain and northern Sweden, wealthy areas, and poor regions such as Puglia in Italy). Conducted in homes and cafes in different regions of each country, by native speakers of the national language, the data incorporate the perspectives of parents and adult children in the same families wherever it proved possible and in different families where it was regarded as a breach of privacy to contact both parent and child in the same family.[5]

Table 24.1 presents a description of the interview sample. In the "delayed departure" countries of Spain, Italy, and Japan, the general emphasis was placed on sampling parents with adult children over the age of 22 in residence[6] and children who live at home, while a smaller proportion of the sample exemplifies the nonnormative status of independent children and their parents. The reverse was the case in the Nordic countries of Sweden and Denmark, where the majority of the sample consisted of nonresident children over the age of 22 and their parents and a "minority" population of resident children over 22 and their parents.[7]

SIGNS OF METAMORPHOSIS

The three countries I studied, where adults in their late 20s and early 30s are increasingly remaining in their natal homes—Spain, Italy, and Japan—share a striking similarity. Parents' memories of their own transition to adulthood suggest an abrupt transformation. But children's perceptions of the same process suggest a slow, undifferentiated metamorphosis. For the parents, there was a before (child-

TABLE 24.1 ***Sample Description***

	Italy	*Spain*	*Japan*	*Denmark*	*Sweden*
Total sample	52	50	50	49	51
Co-Residing Respondents					
Parents who live with adult children	9	22	19	2	5
Proportion of all parents	35%	88%	76%	8%	19%
Proportion of co-resident who are female	67%	68%	50%	100%	100%
Children who live with parents	9	17	20	4	4
Proportion of all children	35%	68%	80%	16%	16%
Proportion of co-residents who are female	33%	53%	58%	25%	75%
Independent Respondents					
Parents who live independently of adult children	17	3	6	22	21
Proportion of all parents	65%	12%	24%	92%	81%
Children who live independently of parents	17	8	5	21	21
Proportion of all children	65%	32%	20%	84%	84%
Ages of Respondents					
Mean age of all children*	28.5	27.1	27.8	25.7	22.4
Mean age of co-residing children	28.2	26.7	26.8	26.3	21.7
Mean age of independent children	28.7	28.0	31.6	25.6	22.5
Mean age of all parents**	57.2	54.9	56.5	53.1	57.3
Mean age of co-residing parents	56.1	55.1	55.4	61.0	50.0
Mean age of independent parents	57.8	53.7	60.2	52.7	57.8

*Age of children missing for 1/25 in Spain and 4/25 in Sweden.

**Age of parents missing for 3/25 in Spain; 1/24 in Denmark; 9/26 in Sweden.

hood) and an after (adulthood) that was marked by clear behavioral changes in their lives. For both mothers and fathers in Spain, marriage, full-time employment, and childbearing were the dividing lines.

> *Interviewer:* When you were young, what marked the change of growing up?
>
> *Respondent:* Having a job and . . . and getting independence. As soon as you had a job you were partly independent, obviously . . . The thing is that these days you are not independent because the money you earn doesn't allow you to pay for a house. And so you always have to depend on third parties, family members who have to help you. In the past they also had to help you, but not in the same way people have lo do it these days (Spain, Age 59, Male).

Another said:

> *Respondent:* I was marked by marriage. Totally. I married at 20, and that changed my life.
>
> *Interviewer:* That implied a change in your life.
>
> *Respondent:* Yes, totally. It was . . . the biggest change in my life; I think so, yes. (Spain, Age 45, Female)

In Japan as well, older men and women understood their lives as a set of marked status transitions with very clear lines that separated their youthful lives from their adult lives. Marriage was the essential boundary condition.

> Adulthood means that one can live a respectable life. For example, to fulfill social responsibilities. Only if one was raising children and leading a married life respectably, could one be considered an adult. (Japan, Age 69, Male)

Another said:

> Marriage was the only pathway for us to be an adult. Since marriage meant to leave your parents' home and become independent, in a sense, to live on your own. At that time, there were not many women who gained jobs. (Japan, Age 60, Female)

What does adulthood mean to the younger generation of mature adults who are living with their parents in these countries? How do they mark the transition to adulthood when many of the traditional markers—full-time jobs, independent residence, marriage are years off? First, they argued that there were no longer any behavioral markers of adulthood at all. Maturity is more of a feeling, a capacity to make decisions or take some greater degree of responsibility for their actions. Such a feeling can arise even inside the natal home where some of the more demanding responsibilities that come with economic independence are years away.

> *Interviewer:* So for you a person can be an adult, even if he lives with his parents . . .
>
> *Respondent:* He can be an adult, of course . . . Because in many cases you can't get independence before 30. I don't consider that they aren't adults. The main thing is that you take your responsibilities, that you assume your actions, and that you don't depend on your parents for everything. (Spain, Age 25, Male)

The transition to adulthood has many more stages and none are canonical or socially recognized. The "fits and starts" quality of the change leaves a great deal of room for ambiguity and, indeed, ambiguity is the pronounced cultural ethos. Our interviewees in their 20s and 30s are aware that their parents' generation could rely on publicly acknowledged markers of status transitions and cannot completely shake the notion that they should have some as well, even if they are different in kind. But they do not have them and, as a result, Spanish and Japanese people in their late 20s are unsure about how to locate themselves along the adolescent/adulthood continuum. They know they are not teenagers any more; but they do not see themselves as full fledged grownups either.

"When I was in high school," a Japanese woman of 28 told us, "college students seemed to be very adult . . ."

> But when I became a college student, I did not feel I was an adult in particular. Then I thought if I began work, I might feel that I was an adult. But after actually beginning work, I still do not feel I am an adult. Of course I think having social responsibility means adulthood, and in that sense I now have that responsibility. And I look like an adult in appearance, but I do not have any sense that I am an adult.

The mix of roles she inhabits (a worker, who is old enough to be a mother, but one who is unmarried and lives at home) leads to an ambiguous placement in the spectrum of roles in a society that has, until her generation, had very clear criteria for social placement.

Given the structural barriers that prevent Japanese and Spanish young people from striking out on their own, we might imagine that the opposite situation would prevail in the Nordic countries. After all, early departure from the family home is the norm and none of our informants indicated it was a high hurdle. Educational benefits are generous, transitional housing (dormitories, rental housing, public housing) is plentiful, and the expectations for residential autonomy are widespread. Parents rarely express any reservations about letting their children fly from the nest. If anything, they are urged to strike out on their own and people who remain with their parents after the age of 18 are regarded as oddballs. "The safety nets we have developed through the Nordic welfare political approach have really made a difference," one 50-year-old Swedish mother explained.

> I guess that is an incentive for our whole welfare politics, that you don't have to be dependent over the generations . . . According to our values, you shouldn't stay at home too long. You're supposed to go out and support your self, live on your own.

She knows what she is talking about because she, too, left home at an early age. Unlike the Japanese or the Spaniards, for whom the parental experience of independence (early residential autonomy following early marriage) was very different from that of their adult children (late residential independence and very late marriage), the Nordic model has been in place for at least three generations, if not even longer. In the period before World War II, when Sweden was a more agrarian society than it is today, remaining at home until marriage—which came fairly late—was normative. But Swedish society is far more urbanized today and has been for decades now. The welfare state supports that underwrite experiments in youthful independence have been in place a long time and hence the experience of the adjacent generations interviewed for this project is very similar.

Given this continuity, one might expect a similar conception of the transition to adulthood to hold across the living generations. Not so fast. Our interviews suggest that in Sweden and Denmark, the younger generation is closer to their age mates in Japan and Spain: migrating slowly toward a sense of independence, rather than experiencing a sharp before and after. Despite a very high rate of residential autonomy, Nordic 20-somethings still feel that they are gradually—and through many undetermined stages migrating toward adulthood. Why the similarity with societies that throw structural roadblocks in the way of residential independence?

First, our interviews made it clear that though Danish and Swedish young people move out, they do not necessarily move very far. Many Scandinavian young adults live near their natal homes, even if they inhabit separate dwellings. Often, they live across the street and continue to take meals with their families, particularly in the 18–20-year-old period. Second, Nordic countries are among the world's most generous "education states," and keep their young people in school for a longer period of time than virtually any other part of the world (Nilsson and Strandh, 1999). As Figure 24. 4 shows, the Netherlands, Denmark, Sweden, Finland, and Norway have the highest proportion of people in the 18–24 age group in school compared to rest of Europe. To the extent that being a student is a disqualification for adulthood, it is little surprise that they see themselves as autonomous from their families, but not fully responsible for themselves.

Yet it would be a mistake to fully equate the southern and northern Europeans in the way they think about adulthood, for in a number of critical ways they experience the slow movement toward independence differently. In the south, dependence on the family for one's economic survival is very pronounced, while in the north, this tie is far weaker, replaced by part-time earnings and reliance on the state (in the form of education aid). Figure 24.5 shows very high and increasing—levels of economic dependence of 18–24-year-olds on parental support in the south, while extremely low and in two cases falling levels of parental responsibility for children's support in the Nordic countries. Moreover, as Figure 24.6 makes clear, partnership (mainly cohabitation) is much higher in the north than the south, again suggesting a greater degree of separation from the natal home, but one that occurs in a gradual fashion in terms of individual economic self-reliance.

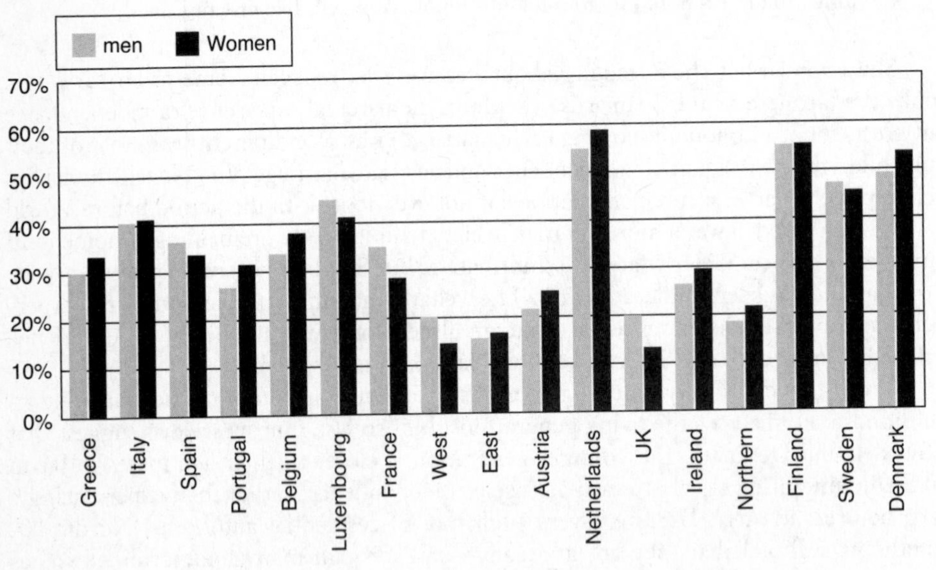

FIGURE 24.4 ***Percentage of 18–24-year-olds who are students in 2001, by sex.***

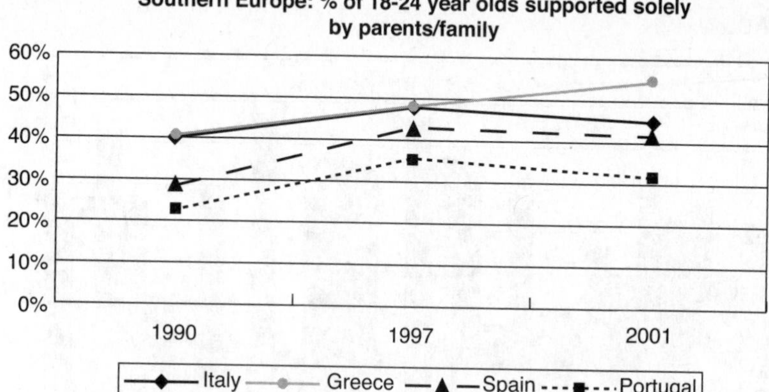

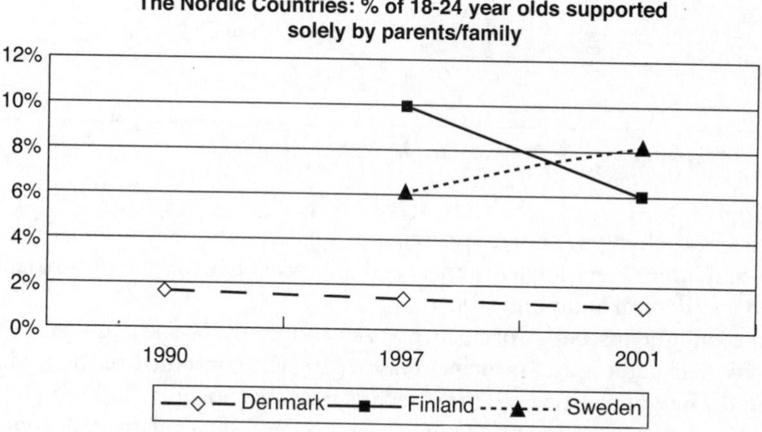

FIGURE 24.5 ***Percentage of 18–24-year-olds supported solely by parents/family: southern Europe versus Nordic countries.***

WHY DID EVERYTHING CHANGE?

Having established that there are significant differences "on the ground" in the process and pace of the movement toward adulthood, it remains to understand why the change took place. The demographic facts point toward an overdetermined outcome as has already been explained. But the subjective explanation for the change is another matter.

The Spanish parents in this study grew up under Francisco Franco, whose traditional, authoritarian rule forms a vivid backdrop to the present. Under Franco, birth control was illegal, as was cohabitation. Early marriage and childbearing, supported by the Catholic Church and the government, was expected and no alternatives were acceptable. Franco's death, in 1975, brought this period to an end, but bequeathed to the modern era

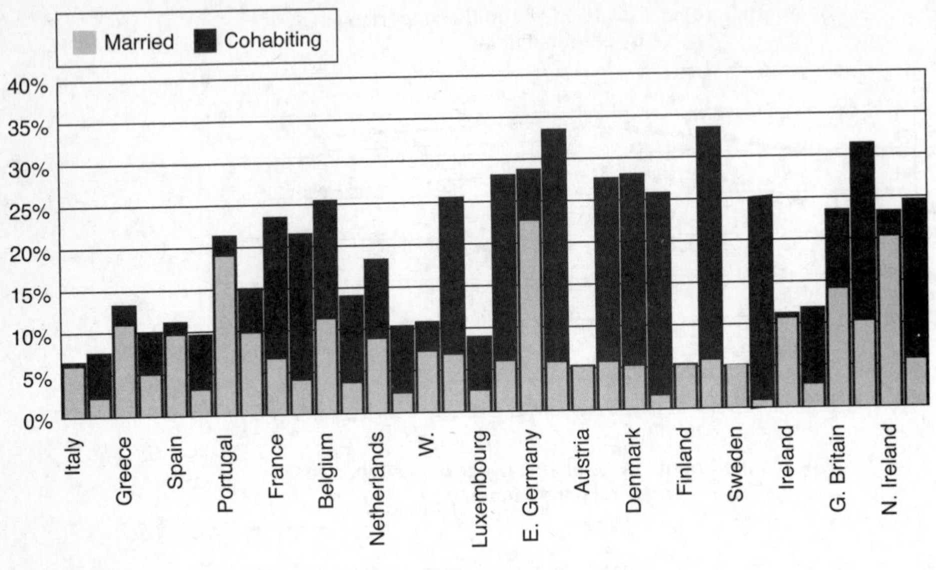

FIGURE 24.6 ***Partnership among 18–24-year-olds in 1990 and 2001.***

two fundamental cultural changes: (1) an appreciation for flexibility and intimacy (as opposed to rigidity and intergenerational distance) and (2) a tendency to explain personal experience through a structural and political lens.

The growing economic insecurity of Spain's workers in their 20s and 30s is recognized very clearly by their parents as a principal reason for their continued residence in the family home. And what, in turn, caused the insecurity? As this Spanish mother in her late 50s explained, it was the government. "When I was young," she explained, "people got independence earlier."

> As soon as you entered a slightly strong company, you already knew that you had . . . [security] like a civil servant. You could search for housing in a particular area, because you knew "I work here." But nowadays you never know. Perhaps you're working one year and perhaps on the next year you are on a different job. And with these rubbish contracts, people can never get independence. You find people in their 30's and 40's at home. But it is not because they don't want to . . . It is only because you can't leave.

The "rubbish contracts" she derides did not come out of thin air; they resulted from legislation passed by the Spanish government intent on providing firms greater flexibility as a way of responding to globalization pressures. An elongated system of higher education that is not matched by professional job opportunities leaves Spanish workers overqualified for the jobs that are available and frustrated by the gap between their expectations and the realities coming their way.

Neither the parents nor the adult children turn inward to discover the cause of their distress; they look over their shoulders to the government, the corporate world, to elites and other powerful actors who have shaped their options from the top down. Indeed, in 2007, there were sit-down strikes in the middle of Madrid protesting high housing prices and demanding government intervention on behalf of young people who are on the losing end of a ferociously expensive housing market.

The Japanese explanation for the prolonged dependence could not be more divergent. Despite the fact that Japan experienced a bubble economy that contracted sharply, raising unemployment and creating the conditions for the emergence of the temporary worker—the freeter noted earlier—the narratives that account for changing patterns of adulthood make virtually no reference to these structural conditions.

Instead, like the Americans profiled by Newman (1993) 15 years ago, who were trying to explain intergenerational downward mobility and the "failure" of young people to become more autonomous from their parents, the Japanese turn to a moral narrative of blame. Mothers and fathers argued that the younger generation is spoiled by affluence, paralyzed by a surplus of choices, and has emerged into their late 20s in defective condition. How did this sorry state of affairs come to be? "We did it," answer the baby boom parents.

> Because our time was very tough, our generation has spoiled our children, in disciplining and educating them at home. What we see in society now is the result of that. We baby boomers went through a hard time. So we wanted to make the life of our children easy—I think this was true in any family. I think that the major portion of the problems of youth now is derived from our generation. We are responsible for it, for example, in terms of disciplining at home. (Japan, Age 57, Male)

The postwar United States experienced its most sustained period of economic prosperity in the country's modern history; however, the Japanese economy took much longer to recover from the ravages of World War II. As such, the baby boom generation in Japan grew up in hardship, only to emerge into a stunning period of economic growth in adulthood. As this father explains, they wanted to shield their children from what they had experienced and, in his view, took their concern too far: they spoiled their kids and failed to provide them with the kind of discipline necessary to achieve adulthood in the contemporary era.

From the boomer parents' perspective, young people in Japan are no longer willing to buckle down to the demands of society and take their place in the social structure. Women no longer wish to serve their husband's parents, as was the absolute norm in the past. Young men are unwilling to chain themselves to the corporation. And both men and women are more self-centered and less other-directed. As one middle-aged Japanese woman explained: "If they are to raise children, [young adults] will not have sufficient free time for themselves . . . ."

The period of rising economic success in Japan was accompanied by the emergence of the well-known workaholic, the "salaryman." While mothers stayed home to raise their children, fathers in the primary, corporate sector gave their lives over to the firm. The specter of fathers who "worked to death," spent 6 days a week far from home, and their evening hours drinking in the company of male friends from the workplace, has led to a retrospective sense that the "absent father" is responsible for the decaying moral center of today's 30-somethings. "While fathers were working hard in pursuit of economic growth," one 57-year-old mother explained, "they never looked back on their family."

> They didn't know what was going on with their children and this is the case for my family . . . There was no place in the family where the father could convey their dignity or their way of living to form the basis of human character for their children. That is, as 1 said before, affecting young people, making their spirit hollow. (Japan, Age 57, Female)

The absent father and the lonely mother are less central to the popular diagnosis of fault lines in the Japanese family structure (at least not as central as the "parasite singles" [Genda, 2000; Lunsing, 2003] or "freeters"), but they emerge in our interviews as explanations for why today's young adults are abandoning established pathways toward responsible adulthood. Parents see that a retrospective critique of the traditional postwar family is gathering force among their children, one that casts a troubling light on the marriages of the elders. "I wonder if our married life did not look so happy to [my daughter]" mused a 60-year-old Japanese mother. "That may be the reason why she could not decide on getting married . . ."

> I worked hard at mothering and was playing the role of a daughter-in-law and a wife. 1 was thinking that I was very happy. But perhaps, [my daughter] was really looking at the inside. [laugh] She was seeing through the reality. So now I think maybe we weren't that happy. That is the reason why she could not have hopes, or dreams for marriage . . . . There are many situations where parents are deceiving each other about their marital life. I think children are watching that, and that may be the reason why there are many young people who do not get married. (Japanese, Age 60, Female)

In sharp contrast to the Spanish or Italian interviews, which emphasize the difficulties young people face in finding good jobs or affordable housing, Japanese informants equate intergenerational change with moral dilemmas and failings catalyzed by the internal climate of the family or the questionable socialization practices of the senior generation.

At times, these moralistic interpretations verge on social hysteria as interviewees describe the country's very social structure as crumbling under the weight of change.[8] They speak in dire tones of disintegrating solidarity and traumas unheard of in the past becoming commonplace. The emergence of the *hikkimori*, young men who have shut themselves into their bedrooms and refused to come out—for years—has captured the dark side of the Japanese imagination. Examples of unspeakable crime committed within families are the focus of an avalanche of press coverage. Why are these forms of deviance becoming so common? This 66-year-old Japanese mother understands exactly what has happened.

> Let's say the father is a corporate man and does not concern himself with his family. His family can live on his salaries, but children do not grow up just by money. In this way, children cannot grow up properly. That is why things like "*hikikomori*" [shut-ins] are happening, or even if young people get a job they stop going to work. When the child is small, this is manifested in their refusal to go to school. In other words, children are victims. Additionally, what is quite noticeable these days is domestic violence, murdering of family members. I think that the root problems lie there [weakening family relationships].

A father in his late 50s concurs, with his own apocalyptic vision.

> [Young adults] treat human life lightly . . . There are news reports that they buried someone while she or he was alive, or they murdered someone—there are so many incidents like that. That is because they see other human beings only as things. (Japan, Age 59, Male)

Baby boom parents are not alone in their fearful sense of social collapse. Their children see the situation in similar terms.

> There was an incident in Japan recently, a girl was making her mother drink poison, and she was keeping a diary of her observations of her mother. Young people are confused about the real world and the world of fantasy they create. The number of children, or youth, who cannot tell the difference between the virtual and the real, seems to be increasing. (Japan, Age 28, Female)

In none of the other interview samples did we find evidence of such concern for the very fabric of the society, not even in the south of Italy where daily violence is more than an occasional possibility. In Japan, we see real worry over the country's future and a moralistic account of how these problems developed in the first place: they were created by the parents themselves.

SILVER LININGS

Although remaining in the natal nest means that genuine independence is a distant goal, the parent-child bond is nonetheless evolving toward a different state than the typical "top-down" relationship characteristic of adolescence. Somewhere between adult autonomy and child-like dependency lies the middling state of "in house adulthood," a more egalitarian relationship that enables the adult child to come and go or develop intimate relations with others, while maintaining a close bond with his or her parents. This evolution can be smooth or bumpy, depending on how much autonomy the son or daughter demands and the comfort level of their parents with this "new creature" in their midst. It can also become a source of genuine pleasure for both parties, even when forms of economic coercion (a poor job market, short-term contracts, exorbitant housing costs) have necessitated the arrangement.

The pleasure often derives from a contrastive experience that the older generation remembers all too well from their own childhood. As they look backward, they remember their relations with their fathers as ones of emotional distance, a mixture of respect and fear. A Spanish mother in her early 60s recalled that her father was rarely at home and when he was, she stayed out of his way in order to avoid disapproval. "My father never put his hand on us," she acknowledged," but with a single gaze from my father we could be dead." She did not want that kind of relationship with her own children. Instead, she wanted to be sure that they could confide in her and their father and felt emotionally close. "This [fear] has never existed in my children's generation," she noted with a degree of pride. "I didn't want it to exist and my husband didn't either."

That desire for a closer relationship helps sustain a more flexible bond as the adult child's role in the household shifts with age. Instead of the parents feeling as though they are suffocating the adult child, they see the silver lining in their continued affection and closeness. "I've seen my children much at home here, very happy," explained a 53-year-old Spanish mother.

> I haven't felt they were inhibited nor daunted, nor ... for example, angry about being still here at home. They know that ... here the door is always open. The chair and the table to sit and talk . . . I understand that it may be a problem in certain homes . . . because . . . living together may be difficult for them, [but] . . . My children have never disturbed me, nor will they ever do, I believe. Just the opposite.

Her daughter, in her late 20s, saw the relationship in very similar, egalitarian terms.

> We have a more personal relationship with our parents. We can tell them many more things, I think they know us much better than their parents knew them . . . We may be influenced by our parents' opinion, but it is not an imposition as it was in the past. Like my parents perhaps went to buy a house and that is something they also had to discuss with my grandparents. And I don't think that's the case any longer.

Japanese parents reported the same kind of softening in their relations with their children and felt the same contrast with their own experience of a childhood under the thumb of more austere and distant fathers. Some agreed with their Spanish counterparts that the modern approach of empathy and support from parent to child was a blessing.

Others were not so sure. Equality may lead to lack of respect according to many Japanese boomers. "Parents do not face their children with confidence," according to a 51-year-old Tokyo mother who seems to lament the passing of the patriarchal model.

> The father used to be called the mainstay of the family—there was one person in the family whom the children could not disobey. There are still families like that, but generally, parents and children relate to each other as though they are friends. What derives from that kind of relationship is that children begin to think whatever they say will be accepted. They become impatient.

NORDIC BLUES

For Americans, the Nordic countries appear, at first blush, to be something close to nirvana. Decisions that pose major challenges to adults and youth in other societies—whether to go to university, live independently, place a child in daycare, find care for an aging parent—are barely constrained by finances. The generosity of the welfare state in Sweden and Denmark removes these concerns. Indeed, the major responsibility parents and their children feel involves checking to be sure whether state-provided services are being properly administered (not whether they are affordable). University education is free, healthcare is universal and inexpensive, child-and eldercare are plentiful and largely free. The social democracies are particularly generous to their youth, providing extensive educational benefits and underwriting among the longest average period of higher education in the Western world.

This exceptional support is delivered through a direct relationship between the citizen[9] and the state. While the southern European states direct whatever social welfare benefits their people are entitled to through the head of the household, the northern states developed a different tradition. Every resident is entitled to particular benefits regardless of his or her household configuration or marital status and these resources are delivered to them as individuals rather than as daughters, sons, or wives.

It is hard for Americans, or southern Europeans, to imagine that anything could be troubling Scandinavians about their social system (apart, perhaps, from the high taxes they pay to make it run). Yet the interviews with Swedish and Danish parents and their adult children, the vast majority of whom have lived independently of one another since the younger generation turned 18, suggests that the absence of dependence can weaken the affective bonds between generations. This might be regarded as a virtue because children are not forced back into the arms of their parents to survive economically. Instead, they can elect the level of interaction they have with their families. Yet the young people in our sample worry that their culture has become too distant, as if lack of financial dependency has created emotional distance that is not healthy.

"In comparison to others," a young woman (age 22) explained, "Danes are a bunch of rootless creatures."

> [This is] due to the fact that we leave home so early, but also due to the fact that we are individualists. I don't know whether it would be different if we didn't move out so soon. . . . Maybe if you stayed with your parents for a longer while, you wouldn't feel like you didn't get enough love.

When asked why Denmark is so different from Italy in the pattern of home leaving, a young man (age 25) explained that in southern countries "people care more about being with their families." And they do not mind living close to each other. He saw his own culture as intolerant of that kind of intimacy, almost running from it. "In Denmark," he remarked, "people probably wouldn't want to share a room with a sibling.". . .

Notes

1. These data come from Raymo (2003).
2. This is the title of the Russell Sage volume in which the data presented in this section first appeared. See Newman and Aptekar (2008).
3. I am immensely grateful to my interviewers, Emanuela Zilio (Italy), Katarina Andersssen (Sweden), Marie Kappel (Denmark), Maria Gomez Garrido (Spain), and Noriko Matsumoto (Japan), whose dedication to the difficult task of creating the sample and conducting the interviews made this research possible.
4. The snowball sample was recruited by research assistants born and raised in each country who relied on distant parts of their personal networks to begin with (e.g., friends of their siblings they did not know well, friends of acquaintances, etc.). They gathered names from their initial informants and selected one at most to pursue and snowballed in a similar fashion with each interview. Much of the information gathered was sensitive and anyone closer than this might have been very hesitant to share it if they thought there was any chance their replies would filter back to their children/parents.
5. In our experience, Japanese parents were unwilling to be interviewed if their own children were contacted and vice versa. Spanish and Italian parents and children were not only comfortable with the idea that both generations would be interviewed, but often insisted that the interviews take place in the family home and seemed unconcerned about privacy. The norm for Nordic parents and their children is to live apart from one another and hence while the interviews often encompassed different generations of the same family, there was little concern about privacy between them because they are already autonomous.

6. This age bar was set to try to capture an average postcollege-age child, but this proved more difficult to judge than originally expected because in many European countries (including the Nordic social democracies), the duration of education is elongating rather dramatically partly in response to weaker labor market opportunities and an effort to reduce social exclusion.
7. By focal child, I mean the adult child who is either the informant or the child on whom we are focusing attention in the parent interviews. Parents in our sample often had more than one child, but our questions pertained to one particular child over the age of 22.
8. For a much more detailed treatment of Japanese preoccupations with social collapse, see David Leheny (2006).
9. Much of it is available to all residents, regardless of citizenship.

References

Cherlin, Andrew J., Eugenia Scabini, and Giovanna Rossi. 1997 "Still in the Nest: Delayed Home Leaving in Europe and the United States," *Journal of Family Issues* 18: 6: 572–575.

Cook, Thomas D., and Frank F. Furstenberg Jr. 2002. "Explaining Aspects of the Transition to Adulthood in Italy, Sweden, Germany, and the United States: A Cross-Disciplinary, Case Synthesis Approach," *ANNALS:* AAPSS 580.

Genda, Yuji. 2000. "Youth Employment and Parasite Singles," *Japan Labour Bulletin* 39: 3.

Golsch, Kutrin. 2003. "Employment Flexibility in Spain and its Impact on Transitions to Adulthood," *Work, Employment and Society* 17: 4: 691–718.

Holdsworth, Clare. 2000. "Leaving Home in Britain and Spain," *European Sociological Review* 16: 2: 201–222.

Holdsworth, Clare, and Mariana Irazoqui Solda. 2002. "First Housing Moves in Spain: An Analysis of Leaving Home and First Housing Acquisition," *European Journal of Population* 18: 1–19.

Jurado Guerrero, Teresa. 2001. *Youth in Transition: Housing, Employment, Social Policies and Families in France and Spain.* Aldershot/Hants: Ashgate.

Katsumata, Y. 2003. "Have We Really Reached the Western Standard of Retired Income Security? From the Viewpoints of Public and Private Pension Schemes," Paper presented at the ISSA Research Conference on Social Security in a Long Life Society, Antwerp, May.

Kosugi, Reiko. 2004. "The Transition from School to Work in Japan: Understanding the Increase in Freeter and Jobless Youth," *Japan Labor Review* 1:1.

Leheny, David. 2006. *Think Global, Fear Local: Sex. Violence and Anxiety in Contemporary Japan.* Ithaca, NY: Cornell University Press.

Lunsing, Wim. 2003. "'Parasite' and 'Non-Parasite' Singles: Japanese Journalists and Scholars Taking Positions," *Social Science Japan Journal* 6: 2: 261–265.

Ministry of International Affairs and Communication. 2007. "Marriage and Divorce." Retrieved June 1, 2008 (http://www.stat.go.jp/english/data/handbook/c02cont.htm).

Mulder, Clara H., and Pieter Hooimeijer. 2002. "Leaving Home in the Netherlands: Timing and First Housing," *Journal of Housing and the Built Environment* 17: 237–268.

Mulder, Clara H., and Dorien Manting. 1994. "Strategies of Nest-Leavers: 'Settling Down' Versus Flexibility," *European Sociological Review* 10: 2: 155–172.

Newman, Katherine. 1993. *Declining Fortunes: The Withering of the American Dream.* New York: Basic Books.

Newman, Katherine, and Sofya Aptekar. 2008. "Sticking Around: Delayed Departure from the Parental Nest in Western Europe," In Sheldon Danziger and Cecilia Rouse (eds.), *The Price of Independence*, pp. 207–230. New York: Russell Sage Foundation.

Nilsson, Karina, and Mattias Strandh. 1999. "Nest Leaving in Sweden: The Importance of Early Educational and Labor Market Careers," *Journal of Marriage and the Family* 61: 4: 1068–1079.

Raymo, James M. 2003. "Premarital Living Arrangements and the Transition to First Marriage in Japan," *Journal of Marriage and the Family* 65: 302–315.

Westoff, Charles F., and Tomas Frejka. 2007. "Religiousness and Fertility Among European Muslims," *Population and Development Review* 33: 4: 785–809.

PART IV

Families in Society

A decade into the twenty-first century, Americans still tend to judge families by the standards of sixty years ago. During the 1950s and 1960s, family scholars and the mass media presented an image of the typical, normal, or model U.S. family. It included a father, a mother, and two or three children living a middle-class existence in a single-family home in an area neither rural nor urban. Father was the breadwinner, and mother was a full-time homemaker. Both were white, as were virtually all families portrayed in the mass media.

No one denied that many families and individuals fell outside the standard nuclear model. Single persons, one-parent families, two-parent families in which both parents worked, three-generation families, and childless couples abounded. Three- or four-parent families were not uncommon, as one or both divorced spouses often remarried. Many families, moreover, neither white nor well-off, also varied from the dominant image. The image scarcely reflected the increasing ratio of older people in the empty nest and retirement stages of the life cycle. But like poverty, before its "discovery" in the mid-1960s, family complexity and variety existed on some dim fringe of semi-awareness.

When they were discussed, individuals or families who departed from the standard model were analyzed in the context of pathology. Studies of one-parent families or working mothers, for example, focused on the harmful effects to children of such "deviant" situations. Couples who were childless by choice were assumed to possess some basic personality inadequacies. Single persons were similarly interpreted, or else thought to be homosexual. Homosexuals symbolized evil, depravity, degradation, and mental illness.

Curiously, although social scientists have always emphasized the diversity of U.S. society in terms of ethnic groups, religion, and geographic region, the concept of diversity had rarely been applied to the family. In the wake of the social upheavals of the 1960s and 1970s, middle-class "mainstream" attitudes toward women's roles, sexuality, and the family were transformed. U.S. families became increasingly diverse, and Americans were increasingly willing to accept nontraditional family patterns. In fact, there is now a tendency to exaggerate how much families have changed. This is probably because politicians and the media focus on divorce, single-parent families, teen pregnancy and other problems, rather than ordinary families leading ordinary lives.

The selections in this part of the book discuss not only diversity in families, but also the reality that families are both embedded in and sensitive to changes in the social structure and economics of U.S. life. The great recession of 2008 has hit American families hard—because of joblessness, pay cuts, foreclosures, lost pensions, and investments. But economic pressures on families have been increasing since the mid-1970s and have done as much as feminism to draw women into the paid workforce. The two-parent family in which both parents work is the form that now comes closest to being the "typical" American family. In the 1950s, the working mother was considered deviant, even though many women were employed in the labor force. It was taken for granted that maternal employment must be harmful to children; much current research on working mothers still takes this "social problem" approach to the subject.

What really does happen in the family as women share the role of the family breadwinner with their husbands? Arlie Hochschild and Anne Machung take a close look at the emotional dynamics inside the family when both parents work full time and the "second shift"—the work of caring for children and maintaining the home—is not shared equitably. The selection from their book portrays a painful dilemma common to many couples in their study: The men saw themselves as having equal marriages; they were doing more work around the house than their fathers had done and more than they thought other men did. The women, whose lives were different from their own mothers', saw their husbands' contributions as falling far short of true equality. They resented having to carry more than their share of the "second shift," yet they stifled their angry feelings in order to preserve their marriages. Still, this strategy took its toll on love and intimacy.

Despite the great changes in women's lives and the rise of the two-earner family, most workplaces still adhere to the old model of the ideal worker as someone without responsibilities outside the job. This lack of flexibility in the workplace is one source of what has been called the "the opt-out revolution"—professional women supposedly leaving the workplace in droves to become full-time mothers. Pamela Stone's research was aimed at understanding the reality behind the rhetoric. Were professional women really choosing to "opt-out"? Were they really trying to return to "the feminine mystique" model of the family? Stone found a more complicated reality. Rather than "choosing" to become full-time homemakers, she discovered that these women actually faced a "choice gap": The kind of work-and-family balance they really wanted was simply not available to them. Instead, they were caught between the demands of "intensive mothering"—the new higher standards of middle-class childrearing—and the demands of today's high-pressure workplaces. Stone concludes that the opting-out notion is a myth that harms not just women, but society. Employers need the skills of high-achieving women, but they have created toxic work environments that are incompatible with family life. Of course, it's not only professionals facing the pressures of the new economy. Lillian B. Rubin finds that words such as downsizing, restructuring, and reengineering have become all too familiar and even terrifying to today's blue-collar workers and their families. Rubin carried out a similar study of working-class families in the 1970s. She found then that while these families were never entirely secure, they felt they had a grasp of the American dream. Most owned their own homes and expected that their children would do even better. In the more recent study, the people Rubin interviewed perceived a discontinuity between past and present—a sense that something had gone very wrong in the country. Thirty-five percent of the men in the study were either unemployed at the time or had experienced bouts of unemployment. Parents and children had given up hope of upward mobility, or even the hope that the children could own homes comparable to the ones they had grown up in. The families, particularly the men, were angry, yet perplexed about who or what to blame—the government, high taxes, immigrants, minorities, women—for displacing them from the jobs they once had.

About two out of five working Americans—40 percent of our labor force—face additional pressures from their nonstandard work schedules. As Harriet Presser explains, today's nonstop 24/7 economy makes it necessary for millions of mostly lower-income people to work through the night, on weekends, or on shifts 12 or more hours long. This work pattern has some advantages for families, but it also puts a heavy burden on them. Nonstandard schedules are particularly hard on single mothers and married couples with children.

In their article here, Katherine S. Newman and Victor Tan Chen tell the story of Valerie Rushing, a 33-year-old mother of one. She works from midnight to 8 AM and then does another shift from 8 AM to 4 PM. She cleans toilets on a commuter train, but she likes her job because it "pays the bills." Valerie Rushing works nonstandard hours, and she is also an example of what Newman and Chen call "the missing class." While the media and politicians focus on the desperately poor, they largely ignore the struggles of a much larger part of the population—the "near poor." These are people who work hard to keep themselves above the poverty line, but they are not middle class, either. Many of the "missing class" work in white-collar settings like health clinics, schools and offices, but they earn less, have fewer benefits, and have less security than blue-collar, unionized workers did in the past. And while they work hard to achieve the American dream, their devotion to work takes a toll on their family lives. Their lives contradict the "sacred promise" of America—if you work hard, you will achieve a better life for yourself and your children. Newman and Chen describe the government policies that are desperately needed by "missing class" families.

Not even the solid middle class is immune from the stresses of the current economy. Millions of employed, educated, and home-owning Americans are in financial trouble, having mortgages foreclosed and filing for bankruptcy. In 2004, more families filed for bankruptcy than for divorce. In their article, Elizabeth Warren and Amelia Warren Tyagi debunk what they call "the over-consumption myth"—the idea that Americans are spending themselves into financial ruin for luxuries they don't really need. Instead, the rising costs of housing, decent elementary schools, and college tuition have placed middle-class parents at greater risk than in earlier generations.

The next group of articles addresses family diversity along several dimensions–economic status, race, ethnicity, age, and sexual orientation. In recent years, family researchers have recognized that diversity is more complicated than previously thought. It's too simple to sort people into distinct categories—African Americans, Latinos, Asian Americans, European Americans, or gays. These aspects of diversity cross-cut one another, along with many other aspects of difference, such as social class, religion, region, family structure (e.g., stepfamilies), and many more.

There is also great diversity within groups. In his article, Ronald L. Taylor explores diversity among African American families. He recalls being troubled that the stereotypes of African Americans, who appeared in the media as well as in social science did not reflect the families he knew growing up in a small southern city. The dominant image of African American families remains the low-income, single-parent family living in a crime-ridden inner-city neighborhood. Yet only a quarter of African American families fit that description. All African Americans share a common history of slavery and segregation, and they still face discrimination in housing and employment. Taylor discusses the impact of these past and present features on African American family life.

Latino families are now emerging as America's largest "minority." They are more diverse than other groups, as Maxine Baca Zinn and Barbara Wells show in their article. Mexican Americans are the largest group among Latinos and have been the most studied, but Puerto Ricans, Cubans, and Central and South Americans differ from those of Mexican background and among themselves. These differences are not only cultural, but also reflect the immigrants' social and economic statuses in their home countries as well as the reasons for and the timing of their departures for the United States.

In her reading, Min Zhou examines the often difficult parent–child relations in today's Chinese immigrant families. The pattern of Chinese immigration to the U.S. was changed dramatically by the new immigration law passed by Congress in 1965. The law ended tight limits on Chinese immigration and allowed for family reunification. As a result, Chinese communities shifted from being "bachelor" to family societies. The new Chinese immigrants are no longer mainly poor as was the older wave, and are more spread out in mainstream American society. As a result, there is more of a generation gap now. Young Chinese are freer to "become American" and to rebel against their parents' traditional ways. Many describe their homes as "pressure cookers," with conflicts over their parents' expectations of obedience and good grades at school. Parents typically view dating as a waste of time and especially dangerous to the reputations of daughters. But the many community institutions, such as schools that teach the language and customs of China, help to resolve parent–child conflicts.

The new wave of immigration from Latin America as well as Asia and other non-European regions has contributed to what demographers have called the "browning" of America. The nation is also "graying" as the aging population continues to grow. By 2030, people over 65 are expected to grow to 20 percent of the American population. As Rona J. Karasik and Raeann R. Hamon point out in their article, it is also becoming an increasingly diverse population. Thus far, there has been relatively little research focusing on the intersection of race, ethnicity, and culture in aging families. Karasik and Hamon review what is known about diversity in late-life families. They examine cultural differences in marriage, sibling relationships, and grandparenthood. They conclude by suggesting that researchers and professionals dealing with the aging populations adopt an attitude of "cultural humility."

Diversity in American family life is not new, but gay and lesbian families are a new addition to the mix. For some people, especially religious conservatives, homosexuality is immoral and unnatural. As Judith Stacey makes clear in her article, families with same-sex parents are here to stay. Stacey traces the emergence of these families in the wake of the gay liberation movements of the 1970s, the growing willingness of courts and legislatures to grant legal recognition to gay families, and the fierce backlash against such efforts. Stacey argues that children in both gay and heterosexual families would benefit if both law and society would be more accepting of diversity in American family life.

In the final chapter, we look at three kinds of family trouble. First, we consider an issue that is rarely thought of as a family problem: the huge spike in the prison population in recent decades due to the "war on drugs" and other get-tough-on-crime policies. The United States now locks up a higher proportion of its citizens than any other country in the world. People who commit violent crimes should go to prison, both as punishment and to protect the community, but about half those now in prison for long sentences are not there for violent acts. As Jeremy Travis points out, prison places a huge burden on the families of prisoners, especially on their relationships with partners and children. He also spells out the ripple effects that high rates of imprisonment have on poor and minority communities—for example, creating a shortage of marriageable men.

Travis partially answers the questions that Katherine Edin and Maria Kefalas address in their article on poor unmarried young mothers. Why do they have babies when they know they will have to struggle to support them? Have they given up the marriage norm? When George W. Bush was in power, his administration funded efforts to promote marriage as a poverty policy, on the theory that if low-income people marry they will no longer be poor. In contrast, Edin and Kefalas find that this kind of thinking is backward—their research shows that these women revere marriage, and about 70 percent will eventually marry. But in America's poor neighborhoods, plagued by joblessness, drug and alcohol abuse, as well as high rates of crime and imprisonment, a good man is hard to find. Edin and Kefalas conclude that the real cure for poverty and "too-early" motherhood is access to good jobs for both men and women.

Chapter

9

Work and Family Life

READING 25

The Second Shift: Working Parents and the Revolution at Home

Arlie Hochschild, with Anne Machung

Between 8:05 A.M. and 6:05 P.M., both Nancy and Evan are away from home, working a "first shift" at full-time jobs. The rest of the time they deal with the varied tasks of the second shift: shopping, cooking, paying bills; taking care of the car, the garden, and yard; keeping harmony with Evan's mother who drops over quite a bit, "concerned" about Joey, with neighbors, their voluble babysitter, and each other. And Nancy's talk reflects a series of second-shift thoughts: "We're out of barbecue sauce. . . . Joey needs a Halloween costume. . . . The car needs a wash. . . ." and so on. She reflects a certain "second-shift sensibility," a continual attunement to the task of striking and restriking the right emotional balance between child, spouse, home, and outside job.

When I first met the Holts, Nancy was absorbing far more of the second shift than Evan. She said she was doing 80 percent of the housework and 90 percent of the childcare. Evan said she did 60 percent of the housework, 70 percent of the childcare. Joey said, "I vacuum the rug, and fold the dinner napkins," finally concluding, "Mom and I do it all." A neighbor agreed with Joey. Clearly, between Nancy and Evan, there was a "leisure gap": Evan had more than Nancy. I asked both of them, in separate interviews, to explain to me how they had dealt with housework and childcare since their marriage began.

One evening in the fifth year of their marriage, Nancy told me, when Joey was two months old and almost four years before I met the Holts, she first seriously raised the issue with Evan. "I told him: 'Look, Evan, it's not working. I do the housework, I take the major care of Joey, *and* I work a full-time job. I get pissed. This is *your* house too. Joey is *your* child too. It's not all *my* job to care for them.' When I cooled down I put to him, 'Look, how about this: I'll cook Mondays, Wednesdays, and Fridays. You cook Tuesdays, Thursdays, and, Saturdays. And we'll share or go out Sundays.'"

According to Nancy, Evan said he didn't like "rigid schedules." He said he didn't necessarily agree with her standards of housekeeping, and didn't like that standard "imposed" on him, especially if she was "sluffing off" tasks on him which from time to time he felt she was. But he went along with the idea in principle. Nancy said the first week of the new plan went as follows: On Monday, she cooked. For Tuesday, Evan planned a meal that required shopping for a few ingredients, but on his way home he forgot to shop for them. He came home, saw nothing he could use in the refrigerator or in the cupboard and suggested to Nancy that they go out for Chinese food. On Wednesday, Nancy cooked. On Thursday morning, Nancy reminded Evan, "Tonight it's your turn." That night Evan fixed hamburgers and french fries and Nancy was quick to praise him. On Friday, Nancy cooked. On Saturday, Evan forgot again.

As this pattern continued, Nancy's reminders became sharper. The sharper they became, the more actively Evan forgot—perhaps anticipating even sharper reprimands if he resisted more directly. This cycle of passive refusal followed by disappointment and anger gradually tightened, and before long the struggle had spread to the task of doing the laundry. Nancy said it was only fair that Evan share the laundry. He agreed in principle, but anxious that Evan would not share, Nancy wanted a clear, explicit agreement. "You ought to wash and fold every other load," she had told him. Evan experienced this "plan" as a yoke around his neck. On many weekdays, at this point, a huge pile of laundry sat like a disheveled guest on the living-room couch.

In her frustration, Nancy began to make subtle emotional jabs at Evan. "I don't know *what's* for dinner," she would say with a sigh. Or "I can't cook now, I've got to deal with this pile of laundry." She tensed at the slightest criticism about household disorder; if Evan wouldn't do the housework, he had absolutely *no* right to criticize how she did it. She would burst out angrily at Evan. She recalled telling him: "After work *my* feet are just as tired as *your* feet. I'm just as wound up as you are. I come home. I cook dinner. I wash and I clean. Here we are, planning a second child, and I can't cope with the one we have."

About two years after I first began visiting the Holts, I began to see the problem in a certain light: as a conflict between their two gender ideologies. Nancy wanted to be the sort of woman who was needed and appreciated both at home and at work—like Lacey, she told me, on the television show "Cagney and Lacey." She wanted Evan to appreciate her for being a caring social worker, a committed wife, and a wonderful mother. But she cared just as much that she be able to appreciate *Evan* for what *he* contributed at home, not just for how he supported the family. She would feel proud to explain to women friends that she was married to one of these rare "new men."

A gender ideology is often rooted in early experience, and fueled by motives formed early on and such motives can often be traced to some cautionary tale in early life. So it was for Nancy. Nancy described her mother:

> My mom was wonderful, a real aristocrat, but she was also terribly depressed being a housewife. My dad treated her like a doormat. She didn't have any self-confidence. And growing up, I can remember her being really depressed. I grew up bound and determined not to be like her and not to marry a man like my father. As long as Evan doesn't do the

housework, I feel it means he's going to be like my father—coming home, putting his feet up, and hollering at my mom to serve him. That's my biggest fear. I've had *bad* dreams about that.

Nancy thought that women friends her age, also in traditional marriages, had come to similarly bad ends. She described a high school friend: "Martha barely made it through City College. She had no interest in learning anything. She spent nine years trailing around behind her husband [a salesman]. It's a miserable marriage. She hand washes all his shirts. The high point of her life was when she was eighteen and the two of us were running around Miami Beach in a Mustang convertible. She's gained seventy pounds and she hates her life." To Nancy, Martha was a younger version of her mother, depressed, lacking in self-esteem, a cautionary tale whose moral was "if you want to be happy, develop a career and get your husband to share at home." Asking Evan to help again and again felt like "hard work" but it was essential to establishing her role as a career woman.

For his own reasons, Evan imagined things very differently. He loved Nancy and if Nancy loved being a social worker, he was happy and proud to support her in it. He knew that because she took her caseload so seriously, it was draining work. But at the same time, he did not see why, just because she chose this demanding career, *he* had to change *his own* life. Why should her personal decision to work outside the home require him to do more inside it? Nancy earned about two-thirds as much as Evan, and her salary was a big help, but as Nancy confided, "If push came to shove, we could do without it." Nancy was a social worker because she loved it. Doing daily chores at home was thankless work, certainly not something Evan needed her to appreciate about him. Equality in the second shift meant a loss in his standard of living, and despite all the high-flown talk, he felt he hadn't *really* bargained for it. He was happy to help Nancy at home if she needed help; that was fine. That was only decent. But it was too risky a matter "committing" himself to sharing.

Two other beliefs probably fueled his resistance as well. The first was his suspicion that if he shared the second shift with Nancy, she would "dominate him." Nancy would ask him to do this, ask him to do that. It felt to Evan as if Nancy had won so many small victories that he had to draw the line somewhere. Nancy had a declarative personality; and as Nancy said, "Evan's mother sat me down and told me once that I was too forceful, that Evan needed to take more authority." Both Nancy and Evan agreed that Evan's sense of career and self was in fact shakier than Nancy's. He had been unemployed. She never had. He had had some bouts of drinking in the past. Drinking was foreign to her. Evan thought that sharing housework would upset a certain balance of power that felt culturally "right." He held the purse strings and made the major decisions about large purchases (like their house) because he "knew more about finances" and because he'd chipped in more inheritance than she when they married. His job difficulties had lowered his self-respect, and now as a couple they had achieved some ineffable "balance"—tilted in his favor, she thought—which, if corrected to equalize the burden of chores, would result in his giving in "too much." A certain driving anxiety behind Nancy's strategy of actively renegotiating roles had made Evan see agreement as "giving in." When he wasn't feeling good about work, he dreaded the idea of being under his wife's thumb at home.

Underneath these feelings; Evan perhaps also feared that Nancy was avoiding taking care of *him*. His own mother, a mild-mannered alcoholic, had by imperceptible steps phased herself out of a mother's role, leaving him very much on his own. Perhaps a personal motive to prevent that happening in his marriage—a guess on my part, and unarticulated on his—underlay his strategies of passive resistance. And he wasn't altogether wrong to fear this. Meanwhile, he felt he was "offering" Nancy the chance to stay home, or cut back her hours, and that she was refusing his "gift;" while Nancy felt that, given her feelings about work, this offer was hardly a gift.

In the sixth year of her marriage, when Nancy again intensified her pressure on Evan to commit himself to equal sharing, Evan recalled saying, "Nancy, why don't you cut back to half time, that way you can fit everything in." At first Nancy was baffled: "We've been married all this time, and you *still* don't get it. Work is important to me. I worked *hard* to get my MSW. Why *should* I give it up?" Nancy also explained to Evan and later to me, "I think my degree and my job has been my way of reassuring myself that I won't end up like my mother." Yet she'd received little emotional support in getting her degree from either her parents or in-laws. (Her mother had avoided asking about her thesis, and her in-laws, though invited, did not attend her graduation, later claiming they'd never been invited.)

In addition, Nancy was more excited about seeing her elderly clients in tenderloin hotels than Evan was about selling couches to furniture salesmen with greased-back hair. Why shouldn't Evan make as many compromises with his career ambitions and his leisure as she'd made with hers? She couldn't see it Evan's way, and Evan couldn't see it hers.

In years of alternating struggle and compromise, Nancy had seen only fleeting mirages of cooperation, visions that appeared when she got sick or withdrew and disappeared when she got better or came forward.

After seven years of loving marriage, Nancy and Evan had finally come to a terrible impasse. Their emotional standard of living had drastically declined, they began to snap at each other, to criticize, to carp. Each felt taken advantage of. Evan, because his offering of a good arrangement was deemed unacceptable, and Nancy, because Evan wouldn't do what she deeply felt was "fair."

This struggle made its way into their sexual life—first through Nancy directly, and then through Joey. Nancy had always disdained any form of feminine wiliness or manipulation. Her family saw her as "a flaming feminist" and that was how she saw herself. As such, she felt above the underhanded ways traditional women used to get around men. She mused, "When I was a teenager, I vowed I would *never* use sex to get my way with a man. It is not self-respecting; it's demeaning. But when Evan refused to carry his load at home, I did, I used sex, I said, 'Look, Evan, I would not be this exhausted and asexual every night if I didn't have so much to face every morning.'" She felt reduced to an old "strategy," and her modern ideas made her ashamed of it. At the same time, she'd run out of other, modern ways.

The idea of a separation arose, and they became frightened. Nancy looked at the deteriorating marriages and fresh divorces of couples with young children around them. One unhappy husband they knew had become so uninvolved in family life (they didn't know whether his unhappiness made him uninvolved, or whether his lack of involvement had caused his wife to be unhappy) that his wife left him. In another case, Nancy felt the wife had "nagged" her husband so much that he abandoned her for another woman. In both cases, the couple was less happy after the divorce than before, and both wives took the children and struggled desperately to survive financially. Nancy took stock. She asked herself, "Why wreck a marriage over a dirty frying pan?" Is it really worth it?

UPSTAIRS-DOWNSTAIRS: A FAMILY MYTH AS "SOLUTION"

Not long after this crisis in the Holts' marriage, there was a dramatic lessening of tension over the issue of the second shift. It was as if the issue was closed. Evan had won. Nancy would do the second shift. Evan expressed vague guilt but beyond that he had nothing to say. Nancy had wearied of continually raising the topic, wearied of the lack of resolution. Now in the exhaustion of defeat, she wanted the struggle to be over too. Evan was "so good" in *other* ways, why debilitate their marriage by continual quarreling. Besides, she told me, "Women always adjust more, don't they?"

One day, when I asked Nancy to tell me who did which tasks from a long list household chores, she interrupted me with a broad wave of her hand and said, "I do the upstairs, Evan does the downstairs." What does that mean? I asked. Matter-of-factly, she explained that the upstairs included the living room, the dining room, the kitchen, two bedrooms, and two baths. The downstairs meant the garage, a place for storage and hobbies—Evan's hobbies. She explained this was a "sharing" arrangement, without humor or irony—just as Evan did later. Both said they had agreed it was the best solution to their dispute. Evan would take care of the car, the garage, and Max, the family dog. As Nancy explained, "the dog is all Evan's problem. I don't have to deal with the dog." Nancy took care of the rest.

For purposes of accommodating the second shift, then, the Holts' garage was elevated to the full moral and practical equivalent of the rest of the home. For Nancy and Evan, "upstairs and downstairs," "inside and outside," were vaguely described like "half and half," a fair division of labor based on a natural division of their house.

The Holts presented their upstairs-downstairs agreement as a perfectly equitable solution to a problem they "once had." This belief is what we might call "family myth," even a modest delusional system. Why did they believe it? I think they believed it because they needed to believe it, because it solved a terrible problem. It allowed Nancy to continue thinking of herself as the sort of woman whose husband didn't abuse her—a self-conception that mattered a great deal to her. And it avoided the hard truth that, in his stolid, passive way, Evan had refused to share. It avoided the truth, too, that in their showdown, Nancy was more afraid of divorce than Evan was. This outer cover to their family life, this family myth was jointly devised. It was an attempt to agree that there was no conflict over the second shift, no tension between their versions of manhood and womanhood, that the powerful crisis that had arisen was temporary and minor.

The wish to avoid such a conflict is natural enough. But their avoidance tacitly supported by the surrounding culture, especially the image of the woman with the flying hair. After all, this admirable woman also proudly does the "upstairs" each day without a husband's help and without conflict.

After Nancy and Evan reached their upstairs-downstairs agreement, the confrontations ended. They were nearly forgotten. Yet, as she described daily life months after the agreement, Nancy's resentment still seemed alive and well. For example, she said:

> Evan and I eventually divided the labor so that I do the upstairs and Evan does the downstairs and the dog. So the dog is my husband's problem. But when I was getting the dog outside and getting Joey ready for childcare, and cleaning up the mess, feeding the cat,

> and getting the lunches together, and having my son wipe his nose on my outfit so I would have to change—then I was pissed! I felt that I was doing *everything*. All Evan was doing was getting up, having coffee, reading the paper, saying, "Well, I have to go now," and often forgetting the lunch I'd bothered to make.

She also mentioned that she had fallen into the habit of putting Joey to bed in a certain way: he asked to be swung around by the arms, dropped on the bed and nuzzled and hugged, whispered to in his ear. Joey waited for her attention. He didn't go to sleep without it. But, increasingly, when Nancy tried it at eight and nine, the ritual didn't put Joey to sleep. On the contrary, it woke him up. It was then that Joey began to say he could only go to sleep in his parents' bed, that he began to sleep in their bed and to encroach on their sexual life.

Near the end of my visits, it struck me that Nancy was putting Joey to bed in an "exciting" way, later and later at night, in order to tell Evan something important: "You win, I'll go on doing all the work at home, but I'm angry about it and I'll make you pay." Evan had won the battle but lost the war. According to the family myth, all was well: the struggle had been resolved by the upstairs-downstairs agreement. But suppressed in one area of their marriage, this struggle lived on in another—as Joey's Problem, and as theirs.

NANCY'S "PROGRAM" TO SUSTAIN THE MYTH

There was a moment, I believe, when Nancy seemed to *decide* to give up on this one. She decided to try not to resent Evan. Whether or not other women face a moment just like this, at the very least they face the need to deal with all the feelings that naturally arise from a clash between a treasured ideal and an incompatible reality. In the age of a stalled revolution, it is a problem a great many women face.

Emotionally, Nancy's compromise from time to time slipped; she would forget and grow resentful again. Her new resolve needed maintenance. Only half aware that she was doing so, Nancy went to extraordinary lengths to maintain it. She could tell me now, a year or so after her "decision," in a matter-of-fact and noncritical way: "Evan likes to come home to a hot meal. He doesn't like to clear the table. He doesn't like to do the dishes. He likes to go watch TV. He likes to play with his son when he feels like it and not feel like he should be with him more." She seemed resigned.

Everything was "fine." But it had taken an extraordinary amount of complex "emotion work"—the work of *trying* to feel the "right" feeling, the feeling she wanted to feel—to make and keep everything "fine." Across the nation at this particular time in history, this emotion work is often all that stands between the stalled revolution on the one hand, and broken marriages on the other.

HOW MANY HOLTS?

In one key way the Holts were typical of the vast majority of two-job couples: their family life had become the shock absorber for a stalled revolution whose origin lay far outside it—in economic and cultural trends that bear very differently on men and women.

Nancy was reading books, newspaper articles, and watching TV programs on the changing role of women. Evan wasn't. Nancy felt benefited by these changes; Evan didn't. In her ideals and in reality, Nancy was more different from her mother than Evan was from his father, for the culture and economy were in general pressing change faster upon women like her than upon men like Evan. Nancy had gone to college; her mother hadn't. Nancy had a professional job; her mother never had. Nancy had the idea that she should be equal with her husband; her mother hadn't been much exposed to that idea in her day. Nancy felt she should share the job of earning money, and that Evan should share the work at home; her mother hadn't imagined that was possible. Evan went to college, his father (and the other boys in his family, though not the girls) had gone too. Work was important to Evan's identity as a man as it had been for his father before him. Indeed, Evan felt the same way about family roles as his father had felt in his day. The new job opportunities and the feminist movement of the 1960s and '70s had transformed Nancy but left Evan pretty much the same. And the friction created by this difference between them moved to the issue of second shift as metal to a magnet. By the end, Evan did less housework and childcare than most men married to working women—but not much less. Evan and Nancy were also typical of nearly 40 percent of the marriages studied in their clash of gender ideologies and their corresponding difference is a notion about what constituted a "sacrifice" and what did not. By far the most common form of mismatch was like that between Nancy, an egalitarian, and Evan, a transitional.

But for most couples, the tensions between strategies did not move so quickly and powerfully to issues of housework and childcare. Nancy pushed harder than most women to get her husband to share the work at home, and she also lost more overwhelmingly than the few other women who fought that hard. Evan pursued his strategy of passive resistance with more quiet tenacity then most men, and he allowed himself to become far more marginal to his son's life than most other fathers. The myth of the Holts' "equal" arrangement seems slightly more odd than other family myths that encapsulated equally powerful conflicts.

Beyond their upstairs-downstairs myth, the Holts tell us a great deal about the subtle ways a couple can encapsulate the tension caused by a struggle over the second shift without resolving the problem or divorcing. Like Nancy Holt, many women struggle to avoid, suppress, obscure, or mystify a frightening conflict over the second shift. They do not struggle like this because they start off wanting to, or because such struggle is inevitable or because women inevitably lose, but because they are forced to choose between equality and marriage. And they choose marriage. When asked about "ideal" relations between men and women in general, about what they want for their daughters or about what "ideally" they'd like in their own marriage, most working mothers "wished" their men would share the work at home.

But many "wish" it instead of "want" it. Other goals—like keeping peace at home—come first. Nancy Holt did some extraordinary behind-the-scenes emotion work to prevent her ideals from clashing with her marriage. In the end she had confined and miniaturized her ideas of equality successfully enough to do two things she badly wanted to do: feel like a feminist, and live at peace with a man who was not. Her program had "worked." Evan won on the reality of the situation, because Nancy did the second shift. Nancy won on the cover story, they would talk about it as if they shared.

Nancy wore the upstairs-downstairs myth as an ideological cloak to protect her from the contradictions in her marriage and from the cultural and economic forces that press upon it. Nancy and Evan Holt were caught on opposite sides of the gender revolution occurring all around them. Through the 1960s, 1970s, and 1980s masses of women entered the public world of work—but went only so far up the occupational ladder. They tried for "equal" marriages, but got only so far in achieving it. They married men who liked them to work at the office and who wouldn't share the extra month a year at home. When confusion about the identity of the working woman created a cultural vacuum in the 1970s and 1980s, the image of the supermom quietly glided in. She made the "stall" seem normal and happy. But beneath the happy image of the woman with the flying hair are modern marriages like the Holts', reflecting intricate webs of tension, and the huge, hidden emotional cost to women, men, and children of having to "manage" inequality. Yet on the surface, all we might see would be Nancy Holt bounding confidently out the door at 8:30 A.M. briefcase in one hand, Joey in the other. All we might hear would be Nancy's and Evan's talk about their marriage as happy, normal, even "equal"—because equality was so important to Nancy.

READING 26

The Rhetoric and Reality of "Opting Out"

Pamela Stone

As a senior publicist at a well-known media conglomerate, Regina Donofrio had one of the most coveted, glamorous jobs in New York. A typical workday might include riding around Manhattan in limousines with movie stars. She loved her job, had worked "a long time," and felt "comfortable" in it. So when the time came to return to work after the birth of her first child, Regina did not hesitate. "I decided I would go back to work, because the job was great, basically," she told me. Before long, Regina found herself "crying on the train," torn between wanting to be at home with her baby and wanting to keep up her successful, exciting career. She started feeling she was never in the right place at the right time. "When I was at work, I should have been at home. When I was at home, I felt guilty because I had left work a little early to see the baby, and I had maybe left some things undone." Ever resourceful, she devised a detailed job-share plan with a colleague who was also a first-time mother. But their proposal was denied. Instead, Regina's employer offered her more money to stay and work full time, and Regina left in a huff, incensed that her employer, with whom she had a great track record, would block her from doing what she wanted to do—continue with her career and combine it with family.

Despite mainstream media portrayals to the contrary, Regina's reasons for quitting are all too typical of what I found in my study of high-achieving, former professionals who are now at-home moms. While Regina did, in fact, feel a strong urge to care for her baby, she decided to quit because of an inflexible workplace, not because of her attraction to home and hearth. She gave up her high-powered career as a last resort, after agonized soul-searching and exhausting her options. Her story differs from the popular depiction of similar, high-achieving, professional women who have headed home. Media stories typically frame these women's decisions as choices about family and see them as symptomatic of a kind of sea-change among the daughters of the feminist revolution, a return to traditionalism and the resurgence of a new feminine mystique. The quintessential article in this prevailing story line (and the one that gave the phenomenon its name) was published in 2003 by the *New York Times*'s work-life columnist, Lisa Belkin, titled "The Opt-Out Revolution." "Opting out" is redolent with overtones of lifestyle preference and discretion, but Regina's experience counters this characterization; her decision to quit was not a lifestyle preference, nor a change in aspirations, nor a desire to return to the 1950s family. Regina did not "opt out" of the workplace because she chose to, but for precisely the opposite reason: because she had no real options and no choice.

High-achieving women's reasons for heading home are multilayered and complex, and generally counter the common view that they quit because of babies and family. This is what I found when I spoke to scores of women like Regina: highly educated, affluent, mostly white, married women with children who had previously worked as professionals or managers and whose husbands could support their being at home. Although many of these women speak the language of choice and privilege, their stories reveal a choice gap—the disjuncture between the rhetoric of choice and the reality of constraints like those Regina encountered. The choice gap reflects the extent to which high achieving women like Regina are caught in a double bind: spiraling parenting (read "mothering") demands on the home front collide with the increasing pace of work in the gilded cages of elite professions.

SOME SKEPTICISM

I approached these interviews with skepticism tempered by a recognition that there might be some truth to the popular image of the "new traditionalist." But to get beyond the predictable "family" explanation and the media drumbeat of choice, I thought it was important to interview women in some depth and to study women who, at least theoretically, could exercise choice. I also gave women full anonymity, creating fictitious names for them so they would speak to me as candidly as possible. The women I interviewed had outstanding educational credentials; more than half had graduate degrees in business, law, medicine, and other professions, and had once had thriving careers in which they had worked about a decade. By any measure, these were work-committed women, with strong reasons to continue with the careers in which they had invested so much. Moreover, they were in high-status fields where they had more control over their jobs and enjoyed (at least relative to workers in other fields) more family-friendly benefits.

While these women had compelling reasons to stay on the job, they also had the option not to, by virtue of their own past earnings and because their husbands were also high earners. To counter the potential criticism that they were quitting or being let go because they were not competent or up to the job, I expressly chose to study women with impeccable educational credentials, women who had navigated elite environments with competitive entry requirements. To ensure a diversity of perspectives, I conducted extensive, in-depth interviews with 54 women in a variety of professions—law, medicine, business, publishing, management consulting, nonprofit administration, and the like—living in major metropolitan areas across the country, roughly half of them in their 30s, half in their 40s.

To be sure, at-home moms are a distinct minority. Despite the many articles proclaiming a trend of women going home, among the demographic of media scrutiny—white, college-educated women, 30–54 years old—fully 84 percent are now in the workforce, up from 82 percent 20 years ago. And the much-discussed dip in the labor-force participation of mothers of young children, while real, appears to be largely a function of an economic downturn, which depresses employment for all workers.

Nevertheless, these women are important to study. Elite, educated, high-achieving women have historically been cultural arbiters, defining what is acceptable for all women in their work and family roles. This group's entrance into high-status, formerly male professions has been crucial to advancing gender parity and narrowing the wage gap, which stubbornly persists to this day. At home, moreover, they are rendered silent and invisible, so that it is easy to project and speculate about them. We can see in them whatever we want to, and perhaps that is why they have been the subject of endless speculation—about mommy wars, a return to traditionalism, and the like. While they do not represent all women, elite women's experiences provide a glimpse into the work-family negotiations that all women face. And their stories lead us to ask, "If the most privileged women of society cannot successfully combine work and family, who can?"

MOTHERHOOD PULLS

When Regina initially went back to work, she had "no clue" that she would feel so torn. She advises women not to set "too much in stone," because "you just don't know, when a human being comes out of your body, how you're going to feel." For some women, the pull of children was immediate and strong. Lauren Quattrone, a lawyer, found herself "absolutely besotted with this baby. . . . I realized that I just couldn't bear to leave him." Women such as Lauren tended to quit fairly soon after their first child was born. For others, like Diane Childs, formerly a nonprofit executive, the desire to be home with the kids came later. "I felt that it was easy to leave a baby for twelve hours a day. That I could do. But to leave a six-year-old, I just thought, was a whole different thing."

But none of these women made their decisions to quit in a vacuum. In fact, they did so during a cultural moment when norms and practices for parents—mothers—are very demanding. These women realized they would rear children very differently from the way their own mothers raised them, feeling an external, almost competitive pressure to do so. Middle- and upper-middle-class women tend to be particularly mindful of expert advice, and these women were acutely aware of a well-documented intensification in raising children, which sociologist Sharon Hays calls an "ideology of intensive mothering." This cultural imperative, felt by women of all kinds, "advises mothers to expend a tremendous amount of time, energy and money in raising their children."

A corollary is what Annette Lareau terms "concerted cultivation," a nonstop pace of organized activities scheduled by parents for school-age children. Among the women

I spoke to, some, like Diane, felt the urgency of "concerted cultivation" and reevaluated their childcare as the more sophisticated needs of their older children superseded the simpler, more straightforward babysitting and physical care required for younger children. Marina Isherwood, a former executive in the health care industry, with children in the second and fourth grades, became convinced that caregivers could not replace her own parental influence:

> There isn't a substitute, no matter how good the childcare. When they're little, the fact that someone else is doing the stuff with them is fine. It wasn't the part that I loved anyway. But when they start asking you questions about values, you don't want your babysitter telling them. . . . Our children come home, and they have all this homework to do, and piano lessons and this and this, and it's all a complicated schedule. And, yes, you could get an au pair to do that, to balance it all, but they're not going to necessarily teach you how to think about math. Or help you come up with mnemonic devices to memorize all of the countries in Spain or whatever.

Because academic credentials were so important to these women's (and their husband's) career opportunities, formal schooling was a critical factor in their decisions to quit. For some, the premium they placed on education and values widened the gap between themselves and their less educated caregivers.

Depending on the woman, motherhood played a larger or smaller role in her decision whether and when to quit. Children were the main focus of women's caregiving, but other family members needed care as well, for which women felt responsible. About 10 percent of the women spoke of significant elder-care responsibilities, the need for which was especially unpredictable. This type of caregiving and mothering made up half of the family/career double bind. More important, though, motherhood influenced women's decision to quit as they came to see the rhythms and values of the workplace as antagonistic to family life.

WORKPLACE PUSHES

On top of their demanding mothering regime, these women received mixed messages from both their husbands and their employers. Husbands offered emotional support to wives who were juggling career and family. Emily Mitchell, an accountant, described her marriage to a CPA as "a pretty equal relationship," but when his career became more demanding, requiring long hours and Saturdays at work, he saw the downside of egalitarianism:

> I think he never minded taking my daughter to the sitter, that was never an issue, and when he would come home, we have a pretty equal relationship on that stuff. But getting her up, getting her ready, getting himself ready to go into work, me coming home, getting her, getting her to bed, getting unwound from work, and then he would come home, we'd try to do something for dinner, and then there was always something else to do—laundry, cleaning, whatever—I think he was feeling too much on a treadmill.

But husbands did little to share family responsibilities, instead maintaining their own demanding careers full-speed ahead.

Similarly, many workplaces claimed to be "family friendly" and offered a variety of supports. But for women who could take advantage of them, flexible work schedules (which usually meant working part-time) carried significant penalties. Women who shifted to part-time work typically saw their jobs gutted of significant responsibilities and the once-flourishing careers derailed. Worse, part-time hours often crept up to the equivalent of full time. When Diane Childs had children, she scaled back to part time and began to feel the pointlessness of continuing:

> And I'm never going to get anywhere—you have the feeling that you just plateaued professionally because you can't take on the extra projects; you can't travel at a moment's notice; you can't stay late; you're not flexible on the Friday thing because that could mean finding someone to take your kids. You really plateau for a much longer period of time than you ever realize when you first have a baby. It's like you're going to be plateaued for thirteen to fifteen years.

Lynn Hamilton, an M.D., met her husband at Princeton, where they were both undergraduates. Her story illustrates how family pulls and workplace pushes (from both her career and her husband's) interacted in a marriage that was founded on professional equality but then devolved to the detriment of her career:

> We met when we were 19 years old, and so, there I was, so naive, I thought, well, here we are, we have virtually identical credentials and comparable income earnings. That's an opportunity. And, in fact, I think our incomes were identical at the time I quit. To the extent to which we have articulated it, it was always understood, well, with both of us working, neither of us would have to be working these killer jobs. So, what was happening was, instead, we were both working these killer jobs. And I kept saying, "We need to reconfigure this." And what I realized was, he wasn't going to.

Meanwhile, her young daughter was having behavioral problems at school, and her job as a medical director for a biomedical start-up company had "the fax machine going, the three phone lines upstairs, they were going." Lynn slowly realized that the only reconfiguration possible, in the face of her husband's absence, was for her to quit.

Over half (60 percent) of the women I spoke to mentioned their husbands as one of the key reasons why they quit. That not all women talked about their husbands' involvement, or lack thereof, reveals the degree to which they perceived the work-family balancing act to be their responsibility alone. But women seldom mentioned their husbands for another reason: they were, quite literally, absent.

Helena Norton, an educational administrator who characterized her husband as a "workaholic," poignantly described a scenario that many others took for granted and which illustrates a pattern typical of many of these women's lives: "He was leaving early mornings; 6:00 or 6:30 before anyone was up, and then he was coming home late at night. So I felt this real emptiness, getting up in the morning to, not necessarily an empty house, because my children were there, but I did, I felt empty, and then going to bed, and he wasn't there."

In not being there to pick up the slack, many husbands had an important indirect impact on their wives' decisions to quit. Deferring to their husbands' careers and exempting them from household chores, these women tended to accept this situation. Indeed, privileging their husbands' careers was a pervasive, almost tacit undercurrent of their stories.

When talking about their husbands, women said the same things: variations on "he's supportive," and that he gave them a "choice." But this hands-off approach revealed husbands to be bystanders, not participants, in the work family bind. "It's your choice" was code for "it's your problem." And husbands' absences, a direct result of their own high-powered careers, put a great deal of pressure on women to do it all, thus undermining the façade of egalitarianism.

Family pulls—from children and, as a result of their own long work hours, their husbands—exacerbated workplace pushes; and all but seven women cited features of their jobs—the long hours, the travel—as another major motivation in quitting. Marketing executive Nathalie Everett spoke for many women when she remarked that her full-time workweek was "really 60 hours, not 40. Nobody works nine-to-five anymore."

Surprisingly, the women I interviewed, like Nathalie, neither questioned nor showed much resentment toward the features of their jobs that kept them from fully integrating work and family. They routinely described their jobs as "all or nothing" and appeared to internalize what sociologists call the "ideal worker" model of a (typically male) worker unencumbered by family demands. This model was so influential that those working part time or in other flexible arrangements often felt stigmatized. Christine Thomas, a marketing executive and job-sharer, used imagery reminiscent of *The Scarlet Letter* to describe her experience: "When you job share, you have 'MOMMY' stamped in huge letters on your forehead."

While some women's decisions could be attributed to their unquestioning acceptance of the status quo or a lack of imagination, the unsuccessful attempts of others who tried to make it work by pursuing alternatives to full-time, like Diane, serve as cautionary tales. Women who made arrangements with bosses felt like they were being given special favors. Their part-time schedules were privately negotiated, hence fragile and unstable, and were especially vulnerable in the context of any kind of organizational restructuring such as mergers.

THE CHOICE GAP

Given the incongruity of these women's experiences—they felt supported by "supportive" yet passive husbands and pushed out by workplaces that once prized their expertise—how did these women understand their situation? How did they make sense of professions that, on the one hand, gave them considerable status and rewards, and, on the other hand, seemed to marginalize them and force them to compromise their identity as mothers?

The overwhelming majority felt the same way as Melissa Wyatt, the 34-year-old who gave up a job as a fund-raiser: "I think today it's all about choices, and the choices we want to make. And I think that's great. I think it just depends where you want to spend your time." But a few shared the outlook of Olivia Pastore, a 42-year-old ex-lawyer:

> I've had a lot of women say to me, "Boy, if I had the choice of, if I could balance, if I could work part-time, if I could keep doing it." And there are some women who are going to stay home full-time no matter what and that's fine. But there are a number of women, I think, who are home because they're caught between a rock and a hard place. . . . There's

> a lot of talk about the individual decisions of individual women. "Is it good? Is it bad? She gave it up. She couldn't hack it." . . . And there's not enough blame, if you will, being laid at the feet of the culture, the jobs, society.

My findings show that Olivia's comments—about the disjuncture between the rhetoric of choice and the reality of constraint that shapes women's decisions to go home—are closer to the mark. Between trying to be the ideal mother (in an era of intensive mothering) and the ideal worker (a model based on a man with a stay-at-home wife), these high-flying women faced a double bind. Indeed, their options were much more limited than they seemed. Fundamentally, they faced a "choice gap": the difference between the decisions women could have made about their careers if they were not mothers or caregivers and the decisions they had to make in their circumstances as mothers married to high-octane husbands in ultimately unyielding professions. This choice gap obscures individual preferences, and thus reveals the things Olivia railed against—culture, jobs, society—the kinds of things sociologists call "structure."

Overall, women based their decisions on mutually reinforcing and interlocking factors. They confronted, for instance, two sets of trade-offs: kids versus careers, and their own careers versus those of their husbands. For many, circumstances beyond their control strongly influenced their decision to quit. On the family side of the equation, for example, women had to deal with caregiving for sick children and elderly parents, children's developmental problems, and special care needs. Such reasons figured in one-third of the sample. On the work side, women were denied part-time arrangements, a couple were laid off, and some had to relocate for their own careers or their husbands'. A total of 30 women, a little more than half the sample, mentioned at least one forced-choice consideration.

But even before women had children, the prospect of pregnancy loomed in the background, making women feel that they were perceived as flight risks. In her first day on the job as a marketing executive, for example, Patricia Lambert's boss asked her: "So, are you going to have kids?" And once women did get pregnant, they reported that they were often the first in their office, which made them feel more like outsiders. Some remarked that a dearth of role models created an atmosphere unsympathetic to work-family needs. And as these women navigated pregnancy and their lives beyond, their stories revealed a latent bias against mothers in their workplaces. What some women took from this was that pregnancy was a dirty little secret not to be openly discussed. The private nature of pregnancy thus complicated women's decisions regarding their careers once they became mothers, which is why they often waited until the last minute to figure out their next steps. Their experiences contrasted with the formal policies of their workplaces, which touted themselves as "family friendly."

THE RHETORIC OF CHOICE

Given the indisputable obstacles—hostile workplaces and absentee husbands—that stymied a full integration of work and family, it was ironic that most of the women invoked "choice" when relating the events surrounding their decision to exit their careers. Why were there not more women like Olivia, railing against the tyranny of an outmoded workplace that favored a 1950s-era employee or bemoaning their husbands' drive for achievement at the expense of their own?

I found that these women tended to use the rhetoric of choice in the service of their exceptionality. Women associated choice with privilege, feminism, and personal agency, and internalized it as a reflection of their own perfectionism. This was an attractive combination that played to their drive for achievement and also served to compensate for their loss of the careers they loved and the professional identities they valued. Some of these women bought into the media message that being an at-home mom was a status symbol, promoted by such cultural arbiters as *New York Magazine* and the *Wall Street Journal.* Their ability to go home reflected their husbands' career success, in which they and their children basked. Living out the traditional lifestyle, male breadwinner and stay-at-home-mom, which they were fortunate to be able to choose, they saw themselves as realizing the dreams of third-wave feminism. The goals of earlier, second-wave feminism, economic independence and gender equality, took a back seat, at least temporarily.

CHALLENGING THE MYTH

These strategies and rhetoric, and the apparent invisibility of the choice gap, reveal how fully these high-achieving women internalized the double bind and the intensive mothering and ideal-worker models on which it rests. The downside, of course, is that they blamed themselves for failing to "have it all" rather than any actual structural constraints. That work and family were incompatible was the overwhelming message they took from their experiences. And when they quit, not wanting to burn bridges, they cited family obligations as the reason, not their dissatisfaction with work, in accordance with social expectations. By adopting the socially desirable and gender-consistent explanation of "family," women often contributed to the larger misunderstanding surrounding their decision. Their own explanations endorsed the prevalent idea that quitting to go home is a choice. Employers rarely challenged women's explanations. Nor did they try to convince them to stay, thus reinforcing women's perception that their decision was the right thing to do as mothers, and perpetuating the reigning media image of these women as the new traditionalists.

Taken at face value, these women do seem to be traditional. But by rejecting an intransigent workplace, their quitting signifies a kind of silent strike. They were not acquiescing to traditional gender roles by quitting, but voting with their feet against an outdated model of work. When women are not posing for the camera or worried about offending former employers (from whom they may need future references), they are able to share their stories candidly. From what I found, the truth is far different and certainly more nuanced than the media depiction.

The vast majority of the type of women I studied do not want to choose between career and family. The demanding nature of today's parenting puts added pressure on women. Women do indeed need to learn to be "good enough" mothers, and their husbands need to engage more equally in parenting. But on the basis of what they told me, women today "choose" to be home full-time not as much because of parenting overload as because of work overload, specifically long hours and the lack of flexible options in their high-status jobs. The popular media depiction of a return to traditionalism is wrong and misleading. Women are trying to achieve the feminist vision of a fully integrated life combining family and work. That so many attempt to remain in their careers when they do not "have to work" testifies strongly to their commitment to their careers, as does the difficulty they experience over their subsequent loss of identity. Their attempts at juggling and their plans to return to work in the future also indicate that their careers were not meant to be ephemeral and should not be treated as such. Rather, we should regard their exits as the miner's canary—a frontline indication that something is seriously amiss in many workplaces. Signs of toxic work environments and white-collar sweatshops are ubiquitous. We can glean from these women's experiences the true cost of these work conditions, which are personal and professional, and, ultimately, societal and economic.

Our current understanding of why high-achieving women quit—based as it is on choice and separate spheres—seriously undermines the will to change the contemporary workplace. The myth of opting out returns us to the days when educated women were barred from entering elite professions because "they'll only leave anyway." To the extent that elite women are arbiters of shifting gender norms, the opting out myth also has the potential to curtail women's aspirations and stigmatize those who challenge the separate-spheres ideology on which it is based. Current demographics make it clear that employers can hardly afford to lose the talents of high-achieving women. They can take a cue from at-home moms like the ones I studied: Forget opting out; the key to keeping professional women on the job is to create better, more flexible ways to work.

Recommended Resources

Mary Blair-Loy. *Competing Devotions: Career and Family among Women Executives* (Harvard University Press, 2003). Argues for a cultural, less materialist, understanding of contemporary work-family conflict among high-achieving working women.

Sharon Hays. *The Cultural Contradictions of Motherhood* (Yale University Press, 1995). Describes the historical emergence and contemporary internalization of motherhood norms that are at odds with the realities of women's changing lives, with powerful theorizing as to why.

Arlie Hochschild. *The Second Shift* (Viking, 1989). Still the defining classic of the work-family field, identifying in women's work at home another problem that had no name.

Jerry A. Jacobs and Kathleen Gerson. *The Time Divide: Work, Family and Gender Inequality* (Harvard University Press, 2004). Makes the case for time as the newly emerging basis of gender and class inequality, with lots of hard-to-find facts and good policy prescriptions.

Phyllis Moen and Patricia Roehling. *The Career Mystique: Cracks in the American Dream* (Rowman and Littlefield, 2005). A masterful exploration of the creation, maintenance, and consequences of the high-demand, all-consuming workplace, whose title consciously echoes Friedan's *The Feminine Mystique*.

Chapter

10

Family and the Economy

READING 27

Families on the Fault Line

Lillian B. Rubin

THE BARDOLINOS

It has been more than three years since I first met the Bardolino family, three years in which to grow accustomed to words like *downsizing*, *restructuring*, or the most recent one, *reengineering;* three years in which to learn to integrate them into the language so that they now fall easily from our lips. But these are no ordinary words, at least not for Marianne and Tony Bardolino.

The last time we talked, Tony had been unemployed for about three months and Marianne was working nights at the telephone company and dreaming about the day they could afford a new kitchen. They seemed like a stable couple then—a house, two children doing well in school, Marianne working without complaint, Tony taking on a reasonable share of the family work. Tony, who had been laid off from the chemical plant where he had worked for ten years, was still hoping he'd be called back and trying to convince himself their lives were on a short hold, not on a catastrophic downhill slide. But instead of calling workers back, the company kept cutting its work force. Shortly after our first meeting, it became clear: There would be no recall. Now, as I sit in the little cottage Marianne shares with her seventeen-year-old daughter, she tells the story of these last three years.

"When we got the word that they wouldn't be calling Tony back, that's when we really panicked; I mean *really* panicked. We didn't know what to do. Where was Tony going to find another job, with the recession and all that? It was like the bottom really dropped out. Before that, we really hoped he'd be called back any day. It wasn't just crazy; they told the guys when they laid them off, you know, that it would be three, four months at most. So we hoped. I mean, sure we worried; in these times, you'd be crazy not to worry. But he'd been laid off for a couple of months before and called back, so we thought maybe it's the same thing. Besides, Tony's boss was so sure the guys would be coming back in a couple of months; so you tried to believe it was true."

She stops speaking, takes a few sips of coffee from the mug she holds in her hand, then says with a sigh, "I don't really know where to start." So much happened, and sometimes you can't even keep track. Mostly what I remember is how scared we were. Tony started to look for a job, but there was nowhere to look. The union couldn't help; there were no jobs in the industry. So he looked in the papers, and he made the rounds of all the places around here. He even went all the way to San Francisco and some of the places down near the airport there. But there was nothing.

"At first, I kept thinking, *Don't panic; he'll find something*. But after his unemployment ran out, we couldn't pay the bills, so then you can't help getting panicked, can you?"

She stops again, this time staring directly at me, as if wanting something. But I'm not sure what, so I sit quietly and wait for her to continue. Finally, she demands, "Well, can you?"

I understand now; she wants reassurance that her anxiety wasn't out of line, that it's not she who's responsible for the rupture in the family. So I say, "It sounds as if you feel guilty because you were anxious about how the family would manage."

"Yeah, that's right," she replies as she fights her tears. "I keep thinking maybe if I hadn't been so awful, I wouldn't have driven Tony away." But as soon as the words are spoken, she wants to take them back. "I mean, I don't know, maybe I wasn't that bad." We were both so depressed and scared, maybe there's nothing I could have done. But I think about it a lot, and I didn't have to blame him so much and keep nagging at him about how worried I was. It wasn't his fault; he was trying.

"It was just that we looked at it so different. I kept thinking he should take anything, but he only wanted a job like the one he had. We fought about that a lot. I mean, what difference does it make what kind of job it is? No, I don't mean that; I know it makes a difference. But when you have to support a family, that should come first, shouldn't it?"

As I listen, I recall my meeting with Tony a few days earlier and how guiltily he, too, spoke about his behavior during that time. "I wasn't thinking about her at all," he explained. "I was just so mad about what happened; it was like the world came crashing down on me. I did a little too much drinking, and then I'd just crawl into a hole, wouldn't even know whether Marianne or the kids were there or not. She kept saying it was like I wasn't there. I guess she was right, because I sure didn't want to be there, not if I couldn't support them."

"Is that the only thing you were good for in the family?" I asked him.

"Good point," he replied laughing. "Maybe not, but it's hard to know what else you're good for when you can't do that."

I push these thoughts aside and turn my attention back to Marianne. "Tony told me that he did get a job after about a year," I remark.

"Yeah, did he tell you what kind of job it was?"

"Not exactly, only that it didn't work out."

"Sure, he didn't tell you because he's still so ashamed about it. He was out of work so long that even he finally got it that he didn't have a choice. So he took this job as a dishwasher in this restaurant. It's one of those new kind of places with an open kitchen, so there he was, standing there washing dishes in front of everybody. I mean, we used to go there to eat sometimes, and now he's washing the dishes and the whole town sees him doing it. He felt so ashamed, like it was such a comedown, that he'd come home even worse than when he wasn't working."

"That's when the drinking really started heavy. Before that he'd drink, but it wasn't so bad. After he went to work there, he'd come home and drink himself into a coma. I was working days by then, and I'd try to wait up until he came home. But it didn't matter; all he wanted to do was go for that bottle. He drank a lot during the day, too, so sometimes I'd come home and find him passed out on the couch and he never got to work that day. That's when I was maddest of all. I mean, I felt sorry for him having to do that work. But I was afraid he'd get fired."

"Did he?"

"No, he quit after a couple of months. He heard there was a chemical plant down near L.A. where he might get a job. So he left. I mean, we didn't exactly separate, but we didn't exactly not. He didn't ask me and the kids to go with him; he just went. It didn't make any difference. I didn't trust him by then, so why would I leave my job and pick up the kids and move when we didn't even know if he'd find work down there?

"I think he went because he had to get away. Anyway, he never found any decent work there either. I know he had some jobs, but I never knew exactly what he was doing. He'd call once in awhile, but we didn't have much to say to each other then. I always figured he wasn't making out so well because he didn't send much money the whole time he was gone."

As Tony tells it, he was in Los Angeles for nearly a year, every day an agony of guilt and shame. "I lived like a bum when I was down there. I had a room in a place that wasn't much better than a flop house, but it was like I couldn't get it together to go find something else. I wasn't making much money, but I had enough to live decent. I felt like what difference did it make how I lived?"

He sighs—a deep, sad sound—then continues, "I couldn't believe what I did, I mean that I really walked out on my family. My folks were mad as hell at me. When I told them what I was going to do, my father went nuts, said I shouldn't come back to his house until I got some sense again. But I couldn't stay around with Marianne blaming me all the time."

He stops abruptly, withdraws to someplace inside himself for a few moments, then turns back to me. "That's not fair. She wasn't the only one doing the blaming. I kept beating myself up, too, you know, blaming myself, like I did something wrong.

"Anyhow, I hated to see what it was doing to the kids; they were like caught in the middle with us fighting and hollering, or else I was passed out drunk. I didn't want them to have to see me like that, and I couldn't help it. So I got out."

For Marianne, Tony's departure was both a relief and a source of anguish. "At first I was glad he left; at least there was some peace in the house. But then I got so scared; I didn't know if I could make it alone with the kids. That's when I sold the house. We were behind in our payments, and I knew we'd never catch up. The bank was okay; they said they'd give us a little more time. But there was no point.

"That was really hard. It was our home; we worked so hard to get it. God, I hated to give it up. We were lucky, though. We found this place here. It's near where we used to live, so the kids didn't have to change schools, or anything like that. It's small, but at least it's a separate little house, not one of those grungy apartments." She interrupts herself with a laugh, "Well, 'house' makes it sound a lot more than it is, doesn't it?"

"How did your children manage all this?"

"It was real hard on them. My son had just turned thirteen when it all happened, and he was really attached to his father. He couldn't understand why Tony left us, and he was real angry for a long time. At first, I thought he'd be okay, you know, that he'd get over it. But then he got into some bad company. I think he was doing some drugs, although he still won't admit that. Anyway, one night he and some of his friends stole a car. I think they just wanted to go for a joyride; they didn't mean to really steal it forever. But they got caught, and he got sent to juvenile hall.

"I called Tony down in L.A. and told him what happened. It really shocked him; he started to cry on the phone. I never saw him cry before, not with all our trouble. But he just cried and cried. When he got off the phone, he took the first plane he could get, and he's been back up here ever since.

"Jimmy's trouble really changed everything around. When Tony came back, he didn't want to do anything to get Jimmy out of juvy right away. He thought he ought to stay there for a while; you know, like to teach him a lesson. I was mad at first because Jimmy wanted to come home so bad; he was so scared. But now I see Tony was right.

"Anyhow, we let Jimmy stay there for five whole days, then Tony's parents lent us the money to bail him out and get him a lawyer. He made a deal so that if Jimmy pleaded guilty, he'd get a suspended sentence. And that's what happened. But the judge laid down the law, told him if he got in one little bit of trouble again, he'd go to jail. It put the fear of God into the boy."

For Tony, his son's brush with the law was like a shot in the arm. "It was like I had something really important to do, to get that kid back on track. We talked it over and Marianne agreed it would be better if Jimmy came to live with me. She's too soft with the kids; I've got better control. And I wanted to make it up to him, too, to show him he could count on me again. I figured the whole trouble came because I left them, and I wanted to set it right.

"So when he got out of juvy, he went with me to my folks' house where I was staying. We lived there for awhile until I got this job. It's no great shakes, a kind of general handyman. But it's a job, and right from the start I made enough so we could move into this here apartment. So things are going pretty good right now."

"Pretty good" means that Jimmy, now sixteen, has settled down and is doing well enough in school to talk about going to college. For Tony, too, things have turned around. He set up his own business as an independent handyman several months ago and, although the work isn't yet regular enough to allow him to quit his job, his reputation as a man who can fix just about anything is growing. Last month the business actually made enough money to pay his bills. "I'll hang onto the job for a while, even if the business gets going real good, because we've got a lot of catching up to do. I don't mind working hard; I like it. And being my own boss, boy, that's really great," he concludes exultantly.

"Do you think you and Marianne will get together again?"

"I sure hope so; it's what I'm working for right now. She says she's not sure, but she's never made a move to get a divorce. That's a good sign, isn't it?"

When I ask Marianne the same question, she says, "Tony wants to, but I still feel a little scared. You know, I never thought I could manage without him, but then when I was forced to, I did. Now, I don't know what would happen if we got together again. It wouldn't be like it was before. I just got promoted to supervisor, so I have a lot of responsibility on my job. I'm a different person, and I don't know how Tony would like that. He says he likes it fine, but I figure we should wait a while and see what happens. I mean, what if things get tough again for him? I don't ever want to live through anything like these last few years."

"Yet you've never considered divorce."

She laughs, "You sound like Tony." Then more seriously, "I don't want a divorce if I can help it. Right now, I figure if we got through these last few years and still kind of like each other, maybe we've got a chance."

* * *

When the economy falters, families tremble. The Bardolinos not only trembled, they cracked. Whether they can patch up the cracks and put the family back together again remains an open question. But the experience of families like those on the pages of this book provides undeniable evidence of the fundamental link between the public and private arenas of modern life.

No one has to tell the Bardolinos or their children about the many ways the structural changes in the economy affect family life. In the past, a worker like Tony Bardolino didn't need a high level of skill or literacy to hold down a well-paying semiskilled job in a steel mill or an automobile plant. A high school education, often even less, was enough. But an economy that relies most heavily on its service sector needs highly skilled and educated workers to fill its better-paying jobs, leaving people like Tony scrambling for jobs at the bottom of the economic order.

The shift from the manufacturing to the service sector, the restructuring of the corporate world, the competition from low-wage workers in underdeveloped countries that entices American corporations to produce their goods abroad, all have been going on for decades; all are expected to accelerate through the 1990s. The manufacturing sector, which employed just over 26 percent of American workers in 1970, already had fallen to nearly 18 percent by 1991. And experts predict a further drop to 12.5 percent by the year 2000. "This is the end of the post-World War boom era. We are never going back to what we knew," says employment analyst Dan Lacey, publisher of the newsletter *Workplace Trends.*

Yet the federal government has not only failed to offer the help working-class families need, but as a sponsor of a program to nurture capitalism elsewhere in the world it has become party to the exodus of American factories to foreign lands. Under the auspices of the U.S. Agency for International Development (AID), for example, Decaturville

Sportswear, a company that used to be based in Tennessee, has moved to El Salvador. AID not only gave grants to trade organizations in El Salvador to recruit Decaturville but also subsidized the move by picking up the $5 million tab for the construction of a new plant, footing the bill for over $1 million worth of insurance, and providing low-interest loans for other expenses involved in the move.

It's a sweetheart deal for Decaturville Sportswear and the other companies that have been lured to move south of the border under this program. They build new factories at minimal cost to themselves, while their operating expenses drop dramatically. In El Salvador, Decaturville is exempted from corporate taxes and shipping duties. And best of all, the hourly wage for factory workers there is forty-five cents an hour; in the United States the minimum starting wage for workers doing the same job is $4.25.

True, like Tony Bardolino, many of the workers displaced by downsizing, restructuring, and corporate moves like these will eventually find other work. But like him also, they'll probably have to give up what little security they knew in the past. For the forty-hour-a-week steady job that pays a decent wage and provides good benefits is quickly becoming a thing of the past. Instead, as part of the new lean, clean, mean look of corporate America, we now have what the federal government and employment agencies call "contingent" workers—a more benign name for what some labor economists refer to as "disposable" or "throwaway" workers.

It's a labor strategy that comes in several forms. Generally, disposable workers are hired in part-time or temporary jobs to fill an organizational need and are released as soon as the work load lightens. But when union contracts call for employees to join the union after thirty days on the job, some unscrupulous employers fire contingent workers on the twenty-ninth day and bring in a new crew. However it's done, disposable workers earn less than those on the regular payroll and their jobs rarely come with benefits of any kind. Worse yet, they set off to work each morning fearful and uncertain, not knowing how the day will end, worrying that by nightfall they'll be out of a job.

The government's statistics on these workers are sketchy, but Labor Secretary Robert Reich estimates that they now make up nearly one-third of the existing work force. This means that about thirty-four million men and women, most of whom want steady, full-time work, start each day as contingent and/or part-time workers. Indeed, so widespread is this practice now that in some places temporary employment agencies are displacing the old ones that sought permanent placements for their clients.

Here again, class makes a difference. For while it's true that managers and professionals now also are finding themselves disposable, most of the workers who have become so easily expendable are in the lower reaches of the work order. And it's they who are likely to have the fewest options. These are the workers, the unskilled and the semiskilled—the welders, the forklift operators, the assemblers, the clerical workers, and the like—who are most likely to seem to management to be interchangeable. Their skills are limited; their job tasks are relatively simple and require little training. Therefore, they're able to move in and perform with reasonable efficiency soon after they come on the job. Whatever lost time or productivity a company may suffer by not having a steady crew of workers is compensated by the savings in wages and benefits the employment of throwaway workers permits. A resolution that brings short-term gains for the company at the long-term expense of both the workers and the nation. For when a person can't count on a permanent job, a critical element binding him or her to society is lost.

THE TOMALSONS

When I last met the Tomalsons, Gwen was working as a clerk in the office of a large Manhattan company and was also a student at a local college where she was studying nursing. George Tomalson, who had worked for three years in a furniture factory, where he laminated plastic to wooden frames, had been thrown out of a job when the company went bankrupt. He seemed a gentle man then, unhappy over the turn his life had taken but still wanting to believe that it would come out all right.

Now, as he sits before me in the still nearly bare apartment, George is angry. "If you're a black man in this country, you don't have a chance, that's all, not a chance. It's like no matter how hard you try, you're nothing but trash. I've been looking for work for over two years now, and there's nothing. White people are complaining all the time that black folks are getting a break. Yeah, well, I don't know who those people are, because it's not me or anybody else I know. People see a black man coming, they run the other way, that's what I know."

"You haven't found any work at all for two years?" I ask.

"Some temporary jobs, a few weeks sometimes, a couple of months once, mostly doing shit work for peanuts. Nothing I could count on."

"If you could do any kind of work you want, what would you do?"

He smiles, "That's easy; I'd be a carpenter. I'm good with my hands, and I know a lot about it," he says, holding his hands out, palms up, and looking at them proudly. But his mood shifts quickly; the smile disappears; his voice turns harsh. "But that's not going to happen. I tried to get into the union, but there's no room there for a black guy. And in this city, without being in the union, you don't have a chance at a construction job. They've got it all locked up, and they're making sure they keep it for themselves."

When I talk with Gwen later, she worries about the intensity of her husband's resentment. "It's not like George; he's always been a real even guy. But he's moody now, and he's so angry, I sometimes wonder what he might do. This place is a hell hole," she says, referring to the housing project they live in. "It's getting worse all the time; kids with guns, all the drugs, grown men out of work all around. I'll bet there's hardly a man in this whole place who's got a job, leave alone a good one."

"Just what is it you worry about?"

She hesitates, clearly wondering whether to speak, how much to tell me about her fears, then says with a shrug, "I don't know, everything, I guess. There's so much crime and drugs and stuff out there. You can't help wondering whether he'll get tempted." She stops herself, looks at me intently, and says, "Look, don't get me wrong; I know it's crazy to think like that. He's not that kind of person. But when you live in times like these, you can't help worrying about everything.

"We both worry a lot about the kids at school. Every time I hear about another kid shot while they're at school, I get like a raving lunatic. What's going on in this world that kids are killing kids? Doesn't anybody care that so many black kids are dying like that? It's like a black child's life doesn't count for anything. How do they expect our kids to grow up to be good citizens when nobody cares about them?

"It's one of the things that drives George crazy, worrying about the kids. There's no way you can keep them safe around here. Sometimes I wonder why we send them to school. They're not getting much of an education there. Michelle just started, but Julia's in the fifth grade, and believe me she's not learning much.

"We sit over her every night to make sure she does her homework and gets it right. But what good is it if the people at school aren't doing their job. Most of the teachers there don't give a damn. They just want the paycheck and the hell with the kids. Everybody knows it's not like that in the white schools; white people wouldn't stand for it.

"I keep thinking we've got to get out of here for the sake of the kids. I'd love to move someplace, anyplace out of the city where the schools aren't such a cesspool. But, she says dejectedly, "we'll never get out if George can't find a decent job." I'm just beginning my nursing career, and I know I've got a future now. But still, no matter what I do or how long I work at it, I can't make enough for that by myself."

George, too, has dreams of moving away, somewhere far from the city streets, away from the grime and the crime. "Look at this place," he says, his sweeping gesture taking in the whole landscape. "Is this any place to raise kids? Do you know what my little girls see every day they walk out the door? Filth, drugs, guys hanging on the corner waiting for trouble.

"If I could get any kind of a decent job, anything, we'd be out of here, far away, someplace outside the city where the kids could breathe clean and see a different life. It's so bad here, I take them over to my mother's a lot after school; it's a better neighborhood. Then we stay over there and eat sometimes. Mom likes it; she's lonely, and it helps us out. Not that she's got that much, but there's a little pension my father left."

"What about Gwen's family? Do they help out, too?"

"Her mother doesn't have anything to help with since her father died. He's long gone; he was killed by the cops when Gwen was a teenager," he says as calmly as if reporting the time of day.

"Killed by the cops." The words leap out at me and jangle my brain. But why do they startle me so? Surely with all the discussion of police violence in the black community in recent years, I can't be surprised to hear that a black man was "killed by the cops."

It's the calmness with which the news is relayed that gets to me. And it's the realization once again of the distance between the lives and experiences of blacks and others, even poor others. Not one white person in this study reported a violent death in the family. Nor did any of the Latino and Asian families, although the Latinos spoke of a difficult and often antagonistic relationship with Anglo authorities, especially the police. But four black families (13 percent) told of relatives who had been murdered, one of the families with two victims—a teenage son and a twenty-two-year-old daughter, both killed in violent street crimes.

But I'm also struck by the fact that Gwen never told me how her father died. True, I didn't ask. But I wonder now why she didn't offer the information. "Gwen didn't tell me," I say, as if trying to explain my surprise.

"She doesn't like to talk about it. Would you?" he replies somewhat curtly.

It's a moment or two before I can collect myself to speak again. Then I comment, "You talk about all this so calmly."

He leans forward, looks directly at me, and shakes his head. When he finally speaks, his voice is tight with the effort to control his rage. "What do you want? Should I rant and rave? You want me to say I want to go out and kill those mothers? Well, yeah, I do. They killed a good man just because he was black. He wasn't a criminal; he was a hard-working guy who just happened to be in the wrong place when the cops were looking for someone to shoot," he says, then sits back and stares stonily at the wall in front of him.

We both sit locked in silence until finally I break it. "How did it happen?"

He rouses himself at the sound of my voice. "They were after some dude who robbed a liquor store, and when they saw Gwen's dad, they didn't ask questions; they shot. The bastards. Then they said it was self-defense, that they saw a gun in his hand. That man never held a gun in his life, and nobody ever found one either. But nothing happens to them; it's no big deal, just another dead nigger," he concludes, his eyes blazing.

It's quiet again for a few moments, then, with a sardonic half smile, he says, "What would a nice, white middle-class lady like you know about any of that? You got all those degrees, writing books and all that. How are you going to write about people like us?"

"I was poor like you once, very poor," I say somewhat defensively.

He looks surprised, then retorts, "Poor and white; it's a big difference."

* * *

Thirty years before the beginning of the Civil War, Alexis de Tocqueville wrote: "If ever America undergoes great revolutions, they will be brought about by the presence of the black race on the soil of the United States; that is to say they will owe their origin, not to the equality, but to the inequality of condition." One hundred and sixty years later, relations between blacks and whites remain one of the great unresolved issues in American life, and "the inequality of condition" that de Tocqueville observed is still a primary part of the experience of black Americans.

I thought about de Tocqueville's words as I listened to George Tomalson and about how the years of unemployment had changed him from, as Gwen said, "a real even guy" to an angry and embittered one. And I was reminded, too, of de Tocqueville's observation that "the danger of conflict between the white and black inhabitants perpetually haunts the imagination of the [white] Americans, like a painful dream." Fifteen generations later we're still paying the cost of those years when Americans held slaves—whites still living in fear, blacks in rage. "People see a black man coming, they run the other way," says George Tomalson.

Yet however deep the cancer our racial history has left on the body of the nation, most Americans, including many blacks, believe that things are better today than they were a few decades ago—a belief that's both true and not true. There's no doubt that in ending the legal basis for discrimination and segregation, the nation took an important step toward fulfilling the promise of equality for all Americans. As more people meet as equals in the workplace, stereotypes begin to fall away and caricatures are transformed into real people. But it's also true that the economic problems of recent decades have raised the level of anxiety in American life to a new high. So although virtually all whites today give verbal assent to the need for racial justice and equality, they also find ways to resist the implementation of the belief when it seems to threaten their own status or economic well-being.

Our schizophrenia about race, our capacity to believe one thing and do another, is not new. Indeed, it is perhaps epitomized by Thomas Jefferson, the great liberator. For surely, as Gordon Wood writes in an essay in the *New York Review of Books*, "there is no greater irony in American history than the fact that America's supreme spokesman for liberty and equality was a lifelong aristocratic owner of slaves."

Jefferson spoke compellingly about the evils of slavery, but he bought, sold, bred, and flogged slaves. He wrote eloquently about equality but he was convinced that blacks were an inferior race and endorsed the racial stereotypes that have characterized African-Americans since their earliest days on this continent. He believed passionately in individual liberty, but he couldn't imagine free blacks living in America, maintaining instead that if the nation considered emancipating the slaves, it must also prepare for their expulsion.

No one talks seriously about expulsion anymore. Nor do many use the kind of language to describe African-Americans that was so common in Jefferson's day. But the duality he embodied—his belief in justice, liberty, and equality alongside his conviction of black inferiority—still lives.

THE RIVERAS

Once again Ana Rivera and I sit at the table in her bright and cheerful kitchen. She's sipping coffee; I'm drinking some bubbly water while we make small talk and get reacquainted. After a while, we begin to talk about the years since we last met. "I'm a grandmother now," she says, her face wreathed in a smile. "My daughter Karen got married and had a baby, and he's the sweetest little boy, smart, too. He's only two and a half, but you should hear him. He sounds like five."

"When I talked to her the last time I was here, Karen was planning to go to college. What happened?" I ask.

She flushes uncomfortably. "She got pregnant, so she had to get married. I was heartbroken at first. She was only nineteen, and I wanted her to get an education so bad. It was awful; she had been working for a whole year to save money for college, then she got pregnant and couldn't go."

"You say she had to get married. Did she ever consider an abortion?"

"I don't know; we never talked about it. We're Catholic," she says by way of explanation. "I mean, I don't believe in abortion." She hesitates, seeming uncertain about what more she wants to say, then adds, "I have to admit, at a time like that, you have to ask yourself what you really believe. I don't think anybody's got the right to take a child's life. But when I thought about what having that baby would do to Karen's life, I couldn't help thinking, *What if* . . . ?" She stops, unable to bring herself to finish the sentence.

"Did you ever say that to Karen?"

"No, I would *never* do that. I didn't even tell my husband I thought such things. But, you know," she adds, her voice dropping to nearly a whisper, "if she had done it, I don't think I would have said a word."

"What about the rest of the kids?"

"Paul's going to be nineteen soon; he's a problem," she sighs. "I mean, he's got a good head, but he won't use it. I don't know what's the matter with kids these days; it's like they want everything but they're not willing to work for anything. He hardly finished high school, so you can't talk to him about going to college. But what's he going to do? These days if you don't have a good education, you don't have a chance. No matter what we say, he doesn't listen, just goes on his smart-alecky way, hanging around the neighborhood with a bunch of no-good kids looking for trouble.

"Rick's so mad, he wants to throw him out of the house. But I say no, we can't do that because then what'll become of him? So we fight about that a lot, and I don't know what's going to happen."

"Does Paul work at all?"

"Sometimes, but mostly not. I'm afraid to think about where he gets money from. His father won't give him a dime. He borrows from me sometimes, but I don't have much to give him. And anyway, Rick would kill me if he knew."

I remember Paul as a gangly, shy sixteen-year-old, no macho posturing, none of the rage that shook his older brother, not a boy I would have thought would be heading for trouble. But then, Karen, too, had seemed so determined to grasp at a life that was different from the one her parents were living. What happens to these kids?

When I talk with Rick about these years, he, too, asks in bewilderment: What happened? "I don't know; we tried so hard to give the kids everything they needed. I mean, sure, we're not rich, and there's a lot of things we couldn't give them. But we were always here for them; we listened; we talked. What happened? First my daughter gets pregnant and has to get married; now my son is becoming a bum."

"Roberto—that's what we have to call him now," explains Rick, "he says it's what happens when people don't feel they've got respect. He says we'll keep losing our kids until they really believe they really have an equal chance. I don't know; I knew I had to *make* the Anglos respect me, and I had to make my chance. Why don't my kids see it like that?" he asks wearily, his shoulders seeming to sag lower with each sentence he speaks.

"I guess it's really different today, isn't it?" he sighs. "When I was coming up, you could still make your chance. I mean, I only went to high school, but I got a job and worked myself up. You can't do that anymore. Now you need to have some kind of special skills just to get a job that pays more than the minimum wage.

"And the schools, they don't teach kids anything anymore. I went to the same public schools my kids went to, but what a difference. It's like nobody cares anymore."

"How is Roberto doing?" I ask, remembering the hostile eighteen-year-old I interviewed several years earlier.

"He's still mad; he's always talking about injustice and things like that. But he's different than Paul. Roberto always had some goals. I used to worry about him because he's so angry all the time. But I see now that his anger helps him. He wants to fight for his people, to make things better for everybody. Paul, he's like the wind; nothing matters to him.

"Right now, Roberto has a job as an electrician's helper, learning the trade. He's been working there for a couple of years; he's pretty good at it. But I think—I hope—he's going to go to college. He heard that they're trying to get Chicano students to go to the university, so he applied. If he gets some aid, I think he'll go," Rick says, his face radiant at the thought that at least one of his children will fulfill his dream. "Ana and me, we tell him even if he doesn't get aid, he should go. We can't do a lot because we have to help Ana's parents and that takes a big hunk every month. But we'll help him, and he could work to make up the rest. I know it's hard to work and go to school, but people do it all the time, and he's smart; he could do it."

His gaze turns inward; then, as if talking to himself, he says, "I never thought I'd say this but I think Roberto's right. We've got something to learn from some of these kids. I told that to Roberto just the other day. He says Ana and me have been trying to pretend we're one of them all of our lives. I told him, 'I think you're right.' I kept thinking if I did everything right, I wouldn't be a 'greaser.' But after all these years, I'm still a 'greaser' in their eyes. It took my son to make me see it. Now I know. If I weren't I'd be head of the shipping department by now, not just one of the supervisors, and maybe Paul wouldn't be wasting his life on the corner."

* * *

We keep saying that family matters, that with a stable family and two caring parents children will grow to a satisfactory adulthood. But I've rarely met a family that's more constant or more concerned than the Riveras. Or one where both parents are so involved with their children. Ana was a full-time homemaker until Paul, their youngest, was twelve. Rick has been with the same company for more than twenty-five years, having worked his way up from clerk to shift supervisor in its shipping department. Whatever the conflicts in their marriage, theirs is clearly a warm, respectful, and caring relationship. Yet their daughter got pregnant and gave up her plans for college, and a son is idling his youth away on a street corner.

Obviously, then, something more than family matters. Growing up in a world where opportunities are available makes a difference. As does being able to afford to take advantage of an opportunity when it comes by. Getting an education that broadens horizons and prepares a child for a productive adulthood makes a difference. As does being able to find work that nourishes self-respect and pays a living wage. Living in a world that doesn't judge you by the color of your skin makes a difference. As does feeling the respect of the people around you.

This is not to suggest that there aren't also real problems inside American families that deserve our serious and sustained attention. But the constant focus on the failure of family life as the locus of both our personal and social difficulties has become a mindless litany, a dangerous diversion from the economic and social realities that make family life so difficult today and that so often destroy it.

THE KWANS

It's a rare sunny day in Seattle, so Andy Kwan and I are in his backyard, a lovely showcase for his talents as a landscape gardener. Although it has been only a few years since we first met, most of the people to whom I've returned in this round of interviews seem older, grayer, more careworn. Andy Kwan is no exception. The brilliant afternoon sunshine is cruel as it searches out every line of worry and age in his angular face. Since I interviewed his wife the day before, I already know that the recession has hurt his business. So I begin by saying, "Carol says that your business has been slow for the last couple of years."

"Yes," he sighs. "At first when the recession came, it didn't hurt me. I think Seattle didn't really get hit at the beginning. But the summer of 1991, that's when I began to feel it. It's as if everybody zipped up their wallets when it came to landscaping.

"A lot of my business has always been when people buy a new house. You know, they want to fix up the outside just like they like it. But nobody's been buying houses lately, and even if they do, they're not putting any money into landscaping. So it's been tight, real tight."

"How have you managed financially?"

"We get by, but it's hard. We have to cut back on a lot of stuff we used to take for granted, like going out to eat once in a while, or going to the movies, things like that. Clothes, nobody gets any new clothes anymore.

"I do a lot of regular gardening now—you know, the maintenance stuff. It helps; it takes up some of the slack, but it's not enough because it doesn't pay much. And the competition's pretty stiff, so you've got to keep your prices down. I mean, everybody knows that it's one of the things people can cut out when things get tough, so the gardeners around here try to hold on by cutting their prices. It gets pretty hairy, real cutthroat."

He gets up, walks over to a flower bed, and stands looking at it. Then, after a few quiet moments, he turns back to me and says, "It's a damned shame. I built my business like you build a house, brick by brick, and it was going real good. I finally got to the point where I wasn't doing much regular gardening anymore. I could concentrate on landscaping, and I was making a pretty good living. With Carol working, too, we were doing all right. I even hired two people and was keeping them busy most of the time. Then all of a sudden, it all came tumbling down.

"I felt real bad when I had to lay off my workers. They have families to feed, too. But what could I do? Now it's like I'm back where I started, an ordinary gardener again and even worrying about how long that'll last," he says disconsolately.

He walks back to his seat, sits down, and continues somewhat more philosophically, "Carol says I shouldn't complain because, with all the problems, we're lucky. She still has her job, and I'm making out. I mean, it's not great, but it could be a lot worse." He pauses, looks around blankly for a moment, sighs, and says, "I guess she's right. Her sister worked at Boeing for seven years and she got laid off a couple of months ago. No notice, nothing; just the pink slip. I mean, everybody knew there'd be layoffs there, but you know how it is. You don't think it's really going to happen to you.

"I try not to let it get me down. But it's hard to be thankful for not having bigger trouble than you've already got," he says ruefully. Then, a smile brightening his face for the first time, he adds, "But there's one thing I can be thankful for, and that's the kids; they're doing fine. I worry a little bit about what's going to happen, though. I guess you can't help it if you're a parent. Eric's the oldest; he's fifteen now, and you never know. Kids get into all kinds of trouble these days. But so far, he's okay. The girls, they're good kids. Carol worries about what'll happen when they get to those teenage years. But I think they'll be okay. We teach them decent values; they go to church every week. I have to believe that makes a difference."

"You say that you worry about Eric but that the girls will be fine because of the values of your family. Hasn't he been taught the same values?"

He thinks a moment, then says, "Did I say that? Yeah, I guess I did. I think maybe there's more ways for a boy to get in trouble than a girl." He laughs and says again, "Did I say *that?*" Then, more thoughtfully, "I don't know. I guess I worry about them all, but if you don't tell yourself that things'll work out okay, you go nuts. I mean, so much can go wrong with kids today.

"It used to be the Chinese family could really control the kids. When I was a kid, the family was law. My father was Chinese-born; he came here as a kid. My mother was born right here in this city. But the grandparents were all immigrants; everybody spoke Chinese at home; and we never lived more than a couple of blocks from both sides of the family. My parents were pretty Americanized everywhere but at home, at least while their parents were alive. My mother would go clean her mother's house for her because that's what a Chinese daughter did."

"Was that because your grandmother was old or sick?"

"No," he replies, shaking his head at the memory. "It's because that's what her mother expected her to do; that's the way Chinese families were then. We talk about that, Carol and me, and how things have changed. It's hard to imagine it, but that's the kind of control families had then.

"It's all changed now. Not that I'd want it that way. I want my kids to know respect for the family, but they shouldn't be servants. That's what my mother was, a servant for her mother.

"By the time my generation came along, things were already different. I couldn't wait to get away from all that family stuff. I mean, it was nice in some ways; there was always this big, noisy bunch of people around, and you knew you were part of something. That felt good. But Chinese families, boy, they don't let go. You felt like they were choking you.

"Now it's *really* different; it's like the kids aren't hardly Chinese any more. I mean, my kids are just like any other American kids. They never lived in a Chinese neighborhood like the one I grew up in, you know, the kind where the only Americans you see are the people who come to buy Chinese food or eat at the restaurants."

"You say they're ordinary American kids. What about the Chinese side? What kind of connection do they have to that?"

"It's funny," he muses. "We sent them to Chinese school because we wanted them to know about their history, and we thought they should know the language, at least a little bit. But they weren't really interested; they wanted to be like everybody else and eat peanut butter and jelly sandwiches. Lately it's a little different, but that's because they feel like they're picked on because they're Chinese. I mean, everybody's worrying about the Chinese kids being so smart and winning all the prizes at school, and the kids are angry about that, especially Eric. He says there's a lot of bad feelings about Chinese kids at school and that everybody's picking on them—the white kids and the black kids, all of them.

"So all of a sudden, he's becoming Chinese. It's like they're making him think about it because there's all this resentment about Asian kids all around. Until a couple of years ago, he had lots of white friends. Now he hangs out mostly with other Asian kids. I guess that's because they feel safer when they're together."

"How do you feel about this?"

The color rises in his face; his voice takes on an edge of agitation. "It's too bad. It's not the way I wanted it to be. I wanted my kids to know they're Chinese and be proud of it, but that's not what's going on now. It's more like . . .," he stops, trying to find the words, then starts again. "It's like they have to defend themselves *because* they're Chinese. Know what I mean?" he asks. Then without waiting for an answer, he explains, "There's all this prejudice now, so then you can't forget you're Chinese.

"It makes me damn mad. You grow up here and they tell you everybody's equal and that any boy can grow up to be president. Not that I ever thought a Chinese kid could ever be president; any Chinese kid knows that's fairy tale. But I did believe the rest of it, you know, that if you're smart and work hard and do well, people will respect you and you'll be successful. Now, it looks like the smarter Chinese kids are, the more trouble they get."

"Do you think that prejudice against Chinese is different now than when you were growing up?"

"Yeah, I do. When I was a kid like Eric, nobody paid much attention to the Chinese. They left us alone, and we left them alone. But now all these Chinese kids are getting in the way of the white kids because there's so many of them, and they're getting better grades, and things like that. So then everybody gets mad because they think our kids are taking something from them."

He stops, weighs his last words, then says, "I guess they're right, too. When I was growing up, Chinese kids were lucky to graduate from high school, and we didn't get in anybody's way. Now so many Chinese kids are going to college that they're taking over places white kids used to have. I can understand that they don't like that. But that's not our problem; it's theirs. Why don't they work hard like Chinese kids do?

"It's not fair that they've got quotas for Asian kids because the people who run the colleges decided there's too many of them and not enough room for white kids. Nobody ever worried that there were too many white kids, did they?"

* * *

"It's not fair"—a cry from the heart, one I heard from nearly everyone in this study. For indeed, life has not been fair to the working-class people of America, no matter what their color or ethnic background. And it's precisely this sense that it's not fair, that there isn't enough to go around, that has stirred the racial and ethnic tensions that are so prevalent today.

In the face of such clear class disparities, how is it that our national discourse continues to focus on the middle class, denying the existence of a working class and rendering them invisible?

Whether a family or a nation, we all have myths that play tag with reality—myths that frame our thoughts, structure our beliefs, and organize our systems of denial. A myth encircles reality, encapsulates it, controls it. It allows us to know some things and to avoid knowing others, even when somewhere deep inside we really know what we don't want to know. Every parent has experienced this clash between myth and reality. We see signals that tell us a child is lying and explain them away. It isn't that we can't know; it's that we won't, that knowing is too difficult or painful, too discordant with the myth that defines the relationship, the one that says: *My child wouldn't lie to me.*

The same is true about a nation and its citizens. Myths are part of our national heritage, giving definition to the national character, offering guidance for both public and private behavior, comforting us in our moments of doubt. Not infrequently our myths trip over each other, providing a window into our often contradictory and ambivalently held beliefs. The myth that we are a nation of equals lives side-by-side in these United States with the belief in white supremacy. And, unlikely as it seems, it's quite possible to believe both at the same time. Sometimes we manage the conflict by shifting from one side to the other. More often, we simply redefine reality. The inequality of condition between whites and blacks isn't born in prejudice and discrimination, we insist; it's black inferiority that's the problem. Class distinctions have nothing to do with privilege, we say; it's merit that makes the difference.

It's not the outcome that counts, we maintain; it's the rules of the game. And since the rules say that everyone comes to the starting line equal, the different results are merely products of individual will and wit. The fact that working-class children usually grow up to be working-class parents doesn't make a dent in the belief system, nor does it lead to questions about why the written rule and the lived reality are at odds. Instead, with perfect circularity, the outcome reinforces the reasoning that says they're deficient, leaving those so labeled doubly wounded—first by the real problems in living they face, second by internalizing the blame for their estate.

Two decades ago, when I began the research for *Worlds of Pain*, we were living in the immediate aftermath of the civil rights revolution that had convulsed the nation since the mid-1950s. Significant gains had been won. And despite the tenacity with which this headway had been resisted by some, most white Americans were feeling good about themselves. No one expected the nation's racial problems and conflicts to dissolve easily or quickly. But there was also a sense that we were moving in the right direction, that there was a national commitment to redressing at least some of the worst aspects of black-white inequality.

In the intervening years, however, the national economy buckled under the weight of three recessions, while the nation's industrial base was undergoing a massive restructuring. At the same time, government policies requiring preferential treatment were enabling African-Americans and other minorities to make small but visible inroads into what had been, until then, largely white terrain. The sense of scarcity, always a part of American life but intensified sharply by the history of these economic upheavals, made minority gains seem particularly threatening to white working-class families.

It isn't, of course, just working-class whites who feel threatened by minority progress. Wherever racial minorities make inroads into formerly all-white territory, tensions increase. But it's working-class families who feel the fluctuations in the economy most quickly and most keenly. For them, these last decades have been like a bumpy roller coaster ride. "Every time we think we might be able to get ahead, it seems like we get knocked down again," declares Tom Ahmundsen, a forty-two-year-old white construction worker. "Things look a little better; there's a little more work; then all of a sudden, boom, the economy falls apart and it's gone. You can't count on anything; it really gets you down."

This is the story I heard repeatedly: Each small climb was followed by a fall, each glimmer of hope replaced by despair. As the economic vise tightened, despair turned to anger. But partly because we have so little concept of class resentment and conflict in America, this anger isn't directed so much at those above as at those below. And when whites at or near the bottom of the ladder look down in this nation, they generally see blacks and other minorities.

True, during all of the 1980s and into the 1990s, white ire was fostered by national administrations that fanned racial discord as a way of fending off white discontent—of diverting anger about the state of the economy and the declining quality of urban life to the foreigners and racial others in our midst. But our history of racial animosity coupled with our lack of class consciousness made this easier to accomplish than it might otherwise have been.

The difficult realities of white working-class life not withstanding, however, their whiteness has accorded them significant advantages—both materially and psychologically—over people of color. Racial discrimination and segregation in the workplace have kept competition for the best jobs at a minimum. They do, obviously, have to compete with each other for the resources available. But that's different. It's a competition among equals; they're all white. They don't think such things consciously, of course; they don't have to. It's understood, rooted in the culture and supported by the social contract that says they are the superior ones, the worthy ones. Indeed, this is precisely why, when the courts or the legislatures act in ways that seem to contravene that belief, whites experience themselves as victims.

From the earliest days of the republic, whiteness has been the ideal, and freedom and independence have been linked to being white. "Republicanism," writes labor historian David Roediger, "had long emphasized that the strength, virtue and resolve of a people guarded them from enslavement." And it was whites who had these qualities in abundance, as was evident, in the peculiarly circuitous reasoning of the time, in the fact that they were not slaves.

By this logic, the enslavement of blacks could be seen as stemming from their "slavishness" rather than from the institution of slavery. Slavery is gone now, but the reasoning lingers on in white America, which still insists that the lowly estate of people of color is due to their deficits, whether personal or cultural, rather than to the prejudice, discrimination, and institutionalized racism that has barred them from full participation in the society.

This is not to say that culture is irrelevant, whether among black Americans or any other group in our society. The lifeways of a people develop out of their experiences—out of the daily events, large and small, that define their lives; out of the resources that are available to them to meet both individual and group needs; out of the place in the social, cultural, and political systems within which group life is embedded. In the case of a significant proportion of blacks in America's inner cities, centuries of racism and economic discrimination have produced a subculture that is both personally and socially destructive. But to fault culture or the failure of individual responsibility without understanding the larger context within which such behaviors occur is to miss a vital piece of the picture. Nor does acknowledging the existence of certain destructive subcultural forms among some African-Americans disavow or diminish the causal connections between the structural inequalities at the social, political, and economic levels and the serious social problems at the community level.

In his study of "working-class lads" in Birmingham, England, for example, Paul Willis observes that their very acts of resistance to middle-class norms—the defiance with which these young men express their anger at class inequalities—help to reinforce the class structure by further entrenching them in their working-class status. The same can be said for some of the young men in the African-American community, whose active rejection of white norms and "in your face" behavior consigns them to the bottom of the American economic order.

To understand this doesn't make such behavior, whether in England or the United States, any more palatable. But it helps to explain the structural sources of cultural forms and to apprehend the social processes that undergird them. Like Willis's white "working-class lads," the hip-hoppers and rappers in the black community who are so determinedly "not white" are not just making a statement about black culture. They're also expressing their rage at white society for offering a promise of equality, then refusing to fulfill it. In the process, they're finding their own way to some accommodation and to a place in the world they can call their own, albeit one that ultimately reinforces their outsider status.

But, some might argue, white immigrants also suffered prejudice and discrimination in the years after they first arrived, but they found more socially acceptable ways to accommodate. It's true—and so do most of today's people of color, both immigrant and native born. Nevertheless, there's another truth as well. For wrenching as their early experiences were for white ethnics, they had an out. Writing about the Irish, for example, Roediger shows how they were able to insist upon their whiteness and to prove it by adopting the racist attitudes and behaviors of other whites, in the process often becoming leaders in the assault against blacks. With time and their growing political power, they won the prize they sought—recognition as whites. "The imperative to define themselves as white," writes Roediger, "came from the particular 'public and psychological wages' whiteness offered to a desperate rural and often preindustrial Irish population coming to labor in industrializing American cities."

Thus does whiteness bestow its psychological as well as material blessings on even the most demeaned. For no matter how far down the socioeconomic ladder whites may fall, the one thing they can't lose is their whiteness. No small matter because, as W. E. B. DuBois observed decades ago, the compensation of white workers includes a psychological wage, a bonus that enables them to believe in their inherent superiority over nonwhites.

It's also true, however, that this same psychological bonus that white workers prize so highly has cost them dearly. For along with the importation of an immigrant population, the separation of black and white workers has given American capital a reserve labor force to call upon whenever white workers seemed to them to get too "uppity." Thus, while racist ideology enables white workers to maintain the belief in their superiority, they have paid for that conviction by becoming far more vulnerable in the struggle for decent wages and working conditions than they might otherwise have been. . . .

READING 28

The Economy That Never Sleeps

Harriet B. Presser

Forty percent of the American labor force works mostly during nonstandard times—in the evenings, overnight, on rotating or variable shifts, or on weekends. These schedules challenge American families, particularly those with children. Research suggests that such schedules undermine the stability of marriages, increase the amount of housework to be done, reduce family cohesiveness, and require elaborate child-care arrangements.

Nonstandard work schedules also have some benefits. Most notably, when fathers and mothers work different shifts, fathers and children typically spend more time together and child care costs less. Parents of school-aged children who work late shifts can see their children off to school and welcome them home. However, the advantages and disadvantages of nonstandard work hours are not evenly distributed. Some kinds of families and workers feel the downside more than others. And all off-hour workers and families need more attention than they are now getting.

Late and rotating work shifts are certainly not new. Some people have always worked at all hours of the day and night. While official data on which hours people work have only recently become available, in recent decades the number of people working nonstandard schedules seems to have increased. A central factor is the remarkable growth of the service economy—particularly in the food, recreation, travel and medical care industries—all of which require more round-the-clock employees than does manufacturing. Consumers are clamoring for continuously available services as well. We see these trends in the newly common phrase "24/7" and in the extension of store hours. Indeed, the 7-Eleven convenience stores, once considered unusual for opening at 7 A.M. and closing at 11 P.M., are anachronistically named: almost all of them are now open around the clock.

At the same time, families themselves are changing. With the growth of female employment, spouses increasingly both work. Also, increasingly many employed mothers are single parents. The "Ozzie and Harriet" family—in which the father works outside the home full time and the mother is a full-time homemaker—has become more and more of an exception. Although we have belatedly come to acknowledge this change, we still tend to think of employed parents as working in the daytime and home with their children in the evening and at night. This remains the case for most parents, but not for a substantial minority.

With more employed mothers—married or single—and more diverse work schedules, the rhythm of family life is changing for millions of Americans. We need to discuss whether employers and government can and should do more to ease the social and physical stresses that many families experience. Moreover, employees need to be aware of the risks of working late and rotating hours so that they can make more informed decisions before accepting such a job—assuming, of course, they have a genuine choice in the matter.

WHO WORKS NONSTANDARD SCHEDULES?

Nonstandard work schedules are surprisingly common. One out of five employed Americans work most of their hours outside the range of 8 A.M. to 4 P.M., or have a regularly rotating schedule. Many more work at least some of their hours in the evenings or at night. About one-third of employed Americans work Saturday, Sunday or both. Men are somewhat more likely than women to work nonstandard schedules, and minorities—particularly blacks—are more likely to do so than non-Hispanic whites. (These estimates are based on a large, representative national sample in 1997. More recent numbers, not yet fully analyzed, suggest little change since then.)

Dual-earner married couples are especially likely to have at least one spouse working late or rotating shifts. In 1997, this was so for 28 percent of all such couples, but even more so for those with children: 35 percent of dual-earner couples with a child under 5 had a parent with such a schedule. (Rarely did both spouses work such schedules.) These percentages are yet higher among low-income couples, the families most likely to be under financial stress while juggling a difficult work schedule.

Weekend work among dual-earner couples is also very common. In more than two-fifths of all dual-earner couples, at least one spouse worked on Saturday or Sunday. The ratio was closer to one-half of all dual-earner couples with children under five. And again, low-income couples had especially high rates of weekend work.

Single mothers are more likely than married mothers to work at nonstandard times and to work long hours. About one-fourth of single mothers with children worked late or rotating shifts and more than one-third worked weekends. For single mothers with children under age five, these ratios were one-fourth and two-fifths, respectively—and still higher for those with low incomes.

STRESS ON MARRIAGES

Late and rotating work schedules seem particularly damaging to marriages when the couples have children at home. The competing demands of children and spouses come through in intensive interviews with such couples. In *Families on the Fault Line*, Lillian Rubin writes about one couple working split shifts: "If the arriving spouse gets home early enough, there may be an hour when both are there together. But with the pressures of the workday fresh for one and awaiting for the other, and with children clamoring for parental attention, there isn't a promising moment for serious conversation" (p. 95). From similar interviews in *Halving It All*, Francine Deutsch reports that, although this arrangement allowed both spouses to care for their children themselves and contribute to family income, "the loss of time together was a bitter pill to swallow. The physical separation symbolized a spiritual separation as well" (p. 177).

Large survey studies confirm that dual-earner couples with children have a less satisfactory married life when one spouse works at nonstandard times. I found, in a sample of about 3,500 married couples, that those in which one spouse works a late shift report having substantially less quality time together and more marital unhappiness. Couples with children are also more likely to separate or divorce. Neither working the evening shift nor weekends seemed to endanger the marriages; only night work did. One might think that spouses who choose to work night shifts do so because their marriages have soured, but data suggest the opposite: the schedule is the cause and marital strain is the effect. Spouses who moved into night work after the first interviews were not any less happy with their marriages during those pre-change interviews than were other employed spouses.

FAMILY REACTIONS

When spouses work different shifts, housework expands. Spouses tend to fend for themselves more, adding to the total family work load. Each one may make dinner for him- or herself rather than one cooking for two (as well as for the children). The husbands also do more traditionally female tasks, such as cleaning house, washing, ironing and cooking. These changes emerge for couples both with and without children. Although wives typically still spend considerably more time than husbands doing housework, husbands shoulder a larger share when their wives are not available. Working late shifts may not be the ideal way of achieving gender equality in housework, but it may be considered a good change by many wives in this situation. However, men who have traditional expectations may see it differently, making housework a potential source of friction.

The family dinner is typically the only daily event that allows for meaningful family time. The dinnertime absence of parents who work evening shifts is clearly a cost. (Night shifts and weekend employment do not generally undercut the family dinner, although schedules that rotate around the clock can.) As [Figure 28.1] shows,

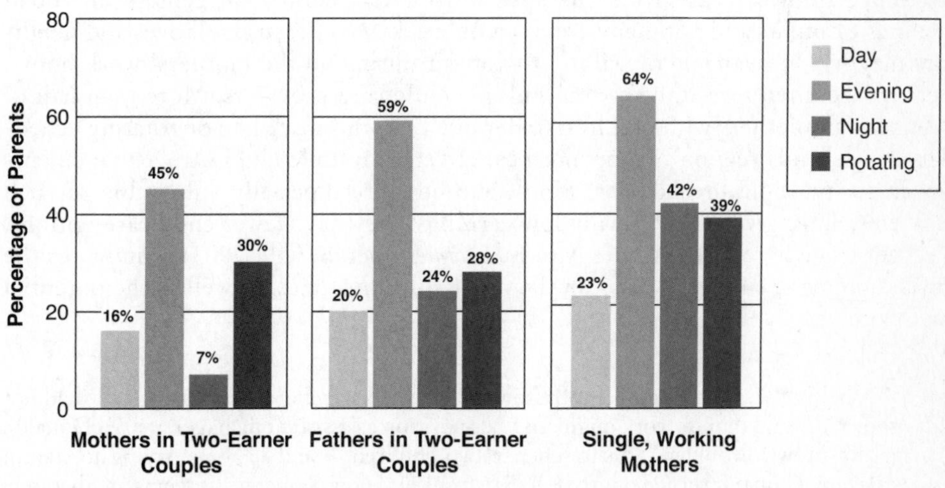

FIGURE 28.1 ***Missing Dinner: Percentage of Parents Who Ate Dinner with Their Children Fewer than 5 Times in the Last Week, According to the Work Shift***

Source: 1987–88 National Survey of Families and Households.

among dual-earner couples with children ages 5 to 13, about 45 percent of the mothers and 59 percent of the fathers who worked evenings had dinner with their children fewer than five days a week. Many of their children at least had one parent available at dinnertime—but not children of single mothers. When single moms worked evenings, fewer than 40 percent ate with their children at least five days a week. Their children may have been eating with other adults, with siblings, or alone—we do not know. (Parents who miss dinner with their children because they work the evening shift do not compensate by having breakfast with them more often.)

Child care also must be negotiated differently. If mothers who work evenings or nights are married, their husbands who work during the day typically assume responsibility for child care during those hours. More than four-fifths of fathers with children under age 5 did so. Child care is also shared when the work schedules of spouses are reversed and the husband works nonstandard hours.

This tag-team arrangement increases father-child interaction. It also reduces the cost of child care. Holding down expenses is especially a concern when married mothers have low-paying jobs. But most married mothers who work evenings, nights or rotating shifts do not say they do it for this reason. Many say it is because the job demands it. Similarly, very few fathers of young children report that they work non-standard schedules for child care reasons, even though they are often caregivers. Many parents simply do not have a choice in their work schedules.

Child care studies show that off-hours workers also rely heavily on relatives, particularly grandparents. Single mothers are especially likely to rely on grandparents, particularly grandmothers, who often work jobs with hours different from their daughters', allowing them to care for their grandchildren in their "off time."

Both single and married mothers have to rely on relatives (as well as neighbors and other informal caregivers) because only a few child care centers are open evenings or nights and not many are open on weekends. Because relatives and neighbors may not be available or willing to babysit during all the mothers' work hours, mothers are often forced to rely on multiple child care providers. More than half of all American mothers with children under age five who work late or rotating schedules or weekends rely on two or more caregivers. Multiple child care arrangements can create multiple breakdowns. Single mothers are especially vulnerable to such problems, since given their usually low earnings, they have fewer child care options. A recent tragedy reported in the *New York Times* (October 19, 2003) illuminates the frustration many single mothers on the night shift must face, as well as the potential for calamity:

> [A]s her night shift neared, Kim Brathwaite faced a hard choice. Her baby sitter had not shown up, and to miss work might end her position as assistant manager at a McDonald's in downtown Brooklyn. So she left her two children, 9 and 1, alone, trying to stay in touch by phone. It turned out to be a disastrous decision. Someone, it seems, deliberately set fire to the apartment. Her children died. And within hours, Ms. Brathwaite was under arrest, charged with recklessly endangering her children . . . and now faces up to 16 years in prison. . . .

HEALTH

Several intensive studies suggest that sleep deprivation is a chronic problem for people who work late at night or rotate their hours around the clock on a regular basis. Parents who forego sleep in order to be available for their children when they are home from school aggravate the toll on their personal health. People with such schedules run higher risks of gastrointestinal disorders, cardiovascular disease and breast cancer. Late and changing work schedules affect our sleep cycles, which in turn are linked to such biological functions as body temperature and hormone levels. Also, being out of sync with the daily rhythms of other family members raises stress and further affects physiological and psychological health.

A PUBLIC DISCUSSION

Clearly, employment in a 24/7 economy challenges American families. Given what we already know—and there is more to learn—we need more public discussion on the role of employers and government. How can we help American workers and families who are feeling the pinch of nonstandard work shifts either to change to day schedules or cope with the odd hours? Low-income parents merit special attention, because they have the fewest work options and suffer the worst financial and emotional stress.

There are several policy options. For instance, we could require higher wages for late shifts to compensate workers for the social and health costs of their schedules, or reduce work hours on late shifts (without a reduction in pay) to minimize the stress on individuals and families. Such reforms could make a major difference for 24/7 workers. Although employment at nonstandard times is pervasive from the worst to the best jobs, one-third of the nonstandard jobs are concentrated in just 10 service-sector occupations, most of which are low paying: cashiers; truck drivers; sales people; waiters and waitresses; cooks; janitors and cleaners; sales supervisors and proprietors; registered nurses; food service and lodging managers; and nursing aides, orderlies, and attendants. Except for registered nurses, the median hourly pay for those in the same occupations who work at nonstandard times is about the same as or less than the pay for people who work daytimes and weekdays only. On the other hand, a financial premium for taking late shifts might tempt more nonparents to compete for those jobs or more low-income parents to take them.

Efforts to enact workshift reforms are constrained by a lack of legal guidelines for adult workers. The Fair Labor Standards Act deals with overtime compensation for working more than 40 hours a week, but does not deal explicitly with work shifts. Pay premiums for shift work are generally negotiated by unions, but only a small minority of American workers are union members. Some unions have negotiated reduced hours at full-time pay for people working late shifts, but this is rare and the pay premiums generally are not large.

Policy could also address the particular difficulties of nonstandard shifts for parents with children by expanding the availability, flexibility and affordability of child care. Little child care is available in the evening and overnight. (Ironically, the people who would provide the care would themselves become part of the problem.) Extra compensation from public sources to providers may be needed. On-site care by employers, as some hospitals provide, and near-site care, as some airports provide, may also help. But many neighborhoods resist the late-night traffic of parents dropping off and picking up their children.

Alternatively, child care subsidies would give more low-income mothers the option of working standard hours while using day care for their young children. As noted earlier, parents who work late shifts rely heavily on multiple child-care arrangements with spouses, relatives and others. Such arrangements for late-hour home care may be financially cheaper than center care, but they may be more costly socially for everyone involved.

Finally, a policy option is to regulate night work, as many other highly industrialized countries do. For example, Belgium has highly restrictive legislation, which generally prohibits work between 8 P.M. and 6 A.M. (exceptions allow for emergency services) and all night workers are entitled by law to substantial pay premiums. However, while European unions fought for such legislation, the restriction of late work shifts does not seem to be high on the agenda of American organized labor. Some voices call for reducing the work week from 40 to 35 hours without reducing pay, but these suggestions treat all hours alike.

If new regulations are pursued, they must avoid discouraging employers from hiring parents of young children. Janet Gornick and Marcia Meyers have proposed the adoption of gender-egalitarian protections that would prevent employers from forcing parents into nonstandard shifts. These protections would expand child care as well, so that parents could switch out of those shifts if they so desire (and presumably not lose their jobs). This is clearly a complex social issue, especially in light of the increasing wariness of protective legislation amid concerns about who is protected by it. In 1990, the International Labor Organization decided to drop its recommended restrictions on women working at night after realizing that the rule had a discriminatory effect: to save those jobs for men. Similarly, in the United States, legislation protective of women was declared by the courts to be invalid under the 1964 Civil Rights Act, which outlawed sex discrimination.

Americans may not be debating these matters because, as consumers, we like stores to be open around the clock, medical services to be available continuously, and people to answer the phone when we make travel reservations late at night. Also, as employees, we may benefit from the expansion of job opportunities in a 24/7 economy. But, again, the economy that never sleeps poses risks to the workers who staff it, and to their families. Given that difficult work schedules are currently a fact of life in our economy, it is obvious that we need to think about how to mitigate their harm. Some employers have tried out shift rotation systems that minimize employee fatigue; others have investigated the use of light to control or change the circadian rhythms of people working late hours. There is also talk about medications that could reset the body's clock. We must consider as well the ethical issues that underlie these manipulations, insofar as they put workers out of sync with family and friends.

When 2 of every 5 working Americans are on nonstandard shifts, employment in a 24/7 economy and its effects on them and their families clearly need to be put higher on the public agenda. The underlying trends that have brought about the great diversity in work schedules among Americans will surely continue, and we need to confront the challenges they pose for American families.

Recommended Resources

Casper, Lynne M. "My Daddy Takes Care of Me!: Fathers as Care Providers." *Current Population Reports.* Washington, D.C.: U.S. Government Printing Office for the U.S. Bureau of the Census, 1997. Casper describes in detail the extent to which American fathers provide child care when mothers are employed.

Deutsch, Francine. *Halving It All: How Equally Shared Parenting Works.* Cambridge, MA: Harvard University Press, 1999. This interview-based study includes a chapter on how some dual-earner couples work different shifts to manage child care.

Presser, Harriet B. *Working in a 24/7 Economy: Challenges for American Families.* New York: Russell Sage Foundation, 2003. This book describes what we know about work shifts in the United States and their consequences for American families.

Presser, Harriet B. "Race-Ethnic and Gender Differences in Nonstandard Work Shifts." *Work and Occupations* 30 (2003): 412–439. I examine how work shifts differ by race, ethnicity and gender.

Wedderburn, Alexander, ed. "Shiftwork and Health." Special issue of *Bulletin of Studies on Time, Vol. 1.* Luxembourg: Office for Official Publications of the European Communities, 2001. Online. http://www.eurofound.ie. This report provides a comprehensive analysis of the relationship between shift work and health.

READING 29

The Missing Class

Katherine S. Newman and Victor Tan Chen

Valerie Rushing starts her shift at midnight. A train pulls into the station, and she hops on it, mop in hand. The thirty-three-year-old mother of one is an employee for the Long Island Rail Road, the busiest commuter railroad in North America, which every morning carries an army of groggy suburbanites to their Manhattan offices, and every night shuttles them back home. When their day ends, hers begins. Most nights she'll mop twenty cars. Tonight it's twice that because she's working a double shift—midnight to 8 A.M., and 8 A.M. to 4 P.M.

Toilet duty, of course, is the worst. Long Islanders are a more slovenly sort than the city's notorious subway riders, Valerie grouses. "You figure that they would have some consideration for the next person that is going to use the bathroom, but they don't. They'll throw their whatevers there in the garbage, in the toilet. . . . And they are the most alcoholic people that I know." Every night, an eclectic assortment of paper-sheathed beer cans and bottles awaits her.

But don't feel sorry for Valerie Rushing. With a union card in her pocket, she makes $13.68 an hour, plus full benefits.[1] Her earlier life at the minimum wage—as a child-care worker, shoe-store employee, and fast-food cashier—is a distant memory.

Two years with the Long Island Rail Road have broadened Valerie's outlook. Before, she hardly ventured into the other boroughs; now she feels comfortable traversing the city and doesn't think twice about heading out to Manhattan to shop. Yes, it's janitorial work, but Valerie doesn't complain. "If it's sweeping, it's sweeping," she says. The point is, it pays the bills.

And Valerie has a lot of bills. She has sole responsibility for her daughter and has custody of her niece's six-year-old son because his own grandmother, Valerie's crack-addled sister, can't be bothered. Valerie sets aside part of every paycheck for the children's clothes, toys, and excursions. She puts aside another part to pay for her $700-a-month Brooklyn apartment, and she stashes away what she can toward that suburban house she hopes to buy someday soon.[2]

Valerie is not poor, but she is not middle class. Instead, she occupies an obscure place between rungs of the nation's social ladder—somewhere between working hard and succeeding, between dreaming big and living in the shadow of her ambitions. People like Valerie don't make the headlines. They aren't invited to focus groups. Blue-ribbon commissions on poverty do not include them. They are a forgotten labor force—too prosperous to be the "working poor," too insecure to be "middle income."

They are America's Missing Class.

They are people like Tomás Linares. A year shy of fifty, he is still clocking in seven days a week at two jobs in centers for people with developmental disabilities, where Tomás spends his days patiently demonstrating to his charges how to brush their teeth, reprimanding them for stealing and scratching, and occasionally wrestling an unruly resident to the floor. For his efforts, he makes a little less than $20,000 a year.

Tomás is not poor, but a look at his rundown Brooklyn apartment might suggest otherwise. He lives in an urban borderland sandwiched between two extremes: the concentrated poverty of rampant drug dealing, sporadic gang violence, and shuttered factories that Tomás has known since his youth and the collateral prosperity that middle-class newcomers and mounting real estate prices bring to Brooklyn these days. Divorced and lacking a college education, Tomás has few prospects for rising much higher in life and no illusion that he'll ever leave his seedy corner.

Gloria Hall is part of the Missing Class as well, but perhaps for not much longer. An employee of the city's health department, she stopped working after falling seriously ill. She has insurance, but her policy won't cover the specialized treatment recommended for her rare form of cancer. So Gloria is a frequent visitor to the local teaching hospital, a drab health-care assembly line where patients like her are nonchalantly wheeled from room to room, waiting interminably for their release. For Gloria, living in near poverty means walking a tightrope over this frayed safety net, unsure of what each new step in her treatment will bring.

It also means worrying about what her deteriorating health will mean for her two adolescent sons, who suffer from the affliction of a deadbeat dad. What will happen to them if she dies? Who will care for them when she's not there? She knows that the odds are stacked against children like hers, those who are unlucky enough to be born black and male and statistically at risk—as crime victims and perpetrators, developmentally disabled and dropouts. Her two boys are unluckier still: they live in a household that is not poor but near poor. "I know some parents that are in worse situations than I am, financially," Gloria says. "And they get everything. Every year their kids go away to summer camp.

"You either got to be on the bottom, or you've got to be on the top."

Thirty-seven million Americans live below the poverty line. We know a lot about them because journalists, politicians, think tanks, and social scientists track their lives in great detail. Every time the poverty rate goes up or down, political parties take credit or blame for this important bellwether.

Yet there is a much larger population of Americans that virtually no one pays attention to: the near poor. Fifty-four million Americans—including 21 percent of the nation's children—live in this nether region above the poverty line but well below a secure station.[3] This "Missing Class" is composed of households earning roughly between $20,000 and $40,000 for a family of four.[4]

The hard-won wages of Missing Class families place them beyond the reach of most policies that speak to the conditions of life among the poor. Yet they are decidedly *not* middle-class Americans. In decades past we might have called them working class, but even that label fails to satisfy, now that many Missing Class workers toil in traditionally white-collar domains like health clinics and schools, even as their incomes, households, and neighborhoods lack the solidity of an earlier generation's blue-collar, union-sheltered way of life. Missing Class families earn less money, have few savings to cushion themselves, and send their kids to schools that are underfunded and crowded. The near poor live in inner-ring suburbs and city centers where many of the social problems that plague the truly poor constrain their lives as well. Crime, drugs, and delinquency are less of a problem in near-poor neighborhoods than they are in blighted ghettos, but they are down the block, within earshot, and close enough to threaten their kids.

Sending Missing Class teens to college, the single most important fault line in determining their long-range prospects, is difficult for the near poor. Many are unaware of the financial aid that might await their children. Parents who have never navigated the shoals of college admission are poorly prepared to offer advice, and the schools that might take over this stewardship are overwhelmed with the task of getting kids to graduate in the first place. Near-poor kids are the ones who work many hours while still in high school, who hardly ever see their guidance counselor, and who struggle to complete homework assignments that no one nearby can help them with.

Yet, because their earnings place them above the poverty line, the Missing Class is rarely on the national radar screen. We just don't think about them. This needs to change. The fate of Missing Class families is a test for this country of what it can offer to those citizens—immigrants and native-born alike—who have pulled themselves off the floor that poverty represents. If they can move up, they clear the way for those coming behind them. If they can at least stay where they are, their example will matter to others. But if their children fail to advance—if they fall back into the hole that the parents labored so hard to escape from—we will have defaulted on the promise of this wealthy nation. We will have seen a temporary respite in a single generation from the problems of poverty, only to see it emerge again in the children of the Missing Class. The danger is real—and growing with every new crack in our increasingly open and vulnerable economy.

Ironically, some of their problems stem from what most would agree is an entirely positive aspect of Missing Class life. Near-poor parents are firmly attached to the world of work. While many arrived in the Missing Class as graduates from the ranks of the welfare dependent, they are now lodged in jobs as transit workers, day-care providers, hospital attendants, teachers' aides, and clerical assistants. They pay their taxes and struggle to keep afloat on wages that are better than the minimum—if not by a huge margin. Yet even as these men and women dutifully turn the wheels of the national economy, their devotion to work takes a toll on their family life, especially on their children, who spend long hours in substandard day care or raise themselves in their teen years.

Of necessity, Missing Class families live fairly close to the margins. They have a hard time saving to buffer themselves from downturns in the economy because a large portion of their income disappears into the pockets of landlords and cash registers of grocery stores every month. As long as the adults—and many of the teens—stay on the job, they can manage. But the slightest push can send them hurtling down the income ladder again. In fact, even in the prosperous years of 1996–2002, about 16 percent of the nation's near-poor families lost a tenth or more of their income. It is important to recognize that the majority actually went in the other direction: they gained income in excess of 30 percent. These upwardly mobile families are headed out of the Missing Class for something much better. Nonetheless, the group that slides is not insignificant, and its ranks have probably grown, now that the economy has cooled.[5]

Missing Class Americans live in safer communities than the truly poor. Indeed, many look out upon their neighborhoods in amazement because they are barely recognizable from the destitute and crime-ridden days of yore. As gentrification has taken root in overheated real estate markets, once-affordable enclaves are now almost beyond the reach of the Missing Class. The arrival of affluent new neighbors brings with it more attention from city officials and the police, more investment in the aesthetics of the community, and something closer to a rainbow of complexions on the streets. For the African Americans, Dominicans, and Puerto Ricans who used to "own" these neighborhoods, this is mainly a blessing. Still, some wonder whether they still belong— whether they are still welcome on their own turf.

Sixty-eight percent of Americans are now the proud owners of their own homes. The near poor must struggle to join their ranks. Many of them missed out on the great run-up in housing prices that created so much wealth in the 1990s and the first five years of this decade. Trapped in a renter's limbo, the Missing Class cannot feather its nest for retirement or borrow against houses to pay for children's college educations. What's more, the children won't enjoy anything approaching the inheritance—in property, cash, or other assets—that their middle-class counterparts will surely reap. These wealth differences are crucial: savings are the safety net that catches you when you falter, but Missing Class families have no such bulwark.[6] As a result, they experience an odd fusion of optimism and insecurity: the former from their upward mobility, the latter from the nagging concern that it could all disappear if just one thing goes wrong. One uninsured child sick enough to pull a parent off the job; one marriage spiraling into divorce; one layoff that shuts off the money spigot.

Like most American consumers, the Missing Class is impatient for just rewards. No one wants to sit on a couch with holes in it, but for the near poor, a new couch is beyond their means. The answer, too often, is debt. Missing Class families are generally uneducated in the ways of credit, and credit card companies are all too happy to indulge them.

They deluge the mailboxes of Missing Class families with offers; they avert their eyes as Missing Class households rack up outrageous bills. (In 2005 Congress passed bankruptcy laws that prevent consumers from shielding their assets from creditors, making this kind of debt even more lethal.)[7] What's more, Missing Class families live in neighborhoods that are chronically underserved by financial institutions and scrupulously avoided by grocery chains and other major retail outlets. Denied even the most basic infrastructure for savings or loans at reasonable rates and forced to pay a premium on virtually everything they buy, these harried workers turn to check-cashing stores that exact a cut before handing over their wages. They purchase their food, household goods, and furniture at corner bodegas and other small shops with high margins.

At the same time that the pull of rising wages and the push of welfare reform have drawn millions of low-income parents deeper into the labor market, new policies governing the lives of their children have emerged that clash with the demands of the adult work world. The No Child Left Behind Act has thrust the burly arm of the state into third-grade classrooms, where kids used to the demands of finger paints and Autoharps are now sweating high-stakes tests every year. Eight-year-olds wake up with stomachaches because they are afraid of being held back in school if they cannot pass these exams. Missing Class kids do not fret needlessly; the failure rates on statewide tests are high in their neighborhoods.

School district officials have their own problems to contend with. If their charges do not show significant improvement every year, they find their schools on watch lists, threatened with the loss of funds. How do they exact these improvements? Not by themselves. School systems see parents as an auxiliary teaching force. Notes come home every day explaining to parents that they must take their children to the library, read to them, and drill them on their arithmetic. For those who have the time and the skills to tutor their kids, this is not an onerous task. For the immigrant factory worker who leaves home at 7 A.M., commutes ninety minutes each way to a bottle-packing plant, and works a back-breaking eight-hour shift on an assembly line, the additional burden of helping her son with his reading every day is simply too much. All this "neglect" adds up in the end and yields dismal outcomes on high-stakes tests. For teenagers, it also means a license to misbehave. When Mom and Dad are working every hour they can find, no one is around to make sure that Johnny is doing his homework, and now that he's fourteen, there is no longer an after-school program to occupy him. Johnny may live in a safer, higher-income community than his poorer cousins, but chances are his neighborhood abuts rougher enclaves.[8] This sets up temptations and risks that snare many a Missing Class teen.

The kinds of jobs that sustain the near poor may not come with health insurance or retirement benefits attached. For the more fortunate whose employers do bestow these perks, the versions they enjoy are likely to be of lower quality than the middle-class kind. Medical insurance often comes with very high deductibles, amounting to something closer to catastrophic coverage.[9] It's a big step beyond no insurance at all, but it often exposes the Missing Class to medicine of middling quality, not to mention a host of bureaucratic complications not unlike what the uninsured face, including delayed care and expensive emergency-room treatment. And yet Missing Class families, more so than their wealthier counterparts, *need* first-rate health care. They live in apartments laden with lead paint and plagued by roaches. Asthma is epidemic in low-income neighborhoods in part because the housing there is in shambles and situated near highways belching out exhaust fumes.[10] When it comes to health, the near poor and the real poor can be hard to tell apart.

Every family has its own way of making decisions about finances and responsibilities, but among the fragile households of the Missing Class the negotiations are especially contentious and complex.[11] Figuring out who does what and for whom is no easy matter where "recombinant families"—made up of stepparents and children by different fathers—are concerned. What is a stepfather's financial responsibility for his wife's child from an earlier relationship? Is he supposed to buy him new Nikes? Or is that the responsibility of the boy's "real" father? What is a mother to do if her new man doesn't feel like paying for a school uniform? Should she take some of the money that he gives her for the phone bill to cover the cost? And how, exactly, should a mother feel when her tight household budget has to stretch even further because her husband has obligations to the children he had with his first wife?

Millions of divorced Americans cope with these sticky questions, albeit with difficulty. But many Missing Class families have only enough to get by, even when two parents are working. The stress of their dicey finances never bodes well for their marriages. Secrecy is rife. Husbands don't tell their wives what they make; they just dole out money for approved purposes. Working wives keep their earnings to themselves as well. Single mothers lean on boyfriends for help and may make their continued affection contingent on some form of support. Men who live alone make regular cash donations to their girlfriends. Thrusting monetary considerations into relationships of intimacy can lead to mutual wariness, even distrust. It is one of the many ways that life in the Missing Class is so delicately held together, even if it is clearly more comfortable than living below the poverty line.

With all these complexities and uncertainties, one might imagine that being near poor is a bleak existence. Not so. Missing Class families know far too many people who are genuinely mired in hardship to think that they deserve pity. In general, they see a good deal of promise in their lives. Comparisons with others who are in distress are always at hand because the near poor live cheek by jowl with the real poor. Chances are good that the less well-off members of their own extended family are among the truly disadvantaged.[12] The Missing Class sees itself as a success story from this vantage point—albeit one hanging on by its fingernails. In many respects, they represent hopeful evidence of upward mobility. As this book shows clearly, the problems of the near poor are not the same as those who live below the poverty line. They are not living in socially isolated neighborhoods, working jobs that have no future, or standing on the welfare lines. They are as likely to stroll past the gleaming new espresso bar on the corner as they are to be frequenting the seamy check-cashing storefront on the other side of the street. Indeed, these are the families for whom the nation's promise of opportunity has actually worked. But did it work well enough? Have they graduated from poverty for good? The question for the Missing Class is not whether they are doing better than their counterparts in the income bracket below them. The question is whether the gains they have made will endure, or disappear in the maelstrom of an increasingly uncertain economy.

READING 30

Why Middle-Class Mothers and Fathers Are Going Broke

Elizabeth Warren and Amelia Warren Tyagi

During the past generation, a great myth has swept through America. Like all good myths, the Over-Consumption Myth tells a tale to explain a confusing world. Why are so many Americans in financial trouble? Why are credit card debts up and savings down? Why are millions of mothers heading into the labor force and working overtime? The myth is so deeply embedded in our collective understanding that it resists even elementary questioning: Families have spent too much money buying things they don't need. Americans have a new character flaw—"the urge to splurge"[1]—and it is driving them to spend, spend, spend like never before.

The drive for all that spending is almost mystical in origin. John de Graaf and his coauthors explain in *Affluenza: The All-Consuming Epidemic*, "It's as if we Americans, despite our intentions, suffer from some kind of Willpower Deficiency Syndrome, a breakdown in affluenza immunity."[2] Economist Juliet Schor blames "the newer consumerism," but the results are the same. She points to "mass 'overspending' within the middle class [in which] large numbers of Americans spend more than they say they would like to, and more than they have. That they spend more than they realize they are spending, and more than is fiscally prudent.[3]

Many maladies are explained away by the Over-Consumptive Myth. Why are Americans in debt? Sociologist Robert Frank claims that America's newfound "Luxury Fever" forces middle-class families "to finance their consumption increases largely by reduced savings and increased debt."[4] Why are schools failing and streets unsafe? Juliet Schor cites "competitive spending" as a major contributor to "the deterioration of public goods" such as "education, social services, public safety, recreation, and culture."[5] Why are Americans unhappy? *Affluenza* sums it up: "The dogged pursuit for more" accounts for Americans' "overload, debt, anxiety, and waste."[6] Everywhere we turn, it seems that over-consumption is tearing at the very fabric of society.

The Over-Consumption Myth rests on the premise that families spend their money on things they don't really need. Over-consumption is not about medical care or basic housing; it is, in the words of Juliet Schor, about "designer clothes, a microwave, restaurant meals, home and automobile air conditioning, and, of course, Michael Jordan's ubiquitous athletic shoes, about which children and adults both display near-obsession."[7] And it isn't about buying a few goodies with extra income; it is about going deep into debt to finance consumer purchases that sensible people could do without.

The beauty of the Over-Consumption Myth is that it squares neatly with our own intuitions. We see the malls packed with shoppers. We receive catalogs filled with outrageously expensive gadgets. We think of that overpriced summer dress that hangs in the back of the closet or those power tools gathering dust in the garage. The conclusion seems indisputable: The "urge to splurge" is driving folks into economic ruin.

But is it true? Intuitions and anecdotes are no substitute for hard data, so we searched deep in the recesses of federal archives, where we found detailed information on Americans' spending patterns since the early 1970s, carefully sorted by spending categories and family size.[8] If families really are blowing their paychecks on designer clothes and restaurant meals, then the expenditure data should show that today's families are spending more on these frivolous items than ever before. (Throughout our discussion, in this [reading] . . . all figures will be adjusted for the effects of inflation.[9]) But we found that the numbers pointed in a very different direction, demonstrating that the over-consumption explanation is just a myth.

Consider clothing. *Newsweek* recently ran a multipage cover story about Americans drowning in debt. The reason for widespread financial distress and high bankruptcy rates? "Frivolous shopping is part of the problem: many debtors blame their woes squarely on Tommy, Ralph, Gucci, and Prada."[10] That certainly sounds reasonable. After all, Banana Republic is so crowded with shoppers we can barely find an empty fitting room, Adidas and Nike clad the feet of every teenager we meet, and designer shops rake in profits selling nothing but underwear or sunglasses. Even little children's clothes now carry hip brand names, and babies sport "GAP" or "YSL" on their T-shirts and sleepers.

And yet, when it is all added up, including the Tommy sweatshirts and Ray-Ban sunglasses, the average family of four today spends 21 percent *less* (inflation adjusted) on clothing than a similar family did in the early 1970s. How can this be? What the finger-waggers have forgotten are the things families *don't* spend money on anymore. I (Elizabeth) recall the days of rushing off to Stride Rite to buy two new pairs of sensible leather shoes for each of my children every three months (one for church and one for everyday) plus a pair of sneakers for play. Today, Amelia's toddler owns nothing but a pair of $5 sandals from Wal-Mart. Suits, ties, and pantyhose have been replaced by cotton trousers and knit tops, as "business casual" has swept the nation. New fabrics, new technology, and cheap labor have lowered prices. And discounters like Target and Marshall's have popped up across the country, providing reasonable, low-cost clothes for today's families. The differences add up. In 1973, Sunday dresses, wool jackets, and the other clothes for a family of four claimed nearly $750 more a year from the family budget than all the name-brand sneakers and hip T-shirts today's families are buying.[11]

OK, so if Americans aren't blowing their paychecks on clothes, then they must be overspending on food. Designer brands have hit the grocery shelves as well, with far more prepared foods, high-end ice creams, and exotic juices. Families even buy bottles of *water*, a purchase that would have shocked their grandparents. Besides, who cooks at home anymore? With Mom and Dad both tied up at work, Americans are eating out (or ordering in) more than ever before. The authors of *Affluenza* grumble, "City streets and even suburban malls sport a United Nations of restaurants. . . . Eating out used to be a special occasion. Now we spend more money on restaurant food than on the food we cook ourselves."[12]

They are right, but only to a point. The average family of four spends more at restaurants than it used to, but it spends less at the grocery store—a lot less. Families are saving big bucks by skipping the T-bone steaks, buying their cereal in bulk at Costco, and opting for generic paper towels and canned vegetables. Those savings more than compensate for all that restaurant eating—so much so that today's family of four is actually spending 22 percent *less* on food (at-home and restaurant eating combined) than its counterpart of a generation ago.[13]

Outfitting the home? *Affluenza* rails against appliances "that were deemed luxuries as recently as 1970, but are now found in well over half of U.S. homes, and thought of by a majority of Americans as necessities: dishwashers, clothes dryers, central heating and air conditioning, color and cable TV."[14] These handy gadgets may have captured a new place in Americans' hearts, but they aren't taking up much space in our wallets. Manufacturing costs are down, and durability is up. When the microwave oven, dishwasher, and clothes dryer are combined with the refrigerator, washing machine, and stove, families are actually spending 44 percent *less* on major appliances today than they were a generation ago.[15]

Vacation homes are another big target. A financial columnist for *Money* magazine explains how life has changed. A generation ago, the dream vacation was a modest affair: "Come summer, the family piled into its Ford country wagon (with imitation woodpanel doors) and tooled off to Lake Watchamasakee for a couple of weeks." Now, laments the columnist, things have changed. "The rented cabin on the lake gave way to a second home high on an ocean dune."[16] But the world he describes does not exist, at least not for the middle-class family. Despite the rhetoric, summer homes remain the fairly exclusive privilege of the well-to-do. In 1973, 3.2 percent of families reported expenses associated with owning a vacation home; by 2000, the proportion had inched up to 4 percent.[17]

That is not to say that middle-class families never fritter away any money. A generation ago no one had cable, big-screen televisions were a novelty reserved for the very rich, and DVD and TiVo were meaningless strings of letters. So how much more do families spend on "home entertainment," premium channels included? They spend 23 percent more—a whopping extra $170 annually. Computers add another $300 to the annual family budget.[18] But even that increase looks a little different in the context of other spending. The extra money spent on cable, electronics, and computers is more than offset by families' savings on major appliances and household furnishings.

The same balancing act holds true in other areas. The average family spends more on airline travel than it did a generation ago, but it spends less on dry cleaning. More on telephone services, but less on tobacco. More on pets, but less on carpets.[19] And, when we add it all up, increases in one category are offset by decreases in another. In other words, there seems to be about as much frivolous spending today as there was a generation ago.

Yet the myth remains rock solid: Middle-class families are rushing headlong into financial ruin because they are squandering too much money on Red Lobster, Gucci, and trips to the Bahamas. Americans cling so tightly to the myth not because it is supported by hard evidence, but because it is a comforting way to explain away some very bad news. If families are in trouble because they squander their money, then those of us who shop at Costco and cook our own pasta have nothing to worry about. Moreover, if families are to blame for their own failures, then the rest of us bear no responsibility for helping those who are in trouble. Their fault, their problem. We can join the chorus of experts advising the financial failures to "simplify"—stay away from Perrier and Rolex. Follow this sensible advice, and credit card balances will vanish, bankruptcy filings will disappear, and mortgage foreclosures will cease to plague America.

Reality is not nearly so neat. Sure, there are some families who buy too much stuff, but there is no evidence of any "epidemic" in overspending—certainly nothing that could explain a 255 percent increase in the foreclosure rate, a 430 percent increase in the bankruptcy rolls, and a 570 percent increase in credit card debt.[20] A growing number of families are in terrible financial trouble, but no matter how many times the accusation is hurled, Prada and HBO are not the reason.

WHERE DID THE MONEY GO?

If they aren't spending themselves into oblivion on designer water and DVDs, how did middle-class families get into so much financial trouble? The answer starts, quite literally, at home.

We could pile cliché on cliché about the home, but we will settle for this observation: The home is the most important purchase for the average middle-class family. To the overwhelming majority of Americans, home ownership stands out as the single most important component of "the good life."[21] Homes mark the lives of their children, setting out the parameters of their universe. The luck of location will determine whether there are computers in their classrooms, whether there are sidewalks for them to ride bikes on, and whether the front yard is a safe place to play. And a home will consume more of the family's income than any other purchase—more than food, more than cars, more than health insurance, more than child care.

As anyone who has read the newspapers or purchased a home knows, it costs a lot more to buy a house than it used to.[22] (Since the overwhelming majority of middle-class parents are homeowners, we focus this discussion on the costs of owning, rather than renting.[23]) What most of us have forgotten, however, is that today's home prices are not the product of some inevitable demographic force that has simply rolled its way across America. Quite the opposite. In the late 1980s, several commentators predicted a spectacular collapse in the housing market. Economists reasoned that the baby boomers were about to become empty nesters, so pressure on the housing market would undergo a sharp reversal. According to these experts, housing prices would reverse their forty-year upward trend and drop during the 1990s and 2000s—anywhere from 10 to 47 percent.[24]

Of course, the over-consumption critics have a ready explanation for why housing prices shot up despite expert predictions: Americans are bankrupting themselves to buy over-gadgeted, oversized "McMansions." *Money* magazine captures this view: "A generation or so ago . . . a basic, 800-square-foot, $8,000 Levittown box with a carport was heaven. . . . By the 1980s, the dream had gone yupscale. Home had become a 6,000-square-foot contemporary on three acres or a gutted and rehabbed townhouse in a gentrified ghetto."[25]

Where did so many people get this impression? Perhaps from the much ballyhooed fact that the average size of a new home has increased by nearly 40 percent over the past generation (though it is still less than 2,200 square feet).[26] But before the over-consumption camp declares victory, there are a few more details to consider. The overwhelming majority of middle-income families don't live in one of those spacious new homes. Indeed, the proportion of families living in older homes has increased by nearly 50 percent over the past generation, leaving a growing number of homeowners grappling with deteriorating roofs, peeling paint, and old wiring. Today, nearly six out of ten families own a home that is more than twenty-five years old, and nearly a quarter own a house that is more than fifty years old.[27]

Despite all the hoopla over the highly visible status symbols of the well-to-do, the size and amenities of the average middle-class family home have increased only modestly. The median owner-occupied home grew from 5.7 rooms in 1975 to 6.1 rooms in the late 1990s—an increase of less than half of a room in more than two decades.[28] What was this half a room used for? Was it an "exercise room," a "media room," or any of the other exotic uses of space that critics have so widely mocked? No. The data show that most often that extra room was a second bathroom or a third bedroom.[29] These are meaningful improvements, to be sure, but the average middle-class family in a six-room house has hardly rocketed to McMansion status.

FOR THE CHILDREN

The finger-waggers missed another vital fact: The rise in housing costs has become a *family* problem. Home prices have grown across the board, but the brunt of the price increases has fallen on families with children. Data from the Federal Reserve show that the median home value for the average childless individual increased by 23 percent between 1983 and 1998—an impressive rise in just fifteen years.[30] (Again, these and all other figures are adjusted for inflation.) For married couples with children, however, housing prices shot up 79 percent—*more than three times faster.*[31] To put this in dollar terms, compare the single person without children to a married couple with children. In 1983 the average childless individual bought a $73,000 house, compared with a $90,000 house today (adjusted for inflation). In 1983 the average married couple with children owned a house worth $98,000. Just fifteen years later, a similar family with children bought a house worth $175,000. The growing costs made a big dent in the family budget, as monthly mortgage costs made a similar jump, despite falling interest rates.[32] No matter how the data are cut, couples with children are spending more than ever on housing.

Why would the average parent spend so much money on a home? The over—consumption theory doesn't offer many insights. We doubt very much that families with children have a particular love affair with "bathroom spas" and "professional kitchens" while the swinging singles are perfectly content to live in Spartan apartments with outdated kitchens and closet sized bathrooms.

No, the real reason lies elsewhere. For many parents, the answer came down to two words so powerful that families would pursue them to the brink of bankruptcy: *safety* and *education.* Families put Mom to work, used up the family's economic reserves, and took on crushing debt loads in sacrifice to these twin gods, all in the hope of offering their children the best possible start in life.

The best possible start begins with good schools, but parents are scrambling to find those schools. Even politicians who can't agree on much of anything agree that there is a major problem in America's public schools. In the 2000 election campaign, for example, presidential candidates from both political parties were tripping over each other to promote their policies for new educational programs. And they had good reason. According to a recent poll, education now ranks as voters' single highest priority for increased federal spending—higher than health care, research on AIDS, environmental protection, and fighting crime.[33]

Everyone has heard the all-too-familiar news stories about kids who can't read, gang violence in the schools, classrooms without textbooks, and drug dealers at the school doors. For the most part, the problems aren't just about flawed educational policies; they are also depicted as the evils associated with poverty.[34] Even President Bush (who didn't exactly run on a Help-the-Poor platform) focused on helping "failing" schools, which, by and large, translates into help for schools in the poorest neighborhoods.

So what does all this have to do with educating middle-class children, most of whom have been lucky enough to avoid the worst failings of the public school system? The answer is simple—money. Failing schools impose an enormous cost on those children who are forced to attend them, but they also inflict an enormous cost on those who don't.

Talk with an average middle-class parent in any major metropolitan area, and she'll describe the time, money, and effort she devoted to finding a slot for her offspring in a decent school. In some cases, the story will be about mastering the system: "we put Joshua on the wait-list for the Science Magnet School the day he was born." In other cases, it will be one of leaving the public school system altogether, as middle-class parents increasingly opt for private, parochial, or home schooling. "My husband and I both went to public schools, but we just couldn't see sending Erin to the [local] junior high." But private schools and strategic maneuvering go only so far. For most middle-class parents, ensuring that their children get a decent education translates into one thing: snatching up a home in the small subset of school districts that have managed to hold on to a reputation of high quality and parent confidence.

Homes can command a premium for all sorts of amenities, such as a two-car garage, proximity to work or shopping, or a low crime rate. A study conducted in Fresno (a midsized California metropolis with 400,000 residents) found that, for similar homes, school quality was *the single most important determinant of neighborhood prices*—more important than racial composition of the neighborhood, commute distance, crime rate, or proximity to a hazardous waste site.[35] A study in suburban Boston showed the impact of school boundary lines. Two homes located less than half a mile apart and similar in nearly every aspect, will command significantly different prices if they are in different elementary school zones.[36] Schools that scored just 5 percent higher on fourth-grade math and reading tests added a premium of nearly $4,000 to nearby homes, even though these homes were virtually the same in terms of neighborhood character, school spending, racial composition, tax burden, and crime rate.

By way of example, consider University City, the West Philadelphia neighborhood surrounding the University of Pennsylvania. In an effort to improve the area, the university committed funds for a new elementary school. The results? At the time of the announcement, the median home value in the area was less than $60,000. Five years later, "homes within the boundaries go for about $200,000, even if they need to be totally renovated."[37] The neighborhood is otherwise pretty much the same: the same commute to work, the same distance from the freeways, the same old houses. And yet, in five years families are willing to pay more than *triple* the price for a home, just so they can send their kids to a better public elementary school. Real estate agents have long joked that the three things that matter in determining the price of a house are "location, location, location." Today, that mantra could be updated to "schools, schools, schools."

This phenomenon isn't new, but the pressure has intensified considerably. In the early 1970s, not only did most Americans believe that the public schools were functioning reasonably well, a sizable majority of adults thought that public education had actually *improved* since they were kids. Today, only a small minority of Americans share this optimistic view. Instead, the majority now believes that schools have gotten significantly worse.[38] Fully half of all Americans are dissatisfied with America's public education system, a deep concern shared by black and white parents alike.[39]

Even Juliet Schor, a leading critic of over-consumption, acknowledges the growing pressure on parents. For all that she criticizes America's love affair with granite countertops and microwave ovens, she recognizes that parents can find themselves trapped by the needs of their children:

> Within the middle class, and even the upper middle class, many families experience an almost threatening pressure to keep up, both for themselves and their children. They are deeply concerned about the rigors of the global economy, and the need to have their children attend "good" schools. This means living in a community with relatively high housing costs.[40]

In other words, the only way to ensure that a beloved youngster gets a solid education is to spring for a three-bedroom Colonial with an hour-long commute to a job in the city.

Today's parents must also confront another frightening prospect as they consider where their children will attend school: the threat of school violence. The widely publicized rise in shootings, gangs, and dangerous drugs at public schools sent many parents in search of a safe haven for their sons and daughters: Violent incidents can happen anywhere, as the shootings at lovely suburban Columbine High School in Colorado revealed to a horrified nation. But the statistics show that school violence is not as random as it might seem. According to one study, the incidence of serious violent crime—such as robbery, rape, or attack with a weapon—is more than three times higher in schools characterized by high poverty levels than those with predominantly middle- and upper-income children.[41] Similarly, urban children are more than twice as likely as suburban children to fear being attacked on the way to or from school.[42] The data expose a harsh reality: Parents who can get their kids into a more *economically* segregated neighborhood really improve the odds that their sons and daughters will make it through school safely.

Newer, more isolated suburbs with restrictive zoning also promise a refuge from the random crimes that tarnish urban living.[43] It may seem odd that families would devote so much attention to personal safety—or the lack thereof—when the crime rate in the United States has fallen sharply over the past decade.[44] But national statistics mask differences among communities, and disparities have grown over time. In many cities, the urban centers have grown more dangerous while outlying areas have gotten safer—further intensifying the pressure parents feel to squeeze into a suburban refuge.[45] In Baltimore and Philadelphia, for example, the crime rate fell in the surrounding suburbs just as it increased in the center city. The disparities are greatest for the most frightening violent crimes. Today a person is *ten times* more likely to be murdered in center city Philadelphia than in its surrounding suburbs, and twelve times more likely to be killed in central Baltimore.[46]

Dyed-in-the-wool urbanites would be quick to remind us that although the crime rate may have climbed in many urban areas, the average family faces only minuscule odds of being killed in a random act of violence in downtown Baltimore or any other city. That may be true, but it is beside the point, because it ignores a basic fact of parental psychology—worry. Parents are constantly mindful of the vulnerability of their children, and no amount of statistical reasoning can persuade them to stop worrying.

Emily Cheung tells a story that resonates with millions of parents. A psychotherapist and longtime city dweller, Emily had rented an apartment in a working-class neighborhood. For years, she sang the praises of city living. But as her boys got older, her views began to change. "We were close to The Corner and I was scared for [my sons]. I didn't want them to grow up there." After a series of break-ins on her block, Emily started looking for a new place for her family to live. "I wasn't looking to buy a house, but I wanted to rent something away from [this neighborhood] to get my boys out to better schools and a safer place." It wasn't as easy as she had hoped. Emily couldn't find any apartments in the neighborhood she wanted to live in. When her real estate agent convinced her that she could qualify for a mortgage, she jumped at the chance to move to the suburbs.

> The first night in the house, I just walked around in the dark and was so grateful. . . . At this house, it was so nice and quiet. [My sons] could go outdoors and they didn't need to be afraid. [She starts crying.] I thought that if I could do this for them, get them to a better place, what a wonderful gift to give my boys. I mean, this place was three thousand times better. It is safe with a huge front yard and a back yard and a driveway. It is wonderful. I had wanted this my whole life.

Emily took a huge financial gamble buying a house that claimed nearly half of her monthly income, but she had made up her mind to do whatever she could to keep her boys safe.

Families like Emily's have long acknowledged crime as an unfortunate fact of life, but the effect on parents has changed. A generation ago, there just wasn't much that average parents could do to escape these hazards. A family could buy a guard dog or leave the lights on, but if the suburbs were about as troubled as the cities—or if crime wasn't framed as a *city* problem—then the impetus to move wasn't very compelling. Today, however, cities and suburbs seem to present two very distinct alternatives. When the car is stolen or the news features a frightening murder on a nearby street, families are more inclined to believe that the suburbs will offer them a safer alternative. According to one study, more than one-third of families who had left central Baltimore and over half of families who had considered leaving "were moved to do so by their fear of crime."[47]

Ultimately, however, it did not matter whether there was a meaningful gap between the schools in the center cities and those in the surrounding suburbs, or whether the streets really were safer far away from the big city. It didn't even matter whether there really was a crisis in public education, as the politicians and the local news might insist. What mattered was that parents *believed* that there was an important difference—and that the difference was growing.[48] The only answer for millions of loving parents was to buy their way into a decent school district in a safe neighborhood—whatever the cost.

BIDDING WAR IN THE SUBURBS

And so it was that middle-class families across America have been quietly drawn into an all-out war. Not the war on drugs, the war about creationism, or the war over sex education. Their war has received little coverage in the press and no attention from politicians, but it has profoundly altered the lives of parents everywhere, shaping every economic decision they make. Their war is a bidding war. The opening shots in this war were fired in the most ordinary circumstances. Individual parents sought out homes they thought were good places to bring up kids, just as their parents had done before them. But as families saw urban centers as increasingly unattractive places to live, the range of desirable housing options began to shrink and parents' desire to escape from failing schools began to take on new urgency. Millions of parents joined in the search for a house on a safe street with a good school nearby. Over time, demand heated up for an increasingly narrow slice of the housing stock.

This in itself would have been enough to trigger a bidding war for suburban homes in good school districts. But a growing number of families brought new artillery to the war: a second income. In an era when the overwhelming majority of mothers are bringing home a paycheck and covering a big part of the family's bills, it is easy to forget that just one generation ago most middle-class mothers—including those in the workforce—made only modest contributions to the family's regular expenses. A generation ago, the average working wife contributed just one-quarter of the family's total income.[49] In many families, Mom's earnings were treated as "pin money" to cover treats and extras, not mortgages and car payments. Unenlightened husbands weren't the only ones to foster this attitude. Banks and loan companies routinely ignored women's earnings in calculating whether to approve a mortgage, on the theory that a wife might leave the workforce at any moment to pursue full-time homemaking.[50]

In 1975 Congress passed an important law with far-reaching consequences for families' housing choices. The Equal Craft Opportunity Act stipulated, among other things, that lenders could no longer ignore a wife's income when judging whether a family earned enough to qualify for a mortgage.[51] By the early 1980s, women's participation in the labor force had become a significant factor in whether a married couple could buy a home.[52] Both families and banks had started down the path of counting Mom's income as an essential part of the monthly budget.

This change may not sound revolutionary today, but it represents a seismic shift in family economics. No longer were families constrained by Dad's earning capacity. When Mom wanted a bigger yard or Dad wanted a better school for the kids, families had a new answer: Send Mom to work and use her paycheck to buy that nice house in the suburbs.

The women's movement contributed to this trend, opening up new employment possibilities and calling on mothers to reconsider their lifetime goals. For some women, the decision to head into the workplace meant personal fulfillment and expanded opportunities to engage in interesting, challenging occupations. For many more, the sense of independence that accompanied a job and a paycheck provided a powerful incentive. But for most middle-class women, the decision to get up early, drop the children off at day care, and head to the office or factory was driven, at least in part, by more prosaic reasons. Millions of women went to work in a calculated attempt to give their families an economic edge.[53]

The transformation happened gradually, as hundreds of thousands of mothers marched into the workforce year after year. But over the course of a few decades, the change has been nothing short of revolutionary. As recently as 1976 a married mother was more than twice as likely to stay home with her children as to work full-time. By 2000, those figures had almost reversed: The modern married mother is now nearly twice as likely to have a full-time job as to stay home.[54] The transformation can be felt in other ways. In 1965 only 21 percent of working women were back at their jobs within 6 months of giving birth to their first child. Today, that figure is higher than 70 percent. Similarly, a modern mother with a three-month-old infant is more likely to be working outside the home than was a 1960s woman with a five-year-old child.[55] As a claims adjuster with two children told us, "It never even occurred to me not to work, even after Zachary was born. All the women I know have a job."

Even these statistics understate the magnitude of change among middle-class mothers. Before the 1970s, large numbers of older women, lower-income women, and childless women were in the workforce.[56] But middle-class mothers were far more likely to stay behind, holding on to the more traditional role of full-time homemaker long after many of their sisters had given it up. Over the past generation, middle-class mothers flooded into offices, shops, and factories, undergoing a greater increase in workforce participation than either their poor or their well-to-do sisters.[57] Attitudes changed as well. In 1970, when the women's revolution was well under way, 78 percent of younger married women thought that it was "better for wives to be homemakers and husbands to do the breadwinning."[58] Today, only 38 percent of women believe that it is "ideal" for one parent to be home full-time, and nearly 70 percent of Americans believe it doesn't matter whether it is the husband or the wife who stays home with the children.[59]

It is also the middle-class family whose finances have been most profoundly affected by women's entry into the workforce. Poorer, less educated women have seen small gains in real wages over the past generation. Wealthy women have enjoyed considerable increases, but those gains were complemented by similar increases in their husbands' rapidly rising incomes.[60] For the middle class, however, women's growing paychecks have made all the difference, compensating for the painful fact that their husbands' earnings have stagnated over the past generation.[61]

For millions of middle-class families hoping to hold on to a more traditional mother-at-home lifestyle, the bidding wars crushed those dreams. A group of solidly middle-class Americans—our nation's police officers—illustrate the point. A recent study showed that the average police officer could not afford a median priced home in *two-thirds* of the nation's metropolitan areas on the officer's income alone.[62] The same is true for elementary school teachers. Nor is this phenomenon limited to high-cost cities such as New York and San Francisco. Without a working spouse, the family of a police officer or teacher is forced to rent an apartment or buy in a marginal neighborhood even in more modestly priced cities such as Nashville, Kansas City, and Charlotte. These families have found that in order to hold on to all the benefits of a stay-at-home mom . . ., they will be shoved to the bottom rungs of the middle class.

What about those families with middle-class aspirations who earned a little less than average or those who lived in a particularly expensive city? Even with both parents in the workforce, they have fallen behind. Rather than drop out of the bidding war and resign themselves to sending their kids to weaker schools, many middle-class couples have seized on another way to fund their dream home: take on a bigger mortgage. In 1980, the mortgage lending industry was effectively deregulated. . . . As a result, average families could find plenty of banks willing to issue them larger mortgages relative to their incomes. As the bidding war heated up, families took on larger and larger mortgages just to keep up, committing themselves to debt loads that were unimaginable just a generation earlier.

With extra income from Mom's paycheck and extra mortgage money from the bank, the usual supply and demand in the market for homes in desirable areas exploded into an all-out bidding war. As millions of families sent a second earner into the workforce, one might expect that they would spend *less* on housing as a proportion of total income. Instead, just the opposite occurred. A growing number of middle-class families now spend *more* on housing relative to family income.[63] As demand for the limited stock of desirable family housing continued to grow, prices did not reach the natural limit that would have been imposed by the purchasing power of the single-income family confined to a conventional 80 percent mortgage. Instead, monthly mortgage expenses took a leap of *69 percent* at a time that other family expenditures—food, clothing, home furnishings, and the like—remained steady or fell.[64]

Parents were caught. It may have been their collective demand for housing in family neighborhoods that drove prices up, but each individual family that wanted one of those houses had no choice but to join in the bidding war. If one family refused to pay, some other family would snatch up the property. No single family could overcome the effects of millions of other families wanting what it wanted.

Each year, a growing number of stay-at-home mothers made the move into the workforce, hoping to put their families into solidly middle-class neighborhoods. But the rules quietly changed. Today's mothers are no longer working to get ahead; now they must work just to keep up. Somewhere along the way, they fell into a terrible trap.

. . . Short of buying a new home, parents currently have only one way to escape a failing public school: Send the kids to private school. But there is another alternative, one that would keep much-needed tax dollars inside the public school system while still reaping the advantages offered by a voucher program. Local governments could enact meaningful reform by enabling parents to choose from among *all* the public schools in a locale, with no presumptive assignment based on neighborhood. Under a public school voucher program, parents, not bureaucrats, would have the power to pick schools for their children—and to choose which schools would get their children's vouchers. Students would be admitted to a particular public school on the basis of their talents, their interests, or even their lottery numbers; their zip codes would be irrelevant. Tax dollars would follow the children, not the parents' home addresses, and children who live in a $50,000 house would have the same educational opportunities as those who live in a $250,000 house.

Children who required extra resources, such as those with physical or learning disabilities, could be assigned proportionately larger vouchers, which would make it more attractive for schools to take on the more challenging (and expensive) task of educating these children. It might tales some re-jiggering to settle on the right amount for a public school voucher, but eventually every child would have a valuable funding ticket to be used in any school in the area. To collect those tickets, schools would have to provide the education parents want. And parents would have a meaningful set of choices, *without* the need to buy a new home or pay private school tuition. Ultimately, an all-voucher system would diminish the distinction between public and private schools, as parents were able to exert more direct control over their children's schools.[65]

Of course, public school vouchers would not entirely eliminate the pressure parents feel to move into better family neighborhoods. Some areas would continue to have higher crime rates or better parks, and many parents might still prefer to live close to their children's schools. But a fundamental revision of school assignment policies would broaden the range of housing choices families would consider. Instead of limiting themselves to homes within one or two miles of a school, parents could choose a home five or even ten miles away—enough distance to give them several neighborhoods to choose from, with a broad range of price alternatives.

School change, like any other change, would entail some costs. More children might need to take a bus to school, pushing up school transportation expenses. On the other hand many parents might actually shorten their own commutes, since they would no longer be forced to live in far-flung suburbs for the sake of their children. The net costs could be positive or negative.

An all-voucher system would be a shock to the educational system, but the shakeout might be just what the system needs. In the short run, a large number of parents would likely chase a limited number of spots in a few excellent schools. But over time, the whole concept of "the Beverly Hills schools" or "Newton schools" would die out, replaced in the hierarchy by schools that offer a variety of programs that parents want for their children, regardless of the geographic boundaries. By selecting where to send their children (and where to spend their vouchers), parents would take control over schools' tax dollars, making them the de facto owners of those schools. Parents, not administrators, would decide on programs, student-teacher ratios, and whether to spend money on art or sports. Parents' competitive energies could be channeled toward signing up early or improving their children's qualifications for a certain school, not bankrupting themselves to buy homes they cannot afford.

If a meaningful public school voucher system were instituted, the U.S. housing market would change forever. These changes might dampen, and perhaps even depress, housing prices in some of today's most competitive neighborhoods. But these losses would be offset by other gains. Owners of older homes in urban centers might find more willing buyers, and the urge to flee the cities might abate. Urban sprawl might slow down as families recalculate the costs of living so far from work. At any rate, the change would cause a one-time readjustment. The housing market would normalize, with supply and demand more balanced and families freed from ruinous mortgages.

THE PRICE OF EDUCATION

Even with that perfect house in a swanky school district parents still are not covered when it comes to educating their kids—not by a long shot. The notion that taxpayers foot the bill for educating middle-class children has become a myth in yet another way. The two ends of the spectrum—everything that happens before a child shows up for his first day of kindergarten and after he is handed his high-school diploma—fall directly on the parents. Preschool and college, which now account for one-third (or more) of the years a typical middle-class kid spends in school, are paid for almost exclusively by the child's family.

Preschool has always been a privately funded affair, at least for most middle-class families. What has changed is its role for middle-class children. Over the past generation, the image of preschool has transformed from an optional stopover for little kids to a "prerequisite" for elementary school. Parents have been barraged with articles telling them that early education is important for everything from "pre-reading" skills to social development. As one expert in early childhood education observes, "In many communities around the country, kindergarten is no longer aimed at the entry level. And the only way Mom and Dad feel they can get their child prepared is through a pre-kindergarten program."[66]

Middle-class parents have stepped into line with the experts' recommendations. Today, nearly two-thirds of America's three- and four-year-olds attend preschool, compared with just 4 percent in the mid-1960s.[67] This isn't just the by-product of more mothers entering the workforce; nearly half of all stay-at-home moms now send their kids to a prekindergarten program.[68] As *Newsweek* put it, "The science says it all: preschool programs are neither a luxury nor a fad, but a real necessity."[69]

As demand has heated up, many families have found it increasingly difficult to *find* a prekindergarten program with an empty slot. Author Vicki Iovine describes the struggle she experienced trying to get her children into preschool in southern California:

> Just trying to get an application to any old preschool can be met with more attitude than the maitre d' at Le Cirque. If you should be naïve enough to ask if there will be openings in the next session, you may be reminded that there are always more applicants than openings, or the person might just laugh at you and hang up.[70]

Ms. Iovine's remarks are tongue-in-cheek, and pundits love to mock the parent who subscribes to the theory that "if little Susie doesn't get into the right preschool she'll never make it into the right medical school." But the shortage of quality preschool programs is very real. Child development experts have rated day-care centers, and the news is not good. The majority are lumped in the "poor to mediocre" range.[71] Not surprisingly, preschools with strong reputations often have long waiting lists.[72]

Once again, today's parents find themselves caught in a trap. A generation ago, when nursery school was regarded as little more than a chance for Mom to take a break, parents could consider the economics in a fairly detached way, committing to pay no more than what they could afford. And when only a modest number of parents were shopping for those preschool slots, the prices had to remain low to attract a full class. Today, when scores of experts routinely proclaim that preschool is decisive in a child's development, but a slot in a preschool—any preschool—can be hard to come by, parents are in a poor position to shop around for lower prices.

The laws of supply and demand take hold in the opposite direction, eliminating the pressure for preschool programs to keep prices low as they discover that they can increase fees without losing pupils. A full-day program in a prekindergarten offered by the Chicago *public* school district costs $6,500 a year—more than the cost of a year's tuition at the University of Illinois.[73] High? Yes, but that hasn't deterred parents: At just one Chicago public school, there are ninety-five kids on a waiting list for twenty slots. That situation is fairly typical. According to one study, the annual cost for a four-year-old to attend a child care center in an urban area is more than *double* the price of college tuition in fifteen states.[74] And so today's middle-class families simply spend and spend, stretching their budgets to give their child the fundamentals of a modern education.

Notes

1. John de Graaf, David Waan, and Thomas H. Naylor, *Affluenza: The All-Consuming Epidemic* (San Francisco: Barrett-Koehler, 2001), p. 13.
2. Graaf, Waan, and Naylor, *Affluenza*, p. 13.
3. Juliet B. Sehor, *The Overspent American: Upscaling, Downshifting, and the New Consumer* (New York: Basic Books, 1998), p. 20.
4. Robert H. Frank, *Luxury Fever: Why Money Fails to Satisfy in an Era of Excess* (New York: Free Press, 1999), p. 45.
5. Sehor, *The Overspent American*, p. 21.
6. Graaf, Waan, and Naylor, *Affluenza*, back cover.
7. Sehor, *The Overspent American*, p. 11.
8. The Bureau of Labor Statistics maintains the Consumer Expenditure Survey (CES), a periodic set of interviews and diary entries that analyze the spending behavior of over 20,000 consumer units. For much of our analysis we compare the results of the 1972–1973 CES with those of the 2000 CES. In some instances, we use prepublished tables from the 1980 or the 2000 survey in order to use the most comparable data available. We gratefully acknowledge the valuable assistance of Eric Keil, an economist at the Bureau of Labor Statistics, in locating and interpreting these data.
9. All comparisons of expenditures and income are adjusted for inflation using the Inflation Calculator, U.S. Department of Labor, Bureau of Labor Statistics. Available at www.bls.gov/cpi/home.htm [1/22/2003].
10. Daniel McGinn, "Maxed Out," *Newsweek*, August 27, 2001, p. 37.
11. U.S. Department of Labor, Bureau of Labor Statistics (BLS), *Consumer Expenditure Survey: Interview Survey, 1972–1973* (1997), Table 5, Selected Family Characteristics, Annual Expenditures, and Sources of Income Classified by Family Income Before Taxes for Four Person Families; *Consumer Expenditures in 2000*, BLS Report 958 (April 2002), Table 4, Size of Consumer Unit: Average Annual Expenditures and Characteristics, Consumer Expenditure Survey 2000 (data are for four-person families). See also Mark Lino, "USDA's Expenditures on Children by Families Project. Uses and Changes Over Time," *Family Economics and Nutrition Review* 13, no. 1 (2001): 81–86. According to USDA estimates, the total amount of money an average family will spend on

clothing for a child between birth and age eighteen decreased 38 percent between 1960 and 2000 (Lino, p. 84).

12. Graaf, Waan, and Naylor, *Affluenza*, p. 28.
13. BLS, *Consumer Expenditure Survey: Interview Survey, 1972–1973*, Table 5; *Consumer Expenditures in 2000*, Table 4. See also Eva Jacobs and Stephanie Shipps, "How Family Spending Has Changed in the U.S.," *Monthly Labor Review 113* (March 1990): 20–27.
14. Graaf, Waan, and Naylor, *Affluenza*, p. 28.
15. BLS, *Consumer Expenditure Survey: Interview Survey, 1972–1973*, Table 5; *Consumer Expenditure Survey, 2000* (prepublished data), Table 1400, Size of Consumer Unit: Average Annual Expenditures and Characteristics (data are for four-person families).
16. Walter L. Updegrave, "How Are We Doing? So Far, So Good. But Prosperity in the '90s Means Meeting Seven Basic Goals," *Money*, Fall 1990, p. 20.
17. BLS, *Consumer Expenditure Survey: Interview Survey, 1972–1973*, Table 5; *Consumer Expenditure Survey, 2000*, Table 1400.
18. BLS, *Consumer Expenditure Survey: Interview Survey, 1972–1973*, Table 5; *Consumer Expenditure Survey, 2000*, Table 1400. Electronics comparison includes expenditures on televisions, radios, musical instruments, and sound equipment. Computer calculation includes computer hardware and software.
19. For example, in 2000 the average family of four spent an extra $290 on telephone services. On the other hand, the average family spent nearly $200 less on floor coverings, $210 less on dry cleaning and laundry supplies, and $240 less on tobacco products and smoking supplies. *BLS, Consumer Expenditure Survey: Interview Survey, 1972–1973*, Table 5; *Consumer Expenditure Survey, 2000*, Table 1400.
20. Total revolving debt (which is predominantly credit card debt) increased from $64,500,000 in 1981 to $692,800,000 in 2000. SMR Research Corporation, *The New Bankruptcy Epidemic: Forecasts, Causes, and Risk Control* (Hackettstown, NJ, 2001), p. 14. Bankruptcy data calculated from data reported by Administrative Office of the United States Courts, Table F2 (total nonbusiness filings), 1980–2002.
21. Carolyn Setlow, "Home: The 'New' Destination," *Point of Purchase*, July 1, 2002.
22. Today the median sale price for an existing home is more than $150,000—up 32 percent in inflation-adjusted dollars from 1975. Joint Center for Housing Studies, Harvard University, *The State of the Nation's Housing, 2002* (Cambridge, MA, 2002), Table A-1, Housing Market Indicators, 1975–2001.
23. In 2001, 78.8 percent of married couples with children were homeowners. U.S. Department of Housing and Urban Development, Office of Policy Development and Research. U.S. Housing Market Conditions (Fourth Quarter, 2002), Table 30, Homeownership Rates by Household Type, 1983–Present. Although the data are not reported for subgroups, presumably this rate was lower for low-income families, and even higher for middle- and upper-income families. In the general population, middle-income households are 34 percent more likely than low-income households to own a home. Calculated from Joint Center for Housing Studies, *State of the Nation's Housing*, Table A-9.
24. Patric H. Hendershott, "Are Real House Prices Likely to Decline by 47 Percent?" *Regional Science and Urban Economics* 21, no. 4 (1991): 553–563. See also N. Gregory Mankiw and David N. Weil, "The Baby Boom, the Baby Bust, and the Housing Market," *Regional Science and Urban Economics* 19, no. 2 (1989): 235–258. Jonathan R. Laing, "Crumbling Castles: The Recession in Real Estate Has Ominous Implications," *Barron's*, December 18, 1989.
25. Updegrave, How Are We Doing?" p. 20.
26. Joint Center for Housing Studies, *State of the Nation's Housing*, Table A-1.
27. The proportion of owner-occupied houses twenty-five years or older grew from 40 percent in 1975 to 59 percent in 1999. U.S. Department of Commerce, Bureau of the Census, *American Housing Survey, 1999*, Current Housing Reports, H150/99 (October 2000), Table 3-1, Introductory Characteristics—Owner Occupied Units; *American Housing Survey: 1975, General Housing Characteristics*, Current Housing Reports, H-150-75A (April 1977), Table A1, Characteristics of the Housing Inventory, 1975 and 1970.

28. Bureau of the Census, *American Housing Survey: 1975, General Housing Characteristics*, Current Housing Reports, H-150-75A, Table A1; *American Housing Survey, 1997*, Current Housing Reports, H150/97 (October 2000), Table 3-3, Size of Unit and Lot—Owner Occupied Units.
29. Bureau of the Census, *American Housing Survey: 1975, General Housing Characteristics*, Current Housing Reports, H-150-75A, Table A1; *American Housing Survey, 1999*, Current Housing Reports, H150/99, Table 3-3.
30. Federal Reserve Board, *Survey of Consumer Finances, 1998 Full Public Dataset*, available at http://www.federalreserve.gov/pubs/oss/oss2/98/scf98home.html [1/5/2003]; Arthur Kennickell and Janice Shack-Marquez, "Changes in Family Finances from 1983 to 1989: Evidence from the Survey of Consumer Finances," *Federal Reserve Bulletin* 78 (January 1992), Table 7, Median Amount of Non-Financial Assets of Families Holding Such Assets, by Selected Characteristics of Families, 1983 and 1989 (data are for home-owning individuals under age fifty-five). We note that the American Housing Survey does not report a substantial difference in the increase in housing prices between families with and without children. Those data are likely skewed by the fact that a growing number of families with children are headed by single mothers, who live in much smaller and less expensive homes than their married counterparts, thus reducing the average amount spent by households with children. When we focus on married couples with children, a demographic group reported on by the Federal Reserve and the Consumer Expenditure Survey, the picture facing two-parent families comes into sharp focus.
31. Federal Reserve Board, *Survey of Consumer Finances, 1998 Full Public Dataset*, Kennickell and Shack-Marquez. Data are for home-owning households in which the head of household is under age fifty-five. Married couples under fifty-five with no minor children also saw an increase in home values, of 84 percent. This statistic is somewhat misleading, however, because it mixes together couples who never planned to have children, couples who bought homes in anticipation of having children, and couples whose children are now eighteen or older. Nearly nine out of ten married women will have children at some point in their lives, so we believe it is reasonable to assume that a large proportion of this group made their housing choices with their children in mind. Bureau of the Census, Current Population Survey (June 2000), Table H2, Distribution of Women 40 to 44 Years Old by Number of Children Ever Born and Marital Status: June 1970 to June 2000. The data also reflect a growing number of couples' decisions to commit both spouses' incomes to purchase housing, even among those who never have children.
32. BLS, *Consumer Expenditure Survey, 1980*, prepublished Table 5, Selected Characteristics and Annual Expenditures of All Consumer Units Classified by Composition of Consumer Unit, Interview Survey, 1980; *Consumer Expenditure Survey*, 1999 (prepublished data), Table 1500, Composition of Consumer Unit: Average Annual Expenditures and Characteristics (data are for husband and wife with children).
33. "Americans Put Education at Top of Federal Spending Priorities," *Public Agenda Online*, April 2001. Available at http://www.publicagenda.org/issues/majprop.cfm?issue_type=education [1/20/2003].
34. See, for example, Arthur Levine, "American Education: Still Separate, Still Unequal," *Los Angeles Times*, February 2, 2003, p. M1.
35. David E. Clark and William E. Herrin, "The Impact of Public School Attributes on Home Sale Prices in California," *Growth and Change* 31 (Summer 2000): 385–407. "The elasticity of teacher-student ratio is nearly 8 times that of murder rate and just over 10 times that of the largest environmental quality measure [proximity to interstate]."
36. Sandra E. Black, "Do Better Schools Matter? Parental Valuation of Elementary Education," *Quarterly Journal of Economics* 114 (May 1999): 577–599.
37. The University of Pennsylvania made other modest investments in the neighborhood, including hiring trash collectors to remove litter from the streets and employing neighborhood safety "ambassadors." Those initiatives, however, did not represent major changes, since the university had already been policing the area for several years; many locals agree that the new elementary school was by far the most important change. Caitlin Francke, "Penn Area Revival Lures Many, Pushes Others Out," *Philadelphia Inquirer*, February 24, 2003.
38. George H. Gallup, "The Eleventh Annual Gallup Poll of the Public's Attitudes Toward the Public Schools," *Phi Delta Kappan* (September 1979), p. 37. "More Than Half of Americans Say Public

Education Is Worse Today Than When They Were Students," *Public Agenda Online* (April 2000), available at http://www.publicagenda.org/issues/pcc_detail.cfm?issue_type=education&list=16 [1/20/2003].

39. Black parents are almost three times more likely than other parents to report that they are "completely dissatisfied" with the quality of their children's schools. Lydia Saad, "Grade School Receives Best Parent Ratings, Education Nationally Gets Modest Ratings," *Gallup Poll Analyses*, September 4, 2002.
40. Juliet Schor, *Do Americans Shop Too Much?* (Boston: Beacon Press, 2000), p. 11.
41. Thomas D. Snyder and Charlene M. Hoffman, *Digest of Education Statistics*, 2001, NCES 2001-130 (U.S. Department of Education, National Center for Education Statistics, February 2002), Table 150, Percent of Public Schools Reporting Crime Incidents and the Seriousness of Crime Incidents Reported, by School Characteristics, 1996–1997.
42. U.S. Department of Justice, Bureau of Justice Statistics, *Sourcebook of Criminal Justice, 2000*, NCJ 190251 (December 2001), Table 2.0001, Students Age 12 to 18 Reporting Fear of School-Related Victimization.
43. For a discussion of the financial effects of restrictive zoning, see Michael Schill, "Regulatory Barriers to Housing Development in the United States," in *Land Law in Comparative Perspective*, edited by Maria Elena Sanchez Jordan and Antonio Gambara (The Hague: Kluwer Law International, 2002), pp. 101–120.
44. "Violent Crime Fell 9% in '01, Victim Survey Shows," *New York Times*, September 9, 2002; the article cites a 50 percent decline in violent crime since 1993.
45. U.S. Department of Justice, 1995 *Uniform Crime Reports* (1996), cited in Setha M. Low, "The Edge and the Center: Gated Communities and the Discourse of Urban Fear," *American Anthropologist* 103 (March 2001): 45–58. In a 1975 survey of homeowners, the U.S. Census Bureau found that people living in city centers were 38 percent more likely to complain of crime in their neighborhoods than their suburban counterparts. Today urban dwellers are 125 percent more likely than suburbanites to cite crime in their neighborhoods. Bureau of the Census, *American Housing Survey: 1975*, *Indicators of Housing and Neighborhood Quality*, Current Housing Reports, H-150-75B (February 1977), Table A-4, Selected Neighborhood Characteristics, 1975; *American Housing Survey, 1999*, Current Housing Reports, H150/99 (October 2000), Table 3-8, Neighborhood—Owner Occupied Units.
46. Dando Yanich, Location, Location, Location: Urban and Suburban Crime on Local TV News," *Journal of Urban Affairs* 23, no. 3–4 (2001): 221–241, Table 2, Rates of Selected Crimes in Baltimore and Philadelphia, 1977 and 1996.
47. Yanich, "Location, Location, Location," p. 222.
48. While this is not exclusively an urban-suburban dichotomy, urban dwellers are more than twice as likely as suburbanites to say that the public elementary schools are so bad that they would like to move. Similarly, parents who have young children and own homes in urban areas are almost 70 percent more likely to be unsatisfied with the public elementary schools in their neighborhoods than those living in the suburbs. Bureau of the Census, *American Housing Survey, 1999*, Current Housing Reports, H150/99, Table 3-8.
49. Lawrence Mishel, Jared Bernstein, and Heather Boushey, *The State of Working America, 2002–03* (Ithaca, NY: Cornell University Press, 2003) p. 103.
50. See, for example, Congressional Research Service, *Women and Credit: Synopsis of Prospective Findings of Study on Available Legal Remedies Against Sex Discrimination in the Granting of Credit and Possible State Statutory Origins of Unequal Treatment Based Primarily on the Credit Applicant's Sex or Marital Status.* Prepared for the Subcommittee on Consumer Affairs, House Committee on Banking and Currency; *Hearings on Credit Discrimination*, by Sylvia L. Beckey, U.S. House of Representatives, 93rd Congress, 2nd sess., May 2, 1974; and Margaret J. Gates, "Credit Discrimination Against Women: Causes and Solutions," *Vanderbilt Law Review* 27 (1974): 409–441.
51. Federal Trade Commission, *Equal Credit Opportunity*. Information sheet for consumers, available at http://www.ftc.gov/bcp/conline/pubs/credit/ecoa.htm [1/20/03].
52. Mark Evan Edwards, "Home Ownership, Affordability, and Mothers' Changing Work and Family Roles," *Social Science Quarterly* 82 (June 2001): 369–383; Sharon Danes and Mary Winter, "The

Impact of the Employment of the Wife on the Achievement of Home Ownership," *Journal of Consumer Affairs* 24, no. 1 (1990): 148–169.

53. In a survey of 1,000 working mothers, 80 percent reported that their main reason for working was to support their families. Carin Rubenstein, "The Confident Generation: Working Moms Have a Brand New Attitude," *Working Mother*, May 1994, p. 42.
54. Calculated from Bureau of the Census, *Historical Income Tables—Families*, Current Population Survey, various Annual Demographic Supplements, Table F-14, Work Experience of Husband and Wife—All Married-Couple Families, by Presence of Children Under 18 Years Old and Median and Mean Income: 1976 to 2000.
55. Kristin Smith, Barbara Downs, and Martin O'Connell, "Maternity Leave and Patterns: 1961–1995," *Household Economic Studies*, U.S. Census Bureau, November 2001, Table 1, Women Working at a job, by Monthly Interval After First Birth, 1961–65 to 1991–94.
56. Stephanie Coontz, *The Way We Never Were: American Families and the Nostalgia Trap* (New York: Basic Books, 1992), p. 162.
57. Between 1979 and 2000, married mothers at all income levels increased their hours in the workforce. However, women whose husbands were in the bottom quintile added 334 hours per year, and those in the top quintile added just 315 hours per year, compared with an average increase of 428 hours per year for women in the middle three quintiles. Calculated from *The State of Working America 2002–2003*, Table 1.32, Annual Hours, Wives in Prime-Age, Married-Couple Families with Children, and Contributions to Change, 1979–2000, Sorted by Husband's Income.
58. Coontz, *The Way We Never Were*, p. 168.
59. Chris McComb, "Few Say It's Ideal for Both Parents to Work Full Time Outside of Home," Gallup News Service, April 20–22, 2001.
60. Both women and men who did not finish high school saw declines in real wages over the past twenty years. By contrast, among college graduates, women's earnings have increased 30 percent since 1979, while men's earnings have increased by 17 percent. U.S. Department of Labor, "Highlights of Women's Earnings in 2000," Report 952, August 2001, Table 15, Median Usual Weekly Earnings of Full-Time Wage and Salary Workers 25 and Over in Constant (2000) Dollars, by Sex and Educational Attainment, 1979–2000 Annual Averages.
61. Median earnings, which are the best measure of middle-class wages, have risen less than 1 percent for men since the early 1970s, while women's earnings have increased by more than one-third. Bureau of the Census, *Historical Income Tables—People*, Current Population Survey, various Annual Demographic Supplements. Available at http://www.census.gov/hhes/income/histinc/incperdet.html [1/5/2003], Table P-36, Full-Time, Year-Round Workers (All Races) by Median Income and Sex, 1955 to 2000.
62. Barbara J. Lipman, Center for Housing Policy, "Paycheck to Paycheck: Working Families and the Cost of Housing in America," *New Century Housing 2* (June 2001): 24–26.
63. [T]he proportion of middle-income families who would be considered "house poor" has doubled since 1975. Bureau of the *Census, Annual Housing Survey for the United States and Regions, 1975, Part C, Financial Characteristics of the Housing Inventory*, Annual Survey (1977), Table A-1, Income of Families and Primary Individuals in Owner and Renter Occupied Housing Units, 1975. Available at http://www.census.gov/prod/www/abs/h150.html [3/10/2003]; *American Housing Survey for the United States: 2001*, Annual Survey (2001), Table 2–20, Income of Families and Primary Individuals by Selected Characteristics—Occupied Units. Available at http://www.census.gov/hhes/www/housing/abs/ahs01/tab313.html [3/4/2003]. In addition, the Consumer Expenditure Survey indicates that mortgage payments as a proportion of income has increased considerably since the early 1970s. Many indexes that measure housing affordability have shown no clear trend. These indices, however, typically calculate a *theoretical* housing cost, based on such factors as current mortgage rates and an imputed down payment amount. As a result, the indices are extremely sensitive to fluctuations in interest rates, ignoring the fact that many families have fixed-rate mortgages and do not refinance during periods of high interest. Similarly, these indexes typically assume that all buyers get a conventional mortgage, which ignores the extraordinary rise in high-cost subprime mortgages in recent years. Furthermore, they assume that the typical down payment has held constant over the past generation, when in fact first-time home buyers are

putting down far smaller down payments today than twenty years ago. See, for example, Bureau of the Census, "Who Could Afford to Buy a House in 1995?" Table 4-2, Affordability Status of Families and Unrelated Individuals for a Modestly Priced Home, by Current Tenure and Type of Financing, United States, 1984, 1988, 1991, 1993, and 1995. See also Joint Center for Housing Studies, *State of the Nation's Housing*, Table A-3. We continue to believe that the best evidence of real housing costs is the direct data on what families report they are actually paying.

64. BLS, *Consumer Expenditure Survey: Interview Survey, 1972–1973*, Table 5; *Consumer Expenditure Survey, 2000*, Table 1400. Note that in 2000, 74 percent of married couples with children owned their own homes; in 1972/73 this figure was 71 percent. In order to isolate the effects of changing supply and demand for owner-occupied housing, this calculation only accounts for changes in mortgage expenditures (including both interest and principal) by families who owned their own homes. Federal Reserve data produce similar results (see above).
65. Martha Minow argues that "daring changes" are needed to increase parental involvement and promote accountability in the schools. *Partners, Not Rivals: Privatization and the Public Good* (Boston: Beacon Press, 2003).
66. Laurent Belsie, "Preschools Are Popping at the Seams," *Christian Science Monitor*, July 9, 2002, p. 13.
67. Belsie, "Preschools Are Popping at the Seams," p. 13.
68. Children's Defense Fund, *Key Facts: Essential Information About Child Care, Early Education, and School-Age Care* (Washington, DC: CDF, 2000).
69. Anna Quindlen, "Building Blocks for Every Kid," *Newsweek*, February 12, 2001.
70. Vicki Iovine, *The Girlfriends' Guide to Toddlers: A Survival Manual to the "Terrible Twos" (and Ones and Threes) from the First Step, the First Potty, and the First Word ("No") to the Last Blankie* (New York: Berkley Publishing Group, 1999): 240.
71. Suzanne Helburn et al., *Cost, Quality, and Child Care Outcomes in Child Care Centers* (Denver: Center for Research in Economic and Social Policy, University of Colorado at Denver, 1995).
72. National Council of Jewish Women, *Opening a New Window on Child Care: A Report on the Status of Child Care in the Nation Today* (New York: NCJW, 1999), p. 6.
73. Kate N. Grossman, "Pre-kindergarten Lures Middle Class to Public School," *Chicago Sun-Times*, June 10, 2002; in-state tuition and fees at the University of Illinois are $5,748. University of -Illinois Web site, at http://www.oar.uiuc.edu/current/tuit.html [12/19/2002].
74. Karen Schulman, *The High Cost of Child Care Puts Quality Care Out of Reach for Many Families* (Washington, DC: Children's Defense Fund, 2000), Table A-1, Comparison of Average Annual Child Care Costs in Urban Area Centers to Average Annual Public College Tuition Costs.

Chapter

11

Dimensions of Diversity

READING 31

Diversity within African American Families

Ronald L. Taylor

PERSONAL REFLECTIONS

My interest in African American families as a topic of research was inspired more than two decades ago by my observation and growing dismay over the stereotypical portrayal of these families presented by the media and in much of the social science literature. Most of the African American families I knew in the large southern city in which I grew up were barely represented in the various "authoritative" accounts I read and other scholars frequently referred to in their characterizations and analyses of such families. Few such accounts have acknowledged the regional, ethnic, class, and behavioral diversity within the African American community and among families. As a result, a highly fragmented and distorted public image of African American family life has been perpetuated that encourages perceptions of African American families as a monolith. The 1986 television documentary *A CBS Report: The Vanishing Family: Crisis in Black America*, hosted by Bill Moyers, was fairly typical of this emphasis. It focused almost exclusively on low-income, single-parent households in inner cities, characterized them as "vanishing" non-families, and implied that such families represented the majority of African American families in urban America. It mattered little that poor, single-parent households in the inner cities made up less than a quarter of all African American families at the time the documentary was aired.

As an African American reared in the segregated South, I was keenly aware of the tremendous variety of African American families in composition, lifestyle, and socioeconomic status. Racial segregation ensured that African American families, regardless of means or circumstances, were constrained to live and work in close proximity to one another. Travel outside the South made me aware of important regional differences among African American families as well. For example, African American families in the Northeast appeared far more segregated by socioeconomic status than did families in many parts of the South with which I was familiar. As a graduate student at Boston University during the late 1960s, I recall the shock I experienced upon seeing the level of concentrated poverty among African American families in Roxbury, Massachusetts, an experience duplicated in travels to New York, Philadelphia, and Newark. To be sure, poverty of a similar magnitude was prevalent throughout the South, but was far less concentrated and, from my perception, far less pernicious.

As I became more familiar with the growing body of research on African American families, it became increasingly clear to me that the source of a major distortion in the portrayal of African American families in the social science literature and the media was the overwhelming concentration on impoverished inner-city communities of the Northeast and Midwest to the near exclusion of the South, where more than half the African American families are found and differences among them in family patterns, lifestyles, and socioeconomic characteristics are more apparent.

In approaching the study of African American families in my work, I have adopted a *holistic* perspective. This perspective, outlined first by DuBois (1898) and more recently by Billingsley (1992) and Hill (1993), emphasizes the influence of historical, cultural, social, economic, and political forces in shaping contemporary patterns of family life among African Americans of all socioeconomic backgrounds. Although the impact of these external forces is routinely taken into account in assessing stability and change among white families, their effects on the structure and functioning of African American families are often minimized. In short, a holistic approach undertakes to study African American families *in context*. My definition of the *family*, akin to the definition offered by Billingsley (1992), views it as an intimate association of two or more persons related to each other by blood, marriage, formal or informal adoption, or appropriation. The latter term refers to the incorporation of persons in the family who are unrelated by blood or marital ties but are treated as though they are family. This definition is broader than other dominant definitions of families that emphasize biological or marital ties as defining characteristics.

This [reading] is divided into three parts. The first part reviews the treatment of African American families in the historical and social sciences literatures. It provides a historical overview of African American families, informed by recent historical scholarship, that corrects many of the misconceptions about the nature and quality of family life during and following the experience of slavery. The second part examines contemporary patterns of marriage, family, and household composition among African Americans in response to recent social, economic, and political developments in the larger society. The third part explores some of the long-term implications of current trends in marriage and family behavior for community functioning and individual well-being, together with implications for social policy.

THE TREATMENT OF AFRICAN AMERICAN FAMILIES IN AMERICAN SCHOLARSHIP

As an area of scientific investigation, the study of African American family life is of recent vintage. As recently as 1968, Billingsley, in his classic work *Black Families in White America*, observed that African American family life had been virtually ignored in family studies and studies of race and ethnic relations. He attributed the general lack of interest among white social scientists, in part, to their "ethnocentrism and intellectual commitment to peoples and values transplanted from Europe" (p. 214). Content analyses of key journals in sociology, social work, and family studies during the period supported Billingsley's contention. For example, a content analysis of 10 leading journals in sociology and social work by Johnson (1981) disclosed that articles on African American families constituted only 3% of 3,547 empirical studies of American families published between 1965 and 1975. Moreover, in the two major journals in social work, only one article on African American families was published from 1965 to 1978. In fact, a 1978 special issue of the *Journal of Marriage and the Family* devoted to African American families accounted for 40% of all articles on these families published in the 10 major journals between 1965 and 1978.

Although the past two decades have seen a significant increase in the quantity and quality of research on the family lives of African Americans, certain features and limitations associated with earlier studies in this area persist (Taylor, Chatters, Tucker, & Lewis, 1990). In a review of recent research on African American families, Hill (1993) concluded that many studies continue to treat such families in superficial terms; that is, African American families are not considered to be an important unit of focus and, consequently, are treated peripherally or omitted altogether. The assumption is that African American families are automatically treated in all analyses that focus on African Americans as individuals; thus, they are not treated in their own right. Hill noted that a major impediment to understanding the functioning of African American families has been the failure of most analysts to use a theoretical or conceptual framework that took account of the totality of African American family life. Overall, he found that the preponderance of recent studies of African American families are

> (a) fragmented, in that they exclude the bulk of Black families by focusing on only a subgroup; (b) ad hoc, in that they apply arbitrary explanations that are not derived from systematic theoretical formulations that have been empirically substantiated; (c) negative, in that they focus exclusively on the perceived weaknesses of Black families; and (d) internally oriented, in that they exclude any systematic consideration of the role of forces in the wider society on Black family life. (p. 5)

THEORETICAL APPROACHES

The study of African American families, like the study of American families in general, has evolved through successive theoretical formulations. Using white family structure as the norm, the earliest studies characterized African American families as impoverished versions of white families in which the experiences of slavery, economic deprivation, and racial discrimination had induced pathogenic and dysfunctional features (Billingsley, 1968). The classic statement of this perspective was presented by Frazier, whose study, *The Negro Family in the United States* (1939), was the first comprehensive analysis of African American family life and its transformation under various historical conditions—slavery, emancipation, and urbanization (Edwards, 1968).

It was Frazier's contention that slavery destroyed African familial structures and cultures and gave rise to a host of dysfunctional family features that continued to undermine the stability and well-being of African American families well into the 20th century. Foremost among these features was the supposed emergence of the African American "matriarchal" or maternal family system, which weakened the economic position of African American men and their authority in the family. In his view, this family form was inherently unstable and produced pathological outcomes in the family unit, including high rates of poverty, illegitimacy, crime, delinquency, and other problems associated with the socialization of children. Frazier concluded that the female-headed family had become a common tradition among large segments of lower-class African American migrants to the North during the early 20th century. The two-parent male-headed household represented a second tradition among a minority of African Americans who enjoyed some of the freedoms during slavery, had independent artisan skills, and owned property.

Frazier saw an inextricable connection between economic resources and African American family structure and concluded that as the economic position of African Americans improved, their conformity to normative family patterns would increase. However, his important insight regarding the link between family structure and economic resources was obscured by the inordinate emphasis he placed on the instability and "self-perpetuating pathologies" of lower-class African American families, an emphasis that powerfully contributed to the pejorative tradition of scholarship that emerged in this area. Nonetheless, Frazier recognized the diversity of African American families and in his analyses, "consistently attributed the primary sources of family instability to external forces (such as racism, urbanization, technological changes and recession) and not to internal characteristics of Black families" (Hill, 1993, pp. 7–8).

During the 1960s, Frazier's characterization of African American families gained wider currency with the publication of Moynihan's *The Negro Family: The Case for National Action* (1965), in which weaknesses in family structure were identified as a major source of social problems in African American communities. Moynihan attributed high rates of welfare dependence, out-of-wedlock births, educational failure, and other problems to the "unnatural" dominance of women in African American families. Relying largely on the work of Frazier as a source of reference, Moynihan traced the alleged "tangle of pathology" that characterized urban African American families to the experience of slavery and 300 years of racial oppression, which, he concluded, had caused "deep-seated structural distortions" in the family and community life of African Americans.

Although much of the Moynihan report, as the book was called, largely restated what had become conventional academic wisdom on African American families during the 1960s, its generalized indictment of all African American families ignited a firestorm of criticism and debate and inspired a wealth of new research and writings on the nature and quality of African American family life in the United States (Staples & Mirande, 1980). In fact, the 1970s saw the beginning of the most prolific period of research on African American families, with more than 50 books and 500 articles published during that decade alone, representing a fivefold increase over the literature produced in all the years since the publication of DuBois's (1909) pioneering study of African American family life (Staples & Mirande, 1980). To be sure, some of this work was polemical and defensively apologetic, but much of it sought to replace ideology with research and to provide alternative perspectives for interpreting observed differences in the characteristics of African American and white families (Allen, 1978).

Critics of the deficit or pathology approach to African American family life (Scanzoni, 1977; Staples, 1971) called attention to the tendency in the literature to ignore family patterns among the majority of African Americans and to overemphasize findings derived from studies of low-income and typically problem-ridden families. Such findings were often generalized and accepted as descriptive of the family life of all African American families, with the result that popular but erroneous images of African American family life were perpetuated. Scrutinizing the research literature of the 1960s, Billingsley (1968) concluded that when the majority of African American families was considered, evidence refuted the characterization of African American family life as unstable, dependent on welfare, and matriarchal. In his view, and in the view of a growing number of scholars in the late 1960s and early 1970s, observed differences between white and African American families were largely the result of differences in socioeconomic position and of differential access to economic resources (Allen, 1978; Scanzoni, 1977).

Thus, the 1970s witnessed not only a significant increase in the diversity, breadth, and quantity of research on African American families, but a shift away from a social pathology perspective to one emphasizing the resilience and adaptiveness of African American families under a variety of social and economic conditions. The new emphasis reflected what Allen (1978) referred to as the "cultural variant" perspective, which treats African American families as different but legitimate functional forms. From this perspective, "Black and White family differences [are] taken as given, without the presumption of one family form as normative and the other as deviant" (Farley & Allen, 1987, p. 162). In accounting for observed racial differences in family patterns, some researchers have taken a *structural perspective*, emphasizing poverty and other socioeconomic factors as key processes (Billingsley, 1968). Other scholars have taken a *cultural approach*, stressing elements of the West African cultural heritage, together with distinctive experiences, values, and behavioral modes of adaptation developed in this country, as major determinants (Nobles, 1978; Young, 1970). Still others (Collins, 1990; Sudarkasa, 1988) have pointed to evidence supporting both interpretations and have argued for a more comprehensive approach.

Efforts to demythologize negative images of African American families have continued during the past two decades, marked by the development of the first national sample of adult African Americans, drawn to reflect their distribution throughout the United States (Jackson, 1991), and by the use of a variety of conceptualizations, approaches, and methodologies in the study of African American family life (Collins, 1990; McAdoo, 1997). Moreover, the emphasis in much of the recent work

> has not been the defense of African American family forms, but rather the identification of forces that have altered long-standing traditions. The ideological paradigms identified by Allen (1978) to describe the earlier thrust of Black family research—cultural equivalence, cultural deviance, and cultural variation—do not fully capture the foci of this new genre of work as a whole. (Tucker & Mitchell-Kernan, 1995, p. 17)

Researchers have sought to stress balance in their analyses, that is, to assess the strengths and weaknesses of African American family organizations at various socioeconomic levels, and the need for solution-oriented studies (Hill, 1993). At the same time, recent historical scholarship has shed new light on the relationship of changing historical circumstances to characteristics of African American family organization and has underscored the relevance of historical experiences to contemporary patterns of family life.

AFRICAN AMERICAN FAMILIES IN HISTORICAL PERSPECTIVE

Until the 1970s, it was conventional academic wisdom that the experience of slavery decimated African American culture and created the foundation for unstable female—dominated households and other familial aberrations that continued into the 20th century. This thesis, advanced by Frazier (1939) and restated by Moynihan (1965), was seriously challenged by the pioneering historical research of Blassingame (1972), Furstenberg, Hershberg, and Modell (1975), and Gutman (1976), among others. These works provide compelling documentation of the centrality of family and kinship among African Americans during the long years of bondage and how African Americans created and sustained a rich cultural and family life despite the brutal reality of slavery.

In his examination of more than two centuries of slave letters, autobiographies, plantation records, and other materials, Blassingame (1972) meticulously documented the nature of community, family organization, and culture among American slaves. He concluded that slavery was not "an all-powerful, monolithic institution which strip[ped] the slave of any meaningful and distinctive culture, family life, religion or manhood" (p. vii). To the contrary, the relative freedom from white control that slaves enjoyed in their quarters enabled them to create and sustain a complex social organization that incorporated "norms of conduct, defined roles and behavioral patterns" and provided for the traditional functions of group solidarity, defense, mutual assistance, and family organization. Although the family had no legal standing in slavery and was frequently disrupted, Blassingame noted its major role as a source of survival for slaves and as a mechanism of social control for slaveholders, many of whom encouraged "monogamous mating arrangements" as insurance against runaways and rebellion. In fashioning familial and community organization, slaves drew upon the many remnants of their African heritage (e.g., courtship rituals, kinship networks, and religious beliefs), merging those elements with American forms to create a distinctive culture, features of which persist in the contemporary social organization of African American family life and community.

Genovese's (1974) analysis of plantation records and slave testimony led him to similar conclusions regarding the nature of family life and community among African

Americans under slavery. Genovese noted that, although chattel bondage played havoc with the domestic lives of slaves and imposed severe constraints on their ability to enact and sustain normative family roles and functions, the slaves "created impressive norms of family, including as much of a nuclear family norm as conditions permitted and . . . entered the postwar social system with a remarkably stable base" (p. 452). He attributed this stability to the extraordinary resourcefulness and commitment of slaves to marital relations and to what he called a "paternalistic compromise," or bargain between masters and slaves that recognized certain reciprocal obligations and rights, including recognition of slaves' marital and family ties. Although slavery undermined the role of African American men as husbands and fathers, their function as role models for their children and as providers for their families was considerably greater than has generally been supposed. Nonetheless, the tenuous position of male slaves as husbands and fathers and the more visible and nontraditional roles assumed by female slaves gave rise to legends of matriarchy and emasculated men. However, Genovese contended that the relationship between slave men and women came closer to approximating gender equality than was possible for white families.

Perhaps the most significant historical work that forced revisions in scholarship on African American family life and culture during slavery was Gutman's (1976) landmark study, *The Black Family in Slavery and Freedom.* Inspired by the controversy surrounding the Moynihan report and its thesis that African American family disorganization was a legacy of slavery, Gutman made ingenious use of quantifiable data derived from plantation birth registers and marriage applications to re-create family and kinship structures among African Americans during slavery and after emancipation. Moreover, he marshaled compelling evidence to explain how African Americans developed an autonomous and complex culture that enabled them to cope with the harshness of enslavement, the massive relocation from relatively small economic units in the upper South to vast plantations in the lower South between 1790 and 1860, the experience of legal freedom in the rural and urban South, and the transition to northern urban communities before 1930.

Gutman reasoned that, if family disorganization (fatherless, matrifocal families) among African Americans was a legacy of slavery, then such a condition should have been more common among urban African Americans closer in time to slavery—in 1850 and 1860—than in 1950 and 1960. Through careful examination of census data, marriage licenses, and personal documents for the period after 1860, he found that stable, two-parent households predominated during slavery and after emancipation and that families headed by African American women at the turn of the century were hardly more prevalent than among comparable white families. Thus "[a]t all moments in time between 1860 and 1925 . . . the typical Afro-American family was lower class in status and headed by two parents. That was so in the urban and rural South in 1880 and 1900 and in New York City in 1905 and 1925" (p. 456). Gutman found that the two-parent family was just as common among the poor as among the more advantaged, and as common among southerners as those in the Northeast. For Gutman, the key to understanding the durability of African American families during and after slavery lay in the distinctive African American culture that evolved from the cumulative slave experiences that provided a defense against some of the more destructive and dehumanizing aspects of that system.

Among the more enduring and important aspects of that culture are the enlarged kinship network and certain domestic arrangements (e.g., the sharing of family households with nonrelatives and the informal adoption of children) that, during slavery, formed the core of evolving African American communities and the collective sense of interdependence.

Additional support for the conclusion that the two-parent household was the norm among slaves and their descendants was provided by Furstenberg et al. (1975) from their study of the family composition of African Americans, native-born whites, and immigrants to Philadelphia from 1850 to 1880. From their analysis of census data, Furstenberg et al. found that most African American families, like those of other ethnic groups, were headed by two parents (75% for African Americans versus 73% for native whites). Similar results are reported by Pleck (1973) from her study of African American family structure in late 19th-century Boston. As these and other studies (Jones, 1985; White, 1985) have shown, although female-headed households were common among African Americans during and following slavery, such households were by no means typical. In fact, as late as the 1960s, three fourths of African American households were headed by married couples (Jaynes & Williams, 1989; Moynihan, 1965).

However, more recent historical research would appear to modify, if not challenge, several of the contentions of the revisionist scholars of slavery. Manfra and Dykstra (1985) and Stevenson (1995), among others, found evidence of considerably greater variability in slave family structure and in household composition than was reported in previous works. In her study of Virginia slave families from 1830 to 1860, Stevenson (1995) discovered evidence of widespread matrifocality, as well as other marital and household arrangements, among antebellum slaves. Her analysis of the family histories of slaves in colonial and antebellum Virginia revealed that many slaves did not have a nuclear "core" in their families. Rather, the "most discernible ideal for their principal kinship organization was a malleable extended family that provided its members with nurture, education, socialization, material support, and recreation in the face of the potential social chaos the slavemasters' power imposed" (1995, p. 36).

A variety of conditions affected the family configurations of slaves, including cultural differences among the slaves themselves, the state or territory in which they lived, and the size of the plantation on which they resided. Thus, Stevenson concluded that

> the slave family was not a static, imitative institution that necessarily favored one form of family organization over another. Rather, it was a diverse phenomenon, sometimes assuming several forms even among the slaves of one community. . . . Far from having a negative impact, the diversity of slave marriage and family norms, as a measure of the slave family's enormous adaptive potential, allowed the slave and the slave family to survive. (p. 29)

Hence, "postrevisionist" historiography emphasizes the great diversity of familial arrangements among African Americans during slavery. Although nuclear, matrifocal, and extended families were prevalent, none dominated slave family forms. These postrevisionist amendments notwithstanding, there is compelling historical evidence that African American nuclear families and kin-related households remained relatively intact and survived the experiences of slavery, Reconstruction, the Great Depression, and the transition to northern urban communities. Such evidence underscores the importance of considering recent developments and conditions in accounting for changes in family patterns among African Americans in the contemporary period.

CONTEMPORARY AFRICAN AMERICAN FAMILY PATTERNS

Substantial changes have occurred in patterns of marriage, family, and household composition in the United States during the past three decades, accompanied by significant alterations in the family lives of men, women, and children. During this period, divorce rates have more than doubled, marriage rates have declined, fertility rates have fallen to record levels, the proportion of "traditional" families (nuclear families in which children live with both biological parents) as a percentage of all family groups has declined, and the proportion of children reared in single-parent households has risen dramatically (Taylor, 1997).

Some of the changes in family patterns have been more rapid and dramatic among African Americans than among the population as a whole. For example, while declining rates of marriage and remarriage, high levels of separation and divorce, and higher proportions of children living in single-parent households are trends that have characterized the U.S. population as a whole during the past 30 years, these trends have been more pronounced among African Americans and, in some respects, represent marked departures from earlier African American family patterns. A growing body of research has implicated demographic and economic factors as causes of the divergent marital and family experiences of African Americans and other populations.

In the following section, I examine diverse patterns and evolving trends in family structure and household composition among African Americans, together with those demographic, economic, and social factors that have been identified as sources of change in patterns of family formation.

Diversity of Family Structure

Since 1960, the number of African American households has increased at more than twice the rate of white households. By 1995, African American households numbered 11.6 million, compared with 83.7 million white households. Of these households, 58.4 million white and 8.0 million African American ones were classified as family households by the U.S. Bureau of the Census (1996), which defines a *household* as the person or persons occupying a housing unit and a *family* as consisting of two or more persons who live in the same household and are related by birth, marriage, or adoption. Thus, family households are households maintained by individuals who share their residence with one or more relatives, whereas nonfamily households are maintained by individuals with no relatives in the housing unit. In 1995, 70% of the 11.6 million African American households were family households, the same proportion as among white households (U.S. Bureau of the Census, 1996). However, nonfamily households have been increasing at a faster rate than family households among African Americans because of delayed marriages among young adults, higher rates of family disruption (divorce and separation), and sharp increases in the number of unmarried cohabiting couples (Cherlin, 1995; Glick, 1997).

Family households vary by type and composition. Although the U.S. Bureau of the Census recognizes the wide diversity of families in this country, it differentiates between three broad and basic types of family households: married-couple or husband-wife families, families with female householders (no husband present), and families with male householders (no wife present). Family composition refers to whether the household is *nuclear*, that is, contains parents and children only, or extended, that is, nuclear plus other relatives.

To take account of the diversity in types and composition of African American families, Billingsley (1968; 1992) added to these conventional categories *augmented* families (nuclear plus nonrelated persons), and modified the definition of nuclear family to include *incipient* (a married couple without children), *simple* (a couple with children), and *attenuated* (a single parent with children) families. He also added three combinations of augmented families: *incipient extended augmented* (a couple with relatives and nonrelatives), *nuclear extended augmented* (a couple with children, relatives, and nonrelatives), and *attenuated extended augmented* (a single parent with children, relatives, and nonrelatives). With these modifications, Billingsley identified 32 different kinds of nuclear, extended, and augmented family households among African Americans. His typology has been widely used and modified by other scholars (see, for example, Shimkin, Shimkin, & Frate, 1978; Stack, 1974). For example, on the basis of Billingsley's typology, Dressler, Haworth-Hoeppner, and Pitts (1985) developed a four-way typology with 12 subtypes for their study of household structures in a southern African American community and found a variety of types of female-headed households, less than a fourth of them consisting of a mother and her children or grandchildren.

However, as Staples (1971) pointed out, Billingsley's typology emphasized the household and ignored an important characteristic of such families—their "extendedness." African Americans are significantly more likely than whites to live in extended families that "transcend and link several different households, each containing a separate . . . family" (Farley & Allen, 1987, p. 168). In 1992, approximately 1 in 5 African American families was extended, compared to 1 in 10 white families (Glick, 1997). The greater proportion of extended households among African Americans has been linked to the extended family tradition of West African cultures (Nobles, 1978; Sudarkasa, 1988) and to the economic marginality of many African American families, which has encouraged the sharing and exchange of resources, services, and emotional support among family units spread across a number of households (Stack, 1974).

In comparative research on West African, Caribbean, and African American family patterns some anthropologists (Herskovits, 1958; Sudarkasa, 1997) found evidence of cultural continuities in the significance attached to coresidence, formal kinship relations, and nuclear families among black populations in these areas. Summarizing this work, Hill (1993, pp. 104–105) observed that, with respect to

> co-residence, the African concept of family is not restricted to persons living in the same household, but includes key persons living in separate households. . . . As for defining kin relationships, the African concept of family is not confined to relations between formal

> kin, but includes networks of unrelated [i.e., "fictive kin"] as well as related persons living in separate households. . . . [According to] Herskovits (1941), the African nuclear family unit is not as central to its family organization as is the case for European nuclear families: "The African immediate family, consisting of a father, his wives, and their children, is but a part of a larger unit. This immediate family is generally recognized by Africanists as belonging to a local relationship group termed the 'extended family.'"

Similarly, Sudarkasa (1988) found that unlike the European extended family, in which primacy is given to the conjugal unit (husband, wife, and children) as the basic building block, the African extended family is organized around blood ties (consanguineous relations).

In their analysis of data from the National Survey of Black Americans (NSBA) on household composition and family structure, Hatchett, Cochran, and Jackson (1991) noted that the extended family perspective, especially kin networks, was valuable in describing the nature and functioning of African American families. They suggested that the "extended family can be viewed both as a family network in the physical-spatial sense and in terms of family relations or contact and exchanges. In this view of extendedness, family structure and function are interdependent concepts" (p. 49). Their examination of the composition of the 2,107 households in the NSBA resulted in the identification of 12 categories, 8 of which roughly captured the "dimensions of household family structure identified in Billingsley's typology of Black families (1968)—the incipient nuclear family, the incipient nuclear extended and/or augmented nuclear family, the simple nuclear family, the simple extended and/or augmented nuclear family, the attenuated nuclear family, and the attenuated extended and/or augmented family, respectively" (p. 51). These households were examined with respect to their *actual kin networks*, defined as subjective feelings of emotional closeness to family members, frequency of contact, and patterns of mutual assistance, and their *potential kin networks*, defined as the availability or proximity of immediate family members and the density or concentration of family members within a given range.

Hatchett et al. (1991) found that approximately 1 in 5 African American households in the NSBA was an extended household (included other relatives—parents and siblings of the household head, grandchildren, grandparents, and nieces and nephews). Nearly 20% of the extended households with children contained minors who were not the head's; most of these children were grandchildren, nieces, and nephews of the head. The authors suggested that "[t]hese are instances of informal fostering or adoption—absorption of minor children by the kin network" (p. 58).

In this sample, female-headed households were as likely to be extended as male-headed households. Hatchett et al. (1991) found little support for the possibility that economic hardship may account for the propensity among African Americans to incorporate other relatives in their households. That is, the inclusion of other relatives in the households did not substantially improve the overall economic situation of the households because the majority of other relatives were minor children, primarily grandchildren of heads who coresided with the household heads' own minor and adult children. Moreover, they stated, "household extendedness at both the household and extra-household levels appears to be a characteristic of black families, regardless of socioeconomic level" (p. 81), and regardless of region of the country or rural or urban residence.

The households in the NSBA were also compared in terms of their potential and actual kin networks. The availability of potential kin networks varied by the age of the respondent, by the region and degree of urban development of the respondent's place of residence, and by the type of household in which the respondent resided (Hatchett et al., 1991). For example, households with older heads and spouses were more isolated from kin than were younger households headed by single mothers, and female-headed households tended to have greater potential kin networks than did individuals in nuclear households. With respect to region and urbanicity, the respondents in the Southern and North Central regions and those in rural areas had a greater concentration of relatives closer at hand than did the respondents in other regions and those in urban areas. However, proximity to relatives and their concentration nearby did not translate directly into actual kin networks or extended family functioning:

> Complex relationships were found across age, income, and type of household. From these data came a picture of the Black elderly with high psychological connectedness to family in the midst of relative geographical and interactional isolation from them. The image of female single-parent households is, on the other hand, the reverse or negative of this picture. Female heads were geographically closer to kin, had more contact with them, and received more help from family but did not perceive as much family solidarity or psychological connectedness. (Hatchett et al., 1991, p. 81)

The nature and frequency of mutual aid among kin were also assessed in this survey. More than two thirds of the respondents reported receiving some assistance from family members, including financial support, child care, goods and services, and help during sickness and at death. Financial assistance and child care were the two most frequent types of support reported by the younger respondents, whereas goods and services were the major types reported by older family members. The type of support the respondents received from their families was determined, to some extent, by needs defined by the family life cycle.

In sum, the results of the NSBA document the wide variety of family configurations and households in which African Americans reside and suggest, along with other studies, that the diversity of structures represents adaptive responses to the variety of social, economic, and demographic conditions that African Americans have encountered over time (Billingsley, 1968; Farley & Allen, 1987).

Although Hatchett et al. (1991) focused on extended or augmented African American families in their analysis of the NSBA data, only 1 in 5 households in this survey contained persons outside the nuclear family. The majority of households was nuclear, containing one or both parents with their own children.

Between 1970 and 1990, the number of all U.S. married-couple families with children dropped by almost 1 million, and their share of all family households declined from 40% to 26% (U.S. Bureau of the Census, 1995). The proportion of married-couple families with children among African Americans also declined during this period, from 41% to 26% of all African American families. In addition, the percentage of African American families headed by women more than doubled, increasing from 33% in 1970 to 57% in 1990. By 1995, married-couple families with children constituted 36% of all African

American families, while single-parent families represented 64% (U.S. Bureau of the Census, 1996). The year 1980 was the first time in history that African American female-headed families with children outnumbered married-couple families. This shift in the distribution of African American families by type is associated with a number of complex, interrelated social and economic developments, including increases in age at first marriage, high rates of separation and divorce, male joblessness, and out-of-wedlock births.

Marriage, Divorce, and Separation

In a reversal of a long-time trend, African Americans are now marrying at a much later age than are persons of other races. Thirty years ago, African American men and women were far more likely to have married by ages 20–24 than were white Americans. In 1960, 56% of African American men and 36% of African American women aged 20–24 were never married; by 1993, 90% of all African American men and 81% of African American women in this age cohort were never married (U.S. Bureau of the Census, 1994).

The trend toward later marriages among African Americans has contributed to changes in the distribution of African American families by type. Delayed marriage tends to increase the risk of out-of-wedlock childbearing and single parenting (Hernandez, 1993). In fact, a large proportion of the increase in single-parent households in recent years is accounted for by never-married women maintaining families (U.S. Bureau of the Census, 1990).

The growing proportion of never-married young African American adults is partly a result of a combination of factors, including continuing high rates of unemployment, especially among young men; college attendance; military service; and an extended period of cohabitation prior to marriage (Glick, 1997; Testa & Krogh, 1995; Wilson, 1987). In their investigation of the effect of employment on marriage among African American men in the inner city of Chicago, Testa and Krogh (1995) found that men in stable jobs were twice as likely to marry as were men who were unemployed, not in school, or in the military. Hence, it has been argued that the feasibility of marriage among African Americans in recent decades has decreased because the precarious economic position of African American men has made them less attractive as potential husbands and less interested in becoming husbands, given the difficulties they are likely to encounter in performing the provider role in marriage (Tucker & Mitchell-Kernan, 1995).

However, other research has indicated that economic factors are only part of the story. Using census data from 1940 through the mid-1980s, Mare and Winship (1991) sought to determine the impact of declining employment opportunities on marriage rates among African Americans and found that although men who were employed were more likely to marry, recent declines in employment rates among young African American men were not large enough to account for a substantial part of the declining trend in their marriage rates. Similarly, in their analysis of data from a national survey of young African American adults, Lichter, McLaughlin, Kephart, and Landry (1992) found that lower employment rates among African American men were an important contributing factor to delayed marriage—and perhaps to nonmarriage—among African American women. However, even when marital opportunities were taken into account, the researchers found that the rate of marriage among young African American women in the survey was only 50% to 60% the rate of white women of similar ages.

In addition to recent declines in employment rates, an unbalanced sex ratio has been identified as an important contributing factor to declining marriage rates among African Americans. This shortage of men is due partly to high rates of mortality and incarceration of African American men (Kiecolt & Fossett, 1995; Wilson & Neckerman, 1986). Guttentag and Secord (1983) identified a number of major consequences of the shortage of men over time: higher rates of singlehood, out-of-wedlock births, divorce, and infidelity and less commitment among men to relationships. Among African Americans, they found that in 1980 the ratio of men to women was unusually low; in fact, few populations in the United States had sex ratios as low as those of African Americans. Because African American women outnumber men in each of the age categories 20 to 49, the resulting "marriage squeeze" puts African American women at a significant disadvantage in the marriage market, causing an unusually large proportion of them to remain unmarried. However, Glick (1997) observed a reversal of the marriage squeeze among African Americans in the age categories 18 to 27 during the past decade: In 1995, there were 102 African American men for every 100 African American women in this age range. Thus, "[w]hereas the earlier marriage squeeze made it difficult for Black women to marry, the future marriage squeeze will make it harder for Black men" (Glick, 1997, p. 126). But, as Kiecolt and Fossett (1995) observed, the impact of the sex ratio on marital outcomes for African Americans may vary, depending on the nature of the local marriage market. Indeed, "marriage markets are local, as opposed to national, phenomena which may have different implications for different genders . . . [for example,] men and women residing near a military base face a different sex ratio than their counterparts attending a large university" (Smith, 1995, p. 137).

African American men and women are not only delaying marriage, but are spending fewer years in their first marriages and are slower to remarry than in decades past. Since 1960, a sharp decline has occurred in the number of years African American women spend with their first husbands and a corresponding rise in the interval of separation and divorce between the first and second marriages (Espenshade, 1985; Jaynes & Williams, 1989). Data from the National Fertility Surveys of 1965 and 1970 disclosed that twice as many African American couples as white couples (10% versus 5%) who reached their 5th wedding anniversaries ended their marriages before their 10th anniversaries (Thornton, 1978), and about half the African American and a quarter of the white marriages were dissolved within the first 15 years of marriage (McCarthy, 1978). Similarly, a comparison of the prevalence of marital disruption (defined as separation or divorce) among 13 racial-ethnic groups in the United States based on the 1980 census revealed that of the women who had married for the first time 10 to 14 years before 1980, 53% of the African American women, 48% of the Native American women, and 37% of the non-Hispanic white women were separated or divorced by the 1980 census (Sweet & Bumpass, 1987).

Although African American women have a higher likelihood of separating from their husbands than do non-Hispanic white women, they are slower to obtain legal divorces (Chertin, 1996). According to data from the 1980 census, within three years of separating from their husbands, only 55% of the African American women had obtained divorces, compared to 91% of the non-Hispanic white women (Sweet & Bumpass, 1987). Cherlin speculated that, because of their lower expectations of remarrying, African American women may be less motivated to obtain legal divorces. Indeed, given the shortage of African American men in each of the age categories from 20 to 49, it is not surprising that the proportion of divorced women who remarry is lower among African American than among non-Hispanic white women (Glick, 1997). Overall, the remarriage rate among African Americans is about one fourth the rate of whites (Staples & Johnson, 1993).

Cherlin (1996) identified lower educational levels, high rates of unemployment, and low income as importance sources of differences in African American and white rates of marital dissolution. However, as he pointed out, these factors alone are insufficient to account for all the observed difference. At every level of educational attainment, African American women are more likely to be separated or divorced from their husbands than are non-Hispanic white women. Using data from the 1980 census, Jaynes and Williams (1989) compared the actual marital-status distributions of African Americans and whites, controlling for differences in educational attainment for men and women and for income distribution for men. They found that when differences in educational attainment were taken into account, African American women were more likely to be "formerly married than White women and much less likely to be living with a husband" (p. 529). Moreover, income was an important factor in accounting for differences in the marital status of African American and white men. Overall, Jaynes and Williams found that socioeconomic differences explained a significant amount of the variance in marital status differences between African Americans and whites, although Bumpass, Sweet, and Martin (1990) noted that such differences rapidly diminish as income increases, especially for men. As Glick (1997) reported, African American men with high income levels are more likely to be in intact first marriages by middle age than are African American women with high earnings. This relationship between income and marital status, he stated, is strongest at the lower end of the income distribution, suggesting that marital permanence for men is less dependent on their being well-to-do than on their having the income to support a family.

As a result of sharp increases in marital disruption and relatively low remarriage rates, less than half (43%) the African American adults aged 18 and older were currently married in 1995, down from 64% in 1970 (U.S. Bureau of the Census, 1996). Moreover, although the vast majority of the 11.6 million African Americans households in 1995 were family households, less than half (47%) were headed by married couples, down from 56% in 1980. Some analysts expect the decline in marriage among African Americans to continue for some time, consistent with the movement away from marriage as a consequence of modernization and urbanization (Espenshade, 1985) and in response to continuing economic marginalization. But African American culture may also play a role. As a number of writers have noted (Billingsley, 1992; Cherlin, 1996), blood ties and extended families have traditionally been given primacy over other types of relationships, including marriage, among African Americans, and this emphasis may have influenced the way many African Americans responded to recent shifts in values in the larger society and the restructuring of the economy that struck the African American community especially hard.

Such is the interpretation of Cherlin (1992, p. 112), who argued that the institution of marriage has been weakened during the past few decades by the increasing economic independence of women and men and by a cultural drift "toward a more individualistic ethos, one which emphasized self-fulfillment in personal relations." In addition, Wilson (1987) and others described structural shifts in the economy (from manufacturing to service industries as a source of the growth in employment) that have benefited African American women more than men, eroding men's earning potential and their ability to support families. According to Cherlin, the way African Americans responded to such broad sociocultural and economic changes was conditioned by their history and culture:

> Faced with difficult times economically, many Blacks responded by drawing upon a model of social support that was in their cultural repertoire. . . . This response relied heavily on extended kinship networks and deemphasized marriage. It is a response that taps a traditional source of strength in African-American society: cooperation and sharing among a large network of kin. (p. 113)

Thus, it seems likely that economic developments and cultural values have contributed independently and jointly to the explanation of declining rates of marriage among African Americans in recent years (Farley & Allen, 1987).

Single-Parent Families

Just as rates of divorce, separation, and out-of-wedlock childbearing have increased over the past few decades, so has the number of children living in single-parent households. For example, between 1970 and 1990, the number and proportion of all U.S. single-parent households increased threefold, from 1 in 10 to 3 in 10. There were 3.8 million single-parent families with children under 18 in 1970, compared to 11.4 million in 1994. The vast majority of single-parent households are maintained by women (86% in 1994), but the number of single-parent households headed by men has more than tripled: from 393,000 in 1970 to 1.5 million in 1994 (U.S. Bureau of the Census, 1995).

Among the 58% of African American families with children at home in 1995, more were one-parent families (34%) than married-couple families (24%). In 1994, single-parent families accounted for 25% of all white family groups with children under age 18, 65% of all African American family groups, and 36% of Hispanic family groups (U.S. Bureau of the Census, 1995).

Single-parent families are created in a number of ways: through divorce, marital separation, out-of-wedlock births, or death of a parent. Among adult African American women aged 25–44, increases in the percentage of never-married women and disrupted marriages are significant contributors to the rise in female-headed households; for white women of the same age group, marital dissolution or divorce is the most important factor (Demo, 1992; Jaynes & Williams, 1989). Moreover, changes in the living arrangements of women who give birth outside marriage or experience marital disruption have also been significant factors in the rise of female-headed households among African American and white women. In the past, women who experienced separation or divorce, or bore children out of wedlock were more likely to move in with their parents or other relatives, creating subfamilies; as a result, they were not classified as female headed. In recent decades, however, more and more of these women have established their own households (Parish, Hao, & Hogan, 1991).

An increasing proportion of female-headed householders are unmarried teenage mothers with young children. In 1990, for example, 96% of all births to African American teenagers occurred outside marriage; for white teenagers, the figure was 55% (National Center for Health Statistics, 1991). Although overall fertility rates among teenage women declined steadily from the 1950s through the end of the 1980s, the share of births to unmarried women has risen sharply over time. In 1970, the proportion of all births to unmarried teenage women aged 15–19 was less than 1 in 3; by 1991, it had increased to 2 in 3.

Differences in fertility and births outside marriage among young African American and white women are accounted for, in part, by differences in sexual activity, use of contraceptives, the selection of adoption as an option, and the proportion of premarital pregnancies that are legitimated by marriage before the children's births (Trusell, 1988). Compared to their white counterparts, African American teenagers are more likely to be sexually active and less likely to use contraceptives, to have abortions when pregnant, and to marry before the babies are born. In consequence, young African American women constitute a larger share of single mothers than they did in past decades. This development has serious social and economic consequences for children and adults because female-headed households have much higher rates of poverty and deprivation than do other families (Taylor, 1991b).

Family Structure and Family Dynamics

As a number of studies have shown, there is a strong correspondence between organization and economic status of families, regardless of race (Farley & Allen, 1987). For both African Americans and whites, the higher the income, the greater the percentage of families headed by married couples. In their analysis of 1980 census data on family income and structure, Farley and Allen (1987) found that "there were near linear decreases in the proportions of households headed by women, households where children reside with a single parent, and extended households with increases in economic status" (p. 185). Yet, socioeconomic factors, they concluded, explained only part of the observed differences in family organization between African Americans and whites. "Cultural factors—that is, family preferences, notions of the appropriate and established habits—also help explain race differences in family organization" (p. 186).

One such difference is the egalitarian mode of family functioning in African American families, characterized by complementarity and flexibility in family roles (Billingsley, 1992; Hill, 1971). Egalitarian modes of family functioning are common even among low-income African American families, where one might expect the more traditional patriarchal pattern of authority to prevail. Until recently, such modes of family functioning were interpreted as signs of weakness or pathology because they were counternormative to the gender-role division of labor in majority families (Collins, 1990). Some scholars have suggested that role reciprocity in African American families is a legacy of slavery, in which the traditional gender division of labor was largely ignored by slaveholders, and Black men and women were "equal in the sense that neither sex wielded economic power over the other" (Jones, 1985, p. 14). As a result of historical experiences and economic conditions, traditional gender distinctions in the homemaker and provider roles have been less rigid in African American families than in white families (Beckett & Smith, 1981). Moreover, since African American women have historically been involved in the paid labor force in greater numbers than have white women and because they have had a more significant economic role in families than their white counterparts, Scott-Jones and Nelson-LeGall (1986, p. 95) argued that African Americans "have not experienced as strong an economic basis for the subordination of women, either in marital roles or in the preparation of girls for schooling, jobs, and careers."

In her analysis of data from the NSBA, Hatchett (1991) found strong support for an egalitarian division of family responsibilities and tasks. With respect to attitudes toward the sharing of familial roles, 88% of the African American adults agreed that women and men should share child care and housework equally, and 73% agreed that both men and women should have jobs to support their families. For African American men, support for an egalitarian division of labor in the family did not differ by education or socioeconomic level, but education was related to attitudes toward the sharing of family responsibilities and roles among African American women. College-educated women were more likely than were women with less education to support the flexibility and interchangeability of family roles and tasks.

Egalitarian attitudes toward familial roles among African Americans are also reflected in child-rearing attitudes and practices (Taylor, 1991a). Studies have indicated that African American families tend to place less emphasis on differential gender-role socialization than do other families (Blau, 1981). In her analysis of gender-role socialization among southern African American families, Lewis (1975) found few patterned differences in parental attitudes toward male and female roles. Rather, age and relative birth order were found to be more important than gender as determinants of differential treatment and behavioral expectations for children. Through their socialization practices, African American parents seek to inculcate in both genders traits of assertiveness, independence, and self-confidence (Boykin & Toms, 1985; Lewis, 1975). However, as children mature, socialization practices are adapted to reflect "more closely the structure of expectations and opportunities provided for Black men and women by the dominant society" (Lewis, 1975, p. 237)—that is, geared to the macrostructural conditions that constrain familial role options for African American men and women.

However, such shifts in emphasis and expectations often lead to complications in the socialization process by inculcating in men and women components of gender-role definitions that are incompatible or noncomplementary, thereby engendering a potential source of conflict in their relationships. Franklin (1986) suggested that young African American men and women are frequently confronted with contradictory messages and dilemmas as a result of familial socialization. On the one hand, men are socialized to embrace an androgynous gender role within the African American community, but, on the other hand, they are expected to perform according to the white masculine gender-role paradigm in some contexts. According to Franklin, this dual orientation tends to foster confusion in some young men and difficulties developing an appropriate gender identity. Likewise, some young African American women may receive two different and contradictory messages: "One message states, 'Because you will be a Black woman, it is imperative that you learn to take care of yourself because it is hard to find a Black man who will take care of you.' A second message . . . that conflicts with the first . . . is 'your ultimate achievement will occur when you have snared a Black man who will take care of you'" (Franklin, 1986, p. 109). Franklin contended that such contradictory expectations and mixed messages frequently lead to incompatible gender-based behaviors among African American men and women and conflicts in their relationships.

Despite the apparently greater acceptance of role flexibility and power sharing in African American families, conflict around these issues figures prominently in marital instability. In their study of marital instability among African American and white couples in early marriages, Hatchett, Veroff, and Douvan (1995) found young African American couples at odds over gender roles in the family. Anxiety over their ability to function in the provider role was found to be an important source of instability in the marriages for African American husbands, but not for white husbands. Hatchett (1991) observed that marital instability tended to be more common among young African American couples if the husbands felt that their wives had equal power in the family and if the wives felt there was not enough sharing of family tasks and responsibilities. Hatchett et al. (1991) suggested that African American men's feelings of economic anxiety and self-doubt may be expressed in conflicts over decisional power and in the men's more tenuous commitment to their marriages vis-à-vis African American women. Although the results of their study relate to African American couples in the early stages of marriage, the findings may be predictive of major marital difficulties in the long term. These and other findings (see, for example, Tucker & Mitchell-Kernan, 1995) indicate that changing attitudes and definitions of familial roles among young African American couples are tied to social and economic trends (such as new and increased employment opportunities for women and new value orientations toward marriage and family) in the larger society.

African American Families, Social Change, and Public Policy

Over the past three decades, no change in the African American community has been more fundamental and dramatic than the restructuring of families and family relationships. Since the 1960s, unprecedented changes have occurred in rates of marriage, divorce, and separation; in the proportion of single and two-parent households and births to unmarried mothers; and in the number of children living in poverty. To be sure, these changes are consistent with trends for the U.S. population as a whole, but they are more pronounced among African Americans, largely because of a conflux of demographic and economic factors that are peculiar to the African American community.

In their summary of findings from a series of empirical studies that investigated the causes and correlates of recent changes in patterns of African American family formation, Tucker and Mitchell-Kernan (1995) came to several conclusions that have implications for future research and social policy. One consistent finding is the critical role that sex ratios—the availability of mates—play in the formation of African American families.

Analyzing aggregate-level data on African American sex ratios in 171 U.S. cities, Sampson (1995) found that these sex ratios were highly predictive of female headship, the percentage of married couples among families with school-age children, and the percentage of African American women who were single. In assessing the causal effect of sex ratios on the family structure of African Americans and whites, he showed that the effect is five times greater for the former than the latter. Similarly, Kiecolt and Fossett's (1995) analysis of African American sex ratios in Louisiana cities and counties disclosed that they had strong positive effects on the percentage of African American women who were married and had husbands present, the rate of marital births per thousand African American women aged 20–29, the percentage of married-couple families, and the percentage of children living in two-parent households.

Another consistent finding is the substantial and critical impact of economic factors on African American family formation, especially men's employment status. Analyses by Sampson (1995) and Darity and Myers (1995) provided persuasive evidence that economic factors play a major and unique role in the development and maintenance of African American families. Using aggregate data, Sampson found that low employment rates for African American men in cities across the United States were predictive of female headship, the percentage of women who were single, and the percentage of married-couple families among family households with school-age children. Moreover, comparing the effect of men's employment on the family structure of African American and white families, he found that the effect was 20 times greater for African Americans than for whites. Similar results are reported by Darity and Myers, who investigated the effects of sex ratio and economic marriageability—Wilson and Neckerman's (1986) Male Marriageability Pool Index—on African American family structure. They found that, although both measures were independently predictive of female headship among African Americans, a composite measure of economic and demographic factors was a more stable and effective predictor. Moreover, Sampson found that the strongest independent effect of these factors on family structure was observed among African American families in poverty. That is, "the lower the sex ratio and the lower the male employment rate the higher the rate of female-headed families with children and in poverty" (p. 250). It should be noted that neither rates of white men's employment nor white sex ratios was found to have much influence on white family structure in these analyses, lending support to Wilson's (1987) hypothesis regarding the structural sources of family disruption among African Americans.

Although the findings reported here are not definitive, they substantiate the unique and powerful effects of sex ratios and men's employment on the marital behavior and family structure of African Americans and point to other problems related to the economic marginalization of men and family poverty in African American communities. Some analysts have predicted far-reaching consequences for African Americans and for society at large should current trends in marital disruption continue unabated. Darity and Myers (1996) predicted that the majority of African American families will be headed by women by the beginning of the next decade if violent crime, homicide, incarceration, and other problems associated with the economic marginalization of African American men are allowed to rob the next generation of fathers and husbands. Moreover, they contended, a large number of such families are likely to be poor and isolated from the mainstream of American society.

The growing economic marginalization of African American men and their ability to provide economic support to families have contributed to their increasing estrangement from family life (Bowman, 1989; Tucker & Mitchell-Kernan, 1995) and are identified as pivotal factors in the development of other social problems, including drug abuse, crime, homicide, and imprisonment, which further erode their prospects as marriageable mates for African American women.

In addressing the structural sources of the disruption of African American families, researchers have advanced a number of short- and long-term proposals. There is considerable agreement that increasing the rate of marriage alone will not significantly improve the economic prospects of many poor African American families. As Ehrenreich (1986) observed, given the marginal economic position of poor African American men, impoverished African American women would have to be married to three such men—simultaneously—to achieve an average family income! Thus, for many African American women, increasing the prevalence of marriage will not address many of the problems they experience as single parents.

With respect to short-term policies designed to address some of the more deleterious effects of structural forces on African American families, Darity and Myers (1996) proposed three policy initiatives that are likely to produce significant results for African American communities. First, because research has indicated that reductions in welfare benefits have failed to stem the rise in female-headed households, welfare policy should reinstate its earlier objective of lifting the poor out of poverty. In Darity and Myers's view, concerns about the alleged disincentives of transfer payments are "moot in light of the long-term evidence that Black families will sink deeper into a crisis of female headship with or without welfare. Better a world of welfare-dependent, near-poor families than one of welfare-free but desolate and permanently poor families" (p. 288). Second, programs are needed to improve the health care of poor women and their children. One major potential benefit of such a strategy is an improvement in the sex ratio because the quality of prenatal and child care is one of the determinants of sex ratios. "By assuring quality health care now, we may help stem the tide toward further depletion of young Black males in the future" (p. 288). A third strategy involves improvements in the quality of education provided to the poor, which are key to employment gains.

Although these are important initiatives with obvious benefits to African American communities, in the long term, the best strategy for addressing marital disruptions and other family-related issues is an economic-labor market strategy. Because much of current social policy is ideologically driven, rather than formulated on the basis of empirical evidence, it has failed to acknowledge or address the extent to which global and national changes in the economy have conspired to marginalize significant segments of the African American population, both male and female, and deprive them of the resources to form or support families. Although social policy analysts have repeatedly substantiated the link between the decline in marriages among African Americans and fundamental changes in the U.S. postindustrial economy, their insights have yet to be formulated into a meaningful and responsive policy agenda. Until these structural realities are incorporated into governmental policy, it is unlikely that marital disruption and other adverse trends associated with this development will be reversed.

There is no magic bullet for addressing the causes and consequences of marital decline among African Americans, but public policies that are designed to improve the economic and employment prospects of men and women at all socioeconomic levels have the greatest potential for improving the lot of African American families. Key elements of such policies would include raising the level of education and employment training among African American youth, and more vigorous enforcement of antidiscrimination laws, which would raise the level of employment and earnings and contribute to higher rates of marriage among African Americans (Burbridge, 1995). To be sure, many of the federally sponsored employment and training programs that were launched during the 1960s and 1970s were plagued by a variety of administrative and organizational problems, but the effectiveness of some of these programs in improving the long-term employment prospects and life chances of disadvantaged youth and adults has been well documented (Taylor et al., 1990).

African American families, like all families, exist not in a social vacuum but in communities, and programs that are designed to strengthen community institutions and provide social support to families are likely to have a significant impact on family functioning. Although the extended family and community institutions, such as the church, have been important sources of support to African American families in the past, these community support systems have been overwhelmed by widespread joblessness, poverty, and a plethora of other problems that beset many African American communities. Thus, national efforts to rebuild the social and economic infrastructures of inner-city communities would make a major contribution toward improving the overall health and well-being of African American families and could encourage more young people to marry in the future.

Winning support for these and other policy initiatives will not be easy in a political environment that de-emphasizes the role of government in social policy and human welfare. But without such national efforts, it is difficult to see how many of the social conditions that adversely affect the structure and functioning of African American families will be eliminated or how the causes and consequences of marital decline can be ameliorated. If policy makers are serious about addressing conditions that destabilize families, undermine communities, and contribute to a host of other socially undesirable outcomes, new policy initiatives, such as those just outlined, must be given higher priority.

References

Allen, W. (1978). The search for applicable theories of black family life. *Journal of Marriage and the Family, 40,* 117–129.

Beckett, J., & Smith, A. (1981). Work and family roles: Egalitarian marriage in black and white families. *Social Service Review, 55,* 314–326.

Billingsley, A. (1968). *Black families in white America.* Englewood Cliffs, NJ: Prentice Hall.

Billingsley, A. (1992). *Climbing Jacob's ladder: The enduring legacy of African American families.* New York: Simon & Schuster.

Blassingame, J. (1972). *The slave community.* New York: Oxford University Press.

Blau, Zena. (1981). *Black children/white socialization.* New York: Free Press.

Bowman, P. J. (1989). Research perspectives on black men: Role strain and adaptation across the life cycle. In R. L. Jones (Ed.), *Black adult development and aging* (pp. 117–150). Berkeley, CA: Cobb & Henry.

Bowman, P. J. (1995). Commentary. In M. B. Tucker & C. Mitchell-Kernan (Eds.), *The decline in marriage among African Americans* (pp. 309–321). New York: Russell Sage Foundation.

Boykin, A. W., & Toms, F. D. (1985). Black child socialization: A conceptual framework. In H. P. McAdoo & J. L. McAdoo (Eds.), *Black children* (pp. 33–54). Beverly Hills, CA: Sage.

Bumpass, L., Sweet, J., & Martin, T. C. (1990). Changing patterns of remarriage. *Journal of Marriage and the Family, 52*, 747–756.

Burbridge, L. C. (1995). Policy implications of a decline in marriage among African Americans. In M. B. Tucker & C. Mitchell-Kernan (Eds.), *The decline in marriage among African Americans* (pp. 323–344). New York: Russell Sage Foundation.

Cherlin, A. (1992). *Marriage, divorce, remarriage* (rev. ed.). Cambridge, MA: Harvard University Press.

Cherlin, A. (1995). Policy issues of child care. In P. Chase-Lansdale & J. Brooks-Gunn (Eds.), *Escape from poverty* (pp. 121–137). New York: Cambridge University Press.

Cherlin, A. (1996). *Public and private families.* New York: McGraw-Hill.

Collins, P. (1990). *Black feminist thought.* Boston, MA: Unwin Hyman.

Darity, W., & Myers, S. (1995). Family structure and the marginalization of black men: Policy implications. In M. B. Tucker & C. Mitchell-Kernan (Eds.), *The decline in marriage among African Americans* (pp. 263–308). New York: Russell Sage Foundation.

Demo, D. (1992). Parent-child relations: Assessing recent changes. *Journal of Marriage and the Family, 54*, 104–117.

Dressler, W., Haworth-Hoeppner, S., & Pitts, B. (1985). Household structure in a southern black community. *American Anthropologist, 87*, 853–862.

DuBois, W. E. B. (1898). The study of the Negro problem. *Annals, 1*, 1–23.

DuBois, W. E. B. (1909). *The Negro American family.* Atlanta: Atlanta University Press.

Edwards, G. F. (1968). *E. Franklin Frazier on race relations.* Chicago: University of Chicago Press.

Ehrenreich, B. (1986, July-August). Two, three, many husbands. *Mother Jones*, 8–9.

Espenshade, T. (1985). Marriage trends in America: Estimates, implications, and underlying causes. *Population and Development Review, 11*, 193–245.

Farley, R., & Allen, W. (1987). *The color line and the quality of life in America.* New York: Oxford University Press.

Franklin, C. (1986). Black male-Black female conflict: Individually caused and culturally nurtured. In R. Staples (Ed.), *The black family* (3rd ed., pp. 106–113). Belmont, CA: Wadsworth.

Frazier, E. F. (1939). *The Negro family in the United States.* Chicago: University of Chicago Press.

Furstenberg, F., Hershberg, T., & Modell, J. (1975). The origins of the female-headed black family: The impact of the urban experience. *Journal of Interdisciplinary History, 6*, 211–233.

Genovese, E. (1974). *Roll Jordan roll: The world slaves made.* New York: Pantheon.

Glick, P. (1997). Demographic pictures of African American families. In H. McAdoo (Ed.), *Black families* (3rd ed., pp. 118–138). Thousand Oaks, CA: Sage.

Gutman, H. (1976). *The black family in slavery and freedom, 1750–1925.* New York: Pantheon.

Guttentag, M., & Secord, P. F. (1983). *Too many women.* Beverly Hills, CA: Sage.

Hatchett, S. (1991). Women and men. In J. Jackson (Ed.), *Life in black America* (pp. 84–104). Newbury Park, CA: Sage.

Hatchett, S., Cochran, D., & Jackson, J. (1991). In J. Jackson (Ed.), *Life in black America* (pp. 46–83). Newbury Park, CA: Sage.

Hatchett, S., Veroff, J., & Douvan, E. (1995). Marital instability among black and white couples in early marriage. In M. B. Tucker & C. Mitchell-Kernan (Eds.), *The decline in marriage among African Americans* (pp. 177–218). New York: Russell Sage Foundation.

Hernandez, D. J. (1993). *America's children.* New York: Russell Sage.

Herskovits, M. J. (1958). *The myth of the Negro past* (Beacon Paperback No. 69). Boston: Beacon Press.

Hill, R. (1971). *The strengths of black families.* New York: Emerson Hall.

Hill, R. (1993). *Research on the African American family: A holistic perspective.* Westport, CT: Auburn House.

Jackson, J. (Ed.). (1991). *Life in black America.* Newbury Park, CA: Sage.

Jaynes, G., & Williams, R. (1989). *A common destiny: Blacks and American society.* Washington, DC: National Academy Press.

Johnson, L. B. (1981). Perspectives on black family empirical research: 1965–1978. In H. P. McAdoo (Ed.), *Black families* (pp. 252–263). Beverly Hills, CA: Sage.

Jones, J. (1985). *Labor of love, labor of sorrow: Black women, work, and the family from slavery to the present.* New York: Basic Books.

Kiecolt, K., & Fossett, M. (1995). Mate availability and marriage among African Americans: Aggregate- and individual-level analysis. In M. B. Tucker & C. Mitchell-Kernan (Eds.), *The decline in marriage among African Americans* (pp. 121–135). New York: Russell Sage Foundation.

Lewis, D. (1975). The black family: Socialization and sex roles. *Phylon, 36,* 221–237.

Lichter, D. T., McLaughlin, D. K., Kephart, G., & Landry, G. (1992). Race and the retreat from marriage: A shortage of marriageable men? *American Sociological Review, 57,* 781–799.

Manfra, J. A. & Dykstra, R. P. (1985). Serial marriage and the origins of the black stepfamily: The Rowanty evidence. *Journal of American History,* 7, 18–44.

Mare, R., & Winship, C. (1991). Socioeconomic change and the decline of marriage for blacks and whites. In C. Jencks & P. E. Peterson (Eds.), *The urban underclass* (pp. 175–204). Washington, DC: Brookings Institute.

McAdoo, H. P. (Ed.). (1997). *Black families* (3rd ed.). Thousand Oaks, CA: Sage.

McCarthy, J. (1978). A comparison of the probability of the dissolution of first and second marriages. *Demography, 15,* 345–359.

Moynihan, D. P. (1965). *The Negro family: The case for national action.* Washington, DC: U.S. Government Printing Office.

National Center for Health Statistics. (1991). *Monthly Vital Statistics Report* (Vol. 35, No. 4, Suppl.). Washington, DC: U.S. Department of Health and Human Services.

Nobles, W. (1978). Toward an empirical and theoretical framework for defining black families. *Journal of Marriage and the Family, 40,* 679–688.

Parish, W. L., Hao, L., & Hogan, D. P. (1991). Family support networks, welfare, and work among young mothers. *Journal of Marriage and the Family, 53,* 203–215.

Pleck, E. (1973). The two-parent household: Black family structure in late nineteenth-century Boston. In M. Gordon (Ed.), *The American family in socio-historical perspective* (pp. 152–178). New York: St. Martin's Press.

Sampson, R. J. (1995). Unemployment and unbalanced sex ratios: Race-specific consequences for family structure and crime. In M. B. Tucker & C. Mitchell-Keman (Eds.), *The decline in marriage among African Americans* (pp. 229–254). New York: Russell Sage Foundation.

Scanzoni, J. (1977). *The black family in modern society.* Chicago: University of Chicago Press.

Scott-Jones, D., & Nelson-LeGall, S. (1986). Defining black families: Past and present. In E. Seidman & J. Rappaport (Eds.), *Redefining social problems* (pp. 83–100). New York: Plenum.

Shimkin, D., Shimkin, E. M., & Frate, D. A. (Eds.). (1978). *The extended family in black societies.* The Hague, the Netherlands: Mouton.

Smith, A. W. (1995). Commentary. In M. B. Tucker & C. Mitchell-Kernan (Eds.), *The decline in marriage among African Americans* (pp. 136–141). New York: Russell Sage Foundation.

Stack, C. (1974). *All our kin.* New York: Harper & Row.

Staples, R. (1971). Toward a sociology of the black family: A decade of theory and research. *Journal of Marriage and the Family, 33,* 19–38.

Staples, R., & Johnson, L. B. (1993). *Black families at the crossroads.* San Francisco: Jossey-Bass.

Staples, R., & Mirande, A. (1980). Racial and cultural variations among American families: A decennial review of the literature on minority families. *Journal of Marriage and the Family, 42,* 157–173.

Stevenson, B. (1995). Black family structure in colonial and antebellum Virginia: Amending the revisionist perspective. In M. B. Tucker & C. Mitchell-Kernan (Eds.), *The decline in marriage among African Americans* (pp. 27–56). New York: Russell Sage Foundation.

Sudarkasa, N. (1988). Interpreting the African heritage in Afro-American family organization. In H. P. McAdoo (Ed.), *Black families* (pp. 27–42). Newbury Park, CA: Sage.

Sudarkasa, N. (1997). African American families and family values. In H. P. McAdoo (Ed.), *Black families* (pp. 9–40). Thousand Oaks, CA: Sage.

Sweet, J., & Bumpass, L. (1987). *American families and households.* New York: Russell Sage Foundation.

Taylor, R. L. (1991a). Child rearing in African American families. In J. Everett, S. Chipungu, & B. Leashore (Eds.), *Child welfare: An Africentric perspective* (pp. 119–155). New Brunswick, NJ: Rutgers University Press.

Taylor, R. L. (1991b). Poverty and adolescent black males: The subculture of disengagement. In P. Edelman & J. Ladner (Eds.), *Adolescence and poverty: Challenge for the 1990s* (pp. 139–162). Washington, DC: Center for National Policy Press.

Taylor, R. L. (1997). Who's parenting? Trends and Patterns. In T. Arendell (Ed.), *Contemporary parenting: Challenges and issues* (pp. 68–91). Thousand Oaks, CA: Sage.

Taylor, R. J., Chatters, L., Tucker, M. B., & Lewis, E. (1990). Developments in research on black families: A decade review. *Journal of Marriage and the Family, 52*, 993–1014.

Testa, M., & Krogh, M. (1995). The effect of employment on marriage among black males in inner-city Chicago. In M. B. Tucker & C. Mitchell-Kernan (Eds.), *The decline in marriage among African Americans* (pp. 59–95). New York: Russell Sage Foundation.

Thornton, A. (1978). Marital instability differentials and interactions: Insights from multivariate contingency table analysis. *Sociology and Social Research, 62*, 572–595.

Trusell, J. (1988). Teenage pregnancy in the United States. *Family Planning Perspectives, 20*, 262–272.

Tucker, M. B., & Mitchell-Kernan, C. (1995). Trends in African American family formation: A theoretical and statistical overview. In M. B. Tucker & C. Mitchell Kernan (Eds.), *The decline in marriage among African Americans* (pp. 3–26). New York: Russell Sage Foundation.

U.S. Bureau of the Census. (1990). Marital status and living arrangements: March 1989. *Current Population Reports* (Series P-20, No. 445). Washington, DC: U.S. Government Printing Office.

U.S. Bureau of the Census. (1994). Marital status and living arrangements: March 1993. *Current Population Reports* (Series P-20, No. 478). Washington, DC: U.S. Government Printing Office.

U.S. Bureau of the Census. (1995). Household and family characteristics: March 1994. *Current Population Reports* (Series P-20, No. 483). Washington, DC: U.S. Government Printing Office.

U.S. Bureau of the Census. (1996). *Statistical abstract of the United States: 1996*. Washington, DC: U.S. Government Printing Office.

White, D. G. (1985). *Ain't I a woman? Female slaves in the plantation South*. New York: W. W. Norton.

Wilson, W. J. (1987). *The truly disadvantaged: The inner city, the underclass and public policy*. Chicago: University of Chicago Press.

Wilson, W. J., & Neckerman K. (1986). Poverty and family structure: The widening gap between evidence and public policy issues. In S. Danziger & D. Weinberg (Eds.), *Fighting poverty: What works and what doesn't* (pp. 232–259). Cambridge, MA: Harvard University Press.

Young, V. H. (1970). Family and childhood in a southern Negro community. *American Anthropologist*, 72, 269–288.

READING 32

Diversity within Latino Families: New Lessons for Family Social Science

Maxine Baca Zinn and Barbara Wells

Who are Latinos? How will their growing presence in U.S. society affect the family field? These are vital questions for scholars who are seeking to understand the current social and demographic shifts that are reshaping society and its knowledge base. Understanding family diversity is a formidable task, not only because the field is poorly equipped to deal with differences at the theoretical level, but because many decentering efforts are themselves problematic. Even when diverse groups are included, family scholarship can distort and misrepresent by faulty emphasis and false generalizations.

Latinos are a population that can be understood only in terms of increasing heterogeneity. Latino families are unprecedented in terms of their diversity. In this [reading], we examine the ramifications of such diversity on the history, boundaries, and dynamics of family life. We begin with a brief look at the intellectual trends shaping Latino family research. We then place different Latino groups at center stage by providing a framework that situates them in specific and changing political and economic settings. Next, we apply our framework to each national origin group to draw out their different family experiences, especially as they are altered by global restructuring. We turn, then, to examine family structure issues and the interior dynamics of family living as they vary by gender and generation. We conclude with our reflections on studying Latino families and remaking family social science. In this [reading], we use interchangeably terms that are commonly used to describe Latino national-origin groups. For example, the terms Mexican American, Mexican, and Mexican-origin population will be used to refer to the same segment of the Latino population. Mexican-origin people may also be referred to as Chicanos.

INTELLECTUAL TRENDS, CRITIQUES, AND CHALLENGES

Origins

The formal academic study of Latino families originated in the late 19th and early 20th centuries with studies of Mexican immigrant families. As the new social scientists of the times focused their concerns on immigration and social disorganization, Mexican-origin and other ethnic families were the source of great concern. The influential Chicago School of Sociology led scholars to believe that Mexican immigration, settlement, and poverty created problems in developing urban centers. During this period, family study was emerging as a new field that sought to document, as well as ameliorate, social problems in urban settings (Thomas & Wilcox, 1987). Immigrant families became major targets of social reform.

Interwoven themes from race relations and family studies gave rise to the view of Mexicans as particularly disorganized. Furthermore, the family was implicated in their plight. As transplants from traditional societies, the immigrants and their children were thought to be at odds with social requirements in the new settings. Their family arrangements were treated as cultural exceptions to the rule of standard family development. Their slowness to acculturate and take on Western patterns of family development left them behind as other families modernized (Baca Zinn, 1995).

Dominant paradigms of assimilation and modernization guided and shaped research. Notions of "traditional" and "modern" forms of social organization joined the new family social science's preoccupation with a standard family form. Compared to mainstream families, Mexican immigrant families were analyzed as traditional cultural forms. Studies of Mexican immigrants highlighted certain ethnic lifestyles that were said to produce social disorganization. Structural conditions that constrained families in the new society were rarely a concern. Instead, researchers examined (1) the families' foreign patterns and habits, (2) the moral quality of family relationships, and (3) the prospects for their Americanization (Bogardus, 1934).

Cultural Preoccupations

Ideas drawn from early social science produced cultural caricatures of Mexican families that became more exaggerated during the 1950s, when structural functionalist theories took hold in American sociology. Like the previous theories, structural functionalism's strategy for analyzing family life was to posit one family type (by no means the only family form, even then) and define it as "the normal family" (Boss & Thorne, 1989). With an emphasis on fixed family boundaries and a fixed division of roles, structural functionalists focused their attention on the group-specific characteristics that deviated from the normal or standard family and predisposed Mexican-origin families to deficiency. Mexican-origin families were analyzed in isolation from the rest of social life, described in simplistic terms of rigid male dominance and pathological clannishness. Although the earliest works on Mexican immigrant families reflected a concern for their eventual adjustment to American society, the new studies virtually abandoned the social realm. They dealt with families as if they existed in a vacuum of backward Mexican traditionalism. Structural functionalism led scholars along a path of cultural reductionism in which differences became deficiencies.

The Mexican family of social science research (Heller, 1966; Madsen, 1964; Rubel, 1966) presented a stark contrast with the mythical "standard family." Although some studies found that Mexican family traditionalism was fading as Mexicans became acculturated, Mexican families were stereotypically and inaccurately depicted as the chief cause of Mexican subordination in the United States.

New Directions

In the past 25 years, efforts to challenge myths and erroneous assumptions have produced important changes in the view of Mexican-origin families. Beginning with a critique of structural functionalist accounts of Mexican families, new studies have successfully challenged the old notions of family life as deviant, deficient, and disorganized.

The conceptual tools of Latino studies, women's studies, and social history have infused the new scholarship to produce a notable shift away from cultural preoccupations. Like the family field in general, research on Mexican-origin families has begun to devote greater attention to the "social situations and contexts that affect Mexican families" (Vega, 1990, p. 1015). This "revisionist" strategy has moved much Latino family research to a different plane—one in which racial-ethnic families are understood to be constructed by powerful social forces and as settings in which different family members adapt in a variety of ways to changing social conditions.

Current Challenges

Despite important advances, notable problems and limitations remain in the study of Latino families. A significant portion of scholarship includes only Mexican-origin groups (Massey, Zambrana, & Bell, 1995) and claims to generalize the findings to other Latinos. This practice constructs a false social reality because there is no Latino population in the same sense that there is an African American population. However useful the terms *Latino* and *Hispanic* may be as political and census identifiers, they mask extraordinary diversity. The category Hispanic was created by federal statisticians to provide data on people of Mexican, Cuban, Puerto Rican, and other Hispanic origins in the United States. There is no precise definition of group membership, and Latinos do not agree among themselves on an appropriate group label (Massey, 1993). While many prefer the term *Latino*, they may use it interchangeably with *Hispanic* to identify themselves (Romero, 1996). These terms are certainly useful for charting broad demographic changes in the United States, but when used as panethnic terms, they can contribute to misunderstandings about family life.

The labels Hispanic or Latino conceal variation in the family characteristics of Latino groups whose differences are often greater than the overall differences between Latinos and non-Latinos (Solis, 1995). To date, little comparative research has been conducted on Latino subgroups. The systematic disaggregation of family characteristics by national-origin groups remains a challenge, a necessary next step in the development of Latino family research.

We believe that the lack of a comprehensive knowledge base should not stand in the way of building a framework to analyze family life. We can use the burgeoning research on Latinos in U.S. social life to develop an analytical, rather than just a descriptive, account of families. The very complexity of Latino family arrangements begs for a unified (but not unitary) analysis. We believe that we can make good generalizations about Latino family diversity. In the sections that follow, we use a structural perspective grounded in intergroup differences. We make no pretense that this is an exhaustive review of research. Instead, our intent is to examine how Latino family experiences differ in relation to socially constructed conditions.

CONCEPTUAL FRAMEWORK

Conventional family frameworks, which have never applied well to racial-ethnic families, are even less useful in the current world of diversity and change. Incorporating multiplicity into family studies requires new approaches. A fundamental assumption guiding our analysis is that Latino families are not merely an expression of ethnic differences but, like all families, are the products of social forces.

Family diversity is an outgrowth of distinctive patterns in the way families and their members are embedded in environments with varying opportunities, resources, and rewards. Economic conditions and social inequalities associated with race, ethnicity, class, and gender place families in different "social locations." These differences are the key to understanding family variation. They determine labor market status, education, marital relations, and other factors that are crucial to family formation.

Studying Latino family diversity means exposing the structural forces that impinge differently on families in specific social, material, and historical contexts. In other words, it means unpacking the structural arrangements that produce and often require a range of family configurations. It also requires analyzing the cross-cutting forms of difference that permeate society and penetrate families to produce divergent family experiences. Several macrostructural conditions produce widespread family variations across Latino groups: (1) the sociohistorical context; (2) the structure of economic opportunity; and (3) global reorganization, including economic restructuring and immigration.

The Sociohistorical Context

Mexicans, Puerto Ricans, Cubans, and other Latino groups have varied histories that distinguish them from each other. The timing and conditions of their arrival in the United States produced distinctive patterns of settlement that continue to affect their prospects for success. Cubans arrived largely between 1960 and 1980; a group of Mexicans indigenous to the Southwest was forcibly annexed into the United States in 1848, and another has been migrating continually since around 1890; Puerto Ricans came under U.S. control in 1898 and obtained citizenship in 1917; Salvadorans and Guatemalans began to migrate to the United States in substantial numbers during the past two decades.

The Structure of Economic Opportunity

Various forms of labor are needed to sustain family life. Labor status has always been the key factor in distinguishing the experiences of Latinos. Mexicans, Puerto Ricans, Cubans, and others are located in different regions of the country where particular labor markets and a group's placement within them determine the kind of legal, political, and social supports available to families. Different levels of structural supports affect family life, often producing various domestic and household arrangements. Additional complexity stems from gendered labor markets. In a society in which men are still assumed to be the primary breadwinners, jobs generally held by women pay less than jobs usually held by men. Women's and men's differential labor market placement, rewards, and roles create contradictory work and family experiences.

Global Reorganization, Including Economic Restructuring and Immigration

Economic and demographic upheavals are redefining families throughout the world. Four factors are at work here: new technologies based primarily on the computer chip, global economic interdependence, the flight of capital, and the dominance of the information and service sectors over basic manufacturing industries (Baca Zinn & Eitzen, 1998). Latino families are profoundly affected as the environments in which they live are reshaped and they face economic and social marginalization because of under-employment and unemployment. Included in economic globalization are new demands for immigrant labor and the dramatic demographic transformations that are "Hispanicizing" the

United States. Family flexibility has long been an important feature of the immigrant saga. Today, "Latino immigration is adding many varieties to family structure" (Moore & Vigil, 1993, p. 36).

The macrostructural conditions described earlier provide the context within which to examine the family experiences of different Latino groups. They set the foundation for comparing family life across Latino groups. These material and economic forces help explain the different family profiles of Mexicans, Puerto Ricans, Cubans, and others. In other words, they enable sociologists to understand how families are bound up with the unequal distribution of social opportunities and how the various national-origin groups develop broad differences in work opportunities, marital patterns, and household structures. However, they do not explain other important differences in family life that cut across national-origin groups. People of the same national origin may experience family differently, depending on their location in the class structure as unemployed, poor, working class or professional; their location in the gender structure as female or male; and their location in the sexual orientation system as heterosexual, gay, lesbian, or bisexual (Baca Zinn & Dill, 1996). In addition to these differences, family life for Latinos is shaped by age, generation living in the United States, citizenship status, and even skin color. All these differences intersect to influence the shape and character of family and household relations.

While our framework emphasizes the social context and social forces that construct families, we do not conclude that families are molded from the "outside in." What happens on a daily basis in family relations and domestic settings also constructs families. Latinos themselves—women, men, and children—have the ability actively to shape their family and household arrangements. Families should be seen as settings in which people are agents and actors, coping with, adapting to, and changing social structures to meet their needs (Baca Zinn & Eitzen, 1996).

Sociohistorical Context for Family Diversity among Mexicans

Families of Mexican descent have been incorporated into the United States by both conquest and migration. In 1848, at the end of the Mexican War, the United States acquired a large section of Mexico, which is now the southwestern United States. With the signing of the Treaty of Guadalupe Hidalgo, the Mexican population in that region became residents of U.S. territory. Following the U.S. conquest, rapid economic growth in that region resulted in a shortage of labor that was resolved by recruiting workers from Mexico. So began the pattern of Mexican labor migration that continues to the present (Portes & Rumbaut, 1990). Some workers settled permanently in the United States, and others continued in cycles of migration, but migration from Mexico has been continuous since around 1890 (Massey et al., 1995).

Dramatic increases in the Mexican-origin population have been an important part of the trend toward greater racial and ethnic diversity in the United States. The Mexican population tripled in size in 20 years, from an estimated 4.5 million in 1970 to 8.7 million in 1980 to 13.5 million in 1990 (Rumbaut, 1995; Wilkinson, 1993). At present, approximately two thirds of Mexicans are native born, and the remainder are foreign born (Rumbaut, 1995). Important differences are consistently found between the social experiences and economic prospects of the native born and the foreign born (Morales & Ong, 1993; Ortiz, 1996). While some variation exists, the typical Mexican migrant to the United States has low socioeconomic status and rural origins (Ortiz, 1995; Portes & Rumbaut, 1990). Recent immigrants have a distinct disadvantage in the labor market because of a combination of low educational attainment, limited work skills, and limited English language proficiency. Social networks are vital for integrating immigrants into U.S. society and in placing them in the social class system (Fernandez-Kelly & Schauffler, 1994). Mexicans are concentrated in barrios that have social networks in which vital information is shared, contacts are made, and job referrals are given. But the social-class context of these Mexican communities is overwhelmingly poor and working class. Mexicans remain overrepresented in low-wage occupations, especially service, manual labor, and low-end manufacturing. These homogeneous lower-class communities lack the high-quality resources that could facilitate upward mobility for either new immigrants or second- and later-generation Mexicans.

The common assumption that immigrants are assimilated economically by taking entry-level positions and advancing to better jobs has not been supported by the Mexican experience (Morales & Ong, 1993; Ortiz, 1996). Today's Mexican workers are as likely as ever to be trapped in low-wage unstable employment situations (Ortiz, 1996; Sassen, 1993). Studies (Aponte, 1993; Morales & Ong, 1993; Ortiz, 1996) have found that high labor force participation and low wages among Mexicans have created a large group of working poor. Households adapt by holding multiple jobs and pooling wages (Velez-Ibañez & Greenberg, 1992).

Mexicans are the largest Latino group in the United States; 6 of 10 Latinos have Mexican origins. This group has low family incomes, but high labor force participation for men and increasing rates for women. Mexicans have the lowest educational attainments and the largest average household size of all Latino groups. (See Table 32.1 and Figure 32.1 for between-group comparisons.)

Table 32.1 Social and Economic Population Characteristics

				Labor Force Participation			
	Median Income	*Poverty*	*% Female Head of Household*	*Male*	*Female*	*High School Graduate*	*Average Household*
Mexican	23,609	29.6	19.9	80.9	51.8	46.5	3.86
Puerto Rican	20,929	33.2	41.2	70.6	47.4	61.3	2.91
Cuban	30,584	13.6	21.3	69.9	50.8	64.7	2.56
Central/ South American	28,558	23.9	25.4	79.5	57.5	64.2	3.54
Other Hispanic	28,658	21.4	29.5			68.4	
All Hispanic	24,313	27.8	24	79.1	52.6	53.4	2.99
All U.S.	38,782	11.6	12	75	58.9	81.7	2.65
	1994	1994	1995	1995	1995	1995	1995

Source: U.S. Bureau of the Census, Statistical Abstract of the United States: 1996 (116th ed.), Washington, D.C.: U.S. Government Printing Office, 1996, Tables 53, 68, 241, 615, 622, 723, 738.

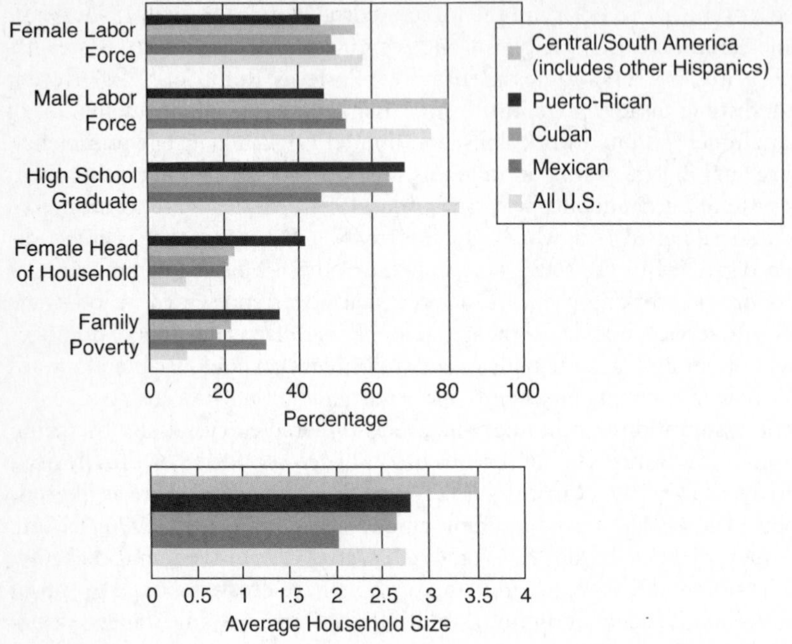

FIGURE 32.1 *Social and Economic Population Characteristics*

Puerto Ricans

The fortunes of Puerto Rico and the United States were joined in 1899 when Puerto Rico became a U.S. possession in the aftermath of Spain's defeat in the Spanish-American War. Puerto Ricans are U.S. citizens and, as such, have the right to migrate to the mainland without regulation. A small stream of migrants increased dramatically after World War II for three primary reasons: high unemployment in Puerto Rico, the availability of inexpensive air travel between Puerto Rico and the United States, and labor recruitment by U.S. companies (Portes & Rumbaut, 1990). Puerto Ricans were concentrated in or near their arrival point—New York City—although migrant laborers were scattered throughout the Northeast and parts of the Midwest. They engaged in a variety of blue-collar occupations; in New York City, they were particularly drawn into the textile and garment industries (Torres & Bonilla, 1993). The unique status of Puerto Rico as a commonwealth of the United States allows Puerto Ricans to engage in a circulating migration between Puerto Rico and the mainland (Feagin & Feagin, 1996).

Puerto Ricans are the most economically disadvantaged of all major Latino groups. The particular context of Puerto Ricans' entry into the U.S. labor market helps explain this group's low economic status. Puerto Ricans with limited education and low occupational skills migrated to the eastern seaboard to fill manufacturing jobs (Ortiz, 1995); their economic well-being was dependent on opportunities for low-skill employment

(Aponte, 1993). The region in which Puerto Ricans settled has experienced a major decline in its manufacturing base since the early 1970s. The restructuring of the economy means that, in essence, the jobs that Puerto Ricans came to the mainland to fill have largely disappeared. Latinos who have been displaced from manufacturing have generally been unable to gain access to higher-wage service sector employment (Carnoy, Daly, & Ojeda, 1993).

Compared to Mexicans and Cubans, Puerto Ricans have the lowest median family incomes and the highest unemployment and poverty rates. Puerto Ricans also have a high rate of female-headed households.

Cubans

The primary event that precipitated the migration of hundreds of thousands of Cubans to the United States was the revolution that brought Fidel Castro to power in 1959. This revolution set off several waves of immigration, beginning with the former economic and political elite and working progressively downward through the class structure. Early Cuban immigrants entered the United States in a highly politicized cold-war context as political refugees from communism. The U.S. government sponsored the Cuban Refugee Program, which provided massive supports to Cuban immigrants, including resettlement assistance, job training, small-business loans, welfare payments, and health care (Dominguez, 1992; Perez-Stable & Uriarte, 1993). By the time this program was phased out after the mid-1970s, the United States had invested nearly $1 billion in assistance to Cubans fleeing from communism (Perez-Stable & Uriarte, 1993, p. 155). Between 1960 and 1980, nearly 800,000 Cubans immigrated to the United States (Dominguez, 1992).

The Cuban population is concentrated in south Florida, primarily in the Miami area, where they have established a true ethnic enclave in which they own businesses; provide professional services; and control institutions, such as banks and newspapers (Perez, 1994). The unique circumstances surrounding their immigration help explain the experience of Cubans. U.S. government supports facilitated the economic successes of early Cuban immigrants (Aponte, 1993; Fernandez-Kelley & Schauffler, 1994). High rates of entrepreneurship resulted in the eventual consolidation of an enclave economy (Portes & Truelove, 1987).

Immigrants, women, and minorities have generally supplied the low-wage, flexible labor on which the restructured economy depends (Morales & Bonilla, 1993). However, Cubans "embody a privileged migration" in comparison to other Latino groups (Morales & Bonilla, 1993, p. 17). Their social-class positions, occupational attainments, and public supports have insulated them from the effects of restructuring. Yet Cubans in Miami are not completely protected from the displacements of the new economic order. As Perez-Stable and Uriarte (1993) noted, the Cuban workforce is polarized, with one segment moving into higher-wage work and the other remaining locked in low-wage employment.

Cuban families have higher incomes and far lower poverty rates than do other major Latino groups. Cubans are the most educated major Latino group and have the smallest average household size.

Other Latinos

In each national-origin group discussed earlier, one finds unique socioeconomic, political and historical circumstances. But the diversity of Latinos extends beyond the differences between Mexican Americans, Cuban Americans, and mainland Puerto Ricans. One finds further variation when one considers the experiences of other Latino national-origin groups. Although research on "other Latinos" is less extensive than the literature cited earlier, we consider briefly contexts for diversity in Central American and Dominican families.

Central Americans. Political repression, civil war, and their accompanying economic dislocations have fueled the immigration of a substantial number of Salvadorans, Guatemalans, and Nicaraguans since the mid-1970s (Hamilton & Chinchilla, 1997). The U.S. population of Central Americans more than doubled between the 1980 and 1990 censuses and now outnumbers Cubans (U.S. Bureau of the Census, 1993). These Latinos migrated under difficult circumstances and face a set of serious challenges in the United States (Dorrington, 1995). Three factors render this population highly vulnerable: (1) a high percentage are undocumented (an estimated 49% of Salvadorans and 40% of Guatemalans), (2) they have marginal employment and high poverty rates, and (3) the U.S. government does not recognize them as political refugees (Lopez, Popkin, & Telles, 1996).

The two largest groups of Central Americans are Salvadorans and Guatemalans, the majority of whom live in the Los Angeles area. Lopez et al.'s (1996) study of Central Americans in Los Angeles illumined the social and economic contexts in which these Latinos construct their family lives. In general, the women and men have little formal education and know little English, but have high rates of labor force participation. Salvadorans and Guatemalans are overrepresented in low-paying service and blue-collar occupations. Salvadoran and Guatemalan women occupy a low-wage niche in private service (as domestic workers in private homes). Central Americans, especially the undocumented who fear deportation and usually have no access to public support, are desperate enough to accept the poorest-quality, lowest-paying work that Los Angeles has to offer. These immigrants hold the most disadvantageous position in the regional economy (Scott, 1996). Lopez et al. predicted that in the current restructured economy, Central Americans will continue to do the worst of the "dirty work" necessary to support the lifestyles of the high-wage workforce.

Dominicans. A significant number of Dominicans began migrating to the U.S. in the mid-1960s. What Grasmuck and Pessar (1996) called the "massive displacement" of Dominicans from their homeland began with the end of Trujillo's 30-year dictatorship and the political uncertainties that ensued. Dominican immigrant families did not fit the conventional image of the unskilled, underemployed peasant. They generally had employed breadwinners who were relatively well educated by Dominican standards; the majority described themselves as having urban middle-class origins (Mitchell, 1992).

The Dominican population is heavily concentrated in New York City. They entered a hostile labor market in which their middle class aspirations were to remain largely unfulfilled because the restructured New York economy offers low-wage, marginal, mostly dead-end employment for individuals without advanced education (Torres

& Bonilla, 1993). Dominicans lacked the English language competence and educational credentials that might have facilitated their upward mobility (Grasmuck & Pessar, 1996). More than two thirds of the Dominican-origin population in the United States is Dominican born. As a group, Dominicans have high rates of poverty and female-headed families. Approximately 4 in 10 family households are headed by women.

THE STRUCTURE OF ECONOMIC OPPORTUNITY

Latino families remain outside the economic mainstream of U.S. society. Their median family income stands at less than two thirds the median family income of all U.S. families (U.S. Bureau of the Census, 1996). But the broad designation of "Latino" obscures important differences among national-origin groups. In this section, we explore variations in the structure of economic opportunity and consider how particular economic contexts shape the lives of different groups of Latino families.

Class, Work, and Family Life

A number of studies (see, for example, Cardenas, Chapa, & Burek, 1993; Grasmuck & Pessar, 1996; Lopez et al., 1996; Ortiz, 1995; Perez, 1994) have documented that diverse social and economic contexts produce multiple labor market outcomes for Latino families. The quality, availability, and stability of wage labor create a socioeconomic context in which family life is constructed and maintained. Cuban American families have fared far better socioeconomically than have other Latino families. Scholars consistently cite the role of the Cuban enclave in providing a favorable economic context with advantages that other groups have not enjoyed (Morales & Bonilla, 1993; Perez, 1994; Perez-Stable & Uriarte, 1993). Cuban families have the highest incomes, educational attainments, and levels of upper-white-collar employment. Puerto Rican, Mexican, and Central American families cluster below Cubans on these socioeconomic indicators, with Puerto Ricans the most disadvantaged group.

The structure of Mexican American economic opportunity stands in sharp contrast to that of Cubans. Betancur, Cordova, and Torres (1993) documented the systematic exclusion of Mexicans from upward-mobility ladders, tracing the incorporation of Mexican Americans into the Chicago economy to illustrate the historic roots of the concentration of Mexicans in unstable, poor-quality work. Throughout the 20th century Mexican migrants have constituted a transient workforce that has been continually vulnerable to fluctuations in the labor market and cycles of recruitment and deportation. Betancur et al.'s study highlighted the significance of the bracero program of contract labor migration in institutionalizing a segmented market for labor. The bracero program limited Mexican workers to specific low-status jobs and industries that prohibited promotion to skilled occupational categories. Mexicans were not allowed to compete for higher-status jobs, but were contracted to fill only the most undesirable jobs. Although formal bracero-era regulations have ended, similar occupational concentrations continue to be reproduced among Mexican American workers.

The effects of these diverging social-class and employment contexts on families are well illustrated by Fernandez-Kelly's (1990) study of female garment workers—Cubans in Miami and Mexicans in Los Angeles—both of whom placed a high value on marriage and family; however, contextual factors shaped differently their abilities to sustain marital relationships over time. Fernandez-Kelly contended that the conditions necessary for maintaining long-term stable unions were present in middle-class families but were absent in poor families. That is, the marriages of the poor women were threatened by unemployment and underemployment. Among these Mexican women, there was a high rate of poor female-headed households, and among the Cuban women, many were members of upwardly mobile families.

Women's Work

Several studies (Chavira-Prado, 1992; Grasmuck & Pessar, 1991; Lamphere, Zavella, Gonzales, & Evans, 1993; Stier & Tienda, 1992; Zavella, 1987) that have explored the intersection of work and family for Latinas have found that Latinas are increasingly likely to be employed. Labor force participation is the highest among Central American women and the lowest among Puerto Rican women, with Mexican and Cuban women equally likely to be employed. Not only do labor force participation rates differ by national origin, but the meaning of women's work varies as well. For example, Fernandez-Kelly's (1990) study demonstrated that for Cuban women, employment was part of a broad family objective to reestablish middle-class status. Many Cuban immigrants initially experienced downward mobility, and the women took temporary jobs to generate income while their husbands cultivated fledgling businesses. These women often withdrew from the workforce when their families' economic positions had been secured. In contrast, Mexican women in Los Angeles worked because of dire economic necessity. They were drawn into employment to augment the earnings of partners who were confined to secondary-sector work that paid less than subsistence wages or worse, to provide the primary support for their households. Thus, whereas the Cuban women expected to work temporarily until their husbands could resume the role of middle-class breadwinner, the Mexican women worked either because their partners could not earn a family wage or because of the breakdown of family relationships by divorce or abandonment.

GLOBAL REORGANIZATION

Economic Restructuring

The economic challenges that Latinos face are enormous. A workforce that has always been vulnerable to exploitation can anticipate the decline of already limited mobility prospects. A recent body of scholarship (see, for example, Lopez et al., 1996; Morales & Bonilla, 1993; Ortiz, 1996) has demonstrated that the restructuring of the U.S. economy has reshaped economic opportunities for Latinos.

Torres and Bonilla's (1993) study of the restructuring of New York City's economy is particularly illustrative because it focused on Puerto Ricans, the Latino group hit hardest by economic transformations. That study found that restructuring in New York City is based on two processes that negatively affect Puerto Ricans. First, stable jobs in both the public and private sectors have eroded since the 1960s because many large corporations that had provided long-term, union jobs for minorities left the New York area and New York City's fiscal difficulties restricted the opportunities for municipal employment. Second, the reorganization of light manufacturing has meant that new jobs offer low wages and poor working conditions; new immigrants who are vulnerable to exploitation by employers generally fill these jobs. The restructuring of the economy has resulted in the exclusion or withdrawal of a substantial proportion of Puerto Ricans from the labor market (Morales & Bonilla, 1993).

Families are not insulated from the effects of social and economic dislocations. Research that has tracked this major social transformation has considered how such changes affect family processes and household composition (Grasmuck & Pessar, 1996; Lopez et al., 1996; Rodriguez & Hagan, 1997). What Sassen (1993) called the "informalization" and "casualization" of urban labor markets will, in the end, shape families in ways that deviate from the nuclear ideal. The marginalization of the Puerto Rican workforce is related not only to high unemployment and poverty rates, but to high rates of nonmarital births and female-headed households (Fernandez-Kelly, 1990; Morrissey, 1987).

Contrasting the experience of Dominicans to that of Puerto Ricans indicates that it is impossible to generalize a unitary "Latino experience" even within a single labor market—New York City. Torres and Bonilla (1993) found that as Puerto Ricans were displaced from manufacturing jobs in the 1970s and 1980s, new Dominican immigrants came into the restructured manufacturing sector to fill low-wage jobs. Dominicans were part of a pool of immigrant labor that entered a depressed economy, was largely ineligible for public assistance, and was willing to accept exploitative employment. Grasmuck and Pessar (1991, 1996) showed how the incorporation of Dominicans into the restructured New York economy has affected families. Although the rate of divorce among early immigrants was high, relationships have become increasingly precarious as employment opportunities have become even more constrained. Currently, rates of poverty and female-headed households for Dominicans approximate those of Puerto Ricans (Rumbaut, 1995).

A Latino Underclass? Rising poverty rates among Latinos, together with the alarmist treatment of female-headed households among "minorities," have led many policy makers and media analysts to conclude that Latinos have joined inner-city African Americans to form part of the "underclass." According to the underclass model, inner-city men's joblessness has encouraged nonmarital childbearing and undermined the economic foundations of the African American family (Wilson, 1987, 1996). Researchers have also been debating for some time whether increases in the incidence of female-headed households and poverty among Puerto Ricans are irreversible (Tienda, 1989). Recent thinking, however, suggests that applying the underclass theory to Latinos obscures more than it reveals and that a different analytical model is needed to understand poverty and family issues in each Latino group (Massey et al., 1995). Not only do the causes of poverty differ across Latino communities, but patterns of social organization at the community and family levels produce a wide range of responses to poverty. According to Moore and Pinderhughes (1993), the dynamics of poverty even in the poorest Latino barrios differ in fundamental ways from the conventional portrait of the under-class. Both African Americans and Puerto Ricans have high rates of female-headed households. However, Sullivan's (1993) research in Brooklyn indicated that Puerto Ricans have high rates of cohabitation and that the family formation processes that lead to these household patterns are different from those of African Americans. Other case studies have underscored the importance of family organization. For example, Velez-Ibañez (1993) described a distinctive family form among poor Mexicans of South Tucson—cross-class household clusters surrounded by kinship networks that stretch beyond neighborhood boundaries and provide resources for coping with poverty.

Immigration

Families migrate for economic reasons, political reasons, or some combination of the two. Immigration offers potential and promise, but one of the costs is the need for families to adapt to their receiving community contexts. A growing body of scholarship has focused on two areas of family change: household composition and gender relations.

Household Composition. Immigration contributes to the proliferation of family forms and a variety of household arrangements among Latinos (Vega, 1995). Numerous studies have highlighted the flexibility of Latino family households. Chavez (1990, 1992) identified transnational families, binational families, extended families, multiple-family households, and other arrangements among Mexican and Central American immigrants. Landale and Fennelly (1992) found informal unions that resemble marriage more than cohabitation among mainland Puerto Ricans, and Guarnizo (1997) found binational households among Dominicans who live and work in both the United States and the Dominican Republic. Two processes are at work as families adapt their household structures. First, family change reflects, for many, desperate economic circumstances (Vega, 1995), which bring some families to the breaking point and lead others to expand their household boundaries. Second, the transnationalization of economies and labor has created new opportunities for successful Latino families; for example, Guarnizo noted that Dominican entrepreneurs sometimes live in binational households and have "de facto binational citizenship" (p. 171).

Immigration and Gender. Several important studies have considered the relationship between immigration and gender (Boyd, 1989; Grasmuck & Pessar, 1991; Hondagneu-Sotelo, 1994). In her study of undocumented Mexican immigrants, Hondagneu-Sotelo (1994) demonstrated that gender shapes migration and immigration shapes gender relations. She found that family stage migration, in which husbands migrate first and wives and children follow later, does not fit the household-strategy model. Often implied in this model is the assumption that migration reflects the unanimous and rational collective decision of all household members. However, as Hondagneu-Sotelo observed, gender hierarchies determined when and under what circumstances migration occurred; that is, men often decided spontaneously, independently, and unilaterally to migrate north to seek employment. When Mexican couples were finally reunited in the United States, they generally reconstructed more egalitarian gender relations. Variation in the form of gender relations in the United States is partially explained by the circumstances surrounding migration, such as the type and timing of migration, access to social networks, and U.S. immigration policy.

FAMILY DYNAMICS ACROSS LATINO GROUPS

Familism

Collectivist family arrangements are thought to be a defining feature of the Latino population. Presumably, a strong orientation and obligation to the family produces a kinship structure that is qualitatively different from that of all other groups. Latino familism, which is said to emphasize the family as opposed to the individual, "is linked to many of the pejorative images that have beset discussions of the Hispanic family" (Vega, 1990, p. 1018). Although themes of Latino familism figure prominently in the social science literature, this topic remains problematic owing to empirical limitations and conceptual confusion.

Popular and social science writing contain repeated descriptions of what amounts to a generic Latino kinship form. In reality, a Mexican-origin bias pervades the research on this topic. Not only is there a lack of comparative research on extended kinship structures among different national-origin groups, but there is little empirical evidence for all but Mexican-origin families. For Mexican-origin groups, studies are plentiful (for reviews, see Baca Zinn, 1983; Vega, 1990, 1995), although they have yielded inconsistent evidence about the prevalence of familism, the forms it takes, and the kinds of supportive relationships it serves.

Among the difficulties in assessing the evidence on extended family life are the inconsistent uses of terms like *familism* and *extended family system*. Seeking to clarify the multiple meanings of familism, Ramirez and Arce (1981) treated familism as a multidimensional concept comprised of such distinct aspects as structure, behavior, norms and attitudes, and social identity, each of which requires separate measurement and analysis. They proposed that familism contains four key components: (1) demographic familism, which involves such characteristics as family size; (2) structural familism, which measures the incidence of multigenerational (or extended) households; (3) normative families, which taps the value that Mexican-origin people place on family unity and solidarity; and (4) behavioral familism, which has to do with the level of interaction between family and kin networks.

Changes in regional and local economies and the resulting dislocations of Latinos have prompted questions about the ongoing viability of kinship networks. Analyzing a national sample of minority families, Rochelle (1997) argued that extended kinship networks are declining among Chicanos, Puerto Ricans, and African Americans. On the other hand, a large body of research has documented various forms of network participation by Latinos. For three decades, studies have found that kinship networks are an important survival strategy in poor Mexican communities (Alvirez & Bean, 1976; Hoppe

& Heller, 1975; Velez-Ibañez, 1996) and that these networks operate as a system of cultural, emotional, and mental support (Keefe, 1984; Mindel, 1980; Ramirez, 1980), as well as a system for coping with socioeconomic marginality (Angel & Tienda, 1982; Lamphere et al., 1993).

Research has suggested, however, that kinship networks are not maintained for socioeconomic reasons alone (Buriel & De Ment, 1997). Familistic orientation among Mexican-origin adults has been associated with high levels of education and income (Griffith & Villavicienco, 1985). Familism has been viewed as a form of social capital that is linked with academic success among Mexican-heritage adolescents (Valenzuela & Dornbusch, 1994).

The research on the involvement of extended families in the migration and settlement of Mexicans discussed earlier (Chavez, 1992; Hondagneu-Sotelo, 1994; Hondagneu-Sotelo & Avila, 1997) is profoundly important. In contrast to the prevailing view that family extension is an artifact of culture, this research helps one understand that the structural flexibility of families is a social construction. Transnational families and their networks of kin are extended in space, time, and across national borders. They are quintessential adaptations—alternative arrangements for solving problems associated with immigration.

Despite the conceptual and empirical ambiguities surrounding the topic of familism, there is evidence that kinship networks are far from monolithic. Studies have revealed that variations are rooted in distinctive social conditions, such as immigrant versus nonimmigrant status and generational status. Thus, even though immigrants use kin for assistance, they have smaller social networks than do second-generation Mexican Americans who have broader social networks consisting of multigenerational kin (Vega, 1990). Studies have shown that regardless of class, Mexican extended families in the United States become stronger and more extensive with generational advancement, acculturation, and socioeconomic mobility (Velez-Ibañez, 1996). Although an assimilationist perspective suggests that familism fades in succeeding generations, Velez-Ibañez found that highly elaborated second- and third-generation extended family networks are actively maintained through frequent visits, ritual celebrations, and the exchange of goods and services. These networks are differentiated by the functions they perform, depending on the circumstances of the people involved.

Gender

Latino families are commonly viewed as settings of traditional patriarchy and as different from other families because of machismo, the cult of masculinity. In the past two decades, this cultural stereotype has been the impetus for corrective scholarship on Latino families. The flourishing of Latina feminist thought has shifted the focus from the determinism of culture to questions about how gender and power in families are connected with other structures and institutions in society. Although male dominance remains a central theme, it is understood as part of the ubiquitous social ordering of women and men. In the context of other forms of difference, gender exerts a powerful influence on Latino families.

New research is discovering gender dynamics among Latino families that are both similar to and different from those found in other groups. Similarities stem from social changes that are reshaping all families, whereas differences emerge from the varied locations of Latino families and the women and men in them. Like other branches of scholarship on Latino families, most studies have been conducted with Mexican-origin populations. The past two decades of research have shown that family life among all Latino groups is deeply gendered. Yet no simple generalizations sum up the essence of power relations.

Research has examined two interrelated areas: (1) family decision making and (2) the allocation of household labor. Since the first wave of "revisionist works" (Zavella, 1987) conducted in the 1970s and 1980s (Baca Zinn, 1980; Ybarra, 1982), researchers have found variation in these activities, ranging from patriarchal role-segregated patterns to egalitarian patterns, with many combinations in between. Studies have suggested that Latinas' employment patterns, like those of women around the world, provide them with resources and autonomy that alter the balance of family power (Baca Zinn, 1980; Coltrane & Valdez, 1993; Pesquera, 1993; Repack, 1997; Williams, 1990; Ybarra, 1982; Zavella, 1987). But, as we discussed earlier, employment opportunities vary widely, and the variation produces multiple work and family patterns for Latinas. Furthermore, women's employment, by itself, does not eradicate male dominance. This is one of the main lessons of Zavella's (1987) study of Chicana cannery workers in California's Santa Clara Valley. Women's cannery work was circumscribed by inequalities of class, race, and gender. As seasonal, part-time workers, the women gained some leverage in the home, thereby creating temporary shifts in their day-to-day family lives, but this leverage did not alter the balance of family power. Fernandez-Kelly and Garcia's (1990) comparative study of women's work and family patterns among Cubans and Mexican Americans found strikingly different configurations of power. Employed women's newfound rights are often contradictory. As Repack's study (1997) of Central American immigrants revealed, numerous costs and strains accompany women's new roles in a new landscape. Family relations often became contentious when women pressed partners to share domestic responsibilities. Migration produced a situation in which women worked longer and harder than in their countries of origin.

Other conditions associated with varying patterns in the division of domestic labor are women's and men's occupational statuses and relative economic contributions to their families. Studies by Pesquera (1993), Coltrane and Valdez (1993), and Coltrane (1996) found a general "inside/outside" dichotomy (wives doing most housework, husbands doing outside work and sharing some child care), but women in middle-class jobs received more "help" from their husbands than did women with lower earnings.

"Family power" research should not be limited to women's roles, but should study the social relations between women and men. Recent works on Latino men's family lives have made important strides in this regard (Coltrane & Valdez, 1993; Shelton & John, 1993). Still, there is little information about the range and variety of Latino men's family experiences (Mirande, 1997) or of their interplay with larger structural conditions. In a rare study of Mexican immigrant men, Hondagneu-Sotelo and Messner (1994) discussed the diminution of patriarchy that comes with settling in the United States. They showed that the key to gender equality in immigrant families is women's and men's relative positions of power and status in the larger society. Mexican immigrant men's status is low owing to racism, economic marginality, and possible undocumented status.

Meanwhile, as immigrant women move into wage labor, they develop autonomy and economic skills. These conditions combine to erode patriarchal authority.

The research discussed earlier suggested some convergences between Latinos and other groups in family power arrangements. But intertwined with the shape of domestic power are strongly held ideals about women's and men's family roles. Ethnic gender identities, values, and beliefs contribute to gender relations and constitute an important but little understood dimension of families. Gender may also be influenced by Latinos' extended family networks. As Lamphere et al. (1993) discovered, Hispanas in Albuquerque were living in a world made up largely of Hispana mothers, sisters, and other relatives. Social scientists have posited a relationship between dense social networks and gender segregation. If this relationship holds, familism could well impede egalitarian relations in Latino families (Coltrane, 1996; Hurtado, 1995).

Compulsory heterosexuality is an important component of both gender and family systems. By enforcing the dichotomy of opposite sexes, it is also a form of inequality in its own right, hence an important marker of social location. A growing literature on lesbian and gay identity among Latinas and Latinos has examined the conflicting challenges involved in negotiating a multiple minority status (Alarcon, Castillo, & Moraga, 1989; Almaguer, 1991; Anzaldúa, 1987; Carrier, 1992; Moraga, 1983; Morales, 1990). Unfortunately, family scholarship on Latinos has not pursued the implications of lesbian and gay identities for understanding family diversity. In fact, there have been no studies in the social sciences in the area of sexual orientation and Latino families (Hurtado, 1995). But although the empirical base is virtually nonexistent and making *families* the unit of analysis no doubt introduces new questions (Demo & Allen, 1996), we can glean useful insights from the discourse on sexual identity. Writing about Chicanos, Almaguer (1991) identified the following obstacles to developing a safe space for forming a gay or lesbian identity: racial and class subordination and a context in which ethnicity remains a primary basis of group identity and survival. "Moreover Chicano *family life* [italics added] requires allegiance to patriarchal gender relations and to a system of sexual meanings that directly mitigate against the emergence of this alternative basis of self identity" (Almaguer, p. 88). Such repeated references to the constraints of ethnicity, gender, and sexual orientation imposed by Chicano families (Almaguer, 1991; Moraga, 1983) raise important questions. How do varied family contexts shape and differentiate the development of gay identities among Latinos? How do they affect the formation of lesbian and gay families among Latinas and Latinos? This area is wide open for research.

Children and Their Parents

Latinos have the highest concentration of children and adolescents of all major racial and ethnic groups. Nearly 40% of Latinos are aged 20 or younger, compared to about 26% of non-Hispanic whites (U.S. Bureau of the Census, 1996). Among Latino subgroups, the highest proportions of children and adolescents are among Mexicans and Puerto Ricans and the lowest among Cubans (Solis, 1995).

Latino socialization patterns have long held the interest of family scholars (Martinez, 1993). Most studies have focused on the child-rearing practices of Mexican families. Researchers have questioned whether Mexican families have permissive or authoritarian styles of child rearing and the relationship of childrearing styles to social class and cultural factors (Martinez, 1993). Patterns of child rearing were expected to reveal the level of acculturation to U.S. norms and the degree of modernization among traditional immigrant families. The results of research spanning the 1970s and 1980s were mixed and sometimes contradictory.

Buriel's (1993) study brought some clarity to the subject of child-rearing practices by situating it in the broad social context in which such practices occur. This study of Mexican families found that child-rearing practices differ by generation. Parents who were born in Mexico had a "responsibility-oriented" style that was compatible with their own life experience as struggling immigrants. U.S.-born Mexican parents had a "concern-oriented" style of parenting that was associated with the higher levels of education and income found among this group and that may also indicate that parents compensate for their children's disadvantaged standing in U.S. schools.

Mainstream theorizing has generally assumed a middle-class European-American model for the socialization of the next generation (Segura & Pierce, 1993). But the diverse contexts in which Latino children are raised suggest that family studies must take into account multiple models of socialization. Latino children are less likely than Anglo children to live in isolated nuclear units in which parents have almost exclusive responsibility for rearing children and the mothers' role is primary. Segura and Pierce contended that the pattern of nonexclusive mothering found in some Latino families shapes the gender identities of Latinos in ways that conventional thinking does not consider. Velez-Ibañez & Greenberg (1992) discussed how the extensive kinship networks of Mexican families influence child rearing and considered the ramifications for educational outcomes. Mexican children are socialized into a context of "thick" social relations. From infancy onward, these children experience far more social interaction than do children who are raised in more isolated contexts. The institution of education—second only to the family as an agent of socialization—is, in the United States, modeled after the dominant society and characterized by competition and individual achievement. Latino students who have been socialized into a more cooperative model of social relations often experience a disjuncture between their upbringing and the expectations of their schools (Velez-Ibañez & Greenberg, 1992).

Social location shapes the range of choices that parents have as they decide how best to provide for their children. Latino parents, who are disproportionately likely to occupy subordinate social locations in U.S. society, encounter severe obstacles to providing adequate material resources for their children. To date, little research has focused on Latino fathers (Powell, 1995). Hondagneu-Sotelo and Avila's (1997) study documented a broad range of mothering arrangements among Latinas. One such arrangement is transnational mothering, in which mothers work in the United States while their children remain in Mexico or Central America; it is accompanied by tremendous costs and undertaken when options are extremely limited. The researchers found that transnational mothering occurred among domestic workers, many of whom were live-in maids or child care providers who could not live with their children, as well as mothers who could better provide for their children in their countries of origin because U.S. dollars stretched further in Central America than in the United States. Other mothering arrangements chosen by Latinas in the study included migrating with their children, migrating alone and later sending for their children, and migrating alone and returning to their children after a period of work.

Intrafamily Diversity

Family scholars have increasingly recognized that family experience is differentiated along the lines of age and gender (Baca Zinn & Eitzen, 1996; Thorne, 1992). Members of particular families—parents and children, women and men—experience family life differently. Scholarship that considers the internal differentiation of Latino families is focused on the conditions surrounding and adaptations following immigration.

While immigration requires tremendous change of all family members, family adaptation to the new context is not a unitary phenomenon. Research has found patterns of differential adjustment as family members adapt unevenly to an unfamiliar social environment (Gold, 1989). Gil and Vega's (1996) study of acculturative stress in Cuban and Nicaraguan families in the Miami area identified significant differences in the adjustment of parents and their children. For example, Nicaraguan adolescents reported more initial language conflicts than did their parents, but their conflicts diminished over time, whereas their parents' language conflicts increased over time. This difference occurred because the adolescents were immediately confronted with their English language deficiency in school, but their parents could initially manage well in the Miami area without a facility with English. The authors concluded that family members experience "the aversive impacts of culture change at different times and at variable levels of intensity" (p. 451).

Differential adjustment creates new contexts for parent-child relations. Immigrant children who are school-aged generally become competent in English more quickly than do their parents. Dorrington (1995) found that Salvadoran and Guatemalan children often assume adult roles as they help their parents negotiate the bureaucratic structure of their new social environment; for example, a young child may accompany her parents to a local utility company to act as their translator.

Immigration may also create formal legal distinctions among members of Latino families. Frequently, family members do not share the same immigration status. That is, undocumented Mexican and Central American couples are likely, over time, to have children born in the United States and hence are U.S. citizens; the presence of these children then renders the "undocumented family" label inaccurate. Chavez (1992, p. 129) used the term *binational family* to refer to a family with both members who are undocumented and those who are citizens or legal residents.

Not only do family members experience family life differently, but age and gender often produce diverging and even conflicting interests among them (Baca Zinn & Eitzen, 1996). Both Hondagneu-Sotelo's (1994) and Grasmuck and Pessar's (1991) studies of family immigration found that Latinas were generally far more interested in settling permanently in the United States than were their husbands. In both studies, the women had enhanced their status by migration, while the men had lost theirs. Hondagneu-Sotelo noted that Mexican women advanced the permanent settlement of their families by taking regular, nonseasonal employment; negotiating the use of public and private assistance;

and forging strong community ties. Grasmuck and Pessar observed that Dominican women tried to postpone their families' return to the Dominican Republic by extravagantly spending money that would otherwise be saved for their return and by establishing roots in the United States.

DISCUSSION AND CONCLUSION

The key to understanding diversity in Latino families is the uneven distribution of constraints and opportunities among families, which affects the behaviors of family members and ultimately the forms that family units take (Baca Zinn & Eitzen, 1996). Our goal in this review was to call into question assumptions, beliefs, and false generalizations about the way "Latino families are." We examined Latino families not as if they had some essential characteristics that set them apart from others, but as they are affected by a complex mix of structural features.

Our framework enabled us to see how diverse living arrangements among Latinos are situated and structured in the larger social world. Although this framework embraces the interplay of macro- and microlevels of analysis, we are mindful that this review devoted far too little attention to family experience, resistance, and voice. We do not mean to underestimate the importance of human agency in the social construction of Latino families, but we could not devote as much attention as we would have liked to the various ways in which women, men, and children actively produce their family worlds. Given the sheer size of the literature, the "non-comparability of most contemporary findings and the lack of a consistent conceptual groundwork" (Vega, 1990, p. 102), we decided that what is most needed is a coherent framework within which to view and interpret diversity. Therefore, we chose to focus on the impact of social forces on family life.

The basic insights of our perspective are sociological. Yet a paradox of family sociology is that the field has tended to misrepresent Latino families and those of other racial-ethnic groups. Sociology has distorted Latino families by generalizing from the experience of dominant groups and ignoring the differences that make a difference. This is a great irony. Family sociology, the specialty whose task it is to describe and understand social diversity, has marginalized diversity, rather than treated it as a central feature of social life (Baca Zinn & Eitzen, 1993).

As sociologists, we wrote this [reading] fully aware of the directions in our discipline that hinder the ability to explain diversity. At the same time, we think the core insight of sociology should be applied to challenge conventional thinking about families. Reviewing the literature for this [reading] did not diminish our sociological convictions, but it did present us with some unforeseen challenges. We found a vast gulf between mainstream family sociology and the extraordinary amount of high-quality scholarship on Latino families. Our review took us far beyond the boundaries of our discipline, making us "cross disciplinary migrants" (Stacey, 1995). We found the new literature in diverse and unlikely locations, with important breakthroughs emerging in the "borderlands" between social science disciplines. We also found the project to be infinitely more complex than we anticipated. The extensive scholarship on three national-origin groups and "others" was complicated by widely varying analytic snapshots. We were, in short, confronted with a kaleidoscope of family diversity. Our shared perspective served us well in managing the task at hand. Although we have different family specializations and contrasting family experiences, we both seek to understand multiple family and household forms that emanate from structural arrangements.

What are the most important lessons our sociological analysis holds for the family field? Three themes offer new directions for building a better, more inclusive, family social science. First, understanding Latino family diversity does not mean simply appreciating the ways in which families are different; rather, it means analyzing how the formation of diverse families is based on and reproduces social inequalities. At the heart of many of the differences between Latino families and mainstream families and the different aggregate family patterns among Latino groups are structural forces that place families in different social environments. What is not often acknowledged is that the same social structures—race, class, and other hierarchies—affect *all* families, albeit in different ways. Instead of treating family variation as the property of group difference, recent sociological theorizing (Baca Zinn, 1994; Dill, 1994; Glenn, 1992; Hill Collins, 1990, 1997) has conceptualized diverse family arrangements in *relational* terms, that is, mutually dependent and sustained through interaction across racial and class boundaries. The point is not that family differences based on race, class, and gender simply coexist. Instead, many differences in family life involve relationships of domination and subordination and differential access to material resources. Patterns of privilege and subordination characterize the historical relationships between Anglo families and Mexican families in the Southwest (Dill, 1994). Contemporary diversity among Latino families reveals *new* interdependences and inequalities. Emergent middle-class and professional lifestyles among Anglos and even some Latinos are interconnected with a new Latino servant class whose family arrangements, in turn, must accommodate to the demands of their labor.

Second, family diversity plays a part in different economic orders and the shifts that accompany them. Scholars have suggested that the multiplicity of household types is one of the chief props of the world economy (Smith, Wallerstein, & Evers, 1985). The example of U.S.-Mexican cross-border households brings this point into full view. This household arrangement constitutes an important "part of the emerging and dynamic economic and technological transformations in the region" (Velez-Ibañez, 1996, p. 143). The structural reordering required by such families is central to regional economic change.

Finally, the incredible array of immigrant family forms and their enormous capacity for adaptation offer new departures for the study of postmodern families. "Binational," "transnational," and "multinational" families, together with "border balanced households" and "generational hopscotching," are arrangements that remain invisible even in Stacey's (1996) compelling analysis of U.S. family life at the century's end. And yet the experiences of Latino families—flexible and plastic—as far back as the late 1800s (Griswold del Castillo, 1984), give resonance to the image of long-standing family fluidity and of contemporary families lurching backward and forward into the postmodern age (Stacey, 1990). The shift to a postindustrial economy is not the only social transformation affecting families. Demographic and political changes sweeping the world are engendering family configurations that are yet unimagined in family social science.

These trends offer new angles of vision for thinking about family diversity. They pose new opportunities for us to remake family studies as we uncover the mechanisms that construct multiple household and family arrangements.

References

Alarcon, N., Castillo, A., & Moraga, C. (Eds.). (1989). *Third woman: The sexuality of Latinas.* Berkeley, CA: Third Woman.

Almaguer, T. (1991). Chicano men: A cartography of homosexual identity and behavior. *Differences: A Journal of Feminist Cultural Studies, 3,* 75–100.

Alvirez, D., & Bean, F. (1976). The Mexican American family. In C. Mindel & R. Habenstein (Eds.), *Ethnic families in America* (pp. 271–292). New York: Elsevier.

Angel, R., & Tienda, M. (1982). Determinants of extended household structure: Cultural pattern or economic need? *American Journal of Sociology, 87,* 1360–1383.

Anzaldúa, G. (1987). *Borderlands/La Frontera: The new meztiza.* San Francisco: Spinsters, Aunt Lute Press.

Aponte, R. (1993). Hispanic families in poverty: Diversity, context, and interpretation. *Families in Society: The Journal of Contemporary Human Services, 36,* 527–537.

Baca Zinn, M. (1980). Employment and education of Mexican American women: The interplay of modernity and ethnicity in eight families. *Harvard Educational Review, 50,* 47–62.

Baca Zinn, M. (1983). Familism among Chicanos: A theoretical review. *Humboldt Journal of Social Relations, 10,* 224–238.

Baca Zinn, M. (1994). Feminist rethinking from racial-ethnic families. In M. Baca Zinn & B. T. Dill (Eds.), *Women of color in U.S. society* (pp. 303–312). Philadelphia: Temple University Press.

Baca Zinn, M. (1995). Social science theorizing for Latino families in the age of diversity. In R. E. Zambrana (Ed.), *Understanding Latino families* (pp. 177–187). Thousand Oaks, CA: Sage.

Baca Zinn, M., & Dill, B. T. (1996). Theorizing difference from multiracial feminism. *Feminist Studies, 22,* 321–332.

Baca Zinn, M., & Eitzen, D. S. (1993). The demographic transformation and the sociological enterprise. *American Sociologist, 24,* 5–12.

Baca Zinn, M., & Eitzen, D. S. (1996). *Diversity in families* (4th ed.). New York: HarperCollins.

Baca Zinn, M., & Eitzen, D. S. (1998). Economic restructuring and systems in inequality. In M. L. Andersen & P. H. Collins (Eds.), *Race, class and gender* (3rd ed., pp. 233–237). Belmont, CA: Wadsworth.

Betancur, J. J., Cordova, T., & Torres, M. L. A. (1993). Economic restructuring and the process of incorporation of Latinos into the Chicago economy. In R. Morales & F. Bonilla (Eds.), *Latinos in a changing U.S. economy: Comparative perspectives on growing inequality* (pp. 109–132). Newbury Park, CA: Sage.

Bogardus, A. (1934). *The Mexican in the United States.* Los Angeles: University of Southern California Press.

Boss, P., & Thorne, B. (1989). Family sociology and family therapy. In M. McGoldrick, C. M. Anderson, & F. Walsh (Eds.), *Women in families* (pp. 78–96). New York: W. W. Norton.

Boyd, M. (1989). Family and personal networks in international migration: Recent developments and new agendas. *International Migration Review, 23,* 638–670.

Buriel, R. (1993). Childrearing orientations in Mexican American families: The influence of generation and sociocultural factors. *Journal of Marriage and the Family, 55,* 987–1000.

Buriel, R., & De Ment, T. (1997). Immigration and sociocultural change in Mexican, Chinese, and Vietnamese American families. In A. Booth, A. C. Crouter, & N. Landale (Eds.), *Immigration and the family: Research and policy on U.S. immigrants* (pp. 165–200). Mahwah, NJ: Lawrence Erlbaum.

Cardenas, G., Chapa, J., & Burek, S. (1993). The changing economic position of Mexican Americans in San Antonio. In R. Morales & F. Bonilla (Eds.), *Latinos in a changing U.S. economy: Comparative perspectives on growing inequality* (pp. 160–183). Newbury Park, CA: Sage.

Carnoy, M., Daley, H. M., & Ojeda, R. H. (1993). The changing economic position of Latinos in the U.S. labor market since 1939. In R. Morales & F. Bonilla (Eds.), *Latinos in a changing U.S. economy: Comparative perspectives on growing inequality* (pp. 28–54). Newbury Park, CA: Sage.

Carrier, J. (1992). Miguel: Sexual life history of a gay Mexican American. In G. Herdt (Ed.), *Gay culture in America* (pp. 202–224). Boston: Beacon Press.

Chavez, L. R. (1990). Coresidence and resistance: Strategies for survival among undocumented Mexicans and Central Americans in the United States. *Urban Anthropology, 19*, 31–61.

Chavez, L. R. (1992). *Shadowed lives: Undocumented immigrants in American society.* Fort Worth, TX: Holt, Rinehart, & Winston.

Chavira-Prado, A. (1992). Work, health, and the family: Gender structure and women's status in an undocumented migrant population. *Human Organization, 51*, 53–64.

Coltrane, S. (1996). *Family man.* New York: Oxford University Press.

Coltrane, S., & Valdez, E. O. (1993). Reluctant compliance: Work-family role allocation in dual earner Chicano families. In J. Hood (Ed.), *Men, work, and family* (pp. 151–175). Newbury Park, CA: Sage.

Demo, D. H., & Allen, K. R. (1996). Diversity within gay and lesbian families: Challenges and implications for family theory and research. *Journal of Social and Personal Relationships, 13*, 415–434.

Dill, B. T. (1994). Fictive kin, paper sons, and compadrazgo: Women of color and the struggle for survival. In M. Baca Zinn & B. T. Dill (Eds.), *Women of color in U.S. society* (pp. 149–169). Philadelphia: Temple University Press.

Dominguez, J. I. (1992). Cooperating with the enemy? U.S. immigration policies toward Cuba. In C. Mitchell (Ed.), *Western hemisphere immigration and United States foreign policy* (pp. 31–88). University Park, PA: Pennsylvania State University Press.

Dorrington, C. (1995). Central American refugees in Los Angeles: Adjustment of children and families. In R. Zambrana (Ed.), *Understanding Latino families: Scholarship, policy, and practice* (pp. 107–129). Thousand Oaks, CA: Sage.

Feagin, J. R., & Feagin, C. B. (1996). *Racial and ethnic relations.* Upper Saddle River, NJ: Prentice Hall.

Fernandez-Kelly, M. P. (1990). Delicate transactions: Gender, home, and employment among Hispanic women. In F. Ginsberg & A. L. Tsing (Eds.), *Uncertain terms* (pp. 183–195). Boston: Beacon Press.

Fernandez-Kelly, M. P., & Garcia, A. (1990). Power surrendered and power restored: The politics of home and work among Hispanic women in southern California and southern Florida. In L. Tilly & P. Gurin (Eds.), *Women and politics in America* (pp. 130–149). New York: Russell Sage Foundation.

Fernandez-Kelly, M. P., & Schauffler, R. (1994). Divided fates: Immigrant children in a restructured U.S. economy. *International Migration Review, 28*, 662–689.

Gil, A. G., & Vega, W. A. (1996). Two different worlds: Acculturation stress and adaptation among Cuban and Nicaraguan families. *Journal of Social and Personal Relationships, 13*, 435–456.

Glenn, E. N. (1992). From servitude to service work: Historical continuities in the racial division of paid reproductive labor. *Signs: Journal of Women in Culture and Society, 18*, 1–43.

Gold, S. J. (1989). Differential adjustment among new immigrant family members. *Journal of Contemporary Ethnography, 17*, 408–434.

Grasmuck, S., & Pessar, P. R. (1991). *Between two islands: Dominican international migration.* Berkeley: University of California Press.

Grasmuck, S., & Pessar, P. R. (1996). Dominicans in the United States: First- and second-generation settlement, 1960–1990. In S. Pedraza & R. G. Rumbaut (Eds.), *Origins and destinies: Immigration, race, and ethnicity in America* (pp. 280–292). Belmont, CA: Wadsworth.

Griffith, J., & Villavicienco, S. (1985). Relationships among culturation, sociodemographic characteristics, and social supports in Mexican American adults. *Hispanic Journal of Behavioral Science, 7*, 75–92.

Griswold del Castillo, R. (1984). *La familia.* Notre Dame, IN: University of Notre Dame Press.

Guarnizo, L. E. (1997). Los Dominicanyorks: The making of a binational society. In M. Romero, P. Hondagneu-Sotelo, & V. Ortiz (Eds.), *Challenging fronteras: Structuring Latina and Latino lives in the U.S.* (pp. 161–174). New York: Routledge.

Hamilton, N., & Chinchilla, N. S. (1997). Central American migration: A framework for analysis. In M. Romero, P. Hondagneu-Sotelo, & V. Ortiz (Eds.), *Challenging fronteras: Structuring Latina and Latino lives in the U.S.* (pp. 81–100). New York: Routledge.

Heller, C. (1996). *Mexican American youth: Forgotten youth at the crossroads.* New York: Random House.

Hill Collins, P. (1990). *Black feminist thought: Knowledge, consciousness and the politics of empowerment.* Boston: Unwin Hyman.

Hill Collins, P. (1997). African-American women and economic justice: A preliminary analysis of wealth, family, and black social class. Unpublished manuscript, Department of African American Studies. University of Cincinnati.

Hondagneu-Sotelo, P. (1994). *Gendered transitions: Mexican experiences of migration.* Berkeley: University of California Press.

Hondagneu-Sotelo, P., & Avila, E. (1997). "I'm here, but I'm there": The meanings of transnational motherhood. *Gender and Society, 11,* 548–571.

Hondagneu-Sotelo, P., & Messner, M. A. (1994). Gender displays and men's power: The "new man" and the Mexican immigrant man. In H. Brod & M. Kaufman (Eds.), *Theorizing masculinities* (pp. 200–218). Newbury Park, CA: Sage.

Hoppe, S. K., & Heller, P. L. (1975). Alienation, familism and the utilization of health services by Mexican-Americans. *Journal of Health and Social Behavior, 16,* 304–314.

Hurtado, A. (1995). Variations, combinations, and evolutions: Latino families in the United States. In R. E. Zambrana (Ed.), *Understanding Latino families* (pp. 40–61). Thousand Oaks, CA: Sage.

Keefe, S. (1984). Deal and ideal extended familism among Mexican Americans and Anglo Americans: On the meaning of "close" family ties. *Human Organization, 43,* 65–70.

Lamphere, L., Zavella, P., & Gonzales F., with Evans, P. B. (1993). *Sunbelt working mothers: Reconciling family and factory.* Ithaca, NY: Cornell University Press.

Landale, N. S., & Fennelly, K. (1992). Informal unions among mainland Puerto Ricans: Cohabitation or an alternative to legal marriage? *Journal of Marriage and the Family, 54,* 269–280.

Lopez, D. E., Popkin, E., & Telles, E. (1996). Central Americans: At the bottom, struggling to get ahead. In R. Waldinger & M. Bozorgmehr (Eds.), *Ethnic Los Angeles* (pp. 279–304). New York: Russell Sage Foundation.

Madsen, W. (1973). *The Mexican-Americans of south Texas.* New York: Holt, Rinehart & Winston.

Martinez, E. A. (1993). Parenting young children in Mexican American/Chicago families. In H. P. McAdoo (Ed.), *Family ethnicity: Strength in diversity* (pp. 184–194). Newbury Park, CA: Sage.

Massey, D. S. (1993). Latino poverty research: An agenda for the 1990s. Items, *Social Science Research Council Newsletter, 47*(l), 7–11.

Massey, D. S., Zambrana, R. E., & Bell, S. A. (1995). Contemporary issues for Latino families: Future directions for research, policy, and practice. In R. E. Zambrana (Ed.), *Understanding Latino families* (pp. 190–204). Thousand Oaks, CA: Sage.

Mindel, C. H. (1980). Extended familism among urban Mexican-Americans, Anglos and blacks. *Hispanic Journal of Behavioral Sciences, 2,* 21–34.

Mirande, A. (1997). *Hombres y machos: Masculinity and Latino culture.* Boulder, CO: Westview Press.

Mitchell, C. (1992). U.S. foreign policy and Dominican migration to the United States. In C. Mitchell (Ed.), *Western hemisphere immigration and United States foreign policy* (pp. 89–123). University Park: Pennsylvania State University Press.

Moore, J. W., & Pinderhughes, R. (Eds.). (1993). *In the barrios: Latinos and the underclass debate.* New York: Russell Sage Foundation.

Moore, J. W., & Vigil, J. D. (1993). Barrios in transition. In J. W. Moore & R. Pinderhughes (Eds.), *In the barrios: Latinos and the underclass debate* (pp. 27–50). New York: Russell Sage Foundation.

Moraga, C. (1983). *Loving in the war years: Lo que nunca paso por sus labios.* Boston: South End Press.

Morales, E. S. (1990). Ethnic minority families and minority gays and lesbians. In F. W. Bozett & M. B. Sussman (Eds.), *Homosexuality and family relations* (pp. 217–239). New York: Harrington Park Press.

Morales, R., & Ong, P. M. (1993). The illusion of progress: Latinos in Los Angeles. In R. Morales & F. Bonilla (Eds.), *Latinos in a changing U.S. economy: Comparative perspectives on growing inequality* (pp. 55–84). Newbury Park, CA: Sage.

Morales, R., & Bonilla, F. (1993). Restructuring and the new inequality. In R. Morales & F. Bonilla (Eds.), *Latinos in a changing U.S. economy: Comparative perspectives on growing inequality* (pp. 1–27). Newbury Park, CA: Sage.

Morrissey, M. (1987). Female-headed families: Poor women and choice. In N. Gerstel & H. Gross (Eds.), Families and work (pp. 302–314). Philadelphia: Temple University Press.

Ortiz, V. (1995). The diversity of Latino families. In R. Zambrana (Ed.), *Understanding Latino families: Scholarship, policy, and practice* (pp. 18–30). Thousand Oaks, CA: Sage.

Ortiz, V. (1996). The Mexican-origin population: Permanent working class or emerging middle class? In R. Waldinger & M. Bozorgmehr (Eds.), *Ethnic Los Angeles* (pp. 247–277). New York: Russell Sage Foundation.

Perez, L. (1994). Cuban families in the United States. In R. L. Taylor (Ed.), *Minority families in the United States: A multicultural perspective.* Englewood Cliffs, NJ: Prentice Hall.

Perez-Stable, M., & Uriarte, M. (1993). Cubans and the changing economy of Miami. In R. Morales & F. Bonilla (Eds.), *Latinos in a changing U.S. economy: Comparative perspectives on growing inequality* (pp. 133–159). Newbury Park, CA: Sage.

Pesquera, B. M. (1993). In the beginning he wouldn't lift even a spoon: The division of household labor. In A. de la Torre & B. M. Pesquera (Eds.), *Building with our hands* (pp. 181–198). Berkeley: University of California Press.

Portes, A., & Rumbaut, R. G. (1990). *Immigrant America: A portrait.* Berkeley: University of California Press.

Portes, A., & Truelove, C. (1987). Making sense of diversity: Recent research on Hispanic minorities in the United States. *Annual Review of Sociology, 13,* 357–385.

Powell, D. R. (1995). Including Latino fathers in parent education and support programs: Development of a program model. In R. E. Zambrana (Ed.), *Understanding Latino families* (pp. 85–106). Thousand Oaks, CA: Sage.

Ramirez, O. (1980, March). Extended family support and mental health status among Mexicans in - Detroit. *Micro, Onda, LaRed, Monthly Newsletter of the National Chicano Research Network,* p. 2.

Ramirez, O., & Arce, C. H. (1981). The contemporary Chicano family: An empirically based review. In A. Baron, Jr. (Ed.), *Explorations in Chicano Psychology* (pp. 3–28). New York: Praeger.

Repack, T. A. (1997). New rules in a new landscape. In M. Romero, P. Hondagneu-Sotelo, & V. Ortiz (Eds.), *Challenging fronteras: Structuring Latina and Latino lives in the U.S.* (pp. 247–257). New York: Routledge.

Rochelle, A. (1997). *No more kin: Exploring race, class, and gender in family networks.* Thousand Oaks, CA: Sage.

Rodriguez, N. P., & Hagan, J. M. (1997). Apartment restructuring and Latino immigrant tenant struggles: A case study of human agency. In M. Romero, P. Hondagneu-Sotelo, & V. Ortiz (Eds.), *Challenging fronteras: Structuring Latina and Latina lives in the U.S.* (pp. 297–309). New York: Routledge.

Romero, M. (1997). Introduction. In M. Romero, P. Hondagneu-Sotelo, & V. Ortiz (Eds.), *Challenging fronteras: Structuring Latina and Latino lives in the U.S.* (pp. xiii-xix). New York: Routledge.

Rubel, A. J. (1966). *Across the tracks: Mexican Americans in a Texas city.* Austin: University of Texas Press.

Rumbaut, R. G. (1995). *Immigrants from Latin America and the Caribbean: A socioeconomic profile* (Statistical Brief No. 6). East Lansing: Julian Samora Research Institute, Michigan State University.

Sassen, S. (1993). Urban transformation and employment. In R. Morales & F. Bonilla (Eds.), *Latinos in a changing U.S. economy: Comparative perspectives on growing inequality* (pp. 194–206). Newbury Park, CA: Sage.

Scott, A. J. (1996). The manufacturing economy: Ethnic and gender divisions of labor. In R. Waldinger & M. Bozorgmehr (Eds.), *Ethnic Los Angeles.* New York: Russell Sage Foundation.

Segura, D. A., & Pierce, J. L. (1993). Chicana/o family structure and gender personality: Chodorow, familism, and psychoanalytic sociology revisited. *Signs, 19,* 62–91.

Shelton, B. A., & John, D. (1993). Ethnicity, race, and difference: A comparison of white, black, and Hispanic men's household labor time. In J. Hood (Ed.), *Men, work, and family* (pp. 1–22). Newbury Park, CA: Sage.

Smith, J., Wallerstein, I., & Evers, H. D. (1985). *The household and the world economy.* Beverly Hills, CA: Sage.

Solis, J. (1995). The status of Latino children and youth: Challenges and prospects. In R. E. Zambrana (Ed.), *Understanding Latino families* (pp. 62–84). Thousand Oaks, CA: Sage.

Stacey, J. (1990). *Brave new families: Stories of domestic upheaval in late twentieth century America.* New York: Basic Books.

Stacey, J. (1995). Disloyal to the disciplines: A feminist trajectory in the border lands. In D. C. Stanton & A. Stewart (Eds.), *Feminisms in the academy* (pp. 311–330). Ann Arbor: University of Michigan Press.

Stacey, J. (1996). *In the name of the family: Rethinking family values in the postmodern age.* Boston: Beacon Press.

Stier, H., & Tienda, M. (1992). Family, work, and women: The labor supply of Hispanic immigrant wives. *International Migration Review, 26,* 1291–1313.

Sullivan, M. L. (1993). Puerto Ricans in Sunset Park, Brooklyn: Poverty amidst ethnic and economic diversity. In J. W. Moore & R. Pinderhughes (Eds.), *In the barrios: Latinos and the underclass debate* (pp. 1–26). New York: Russell Sage Foundation.

Thomas, D., & Wilcox, J. E. (1987). The rise of family theory. In M. B. Sussman & S. Steinmetz (Eds.), *Handbook of marriage and the family* (pp. 81–102). New York: Plenum.

Thorne, B. (1992). Feminism and the family: Two decades of thought. In B. Thorne & M. Yalom (Eds.), *Rethinking the family: Some feminist questions* (pp. 3–30). Boston: Northeastern University Press.

Tienda, M. (1989). Puerto Ricans and the underclass debate. *Annals of the American Association of Political and Social Sciences, 501,* 105–119.

Torres, A., & Bonilla, F. (1993). Decline within decline: The New York perspective. In R. Morales & F. Bonilla (Eds.), *Latinos in a changing U.S. economy: Comparative perspectives on growing inequality* (pp. 85–108). Newbury Park, CA: Sage.

U.S. Bureau of the Census. (1993). *1990 census of the population: Persons of Hispanic origin in the United States.* Washington, DC: U.S. Government Printing Office.

U.S. Bureau of the Census. (1996). *Statistical abstract Of the United States: 1996.* Washington DC: U.S. Government Printing Office.

Valenzuela, A., & Dombusch, S. (1994). Familism and social capital in the academic achievement of Mexican origin and Anglo adolescents. *Social Science Quarterly, 75,* 18–36.

Vega, W. (1990). Hispanic families in the 1980s: A decade of research. *Journal of Marriage and the Family, 52,* 1015–1024.

Vega, W. A. (1995). The study of Latino families: A point of departure. In R. E. Zambrana (Ed.), *Understanding Latino families* (pp. 3–17). Thousand Oaks, CA: Sage.

Velez-Ibañez, C. (1993). U.S. Mexicans in the borderlands: Being poor without the underclass. In J. Moore & R. Pinderhughes (Eds.), *In the barrios: Latinos and the underclass debate* (pp. 195–220). New York: Russell Sage Foundation.

Velez-Ibañez, C. (1996). *Border visions.* Tucson: University of Arizona Press.

Velez-Ibañez, C. G., & Greenberg, J. B. (1992). Formation and transformation of funds of knowledge among U.S.-Mexican households. *Anthropology and Education Quarterly, 23,* 313–335.

Williams, N. (1990). *The Mexican American family: Tradition and change.* Dix Hills, NY: General Hall.

Wilkinson, D. (1993). Family ethnicity in America. In H. P. McAdoo (Ed.), *Family ethnicity: Strength in diversity* (pp. 15–59). Newbury Park, CA: Sage.

Wilson, W. J. (1987). *The truly disadvantaged. The inner city, the underclass, and public policy.* Chicago: University of Chicago Press.

Wilson, W. J. (1996). *When work disappears: The world of the new urban poor.* New York: Alfred A. Knopf.

Ybarra, L. (1982). When wives work: The impact on the Chicano family. *Journal of Marriage and the Family, 44,* 169–178.

Zavella, P. (1987). *Women's work and Chicano families: Cannery workers of the Santa Clara Valley.* Ithaca, NY: Cornell University Press.

READING 33

Conflict, Coping, and Reconciliation: Intergenerational Relations in Chinese Immigrant Families

Min Zhou

Chinese Americans are by far the oldest and largest ethnic group of Asian ancestry in the United States. Their long history of migration and settlement dates back to the late 1840s, including some sixty years of legal exclusion. With the lifting of legal barriers to Chinese immigration during World War II and especially following the 1965 Hart-Celler Act, which abolished the national-origins quota system and emphasized family reunification and the importation of skilled labor, the Chinese American community increased dramatically—from 237,000 in 1960 to more than three million (including half a million mixed-race persons) in 2005. Much of this extraordinary growth is due to immigration. Between 1961 and 2005, more than 1.8 million immigrants were admitted to the United States as permanent residents from China, Hong Kong, and Taiwan.[3] The foreign born accounted for more than two-thirds of the ethnic Chinese population in the United States. Today's second generation is still very young and has not yet come of age in significant numbers.[4] The 2000 Current Population Survey indicates that 44 percent of the U.S.-born Chinese are under the age of eighteen and another 10 percent are between eighteen and twenty-four.[5]

After 1965, the Chinese American community was transformed from a bachelors' society to a family community. There have been other significant changes as well. Unlike earlier Chinese immigrants, post-1965 Chinese arrivals have come not only from mainland China, but also from the greater Chinese Diaspora—Hong Kong, Taiwan, Vietnam, Cambodia, Malaysia, and the Americas. Diverse national origins entail diverse cultural patterns. Linguistically, for example, Chinese immigrants come from a much wider variety of dialect groups than in the past. While all Chinese share a single ancestral written language, they speak numerous regional dialects—Cantonese, Mandarin, Minnanese, Hakkaese, Chaozhounese, and Shanghainese.

Post-1965 Chinese immigrants also have diverse socioeconomic backgrounds. Like those in the past, some arrive in the United States with little money, minimum education, few job skills, and from rural areas, but a significant number now come with considerable family savings, education, and skills far above the levels of average Americans. The 2004 American Community Survey reports that 50 percent of adult Chinese Americans (age twenty-five or older) in the United States have attained four or more years of college education, compared to 30 percent of non-Hispanic whites. Immigrants from Taiwan displayed the highest levels of educational attainment, with nearly two-thirds completing at least four years of college, followed by those from Hong Kong (just shy of half) and from mainland China (about a third). Professional occupations were also more common among Chinese American workers (age sixteen or older) than non-Hispanic white workers (52 percent versus 38 percent). The annual median household income for Chinese Americans was $57,000 in 2003 dollars, compared to $49,000 for non-Hispanic whites. While major socioeconomic indicators are above the national average and above those for non-Hispanic whites, the poverty rate for Chinese Americans was also higher (13 percent) than for non-Hispanic whites (9 percent), and the homeownership rate was lower (63 percent) than for non-Hispanic whites (74 percent).[6]

In terms of settlement patterns, Chinese Americans have continued to concentrate in the western United States and in urban areas. California alone accounts for nearly 40 percent of all Chinese Americans (1.1 million); New York comes in second with 16 percent, followed by Hawaii with 6 percent. At the same time, other states that historically received few Chinese immigrants, such as Texas, New Jersey, Massachusetts, Illinois, Washington, Florida, Maryland, and Pennsylvania, have now witnessed phenomenal growth. Traditional urban enclaves, such as Chinatowns in San Francisco, New York, Los Angeles, Chicago, and Boston, still receive new immigrants, but they are no longer the primary centers of initial settlement now that many new immigrants, especially the affluent and highly skilled, go straight to the suburbs on arrival. Currently, only 2 percent of the Chinese in Los Angeles, 8 percent in San Francisco, and 14 percent in New York City live in old Chinatowns. Half of all Chinese Americans live in suburbs. A good number live in the new multiethnic, immigrant-dominant suburban municipalities, often referred to as "ethnoburbs," that have appeared since the 1980s.[7] In 2000, there were eleven cities in the United States—all in California and all but San Francisco in the suburbs—in which Chinese Americans made up more than 20 percent of the population.

These demographic changes in the Chinese American community have created multiple contexts in which the new second generation (the U.S.-born or -raised children of post-1965 Chinese immigrants) is coming of age. Three main neighborhood contexts—the traditional ethnic enclaves such as inner-city Chinatowns, the ethnoburbs, and the white middle-class suburbs—are particularly important in understanding the challenges confronting new Chinese immigrant families.

COMMUNITY TRANSFORMATIONS AND CONTEXTS

During the era of legal exclusion, most Chinese immigrants were isolated in inner-city ethnic enclaves that were characterized as bachelors' societies. Many Chinatown "bachelor" workers were actually married but had left their wives, children, and parents behind in their villages in China. The few "normal" families in the bachelors' society often were those of merchants or workers who, for immigration purposes, claimed to be partners of merchants. In old Chinatowns, individuals and families were enmeshed in and highly dependent upon the ethnic community for social, economic, and emotional support, while also subject to its control. Chinatown children grew up in an extended family environment surrounded by and under the watchful eyes of many "grandpas" and "uncles" who were not actually related by blood but were part of an intricate system of family, kin or parental friendship associations.

The behavior of both children and parents in old Chinatowns was carefully monitored by a closely knit ethnic community. Children were either "good" kids—loyal, *guai* (obedient), and *you-chu-xi* (promising)—or "bad" kids, disrespectful, *bai-jia-zi* (family failure), and *mei-chu-xi* (good-for-nothing). They grew up speaking fluent Chinese, mostly in local dialects, going to Chinese schools, working in Chinese-owned businesses in the community, and interacting intimately with other Chinese in the ethnic enclave. Many wished to become like other American children but faced resistance from the larger society as well as from their own families. The larger society looked down on the Chinese and set barriers to keep them apart, such as segregation in schools and workplaces. The Chinese family tied children to Chinatown and its ethnic institutions, Chinese school being the most important, to shield them from overt discrimination. Despite considerable adolescent rebellion and generational conflict within the family, the children often found themselves dependent on ethnic networks without much scope to break free.

Whereas members of the old second generation grew up in ethnic enclaves isolated from middle-class America, those of the new second generation come from more diverse socioeconomic backgrounds and have settled in a wider range of neighborhoods. Those who reside in inner-city Chinatowns are generally from low-income families who have recently arrived. Like the old second generation, they speak Chinese fluently, interact primarily with people in a Chinese-speaking environment, and participate in various cultural and social institutions in the ethnic community. However, they no longer live in a hostile environment that socially and legally excludes the Chinese. Even though they may go to neighborhood schools with mostly immigrant Chinese and other minority children, they have more opportunities to interact with non-coethnic children and adults and a wider range of occupational choices.

Members of the new second generation who reside in multiethnic ethnoburbs are mainly from upper- and middle-income families. They generally go to higher-quality suburban public schools. They also have access to ethnic institutions unavailable, or less available, in old Chinatown, such as after-school tutoring (*buxiban*), academic enrichment, sports, and music programs offered by Chinese-owned private businesses. Although they speak Chinese fluently, interact with other Chinese, and are involved with things "Chinese," including food, music, and customs, they also interact regularly with people of diverse racial/ethnic backgrounds.

The children of Chinese immigrants in suburban white middle-class neighborhoods tend to have parents who have achieved high levels of education, occupation, income, and English proficiency and who are bicultural, transnational, cosmopolitan, and highly assimilated. These children attend schools where white students are in the majority and have few primary contacts with coethnic peers. Many grow up speaking only English at home and have mostly white friends.

Overall, compared to the old, pre-1965, second generation, members of the new second generation are growing up in a more open society. They do not face the kinds of legal barriers to educational and occupational attainment that blocked the mobility of the old second generation. They tend to live in family neighborhoods and have more sources of social support beyond the ethnic community. They also have much more freedom to "become American" and more leverage to rebel against their parents if they choose.

They can even report their parents to government authorities if they feel they have been "abused" at home, because social institutions and the legal system in the larger society provide support. And to take another extreme measure, should they decide to run away from home, they have more options to get by. In today's more open society, immigrant parents often find it harder than in the isolated enclave to raise children "the Chinese way" because of the more intense conflicts between the parents' social world and the mainstream society.

CHALLENGES CONFRONTING THE CHINESE IMMIGRANT FAMILY

Post-1965 Chinese immigrants confront profound challenges when they move to America. One such challenge has to do with structural changes in the immigrant family. In Taiwan, Hong Kong, and the mainland, Chinese families are often extended in form, with grandparents or other relatives living in the home or in close contact. When family members arrive in the United States, their extended kin and friendship networks, and the associated support and control mechanisms, are disrupted. When immigrant families locate first in ethnic enclaves or ethnoburbs, they may be able to reconnect to, or rebuild, ethnic networks, but these new ethnic networks tend to be composed of coethnic "strangers" rather than close kin and friends and tend to be more instrumental than emotionally intimate. Those who go to white middle-class suburbs are more detached from the existing ethnic community and have a harder time rebuilding social networks based on common origins and a common cultural heritage. Even though affluent Chinese immigrant families may have less need of ethnic networks and ethnic resources than their working-class counterparts, many find them comforting and, at times, helpful in enforcing traditional Chinese values to which they are still closely attached.

A second challenge is the change in roles within the immigrant family. In most Chinese immigrant families, both parents work full time, and some hold several jobs on different shifts. Because of the disadvantages associated with immigrant status, many Chinese immigrant men experience downward mobility and have difficulty obtaining jobs that enable them to be the main breadwinners. Women have to work outside the home, and many contribute equally, if not more, to the family income while also assuming the principal responsibility for child-rearing. That women work outside the home often creates difficulties for children in the family. Without the help of grandparents, relatives, and other close friends, many of them become latch-key children, staying home alone after school hours. Immigration affects parent-child roles in another way, particularly in families where the parents have low levels of education and job skills and speak little or no English. Often, these parents have to depend on their children as translators and brokers between home and the outside world, which typically diminishes parental authority.

A third challenge is the generation gap between parents and children, which is exacerbated by a cultural divide between the immigrant family and the larger society. There is a pronounced discrepancy in goal orientation—and views of the means of achieving goals—between immigrant parents and their U.S.-born or -raised children.

Most immigrants structure their lives primarily around three goals—as one Chinese immigrant put it, "to live in your own house, to be your own boss, and to send your children to the Ivy League." They try to acculturate or assimilate into American society, but only in ways that facilitate the attainment of these goals. The children, in contrast, want more. They aspire to be fully American. In the words of a U.S.-born high school student in Los Angeles's Chinatown, ". . . Looking cool, going to the ball games, eating hamburgers and french fries, taking family vacations, having fun . . . feeling free to do whatever you like rather than what your parents tell you to."

This cultural gap sets the parents and children apart and increases what are often already-strained parent-child relations. Children frequently view their immigrant parents as *lao-wan-gu* and consciously rebel against familial traditions. The parents, aside from juggling work and household responsibilities that devour most of their waking hours, are worried that their children have too much freedom, too little respect for authority, and too many unfavorable stimuli in school, on the street, and on the television screen at home. They are horrified when their children are openly disrespectful, for example, or aggressively disobey their orders. Intergenerational strains are further intensified because parents have difficulty communicating with their Americanized children. To make matters worse, the parents' customary ways of exercising authority or disciplining children—physical punishment by beating, for example—which were considered normative and acceptable in the old world, have suddenly become obsolete and even illegal, further eroding parental power in parent-child relations.

Immigrant children who arrive in the United States as teenagers have additional problems that affect relations with their parents. They have spent their formative years in a different society, were schooled in a different language, and were immersed in a different youth culture than that of the United States. In their homeland, they played a leading role in defining what was *in*, what was cool, and what was trendy, and many were average students in their schools. However, once in the United States, they find themselves standing out the wrong way, becoming the objects of mockery and ridicule and being referred to derogatively as "FOB" (fresh-off-boat) by their U.S.-born or raised coethnic peers. They also experience problems in school. Because of language difficulties, many are unable to express themselves and are misunderstood by their teachers and fellow students; they are often teased, mocked, or harassed by other students because of their different look, accent, and dress; and they worry that if they bring up these problems at home their parents will get upset or blame them. When their problems are unaddressed by schools or parents, the youth become discouraged. This discouragement is sometimes followed by loss of interest in school and plunging grades, and some eventually drop out and join gangs.

SENSITIVE PRESSURE POINTS

The generation gap between parents and children that I have described is particularly acute in Chinese immigrant families because Chinese cultural norms are so different from those that dominate in the United States and because Chinese parents are often afraid of losing their children to Americanization. Second-generation Chinese, born and raised in the United States, find themselves straddling two social-cultural worlds—Chinese and American—which is at the core of head-on intergenerational conflicts within the Chinese immigrant family. Lacking meaningful connections to their parents' countries of origin, they rarely consider the homeland as a point of reference and generally evaluate themselves against and adopt American standards and values.[8]

This is clearly different for immigrant parents who remain oriented to the homeland and, especially relevant here, to Chinese notions of filial piety. In the Chinese cultural context, filial piety is at the core of parent-child relationships. In its ideal form, the child's filial responsibility is the debt of life owed to parents; a child is expected to suppress his or her own self-interests to satisfy parental needs, whether or not these needs are appropriate or rational.[9] Related to filial piety is the notion of unconditional obedience, or submission, to authority—to the parent, the elder, and the superior. The parent is the authority in the home, as is the teacher in the school. The parent, often the father, is not supposed to show too much affection to his children, to play with them, or treat them as equals. This stone-faced, authoritative image often inhibits children from questioning, much less challenging, their parents. Furthermore, in the traditional Chinese family, there is little room for individualism. All family members are tied to one another, and every act of individual members is considered to bring honor or shame to the whole family. Thus, Chinese parents are expected to bring up their children in ways that honor the family.

Asymmetric filial piety, unconditional submission to authority, and face-saving override other familial values in the traditional Chinese family. Even though modernization has brought changes to the family in China, these traditional influences still loom large among Chinese immigrants. The problem is that in the American context, these practices and values are frowned upon, and children and parents are expected to be independent individuals on equal terms.

The immigrant Chinese family is often referred to by the children as a "pressure cooker," where intense intergenerational conflicts accumulate and sometimes boil to the point of explosion. Issues related to education, work ethic, consumption behavior, and dating, among others, are sensitive pressure points that can create potentially intense conflicts. For example, a young Chinese American who returned to college to complete her associate degree recalled:

> I never felt I was good enough to live up to my parents' expectations. So I fought them non-stop through high school. A war broke out when I got accepted into a few UC [University of California] schools but decided not to enroll in any one of them. I got kicked out of home. I moved in with my white boyfriend and started to work to support myself. I felt that the only way to get back at my parents was to make them feel ashamed. With a rebellious daughter, they had nothing to brag about and they lost the war. It may seem silly now, but at that time I really liked what I did.

Chinese parents who were raised in the Confucian tradition tend to be particularly demanding and unyielding about their children's educational achievement. While education is generally considered a primary means to upward social mobility in all American families, it is emphasized in some unique ways in the immigrant Chinese family. First and foremost, the children's success in school is tied to face-saving for the family. Parents consistently remind their children that achievement is a duty and an obligation to the family goal, and that if they fail they will bring shame to the family. Not surprisingly, children are under tremendous pressure to succeed.

Immigrant parents also have a pragmatic view of education. They see education as not only the most effective means to achieve success in society but also the *only* means. The parents are keenly aware of their own limitations as immigrants and the structural constraints blocking their own mobility—for example, limited family wealth even among middle-income immigrants, lack of access to social networks connecting them to the mainstream economy and various social and political institutions, and entry barriers to certain occupations because of racial stereotyping and discrimination. Their own experience tells them that a good education in certain fields will allow their children to get good jobs in the future. These fields include science, math, engineering, medicine, and, to a lesser extent, business and law. Parents are more concerned with their children's academic coursework, grades, and majors in these preferred fields than with a well-rounded learning experience and extracurricular activities. They actively discourage their children from pursuing interests in history, literature, music, dance, sports, or any subject that they consider unlikely to lead to well-paid, stable jobs. Involvement in these academic fields and extracurricular activities is only encouraged to the extent that it will improve their children's chances of getting into an Ivy League college. The children are often frustrated—sometimes deeply resentful—that their parents choose the type of education they are to pursue and make decisions for their future. At college, many Chinese American students pursue double majors, one in science or engineering for their parents and the other in history, literature, or Asian American studies for themselves.

Another sensitive issue is the work ethic. Immigrant Chinese parents believe that hard work, rather than natural ability or innate intelligence, is the key to educational success. Regardless of socioeconomic background, they tend to think that their children can get A's on all their exams if they just work hard, and if the children get lower grades they will be scolded for not working hard enough. The parents also believe that by working twice as hard it is possible to overcome structural disadvantages associated with immigrant and/or racial minority status. They tend to ignore the fact that not everybody learns English, catches up with school work, and establishes productive relationships with teachers and fellow students at the same rate. As a result, the children often find themselves working at least twice as hard as their American peers and simultaneously feeling that their parents never think that they work hard enough.

A third sensitive issue is related to the value of thrift.[10] Immigrant Chinese parents emphasize savings as a means of effectively deploying available family resources. They often bluntly reject their children's desire for material possessions and view spending money on name-brand clothes, stylish accessories, and fashionable hairstyles as a sign of corruption, or as becoming "too American." At the same time, these parents seldom hesitate to spend money on whatever they consider good for their children, such as books and computer software, after-school programs, Chinese lessons, private tutors, private lessons on the violin or the piano, and other education-oriented activities.

The fourth sensitive issue is dating, particularly at an early age. Chinese parents, especially newer arrivals, consider dating in high school not only a wasteful distraction from academics, but also a sign of unhealthy, promiscuous behavior, especially for girls.

They are concerned about the potential risks of unwanted pregnancy—and that this will interfere with their daughters' educational progress. Over time, parents' attitudes toward dating in high school may grow more ambivalent, and it may be interracial dating, rather than early dating in general, that "freaks them out."

These sensitive pressure points have become the sources of parent-child conflicts as the children rapidly acculturate into American ways, and as parents, in a position of authority, insist on their values and practices. These conflicts seem to be especially severe in the case of working-class Chinese immigrant parents, who are unusually demanding and unbending when it comes to their children's education and behavioral standards because they lack the time, patience, cultural sensitivity, and financial and human capital to be more compromising. Middle-class Chinese immigrant parents are also demanding and have high expectations for their children. But owing to their higher socioeconomic status and higher level of acculturation, they consciously try to be more like American parents in some ways. Some middle-class parents develop a sense of guilt for not being like American parents and become more easygoing and less strict with their children. For example, when a child refuses to do schoolwork on weekends as the father demands, and talks back by saying that "nobody works on weekends," a middle-class suburban Chinese immigrant father might simply shrug and let his child run off with his friends, because he himself doesn't have to work on weekends. A working-class Chinese immigrant father is more likely to get angry and make the child feel guilty about his own sacrifice, since he has to work on weekends to support the family.

ETHNIC NETWORKS AND INSTITUTIONS AS SOURCES OF CONCILIATION AND MEDIATING GROUNDS

Tremendous parental pressures to achieve and behave in the Chinese way can lead children to rebellious behavior, withdrawal from school, and alienation from ethnic networks. Alienated children fall easy prey to street gangs. Even those children who do well in school and hope to make their parents proud are at risk for rebellious and disrespectful behavior and for flouting their parents' rules and regulations. A high school student said, "But that [doing well to make parents happy] never happens. My mother is never satisfied no matter what you do and how well you do it." This remark echoes a frustration felt by many other Chinatown youths, who are torn between wanting to please their parents and succeed educationally, but who feel overwhelmed and constrained by parental pressures, rules, and orders. Tensions in the home may seethe beneath the surface—often to a point that parents and children feel they have no room to breathe.

Yet despite these intense pressures, and the strains between the children and their parents, there is rarely an all-out war between them. And despite severe bicultural conflicts—and the challenges that American popular culture poses to Chinese immigrant parents' values—many Chinese immigrant children, whatever their socioeconomic background, seem to live up to their parents' expectations. Involvement in the Chinese ethnic community is critical in explaining why this is so.

Most remarkable is the educational success of Chinese immigrant children, who significantly outperform other Americans, including non-Hispanic whites. They score exceptionally well on standardized tests and are overrepresented in the nation's elite universities as well as in the top lists of many national or regional academic competitions. They have appeared repeatedly in the top-ten award winners' list of the Westinghouse Science Talent Search, now renamed the Intel Science Talent Search, one of the country's most prestigious high school academic prizes. At the University of California, Los Angeles, where I teach, the proportion of Chinese Americans in the entering class in the past few years has been 18 percent higher than that of blacks and Latinos combined.

Is the extraordinary educational achievement of Chinese Americans a result of the parental pressure for success and enforcement of Confucian values? There is no simple answer. A more appropriate question is: How is it possible for parents in the Chinese immigrant family, plagued with intergenerational strains, to exercise authority and enforce Confucian values on education? Why do children end up doing what their parents expect them to do? My research in the Chinese immigrant community points to the important role of an ethnic institutional environment and multiple ethnic involvements.

In Chinatowns or Chinese ethnoburbs, an ethnic enclave economy and a range of ethnic social and cultural institutions have developed to support the daily needs of Chinese immigrants. As the community changed from a bachelor society to a family community, traditional ethnic institutions also shifted their functions to serve families and children. Among the programs they offer are weekend Chinese schools and a variety of educational and recreational enterprises, such as daily afterschool classes that match formal school curricula, academic tutoring and English enhancement classes, "exam-cram" schools, college prep schools, and music/dance/sports studios.

Consider the Chinese language school. In New York City, the Chinese Language School (*Zhongwen xuexiao*), run by the Chinese Consolidated Benevolent Association (CCBA), is perhaps the largest children- and youth-oriented organization in the nation's Chinatowns.[11] The school enrolls about four thousand Chinese children annually (not including summer), from pre-school to twelfth grade, in its 137 Chinese language classes and other specialty classes (including band, choir, piano, cello, violin, T'ai chi, ikebana, dancing, and Chinese painting). The Chinese language classes run from 3:00 to 6:30 p.m. daily after regular school hours. Students usually spend one hour on regular school homework and two hours on Chinese language or other selected specialties. The school also has English classes for immigrant youths and adult immigrant workers.

As Chinese immigrants have become dispersed residentially, Chinese language schools have also sprung up in the suburbs. As of the mid-1990s, there were approximately 635 Chinese language schools in the United States (with 189 in California alone), enrolling nearly 83,000 students.[12] The Chinese language school provides an ethnically affirming experience for most Chinese immigrant children. In response to the question, "What makes you Chinese?" many Chinese students say that it is "going to Chinese school." In Chinese language school, Chinese immigrant children come to understand that their own problems with their parents are common in

Chinese families and that their parents are simply acting like other Chinese parents. They come to terms with the fact that growing up in Chinese families is different. As Betty Lee Sung observes:

> For Chinese immigrant children who live in New York's Chinatown or in satellite Chinatowns, these [bi-cultural] conflicts are moderated to a large degree because there are other Chinese children around to mitigate the dilemmas that they encounter. When they are among their own, the Chinese ways are better known and better accepted. The Chinese customs and traditions are not denigrated to the degree that they would be if the immigrant child were the only one to face the conflict on his or her own.[13]

Ethnic institutions also allow the children to develop strategies to cope with parental constraints. For example, a girl can tell her parents that she is going out with someone at the Chinese school whom her parents know, while she actually goes to a movie with her white boyfriend. Her friends at the Chinese school will provide cover for her, confirming her story when her parents check. Chinese parents usually trust their children's friends from Chinese schools because they know the parents of the Chinese school friends.

The Chinese schools and various after-school programs not only ensure that the children spend time on homework or other constructive activities, they also help to keep children off the streets and reduce the anxieties and worries of working parents. More important, these ethnic institutions offer some space where children can share their feelings. A Chinese school teacher said, "It is very important to allow youths to express themselves in their own terms without parental pressures. Chinese parents usually have very high expectations of their children. When children find it difficult to meet these expectations and do not have an outlet for their frustration and anxiety, they tend to become alienated and lost on the streets."

Ethnic institutions also serve as a bridge between a seemingly closed immigrant community and the mainstream society. Immigrant parents and the children who live in ethnic enclaves or ethnoburbs are relatively isolated and their daily exposure to the larger American society is limited. Many parents, usually busy working, expect their children to do well in school and have successful careers in the future, but are unable to give specific directions to guide their children's educational and career plans, leaving a gap between high expectations and feasible means of meeting them. Ethnic institutions fill this gap by helping young people to become better aware of their choices and to find realistic means of moving up socioeconomically in mainstream society. After-school programs, tutor services, and test preparation programs are readily available in the ethnic community, making school after school an accepted norm. An educator said, "When you think of how much time these Chinese kids put in their studies after regular school, you won't be surprised why they succeed at such a high rate."

At the same time, ethnic institutions function as cultural centers, where Chinese traditional values and a sense of ethnic identity are nurtured. Students who participate in the after-school programs, especially those born and raised in the United States, often speak English to one another in their Chinese classes, but they learn a limited number of Chinese words each day. In the after-school programs, they are able to relate to

Chinese "stuff" without being teased as they might be in school. They listen to stories and sing songs in Chinese, which reveal different aspects of Chinese history and culture. Children and youths learn to write in Chinese such phrases as "I am Chinese" and "My home country is in China" and to recite classical Chinese poems and Confucian sayings about family values, behavioral and moral guidelines, and the importance of schooling. A Chinese school principal made it clear that "these kids are here because their parents sent them. They are usually not very motivated to learn Chinese per se, and we do not push them too hard. Language teaching is only part of our mission. An essential part of our mission is to enlighten these kids about their own cultural heritage, so that they show respect for their parents and feel proud of being Chinese."

Despite differences in origin, socioeconomic backgrounds, and geographic dispersion, Chinese immigrants have many opportunities to interact with one another as they participate in the ethnic community in multiple ways. Working, shopping, and socializing in the community tie immigrants to a closely knit system of ethnic social relations. Social networks, embedded in the broader Chinese immigrant community, reinforce norms and standards and operate as a means of control over those who are connected to them. Especially pertinent here is that involvement in different types of ethnic institutions also helps children to cope with—and indeed has the effect of alleviating—parental pressure.

CONCLUSION

A complex and often contradictory set of forces affect parents and children in Chinese immigrant families and their relations with each other. Many Chinese immigrant parents expect the children to attain the highest levels of achievement possible and rely on them to move the family into middle-class status as a way to repay parental sacrifices and to honor the family name. Deviation from these cultural values, standards, and expectations is considered shameful or "losing face" and is strongly criticized, indeed censured, by the family and the ethnic community. Still, parents have trouble enforcing these values and behavioral standards—and guaranteeing that familial expectations are met. Both parents and children struggle constantly to negotiate cultural differences, make compromises, and resolve conflicts in order to navigate the "right" way into mainstream American society.

This undertaking is by no means limited to the family arena, nor is it simply a matter of having the right cultural values. As I have emphasized, Chinese immigrant families cannot be viewed in isolation. Many are intricately and closely connected to broader networks in the wider ethnic community. Ethnic educational institutions and children-oriented programs, as I have shown, not only provide tangible resources in the form, for example, of educational training, but also serve as effective mechanisms of social control, thereby reinforcing parental values. At the same time, they give young people a socially accepted place to develop their own coping strategies as well as social relationships with peers experiencing the same dilemmas at home. One of the many factors that set parachute kids apart is their lack of access to these kinds of support and control because they are less connected to the ethnic community than young people in immigrant families. It is also important to stress that the mobilization of educational resources in the immigrant family and community is heavily affected by immigration selectivity, in that those with education, professional skills, and money comprise a significant proportion of the Chinese migrant inflow.

The children of Chinese immigrants are motivated to learn and do well in school because they believe that education is the most effective route for them to do better than their parents—and also a way to free themselves from their parents' control. Whatever the children's motivation, parental pressure—which is supported and strengthened through participation in the ethnic community—reinforces educational goals and often leads to positive outcomes. A community youth program organizer put it this way: "Well, tremendous pressures create problems for sure. However, you've got to realize that we are not living in an ideal environment. Without these pressures, you would probably see as much adolescent rebellion in the family, but a much *larger* proportion of kids failing. Our goal is to get these kids out into college, and for that, we have been very successful."

While intense parent-child and community pressure pushes children to work hard to succeed, there are limits to its effectiveness. Beyond high school, the social capital available in the Chinese-American community is not sufficient to help children choose appropriate academic and career paths. When applying to college, many children of Chinese immigrants are forced by parents to choose institutions close to home, which can limit chances for significant social mobility. At college, the children tend to concentrate in science and engineering because their families want them to and their friends are doing it—even if this is something they are not interested or lack talent in. After graduation from college, they often lack the type of networks that facilitate job placement and occupational mobility.

A whole series of additional issues arise as the children of Chinese immigrants enter adulthood. What will their relationships with their parents be like then? Will the children be grateful to parents for pushing them to succeed? Will sources of conflict prominent in adolescence be less acute in adulthood? Will there be new sources of tension, for example, disagreements with parents over family finances, marriage, and childbearing or child-rearing methods? In the case of the parachute kids, if they stay in the United States and their parents remain in the homeland, will the children become even more emotionally distant from parents—or will some return to their homeland and reestablish close bonds with parents? These are among the many questions that deserve further research.

Notes

1. This chapter draws on my previously published work; see Zhou 1997; 1998; 2006.
2. Foner 1999; Mahalingam 2006.
3. USDHS 2006.
4. Estimated from the Current Population Survey (CPS) data 1998–2000. See Logan et al. 2001.
5. Compared to 8 percent under age eighteen and 8 percent between ages eighteen and twenty-four in the first generation.
6. U.S. Census Bureau 2007.

7. "Ethnoburb" is a term developed by Wei Li (1997) to refer to suburban ethnic clustering of diverse groups with no single racial ethnic group dominating. Los Angeles's Monterey Park is a typical ethnoburb.
8. Gans 1992; Portes and Zhou 1993; Zhou 1997.
9. Yeh and Bedford 2003.
10. Sung 1987.
11. The Chinese Consolidated Benevolent Association (CCBA) is a quasi-government in Chinatown. It used to be an apex group representing some sixty different family and district associations, guilds, tongs, the Chamber of Commerce, and the Nationalist Party, and it has remained the most influential ethnic organization in the Chinese immigrant community.
12. Chao 1996.
13. Sung 1987: 126.

References

Chao, Teresa Hsu. 1996. "Overview." Pp. 7–13 in Xueying Wang (ed.), *A View from Within: A Case Study of Chinese Heritage Community Language Schools in the United States.* Washington, DC: The National Foreign Language Center.

Foner, Nancy. 1999. "The Immigrant Family: Cultural Legacies and Cultural Changes." Pp. 257–74 in C. Hirschman, P. Kasinitz and J. DeWind (eds.), *The Handbook of International Migration: The American Experience.* New York: Russell Sage Foundation.

Gans, Herbert J. 1992. "Second-Generation Decline: Scenarios for the Economic and Ethnic Futures of the Post-1965 American Immigrants." *Ethnic and Racial Studies* 15 (2): 173–92.

Li, Wei. 1997. "Spatial Transformation of an Urban Ethnic Community from Chinatown to Chinese Ethnoburb in Los Angeles." Ph.D. Dissertation, Department of Geography. University of Southern California.

Logan, John R., with Jacob Stowell and Elena Vesselinov. 2001. "From Many Shores: Asians in Census 2000." A report by the Lewis Mumford Center for Comparative Urban and Regional Research, State University of New York at Albany, accessed on October 6, 2001, at http://mumford1.dyndns.org/cen2000/report.html.

Mahalingam, Ram (ed.). 2006. *Cultural Psychology of Immigrants.* Mahwah, NJ: Lawrence Erlbaum.

Portes, Alejandro, and Min Zhou. 1993. "The New Second Generation: Segmented Assimilation and Its Variants." *Annals of the American Academy of Political and Social Science* 530 (November): 74–96.

Sung, Betty Lee. 1987. *The Adjustment Experience of Chinese Immigrant Children in New York City.* New York: Center for Migration Studies.

U.S. Census Bureau. 2007. *The American Community, Asians: 2004.* American Community Survey Reports (acs-05), accessed on September 6, 2007, at http://www.census.gov/prod/2007pubs/acs-05.pdf.

U.S. Department of Homeland Security (USDHS). 2006. *Yearbook of Immigration Statistics, 2006.* Accessed on October 9, 2007, at http://www.dhs.gov/ximgtn/statistics/publications/LPR06.shtm.

Wang, Xueying (ed.). 1996. *A View from Within: A Case Study of Chinese Heritage Community Language Schools in the United States.* Washington, DC: The National Foreign Language Center.

Yeh, Kuang-Hui, and Olwen Bedford. 2003. "Filial Piety and Parent-Child Conflict." Paper presented at the International Conference on Intergenerational Relations in Families' Life Course, co-sponsored by the Institute of Sociology, Academie Sinica, Taiwan, and the Committee on Family Research, International Sociological Association, March 12–14, Taipei.

Zhou, Min. 1992. *Chinatown: The Socioeconomic Potential of an Urban Enclave.* Philadelphia: Temple University Press.

———. 1997. "Social Capital in Chinatown: the Role of Community-Based Organizations and Families in the Adaptation of the Younger Generation." Pp. 181–206 in Lois Weis and Maxine S. Seller (eds.), *Beyond Black and White: New Faces and Voices in U.S. Schools.* Albany, NY: State University of New York Press.

———. 1998. "'Parachute Kids' in Southern California: The Educational Experience of Chinese Children in Transnational Families." *Educational Policy* 12 (6): 682–704.

———. 2006. "Negotiating Culture and Ethnicity: Intergenerational Relations in Chinese Immigrant Families in the United States." Pp. 315–36 in Ram Mahalingam, ed., *Cultural Psychology of Immigrants*. Mahwah, NJ: Lawrence Erlbaum.

Zhou, Min, and Xiyuan Li. 2003. "Ethnic Language Schools and the Development of Supplementary Education in the Immigrant Chinese Community in the United States." Pp. 57–73 in Carola Suarez-Orozco and Irina L.G. Todorova (eds.), *New Directions for Youth Development: Understanding the Social Worlds of Immigrant Youth*. San Francisco: Jossey-Bass.

READING 34

Cultural Diversity and Aging Families

Rona J. Karasik and Raeann R. Hamon

> It is not by the gray of the hair that one knows the age of the heart.
>
> —*Edward G. Bulwer-Lytton*

In thinking about aging and older families, it is important to consider that aging is not a single experience. Many equate aging with the physiological changes our bodies go through over time. Some focus on diseases that, while not age related, are often thought to be associated with old age. Aging, however, is much more than the accumulation of wrinkles, gray hair, and the possibility of one or more chronic health conditions. Aging is also about how we view people (including ourselves) based on how we look and act and even by the number of candles on our birthday cakes. Aging is also about relationships—how they are sustained, how they change, and how new relationships are formed.

We have many stereotypes about aging and older persons. While our expectations are often negative, in reality, there are both positive and negative aspects to aging. The way in which we age is affected by a wide range of personal and social factors. Older persons are a highly heterogeneous group, and the family relationships of older persons are highly diverse as well. This chapter will focus on how culture and ethnicity interplay with a variety of factors to affect aging and older families.

WHY FOCUS ON CULTURAL DIVERSITY IN OLDER FAMILIES?

> We do not grow absolutely, chronologically. We grow sometimes in one dimension, and not in another, unevenly. We grow partially. We are relative. We are mature in one realm, childish in another. The past, present, and future mingle and pull us backward, forward, or fix us in the present.
>
> —*Anaïs Nin*

There are many reasons to try to understand the diverse impact of aging on families. First and foremost is the size and ongoing growth of the older population in the United States. In 2002, 35.6 million persons (12.3 percent of the U.S. population) were aged 65 and older (Administration on Aging, 2003). By 2030, the older population is expected to grow to 20 percent of the U.S. population—roughly 71.5 million persons will be aged 65 and older. Not surprisingly, the U.S. older population is not just growing in size but in ethnic diversity as well. In 2000, 17.2 percent of adults 65 and older in the United States reported being ethnic minorities. African American elders made up the largest ethnic minority elder group (8.1 percent), followed by 2.7 percent identifying as Asian or Pacific Islanders, and less than 1 percent identifying themselves as American Indian or Alaskan Native. Older persons identifying themselves as Hispanic (who may be of any race) composed 5.5 percent of the population, and 0.5 percent of older adults indicated being of two or more races. By 2030, the proportion of ethnic minority elders is expected to grow to 26.4 percent of the older population (Administration on Aging, 2003).

While these demographics clearly reflect a rapidly growing and increasingly diverse older population, numbers do not tell the whole story. Diversity within each racial and ethnic group is considerable. Most data on race and ethnicity, however, are reported in the overly broad categories of White, Black, American Indian/Alaskan Native, Asian or Pacific Islander, and Hispanic (U.S. Bureau of the Census, 2002). Moreover, while the census requests write-in information on a "person's ancestry or ethnic origin," rarely are these data included in descriptions of the aging population. As such, we know very little about how culture and ethnicity affect the aging experiences of many groups in the United States.

Salari (2002), for example, notes the invisibility in aging research of the diverse groups in the United States who have Middle Eastern origins as well as of those who practice Islam. For many groups, religion is a vital concern in how we understand the impact of cultural diversity on aging. Thus, a second reason to explore the cultural diversity of the older population is to understand how factors of culture, ethnicity, and race interplay with the other factors that make aging unique—including religion (Salari, 2002), gender (Conway-Turner, 1999), sexual orientation (Cooney & Dunne, 2001; Orel, 2004), health (Diwan & Jonnalagadda, 2001; Johnson & Smith, 2002; Li & Fries, 2005; Zhan & Chen, 2004), socioeconomic status (Angel, 2003), family relationships (Shawler, 2004), social support (Johnson & Tripp-Reimer, 2001; Jordan-Marsh & Harden, 2005), geographic location (Applewhite & Torres, 2003; Barusch & TenBarge, 2003; Himes, Hogan, & Eggebeen, 1996), and life experiences (Moriarty & Butt, 2004). None of these factors alone makes a person or family. Rather, all are important for us to understand who our older population is and what their increasing numbers will mean.

Finally, considerations for how best to meet the needs of this rapidly growing and changing population are a third reason for exploring the impact of cultural diversity. Many call attention to the need for *cultural competence—a* system that provides appropriate, effective, high-quality services for all persons regardless of racial or ethnic background (Geron, 2002). Defining what constitutes cultural competence and how we can achieve it, however, can be challenging and perhaps a bit overwhelming. Capitman

(2002), therefore, suggests starting with *cultural humility*, where we begin by "acknowledging what we do not know about each other as individuals and members of multiple cultural groups" (p. 12). Such an approach, however, still requires working not only toward understanding the needs of all older adults, but also toward the improved provision of culturally appropriate services. Saying we know little about a group is not enough. We must continuously seek to learn more about the diverse experiences, strengths, and needs of older adults and their families.

THEORETICAL APPROACHES TO UNDERSTANDING CULTURAL DIVERSITY AND AGING FAMILIES

It is theory that decides what can be observed.

—*Albert Einstein*

In selecting a framework to examine cultural diversity in older families, we must be sensitive to how our own expectations and biases affect not only the questions we ask but also the way in which we interpret the responses. Currently, much of the research on diversity in aging takes a preliminary, primarily descriptive approach (e.g., "what?" "who?" and "how many?"). Several studies, however, have taken the next step of grounding their research into a particular theoretical framework.

Many theories focus on the problems experienced by culturally diverse aging families. Sands and Goldberg-Glen (2000), for example, employ stress theory to explore factors that affect levels of stress experienced by grandparents who serve as parents to their grandchildren. Not surprisingly, research conducted under such an approach can result in lists of problems to be "fixed" by programs, services, and more research.

Other studies employ broader theoretical frameworks, such as the life course perspective, where the focus is on age norms and the timing of life transitions (Hagestad & Neugarten, 1985). From this perspective, family life transitions (e.g., marriage, widowhood, grandparenthood) are placed into social and historical context (e.g., as "on-time" or "off-time"). Individual life experiences and their outcomes are then interpreted with regard to the impact of such timing. Some recent studies using this framework have expanded the perspective to include how factors such as race and ethnicity affect the timing and interpretation of such experiences (Burton, 1996).

While also considering changes over the life span, selectivity theory focuses on the evolving function of social interaction and emotional closeness within relationships. Carstensen (2001) suggests that older persons become more selective in their choice of social partners, often directing their attention to, and thus placing more importance on, relationships with available close family and friends. Such an approach may be seen as an adaptive way to deal with shrinking social networks.

Also seeking to focus on positive adaptation, some frame their research in terms of the shared strengths and challenges certain social and historical circumstances bring about. Conway-Turner (1999) uses a feminist perspective to examine the lives of older women of color. Her approach is grounded in the notion that while women of color may come from very different backgrounds, they share experiences of discrimination based on race, ethnicity, gender, and age. Conway-Turner's approach also calls for exploring the cumulative effects of these variables as they both positively and negatively interact with the later-life and family experiences of women of color.

More recently, Pillemer and Lüscher (2004) suggest that "societies, and the individuals within them, are characteristically ambivalent about relationships between parents and children in adulthood" (p. 6). They propose an ambivalence framework "for studying dilemmas and contradictions in late-life families" in an empirical and systematic fashion, both at the sociological and psychological levels. Though it has not yet been explicitly applied to family relationships among ethnically or culturally diverse families, Boss and Kaplan (2004) assert that "the ambiguous loss of a parent with dementia provides fertile ground for increased ambivalence in intergenerational relations" (p. 207), making the model particularly relevant. So, too, ambivalence is a useful construct when considering adult children's filial role or sense of responsibility for the well-being of their aging parents (Lang, 2004).

Finally, Gibson's work (2005) is one of a handful of studies looking at aging families from an Afrocentric perspective. Such an approach "focuses on traditional African philosophical assumptions, which emphasize holistic, interdependent, and spiritual conceptions of people and their environment" and "focuses on family strengths within the culture of people of African descent" (p. 293). Thus, in contrast to a life course perspective that might view the event of grandparents parenting their grandchildren as "off-time," or stress theory, which might look at the negative impact parenting duties have on grandparents (Sands & Goldberg-Glen, 2000), Gibson looks at the positive aspects gained from this "grand-parenting" role and focuses, instead, on ways to strengthen the existing grandparent-as-parent relationships. Similarly, Minkler and Fuller-Thomson (2005) emphasize the value of "theories of intersectionality" or those that stress the connection of class, race, and gender (p. S82), particularly when examining later-life family topics like care provided by grandparents in African American communities.

Each of the above theoretical frameworks has a place in helping us to understand the experiences of culturally diverse older families. Certainly, aging families face many challenges as well as possess unique strengths. These theoretical approaches help to place the current research findings into context as well guide new research questions.

RESEARCH ON DIVERSITY IN LATER-LIFE FAMILIES

> We have become not a melting pot but a beautiful mosaic. Different people, different beliefs, different yearnings, different hopes, different dreams.
>
> —*Jimmy Carter*

Despite the rather large but separate bodies of research on aging families (Allen, Blieszner, & Roberto, 2000; Walker, Manoogian-O'Dell, McGraw, & White, 2001) and diversity in older populations (Capitman, 2002; Harris, 1998) there has been only limited research focusing on the intersections of race, ethnicity, and cultural background in aging families. Thus, much of the research presented here was not specifically designed to address culturally diverse aging families.

Additionally, in examining this research, it is important to recognize that culture and ethnicity do not operate in a vacuum. Time, history, immigration (Wilmoth, 2001), acculturation (Silverstein & Chen, 1999), and societal pressure continuously make and remake culture's role. For example, while Harris (1998) notes that the traditions of many groups (e.g., African American, Asian, Hispanic, Native American) focus on collectivity and interdependence—placing the needs of the family above the needs of the individual—changing societal influences have altered the meaning and outcome of these traditions. Whereas elders in such families might expect to hold central roles (e.g., teacher, guide, tradition bearer), many find themselves in conflict with current societal pressure to focus on youth and individualism. Many also face the paradox of wanting their children and grandchildren to become fully assimilated into the dominant culture and to have a better life than they did, while still adhering to their cultural traditions as well (Patterson, 2003). The goal of this section, therefore, is to highlight areas where culture, ethnicity, and aging families intersect, while also considering how such influences continue to change in today's society.

PARTNERSHIPS IN LATER LIFE

> Newlyweds become oldyweds, and oldyweds are the reasons that families work.
>
> —*Author unknown*

Despite media images of lonely older adults, over half of adults age 65 and over are married. There are, however, significant discrepancies in marital status between men and women. Older women, who outnumber older men by a ratio of 141:100, are much less likely to be married than older men. In fact, in 2002, 73 percent of older men and only 41 percent of older women were currently married (Administration on Aging, 2003). These gender disparities also hold true when looking across broad racial and ethnic categories. While older White males were more likely to be married (74.3 percent) than older Hispanic males (67.5 percent) and older Black males (53.9 percent), males in general were still more likely to be married than females. As such, 42.9 percent of White older women, 38 percent of Hispanic older women, and 25 percent of older Black women were currently married (U.S. Bureau of the Census, 2002).

Conversely, older women (46 percent) were over four times as likely to be widowed as older men (14 percent) (Administration on Aging, 2003). With regard to race and ethnicity, older Black women (54.6 percent) were the most likely to be widowed, followed by White older women (44.4 percent) and Hispanic older women (39.4 percent). Similarly, older Black men (21 percent) were more likely to be widowed than older Hispanic men (15 percent) and older White men (13.9 percent) (U.S. Bureau of the Census, 2002).

Some of the gender difference in marital status has been attributed to the discrepancy in overall numbers and life expectancy between men and women, with women living an average of six years longer than men (Administration on Aging, 2003; Arias,

2004). Life expectancy differences, however, are not the only factor here. Social and cultural expectations about marriage and remarriage, which can vary among different groups, have also been cited in the higher rates of continued widowhood for women. The pool of socially acceptable potential mates for widowed women (their age and older) continues to diminish, while the pool for men (their age and younger) is potentially endless. Social norms about race and acceptable marriage partners may also contribute to this disparity (Pienta, Hayward, & Jenkins, 2000), as well as pervasive media images of older women as unattractive and men as ageless. Regardless of the cause, women of all ethnic groups are much more likely to live alone in later life than men (Administration on Aging, 2003; Himes et al., 1996). Furthermore, older women living alone, particularly older Hispanic women, have the highest rates of poverty among older adults (Administration on Aging, 2003). Factors of education and employment status, however, are also found to interact with marital status and ethnicity in regard to rates of income and poverty (Wilson & Hardy, 2002).

In addition to widowhood, divorce is another factor that places older women of all ethnic backgrounds at higher risk both of living alone and experiencing poverty. In 2002, approximately 10 percent of older persons were currently divorced, a rate that has almost doubled since 1980 (Administration on Aging, 2003). With regard to data on race and ethnicity, however, some gender differences appear, with the percentage of currently divorced older Hispanic women (11.1 percent) being somewhat higher than for older Hispanic men (8.4 percent) and older Black women (8.9 percent) and older Black men (8.4 percent). The number of currently divorced older White women (7.1 percent) was also slightly higher than for older White men (6.0 percent) (U.S. Bureau of the Census, 2002).

Finally, an often overlooked area is the highly diverse group of older adults who have remained ever-single (Cooney & Dunne, 2001), accounting for about 4 percent of older men and 4 percent of older women (Administration on Aging, 2003). Older Black men (9.1 percent) were the most likely group not to marry, followed by older Black women (5.9 percent) and older Hispanic women (5.6 percent). An equal percentage of older White men (3.8 percent) and older Hispanic men (3.8 percent) remained ever-single, while older White women (3.5 percent) were the least likely to never marry. Currently, few studies focus on older ever-singles—and even fewer, if any, focus on culture and ethnicity in older ever-singles. The reasons why a person might remain single, however, and also in who we as a society label as single, are important factors in later-life experiences. Careers, lack of opportunity, and relatively high percentage of Latinos who live in informal unions; these individuals may not appear in demographic studies as married. Similarly, some stay single because marriage is not a legal option, not because they are not involved in a partnership. While growing attention is being given to gay and lesbian partnerships in later life (Grossman, D'Augelli, & Hershberger, 2000; Orel, 2004), few studies focus specifically on issues of culture and ethnicity (McFarland & Sanders, 2003).

Beyond the above demographic descriptions, research directed specifically at the intersections of race, culture, ethnicity, and later-life family partnerships is limited. Pienta et al. (2000) looked at the effects of marriage on health for White, African American, and Latino adults and found that married older adults had better health than widowed and divorced persons, although these findings were less distinct for Whites than for persons of color. Kitson (2000) found similarly complex outcomes looking at how widows adjust to the death of their spouses, with age, race, and cause of death interacting. Of note is that Black widows of spouses who died of suicide expressed more distress than similar White widows, suggesting a greater stigma against suicide among Blacks.

SIBLINGS IN LATER LIFE

> To the outside world we all grow old. But not to brothers and sisters. We know each other as we always were.
>
> —*Clara Ortega*

The sibling relationship is typically one of the longest lasting of all family relationships, with most current older adults having at least one living sibling—something that may change as smaller families become the norm. Later-life sibling relationships tend to decrease in intensity and contact during the childbearing and rearing years, followed by increased contact in the later years (Goetting, 1986). Studies suggest gender, geographic proximity, and individual differences mediate the amount and type of contact siblings have in later life (Connidis & Campbell, 2001). Campbell, Connidis, and Davies (1999) discovered the centrality of the confidant role as well as emotional and instrumental support among siblings; companionship is a less critical function for siblings. So, too, they found that single, childless, and widowed women tend to have greater involvement with their siblings. Gold (1990) found that race also had an impact on later sibling relationships, finding that Black sibling dyads tended to be more positive than White sibling dyads. Other findings that include culture and race, however, are somewhat mixed. For example, many studies find that sister-sister ties hold the strongest bonds (Connidis & Campbell, 2001). John (1991), however, found ties between brothers to be stronger in his study of siblings in the Prairie Band Potawatomi, a Native American tribe.

While few studies focus directly on the impact of culture and ethnicity on later-life sibling relationships, several studies on the social support networks of culturally diverse older adults also find that siblings play an important role. Becker, Beyene, Newsom, and Mayen (2003) found that siblings were an important part of mutual support networks for older African Americans, Latinos, and Filipino Americans. Similarly, Johnson (1999) found strong bonds between older Black men and their siblings. Williams (2001), on the other hand, found that the impoverished older Mexican American men in her sample had little interaction with their extended families, including their siblings.

GRANDPARENTHOOD

> Grandchildren are the dots that connect the lines from generation to generation.
>
> —*Lois Wyse*

While there have always been some who have lived long enough to become grandparents, the evolution of grandparenthood is fairly new. Today's ever-increasing life expectancies have created unprecedented numbers of three-, four-, and even five-generation families. Szinovacz (1998) calls grandparenthood a "near universal experience" (pp. 48–49), with most older adults having an average of five to six grandchildren. Szinovacz also notes, however, that "about 15 percent of Black and Hispanic men report that they are not grandparents" (p. 49). In suggesting that some of these men may be unaware of their grandparent status due to loss of contact with their families (via immigration, divorce, and other means), Szinovacz raises two important concerns.

First, much of the data on grandparenthood is self-reported. Even the census, which recently added questions on the number of grandparents living with grandchildren, relies on measures of self-report (Simmons & Dye, 2003). A second concern is the question of who is a grandparent. Is grandparenthood solely a biological event, or must one acknowledge the bond for it to exist? Also, is a biological bond required? In some groups, the titles "mother" and "grandmother" are used as a sign of respect for all elder women or to designate fictive kin (Gibson, 2005; Jordan-Marsh & Harden, 2005) and is not necessarily reserved for blood kin.

Additionally, the roles grandparents play and their impacts on families are quite varied. Several factors can influence the shape grandparent roles may take, including gender, age, culture, and ethnicity (Bengtson, 1985; Fingerman, 2004). Cherlin and Furstenberg (1992) describe three grandparenting styles—remote, companionate, and involved. Remote relationships were characterized as largely symbolic, with little if any direct contact. Often geographic distance and/or divorce were factors in limiting the amount of grandparent-grandchild contact. Companionate grand-relationships tend to focus more on leisure activities and friendship, while involved grandparents took a more active role in their grandchildren's lives, often taking on a more parental role. Weibel-Orlando (2001) found similar grandparenting styles among Native American elders, adding two additional styles—*ceremonial grandparents*, who lived distant from their grandchildren but had frequent, culturally endowed contact, and *cultural conservator grandparents*, who actively sought contact and temporary coresidence with their grandchildren "for the expressed purpose of exposing them to the American Indian way of life" (p. 143).

In another study, Silverstein and Chen (1999) examined how acculturation, defined as "the erosion of traditional cultural language, values, and practices" (p. 196) affected the quality of the grandparent-grandchild relationship in Mexican American families. Using data from the study of three-generational Mexican American families, Silverstein and Chen found that gaps in cultural values between generations reduced the social interaction and intimacy of these Mexican American grandparents and grandchildren over time. While language barriers appeared to add to this gap, language was not the sole cause of the relationship distance. Of additional note is that while the grandchildren in this study reported a reduction in their grandparent-grandchild relationship, their grandparents did not.

Other research focuses on the small but growing trend involving coresidence among grandparents and grandchildren. The 2000 census found that 3.6 percent of adults (or 5.8 million people) were living with grandchildren under the age of 18 (Simmons & Dye, 2003). Some of these relationships may be characterized as coparenting (where the parent also lives with the grandparent and grandchild) and others (2.4

million, or 42 percent) were described as custodial grandparent caregivers. Census rates of coresidence, either as coparent or as caregiver, varied considerably by racial and ethnic category. Only 2 percent of non-Hispanic Whites reported coresiding with a grandchild, compared with 6 percent of Asian Americans, 8 percent of American Indian and Native Alaskans, 8 percent of people who are Black, 8 percent who are Hispanic, and 10 percent of Pacific Islanders (Simmons & Dye, 2003).

Several researchers have looked at the phenomenon of grandparents raising grandchildren (Erera, 2002). Fuller-Thomson, Minkler, and Driver (1997) note that while custodial grandparenting was not limited to any single group, a disproportionate number of single women, African Americans, recently bereaved parents, and persons with low income were found in this role. African American grandparent caregivers, especially grandmothers, were particularly vulnerable in that they experienced elevated rates of poverty and "were more likely than their noncaregiving peers to report functional limitations" (Minkler & Fuller-Thomson, 2005, p. S90). Examinations of the impact on grandparents providing care for grandchildren suggest that the role involves some level of stress (Musil, 1998), but that a variety of factors, including caregiving context and family support (Sands & Goldberg-Glen, 2000) as well as ethnicity (Goodman & Silverstein, 2002), moderate just how much stress caregiving grandparents experience.

Taking a somewhat different approach, Gibson (2005), focused on the positive impact parenting African American grandparents can have on their grandchildren and identified seven themes or potential strengths of such relationships, including maintaining effective communication, taking a strong role in their grandchildren's education, providing socioemotional support, involving the extended family, involving grandchildren in the community, working with the vulnerabilities of the grandchildren, and acknowledging the absence of the grandchildren's biological parent(s). Strom, Carter, and Schmidt (2004) and Strom, Heeder, and Strom (2005) similarly found that African American grandparents often take a strong role in their grandchildren's lives, particularly with regard to being a teacher and role model. These studies suggest that teaching is a strength of Black grandmothers, and that grandparents should be encouraged to help support the education of their grandchildren.

Taken together, these findings suggest that grandparenthood is an important yet highly variable aspect of later-life families. The range of variables, including cultural and ethnic diversity, that affect grandparent-hood suggest further research with broader samples from a variety of backgrounds is warranted (Fingerman, 2004; Hayslip & Kaminski, 2005).

References

Administration on Aging. (2003). *A profile of older Americans: 2003.* Washington, DC: U.S. Department of Health and Human Services.

Allen, K. R., Blieszner, R., & Roberto, K. A. (2000). Families in the middle and later years: A review and critique of research in the 1990s. *Journal of Marriage and the Family, 62*(4), 911–926.

Angel, J. L. (2003). Devolution and the social welfare of elderly immigrants: Who will bear the burden? *Public Administration Review, 63*(1), 79–89.

Applewhite, S. L., & Torres, C. (2003). Rural Latino elders. *Journal of Gerontological Social Work, 41*(1/2), 151–174.

Arias, E. (2004). United States life tables, 2002. *National Vital Statistics Reports, 53*(6), 1–39.
Barusch, A., & TenBarge, C. (2003). Indigenous elders in rural America. *Journal of Gerontological Social Work, 41*(1/2), 121–136.
Becker, G., Beyene, Y., Newsom, E., & Mayen, N. (2003). Creating continuity through mutual assistance: Intergenerational reciprocity in four ethnic groups. *Journal of Gerontology: Social Sciences, 58B*(3), S151–S159.
Bengtson, V. L. (1985). Diversity and symbolism in grandparental roles. In V. Bengtson & J. Robertson (Eds.), *Grandparenthood* (pp. 11–25). Beverly Hills, CA: Sage.
Boss, P., & Kaplan, L. (2004). Ambiguous loss and ambivalence when a parent has dementia. In K. Pillemer & K. Ldscher (Eds.), *Intergenerational ambivalences: New perspectives on parent-child relations in later life* (pp. 207–224). Amsterdam: Elsevier.
Burton, L. M. (1996). Age norms, the timing of family role transitions, and intergenerational caregiving among African American women. *The Gerontologist, 36*(2), 199–208.
Campbell, L. D., Connidis, I. A., & Davies, L. (1999). Sibling ties in later life: A social network analysis. *Journal of Family Issues, 20*(1), 114–148.
Capitman, J. (2002). Defining diversity: A primer and a review. *Generations, XXVI*(3), 8–14.
Carstensen, L. L. (2001). Selectivity theory: Social activity in life-span context. In A. Walker, M. Manoogian-O'Dell, L. McGraw, & D. White (Eds.), *Families in later life: Connections and transitions* (pp. 265–275). Thousand Oaks, CA: Pine Forge Press.
Cherlin, A., & Furstenberg, F. (1992). *The new American grandparent.* Cambridge, MA: Harvard University Press.
Connidis, I., & Campbell, L. (2001). Closeness, confiding, and contact among siblings in middle and late adulthood. In A. Walker, M. Manoogian-O'Dell, L. McGraw, & D. White (Eds.), *Families in later life: Connections and transitions* (pp. 149–155). Thousand Oaks, CA: Pine Forge Press.
Conway-Turner, K. (1999). Older women of color: A feminist exploration of the intersections of personal, familial and community life. *Journal of Women and Aging, 11*(2–3), 115–130.
Cooney, T. M., & Dunne, K. (2001). Intimate relationships in later life. *Journal of Family Issues, 22*(7), 838–858.
Diwan, S., & Jonnalagadda, S. S. (2001). Social integration and health among Asian Indian immigrants in the United States. *Journal of Gerontological Social Work, 36*(1/2), 45–62.
Erera, P. I. (2002). *Family diversity: Continuity and change in the contemporary family.* Thousand Oaks, CA: Sage.
Fingerman, K. L. (2004). The role of offspring and in-laws in grandparents' ties to their grandchildren. *Journal of Family Issues, 25*(8), 1026–1049.
Fuller-Thomson, E., Minkler, M., & Driver, D. (1997). A profile of grandparents raising grandchildren in the United States. *The Gerontologist, 37*(3), 406–411.
Geron, S. M. (2002). Cultural competency: How is it measured? Does it make a difference? *Generations, XXVI*(3), 39–45.
Gibson, P. A. (2005). Intergenerational parenting from the perspective of African American grandmothers. *Family Relations, 54*(2), 280–297.
Goetting, A. (1986). The developmental tasks of siblingship over the life cycle. *Journal of Marriage and the Family, 48*, 703–714.
Gold, D.T. (1990). Late-life sibling relationships: Does race affect typological distribution? *The Gerontologist, 30*(6), 741–748.
Goodman, C., & Silverstein, M. (2002). Grandmothers raising grandchildren: Family structure and well-being in culturally diverse families. *The Gerontologist, 42*(5), 676–689.
Grossman, A. H., D'Augelli, A. R., & Hershberger, S. L. (2000). Social support networks of lesbian, gay, and bisexual adults 60 years of age and older. *Journal of Gerontology: Psychological Sciences, 55B*, P171–P179.
Hagestad, G., & Neugarten, B. (1985). Age and the life course. In R. Binstock & E. Shanas (Eds.), *Handbook of aging and the social sciences* (2nd ed., pp. 35–61). New York: Van Nostrand Reinhold.
Harris, H. L. (1998). Ethnic minority elders: Issues and interventions. *Educational Gerontology, 24*(4), 309–323.
Hayslip, B., & Kaminski, P. L. (2005). Grandparents raising their grandchildren: A review of the literature and suggestions for practice. *The Gerontologist, 45*(2), 262–269.
Himes, C. L., Hogan, D. P., & Eggebeen, D. J. (1996). Living arrangements of minority elders. *Journal of Gerontology: Psychological Sciences and Social Sciences, 51B*(1), S42–S48.

John, R. (1991). Family support networks among elders in a Native American community. Contact with children and siblings among the Prairie Band Potawatomi. *Journal of Aging Studies, 5*(1), 45–59.

Johnson, C. (1999). Family life of older Black men. *Journal of Aging Studies, 13*(2), 145–160.

Johnson, J. C., & Smith, N. H. (2002). Health and social issues associated with racial, ethnic, and cultural disparities. *Generations, XXVI*(3), 25–32.

Johnson, R. A., & Tripp-Reimer, T. (2001). Aging, ethnicity, and social support. *Journal of Gerontological Nursing, 27*(6), 15–21.

Jordan-Marsh, M., & Harden, J. T. (2005). Fictive kin: Friends and family supporting older adults as they age. *Journal of Gerontological Nursing, 31*(2), 25–31.

Kitson, G. C. (2000). Adjustment to violent and natural deaths in later and earlier life for Black and White widows. *Journal of Gerontology: Social Sciences, 55B*(6), S341–S351.

Lang, F. R. (2004). The filial task in midlife: Ambivalence and the quality of adult children's relationships with their older parents. In K. Pillemer & K. Lüscher (Eds.), *Intergenerational ambivalences: New perspectives on parent-child relations in later life* (pp. 183–206). Amsterdam: Elsevier.

Li, L. W., & Fries, B. E. (2005). Elder disability as an explanation for racial differences in informal home care. *The Gerontologist, 45*(2), 206–215.

McFarland, P. L., & Sanders, S. (2003). A pilot study about the needs of older gays and lesbians: What social workers need to know. *Journal of Gerontological Social W*ork, *40*(3), 67–80.

Minkler, M., & Fuller-Thomson, E. (200S). African American grandparents raising grandchildren: A national study using the census 2000 American Community Survey. *Journal of Gerontology: Social Sciences, 60B*(2), S82–S92.

Moriarty, J., & Butt, J. (2004). Inequalities in quality of life among older people from different ethnic groups. *Ageing and Society, 24*(5), 729–753.

Musil, C. M. (1998). Health, stress, coping, and social support in grandmother care-givers. *Health Care for Women International, 19*, 441–455.

Orel, N. A. (2004). Gay, lesbian, and bisexual elders: Expressed needs and concerns across focus groups. *Journal of Gerontological Social Work, 43*(2–3), 57–77.

Patterson, F. M. (2003). Heeding new voices: Gender-related herstories of Asian and Caribbean-born elderly women. *Affilia, 18*(1), 68–79.

Pienta, A. M., Hayward, M. D., & Jenkins, K. R. (2000). Health consequences of marriage for the retirement years. *Journal of Family Issues, 21*(5), 559–586.

Pillemer, K., & Luscher, K. (2004). Introduction: Ambivalence in parent-child relations in later life. In K. Pillemer & K. Lilscher (Eds.), *Intergenerational ambivalences: New perspectives on parent-child relations in later life* (pp. 1–19). Amsterdam: Elsevier.

Salari, S. (2002). Invisible in aging research: Arab Americans, Middle Eastern immigrants, and Muslims in the United States. *The Gerontologist, 42*(5), 580–588.

Sands, R. G., & Goldberg-Glen, R. S. (2000). Factors associated with stress among grandparents raising their grandchildren. *Family Relations, 49*(1), 97–105.

Shawler, C. (2004). Aging mothers and daughters: Relationship changes over time. *Ageing International, 29*(2), 149–177.

Silverstein, M., & Chen, X. (1999). The impact of acculturation in Mexican American families on the quality of adult grandchild-grandparent relationships. *Journal* of *Marriage and the Family, 61*(1), 188–198.

Simmons, T., & Dye, J. L. (2003). *Grandparents living with grandchildren:* 2000 (Census 2000 Brief). Washington, DC: U.S. Census Bureau.

Strom, R., Carter, T., & Schmidt, K. (2004). African-Americans in senior settings: On the need for educating grandparents. *Educational Gerontology, 30*(4), 287–303.

Strom, R. D., Heeder, S. D., & Strom, P. S. (2005). Performance of Black grandmothers: Perceptions of three generations of females. *Educational Gerontology, 31*(3), 187–205.

Szinovacz, M. (1998). Grandparents today: A demographic profile. *The Gerontologist, 38*(1), 37–52.

U.S. Bureau of the Census. (2002). *Current population survey.* Washington, DC: U.S. Government Printing Office.

Walker, A., Manoogian-O'Dell, M., McGraw, L., & White, D. (Eds.). (2001). *Families in later life: Connections and transitions.* Thousand Oaks, CA: Pine Forge Press.

Weibel-Orlando, J. (2001). Grandparenting styles: Native American perspectives. In A. Walker, M. Manoogian-O'Dell, L. McGraw, & D. White (Eds.), *Families in later life: Connections and transitions* (pp. 139–145). Thousand Oaks, CA: Pine Forge Press.

Williams, N. (2001). Elderly Mexican American men: Work and family patterns. In A. Walker, M. Manoogian-O'Dell, L. McGraw, & D. White (Eds.), *Families in later life: Connections and transitions* (pp. 202–207). Thousand Oaks, CA: Pine Forge Press.

Wilmoth, J. M. (2001). Living arrangements among older immigrants in the United States. *The Gerontologist, 41*(2), 228–238.

Wilson, A. E., & Hardy, M. A. (2002). Racial disparities in income security for a cohort of aging American women. *Social Forces, 80*(4), 1283–1306.

Zhan, L., & Chen, J. (2004). Medication practices among Chinese American older adults. *Journal of Gerontological Nursing, 30*(4), 24–33.

READING 35

Gay and Lesbian Families: Queer Like Us

Judith Stacey

Until recently, gay and lesbian families seemed quite a queer concept, if not oxymoronic, not only to scholars and the general public but even to most lesbians and gay men. The grass roots movement for gay liberation of the late 1960s and early 1970s struggled along with the militant feminist movement of that period to liberate gays and women *from* perceived evils and injustices represented by "the family," rather than *for* access to its blessings and privileges. Early marches for gay pride and women's liberation flaunted provocative, countercultural banners, like "Smash the Family" and "Smash Monogamy." Their legacy is a lasting public association of gay liberation and feminism with family subversion. Today, however, gays and lesbians are in the thick of a vigorous profamily movement of their own.

Gay and lesbian families are indisputably here. By the late 1980s an astonishing "gay-by" boom had swelled the ranks of children living with at least one gay or lesbian parent.[1] *Family Values*, the title of a popular 1993 book by and about a lesbian's successful struggle to become a legal second mother to the son she and his biological mother have coparented since his birth,[2] is also among the most popular themes of contemporary Gay Pride marches. In 1989, Denmark became the first nation in the world to legalize a form of gay marriage, termed "registered partnerships," and its Nordic neighbors, Norway and Sweden, soon followed suit. In April 2001, the Netherlands leap-frogged ahead to become the first nation in the world to grant full legal marriage rights to same-sex couples. Meanwhile, in 1993, thousands of gay and lesbian couples participated in a mass wedding ceremony on the Washington Mall during the largest demonstration for gay rights in U.S. history. That same year, the Hawaiian state supreme court issued a ruling that raised the prospect that Hawaii would become the first state in the United States to legalize same-sex marriage. As a result, controversies over gay and lesbian families began to receive center stage billing in U.S. electoral politics.

Gay and lesbian families come in different sizes, shapes, ethnicities, races, religions, resources, creeds, and quirks, and even engage in diverse sexual practices.[3] The gay and lesbian family label primarily marks the cognitive dissonance, and even emotional threat, that much of the nongay public experiences upon recognizing that gays can participate in family life at all. What unifies such families is their need to contend with the particular array of psychic, social, legal, practical, and even physical challenges to their very existence that institutionalized hostility to homosexuality produces. Paradoxically, the label "gay and lesbian family" might become irrelevant if the nongay population could only "get used to it."

In this [reading] I hope to facilitate such a process of normalization, ironically, perhaps, to make using the marker "gay and lesbian" to depict a family category seem queer—as queer, that is, as it now seems to identify a *family*, rather than an individual or a desire, as heterosexual.[4] I will suggest that this historically novel category of family crystallizes widespread processes of family diversification and change that characterize the postmodern family conditions.[5] Gay and lesbian families represent such a new, embattled, visible, and, necessarily, self-conscious genre of kinship, that they help to expose the widening gap between the complex reality of contemporary family forms and the dated family ideology that still undergirds most public rhetoric, policy, and law concerning families. Nongay families, family scholars, and policymakers alike can learn a great deal from examining the experience, struggles, conflicts, needs, and achievements of contemporary gay and lesbian families.

BRAVE NEW FAMILY PLANNING

History rarely affords a social scientist an opportunity to witness during her own lifetime the origins and evolution of a dramatic and significant cultural phenomenon in her field. For a family scholar, it is particularly rare to be able to witness the birth of a historically unprecedented variety of family life. Yet the emergence of the "genus" gay and lesbian family as a distinct social category, and the rapid development and diversification of its living species, have occurred during the past three decades, less than my lifetime. Same-sex desire and behavior, on the other hand, have appeared in most human societies, including all Western ones, as well as among most mammalian species; homosexual relationships, identities, and communities have much longer histories than most Western heterosexuals imagine; and historical evidence documents the practice of sanctioned and/or socially visible same-sex unions in the West, as well as elsewhere, since ancient times.[6] Nonetheless, the notion of a gay or lesbian family is decidedly a late-twentieth-century development, and several particular forms of gay and lesbian families were literally "inconceivable" prior to recent developments in reproductive technology.

Indeed, before the Stonewall rebellion in 1969, the family lives of gays and lesbians were so invisible, both legally and socially, that one can actually date the appearance of the first identifiable species of gay family life—a unit that includes at least one self-identified gay or lesbian parent and children from a former heterosexual marriage. Only one U.S. child custody case reported before 1950 involved a gay or lesbian parent, and only five more gays or lesbians dared to sue for custody of their children between 1950 and 1969. Then, immediately after Stonewall, despite the predominantly antifamily ethos of the early gay liberation period, gay custody conflicts jumped dramatically, with fifty occurring during the 1970s and many more since then.[7] Courts consistently denied parental rights to these early pioneers, rendering them martyrs to a cause made visible by their losses. Both historically and numerically, formerly married lesbian and gay parents who "came out" after marriage and secured at least shared custody of their children represent the most significant genre of gay families. Such gay parents were the first to level a public challenge against the reigning cultural presumption that the two terms, "gay" and "parent" are antithetical. Their family units continue to comprise the vast majority of contemporary gay families and to manifest greater income and ethnic diversity than newer categories of lesbian and gay parents. Moreover, studies of these families provide the primary data base of the extant research on the effects of gay parenting on child development.

It was novel, incongruous, and plain brave for lesbian and gay parents to struggle for legitimate family status during the height of the antinatalist, antimaternalist, antifamily fervor of grass roots feminism and gay liberation in the early 1970s. Fortunately for their successors, such fervor proved to be quite short-lived. Within very few years many feminist theorists began to celebrate women's historically developed nurturing capacities, not coincidentally at a time when aging, feminist baby-boomers had begun producing a late-life boomlet of their own.[8] During the middle to late seventies, the legacy of sexual revolution and feminist assertions of female autonomy combined with the popularization of alternative reproductive technologies and strategies to embolden a first wave of "out" lesbians to join the burgeoning ranks of women actively choosing to have children outside of marriage.

Fully intentional childbearing outside of heterosexual unions represents one of the only new, truly original, and decidedly controversial genres of family formation and structure to have emerged in the West during many centuries. While lesbian variations on this cultural theme include some particularly creative reproductive strategies, they nonetheless represent not deviant, but vanguard manifestations of much broader late-twentieth-century trends in Western family life. Under postmodern conditions, processes of sexuality, conception, gestation, marriage, and parenthood, which once appeared to follow a natural, inevitable progression of gendered behaviors and relationships, have come unhinged, hurtling the basic definitions of our most taken-for-granted familial categories—like mother, father, parent, offspring, sibling, and, of course, "family" itself—into cultural confusion and contention.

The conservative turn toward profamily and postfeminist sensibilities of the Reagan-Bush era, combined with the increased visibility and confidence of gay and lesbian communities, helped to fuel the "gay-by" boom that escalated rapidly during the 1980s. It seems more accurate to call this a "lesbaby" boom, because lesbians vastly outnumber the gay men who can, or have chosen to, become parents out of the closet. Lesbian "planned parenthood" strategies have spread and diversified rapidly during the past two decades. With access to customary means to parenthood denied or severely limited, lesbians necessarily construct their chosen family forms with an exceptional degree of reflection and intentionality. They have been choosing motherhood within a broad array of kinship structures. Some become single mothers, but many lesbians choose to share responsibility for rearing children with a lover and/or with other coparents, such as sperm donors, gay men, and other friends and relatives. Several states expressly prohibit adoptions and/or foster care by lesbians and gay men, and many states and adoption agencies actively discriminate against them. Consequently, independent adoption provided the first, and still traveled, route to planned lesbian maternity, but increasing numbers of lesbians have been choosing to bear children of their own. In pursuit of sperm, some lesbians resort quite instrumentally to heterosexual intercourse—with or without the knowledge of the man involved—but most prefer alternative insemination strategies, locating known or anonymous donors through personal networks or through private physicians or sperm banks.

Institutionalized heterosexism and married-couple biases pervade the medically controlled fertility market. Many private physicians and many sperm banks in the United States, as well as the Canadian and most European health services, refuse to inseminate unmarried women in general, and lesbians particularly. More than 90 percent of U.S. physicians surveyed in 1979 denied insemination to unmarried women, and a 1988 federal government survey of doctors and clinics reported that homosexuality was one of their top four reasons for refusing to provide this service.[9] Thus, initially, planned lesbian pregnancies depended primarily upon donors located through personal networks, very frequently involving gay men or male relatives who might also agree to participate in child rearing, in varying degrees. Numerous lesbian couples solicit sperm from a brother or male relative of one woman to impregnate her partner, hoping to buttress their tenuous legal, symbolic, and social claims for shared parental status over their "turkey-baster babies."

Despite its apparent novelty, "turkey-baster" insemination for infertility dates back to the late eighteenth century, and, as the nickname implies, is far from a high-tech procedure requiring medical expertise.[10] Nonetheless, because the AIDS epidemic and the emergence of child custody conflicts between lesbians and known sperm donors led many lesbians to prefer the legally sanitized, medical route to anonymous donors, feminist health care activists mobilized to meet this need. In 1975 the Vermont Women's Health Center added donor insemination to its services, and in 1980 the Northern California Sperm Bank opened in Oakland expressly to serve the needs of unmarried, disabled, or nonheterosexual women who want to become pregnant. The clinic ships frozen semen throughout North America, and more than two-thirds of the clinic's clients are not married.[11]

The absence of a national health system in the United States commercializes access to sperm and fertility services. This introduces an obvious class bias into the practice of alternative insemination. Far more high-tech, innovative, expensive, and, therefore, uncommon is a procreative strategy some lesbian couples now are adopting in which an ovum from one woman is fertilized with donor sperm and then extracted and implanted in her lover's uterus. In June 2000, one such couple in San Francisco became the first to receive joint recognition as the biological and legal co-mothers of their infant. The irony of deploying technology to assert a biological, and thereby a legal, social, and emotional claim to maternal and family status throws the contemporary instability of all the relevant categories—biology, technology, nature, culture, maternity, family—into bold relief.

While the advent of AIDS inhibited joint procreative ventures between lesbians and gay men, the epidemic also fostered stronger social and political solidarity between the two populations and stimulated gay men to keener interest in forming families. Their ranks are smaller and newer than those of lesbian mothers, but by the late eighties gay men were also visibly engaged in efforts to become parents, despite far more limited opportunities to do so. Not only do men still lack the biological capacity to derive personal benefits from most alternative reproductive technologies, but social prejudice also severely restricts gay male access to children placed for adoption, or even into foster care. Ever since Anita Bryant's "Save the Children" campaign against gay rights in 1977, right-wing mobilizations in diverse states, including Florida, Utah, New Hampshire, and Massachusetts, have successfully cast gay men, in particular, as threats to children and families and denied them the right to adopt or foster the young. In response, some wishful gay fathers have resorted to private adoption and surrogacy arrangements, accepting the most difficult-to-place adoptees and foster children, or entering into shared social parenting arrangements with lesbian couples or single women. During the 1990s, "Growing Generations," the world's first gay and lesbian-owned surrogacy agency, opened in Los Angeles to serve an international constituency of prospective gay parents.

Compelled to proceed outside conventional channels, lesbian and gay male planned parenthood has become an increasingly complex, creative, and politicized, self-help enterprise. Because gays forge kin ties without established legal protections or norms, relationships between gay parents and their children suffer heightened risks. By the mideighties many lesbians and gays found themselves battling each other, as custody conflicts between lesbian coparents or between lesbian parents and sperm donors and/or other relatives began to reach the dockets and to profoundly challenge family courts.[12] Despite a putative "best interests of the child" standard, a bias favoring the heterosexual family guided virtually all the judges who heard these early cases. Biological claims of kinship nearly always trumped those of social parenting, even in heartrending circumstances of custody challenges to bereaved lesbian "widows" who, with their deceased lovers, had jointly planned for, reared, loved, and supported children since their birth.[13] Likewise, judges routinely honored fathers' rights arguments by favoring parental claims of donors who had contributed nothing more than sperm to their offspring over those of lesbians who had coparented from the outset, *even when these men had expressly agreed to abdicate paternal rights or responsibilities.* The first, and still rare, exception to this rule involved a donor who did not bring his paternity suit until the child was ten years old.[14] While numerous sperm donors have reneged on their prenatal custody agreements with lesbian parents, thus far no lesbian mother has sued a donor to attain parental terms different from those to which he first agreed. On the other hand, in the first case in which a lesbian biological mother sought financial support from her former lesbian partner, a New York court found the nonbiological coparent to be a parent. Here, the state's fiduciary interest rather than gay rights governed the decision.[15]

Perhaps the most poignant paradox in gay and lesbian family history concerns how fervently many lesbians and gay men have had to struggle for family status precisely when forces mobilized in *the name of The Family* conspire to deny this to them. The widely publicized saga of the Sharon Kowalski case, in which the natal family of a lesbian who had been severely disabled in a car crash successfully opposed her guardianship by her chosen life-companion, proved particularly galvanizing in this cause, perhaps because all of the contestants were adults. After eight years of legal and political struggle, Sharon's lover, Karen Thompson, finally won a reversal, in a belated, but highly visible, landmark victory for gay family rights.[16]

Gay family struggles rapidly achieved other significant victories, like the 1989 *Braschi* decision by New York State's top court, which granted protection against eviction to a gay man by explicitly defining family in inclusive, social terms, to rest upon

> the exclusivity and longevity of the relationship, the level of emotional and financial commitment, the manner in which the parties have conducted their everyday lives and held themselves out to society, and the reliance placed upon one another for daily family services . . . it is the totality of the relationship as evidenced by the dedication, caring and self-sacrifice of the parties which should, in the final analysis, control.[17]

More recently, in 2000, Vermont became the first state in the United States to grant same-sex couples the right to enter a civil union, a status that confers all of the legal benefits of marriage except those denied by federal law, and numerous state legislatures will be considering similar proposals. The struggle for second-parent adoption rights, which enable a lesbian or gay man to adopt a lover's children without removing the lover's custody rights, represents one of the most active, turbulent fronts in the struggle for gay family rights. In more than half of the 50 states, individual lesbian and gay male couples have won petitions for second-parent adoptions at the trial court level. However, many trial judges deny such petitions, and only a handful of states have granted this right at the appeals court level. In 2000, a Pennsylvania appeals court decision denied such an appeal, thereby setting back the drive for gay parental rights in that state. Even the Nordic countries explicitly excluded adoption rights when they first legalized gay registered partnerships, but since then the Netherlands, Denmark, and Iceland have granted these rights, and other European and Commonwealth countries are beginning to follow suit.

The highly politicized character of family change in the United States renders struggles for gay parenting rights painfully vulnerable to unfavorable political winds. For example, state barriers to lesbian and gay second-parent adoptions in California rise and fall with the fortunes of Republican and Democratic gubernatorial campaigns. The National Center for Lesbian Rights considers second-parent adoptions right to be so crucial to the lesbian "profamily" cause that it revoked its former policy of abstaining from legal conflicts between lesbians over this issue. Convinced that the long-term, best interests of lesbian parents and their children depend upon defining parenthood in social rather than biological terms, the center decided to represent lesbian parents who are denied custody of their jointly reared children when their former lovers exploit the biological and homophobic prejudices of the judiciary.[18]

Here again, gay family politics crystallize, rather than diverge from, pervasive cultural trends. Gay second-parent adoptions, for example, trek a kin trail blazed by court responses to families reconstituted after divorce and remarriage. Courts first allowed some stepparents to adopt their new spouses' children without terminating the custody rights of the children's former parents. Gay family rights law also bears a kind of second cousin tie to racial kin case law. Gay and lesbian custody victories rely heavily on a milestone race custody case, *Palmore v. Sidoti* (1984), which restored the custody rights of a divorced, white mother who lost her children after she married a black man. Even though *Palmore* was decided on legal principles governing race discrimination, which do not yet apply to gender or sexual discrimination, several successful gay and lesbian custody decisions rely on its logic. The first successful second-parent adoption award to a lesbian couple actually was a "third-parent" adoption on the new model of stepparent adoption after divorce, which Mary Ann Mason discusses in Reading 18. The court granted coparent status to the nonbiological mother without withdrawing it from the sperm donor father, a Native American, in order to honor the shared desires of all three parents to preserve the child's bicultural inheritance.[19]

As U.S. tabloid and talk show fare testify daily, culturally divisive struggles over babies secured or lost through alternative insemination, in vitro fertilization, ovum extraction, frozen embryos, surrogacy, transracial adoption, not to mention mundane processes of divorce and remarriage are not the special province of a fringe gay and lesbian minority. We now inhabit a world in which technology has upended the basic premises of the old nature-nurture debate by rendering human biology more amenable to intervention than human society. Inevitably, therefore, contests between biological and social definitions of kinship, such as depicted in the chapters on adoption and stepfamilies, will continue to proliferate and to rub social nerves raw.

Thus while one can discern a gradual political and judicial trend toward granting parental and family rights to gays, the legal situation in the fifty states remains uneven, volatile, and replete with major setbacks for gay and lesbian parents.[20] Forces opposed to gay parenting continue to introduce statewide initiatives and regulations to rescind such rights. The crucial fact remains that numerous states still criminalize sodomy, supported by the 1986 U.S. Supreme Court decision in *Bowers* v. *Hardwick*, which upheld the constitutionality of this most basic impediment to civil rights for gay relationships. One decade later, however, in May 1996, the court struck down a Colorado antigay rights initiative in *Romer* v. *Evans*, raising the hopes of gays and lesbians that it might soon reconsider the detested *Bowers* ruling. As of 2002, however, such wishes remain unfulfilled.

A MORE, OR LESS, PERFECT UNION?

Much nearer at hand, however, than most ever dared to imagine is the momentous prospect of legal gay marriage. The idea of same-sex marriage used to draw nearly as many jeers from gays and lesbians as from nongays. As one lesbian couple recalls,

> In 1981, we were a very, very small handful of lesbians who got married. We took a lot of flak from other lesbians, as well as heterosexuals. In 1981, we didn't know any other lesbians, not a single one, who had had a ceremony in Santa Cruz, and a lot of lesbians live in that city. Everybody was on our case about it. They said, What are you doing, How heterosexual. We really had to sell it.[21]

Less than a decade later, gay and lesbian couples would proudly announce their weddings and anniversaries, not only in the gay press, which now includes specialized magazines for gay and lesbian couples and parents, like *Partners Magazine*, but even in such mainstream, midwestern newspapers as the Minneapolis *Star Tribune*.[22] Jewish rabbis, Protestant ministers, Quaker meetings, and even some Catholic priests regularly perform gay and lesbian wedding or commitment ceremonies, and the phenomenon has become a fashionable pop culture motif. In December 1995, the long-running, provocative TV sitcom program *Roseanne* featured a gay male wedding, and one month later, the popular sitcom *Friends* aired a lesbian wedding on primetime television. A few years later, a high profile made-for-TV HBO movie starring Vanessa Redgrave, Michelle Williams, Ellen DeGeneres, and Sharon Stone, *If These Walls Could Talk 2*, expanded on the theme by highlighting difficulties experienced by lesbian couples who cannot be legally married. Such popular culture breakthroughs have helped normalize what once seemed inconceivable to gay and straight audiences alike.

Gradually, major corporations, universities, and nonprofit organizations are providing spousal benefits to the domestic mates of their gay and lesbian employees, and a small but growing number of U.S. municipalities, states, and increasing numbers of European and Commonwealth nations have legalized domestic partnerships, which grant legal status and varying rights and responsibilities to cohabiting couples, irrespective of gender or sexual identity.

When the very first social science research collection about gay parents was published in 1987, its editor concluded that however desirable such unions might be, "it is highly unlikely that marriages between same-sex individuals will be legalized in any state in the foreseeable future."[23] Yet, almost immediately thereafter, precisely this specter began to exercise imaginations across the political spectrum. A national poll reported by the *San Francisco Examiner* in 1989 found that 86 percent of lesbians and gay men supported legalizing same-sex marriage.[24] A few years later, the Hawaiian supreme court issued a ruling that made such a prospect seem imminent. Amidst rampant rumors that thousands of mainland gay and lesbian couples were stocking their hope chests with Hawaiian excursion fares, posed to fly to tropical altars the instant the first gay matrimonial bans falter, right-wing Christian groups began actively to mobilize resistance. Utah became the first state to pass legislation refusing recognition to same-sex marriages if they were performed in other states. Soon a majority of states were considering similar bills.

On May 8, 1996, gay marriage galloped onto the nation's center political stage when Republicans introduced the Defense of Marriage Act (DOMA) to define marriage in exclusively heterosexual terms as "a legal union between one man and one woman as husband and wife." Introduced primarily as a "wedge" issue in the Republican 1996 electoral strategy, DOMA passed both houses of Congress in a landslide vote, and President Clinton promptly signed it, despite his personal support for gay rights.

As with child custody, the campaign for gay marriage clings to legal footholds planted by racial justice pioneers. It is startling to recall how recent it was that the Supreme Court finally struck down antimiscegenation laws. Not until 1967, that is only two years before the Stonewall rebellion, did the high court, in *Loving* v. *Virginia*, find state restrictions on interracial marriages to be unconstitutional. (Twenty states still had such restrictions on the books in 1967, a greater number than currently prohibit sodomy.) A handful of gay couples quickly sought to marry in the 1970s through appeals to this precedent, but until three lesbian and gay male couples sued Hawaii in *Baehr* v. *Lewin* for equal rights to choose marriage partners without restrictions on gender, all U.S. courts had dismissed the analogy. In a historic ruling in 1993, the Hawaii Supreme Court remanded this suit to the trial court, requiring the state to demonstrate a "compelling interest" in prohibiting same-sex marriage, a strict scrutiny standard that the state was unable to meet when the case was retried. Significantly, the case was neither argued nor adjudicated as a gay rights issue. Rather, just as ERA opponents once had warned and advocates had denied, passage of an equal rights amendment to Hawaii's state constitution in 1972 paved the legal foundation for *Baehr*.[25]

Although backlash forces succeeded in preventing the legalization of gay marriage in Hawaii, this global struggle keeps achieving milestone victories at a breathless pace. Marriage rights in all but name are now available throughout most of Western Europe and Canada, as well as in Vermont. In 2001, the Netherlands assumed world leadership in fully legalizing same-sex marriage at the national level, and similar developments appear imminent in the Nordic nations, Canada, and perhaps in South Africa. Clearly this issue is on the historical agenda for the twenty-first century. Not all gay activists or legal scholars embrace this prospect with enthusiasm. Although most of their constituents desire the right to marry, gay activists and theorists continue to debate vigorously the politics and effects of this campaign. An articulate, vocal minority seeks not to extend the right to marry, but to dismantle an institution they regard as inherently, and irredeemably, hierarchical, unequal, conservative, and repressive.[26] A second perspective supports legal marriage as one long-term goal of the gay rights movement but voices serious strategic objections to making this a priority before there is sufficient public support to sustain a favorable ruling in any state or the nation. Such critics fear that a premature victory will prove pyrrhic, because efforts to defend it against the vehement backlash it has already begun to incite are apt to fail, after sapping resources and time better devoted to other urgent struggles for gay rights. Rather than risk a major setback for the gay movement, some leaders advocate an incremental approach to establishing legal family status for gay and lesbian kin ties through a multifaceted struggle for "family diversity."[27]

However, the largest, and most diverse, contingent of gay activist voices now supports the marriage rights campaign, perhaps because gay marriage can be perceived as harmonizing with virtually every hue on the gay ideological spectrum. Progay marriage arguments range from profoundly conservative to liberal humanist to radical and deconstructive. Conservatives, like those radicals who still oppose marriage, view it as an institution that promotes monogamy, commitment, and social stability, along with interests in private property, social conformity, and mainstream values.[28] Liberal gays support legal marriage, of course, not only to affirm the legitimacy of their relationships and help sustain them in a hostile world but as a straightforward matter of equal civil rights. They also recognize the social advantages of divorce law. "I used to say, 'Why do we want to get married? It doesn't work for straight people,'" one gay lawyer comments. "But now I say we should care: They have the privilege of divorce and we don't. We're left out there to twirl around in pain."[29]

Some feminist and other critical gay legal theorists craft more radical defenses of gay marriage. Nan Hunter, for example, rejects feminist colleague Nancy Polikoff's belief that marriage is an unalterably sexist and heterosexist institution. Hunter argues that legalized same-sex marriage would have "enormous potential to destabilize the gendered definition of marriage for everyone."[30] Likewise, Evan Wolfson, director of the Marriage Project of the gay legal rights organization Lambda Legal Defense, who served as co-counsel in *Baehr*, argues that marriage is neither inherently equal nor unequal, but depends upon an ever-changing cultural and political context.[31] (Anyone who doubts this need only consider such examples as polygamy, arranged marriage, or the same-sex unions in early Western history documented by the late Princeton historian John Boswell.)

Support for gay marriage, not long ago anathema to radicals and conservatives, gays and nongays alike, now issues forth from ethical and political perspectives as diverse, and even incompatible, as these. The cultural and political context has changed so dramatically since Stonewall that it now seems easier to understand why marriage has come to enjoy overwhelming support in the gay community than to grasp the depth of resistance to the institution that characterized the early movement.

Gay marriage, despite its apparent compatibility with mainstream "family values" sentiment, raises far more threatening questions than does military service about gender relations, sexuality, and family life. Few contemporary politicians, irrespective of their personal convictions, display the courage to confront this contradiction, even when urged to do so by gay conservatives. Gay marriage would strengthen the ranks of those endangered two-parent, "intact," married-couples families whose praises conservative, "profamily" enthusiasts tirelessly sing. Unsurprisingly, however, this case has won few nongay conservative converts to the cause. After all, homophobia is a matter of passion, politics, and prejudice, not logic.

Surveys suggest, however, that while a majority of citizens still oppose legalizing gay marriage, the margin of opposition is declining slowly but surely. In a 1994 *Time* magazine/CNN poll, 64 percent of respondents did not want to legalize gay marriages.[32] A *Newsweek* poll conducted right after the DOMA was introduced in May 1996 reported that public opposition to gay marriage had declined to 58 percent, and a Gallup poll conducted June 2001 indicated a further drop to 52 percent.[33]

Despite the paucity of mainstream political enthusiasm for legalizing gay marriage, there are good reasons to believe that gays and lesbians will eventually win this right and to support their struggle to do so. Legitimizing gay and lesbian marriages would promote a democratic, pluralist expansion of the meaning, practice, and politics of family life in the United States, helping to supplant the destructive sanctity of *The Family* with respect for diverse and vibrant *families*. To begin with, the liberal implications of legal gay marriage are far from trivial, as the rush to nullify them should confirm. For example, legal gay marriage in one state could begin to threaten antisodomy laws in all the others. Policing marital sex would be difficult to legitimate, and differential prosecution of conjugal sex among same-sex couples could violate equal protection legislation. Likewise, if gay marriage were legalized, the myriad of state barriers to child custody, adoption, fertility services, inheritance, and other family rights that lesbians and gay men currently suffer could also become subject to legal challenge. Moreover, it seems hard to overestimate the profound cultural implications for the struggle against the injurious effects of legally condoned homophobia that would ensue were lesbian and gay relationships to be admitted into the ranks of legitimate kinship. In a society that forbids most public school teachers and counselors even the merest expression of tolerance for homosexuality, while lesbian and gay youth attempt suicide at rates estimated to be at least three times greater than other youth,[34] granting full legal recognition to lesbian and gay relationships could have dramatic, and salutary, consequences.

Moreover, while it is unlikely that same-sex marriage can in itself dismantle the patterned gender and sexual injustices of the institution, I believe it could make a potent contribution to those projects, as the research on gay relationships I discuss later seems to indicate. Admitting gays to the wedding banquet invites gays and nongays alike to consider the kinds of place settings that could best accommodate the diverse needs of all contemporary families. Subjecting the conjugal institution to this sort of heightened democratic scrutiny could help it to assume varied, creative, and adaptive contours. If we begin to value the meaning and quality of intimate bonds over their customary forms, people might devise marriage and kinship patterns to serve diverse needs. For example, the "companionate marriage," a much celebrated, but less often realized, ideal of modern sociological lore, could take on new life. Two friends might decide to "marry" without basing their bond on erotic or romantic attachment, as Dorthe, a prominent Danish lesbian activist who had initially opposed the campaign for gay marriage, fantasized after her nation's parliament approved gay "registered partnerships": If I am going to marry it will be with one of my oldest friends in order to share pensions and things like that. But I'd never marry a lover. That is the advantage of being married to a close friend. Then, you never have to marry a lover![35]

While conservative advocates of gay marriage scoff at such radical visions, they correctly realize that putative champions of committed relationships and children who oppose gay marriage can be charged with gross hypocrisy on this score. For access to legal marriage not only would promote long-term, committed intimacy and economic security among gay couples but also would afford invaluable protection to the children of gay parents. Public legitimacy for gay relationships would also provide indirect protection to closeted gay youth who reside with nongay parents. Clearly, only through a process of massive denial of the fact that millions of children living in gay and lesbian families are here, and here to stay, can anyone genuinely concerned with the best interests of children deny their parents the right to marry.

IN THE BEST INTERESTS OF WHOSE CHILDREN?

The most cursory survey of the existing empirical research on gay and lesbian families reveals the depth of sanctioned discrimination they continue to suffer and the absence of evidence to justify this iniquity. To be sure, substantial limitations mar the social science research on this subject, which is barely past its infancy. Mainstream journals, even those specializing in family research, warmed to this subject startlingly late and little, relegating the domain primarily to sexologists, clinicians, and a handful of movement scholars and their sympathizers and opponents. In 1995, a survey of the three leading journals of family research in the United States found only 12 of the 2598 articles published between 1980 and 1993, that is less than .05 percent, focused on the families of lesbians and gay men, which, even by conservative estimates make up at least 3 percent of U.S. families.[36] The research that does exist, moreover, has deficiencies that skew results so as to exaggerate rather than understate any defects of gay and lesbian families. Until very recently, most investigators began with a deviance perspective, seeking, whether homophobically or defensively, to "test" the validity of the popular prejudice that gay parenting is harmful to children. In other words, the reigning premise has been that gay and lesbian families are dangerously, and *prima facie*, "queer" in the pejorative sense, unless proven otherwise. Taking children reared by nongay parents as the unquestioned norm, most studies asymmetrically ask whether lesbian and gay parents hinder their children's emotional, cognitive, gender, or sexual development. Because lesbian and gay "planned parenthood" is so new, and its progeny so young, nearly all of the studies to date sample the ranks of formerly married parents who had children before they divorced and came out of the closet. The studies are generally small-scale and draw disproportionately from urban, white, middle-class populations. Frequently they make misleading comparisons between divorced lesbian and nongay, single-mother households by ignoring the presence or absence of lesbian life partners or other caretakers in the former.[37]

Despite such limitations, psychologists, social psychologists, and sociologists have by now conducted dozens of studies which provide overwhelming support for the "proven otherwise" thesis. Almost without exception they conclude, albeit in defensive tones, that lesbian and gay parents do not produce inferior, nor even particularly different kinds of children than do other parents. Generally they find no significant differences in school achievement, social adjustment, mental health, gender identity, or sexual orientation between the two groups of children. As Joan Laird's overview of research on lesbian and gay parents summarizes:

> a generation of research has failed to demonstrate that gays or lesbians are any less fit to parent than their heterosexual counterparts. Furthermore, a substantial number of studies on the psychological and social development of children of lesbian and gay parents have failed to produce any evidence that children of lesbian or gay parents are harmed or compromised or even differ from, in any significant ways along a host of psychosocial developmental measures, children raised in heterosexual families.[38]

The rare small differences between gay and nongay parents reported tend to favor gay parents, portraying them as somewhat more nurturant and tolerant, and their children, in turn, more tolerant and empathic, and less aggressive than those reared by nongay parents.[39] In April 1995, British researchers published the results of their unusual sixteen-year-long study which followed twenty-five children brought up by lesbian mothers and twenty-one brought up by heterosexual mothers from youth to adulthood. They found that the young adults raised in lesbian households had better relationships with their mothers' lesbian partners than the young adults brought up by heterosexual single mothers had with their mothers' male partners.[40] Published research to date seems to vindicate one ten-year-old girl who, rather apologetically, deems herself privileged to be the daughter of two lesbian parents: "But I think you get more love with two moms. I know other kids have a mom and a dad, but I think that moms give more love than dads. This may not be true, but it's what I think." Her opinion is shared by a six-year-old girl from another lesbian family: "I don't tell other kids at school about my mothers because I think they would be jealous of me. Two mothers is better than one."[41]

In light of the inhospitable, often outrightly hostile climate which gay families typically encounter, this seems a remarkable achievement. One sign that mainstream social scientists have begun to recognize the achievement is the inclusion of Laird's chapter, "Lesbian and Gay Families," in the 1993 edition of a compendium of research, *Normal Family Processes*, whose first edition, in 1982, ignored the subject.[42] Researchers have begun to call for, and to initiate, a mature, creative, undefensive approach to studying the full range of gay and lesbian families. Coming to terms with the realities of the postmodern family condition, such studies begin with a pluralist premise concerning the legitimacy and dignity of diverse family structures. They ask whether and how gay and lesbian families differ, rather than deviate, from nongay families; they attend as much to the differences among such families as to those dividing them from nongays; and they explore the particular benefits as well as the burdens such families bestow on their members.[43]

This kind of research has begun to discover more advantages of gay and lesbian family life for participants and our society than have yet been explored. Most obvious, certainly, are mental health rewards for gay and lesbian youth fortunate enough to come of age in such families. Currently most youth who experience homosexual inclinations either conceal their desires from their immediate kin or risk serious forms of rejection. State hostility to gay parents can have tragic results. In 1994, for example, the Nebraska Department of Social Services adopted a policy forbidding lesbian or gay foster homes, and the next day a seventeen-year-old openly gay foster child committed suicide, because he feared he would be removed from the supportive home of his gay foster parents.[44]

Of course, this speaks precisely to the heart of what homophobes most fear, that public acceptance of lesbian and gay families will spawn an "epidemic" of gay youth. As Pat Robertson so crudely explained to a Florida audience: "That gang of idiots running the ACLU, the National Education Association, the National Organization of Women, they don't want religious principles in our schools. Instead of teaching the Ten Commandments, they want to teach kids how to be homosexuals."[45] Attempting to respond to such anxieties, most defenders of gay families have stressed the irrelevance of parental sexual identity to that of their children. Sympathetic researchers repeatedly, and in my view misguidedly, maintain that lesbian and gay parents are no more likely than nongay parents to rear lesbian and gay children. Laird, for example, laments:

> One of the most prevalent myths is that children of gay parents will themselves grow up gay; another that daughters will be more masculine and sons more feminine than "normal" children. A number of researchers have concluded that the sexual orientations/preferences of children of gay or lesbian parents do not differ from those whose parents are heterosexual.[46]

Increasingly this claim appears illogical, unlikely, and unwittingly anti-gay. Ironically, it presumes the very sort of fixed definition of sexuality that the best contemporary gay and lesbian scholarship has challenged. Although it is clearly true that, until now, nearly all "homosexuals," like almost everyone else, have been reared by nongays, it is equally clear that sexual desire and identity do not represent a singular fixed "trait" that expresses itself free of cultural context. However irresolvable eternal feuds over the relative weight of nature and nurture may forever prove to be, historical and anthropological data leave no doubt that culture profoundly influences sexual meanings and practices. Homophobes are quite correct to believe that environmental conditions incite or inhibit expressions of homosexual desire, no matter its primary source. If culture had no influence on sexual identity, there would not have emerged the movement for gay and lesbian family rights that inspired me to write this [reading].

Contrary to what most current researchers claim, public acceptance of gay and lesbian families should, in fact, slightly expand the percentage of youth who would dare to explore their same-sex desires. In fact, a careful reading of the studies does suggest just this.[47] Children reared by lesbian or gay parents feel greater openness to homosexuality or bisexuality. In January 1996, the researchers who conducted the long-term British study conceded this point, after issuing the obligatory reassurance that, "the commonly held assumption that children brought up by lesbian mothers will themselves grow up to be lesbian or gay is not supported by the findings." Two of the twenty-five young adults in the study who were reared by lesbians grew up to identify as lesbians, but none of the twenty-one who were reared in the comparison group of heterosexual mothers identify as lesbian or gay. More pertinent, in my view, five daughters and one son of lesbian mothers, but none of the children of heterosexual mothers, reported having had a same-sex erotic experience of some sort, prompting the researchers to acknowledge that, "It seems that growing up in an accepting atmosphere enables individuals who are attracted to same-sex partners to pursue these relationships."[48] This prospect should disturb only those whose antipathy to homosexuality derives from deeply held religious convictions or irrational prejudice.

The rest of us could benefit from permission to explore and develop sexually free from the rigid prescriptions of what Adrienne Rich memorably termed "compulsory heterosexuality."[49] Currently, lesbian and gay parents grant their children such permission much more generously than do other parents. Not only do they tend to be less doctrinaire or phobic about sexual diversity than heterosexual parents, but, wishing to spare their children the burdens of stigma, some gay parents actually prefer that their youngsters do not become gay. Indeed, despite the ubiquity of Pat Robertson's sort of alarmist, propagandistic warnings, "advice on how to help your kids turn out gay," as cultural critic Eve Sedgwick sardonically puts it, "not to mention your students, your parishioners, your therapy clients, or your military subordinates, is less ubiquitous than you might think."[50]

Heterosexual indoctrination is far more pervasive and far the greater danger. Contemporary adolescent culture is even more mercilessly homophobic, or perhaps less hypo-critically so, than most mainstream adult prejudices countenance. Verbal harassment, ridicule, hazing, and ostracism of "faggots," "bull-dykes," and "queers"—quotidien features of our popular culture—are particularly blatant among teens. "Sometimes I feel like no one really knows what I'm going through," one fifteen-year-old daughter of a lesbian laments: "Don't get me wrong. I really do love my mom and all her friends, but being gay is just not acceptable to other people. Like at school, people make jokes about dykes and fags, and it really bothers me. I mean I bite my tongue, because if I say anything, they wonder, Why is she sticking up for them?"[51] In a 1995 survey, nearly half the teen victims of reported violent physical assaults identified their sexual orientation as a precipitating factor. Tragically, family members inflicted 61 percent of these assaults on gay youth.[52]

Little wonder such disproportionate numbers of gay youth commit suicide. Studies claim that gay youth commit one-third of all teenage suicide attempts.[53] To evade harassment, most of the survivors suffer their clandestine difference in silent isolation, often at great cost to their self-esteem, social relationships, and to their very experience of adolescence itself. One gay man bought his life partner a Father's Day card, because he "realized that in a lot of ways we've been brother and father to each other since we've had to grow up as adults. Because of homophobia, gay people don't have the same opportunity as heterosexuals to be ourselves when we are teenagers. A lot of times you have to postpone the experiences until you're older, until you come out."[54]

The increased social visibility and community-building of gays and lesbians have vastly improved the quality of life for gay adults. Ironically, however, Linnea Due, author of a book about growing up gay in the nineties, was disappointed to find that this improvement has had contradictory consequences for gay teens. Due expected to find conditions much better for gay youth than when she grew up in the silent sixties. Instead, many teens thought their circumstances had become more difficult, because, as one young man put it, "now they know we're here."[55]

While most youth with homosexual desires will continue to come of age closeted in nongay families into the foreseeable future, they would surely gain some comfort from greater public acceptance of gay and lesbian families. Yet in 1992, when the New York City Board of Education tried to introduce the Rainbow multicultural curriculum guide which advocated respect for lesbian and gay families in an effort "to help increase the tolerance and acceptance of the lesbian/gay community and to decrease the staggering number of hate crimes perpetrated against them," public opposition became so vehement that it contributed to the dismissal of Schools Chancellor Joseph Fernandez.[56]

Indeed, the major documented special difficulties that children in gay families experience derive directly from legal discrimination and social prejudice. As one, otherwise well-adjusted, sixteen-year-old son of a lesbian puts it: "If I came out and said my mom was gay, I'd be treated like an alien."[57] Children of gay parents are vicarious victims of homophobia and institutionalized heterosexism. They suffer all of the considerable economic, legal, and social disadvantages imposed on their parents, sometimes even more harshly. They risk losing a beloved parent or coparent at the whim of a judge. They can be denied access to friends by the parents of playmates. Living in families that are culturally invisible or despised, the children suffer ostracism by proxy, forced continually to negotiate conflicts between loyalty to home, mainstream authorities, and peers.

However, as the Supreme Court belatedly concluded in 1984, when it repudiated discrimination against interracial families in *Palmore* v. *Sidoti*, and as should be plain good sense, the fact that children of stigmatized parents bear an unfair burden provides no critique of their families. The sad *social* fact of prejudice and discrimination indicts the "family values" of the bigoted society, not the stigmatized family. In the words of the

Court: "private biases may be outside the reach of the law, but the law cannot, directly or indirectly, give them effect."[58] Although the strict scrutiny standards that now govern race discrimination do not apply to sexual discrimination, several courts in recent years have relied on the logic of *Palmore* in gay custody cases. These decisions have approved lesbian and gay custody awards while explicitly acknowledging that community disapproval of their parents' sexual identity would require "greater than ordinary fortitude" from the children, but that in return they might more readily learn that, "people of integrity do not shrink from bigots." The potential benefits that children might derive from being raised by lesbian or gay parents which a New Jersey court enumerated could serve as child-rearing ideals for a democracy:

> emerge better equipped to search out their own standards of right and wrong, better able to perceive that the majority is not always correct in its moral judgments, and better able to understand the importance of conforming their beliefs to the requirements of reason and tested knowledge, not the constraints of currently popular sentiment or prejudice.[59]

The testimony of one fifteen-year-old daughter of a lesbian mother and gay father indicates just this sort of outcome:

> I think I am more open-minded than if I had straight parents. Sometimes kids at school make a big deal out of being gay. They say it's stupid and stuff like that. But they don't really know, because they are not around it. I don't say anything to them, but I know they are wrong. I get kind of mad, because they don't know what they are talking about.[60]

However, literature suggests that parents and children alike who live in fully closeted lesbian and gay families tend to suffer more than members of "out" gay families who contend with stigma directly.[61] Of course, gay parents who shroud their families in closets do so for compelling cause. Some judges still make the closet an explicit condition for awarding custody or visitation rights to gay or lesbian parents, at times imposing direct restrictions on their participation in gay social or political activity.[62] Or, fearing judicial homophobia, some parents live in mortal terror of losing their children, like one divorced lesbian in Kansas City whose former, violent husband has threatened an ugly custody battle if anyone finds out about her lesbianism.[63]

Heroically, more and more brave new "queer" families are refusing the clandestine life. If the survey article, "The Families of Lesbians and Gay Men: A New Frontier in Family Research,"[64] is correctly titled, then research on fully planned lesbian and gay families is its vanguard outpost. Researchers estimate that by 1990, between five thousand and ten thousand lesbians in the United States had given birth to chosen children, and the trend has been increasing ever since.[65] Although this represents a small fraction of the biological and adopted children who live with lesbian parents, planned lesbian births, as Kath Weston suggests, soon, "began to overshadow these other kinds of dependents, assuming a symbolic significance for lesbians and gay men disproportionate to their numbers."[66] Lesbian "turkey-baster" babies are equally symbolic to those who abhor the practice. "National Fatherhood Initiative" organizer David Blankenhorn, for example, calls for restricting sperm bank services to infertile married couples in order to inhibit the production of such "radically fatherless children," and similar concerns have been expressed in such popular publications as *U.S. News and World Report* and *Atlantic Monthly*.[67] (Interestingly, restrictions that limit access to donor sperm exclusively to married women remain widespread in Europe, even in most of the liberal Nordic nations.) Because discrimination against prospective gay and lesbian adoptive parents leads most to conceal their sexual identity, it is impossible to estimate how many have succeeded in adopting or fostering children, but this, too, has become a visible form of gay planned parenthood.[68]

Research on planned gay parenting is too young to be more than suggestive, but initial findings give more cause for gay pride than alarm. Parental relationships tend to be more cooperative and egalitarian than among heterosexual parents, child rearing more nurturant, children more affectionate.[69] On the other hand, lesbian mothers do encounter some particular burdens. Like straight women who bear children through insemination, they confront the vexing question of how to negotiate their children's knowledge of and relationship to sperm donors. Some progeny of unknown donors, like many adopted children, quest for contact with their genetic fathers. One ten-year-old girl, conceived by private donor insemination, explains why she was relieved to find her biological father: "I wanted to find my dad because it was hard knowing I had a dad but not knowing who he was. It was like there was a missing piece."[70]

Lesbian couples planning a pregnancy contend with some unique decisions and challenges concerning the relationship between biological and social maternity. They must decide which woman will try to become pregnant and how to negotiate feelings of jealousy, invisibility, and displacement that may be more likely to arise between the two than between a biological mother and father. Struggling to equalize maternal emotional stakes and claims, some couples decide to alternate the childbearing role, others attempt simultaneous pregnancies, and some, as we have seen, employ reproductive technology to divide the genetic and gestational components of procreation. Some nongestational lesbian mothers stimulate lactation, so that they can jointly breastfeed the babies their partners bear, some assume disproportionate responsibility for child care to compensate for their biological "disadvantage," and others give their surnames to their partners' offspring.

Planned lesbian and gay families, however, most fully realize the early planned Parenthood goal, "every child a wanted child," as one twelve-year-old son of a lesbian recognized: "I think that if you are a child of a gay or lesbian, you have a better chance of having a great parent. If you are a lesbian, you have to go through a lot of trouble to get a child, so that child is really wanted."[71] Disproportionately "queer" families choose to reside in and construct communities that support family and social diversity. Partly because fertility and adoption services are expensive and often difficult to attain, intentional gay parents are disproportionately white, better educated, and more mature than other parents. Preliminary research indicates that these advantages more than offset whatever problems their special burdens cause their children.[72] Clearly, it is in the interest of all our children to afford their families social dignity and respect.

If we exploit the research with this aim in mind, deducing a rational wish list for public policy is quite a simple matter. A straightforward, liberal, equal rights agenda for lesbians and gays would seem the obvious and humane course. In the best interests of all children, we would provide lesbian and gay parents equal access to marriage, child custody, adoption, foster placements, fertility services, inheritance, employment, and all social benefits. We would adopt "rainbow" curricula within our schools and our public media that promote the kind of tolerance and respect for family and sexual diversity that Laura Sebastian, an eighteen-year-old reared by her divorced mother and her mother's lesbian lover, advocates:

> A happy child has happy parents, and gay people can be as happy as straight ones. It doesn't matter what kids have—fathers, mothers, or both—they just need love and support. It doesn't matter if you are raised by a pack of dogs, just as long as they love you! It's about time lesbians and gays can have children. It's everybody's right as a human being.[73]

OUR QUEER POSTMODERN FAMILIES

Far from esoteric, the experiences of diverse genres of gay and lesbian "families we choose" bear on many of the most feverishly contested issues in contemporary family politics. They can speak to our mounting cultural paranoia over whether fathers are expendable, to nature-nurture controversies over sexual and gender identities and the gender division of labor, to the meaning and purpose of voluntary marriage, and, most broadly, to those ubiquitous "family values" contests over the relative importance for children of family structure or process, of biological or "psychological" parents.

From the African-American "Million Man March" in October 1995, the stadium rallies of Christian male "Promise Keepers" that popularized the subject of responsible fatherhood in evangelical churches across the nation, and the National Fatherhood Initiative, to congressional hearings on the Father's Responsibility Act in 2001, the nation seems to be gripped by cultural obsession over the decline of dependable dads. Here research on lesbian families, particularly on planned lesbian couple families, could prove of no small import. Thus far, as we have seen, such research offers no brief for Blankenhorn's angst over "radically fatherless children." Also challenging to those who claim that the mere presence of a father in a family confers significant benefits on his children are surprising data reported in a study of youth and violence commissioned by Kaiser Permanente and Children Now. The study of 1000 eleven to seventeen-year-olds and of 150 seven to ten-year-olds found that, contrary to popular belief, 68 percent of the "young people exposed to higher levels of health and safety threats" were from conventional two-parent families. Moreover, poignantly, fathers were among the last people these troubled teens would turn to for help, even when they lived in such families. Only 10 percent of the young people in these two-parent families said they would seek their fathers' advice first, compared with 44 percent who claimed they would turn first to their mothers, and 26 percent who would first seek help from friends. Many more youth were willing to discuss concerns over their health, safety, and sexuality with nurses or doctors.[74] Thus, empirical social science to date, like the historical record, gives us impeccable cause to regard fathers and mothers alike as "expendable." The quality, not the gender, of parenting is what truly matters.

Similarly, research on the relationships of gay male and lesbian couples depicts diverse models for intimacy from which others could profit. "Freed" from normative conventions and institutions that govern heterosexual gender and family relationships, self-consciously "queer" couples and families, by necessity, have had to reflect much more seriously on the meaning and purpose of their intimate commitments. Studies that compare lesbian, gay male, and heterosexual couples find intriguing contrasts in their characteristic patterns of intimacy. Gender seems to shape domestic values and practices more powerfully than sexual identity, so that same-sex couples tend to be more compatible than heterosexual couples. For example, both lesbian and straight women are more likely than either gay or straight men to value their relationships over their work. Yet both lesbian and gay male couples agree that both parties should be employed, while married men are less likely to agree with wives who wish to work. Predictably, same-sex couples share more interests and time together than married couples. Also unsurprising, lesbian couples have the most egalitarian relationships, and married heterosexual couples the least. Lesbian and gay male couples both share household chores more equally and with less conflict than married couples, but they share them differently. Lesbian couples tend to share most tasks equally, while gay males more frequently assign tasks "to each according to his abilities," schedules, and preferences.[75] Each of these modal patterns for intimacy has its particular strengths and vulnerabilities. Gender conventions and gender fluidity alike have advantages and limitations, as Blumstein and Schwartz and other researchers have discussed. Accepting queer families does not mean converting to any characteristic patterns of intimacy, but coming to terms with the collapse of a monolithic cultural regime governing our intimate bonds. It would mean embracing a genuinely pluralist understanding that there are diverse, valid ways to form and sustain these.

Perhaps what is truly distinctive about lesbian and gay families is how unambiguously the substance of their relationships takes precedence over their form, emotional and social commitments over genetic claims. Compelled to exercise "good, old-fashioned American" ingenuity to fulfill familial desires, gays and lesbians improvisationally assemble a patchwork of "blood" and intentional relations—gay, straight, and other—into creative, extended kin bonds."[76] Gay communities more adeptly integrate singles into their social worlds than does mainstream heterosexual society, a social "skill" quite valuable in a world in which divorce, widowhood, and singlehood are increasingly normative. Because "queer" families must continually, self-consciously migrate in and out of the closet, they hone bicultural skills particularly suitable for life in a multicultural society.[77] Self-identified queer families serve on the front lines of the postmodern family condition, commanded directly by its regime of improvisation, ambiguity, diversity, contradiction, self-reflection, and flux.

Even the distinctive, indeed the definitional, burden that pervasive homophobia imposes on lesbian and gay families does not fully distinguish them from other contemporary families. Unfortunately, prejudice, intolerance, and disrespect for "different" or "other" families is all too commonplace in the contemporary world. Ethnocentric familism afflicts the families of many immigrants, interracial couples, single mothers (be they unwed or divorced, impoverished or affluent), remarried couples, childless "yuppie" couples, bachelors and "spinsters," househusbands, working mothers, and the homeless. It even places that vanishing, once-hallowed breed of full-time homemakers on the ("I'm-just-a-housewife") defensive.

Gay and lesbian families simply brave intensified versions of ubiquitous contemporary challenges. Both their plight and their pluck expose the dangerous disjuncture between our family rhetoric and policy, on the one hand, and our family and social realties, on the other. In stubborn denial of the complex, pluralist array of contemporary families and kinship, most of our legal and social policies atavistically presume to serve a singular, "normal" family structure—the conventional, heterosexual, married-couple, nuclear family. In the name of children, politicians justify decisions that endanger children, and in the name of *The Family*, they cause grave harm to our families. It is time to get used to the queer, post-modern family condition we all now inhabit.

Notes

1. An estimate that at least six million children would have a gay parent by 1985 appeared in J. Schulenberg, *Gay Parenting* (New York: Doubleday, 1985) and has been accepted or revised upwards by most scholars since then. See, for example, F. W. Bozett (ed.), *Gay and Lesbian Parents* (New York: Praeger, 1987), 39; C. Patterson, "Children of Lesbian and Gay Parents," *Child Development* 63:1025–1042; K. R. Allen and D. H. Demo, "The Families of Lesbians and Gay Men: A New Frontier in Family Research," *Journal of Marriage and the Family* 57 (February 1995):111–127. Nevertheless, these estimates are based upon problematic assumptions and calculations, so the actual number could be considerably lower—especially if we exclude children whose parents have not acknowledged to anyone else in the family that they are gay or lesbian. Still, even a conservative estimate would exceed one million.
2. P. Burke, *Family Values: A Lesbian Mother's Fight for Her Son* (New York: Random House, 1993).
3. For a sensitive discussion of the definitional difficulties involved in research on gay and lesbian families, see Allen and Demo, "Families of Lesbians and Gay Men," 112–113.
4. Many gay activist groups and scholars, however, have begun to reclaim the term "queer" as a badge of pride, in much the same way that the black power movement of the 1960s reclaimed the formerly derogatory term for blacks.
5. In J. Stacey, *Brave New Families* (New York: Basic Books, 1990), I provide a book-length, ethnographic treatment of postmodern family life in the Silicon Valley.
6. For historical and cross-cultural treatments of same-sex marriages, relationships, and practices in the West and elsewhere, see J. Boswell, *Same-Sex Unions in Premodern Europe* (New York: Villard Books, 1994) and W. N. Eskridge Jr., "A History of Same-Sex Marriage," *Virginia Law Review* 79:1419–1451, 1993.
7. R. R. Rivera, "Legal Issues in Gay and Lesbian Parenting," in Bozett, ed., *Gay and Lesbian Parents.*
8. Among the influential feminist works of this genre were: N. Chodorow, *The Reproduction of Mothering* (Berkeley and Los Angeles: University of California Press, 1978); C. Gilligan, *In a Different Voice* (Cambridge: Harvard University Press, 1982); and S. Ruddick, *Maternal Thinking* (Boston: Beacon Press, 1989).
9. See R. Rosenbloom (ed.), *Unspoken Rules: Sexual Orientation and Women's Human Rights* (San Francisco: International Gay and Lesbian Human Right Commission, 1995), 226 (fn22); and L. Benkov, *Reinventing the Family* (New York: Crown, 1994), 117.
10. D. Wikler and N. J. Wikler, "Turkey-baster Babies: The Demedicalization of Artificial Insemination," *Milbank Quarterly* 69(1):10, 1991.
11. Ibid.
12. The first known custody battle involving a lesbian couple and a sperm donor was *Loftin* v. *Flournoy* in California. For a superb discussion of the relevant case law, see N. Polikoff, "This Child Does Have Two Mothers," *Georgetown Law Journal* 78(1990):459–575.
13. Polikoff, "Two Mothers" provides detailed discussion of the most significant legal cases of custody contests after death of the biological lesbian comother. In both the most prominent cases, higher

courts eventually reversed decisions that had denied custody to the surviving lesbian parent, but only after serious emotional harm had been inflicted on the children and parents alike. See pp. 527–532.

14. V. L. Henry, "A Tale of Three Women," *American Journal of Law & Medicine* XIX, 3:297, 1993.
15. Ibid., 300; Polikoff, "This Child Does Have Two Mothers," 492.
16. J. Griscom, "The Case of Sharon Kowalski and Karen Thompson," in P. S. Rothenberg (ed.), *Race, Class, and Gender in the United States* (New York: St. Martin's Press, 1992).
17. See W. B. Rubenstein (ed.), *Lesbians, Gay Men, and the Law* (New York: New Press, 1993), 452.
18. National Center for Lesbian Rights, "Our Day in Court—Against Each Other," in Rubenstein, 561–562.
19. M. Gil de Lamadrid, "Expanding the Definition of Family: A Universal Issue," *Berkeley Women's Law Journal* v. 8:178, 1993.
20. The Sharon Bottoms case in Virginia is the most prominent of current setbacks. In 1994, Sharon Bottoms lost custody of her two-year-old son because the trial court judge deemed her lesbianism to be immoral and illegal. In April 1995, the Virginia state supreme court upheld the ruling, which at this writing is being appealed to the U.S. Supreme Court.
21. Quoted in S. Sherman (ed.), *Lesbian and Gay Marriage* (Philadelphia: Temple University Press, 1992), 191.
22. Ibid., 173.
23. Bozett, epilogue to *Gay and Lesbian Parents*, 232.
24. Cited in Sherman, *Lesbian and Gay Marriage*, 9 (fn. 6). A more recent poll conducted by *The Advocate* suggests that the trend of support for gay marriage is increasing. See E. Wolfson, "Crossing the Threshhold," *Review of Law & Social Change* XXI, 3:583, 1994–95.
25. The decision stated that the sexual orientation of the parties was irrelevant because same-sex spouses could be of any sexual orientation. It was the gender discrimination involved in limiting one's choice of spouse that violated the state constitution. See Wolfson, "Crossing the Threshold," 573.
26. See, for example, Nancy Polikoff, "We Will Get What We Ask For: Why Legalizing Gay and Lesbian Marriage Will Not 'Dismantle the Legal Structure of Gender in Every Marriage.'" *Virginia Law Review* 79:1549–1550, 1993.
27. Law professor Thomas Coleman, executive director of the "Family Diversity Project" in California, expresses these views in Sherman, 128–129. Likewise, Bob Hattoy, a gay White House aide in the Clinton administration, believed that "to support same-sex marriage at this particular cultural moment in America is a loser." Quoted in Francis X. Clines, "In Gay-Marriage Storm, Weary Clinton Aide Is Buffeted on All Sides," *New York Times*, May 29, 1996, A16.
28. A. Sullivan, "Here Comes the Groom: A Conservative Case for Gay Marriage," *New Republic* 201(9):20–22, August 28, 1989; J. Rauch, "A Pro-Gay, Pro-Family Policy," *Wall Street Journal*, November 29, 1995, A22.
29. Kirk Johnson, quoted in Wolfson, 567.
30. N. D. Hunter, "Marriage, Law and Gender: A Feminist Inquiry," *Law & Sexuality* 1(1):12, 1991.
31. Wolfson, "Crossing the Threshhold."
32. "Some Progress Found in Poll on Gay Rights," *San Francisco Chronicle*, June 20, 1994.
33. "Support for Clinton's Stand on Gay Marriage," *San Francisco Chronicle*, May 25, 1996, A6; Available online at www.gallup.com/poll/releases/pr010604.asp.
34. G. Remafedi (ed.), *Death by Denial* (Boston: Alyson Publications, 1994).
35. Quoted in Miller, *Out in the World*, 350.
36. The three journals were *Journal of Marriage and the Family*, *Family Relations*, and *Journal of Family Issues;* Allen and Demo, "Families of Lesbians and Gay Men," 119.
37. For overviews of the research, see Patterson, "Children of Lesbian and Gay Parents"; J. Laird, "Lesbian and Gay Families," in Walsh (ed.), *Normal Family Processes* 2nd ed. (New York: Guilford Press, 1993), 282–328; Allen and Demo, "Families of Lesbians and Gay Men."
38. Laird, "Lesbian and Gay Families," 316–317.
39. Ibid., 317; D. H. Demo and K. Allen, "Diversity within Lesbian and Gay Families," *Journal of Social and Personal Relationships* 13(3):26, 1996; F. Tasker and S. Golombok, "Adults Raised as Children in Lesbian Families," *American Journal of Orthopsychiatry*, 65:203–215, 1998.

40. Tasker and Golombok, "Adults Raised as Children in Lesbian Families."
41. Quoted in L. Rafkin, *Different Mothers* (Pittsburgh: Cleis Press, 1990), 34.
42. Laird, "Lesbian and Gay Families."
43. See, for example, Patterson; Demo and Allen; Benkov; K. Weston, *Families We Choose* (New York: Columbia University Press, 1991); and L. Peplau, "Research on Homosexual Couples: An Overview," in J. P. De Cecco (ed.), *Gay Relationships* (New York: Hayworth Press, 1988).
44. S. Minter, "U.S.A.," in Rosenbloom (ed.), *Unspoken Rules,* 219.
45. Quoted in Maralee Schwartz & Kenneth J. Cooper, "Equal Rights Initiative in Iowa Attacked," *Washington Post,* Aug 23, 1992, A15.
46. Laird, 315–316.
47. See, for example, Judith Stacey and Timothy Biblarz, "Does the Sexual Orientation of Parents Matter?" *American Sociological Review* 66(2):159–183, April 2001.
48. As Tasker and Golombok concede, "Young adults from lesbian homes tended to be more willing to have a sexual relationship with someone of the same gender if they felt physically attracted to them. They were also more likely to have considered the possibility of developing same-gender sexual attractions or relationships. Having a lesbian mother, therefore, appeared to widen the adolescent's view of what constituted acceptable sexual behavior to include same-gender sexual relationships," 212.
49. A. Rich, "Compulsory Heterosexuality and the Lesbian Continuum," *Signs* 5(4):Summer 1980:631–660.
50. Eve Sedgwick, "How to Bring Your Kids Up Gay," in Warner (ed.), *Fear of a Queer Planet* (Minneapolis: University of Minnesota Press, 1993), 76.
51. Quoted in Rafkin, *Different Mothers,* 64–65.
52. Minter, "U.S.A.," 222.
53. Remafedi, *Death by Denial.*
54. Quoted in Sherman, 70.
55. L. Due, *Joining the Tribe* (New York: Doubleday, 1996).
56. See J. M. Irvine, "A Place in the Rainbow: Theorizing Lesbian and Gay Culture," *Sociological Theory* 12(2):232, July 1994.
57. Quoted in Rafkin, *Different Mothers,* 24.
58. Quoted in Polikoff, "This Child Does Have Two Mothers," 569–570.
59. Quoted in Polikoff, 570.
60. Quoted in Rafkin, 81.
61. Benkov, *Reinventing the Family,* chap. 8.
62. L. Kurdek and J. P. Schmitt, "Relationship Quality of Gay Men in Closed or Open Relationships," *Journal of Homosexuality* 12(2):85–99, 1985; and F. R. Lynch, "Nonghetto Gays: An Ethnography of Suburban Homosexuals," in Herdt (ed.), *Gay Culture in America* (Boston: Beacon Press, 1992), 165–201.
63. Rafkin, 39.
64. Allen and Demo.
65. Polikoff, "This Child Does Have Two Mothers," 461 (fn.2).
66. Weston, "Parenting in the Age of AIDS," 159.
67. D. Blankenhorn, *Fatherless America* (New York: Basic Books, 1995), 233; J. Leo, "Promoting No-Dad Families," *U.S. News and World Report,* May 15, 1995:26; and S. Seligson, "Seeds of Doubt," *Atlantic Monthly,* March 1995:28.
68. Bozett, p. 4 discusses gay male parenthood strategies. Also, available on-line at www.growinggenerations.com.
69. Stacey and Biblarz, "Does the Sexual Orientation of Parents Matter?"; Maureen Sullivan, "Rozzie and Harriet?: Gender and Family Patterns of Lesbian Coparents," *Gender & Society* 10(6):747–767, December 1996.
70. Quoted in Rafkin, 33.
71. Ibid., 53.
72. Stacey and Biblarz, "Does the Sexual Orientation of Parents Matter?" 176.
73. Rafkin, 174.

74. T. Moore, "Fear of Violence Rising among 1990s Youth," *San Francisco Chronicle*, December 7, 1995, A1, A15.
75. L. Kurdek, "The Allocation of Household Labor in Gay, Lesbian, and Heterosexual Married Couples," *Journal of Social Issues* 49(3):127–139, 1993; P. Blumstein and P. Schwartz, *American Couples* (New York: William Morrow, 1983); Peplau, 193; Stacey and Biblarz, "Does the Sexual Orientation of Parents Matter," 173–174; Sullivan, "Rozzie and Harriet?"; Gillian Dunne, "Opting into Motherhood: Lesbians Blurring the Boundaries and Transforming the Meaning of Parenthood and Kinship," *Gender & Society* 14(1):11–35, 2000.
76. See Weston, *Families We Choose*, for an ethnographic treatment of these chosen kin ties.
77. As Allen and Demo suggest, "An aspect of biculturalism is resilience and creative adaptation in the context of minority group oppression and stigma," and this "offers a potential link to other oppressed groups in American society." "Families of Lesbians and Gay Men," 122.

Chapter

12

Trouble in the Family

READING 36

Prisoners' Families and Children

Jeremy Travis

As the nation debates the wisdom of a fourfold increase in our incarceration rate over the past generation, one fact is clear: Prisons separate prisoners from their families. Every individual sent to prison leaves behind a network of family relationships. Prisoners are the children, parents, siblings, and kin to untold numbers of relatives who are each affected differently by a family member's arrest, incarceration, and ultimate homecoming.

Little is known about imprisonment's impact on these family networks. Descriptive data about the children of incarcerated parents only begin to tell the story. During the 1990s, as the nation's prison population increased by half, the number of children who had a parent in prison also increased by half—from 1 million to 1.5 million. By the end of 2002, 1 in 45 minor children had a parent in prison (Mumola 2004).[1] These children represent 2 percent of all minor children in America, and a sobering 7 percent of all African-American children (Mumola 2000). With little if any public debate, we have extended prison's reach to include hundreds of thousands of young people who were not the prime target of the criminal justice policies that put their parents behind bars.

In the simplest human terms, prison places an indescribable burden on the relationships between these parents and their children. Incarcerated fathers and mothers must learn to cope with the loss of normal contact with their children, infrequent visits in inhospitable surroundings, and lost opportunities to contribute to their children's development. Their children must come to terms with the reality of an absent parent, the stigma of parental imprisonment, and an altered support system that may include grandparents, foster care, or a new adult in the home. In addition, in those communities where incarceration rates are high, the experience of having a mother or father in prison is now quite commonplace, with untold consequences for foster care systems, multigenerational households, social services delivery, community norms, childhood development, and parenting patterns.

Imprisonment profoundly affects families in another, less tangible way. When young men and women are sent to prison, they are removed from the traditional rhythms of dating, courtship, marriage, and family formation. Because far more men than women are sent to prison each year, our criminal justice policies have created a "gender imbalance" (Braman 2002), a disparity in the number of available single men and women in many communities. In neighborhoods where incarceration and reentry have hit hardest, the gender imbalance is particularly striking. Young women complain about the shortage of men who are suitable marriage prospects because so many of the young men cycle in and out of the criminal justice system. The results are an increase in female-headed households and narrowed roles for fathers in the lives of their children and men in the lives of women and families in general. As more young men grow up with fewer stable attachments to girlfriends, spouses, and intimate partners, the masculine identity is redefined.

The family is often depicted as the bedrock of American society. Over the years, we have witnessed wave after wave of social policy initiatives designed to strengthen, reunite, or simply create families. Liberals and conservatives have accused each other of espousing policies that undermine "family values." In recent years, policymakers, foundation officers, and opinion leaders have also decried the absence of fathers from the lives of their children. These concerns have translated into a variety of programs, governmental initiatives, and foundation strategies that constitute a "fatherhood movement." Given the iconic stature of the family in our vision of American life and the widespread consensus that the absence of father figures harms future generations, our national experiment with mass incarceration seems, at the very least, incongruent with the rhetoric behind prevailing social policies. At worst, the imprisonment of millions of individuals and the disruption of their family relationships has significantly undermined the role that families could play in promoting our social well-being.

The institution of family plays a particularly important role in the crime policy arena. Families are an integral part of the mechanisms of informal social control that constrain antisocial behavior. The quality of family life (e.g., the presence of supportive parent-child relationships) is significant in predicting criminal delinquency (Loeber and Farrington 1998, 2001). Thus, if families suffer adverse effects from our incarceration policies, we would expect these harmful effects to be felt in the next generation, as children grow up at greater risk of engaging in delinquent and criminal behavior. The institution of marriage is another important link in the mechanism of informal social control. Marriage reduces the likelihood that ex-offenders will associate with peers involved in crime, and generally inhibits a return to crime (Laub, Nagin, and Sampson 1998). In fact, marriage is a stronger predictor of desistance from criminal activity than simple cohabitation, and a "quality" marriage—one based on a strong mutual commitment—is an even stronger predictor (Horney, Osgood, and Marshall 1995). Thus, criminal justice policies that weaken marriage and inhibit spousal commitments are likely to undermine the natural processes of desistance, thereby causing more crime. In short, in developing crime policies, families matter. If our crime policies have harmful consequences for families, we risk undermining the role families can play in controlling criminal behavior.

This [reading] examines the impact of incarceration and reentry on families. We begin by viewing the antecedents to the creation of families—the relationships between young men and young women—in communities where the rates of arrest, removal, incarceration, and reentry are particularly high. Then we discuss imprisonment's impact on relationships between an incarcerated parent and his or her children. Next we examine the effects of parental incarceration on the early childhood and adolescent development of children left behind. We then observe the family's role in reentry. We close with reflections on the impact of imprisonment on prisoners' family life, ways to mitigate incarceration's harmful effects, and ways to promote constructive connections between prisoners and their families.

THE "GENDER IMBALANCE"

To understand the magnitude of the criminal justice system's impact on the establishment of intimate partner relationships, we draw upon the work of Donald Braman (2002, 2004), an anthropologist who conducted a three-year ethnographic study of incarceration's impact on communities in Washington, D.C. In the District of Columbia, 7 percent of the adult African-American male population returns to the community from jail or prison each year. According to Braman's estimates, more than 75 percent of African-American men in the District of Columbia can expect to be incarcerated at some point during their lifetime. One consequence of these high rates of incarceration is what Braman calls a "gender imbalance," meaning simply that there are fewer men than women in the hardest hit communities. Half of the women in the nation's capital live in communities with low incarceration rates. In these communities, there are about 94 men for every 100 women. For the rest of the women in D.C.—whose neighborhoods have higher incarceration rates—the ratio is about 80 men for every 100 women. Furthermore, 10 percent of the District's women live in neighborhoods with the highest incarceration rates, where more than 12 percent of men are behind bars. In these neighborhoods, there are fewer than 62 men for every 100 women.

This gender imbalance translates into large numbers of fatherless families in communities with high rates of incarceration. In neighborhoods with a 2 percent male incarceration rate, Braman (2002) found that fathers were absent from more than one-half of the families. But in the communities with the highest male incarceration rates—about 12 percent—more than three-quarters of the families had a father absent. This phenomenon is not unique to Washington, D.C., however. In a national study, Sabol and Lynch (1998) also found larger numbers of female-headed families in counties receiving large numbers of returning prisoners.

Clearly, mass incarceration results in the substantial depletion in the sheer numbers of men in communities with high rates of imprisonment. For those men who are arrested, removed, and sent to prison, life in prison has profound and long-lasting consequences for their roles as intimate partners, spouses, and fathers. In the following sections, we will document those effects. Viewing this issue from a community perspective, however, reminds us that incarceration also alters the relationships between the men and women who are not incarcerated. In her research on the marriage patterns of low-income mothers, Edin (2000) found that the decision to marry (or remarry) depends, in part, on the economic prospects, social respectability, and reliability of potential husbands—attributes that are adversely affected by imprisonment. Low marriage rates, in turn, affect the life courses of men who have been imprisoned, reducing their likelihood of desistance from criminal activity. Thus, the communities with the highest rates of incarceration are caught in what Western, Lopoo, and McLanahan (2004, 21) call the "high-crime/low-marriage equilibrium." In these communities, women "will be understandably averse to marriage because their potential partners bring few social or economic benefits to the table. Men, who remain unmarried or unattached to stable households, are likely to continue their criminal involvement."

Braman quotes two of his community informants to illustrate these ripple effects of the gender imbalance. "David" described how the shortage of men affected dating patterns:

> Oh, yeah, everybody is aware of [the male shortage]. . . . And the fact that [men] know the ratio, and they feel that the ratio allows them to take advantage of just that statistic. 'Well, this woman I don't want to deal with, really because there are six to seven women to every man.' (2002, 166)

The former wife of a prisoner commented that women were less discerning in their choices of partners because there were so few men:

> Women will settle for whatever it is that their man [wants], even though you know that man probably has about two or three women. Just to be wanted, or just to be held, or just to go out and have a date makes her feel good, so she's willing to accept. I think now women accept a lot of things—the fact that he might have another woman or the fact that they can't clearly get as much time as they want to. The person doesn't spend as much time as you would [like] him to spend. The little bit of time that you get you cherish. (2002, 167)

The reach of our incarceration policies thus extends deep into community life. Even those men and women who are never arrested pay a price. As they are looking for potential partners in marriage and parenting, they find that the simple rituals of dating are darkened by the long shadow of imprisonment.

THE IMPACT OF INCARCERATION ON PARENT-CHILD RELATIONSHIPS

The Family Profile of the Prisoner Population

Before turning to a closer examination of the effects of imprisonment on the relationships between incarcerated parents and their children, we should first describe the family circumstances of the nation's prisoners. In 1997, about half (47 percent) of state prisoners reported they had never been married. Only 23 percent reported they were married

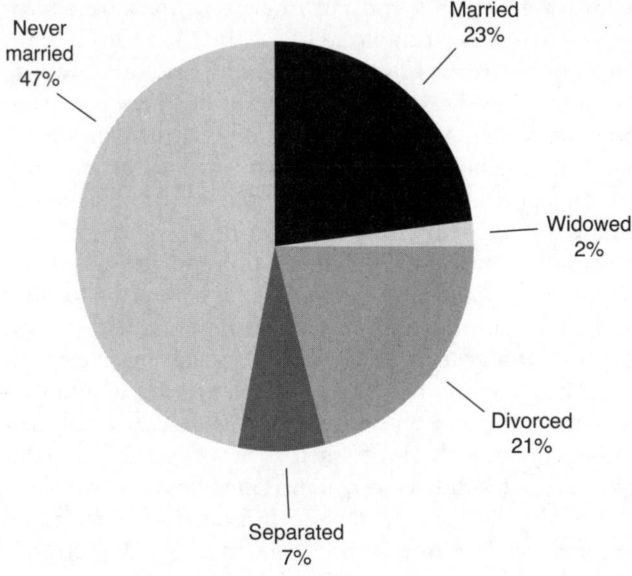

FIGURE 36.1 ***Marital Status of Parents in State Prison, 1997***
Source: Mumola (2000).

at the time of their incarceration, while 28 percent said they were divorced or separated (Figure 36.1). Yet most prisoners are parents. More than half (55 percent) of all state prisoners reported having at least one minor child. Because the overwhelming majority of state prisoners are men, incarcerated parents are predominantly male (93 percent). The number of incarcerated mothers, however, has grown dramatically in the past decade. Between 1991 and 2000, the number of incarcerated mothers increased by 87 percent, compared with a 60 percent increase in the number of incarcerated fathers. Of the men in state prison, 55 percent have children—a total of about 1.2 million—under the age of 18. About 65 percent of women in state prison are mothers to children younger than 18; their children number about 115,500 (Mumola 2000).

A mother's incarceration has a different impact on living arrangements than does that of a father. Close to two-thirds (64 percent) of mothers reported living with their children before incarceration, compared with slightly less than half (44 percent) of fathers in 1997. Therefore, as the percentage of women in prison increases, more children experience a more substantial disruption. We should not conclude, however, that the imprisonment of a nonresident father has little impact on his children. Research has shown that nonresident fathers can make considerable contributions to the development and well-being of their children (Amato and Rivera 1999; Furstenberg 1993). They contribute to their children's financial support, care, and social support even when they are not living in the children's home (Edin and Lein 1997; Hairston 1998; Western and McLanahan 2000). Therefore, a depiction of families' living arrangements only begins to describe the nature of the parenting roles played by fathers before they were sent to prison.

The national data on incarcerated parents also fail to capture the diversity of parent-child relationships. According to research conducted by Denise Johnston (2001) at the Center for Children of Incarcerated Parents, it is not uncommon for both incarcerated fathers and mothers to have children by more than one partner. Furthermore, these parents may have lived with some but not all of their children prior to their incarceration. This perspective leads to another conclusion: Individuals who are incarcerated may also have served as parent figures to children not their own—as stepparents or surrogate parents in families that blend children into one household.

We know little about the nature of these parent-child relationships. As was noted above, even absent fathers can provide emotional and financial support prior to their incarceration. However, the profiles of incarcerated parents also point to indicia of stress and dysfunction within these families. More than three-quarters of parents in state prison reported a prior conviction and, of those, more than half had been previously incarcerated. During the time leading up to their most current arrest and incarceration, nearly half were out of prison on some type of conditional release, such as probation or parole, in 1997. Nearly half (46 percent) of incarcerated fathers were imprisoned for a violent crime, as were one-quarter (26 percent) of the mothers. Mothers in prison were much more likely than fathers to be serving time for drug offenses (35 percent versus 23 percent). Nearly one-third of the mothers reported committing their crime to get either drugs or money for drugs, compared with 19 percent of fathers. More than half of all parents in prison reported using drugs in the month before they were arrested, and more than a third were under the influence of alcohol when they committed the crime. Nearly a quarter of incarcerated mothers (23 percent) and about a tenth (13 percent) of incarcerated fathers reported a history of mental illness (Mumola 2000). Clearly, these individuals were struggling with multiple stressors that, at a minimum, complicated their role as parents.

The portrait of prisoners' extended family networks is also sobering. According to findings from the Urban Institute's *Returning Home* (Visher, La Vigne, and Travis 2004) study in Maryland, these networks exhibit high rates of criminal involvement, substance abuse, and family violence (La Vigne, Kachnowski, et al. 2003). In interviews conducted with a sample of men and women just prior to their release from prison and return to homes in Baltimore, the Institute's researchers found that about 40 percent of the prisoners reported having at least one relative currently serving a prison sentence. Nine percent of the women said they had been threatened, harassed, or physically hurt by their husband, and 65 percent of those who reported domestic violence also reported being victimized by a nonspouse intimate partner. No male respondents reported this kind of abuse. The women reported that, other than their partners, the highest level of abuse came from other women in their families—their mothers, stepmothers, or aunts. Nearly two-thirds of inmates (62 percent) reported at least one family member with a substance abuse or alcohol problem and more than 16 percent listed four or more family members with histories of substance abuse. These characteristics highlight the high levels of risks and challenges in the families prisoners leave behind.

The Strain of Incarceration on Families

We turn next to a discussion of the impact of parental incarceration on the families left behind. One obvious consequence is that the families have fewer financial resources.

According to the Bureau of Justice Statistics, in 1997 most parents in state prison (71 percent) reported either full-time or part-time employment in the month preceding their current arrest (Mumola 2002). Wages or salary was the most common source of income among incarcerated fathers before imprisonment, 60 percent of whom reported having a full-time job. Mothers, on the other hand, were less likely to have a full-time job (39 percent). For them, the most common sources of income were wages (44 percent) or public assistance (42 percent). Very few mothers reported receiving formal child support payments (6 percent) (Mumola 2000). During incarceration, the flow of financial support from the incarcerated parent's job stops, leaving the family to either make do with less or make up the difference, thereby placing added strains on the new caregivers. Eligibility for welfare payments under the TANF (Temporary Assistance for Needy Families) program ceases as soon as an individual is no longer a custodial parent—i.e., upon incarceration. In some cases, a caregiver may continue to receive TANF payments when the incarcerated parent loses eligibility, but because these benefits are now "child-only," they are lower than full TANF benefits. Food stamps are also unavailable to incarcerated individuals.

New caregivers often struggle to make ends meet during the period of parental incarceration. Bloom and Steinhart (1993) found that in 1992 nearly half (44 percent) of families caring for the children of an incarcerated parent were receiving welfare payments under TANF's predecessor program, AFDC (Aid to Families with Dependent Children). Under the recent welfare reform laws, however, TANF support is more limited than in the past, as lifetime eligibility has been capped at 60 months, work requirements have been implemented, and restrictions have been placed on TANF funds for those who have violated probation or parole, or have been convicted of certain drug crimes (Phillips and Bloom 1998). Even under the old AFDC program, most caregivers reported that they did not have sufficient resources to meet basic needs (Bloom and Steinhart 1993). Moreover, these economic strains affect more than the family's budget. According to several studies, financial stress can produce negative consequences for caretakers' behavior, including harsh and inconsistent parenting patterns, which, in turn, cause emotional and behavioral problems for the children (McLoyd 1998).

Other adjustments are required as well. Because most prisoners are men, and 55 percent of them are fathers, the first wave of impact is felt by the mothers of their children. Some mothers struggle to maintain contact with the absent father, on behalf of their children as well as themselves. Others decide that the incarceration of their children's father is a turning point, enabling them to start a new life and cut off ties with the father. More fundamentally, Furstenberg (1993) found that a partner left behind often becomes more independent and self-sufficient during the period of incarceration, changes that may ultimately benefit the family unit or lead to the dissolution of the relationship. At a minimum, however, these changes augur a significant adjustment in roles when the incarcerated partner eventually returns home.

In some cases, the incarceration period can have another, longer-lasting effect on the legal relationships between parents and children. In 1997, Congress enacted the Adoption and Safe Families Act (ASFA) to improve the safety and well-being of children in the foster care system as well as to remove barriers to the permanent placement, particularly adoption, of these children.[2] The ASFA stipulates that "permanency" decisions (determinations about a child's ultimate placement) should be made within 12 months of the initial removal of the child from the home. With limited exceptions, foster care placements can last no longer than 15 months, and if a child has been in foster care for 15 out of the previous 22 months, petitions must be filed in court to terminate parental rights. At least half the states now include incarceration as a reason to terminate parental rights (Genty 2001).

This new legislation has far-reaching consequences for the children of incarcerated parents. According to BJS, 10 percent of mothers in prison, and 2 percent of fathers, have at least one child in foster care (Mumola 2000). Because the average length of time served for prisoners released in 1997 was 28 months (Sabol and Lynch 2001), the short timelines set forth in ASFA establish a legal predicate that could lead to increases in the termination of parental rights for parents in prison (Lynch and Sabol 2001). Philip Genty (2001), a professor at Columbia University Law School, made some rough calculations of ASFA's impact. Looking only at reported cases discoverable through a Lexis search, he found, in the five years following ASFA's enactment, a 250 percent increase in cases terminating parental rights due to parental incarceration, from 260 to 909 cases.

In addition to those legal burdens placed on incarcerated parents, the new family caregivers face challenges in forging relationships with the children left behind. Some of these new caregivers may not have had much contact with the children before the parent's incarceration, so they must establish themselves as de facto parents and develop relationships with the children. Contributing to the trauma of this changing family structure, prisoners' children are sometimes separated from their siblings during incarceration because the new network of caregivers cannot care for the entire sibling group (Hairston 1995).

In short, when the prison gates close and parents are separated from their children, the network of care undergoes a profound realignment. Even two-parent families experience the strain of lost income, feel the remaining parent's sudden sole responsibility for the children and the household, and suffer the stigma associated with imprisonment. However, prisoners' family structures rarely conform to the two-parent model and are more often characterized by nonresident fathers, children living with different parents, and female-headed households. In these circumstances, the ripple effects of a mother or father going to prison reach much farther, and grandparents, aunts and uncles, and the foster care system must step into the breach. In addition, these extended networks feel the financial, emotional, and familial weight of their new responsibilities.

Incarceration has yet one more effect on the structure of prisoners' families. One of the important functions that families perform is to create assets that are passed along to the next generation. These assets are sometimes quite tangible: Money is saved, real estate appreciates in value, and businesses are built. These tangible assets can typically be transferred to one's children. Sometimes the assets are intangible: Social status is achieved, professional networks are cultivated, and educational milestones are reached. These intangible assets can also translate into economic advantage by opening doors for the next generation. Braman asks whether the minimal intergenerational transfer of wealth in black families is related to the high rates of incarceration among black men. Taking a historical view, he concludes:

> The disproportionate incarceration of black men . . . helps to explain why black families are less able to save money and why each successive generation inherits less wealth than

> their white counterparts. Incarceration acts like a hidden tax, one that is visited disproportionately on poor and minority families; and while its costs are most directly felt by the adults closest to the incarcerated family member, the full effect is eventually felt by the next generation as well. (2004, 156)

The ripple effects of incarceration on the family are far-reaching. The gender imbalance disturbs the development of intimate relationships that might support healthy families. Families' financial resources and relationship capabilities are strained at the same time they are scrambling for more assets to support their incarcerated loved one. Yet, despite the hardships of incarceration, families can play an important role in improving outcomes for prisoners and prisoners' children. Several studies have shown that the "quality of care children receive following separation and their ongoing relationships with parents" are "instrumental forces in shaping outcomes for children" (Hairston 1999, 205). According to one study (Sack 1977), the behavioral problems displayed by children of incarcerated fathers diminished once the children got to spend time with their fathers.

On the other hand, in a small percentage of cases, continued parental involvement may not be in the child's best interests. For example, BJS (Greenfeld et al. 1998) reports that 7 percent of prisoners convicted of violent crimes were convicted of intimate partner violence. Even more disturbing are those cases involving child abuse and neglect, where the child's best interests argue against parental involvement. According to BJS, among inmates who were in prison for a sex crime against a child, the child was the prisoner's own child or stepchild in a third of the cases (Langan, Schmitt, and Durose 2003). Yet there has been very little research on the nexus between this form of family violence, incarceration, and reentry.

Discussion of prisoners convicted of violence within the family only raises larger questions—questions not answered by current research—about whether some parent-child relationships are so troubled and so characterized by the patterns of parental substance abuse, criminal involvement, mental illness, and the intrusions of criminal justice supervision that parental removal is a net benefit for the child. It is undoubtedly true that removing a parent involved in certain types of child abuse is better for the child. But we know little about the critical characteristics of the preprison relationships between children and their incarcerated parents, especially as to what kind of parents they were, and how their removal affects their children.

Even without a deeper understanding of the parenting roles played by America's prisoners, we still must face several incontrovertible, troubling facts. First, expanding the use of prison to respond to crime has put more parents in prison. Between 1991 and 1999, a short eight-year period, the number of parents in state and federal prisons increased by 60 percent, from 452,500 to 721,500 (Mumola 2000). By the end of 2002, 3.7 million parents were under some form of correctional supervision (Mumola 2004). Second, many children are left behind when parents are incarcerated. By 1999, 2 percent of all minor children in the United States—about 1.5 million—had a parent in state or federal prison. (If we include parents who are in jail, on probation or parole, or recently released from prison, the estimate of children with a parent involved in the criminal justice system reaches 7 million, or nearly 10 percent of all minor children in America

[Mumola 2000].) Third, the racial disparities in America's prison population translate into substantial, disturbing racial inequities in the population of children affected by our current levels of imprisonment. About 7 percent of all African-American minor children and nearly 3 percent of all Hispanic minor children in America have a parent in prison. In comparison, barely 1 percent of all Caucasian minor children have a parent in prison (Mumola 2000). Finally, most of the children left behind are quite young. Sixty percent are under age 10, while the average child left behind is 8 years old.

In this era of mass incarceration, our criminal justice system casts a wide net that has altered the lives of millions of children, disrupting their relationships with their parents, altering the networks of familial support, and placing new burdens on such governmental services as schools, foster care, adoption agencies, and youth-serving organizations. As Phillips and Bloom succinctly concluded, "by getting tough on crime, the United States has gotten tough on children" (1998, 539). These costs are rarely included in our calculations of the costs of justice.

Parent-Child Relationships during Imprisonment

When a parent is arrested and later incarcerated, the child's world undergoes significant, sometimes traumatic, disruption. Most children are not present at the time of their parent's arrest, and arrested parents typically do not tell the police that they have minor children (ABA 1993). Family members are often reluctant to tell the children that their parent has been incarcerated because of social stigma (Braman 2003). Therefore, the immediate impact of an arrest can be quite traumatizing—a child is abruptly separated from his or her parent, with little information about what happened, why it happened, or what to expect.

The arrest and subsequent imprisonment of a parent frequently results in a significant realignment of the family's arrangements for caring for the child, depicted in Figure 36.2. Not surprisingly, the nature of the new living arrangements depends heavily on which parent is sent to prison. Recall that about two-thirds of incarcerated mothers in state prison lived with their children before they were imprisoned. Following the mother's incarceration, about a quarter (28 percent) of their children remain with their fathers. Most children of incarcerated mothers, however, are cared for by an extended family that is suddenly responsible for another mouth to feed and child to raise. More than half of these children (53 percent) will live with a grandparent, adding burdens to a generation that supposedly has already completed its child-rearing responsibilities. Another quarter of these children (26 percent) will live with another relative, placing new duties on the extended family. Some children have no familial safety net: almost 10 percent of incarcerated mothers reported that their child was placed in foster care (Mumola 2000).[3]

The story for incarcerated fathers is quite different. Less than half (44 percent) lived with their children before prison; once they are sent to prison, most of their children (85 percent) will live with the children's mother. Grandparents (16 percent) and other relatives (6 percent) play a much smaller role in assuming child care responsibilities when a father is incarcerated. Only 2 percent of the children of incarcerated men enter the foster care system. In sum, a child whose father is sent to prison is significantly less likely to experience a life disruption, such as moving in with another family member or placement in a foster home.

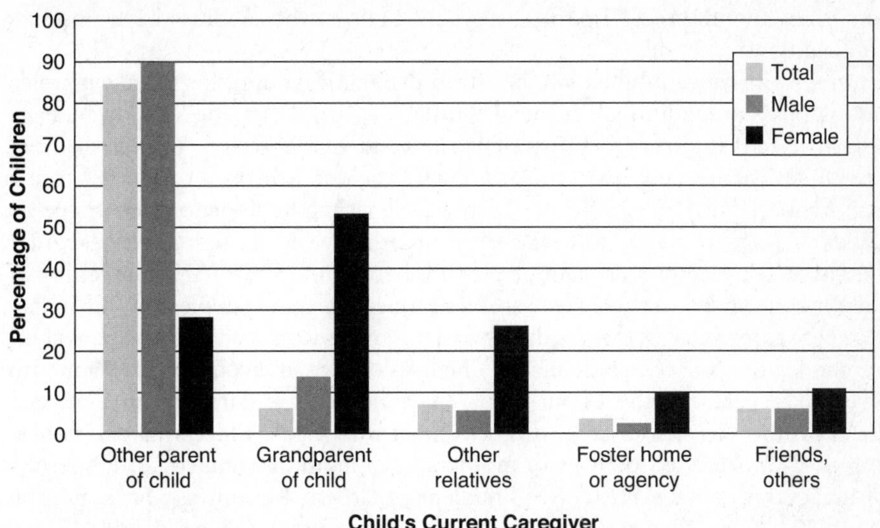

FIGURE 36.2 ***Living Arrangements of Minor Children of State Inmates prior to Incarceration***

Figures do not total 100 percent because some prisoners had children living with multiple caregivers.
Source: Mumola (2000).

The nation's foster care system has become a child care system of last resort for many children with parents in prison. Research by the Center for Children of Incarcerated Parents (Johnston 1999) found that, at any given time, 10 percent of children in foster care currently have a mother—and 33 percent have a father—behind bars. Even more striking, 70 percent of foster children have had a parent incarcerated at one time or another during their time in foster care.

When a parent goes to prison, the separation between parent and child is experienced at many levels. First, there is the simple fact of distance. The majority of state prisoners (62 percent) are held in facilities located more than 100 miles from their homes (Mumola 2000). Because prison facilities for women are scarce, mothers are incarcerated an average of 160 miles away from their children (Hagan and Coleman 2001). The distance between prisoners and their families is most pronounced for District of Columbia residents. As a result of the federal takeover of the District's prison system, defendants sentenced to serve felony time are now housed in facilities that are part of the far-flung network of federal prisons. In 2000, 12 percent of the District's inmates were held in federal prisons more than 500 miles from Washington. By 2002, that proportion had risen to 30 percent. Nineteen percent are in prisons as far away as Texas and California (Santana 2003). Not surprisingly, in an analysis of BJS data, Hairston and Rollin (2003, 68) found a relationship between this distance and family visits: "The distance prisoners were from their homes influenced the extent to which they saw families and friends. The farther prisoners were from their homes, the higher the percentage of prisoners who had no visitors in the month preceding the survey. . . . Those whose homes were closest to the prison had the most visits."

Geographic distance inhibits families from making visits and, for those who make the effort, imposes an additional financial burden on already strained family budgets. Donald Braman tells the story of Lilly, a District resident whose son Anthony is incarcerated in Ohio (Braman 2002). When Anthony was held in Lorton, a prison in Virginia that formerly housed prisoners from the District, she visited him once a week. Since the federal takeover, she manages to make only monthly visits, bringing her daughter, Anthony's sister. For each two-day trip, she spends between $150 and $200 for car rental, food, and a motel. Added to these costs are her money orders to supplement his inmate account and the care packages that she is allowed to send twice a year. She also pays about $100 a month for the collect calls he places. She lives on a fixed income of $530 a month.

Given these realities, the extent of parent-child contact during incarceration is noteworthy. Mothers in prison stay in closer contact with their children than do fathers. According to BJS, nearly 80 percent of mothers have monthly contact and 60 percent have at least weekly contact. Roughly 60 percent of fathers, by contrast, have monthly contact, and 40 percent have weekly contact with their children (Mumola 2000). These contacts take the form of letters, phone calls, and prison visits. Yet, a large percentage of prisoners serve their entire prison sentence without ever seeing their children. More than half of all mothers, and 57 percent of all fathers, never receive a personal visit from their children while in prison.

Particularly disturbing is Lynch and Sabol's finding (2001) that the frequency of contact decreases as prison terms get longer. Between 1991 and 1997, as the length of prison sentences increased, the level of contact of all kinds—calls, letters, and visits—decreased (Figure 36.3). This is especially troubling in light of research showing that the average length of prison sentences is increasing in America, reflecting more stringent sentencing policies. Thus, prisoners coming home in the future are likely to have had fewer interactions with their children, a situation that further weakens family ties and makes family reunification even more difficult.

In addition to the significant burden imposed by the great distances between prisoners and their families, corrections policies often hamper efforts to maintain family ties across the prison walls. The Women's Prison Association (1996) has identified several obstacles to constructive family contacts, some of which could easy be solved. The association found that it is difficult to get simple information on visiting procedures, and correctional administrators provide little help in making visiting arrangements. The visiting procedures themselves are often uncomfortable or humiliating. Furthermore, little attention is paid to mitigating the impact on the children of visiting a parent in prison.

Elizabeth Gaynes, director of the Osborne Association in New York City, tells a story that captures the emotional and psychological impact of a particular correctional policy upon a young girl who had come to visit her father. Because inmates were not allowed to handle money, the prison had drawn a yellow line three feet in front of the soda vending machines. Only visitors could cross that line. The father could not perform the simple act of getting his daughter a soda. If he wanted one, he had to ask his daughter to get it. According to Ms. Gaynes, this interaction represented an unnecessary and damaging role transformation; the child had become the provider, the parent had become the child.[4]

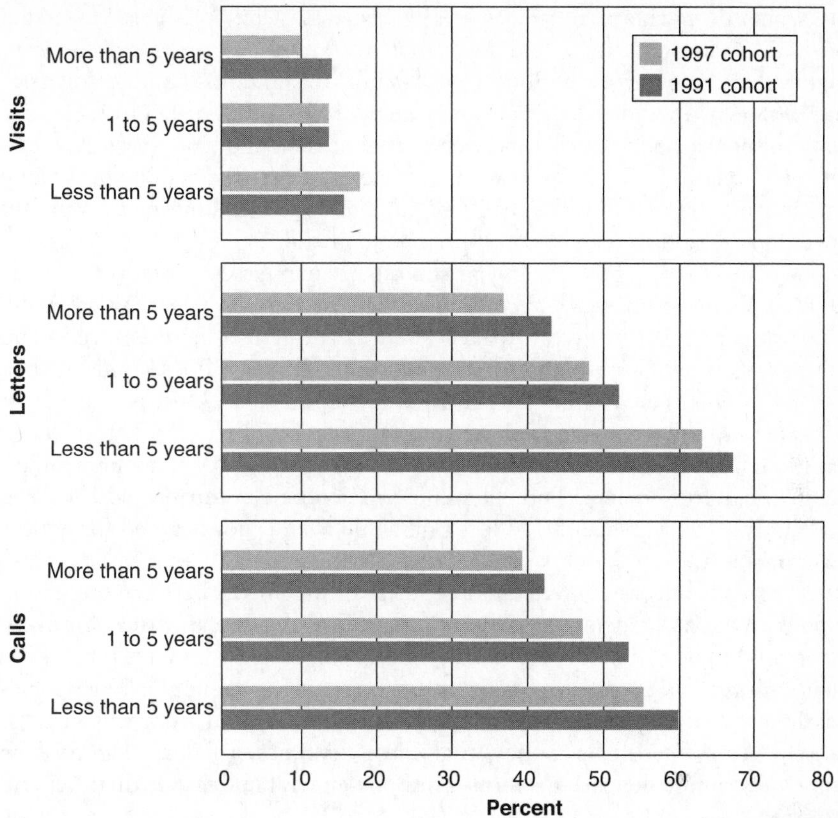

FIGURE 36.3 ***Level of Prisoners' Weekly Contact with Children, by Method and Length of Stay, 1991 and 1997***

Prisoners to be released in the next 12 months.

Source: Lynch and Sabol (2001).

Family Contact during Imprisonment: Obstacles and Opportunities

For a number of reasons, it is difficult to maintain parent-child contact during a period of incarceration. For one thing, many prisons narrowly define the family members who are granted visiting privileges. The State of Michigan's corrections department, for example, promulgated regulations in 1995 restricting the categories of individuals who are allowed to visit a prisoner. The approved visiting list may include minor children under the age of 18, but only if they are the prisoner's children, stepchildren, grandchildren, or siblings. Prisoners who are neither the biological parents nor legal stepparents of the children they were raising do not have this privilege. Finally, a child authorized to visit must be accompanied by either an adult who is an immediate family member of the child or of the inmate, or who is the child's legal guardians.[5] Many prisoners' extended family networks, including girlfriends and boyfriends who are raising prisoners' children, are not recognized in these narrow definitions of "family."[6] Limitations on visiting privileges are commonly justified on security or management grounds, but fail to recognize the complexity of the prisoner's familial networks. Rather than allowing the prisoner to define the "family" relationships that matter most, the arbitrary distinctions of biology or legal status are superimposed on the reality of familial networks, limiting meaningful contact that could make a difference to both prisoner and child.

Telephone contact is also burdened by prison regulations and by controversial relationships between phone companies and corrections departments. Prisoners are typically limited in the number of calls they can make. Their calls can also be monitored. The California Department of Corrections interrupts each call every 20 seconds with a recorded message: "This is a call from a California prison inmate." Most prisons allow prisoners to make only collect calls, and those calls typically cost between $1 and $3 per minute, even though most phone companies now charge less than 10 cents per minute for phone calls in the free society (Petersilia 2003). Telephone companies also charge between $1.50 and $4 just to place the collect call, while a fee is not charged for collect calls outside of prison.

The high price of collect calls reflects sweetheart arrangements between the phone companies and corrections agencies, under which the prisons receive kickbacks for every collect call, about 40 to 60 cents of every dollar. This arrangement translates into a substantial revenue source for corrections budgets. In 2001, for example, California garnered $35 million, based on $85 million of total revenue generated from prison calls. Some states require, by statute or policy, that these revenues pay for programs for inmates. Most states simply deposit this money into the general budget for their department of corrections.

Yet who bears these additional costs for maintaining phone contact with prisoners? The families of prisoners do, of course. In a study conducted by the Florida House of Representatives Corrections Committee (1998), family members reported spending an average amount of $69.19 per month accepting collect phone calls. According to this report, "Several family members surveyed stated that, although they wanted to continue to maintain contact with the inmate, they were forced to remove their names from the inmate's approved calling list because they simply could not afford to accept the calls" (1998, 23).

This monopolistic arrangement between phone companies and prisons makes families the unwitting funders of the prisons holding their loved ones. In essence, the states have off-loaded upwards of hundreds of millions of dollars of prison costs on to prisoners' families. Subsequently, families are placed in the unacceptable position of either agreeing to accept the calls, thereby making contributions to prison budgets, or ceasing phone contact with their loved ones. Of course, there are other, deeper costs attached to this practice. If a family chooses to limit (or stop) these phone calls, then family ties are weakened and the support system that could sustain the prisoner's reintegration is damaged. If the family chooses to pay the phone charges, then those financial resources are not available for other purposes, thereby adding to the strain the household experiences. In recent years, efforts to reform prison telephone policies have been successful in several states.[7] Yet, while these reform efforts are under way, tens of thousands of families are setting aside large portions of their budgets to pay inflated phone bills to stay in touch with their imprisoned family members.

Fortunately, a number of communities have implemented programs designed to overcome the barriers of distance, cost, and correctional practices that reduce contact between prisoners and their families. For example, Hope House, an organization in Washington, D.C., that connects incarcerated fathers with their children in the District, hosts summer camps at federal prisons in North Carolina and Maryland where children spend several hours a day for a week visiting with their fathers in prison. Hope House has also created a teleconference hookup with federal prisons in North Carolina, Ohio, and New Mexico so that children can go to a neighborhood site to talk to their fathers in prison. In another instance, a Florida program called "Reading and Family Ties—Face to Face" also uses technology to overcome distance. Incarcerated mothers and their children transmit live video recordings via the Internet. These sessions occur each week, last an hour, and are available at no cost to the families. In addition, the U.S. Department of Justice in 1992 initiated the Girl Scouts Beyond Bars program, the first mother-daughter visitation program of its kind. Twice a month, more than 500 girls across the country, much like other girls their age, participate in Girl Scout programs, but in this program these Girl Scouts meet their mothers in prison. Finally, in Washington State, the McNeil Island Correction Center has launched a program that teaches incarcerated fathers the skills of active and involved parenting, encourages them to provide financial support for their children, and facilitates events to bring prisoners together with their families.

These programs—and many others like them—demonstrate that, with a little creativity and a fair amount of commitment, corrections agencies can find ways to foster ongoing, constructive relationships between incarcerated parents and their children. It seems particularly appropriate, in an era when technology has overcome geographical boundaries, to harness the Internet to bridge the divide between prisons and families. Yet the precondition for undertaking such initiatives is the recognition that corrections agencies must acknowledge responsibility for maintaining their prisoners' familial relationships. If these agencies embraced this challenge for all inmates—and were held accountable to the public and elected officials for the results of these efforts—the quality of family life for prisoners and their extended family networks would be demonstrably improved.

Notes

1. This is a single-day prevalence and does not take into account minor children whose parents were previously incarcerated; it accounts only for those who are currently incarcerated in state and federal prisons in 2002.
2. Public Law 105-89.
3. Figures do not total 100 percent because some prisoners had children living with multiple caregivers.
4. Elizabeth Gaynes, conversation with the author, June 22, 2004. Cited with permission.
5. The Michigan restrictions were challenged in court as unconstitutional because they violated the Fourteenth Amendment's guarantee of due process, the First Amendment's guarantee of free association, and the Eighth Amendment's prohibition against cruel and unusual punishment. The Supreme Court upheld the regulations, finding that the restrictions "bear a rational relation to

the [department of correction's] valid interests in maintaining internal security and protecting child visitors from exposure to sexual or other misconduct or from accidental injury. . . . To reduce the number of child visitors, a line must be drawn, and the categories set out by these regulations are reasonable" (*Overton v. Bazzetta*, 539 U.S. 94 [2003]).

6. The definition of who can visit or take children to visit is an even bigger problem in light of cultural traditions, i.e., the extended family network and fictive kin arrangements that exist in many African-American families. Family duties and responsibilities are shared among a group of individuals; e.g., a young uncle may be expected to take on the father's role and do things such as take the child to a game or on a prison visit while the grandmother provides day-to-day care and an aunt with a "good" job provides financial subsidies. Apparently this perspective was either not presented or ignored as unimportant in the Michigan case (Personal communication with Creasie Finney Hairston, January 6, 2004).
7. Missouri has announced that its next contract with prison telephone systems will not include a commission for the state. The Ohio prison system entered into a contract that will reduce the cost of prison phone calls by 15 percent. California will reduce most prisoner phone calls by 25 percent. In 2001, the Georgia Public Service Commission ordered telephone providers to reduce the rates for prisoner calls from a $3.95 connection fee and a rate of $0.69 per minute to a $2.20 connection fee and a rate of $0.35 per minute. The new telephone contract for the Pennsylvania Department of Corrections will reduce the average cost of a 15-minute telephone call by 30 percent. And litigation has been initiated in a number of states—including Illinois, Indiana, Kentucky, Ohio, New Hampshire, New Mexico, New York, South Dakota, Washington, Wisconsin, and the District of Columbia—to reduce the cost of prison phone calls and kickbacks to the state (eTc Campaign 2003).

References

Amato, Paul R., and Fernando Rivera. 1999. "Paternal Involvement and Children's Behavior Problems." *Journal of Marriage and the Family* 61(2): 375–84.

American Bar Association. 1993. *ABA Standards for Criminal Justice*. Chicago: American Bar Association.

Bloom, Barbara, and David Steinhart. 1993. *Why Punish the Children? A Reappraisal of the Children of Incarcerated Mothers in America*. San Francisco: National Council on Crime and Delinquency.

Braman, Donald. 2002. "Families and Incarceration." In *Invisible Punishment: The Collateral Consequences of Mass Imprisonment*, edited by Marc Mauer and Meda Chesney-Lind (117–35). New York: The New Press.

———. 2004. *Doing Time on the Outside: Incarceration and Family Life in Urban America*. Ann Arbor: University of Michigan Press.

Edin, Kathryn. 2000. "Few Good Men: Why Poor Mothers Don't Marry or Remarry." *The American Prospect* 11(4): 26–31.

Edin, Kathryn, and Laura Lein. 1997. *Making Ends Meet: How Single Mothers Survive Welfare and Low-Wage Work*. New York: Russell Sage Foundation.

eTc Campaign. 2003. "The Campaign to Promote Equitable Telephone Charges." http://www.curenational.org/~etc/. (Accessed April 5, 2004.)

Florida House of Representatives, Justice Council, Committee on Corrections. 1998. *Maintaining Family Contact When a Family Member Goes to Prison: An Examination of State Policies on Mail, Visiting, and Telephone Access*. http://www.fcc.state.fl.us/fcc/reports/family.pdf. (Accessed February 8, 2005.)

Furstenberg, Frank F. 1993. "How Families Manage Risk and Opportunity in Dangerous Neighborhoods." In *Sociology and the Public Agenda*, edited by William J. Wilson (231–58). Newbury Park, CA: Sage Publications.

Genty, Philip M. 2001. "Incarcerated Parents and the Adoption and Safe Families Act: A Challenge for Correctional Service Providers." *International Community Corrections Association Journal*, 44–47.

Greenfeld, Lawrence A., Michael R. Rand, Diane Craven, Patsy A. Klaus, Craig A. Perkins, Cheryl Ringel, Greg Warchol, Cathy Maston, and James Alan Fox. 1998. "Violence by Intimates:

Analysis of Data on Crimes by Current or Former Spouses, Boyfriends, and Girlfriends." NCJ 167237. U.S. Department of Justice, Bureau of Justice Statistics.

Hagan, John, and Juleigh Petty Coleman. 2001. "Returning Captives of the American War on Drugs: Issues of Community and Family Reentry." *Crime and Delinquency* 47(3): 352–67.

Hairston, Creasie Finne. 1998. "The Forgotten Parent: Understanding the Forces that Influence Incarcerated Fathers' Relationships with Their Children." *Child Welfare: Journal of Polity, Practice and Program* 77(5): 617–39.

———. 1999. "Kinship Care When Parents Are Incarcerated." In *Kinship Care Research: Improving Practice through Research*, edited by James P. Gleeson and Creasie Finney Hairston (189–212). Washington, DC: Child Welfare League of America.

Hairston, Creasie Finney, and James Rollin. 2003. "Social Capital and Family Connections." *Women, Girls & Criminal Justice* 4(5): 67–69.

Horney, Julie, D. Wayne Osgood, and Ineke Haen Marshall. 1995. "Criminal Careers in the Short-Term: Infra-Individual Variability in Crime and Its Relation to Local Life Circumstances." *American Sociological Review* 60(5): 655–73.

Johnston, Denise. 1999. "Children of Criminal Offenders and Foster Care." Presented at the Child Welfare League of America National Conference on Research, Seattle.

———. 2001. "Incarceration of Women and Effects on Parenting." Paper prepared for a conference: *The Effects of Incarceration on Children and Families*, sponsored by the Program on Child, Adolescent, and Family Studies, Institute for Policy Research, Northwestern University, Evanston, IL, May 5.

La Vigne, Nancy G., Vera Kachnowski, Jeremy Travis, Rebecca Naser, and Christy Visher. 2003. *A Portrait of Prisoner Reentry in Maryland*, Washington, DC: The Urban Institute. http://www.urban.org/url.cfm?ID=410655. (Accessed April 5, 2004.)

Langan, Patrick A., Erica L. Schmitt, and Matthew R. Durose. 2003. *Recidivism of Sex Offenders Released from Prison in 1994.* NCJ 198281. Washington, DC: U.S. Department of Justice, Bureau of Justice Statistics.

Laub, John H., Daniel S. Nagin, and Robert J. Sampson. 1998. "Trajectories of Change in Criminal Offending: Good Marriages and the Desistance Process." *American Sociological Review* 63(2): 225–38.

Loeber, Rolf, and David P. Farrington, eds. 1998. *Serious and Violent Juvenile Offenders: Risk Factors and Successful Interventions.* Thousand Oaks, CA: Sage Publications.

Lynch, James P., and William J. Sabol. 2001. *Prisoner Reentry in Perspective.* Crime Policy Report, vol. 3. Washington, DC: The Urban Institute.

McLoyd, Vonnie C. 1998. "Socioeconomic Disadvantage and Child Development." *American Psychologist* 53(2): 185–204.

Mumola, Christopher. 2000. "Incarcerated Parents and Their Children." NCI 182335. Washington, DC: U.S. Department of Justice, Bureau of Justice Statistics.

———. 2002. "Survey of Inmates in State and Federal Correctional Facilities, 2001 Annual Survey of Jails, and the 2001 National Prisoners Statistics Program." Paper presented at the National Center for Children and Families, Washington, DC, October 31.

———. 2004. "Incarcerated Parents and Their Children." Presented at the annual Administration for Children and Families Welfare Research and Evaluation Conference, U.S. Department of Health and Human Services, Washington, DC, May 28.

Petersilia, Joan. 2003. *When Prisoners Come Home: Parole and Prisoner Reentry.* New York: Oxford University Press.

Phillips, Susan, and Barbara Bloom. 1998. "In Whose Best Interest? The Impact of Changing Public Policy on Relatives Caring for Children with Incarcerated Parents." *Child Welfare* 77(5): 531–42.

Sabol, William J., and James P. Lynch. 1998. "Assessing the Longer-run Consequences of Incarceration: Effects on Families and Employment." Paper presented at the 20th Annual APPAM (Association for Public Policy Analysis and Management) Research Conference, New York, October 29–31.

Sack, W. 1977. "Children of Imprisoned Fathers." *Psychiatry* 40: 163–74.

Santana, Arthur. 2003. "Locked Dow and Far From Home." *Washington Post*, April 24.

Visher, Christy, Nancy La Vigne, and Jeremy Travis. 2004. *Returning Home: Understanding the Challenges of Prisoner Reentry: Maryland Pilot Study: Findings from Baltimore.* Washington, DC: The Urban Institute.

Western, Bruce, and Sarah McLanahan. 2000. "Fathers Behind Bars: The Impact of Incarceration on Family Formation." *Contemporary Perspectives in Family Research* 2: 307–22.

Western, Bruce, Leonard M. Lopoo, and Sarah McLanahan. 2004. "Incarceration and the Bonds Between Parents in Fragile Families." In *Imprisoning America: The Social Effects of Mass Incarceration*, edited by Mary Pattillo, David Weiman, and Bruce Western (21–45). New York: Russell Sage Foundation.

Women's Prison Association. 1996. *When a Mother Is Arrested: How the Criminal Justice and Child Welfare Systems Can Work Together More Effectively.* Baltimore: Maryland Department of Human Resources.

READING 37

Unmarried with Children

Kathryn Edin and Maria Kefalas

Jen Burke, a white tenth-grade dropout who is 17 years old, lives with her stepmother, her sister, and her 16-month-old son in a cramped but tidy row home in Philadelphia's beleaguered Kensington neighborhood. She is broke, on welfare, and struggling to complete her GED. Wouldn't she and her son have been better off if she had finished high school, found a job, and married her son's father first?

In 1950, when Jen's grandmother came of age, only 1 in 20 American children was born to an unmarried mother. Today, that rate is 1 in 3—and they are usually born to those least likely to be able to support a child on their own. In our book, *Promises I Can Keep: Why Poor Women Put Motherhood Before Marriage*, we discuss the lives of 162 white, African American, and Puerto Rican low-income single mothers living in eight destitute neighborhoods across Philadelphia and its poorest industrial suburb, Camden. We spent five years chatting over kitchen tables and on front stoops, giving mothers like Jen the opportunity to speak to the question so many affluent Americans ask about them: Why do they have children while still young and unmarried when they will face such an uphill struggle to support them?

ROMANCE AT LIGHTNING SPEED

Jen started having sex with her 20-year-old boyfriend Rick just before her 15th birthday. A month and a half later, she was pregnant. "I didn't want to get pregnant," she claims. "He wanted me to get pregnant." "As soon as he met me, he wanted to have a kid with me," she explains. Though Jen's college-bound suburban peers would be appalled by such a declaration, on the streets of Jen's neighborhood, it is something of a badge of honor. "All those other girls he was with, he didn't want to have a baby with any of them," Jen boasts. "I asked him, 'Why did you choose me to have a kid when you could have a kid with any one of them?' He was like, 'I want to have a kid with you.' " Looking back, Jen says she now believes that the reason "he wanted me to have a kid that early is so that I didn't leave him."

In inner-city neighborhoods like Kensington, where child-bearing within marriage has become rare, romantic relationships like Jen and Rick's proceed at lightning speed. A young man's avowal, "I want to have a baby by you," is often part of the courtship ritual from the beginning. This is more than idle talk, as their first child is typically conceived within a year from the time a couple begins "kicking it." Yet while poor couples' pillow talk often revolves around dreams of shared children, the news of a pregnancy—the first indelible sign of the huge changes to come—puts these still-new relationships into overdrive. Suddenly, the would-be mother begins to scrutinize her mate as never before, wondering whether he can "get himself together"—find a job, settle down, and become a family man—in time. Jen began pestering Rick to get a real job instead of picking up day-labor jobs at nearby construction sites. She also wanted him to stop hanging out with his ne'er-do-well friends, who had been getting him into serious trouble for more than a decade. Most of all, she wanted Rick to shed what she calls his "kiddie mentality"—his habit of spending money on alcohol and drugs rather than recognizing his growing financial obligations at home.

Rick did not try to deny paternity, as many would-be fathers do. Nor did he abandon or mistreat Jen, at least intentionally. But Rick, who had been in and out of juvenile detention since he was 8 years old for everything from stealing cars to selling drugs, proved unable to stay away from his unsavory friends. At the beginning of her seventh month of pregnancy, an escapade that began as a drunken lark landed Rick in jail on a carjacking charge. Jen moved back home with her stepmother, applied for welfare, and spent the last two-and-a-half months of her pregnancy without Rick.

Rick sent penitent letters from jail. "I thought he changed by the letters he wrote me. I thought he changed a lot," she says. "He used to tell me that he loved me when he was in jail. . . . It was always gonna be me and the baby when he got out." Thus, when Rick's alleged victim failed to appear to testify and he was released just days before Colin's birth, the couple's reunion was a happy one. Often, the magic moment of childbirth calms the troubled waters of such relationships. New parents typically make amends and resolve to stay together for the sake of their child. When surveyed just after a child's birth, eight in ten unmarried parents say they are still together, and most plan to stay together and raise the child.

Promoting marriage among the poor has become the new war on poverty, Bush style. And it is true that the correlation between marital status and child poverty is strong. But poor single mothers already believe in marriage. Jen insists that she will walk down the aisle one day, though she admits it might not be with Rick. And demographers still project that more than seven in ten women who had a child outside of marriage will eventually wed someone. First, though, Jen wants to get a good job, finish school, and get her son out of Kensington.

Most poor, unmarried mothers and fathers readily admit that bearing children while poor and unmarried is not the ideal way to do things. Jen believes the best time to become a mother is "after you're out of school and you got a job, at least, when you're like 21. . . . When you're ready to have kids, you should have everything ready, have your house, have a job, so when that baby comes, the baby can have its own room." Yet given their already limited economic prospects, the poor have little motivation to time their births as precisely as their middle-class counterparts do. The dreams of young people like Jen and Rick center on children at a time of life when their more affluent peers plan for college and careers. Poor girls coming of age in the inner city value children highly, anticipate them eagerly, and believe strongly that they are up to the job of mothering—even in difficult circumstances. Jen, for example, tells us, "People outside the neighborhood, they're like, 'You're 15! You're pregnant?' I'm like, it's not none of their business. I'm gonna be able to take care of my kid. They have nothing to worry about." Jen says she has concluded that "some people . . . are better at having kids at a younger age. . . . I think it's better for some people to have kids younger."

WHEN I BECAME A MOM

When we asked mothers like Jen what their lives would be like if they had not had children, we expected them to express regret over foregone opportunities for school and careers. Instead, most believe their children "saved" them. They describe their lives as spinning out of control before becoming pregnant—struggles with parents and peers, "wild," risky behavior, depression, and school failure. Jen speaks to this poignantly. "I was just real bad. I hung with a real bad crowd. I was doing pills. I was really depressed. . . . I was drinking. That was before I was pregnant." "I think," she reflects, "if I never had a baby or anything, . . . I would still be doing the things I was doing. I would probably still be doing drugs. I'd probably still be drinking." Jen admits that when she first became pregnant, she was angry that she "couldn't be out no more. Couldn't be out with my friends. Couldn't do nothing." Now, though, she says, "I'm glad I have a son . . . because I would still be doing all that stuff."

Children offer poor youth like Jen a compelling sense of purpose. Jen paints a before-and-after picture of her life that was common among the mothers we interviewed. "Before, I didn't have nobody to take care of. I didn't have nothing left to go home for. . . . Now I have my son to take care of. I have him to go home for. . . . I don't have to go buy weed or drugs with my money. I could buy my son stuff with my money! . . . I have something to look up to now." Children also are a crucial source of relational intimacy, a self-made community of care. After a nasty fight with Rick, Jen recalls, "I was crying. My son came in the room. He was hugging me. He's 16 months and he was hugging me with his little arms. He was really cute and happy, so I got happy. That's one of the good things. When you're sad, the baby's always gonna be there for you no matter what." Lately she has been thinking a lot about what her life was like back then, before the baby. "I thought about the stuff before I became a mom, what my life was like back then. I used to see pictures of me, and I would hide in every picture. This baby did so much for me. My son did a lot for me. He helped me a lot. I'm thankful that I had my baby."

Around the time of the birth, most unmarried parents claim they plan to get married eventually. Rick did not propose marriage when Jen's first child was born, but when she conceived a second time, at 17, Rick informed his dad, "It's time for me to get married. It's time for me to straighten up. This is the one I wanna be with. I had a baby with her, I'm gonna have another baby with her." Yet despite their intentions, few of these couples actually marry. Indeed, most break up well before their child enters preschool.

I'D LIKE TO GET MARRIED, BUT . . .

The sharp decline in marriage in impoverished urban areas has led some to charge that the poor have abandoned the marriage norm. Yet we found few who had given up on the idea of marriage. But like their elite counterparts, disadvantaged women set a high financial bar for marriage. For the poor, marriage has become an elusive goal—one they feel ought to be reserved for those who can support a "white picket fence" lifestyle: a mortgage on a modest row home, a car and some furniture, some savings in the bank, and enough money left over to pay for a "decent" wedding. Jen's views on marriage provide a perfect case in point. "If I was gonna get married, I would want to be married like my Aunt Nancy and my Uncle Pat. They live in the mountains. She has a job. My Uncle Pat is a state trooper; he has lots of money. They live in the [Poconos]. It's real nice out there. Her kids go to Catholic school. . . . That's the kind of life I would want to have. If I get married, I would have a life like [theirs]." She adds, "And I would wanna have a big wedding, a real nice wedding."

Unlike the women of their mothers' and grandmothers' generations, young women like Jen are not merely content to rely on a man's earnings. Instead, they insist on being economically "set" in their own right before taking marriage vows. This is partly because they want a partnership of equals and they believe money buys say-so in a relationship. Jen explains, "I'm not gonna just get into marrying him and not have my own house! Not have a job! I still wanna do a lot of things before I get married. He [already] tells me I can't do nothing. I can't go out. What's gonna happen when I marry him? He's gonna say he owns me!"

Economic independence is also insurance against a marriage gone bad. Jen explains, "I want to have everything ready, in case something goes wrong. . . . If we got a divorce, that would be my house. I bought that house, he can't kick me out or he can't take my kids from me." "That's what I want in case that ever happens. I know a lot of people that happened to. I don't want it to happen to me." These statements reveal that despite her desire to marry, Rick's role in the family's future is provisional at best. "We get along, but we fight a lot. If he's there, he's there, but if he's not, that's why I want a job . . . a job with computers . . . so I could afford my kids, could afford the house. . . . I don't want to be living off him. I want my kids to be living off me."

Why is Jen, who describes Rick as "the love of my life," so insistent on planning an exit strategy before she is willing to take the vows she firmly believes ought to last "forever?" If love is so sure, why does mistrust seem so palpable and strong? In relationships among poor couples like Jen and Rick, mistrust is often spawned by chronic violence and infidelity, drug and alcohol abuse, criminal activity, and the threat of imprisonment. In these tarnished corners of urban America, the stigma of a failed marriage is far worse than an out-of-wedlock birth. New mothers like Jen feel they must test the relationship over three, four, even five years' time. This is the only way, they believe, to insure that their marriages will last.

Trust has been an enormous issue in Jen's relationship with Rick. "My son was born December 23rd, and [Rick] started cheating on me again . . . in March. He started cheating on me with some girl—Amanda. . . . Then it was another girl, another girl, another girl after. I didn't wanna believe it. My friends would come up to me and be like, 'Oh yeah, your boyfriend's cheating on you with this person.' I wouldn't believe it. . . . I would see him with them. He used to have hickies. He used to make up some excuse that he was drunk—that was always his excuse for everything." Things finally came to a head when Rick got another girl pregnant. "For a while, I forgave him for everything. Now, I don't forgive him for nothing." Now we begin to understand the source of Jen's hesitancy. "He wants me to marry him, [but] I'm not really sure. . . . If I can't trust him, I can't marry him, 'cause we would get a divorce. If you're gonna get married, you're supposed to be faithful!" she insists. To Jen and her peers, the worst thing that could happen is "to get married just to get divorced."

Given the economic challenges and often perilously low quality of the romantic relationships among unmarried parents, poor women may be right to be cautious about marriage. Five years after we first spoke with her, we met with Jen again. We learned that Jen's second pregnancy ended in a miscarriage. We also learned that Rick was out of the picture—apparently for good. "You know that bar [down the street] It happened in that bar. . . . They were in the bar, and this guy was like badmouthing [Rick's friend] Mikey, talking stuff to him or whatever. So Rick had to go get involved in it and start with this guy. . . . Then he goes outside and fights the guy [and] the guy dies of head trauma. They were all on drugs, they were all drinking, and things just got out of control, and that's what happened. He got fourteen to thirty years."

THESE ARE CARDS I DEALT MYSELF

Jen stuck with Rick for the first two and a half years of his prison sentence, but when another girl's name replaced her own on the visitors' list, Jen decided she was finished with him once and for all. Readers might be asking what Jen ever saw in a man like Rick. But Jen and Rick operate in a partner market where the better-off men go to the better-off women. The only way for someone like Jen to forge a satisfying relationship with a man is to find a diamond in the rough or improve her own economic position so that she can realistically compete for more upwardly mobile partners, which is what Jen is trying to do now. "There's this kid, Donny, he works at my job. He works on C shift. He's a supervisor! He's funny, three years older, and he's not a geek or anything, but he's not a real preppy good boy either. But he's not [a player like Rick] and them. He has a job, you know, so that's good. He doesn't do drugs or anything. And he asked my dad if he could take me out!"

These days, there is a new air of determination, even pride, about Jen. The aimless high school dropout pulls ten-hour shifts entering data at a warehouse distribution center Monday through Thursday. She has held the job for three years, and her aptitude and hard work have earned her a series of raises. Her current salary is higher than anyone in her household commands—$10.25 per hour, and she now gets two weeks of paid vacation, four personal days, 60 hours of sick time, and medical benefits. She has saved up the necessary $400 in tuition for a high school completion program that offers evening and weekend classes. Now all that stands between her and a diploma is a passing grade in mathematics, her least favorite subject. "My plan is to start college in January. [This month] I take my math test . . . so I can get my diploma," she confides.

Jen clearly sees how her life has improved since Rick's dramatic exit from the scene. "That's when I really started [to get better] because I didn't have to worry about what he was doing, didn't have to worry about him cheating on me, all this stuff. [It was] then I realized that I had to do what I had to do to take care of my son. . . . When he was there, I think that my whole life revolved around him, you know, so I always messed up somehow because I was so busy worrying about what he was doing. Like I would leave the [GED] programs I was in just to go home and see what he was doing. My mind was never concentrating." Now, she says, "a lot of people in my family look up to me now, because all my sisters dropped out from school, you know, nobody went back to school. I went back to school, you know? . . . I went back to school, and I plan to go to college, and a lot of people look up to me for that, you know? So that makes me happy . . . because five years ago nobody looked up to me. I was just like everybody else."

Yet the journey has not been easy. "Being a young mom, being 15, it's hard, hard, hard, you know." She says, "I have no life. . . . I work from 6:30 in the morning until 5:00 at night. I leave here at 5:30 in the morning. I don't get home until about 6:00 at night." Yet she measures her worth as a mother by the fact that she has managed to provide for her son largely on her own. "I don't depend on nobody. I might live with my dad and them, but I don't depend on them, you know." She continues, "There [used to] be days when I'd be so stressed out, like, 'I can't do this!' And I would just cry and cry and cry. . . . Then I look at Colin, and he'll be sleeping, and I'll just look at him and think I don't have no [reason to feel sorry for myself]. The cards I have I've dealt myself so I have to deal with it now. I'm older. I can't change anything. He's my responsibility—he's nobody else's but mine—so I have to deal with that."

Becoming a mother transformed Jen's point of view on just about everything. She says, "I thought hanging on the corner drinking, getting high—I thought that was a good life, and I thought I could live that way for eternity, like sitting out with my friends. But it's not as fun once you have your own kid. . . . I think it changes [you]. I think, 'Would I want Colin to do that? Would I want my son to be like that. . .?' It was fun to me but it's not fun anymore. Half the people I hung with are either . . . Some have died from drug overdoses, some are in jail, and some people are just out there living the same life that they always lived, and they don't look really good. They look really bad." In the end, Jen believes, Colin's birth has brought far more good into her life than bad. "I know I could have waited [to have a child], but in a way I think Colin's the best thing that could have happened to me. . . . So I think I had my son for a purpose because I think Colin changed my life. He saved my life, really. My whole life revolves around Colin!"

PROMISES I CAN KEEP

There are unique themes in Jen's story—most fathers are only one or two, not five years older than the mothers of their children, and few fathers have as many glaring problems as Rick—but we heard most of these themes repeatedly in the stories of the 161 other poor, single mothers we came to know. Notably, poor women do not reject marriage; they revere it. Indeed, it is the conviction that marriage is forever that makes them think that divorce is worse than having a baby outside of marriage. Their children, far from being liabilities, provide crucial social-psychological resources—a strong sense of purpose and a profound source of intimacy. Jen and the other mothers we came to know are coming of age in an America that is profoundly unequal—where the gap between rich and poor continues to grow. This economic reality has convinced them that they have little to lose and, perhaps, something to gain by a seemingly "ill-timed" birth.

The lesson one draws from stories like Jen's is quite simple: Until poor young women have more access to jobs that lead to financial independence—until there is reason to hope for the rewarding life pathways that their privileged peers pursue—the poor will continue to have children far sooner than most Americans think they should, while still deferring marriage. Marital standards have risen for all Americans, and the poor want the same things that everyone now wants out of marriage. The poor want to marry too, but they insist on marrying well. This, in their view, is the only way to avoid an almost certain divorce. Like Jen, they are simply not willing to make promises they are not sure they can keep.

Recommended Resources

Kathryn Edin and Maria Kefalas. *Promises I Can Keep: Why Poor Women Put Motherhood Before Marriage* (University of California Press, 2005). An account of how low-income women make sense of their choices about marriage and motherhood.

Christina Gibson, Kathryn Edin, and Sara McLanahan. "High Hopes but Even Higher Expectations: A Qualitative and Quantitative Analysis of the Marriage Plans of Unmarried Couples Who Are New Parents." Working Paper 03-06-FF, Center for Research on Child Wellbeing, Princeton University, 2004. Online at http://crcw.princeton.edu/workingpapers/WP03-06-FF-Gibson.pdf. The authors examine the rising expectations for marriage among unmarried parents.

Sharon Hays. *Flat Broke with Children: Women in the Age of Welfare Reform* (Oxford University Press, 2003). How welfare reform has affected the lives of poor moms.

Annette Lareau. *Unequal Childhoods: Class, Race, and Family Life* (University of California Press, 2003). A fascinating discussion of different childrearing strategies among low-income, working-class, and middle-class parents.

Timothy J. Nelson, Susan Clampet-Lundquist, and Kathryn Edin. "Fragile Fatherhood: How Low-Income, Non-Custodial Fathers in Philadelphia Talk About Their Families." In *The Handbook of Father Involvement: Multidisciplinary Perspectives*, ed. Catherine Tamis-LeMonda and Natasha Cabrera (Lawrence Earlbaum Associates, 2002). What poor, single men think about fatherhood.

Credits

pp. 15–27: William J. Goode, "The Theoretical Importance of Family" is from *The Family*, second edition. Copyright © 1982. Reproduced by permission of Pearson Education, Inc., Upper Saddle River, New Jersey.

pp. 27–33: Anthony Giddens, "The Global Revolution in Family and Personal Life" is from *Runaway World: How Globalisation is Reshaping Our Lives*. Copyright © 1999. Reproduced by permission of Routledge, Inc., a division of Informa plc.

pp. 33–40: Erikka Oinonin, "Family in Finland and Spain." from *Families in Converging Europe: A Comparison of Forms, Structures and Ideals*. Palgrave/Macmillan: Houndmills, Basingstoke, Hampshire, England. 2008, pp. 152–160. Reprinted by permission.

pp. 41–60: Sharon Hays, "The Mommy Wars" is from *The Cultural Contradictions of Motherhood* (pp. 131–151). Copyright © 1996. Published by Yale University Press. Reprinted by permission of the publisher.

pp. 60–80: Janet Z. Giele, "Decline of the Family: Conservative, Liberal, and Feminist Views" is from David Popenoe, Jean Bethke Elshtain, and David Blankenhorn (Eds.), Promises to Keep: Decline and Renewal of Marriage in America (pp. 89–115). Copyright © 1996. Reprinted by permission of Rowman & Littlefield.

pp. 87–95: Robert M. Jackson, "Destined for Equality" is from *Destined for Equality: The Inevitable Rise of Women's Status* (pp. 1–23, 157–171). Cambridge, MA.: Harvard University Press. Copyright © 1998 by Robert Max Jackson. Reprinted by permission of the publisher.

pp. 95–102: Gail Collins, "The Ice Cracks" is from *When Everything Changed*. Copyright © 2009. By permission of Little, Brown and Company.

pp. 102–116: Kathleen Gerson, "Falling Back on Plan B: The Children of the Gender Revolution Face Uncharted Territory" from *Families as They Really Are*, edited by Barbara J. Risman. Copyright © 2010 by W. W. Norton & Company, Inc. Used by permission of W. W. Norton & Company, Inc.

pp. 117–134: Beth Bailey, "Sexual Revolution(s)" is from David R. Farber (Ed.), *The Sixties: From Memory to History*. Copyright © 1994 by the University of North Carolina Press. Reprinted by permission of the publisher.

pp. 134–154: Kathleen A. Bogle, "Hooking Up and Dating: A Comparison" from *Hooking Up: Sex Dating and Relationships on Campus*, New York University Press: New York. 208, pp. 158–185. Reprinted by permission of the publisher.

pp. 154–160: Margaret Talbot, "Red Sex, Blue Sex," originally published in The New Yorker, November 3, 2008, pp. 64–69. Copyright © 2008 by Margaret Talbot. Reprinted with permission of The Wylie Agency LLC.

pp. 161–172: Lynne M. Casper and Suzanne M. Bianchi, "Cohabitation" is from *Continuity And Change In The American Family* (pp. 39-66). Copyright © 2001. Published by SAGE Publications, Inc. Reprinted by permission of the publisher.

pp. 172–189: Maria Kefalas, Frank Furstenberg, Patrick Carr, and Laura Napolitano, "Marriage is More than Being Together: Mapping the Meaning of Marriage Among Young Adults), Paper for publication in edited volume (Editors: Douglas Hartmann, Teresa Swartz, and Ruben Rumbaut). Reprinted by permission.

pp. 190–210: Andrew Cherlin, "American Marriage in the Early Twenty-First Century" is from *The Future of Children*, a publication of The Woodrow Wilson School of Public and International Affairs at Princeton University and The Brookings Institution.

pp. 211–220: Arlene Skolnick, "Grounds for Marriage: How Relationships Succeed or Fail" is revised from *Inside the American Couple: New Thinking/New Challenges* edited by Margret Yalom and Laura L. Carstensen. Copyright © 2002, The Regents of the University of California. Used with permission of the University of California Press.

pp. 221–228: Lawrence M. Friedman, "Divorce: The 'Silent Revolution' " is from "Who Are Our Children? Adoption, Custody, and Related Issues" in *Private Lives: Families, Individuals, and the Law* (pp. 96–123). Cambridge, MA: Harvard University Press. Copyright © 2004 by the President and Fellows of Harvard College. Reprinted by permission of the publisher.

pp. 228–239: Virginia E. Rutter, "Divorce in Research vs. Divorce in Media," Sociology Compass, 3/4/2009, pp. 707–720. Reprinted by permission of Wiley-Blackwell.

pp. 239–256: Mary Ann Mason, "The Modern American Stepfamily: Problems and Possibilities" is from Mary Ann Mason, Arlene Skolnick, and Stephen D. Sugarman (Eds.), *All Our Families: New Policies for a New Century* (pp. 96–116). Copyright © 2003. Reprinted by permission of the publisher.

pp. 261–281: Philip Cowan and Carolyn Pape Cowan, "New Families: Modern Couples as New Pioneers" is from Mary Ann Mason, Arlene Skolnick, and Stephen D. Sugarman (Eds.), *All Our Families: New Policies for a New Century* (pp. 196–219). Copyright © 2003. Reprinted by permission of the publisher.

pp. 281–287: William Marsiglio, "Healthy Dads, Healthy Kids." in *Contexts*, *8*(4), pp. 22–27, 2009. Reprinted by permission of The University of California Press.

pp. 289–302: Steven Mintz, "Beyond Sentimentality: American Childhood as a Social and Cultural Construct" is reprinted by permission of the publisher.

pp. 302–313: Annette Lareau, "Unequal Childhoods: Class, Race, and Family Life" is from David Grusky, *Inequality Reader*. Copyright © 2006 David Grusky and Szonja Szelenyi. Reprinted by permission of Westview Press, a member of Perseus Books Group.

pp. 314–331: Frank F. Furstenberg, "Diverging Development: The Not-So-Invisible Hand in the Unmited States" paper presented at the biennial meetings of the Society for Research on Adolescence, San Francisco, March 2006. Reprinted by permission of the author.

pp. 331–348: Katherine S. Newman "Ties that Bind: Cultural Interpretations of Delayed Adulthood in Western Europe and Japan," Sociological Forum: Vol. 23, No. 4, pp. 645–669. Reprinted by permission.

pp. 355–362: Arlie Hochschild and Ann Machung, "The Second Shift: Working Patterns and the Revolution at Home" is from "Joey's Problem: Nancy and Evan Holt" in *The Second Shift*. Copyright © 1989, 2003 by Arlie Hochschild. Used by permission of Viking Penguin, a division of Penguin Group (USA) Inc.

pp. 362–370: Pamela Stone, "The Rhetoric and Reality of 'Opting Out' " is from *Contexts*, *6*(4), pp. 14–19. University of California Press. Reprinted by permission of the publisher.

pp. 371–388: Lillian B. Rubin, "Families on the Fault Line" is from *Families on the Fault Line* (pp. 217–243). Copyright © 1994 Lillian B. Rubin. Published by HarperCollins. Reprinted by permission of the author.

pp. 389–395: Harriet B. Presser, "The Economy That Never Sleeps" is from *Contexts*, *3*(2), pp. 42–49. University of California Press. Reprinted by permission of the publisher.

pp. 395–400: Katherine S. Newman, "The Missing Class." Copyright © 2007 by Katherine Newman and Victor Tan Chen. Reprinted by permission of Beacon Press, Boston.

pp. 401–419: Elizabeth Warren and Amelia Warren Tyagi, "Why Middle-Class Mothers and Fathers Are Going Broke" is from *The Two-Income Trap*. Copyright © 2004 Elizabeth Warren and Amelia Warren Tyagi. Reprinted by permission of Basic Books, a member of Perseus Books Group.

pp. 421–445: Ronald L. Taylor, "Diversity within African-American Families" is from David H. Demo, Katherine R. Allen, and Mark A. Fine (Eds.), *The Handbook of Family Diversity* (pp. 232–251). Copyright © 1999. Reprinted by permission of Oxford University Press.

pp. 445–471: Maxine Baca Zinn and Barbara Wells, "Diversity within Latino Families: New Lessons for Family Social Science" is from David H. Demo, Katherine R. Allen, and Mark A. Fine (Eds.), *The Handbook of Family Diversity* (pp. 252–273). Copyright © 1999. Reprinted by permission of Oxford University Press.

pp. 472–485: Min Zhou, "Conflict, Coping and Reconciliation in Chinese Immigrant Families," In *Across Generations: Immigrant Families in America* edited by Nancy Foner, New York University Press, New York: 2009, pp. 21-45. Reprinted by permission of the publisher.

pp. 485–496: Rona J. Karasik and Raeann R. Hamon, "Cultural Diversity and Aging Families," is from B. S. Trask and R. R. Haman (Eds.), *Cultural Diversity and Families* (pp. 136–146). Copyright © 2007. Reprinted by permission of the publisher.

pp. 496–518: Judith Stacey, "Gay and Lesbian Families: Queer Like Us" is from Mary Ann Mason, Arlene Skolnick, and Stephen D. Sugarman (Eds.), *All Our Families: New Policies for a New Century* (pp. 144–169). Copyright © 2003. Reprinted by permission of Oxford University Press.

pp. 519–536: Jeremy Travis, "Prisoners' Families and Children" is from *But They All Come Back: Facing the Challenges of Prisoner Reentry* (pp. 119–138). Copyright © 2005. Published by Urban Institute Press. Reprinted by permission of the Urban Institute.

pp. 536–542: Kathryn Edin and Maria Kefalas, "Unmarried with Children" is from *Contexts*, *4*(2), pp. 16–22. University of California Press. Reprinted by permission of the publisher.